THE ROUGH GUIDE TO
TRINIDAD & TOBAGO

This seventh edition updated by
Polly Thomas

ROUGH
GUIDES

Contents

Introduction to
Trinidad & Tobago

Sitting pretty just off the coast of the South American mainland it was once part of, the twin-island republic of Trinidad and Tobago (often shortened to "T&T") is one of the Caribbean's most diverse and underexplored destinations. The islands boast spectacular rainforests, waterfalls, savannas and reefs, and the endless undeveloped beaches – from palm-lined white sands fringed by limpid waters to secluded, wave-whipped outcrops – are some of the prettiest in the region. As the home and heart of West Indian Carnival and the place where calypso, soca and steel pan were invented, T&T is also a cultural pacemaker for the Caribbean and a fantastic place to party.

Trinidad and Tobago's economy is the most diversified and industrialized in the English-speaking Caribbean, with an average of around 96,500 barrels of oil and 32 million cubic metres of natural gas produced here each year. Because gas and oil are the main economic earners, both islands remain largely unfettered by the more noxious elements of Caribbean tourism, and are well suited to **independent travellers** without being fully fledged resorts. Visitors are not corralled in all-inclusives or holed up on private beaches – swathes of sand are enjoyed by locals and foreigners alike, with visitors often in the minority. Sun and sea are by no means the only draw here, however: no other Caribbean island offers such a variety of **wildlife and habitats** in so compact an area (roughly half the size of Hawaii Island). In Trinidad, there are tropical rainforests of mahogany and teak patrolled by howler monkeys and ocelots, wetlands harbouring manatees and anacondas, and remote beaches where giant leatherback turtles lay their eggs, while Tobago is best known for its stunning **coral reefs**, favoured by manta rays and shoals of brightly coloured tropical fish. Both islands also offer some brilliant opportunities for birdwatching; with more than 485 recorded species T&T has one of the richest concentrations of birds per square kilometre in the world.

CARONI SWAMP

The crowded and dynamic **towns and cities** are equally engaging, with fretworked "gingerbread" homes sitting side by side with temples, mosques, Catholic cathedrals and Anglican churches. The many ethnic groups brought to labour in the islands after slaves were freed in 1834 have given rise to a remarkably varied populace, hailing from India, China, Portugal and Syria as well as Africa, England, France and Spain. Though racial tensions are inevitably present, Trinbagonians (as they're collectively known) generally coexist with good humour, and are proud of the **multiculturalism** that has so enriched the islands. This easy-going mentality is best expressed in the local propensity for "liming" – taking time out to meet friends and talk, usually over food and a beer or glass of rum.

Both islands share a party-hard ethic, and Trinidad has an electrifying **music scene** that rivals even that of Jamaica. T&T is the birthplace of calypso and the more fast-paced soca, as well as that quintessential sound of the Caribbean, the steel pan; you'll hear plenty of all three year-round, but especially during the republic's most famous party, its annual pre-Lenten **Carnival**. During this unique and explosive event, the no-holds-barred debauchery of the Jouvert "dirty mas" parades is followed by two days of pure joy as 3000-strong bands of intricately costumed revellers take to the streets in a spectacular celebration of life.

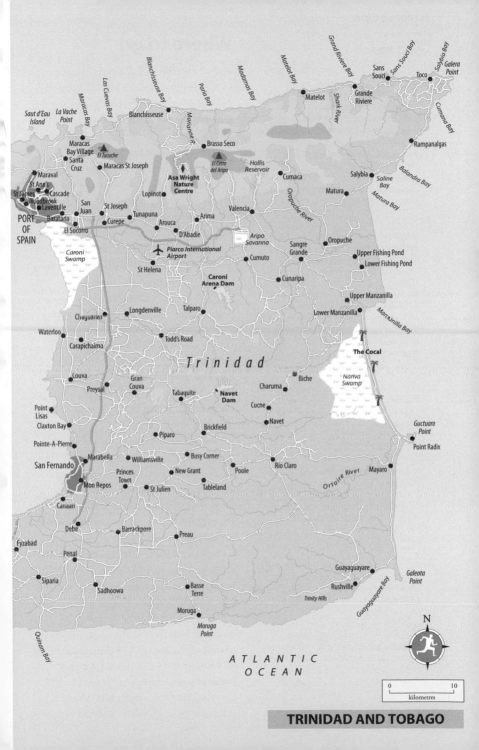

TRINIDAD AND TOBAGO

FACT FILE

- Standing at about 1.36 million, T&T's **population** is around 40 percent Indian, 39 percent black, 18 percent mixed-heritage, 0.6 percent white and 0.4 percent Chinese. Its people are theologically diverse, too: with 26 percent Roman Catholic, 25 percent Protestant, 23 percent Hindu, 6 percent Muslim, 3 percent Presbyterian and 6 percent adhering to African-based **religions** such as Spiritual Baptist and Orisha.

- Go into almost any bar in the world and you'll see a bottle of **Angostura bitters**, produced in Trinidad and an essential ingredient of many classic cocktails. Its aromatic blend of herbs, spices and alcohol is such a guarded secret that no single person is permitted to know the full recipe.

- Trinidad is one of the world's most important nesting sites for the giant **leatherback turtle**, with 18 percent of the total global population laying their eggs here. The highest density of nests is at Grande Riviere in the northeast, with some 500 turtles visiting per night at the height of the season.

- The peculiar **Pitch Lake**, at La Brea on Trinidad's southwestern coast, is the world's largest natural reservoir of asphalt.

- The Kelleston Drain dive site, offshore of Little Tobago, can lay claim to having the largest **brain coral** in the world: 3m high and 5.3m across.

- T&T lie outside the region's **hurricane** belt, and haven't suffered a big blast since Flora in 1963, though minor **earthquakes** occur at an average of one per month.

- Native to southern Trinidad, the **Moruga Scorpion** is officially the second hottest pepper in the world, notching up two million units on the Scoville heat scale, just a fraction less than the Carolina Reaper.

Where to go

Bound together for the convenience of the British Empire, Trinidad and Tobago are vastly different places. **Trinidad** offers culture, ethnic diversity, music, clubs, great food, pristine rainforest and a wealth of undeveloped beaches. **Tobago** is more of a conventional Caribbean resort, its southwest replete with busy strips of white sand and hotels of every stripe, as well as plenty of bars, restaurants and places to dance under the stars. The rest of the island is relatively undeveloped, with plenty of fantastic small-scale guesthouses, but nowhere in Tobago will you find the high-rise hotels and slick resort areas of other islands in the region. It's impossible to get a full picture of T&T without visiting both Trinidad and Tobago, and inexpensive plane and boat services between the two make it easy to see the best of each even during a short stay.

A visit to Trinidad will inevitably begin in the vibrant capital, **Port of Spain**, which with its restaurants, nightlife and accommodation is a natural base from which to explore the rest of the country. To the west, **Chaguaramas** is the capital's playground, with a beachfront boardwalk, walking and mountain biking trails, golf course, kids' amusement park, mini-zoo, zip line and the great Macqueripe Beach at Tucker Valley. Chaguaramas is also the jumping-off point for boat trips to the rocky, wooded islands of the **Bocas**. A sweeping curve of powdery sand and powerful waves, **Maracas Bay** is the first of many lovely beaches along the **north coast**, some reachable by road, others only on foot.

CARNIVAL

Trinidad's **Carnival** is all about participation rather than watching from the sidelines as in Rio – whether young or old, big or small, anyone with a willingness to "wine their waist" and "get on bad" is welcome to sign up with a **masquerade band**, which gets you a costume and the chance to dance through the streets alongside tens of thousands of fellow revellers. Preceded by weeks of all-night outdoor fetes, as parties here are known, as well as competitions for the best steel bands and calypso and soca singers, the main event starts at 4am on Carnival Sunday with **Jouvert** (pronounced "jou-vay"). This anarchic and raunchy street party is pure, unadulterated bacchanalia, with generous coatings of mud, chocolate, oil or body paint – and libations of local rum, of course – helping you lose all inhibitions and slip and slide through the streets until morning in an anonymous mass of dirty, drunken, happy humanity, chipping along to steel bands, sound-system trucks or the traditional "rhythm section" percussionists. Once the sun is fully up, and a sluice down with a hose has dispensed with the worst of the mud, the masquerade bands hit the streets, their costumed followers dancing along in the wake of the pounding soca. Monday is a mere warm-up for the **main parade** the following day, however, when full costumes are worn and the streets are awash with colour. The music trucks are back in earnest and the city reverberates with beats, becoming one giant street party, until "las lap" and total exhaustion closes proceedings for another year.

forested peaks of the **Northern Range** offer excellent hiking and birdwatching opportunities. South of the hills, the **East–West Corridor** provides access to caves, swimmable rivers and waterfalls, the Yerettê hummingbird centre, and the oldest Benedictine monastery in the Caribbean at Mount St Benedict.

The flat agricultural plains of **central Trinidad** provide a fascinating contrast to the north. From the ethereal Waterloo Temple in the Sea and the nearby Hanuman Murti statue at Sri Dattatreya Temple to the busy market town of **Chaguanas**, Indian culture predominates; there's plenty of natural allure too, from the scarlet ibis that inhabit the mangrove labyrinth of **Caroni Swamp** on the west coast to the manatees and monkeys in the protected eastern wetlands at **Nariva**. Also on the east coast, endless swathes of fine brown sand lined by groves of coconut palms make **Manzanilla** and **Mayaro** favourite spots for some beach time, while the burgeoning city of **San Fernando**, in the southwest, is a friendly coastal base from which to explore the largely unvisited "deep south", where modern oil towns such as **Fyzabad** contrast with the spectacular coastline and wetlands around **Cedros** and **Icacos**.

Most people travelling to **Tobago** head for the translucent waters, coral reefs and excellent facilities around **Crown Point** at the low-lying southwestern tip. The vibrant capital, **Scarborough**, with its market and historic fort, offers a more workaday picture of local life, while the rugged windward (or Atlantic) coast is best known for the waterfall and cocoa estate at **Argyle** and the island's finest snorkelling and scuba diving at **Speyside**. The leeward (or Caribbean) coast promises some superb beaches, kicking off with the clear green waters of **Mount Irvine** and the wide sweeps of sand at **Stonehaven Bay** and **Turtle Beach**; further afield there's the twin bays at the laidback mini-resort of **Castara** to the palm-lined swathe of **Englishman's Bay**. At the northeast tip, the pretty village of **Charlotteville** has the sublime Pirate's Bay as well as the none-too-shabby Man O'War Bay.

When to go

Though T&T's **temperatures** remain tropical year-round, most people visit between December and March, when **Carnival** explodes into life, the trees are in bloom and the climate is at its most forgiving – the sun shines, rain is rare and the nights are cool. By May, the lack of rain has parched the formerly lush landscape: greens turn to yellow, dust clouds put the views into soft focus and bush fires spark in Trinidad's hills. Around the end of May, the **rainy season** begins, and the skies open up with dramatic deluges that can last all day. The wet season lasts until November, but there's usually a respite from the downpours in September, a period of hot sunshine and blue skies known as the **petit carem**. It's an excellent time to visit, with flights at low-season rates, though you'll find the resorts a little quiet. Some Tobago hoteliers raise rates during the **high season** (Dec 15–April 15), and those in Trinidad's Grande Riviere do the same during the turtle-laying season (March–Sept), but most of the smaller hotels charge the same year-round in both islands. During Carnival week, however, all Port of Spain hotels and guesthouses boost their rates.

CLIMATE IN PORT OF SPAIN

	Jan	Feb	Mar	Apr	May	Jun	Jul	Aug	Sep	Oct	Nov	Dec
AVERAGE DAILY TEMPERATURE												
Max/min (°C)	31/21	31/20	32/20	32/21	32/22	32/22	31/22	31/22	32/22	32/22	32/22	31/21
Max/min (°F)	87/69	88/68	89/68	90/69	90/71	89/71	88/71	88/71	89/71	89/71	89/71	88/69
AVERAGE RAINFALL												
mm	69	41	46	53	94	193	218	246	193	170	183	125

MARACAS BAY

Author picks

Our author has travelled the length and breadth of T&T, shimmying through the streets at Carnival, body-surfing at the beaches and sampling the best cuisine. Here are her highlights.

Carnival time Arrive in time to check out the panyards (see page 74) and party at the fetes (see page 91), then cover yourself in mud and chip along to a rhythm section for Jouvert (see page 71) and bring out the bling to play mas (see page 70) in the main parades – simply the most fun you will ever have.

Tropical birdlife Whether you view humming-birds up close at Yerettê (see page 127), see the scarlet ibis at Caroni Swamp (see page 152) or spend an afternoon spotting the colourful species at Asa Wright (see page 124), T&T's rich birdlife is not just for the hardened twitcher.

Street food From a hot cup of corn soup to a filled-to-bursting roti, early morning chickpea doubles to paper bags of pholouri dipped into spicy tamarind sauce, T&T's street food (see page 28) is ridiculously moreish.

Go cocoa loco Explore T&T's chocolate revolution with a bean-to-bar tour in Port of Spain (see page 79), at Brasso Seco (see page 123), Grande Riviere (see page 142), San Antonio (see page 160) or Tobago Windward Chocolate Company (see page 237); sample creative cocoa-infused cuisine at Lopinot (see page 131); and take a taste of T&T home via a visit to Cocobel (see page 92), Cocoa Pod (see page 92) or Tobago Chocolate Delights (see page 227).

Swim in a waterfall From floating in cool water under a rainforest canopy to getting a watery massage, waterfalls are a highlight of T&T; Rio Seco (see page 138), Argyle (see page 238), Sombasson (see page 135) and Paria (see page 119) are four of the best.

The deep south There's much more to the south than the Pitch Lake, from beachside palm groves and gorgeous wetlands at Columbus Bay and Icacos Point (see page 183) to history and culture at Moruga (see page 187) – plus a friendly, hospitable and uniquely southside vibe.

> Our author recommendations don't end here. We've flagged up our favourite places – a perfectly sited hotel, an atmospheric café, a special restaurant – throughout the Guide, highlighted with the ★ symbol.

SCARLET IBIS
PARIA WATERFALL

15

things not to miss

It's not possible to see everything that Trinidad and Tobago have to offer in one trip – and we don't suggest you try. What follows gives a taste of the islands' highlights: gorgeous beaches, thrilling nightlife, fine food and exotic wildlife. All highlights are colour-coded by chapter and have a page reference to take you into the Guide, where you can find out more.

1

1 NORTH COAST DRIVE
See page 113
The drive along Trinidad's northern coastline provides glimpses of innumerable rainforest-smothered headlands, and stopoffs at fantastic beaches such as Las Cuevas.

2 HIKING IN THE NORTHERN RANGE
See pages 123 and 134
Trinidad's Northern Range hills offer excellent hiking, with hundreds of trails through the lush forest.

3 CARAPICHAIMA
See page 155
Carapichaima provides a great introduction to Indo-Trinidadian culture, from the Temple in the Sea at Waterloo to the gigantic Hanuman Murti statue at Sri Dattatreya Temple.

4 CARNIVAL
See page 260
Whether you're watching the parade go by or joining a mas band, Carnival is T&T's ultimate party.

5 BIRDWATCHING AT ASA WRIGHT
See page 124
This standout nature centre is one of the best places in T&T for a spot of birdwatching.

6 ESCAPISM AT GRANDE RIVIERE
See page 141
Close to swimmable rivers and rainforest hikes, this remote and unspoiled coastal village is a fabulous place escape the crowds any time of the year.

7 SPEYSIDE DIVING
See page 242
With intricate reefs patrolled by shoals of colourful fish, the waters offshore of Speyside are a delight.

8 TURTLE-WATCHING
See pages 137, 142 and 219
Visit Trinidad's Matura and Grand Riviere beaches and Turtle Beach on Tobago in season and you can watch leatherback turtles lay their eggs in the sand or see the hatchlings make their way to the sea.

9 TOBAGO'S BEACHES
See pages 214 and 233
From the emerald waters of Mount Irvine to the often-deserted Englishman's Bay, Tobago's beaches offer plenty of variety beyond the palm-trees-and-white-sand scene.

10 HUMMINGBIRD ENCOUNTERS
See page 127 and 219
Witness these magical little birds up close as they flit around the sugar-water feeders at Trinidad's Yerettê and Tobago's Adventure Farm.

9

11 TRINIDAD'S EAST COAST
See page 164

Enjoy some Trini-style beach time, drive through the coconut groves of the Cocal or explore the fantastically diverse forests and wetlands of Nariva Swamp.

12 CRUISING ALONG TOBAGO'S COAST
See page 202

A boat ride along the island's Caribbean coast provides a spectacularly different perspective on Tobago's scenery.

13 PORT OF SPAIN NIGHTLIFE
See page 88

From jumping up at an outdoor fete to dancing the night away at a club or bar, there are few reasons to go to bed early in the nation's capital.

14 PANYARDS
See page 74

Take a pre-Carnival tour of Port of Spain's panyards to hear practice sessions for the coveted Panorama prize; most bands practise throughout the year, too.

15 TRINBAGO CUISINE
See page 27, 84, 85 and 209

From delicious doubles from a Port of Spain street cart (pictured) and curry crab and dumpling at Store Bay to gourmet Creole dishes at *Chaud*, T&Ts rich potpourri of influences has created a delicious and unique cuisine.

13

14

15

Itineraries

The itineraries here are designed to give you a taste of Trinidad and Tobago's many and varied attractions. Our week-long tours take in beaches, birdwatching, nature and culture, ticking off the islands' highlights as well as a few lesser-known sights. We've also mapped out an adrenaline-fuelled itinerary, featuring surfing, mountain biking and many other exhilarating experiences across both islands.

A WEEK IN TRINIDAD

❶ Port of Spain From Independence Square, walk up bustling Frederick Street to the National Museum. After lunch at *Buzo Osteria*, stroll around the Savannah to the Botanical Gardens, and sample Ariapita Avenue's restaurants and bars after dark. See page 52

❷ North coast beaches Enjoy sun, sea and surf at Maracas, or take to the calmer waters of Las Cuevas. Recharge with a slap-up dinner at *Buzo Osteria Italiana*. See pages 113, 115 and 87

❸ West coast Make an early start to see the Indian temples at Carapichaima, head south to walk on the weird and wonderful Pitch Lake, and then watch scarlet ibis roost at Caroni. See pages 156, 181 and 152

❹ Yerettê and Mount St Benedict Spend the morning surrounded by dazzling hummingbirds at Yerettê, then check into *Pax Guest House* at Mount St Benedict for old-world charm and fantastic views. See pages 127 and 129

❺ Asa Wright Nature Centre Head into the Northern Range for easy-access birdwatching, swimming in a natural pool and some lovely walks through the forest. See page 124

❻ Northeast Trinidad Drive around Trinidad's eastern tip and walk to Rio Seco waterfall for a swim. Drive on to Grande Riviere via Toco and Galera Point, and spend the night in a beachside hotel. See page 135

❼ East coast Take a scenic drive along the east coast, past sweeping Mayaro and Manzanilla beaches and the Cocal palm grove, and explore the amazing Nariva Swamp. See page 164

A WEEK IN TOBAGO

❶ Crown Point Kick off your holiday at Pigeon Point, enjoying lunch and cocktails right on the sand. End the day with a gourmet dinner at *Kariwak Village*. See pages 202 and 208

❷ Mount Irvine After a morning on the beach, get active with a round of golf or a horse ride through the sea at nearby Buccoo. See pages 214 and 203

❸ Castara Take the Northside Road through the precipitous village of Moriah and view the unravelling coastline from Mount Dillon. Check in to a Castara guesthouse and have sunset cocktails and dinner at *Castara Retreats* hotel. See page 229

❹ Rainforest and Englishman's Bay Take a guided walk into the Tobago Forest Reserve, then spread your towel under a coconut palm. See pages 234 and 233

❺ Scarborough and the windward coast Check out fabulous views from Fort King George, have lunch at the *Blue Crab*, then sample chocolate at Tobago Windward Chocolate Company and swim at Argyle Waterfall. See pages 223, 227 and 236

⑥ Speyside Hop on a glass-bottom boat to see (and snorkel among) pristine reefs and walk on Little Tobago. After lunch at *Jemma's Seaview Kitchen*, take in the view at Flagstaff Hill en route to a Charlotteville guesthouse. See pages 240 and 244

⑦ Charlotteville Spend the morning exploring the village, then cool off with a swim at Pirate's Bay after a seafood lunch at *Suckhole*. See page 244

ADRENALINE TOUR

① Chaguaramas Try your hand at wake-boarding in the Gulf of Paria, then swing through the treetops at the Tucker Valley zip line. Return to the capital for a workout on the dancefloor. See pages 79 and 100

② Blanchisseuse–Matelot bench trail Hike this age-old trail along undeveloped coastline, and take a swim at the gorgeous beach and waterfall at Paria before hopping in a boat back to Blanchisseuse and checking into a seaside guesthouse. See page 118

③ Guanapo Gorge hike Follow the road through the rainforest to walk and swim through the cool confines of this narrow gorge of 30m-high rocks, then hole up at *Pax Guest House*. See page 134

④ El Tucuche From the Maracas–St Joseph Valley, trek through mist-drenched elfin and montane forest to the top of Trinidad's second-highest mountain, or rise to the challenge of mountain biking halfway to the summit. See page 128

⑤ Tobago SUP Hop over to Tobago to see the bioluminescence at Bon Accord Lagoon by night, or take a whole day to paddle along the coast to little-visited beaches and rivers. See page 205

⑥ Surfing at Mount Irvine Check out the breaks at the "Office", the undisputed capital of T&T's surf scene: take a lesson or ride the waves with the locals. See page 214

⑦ Northeast Tobago drift diving Head east to fly like a bird past walls of coral at Sisters Rocks, or let the currents take you through Charlotteville's famous "London Bridge". See page 242

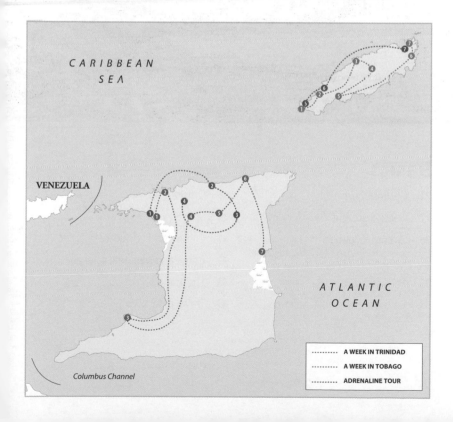

CARIBBEAN
SEA

VENEZUELA

ATLANTIC
OCEAN

Columbus Channel

········· A WEEK IN TRINIDAD

········· A WEEK IN TOBAGO

········· ADRENALINE TOUR

PULLING IN THE SEINES, CASTARA

Basics

Getting there

Though there are far fewer budget flights to Trinidad and Tobago than more touristed Caribbean islands, there are regular international services from the UK, US and Canada, as well as South and Central America and the rest of the Caribbean. And because Trinidad and Tobago are linked by inexpensive twenty-minute domestic services (see page 25), it's worth researching flights to both islands, even if you only plan on spending time on one of them.

If you're visiting just Tobago, booking a **package** might be your best option. There are many specialist companies (see page 22) who can arrange these, often at a lower rate than you'd get booking flight and accommodation independently; for packages and flight-only deals, it's also well worth searching via sites such as 🖥expedia.co.uk, 🖥skyscanner.net, 🖥kayak.co.uk or 🖥momondo.co.uk. As Trinidad is less geared toward tourists, there are fewer deals available beyond birdwatching or Carnival packages, though Tobago-oriented companies sometimes give the option for a few days in Trinidad.

Fares to both islands **peak** during the winter high season (Dec–March), and also rise during the (northern hemisphere) summer school holidays; flights to Trinidad are also at a premium before and after the pre-Lenten Carnival (see page 34).

Flights from the UK and Ireland

To Trinidad, British Airways (🖥britishairways.com) offer five weekly flights from Gatwick (Mon, Tues, Thurs, Fri & Sun, all with a 1hr stopoff in St Lucia). You might also get a good deal by searching for flights to the US (see below), and getting a connecting flight to Trinidad from there. **To Tobago**, British Airways fly twice weekly from Gatwick (Mon & Fri; stopoff in Antigua), while Virgin (🖥virgin-atlantic.com) flights vary seasonally (Sun in summer, Tues & Sat in winter; stopoff in St Lucia). Thomas Cook (🖥thomascook.

com) also fly once a week (Sun) from Manchester to Tobago.

Virgin and BA **fares** to both islands start at around £650 year-round, but hike up to £900–1400-plus during school holidays, Christmas and Carnival season. Thomas Cook are usually a little cheaper, with fares starting at the £500 mark.

There are no flights to T&T **from Ireland**. The best option is to fly to London or the US and then take a direct flight from there.

Flights from the US and Canada

To Trinidad, national carrier Caribbean Airlines (🖥caribbean-airlines.com) offers regular flights from Miami, New York, Toronto, Orlando and Fort Lauderdale; American Airlines (🖥aa.com) operate daily nonstop flights from Miami; and United (🖥united.com) fly daily from Houston. Budget carrier Jet Blue (🖥jetblue.com) also offers daily flights from New York (Newark) and Fort Lauderdale, and during the winter season, West Jet (🖥westjet.com) offer five flights a week from Toronto. **To Tobago**, Caribbean Airlines fly direct from New York (JFK) once a week.

High-season **fares** from Miami average around US$600; low-season fares are around US$100 less. Add around US$100 if you're connecting from other US cities or flying direct from Atlanta. From Canada, you'll pay around Can$700 in low season, Can$1100 in high season.

Flights from the Caribbean and Central/South America

It is possible to visit T&T in conjunction with a trip to another Caribbean island or the South/Central American mainland. Liat (🖥liat.com) and Caribbean Airlines offer a wide range of **inter-island flights**. **To Trinidad**, Caribbean Airlines operate three flights weekly **from Venezuela** and daily **from Guyana**; LIAT also fly (via Barbados) from Guyana daily. **From Suriname**, Caribbean Airlines has weekly flights, while Suriname Airways (🖥flyslm.com) flies twice weekly.

A BETTER KIND OF TRAVEL

At Rough Guides we are passionately committed to travel. We believe it helps us understand the world we live in and the people we share it with – and of course tourism is vital to many developing economies. But the scale of modern tourism has also damaged some places irreparably, and climate change is accelerated by most forms of transport, especially flying. All Rough Guides' flights are carbon-offset.

Flights from Australia and New Zealand

The Caribbean is no bargain destination from **Australia** or **New Zealand**. There are no direct flights to Trinidad and Tobago, so you'll have to fly to one of the main US gateway airports, and pick up onward connections from there. Air New Zealand (Ⓦairnewzealand.com) and Qantas (Ⓦqantas.com.au) have regular services from major cities in Australia and New Zealand to Los Angeles, with connecting flights to New York or Miami on American Airlines or United: return **fares** start at around Aus$1700 or NZ$2000.

AGENTS AND OPERATORS ABROAD

Caradonna US ☎ 1800 330 6611, Ⓦ caradonna.com. Diving and hiking packages to Tobago.

Caribbean Journey US ☎ 1866 828 5424, Ⓦ caribbeanjourney.com. Tailor-made hotel and villa holidays on Tobago.

Caribtours UK ☎ 020 3627 1785, Ⓦ caribtours.co.uk. Specialist operator offering luxurious packages to both Trinidad and Tobago.

CV Villas UK ☎ 020 3811 1894, Ⓦ cvvillas.com. Villa holidays in Tobago.

Geodyssey UK ☎ 020 7281 7788, Ⓦ geodyssey.co.uk. Specialist in T&T and Venezuela, offering excellent tours that take in the cultural and natural highlights of both Trinidad and Tobago, from Carnival or Caroni Swamp to birding in Speyside.

Just Tobago UK ☎ 01373 814 234, Ⓦ www.justtobago.co.uk. Specialist company offering flexible packages to Tobago offering a range of prices and themes, with villa, apartment and hotel accommodation.

Kuoni Worldwide UK ☎ 0800 140 4081, Ⓦ kuoni.co.uk. Package holidays and good family deals to Tobago.

MotMot Travel UK ☎ 01327 359 622, Ⓦ motmottravel.com. Excellent tour operator, with knowledgeable staff and some great tours on both islands, from nature-based trips to birdwatching and diving.

Newmont Travel UK ☎ 020 8920 1155, Ⓦ newmont.co.uk. Caribbean flight specialist offering the best deals out of the UK, as well as accommodation packages.

North South Travel UK ☎ 01245 608 291, Ⓦ northsouthtravel.co.uk. Friendly, competitive travel agency, offering discounted fares worldwide. Profits are used to support projects in the developing world, especially the promotion of sustainable tourism.

Regaldive UK ☎ 01353 659 999, Ⓦ regal-diving.co.uk. Specializes in diving packages to Tobago, including eco-friendly packages, as well as live-aboards.

STA Travel UK ☎ 0333 321 0099, US ☎ 1800 781 4040, Australia ☎ 134 782, New Zealand ☎ 0800 474 400, South Africa ☎ 0861 781 781; Ⓦ statravel.co.uk. Worldwide specialists in independent travel; also student IDs, travel insurance, car rental, rail passes, and more. Good discounts for students and under-26s.

Travel CUTS Canada ☎ 1800 667 2887, Ⓦ travelcuts.com. Youth and student travel firm.

USIT Ireland ☎ 01 602 1906, Australia ☎ 1800 092 499; Ⓦ usit.ie. Ireland's main student and youth travel specialist.

Wildside Nature Tours US ☎ 1888 875 9453, Ⓦ wildsidenaturetours.com. Birding tours of Trinidad and Tobago, as well as a bird/wildlife photography workshop trip led by renowned photographer Roger Neckles.

Wildwings UK ☎ 0117 965 8333, Ⓦ wildwings.co.uk. Excellent birdwatching and eco-tour packages in both Trinidad and Tobago.

Visas and entry requirements

Citizens of the UK, EU countries (as well as Switzerland and Norway), the US and Canada do not require a **visa** for stays of less than three months. Nationals of Australia, New Zealand and South Africa need visas before entering the country. You can apply through the offices listed below or have your travel agent obtain one on your behalf. On arrival, you will have to provide an **address** where you will be staying (hotels and guesthouses are acceptable; take any address from the Guide text if you're not yet sure), and, occasionally, proof that you have a return or onward ticket. Your passport must be valid for six months beyond the period of your proposed visit.

Visa extensions (Ⓦimmigration.gov.tt) are usually for three months, but this depends on your reasons for wanting to stay; extensions are issued by Immigration Offices: 67 Frederick St, Port of Spain (☎625 3571); or Agricola Building, Plymouth Rd, Scarborough (☎635 0430). You must first make an appointment; a one-week wait is typical. Bring your passport and, if you have one, a return ticket, as well as the TT$200 visa fee and TT$100 extension fee.

T&T EMBASSIES AND HIGH COMMISSIONS

Canada High Commission, First Ave, Ottawa, Ontario K1S 2G6 ☎ 613 232 2418, Ⓦ foreign.gov.tt/hcottawa.

UK High Commission, 42 Belgrave Square, London SW1X 8TNT ☎ 020 7245 9351, Ⓦ foreign.gov.tt/hclondon.

US Embassy, 1708 Massachusetts Ave, NW, Washington, DC 20036-1975 ☎ 202 467 6490, Ⓦ foreign.gov.tt/embwashington.

Getting around

T&T's public transportation system can initially seem chaotic and unpredictable, but once you've got the hang of it, getting around these two compact islands is relatively straightforward – if somewhat longwinded if you're using buses or maxi taxis.

Public transport – buses, maxi taxis and route taxis – serves most places covered in the Guide, though a few of the more rural areas have only infrequent services. In populated areas, buses and maxi/route taxis run from around 6am until late evening, but outside commuter hours the waits can be long and having **your own car** is infinitely more convenient. **Private taxis** are always available. Avoid travelling at peak hours (6–8am & 3–6pm), when urban roads are clogged with heavy traffic and maxis and taxis heave with people.

Note also that many of the islands' tour operators (see page 38) offer **airport transfers** and general transportation, such as from Port of Spain to Grande Riviere or Crown Point to Castara and Charlotteville.

By bus and maxi taxi

Bus services in Trinidad and Tobago are divided between large public buses, run by the Public Transport Service Corporation (PTSC; ⦿ ptsc.co.tt) and private services – small minibuses called **maxi taxis**. All public buses and most maxi taxis in **Trinidad** leave from and terminate at City Gate – sometimes referred to as South Quay in official literature – in Port of Spain, the country's main transportation hub; there are also smaller bus depots in San Fernando, Chaguanas, Point Fortin and Sangre Grande. Maxi and bus services between Port of Spain and Arima are especially quick due to the Priority Bus Route, which runs along the course of the old railway line through Trinidad's east–west corridor, and there are now deluxe non-stop bus services running between Port of Spain and both San Fernando and Sangre Grande. In **Tobago**, buses cover the entire island, originating at the Sangster Hill Road terminal, off Milford Road in Scarborough.

Buses and maxis are viable transport options for visitors, and riding in a maxi can often be an entertaining experience as well as a chance to chat to locals; note that when entering, it's normal to greet other passengers with a "good morning" or a "good afternoon". It's also fun to try and spot the most unusual of the "names" splashed over the top of the windscreen – popular standards include the likes of "Problem Child" or "Wotless", perhaps in honour of the notoriously cavalier driving habits of their owners.

By bus

All **public buses** in Trinidad in Trinidad are air-conditioned and reasonably comfortable. **Bus stops** are often small concrete shelters on the side of the road, or sometimes just a sign on a telephone pole. **Tickets** must be bought in advance, either from the main City Gate terminus in Port of Spain, Scarborough's Sangster Hill Road bus terminal or from small general stores around the country – you cannot simply board a bus and buy your fare. Weekly and monthly travel cards are available. **Fares** run from TT$2.50 to TT$8, and services operate from 4.30am to around 9pm. **Bus information** can be obtained online, in person at the bus terminals, or by ringing ⦿623 2341 (Trinidad) and ⦿639 2293 (Tobago).

By maxi taxi

Maxi taxis carry anything from ten to thirty people, and are privately owned but run according to set routes and fares; each area has a different colour-coded stripe, or band. In Trinidad, **yellow-band** vehicles work from in and around Port of Spain to Diego Martin and the western tip; **red bands** in the east; **green bands** in the centre and south; **black bands** in and around Princes Town; and **brown bands** from San Fernando to the southwest. **Blue-band** maxis operate in Tobago, where there is only one set route, from Scarborough to Charlotteville (the rest are for schoolchildren and private tourist charters). Maxis adhere to no fixed timetable, though services are at their most frequent from 6am to 10am, and 3pm to 8pm; after 8pm you can expect a longer wait. Some maxis run intermittently through the night, especially along the east–west corridor and in the major towns. Importantly, maxis can be hailed anywhere along their route – just stick out your hand and if they have space they will pick you up – but it's often quicker to go to a main stand; since maxis wait until they are full before leaving, they may not have free seats until they reach their destination. Once aboard, they will let you off at any point; press the buzzers by the windows to stop the bus. **Fares** range between TT$3 and TT$10; ask fellow passengers if you're not sure, or just give the driver a TT$10/20 note and wait for your change.

By route taxi and private taxi

Route taxis are privately owned cars operating as shared taxis on set routes and depart from stands in all sizeable towns. They hold four to five passengers in addition to the driver and, apart from their H number plates, are indistinguishable from private cars (which have P number plates – although note that some P-licensed cars also operate as route taxis; these are best avoided, as you could be getting into anyone's car). Route taxis don't leave their stand until they're full, but are usually quicker (and slightly more expensive) than maxis as they stop less frequently.

To stop a taxi en route, hail it with a wave of your hand. There is a widely accepted code of hand signals among locals catching taxis; point left or right to indicate which direction you want to take at the next major turn-off. As with maxis, when entering the car, it's normal to greet other passengers. To stop the taxi, just tell your driver you want to get out as you approach your destination. If you're not sure what you should be paying, just hand over a TT$20 note and wait for change; you're unlikely to be overcharged.

Private taxis are unmetered, so a price must be agreed beforehand, and they easily work out just as expensive as a cab in Britain or the US. As with route taxis, vehicles have an H number plate. It is often possible – and more economical – however, to bargain with a route taxi driver to drop you where you want. Kalloos (☎622 9073) offers a 24-hour, island-wide service in Trinidad; **Uber** also arrived in Trinidad in 2017, with the majority of drivers based in Port of Spain and San Fernando; visit ⓦ uber.com/cities for up-to-date coverage and fare estimates. In Tobago, call the Tobago Taxi Co-Op (☎639 2707); drivers also hang out at the airport. Hotels and guesthouses in both islands will be able to recommend a driver.

By car

Driving in T&T requires **patience** and constant **alertness**: you simply cannot take your eyes off the road for one moment, and the packed one-way streets of downtown Port of Spain can seem a nightmare to the unfamiliar. Tobago is easier for drivers, with quieter roads and far less potential for getting lost. Though Trinbagonian drivers are generally courteous, often stopping to let other drivers pull out or offering parking advice, they also habitually stop at short notice, turn without indicating and will happily block traffic to buy doubles or chat with a friend. The best thing to do is accept it; beeping your horn out of irritation will only get you withering stares; **horns** are more frequently used as a thank-you gesture for a courtesy or indication of an intention to overtake. Expect maxis/taxis to pull over at any moment, and always drive defensively. Note also that many local drivers keep full-beam headlights on all the time after dark; keep your eyes to the left verge to avoid being dazzled. **Hand signals** are frequently used: an up-and-down movement indicates that a driver is about to stop (or an

instruction for others to stop due to a hazard ahead); if pulling out into traffic, some still stick out an arm to indicate their intent. Whatever the motivation, slow down.

Trinidad has two **highways** (the Churchill Roosevelt or CRH, between Port of Spain and Arima; and the Uriah Butler/Solomon Hochoy Highway between Grand Bazaar on the CRH and San Fernando), while Tobago's slow Claude Noel Highway runs between Scarborough and Lowlands. Trinidad's highways can feel hair-raising, mostly thanks to high-speed lane-change weaving which looks as though it ought to cause a multiple pile-up (sadly, it often does); left-hand overtaking is also commonplace. Always take extra care, and slow right down in the tropical rains.

Signage is fairly good on both islands. Distances and speed limits are in kilometres, and in Trinidad, most of the tourist sites are marked with brown signs indicating where to turn off from the highways/minor roads. The Waze app is useful for navigation and monitoring the traffic situation, though you'll of course need mobile data to use it.

Traffic lights can be confusing: as well as the usual red/amber/green sequence, you'll see flashing red or yellow lights at junctions; both mean "proceed with caution"; yellow means it's primarily your right of way, red that it's someone else's.

Driving is the **left**, and **seat belts** are compulsory. T&T's drink-driving laws have been tightened up in recent years, though attitudes remain somewhat laidback. The law also demands that drivers be properly attired; men can be charged for driving without a top on ("bareback"), so always keep a T-shirt handy. In Trinidad, the (almost universally ignored) **speed limit** is 100kmph on the Churchill Roosevelt/Uriah Butler highways, 80kmph on all other highways and 50kmph on main roads in built-up areas. Tobago's speed limit is 50kmph, even on the Claude Noel Highway.

A valid international **driving licence** or one issued in the US, Canada, UK, Germany or the Bahamas is required for driving both cars and motorcycles for up to ninety days.

Car rental

All companies require you to be 25 or over and hold a valid driving licence; most ask for a deposit guaranteed by a credit card imprint. You'll be offered a collision damage waiver at extra cost (usually US$5–15/day); without one, you will be liable for damage, but note that you may well be able to arrange CDW cover through your home insurance before you arrive in T&T, which often works out to be much cheaper. Rental prices vary, so shop around; they tend to start at around US$30 per day for the smallest vehicle, inclusive of third-party insurance and unlimited mileage. Check tyres (including the spare) before you drive away, and make sure you're present when existing scratches and bumps are noted; a video record on your phone as you do this is recommended.

CAR RENTAL FIRMS

Econo-Car Trinidad and Tobago ⓦ econocarrentalstt.com/trinidad-car-rentals.html
Europcar Trinidad ⓦ europcar.co.tt
Hertz Trinidad ⓦ hertz.com
Kalloos Trinidad ⓦ kalloos.com
Sheppy's Tobago ⓦ tobagocarrental.com
Sherman's Tobago ⓦ shermansrental.com
Sixt Tobago ⓦ sixt.com
Thrifty Trinidad and Tobago ⓦ thrifty.com

Motorcycle and bicycle rental

Renting a **motorcycle** isn't advisable in Trinidad due to the volume of traffic and unpredictable driving, but a moped or larger bike can be a good way of getting around Tobago's quieter roads; TTBikes (⊕ 338 2377, ⓦ ttbks.com) or Sheppy's (⊕ 639 1543, ⓦ tobagocarrental.com) are reliable outlets. You can rent **bicycles** on both islands, though for the same reason they're not great for getting around Trinidad. In Tobago, try Easy Goers on Airport Rd in Crown Point (⊕ 681 8025 or ⊕ 787 0685, ⓦ easygoersbikes.com). Tour companies on both islands (see pages 38 and page 202) offer guided cycling tours.

By water taxi

Trinidad's **water taxis** (⊕ 624 5137, ⓦ nidco.co.tt) save time and stress on the roads between Port of Spain and San Fernando (45min; TT$15), and are a quick, easy way and fun way to travel (see pages 78 and 178)

Travelling between Trinidad and Tobago

There are two options available if you wish to **travel between the islands**: the plane, quick and relatively inexpensive; and the ferry, a lot cheaper, but slower and a rough ride that's notorious for seasickness. Going by air is a far more pleasant experience, though it does mean that you have to get to and from Piarco airport, which can be a lengthy journey at rush hour; the ferry, by compar-

ison, shuttles between central Port of Spain and Scarborough.

By ferry

T&T's inter-island ferry service has long been plagued by problems, and at the time of writing only one **catamaran**, the *T&T Express*, was in operation; a newly purchased second vessel is due to be put into service sometime in 2018. Journey time between the islands is 4–5 hours.

In Trinidad, ferries arrive and depart from the main **terminal** opposite the Twin Towers on Wrightson Road in Port of Spain; in Tobago, the terminal is on Milford Road in central Scarborough. Sailing **schedules** are available on the Inter-Island Ferry Service website, ⓦ https://ttitferry.com. Bear in mind that the journey can be rough due to strong currents in the Bocas (less so from Tobago to Trinidad); take seasickness tablets, and sit in the middle of the boat rather than the back or the front. Seasoned ferry passengers travel with a sheet or wrap to cover the sometimes less-than-clean seats.

One-way **tickets** are bookable online and cost TT$50; standard car prices are TT$150 one-way (though few rental outfits will let you take their cars on the ferry). For same-day tickets only, the Port of Spain and Scarborough terminal ticket offices are open Monday to Thursday 7.15am to 3pm, 4.15 to 6pm & 7 to 10.30pm, Friday 7.15am to 3pm; be prepared to join the queue at least three hours before the boat leaves. Try to secure tickets as far in advance as possible, particularly during busy periods like Carnival and Easter. For further information, call ⊕ 625 4906 in Trinidad, ⊕ 639 2416 in Tobago.

By plane

National carrier **Caribbean Airlines** (⊕ 625 7200, ⓦ caribbean-airlines.com) makes the twenty-minute **flight** between Trinidad and Tobago up to twenty times a day each way, though bear in mind that services are often subject to delays. **Tickets** cost US$24 one-way and US$48 return; you can book and pay for tickets online, or visit a ticket office in person. The latter are at Piarco Airport (daily 4.15am–7pm), and at Nicholas Tower, Independence Square, Port of Spain (Mon–Fri 8am–4pm, Sat 8am–noon); in Tobago, there's an office opposite departures in Crown Point Airport (daily 5.45am–9.45pm; ⊕ 660 7200). Note that all tickets are flexible: once you've paid, you can change the date and time of your flight online, by phone or at ticket offices.

Accommodation

Though Trinidad and Tobago aren't the most tourist-oriented islands in the Caribbean, there's no shortage of places to stay. Tobago has luxury resorts, cosy guesthouses and private villas, with the largest concentration in the Crown Point area. In Trinidad, there is plenty of accommodation in Port of Spain as well as guesthouses and hotels near most of the better beaches along the north coast. Trinidad's centre and south is less promising; with the exception of Mayaro Bay in the southeast, most options are expensive and geared towards oil workers and business travellers. There are no campsites in T&T, though locals do camp on Trinidad's beaches at holiday times.

It's advisable to **book ahead** during the busy times of Carnival (see page 34) – and Easter on Tobago – but at other times you should have no problem finding suitable accommodation once you've arrived. Bear in mind too that while online accommodation sites such as ⓦbooking.com purport to offer discounted rates, their high surcharges mean that many small properties bump up their base rate for the site, and you'll often get a cheaper stay by cutting out the brokers and **booking directly**.

Accommodation in T&T is **cheaper** than you might expect for the Caribbean, ranging from as little as US$20 (£15) per night in a guesthouse for a bed in a dorm with a fan to US$70–90 (£53–68) for an air-conditioned private room with cable TV, and US$200/£150-plus for the top-notch places. There are a couple of **hidden extras** to watch out for: room tax (ten percent) and service charge (ten percent) are added to quoted room rates at more expensive hotels, though not at guesthouses. It's worth checking whether these charges have been included each time you book. Finally, it's worth knowing that in both islands, almost all accommodation options will have **wi-fi** (denoted with 🛜 in

our accommodation listings), though its reach can be patchy in rural areas.

Hotels

Most of T&T's resort-type **hotels** – and eco-hotels and holistic retreats – cluster around Tobago's southwestern beaches; there are a couple of expansive, landscaped enclaves with private beaches, but most places are eight- to-twelve-room properties, often with a pool, offering rooms and self-contained apartments that tend to feature pastel decor and loud bedspreads. Thankfully, the **all-inclusive** trend that's swept through the rest of the Caribbean hasn't caught on here, and most people stay on a room- or breakfast-only basis at the few places that do offer all-inclusive. Most of Trinidad's smarter hotels cater largely to business travellers, so you won't find much in the way of organized entertainment or a holiday atmosphere – something that you'll find in abundance in Tobago.

Note that many hotels in Tobago offer **free airport pick-ups**.

Guesthouses and Airbnb

T&T's myriad small **guesthouses** are usually friendly, good-value options. Being anything from a couple of rooms tacked on to a private home or a smoothly run nine-room establishment, they generally have fewer facilities than at hotels; many don't have a pool, and you might get a fan instead of air conditioning. There may also be a shared bathroom and homelier decor, though you'll also get a more of a personal touch. Owners are often open to a bit of bargaining. Many guesthouse (and even hotel) rooms include a **kitchen** or kitchenette (the latter consisting of a hot plate, fridge and sometimes a microwave) for roughly the same rate as a standard room. Some guesthouses also have one or two rooms equipped with bunk beds that serve as **dorms**: worth seeking out if you're on a budget.

Many of T&T's guesthouses, alongside a host of private homes, advertise their rooms on **Airbnb**, which lists options throughout both islands. Many are of a very high standard and obviously come with the advantage of the host's local knowledge and expertise on hand. You'll find a similar variety of places, as well as holiday homes and villas, on VRBO (ⓦvrbo.com).

Villas, beach houses and long-term rentals

Most **holiday villas** rented to tourists are in Tobago and tend to have full staff and facilities such as a

---

TOP 5 PLACES TO STAY

Castara Retreats, Castara, Tobago. See page 231
Man-O-War Bay Cottages, Charlotteville, Tobago. See page 246
Mt Plaisir Estate, Grande Riviere, Trinidad. See page 143
Plantation Beach Villas, Stonehaven Bay, Tobago. See page 216
Top O' Tobago, Arnos Vale, Tobago. See page 220

ACCOMMODATION PRICES

Rates quoted in this guide are for a double room with tax and service charges (where applied) taken into account. Rates at most places **in Trinidad** change only at Carnival time – in Port of Spain, for example, they can jump by anywhere from 20 to over 100 percent, depending on the establishment. At other times, business-oriented hotels often charge more in the week than at weekends. **In Tobago**, most places have two rates; one for the summer low season (mid-April to mid-Dec) and another for the winter high season (mid-Dec to mid-April). For accommodation in Tobago, we have used the **high-season** rate, and for Trinidad the standard non-Carnival rate.

Many local hoteliers are open to **bargaining**, however, particularly in the shoulder seasons (mid-April to July and Sept to mid-Dec), or if you plan to stay for more than two or three nights. Trinbagonians always get rooms at a lower rate; this is normal practice, ensuring that resorts get a mix of local people and tourists.

Many hotels and guesthouses quote rates in **US currency**, while others use TT$; we have quoted prices in US$ throughout for ease of comparison. Finally, note that while most places will serve **breakfast**, it isn't always included in room rates; we've noted where it is within the Guide.

kitchen and pool. These options can actually be quite cost-effective if you're travelling in a group; plan on paying US$200 per night for the most basic villa to as much as US$1500 per night for something in the lap of luxury – those around the Mount Irvine golf course, for example. Most are privately owned but represented by websites or agencies such as ⓦvrbo.com; in Tobago, Island Investments are a good resource (☎639 0929, ⓦislreal.com).

In Trinidad, **beach houses** are available in areas such as Mayaro and the Toco coast – generally geared to locals on a weekend break (you may have to bring your own bed linen and so on), though you can get some real bargains by scanning the local papers; many are also listed on Airbnb. If you're planning to stay in Trinidad for a month or more, consider a furnished apartment, again best found via the newspaper classified ads.

Food and drink

A unique and addictive blend of African, Indian, Chinese, European and Latin American influences, the fantastic cuisine of Trinidad and Tobago is a highlight of any visit to the islands. It's hard to overemphasize the centrality of food to local culture; a true Trinbagonian would never lime (the local word for socializing) without a full stomach. Many leisure activities – beach days, river limes – revolve around the preparation and consumption of food and drink, and it's rare to visit a private home without being offered something to eat.

Even in T&T's larger hotels and international-style restaurants, Trinbagonian cuisine hasn't been dumbed down for visitors, and you're likely to be offered dishes from the vast array of **local food**. Due to the islands' diverse heritage, "local" can mean anything from **Indian** curry and roti to **Creole** coocoo and oil down (see page 29) or **Spanish and South American**-style **pastelles** (cornmeal patties filled with ground meat or fish, olives and raisins, steamed in a banana leaf and traditionally eaten at Christmas time).

Cooks in T&T have a far lighter hand with hot pepper than you might expect, preferring the delicate flavours of fresh herbs such as chives (aka spring/green onions), thyme and the ubiquitous coriander-like **chadon beni**. Heat is usually added later at the table, in liberal dashes of fiery **hot-pepper sauce**. If you don't like things too hot, remember to say so when buying takeaway, or your meal may be automatically smothered with pepper sauce. If you like things just a little spicy, ask for "slight pepper".

Eating out

There's a burgeoning **restaurant culture** in **Trinidad**'s urban areas, with Port of Spain and San Fernando in particular replete with everything from casual diners to world-class gourmet establishments, with some stylish places to enjoy Indian, Creole, Chinese and international cuisine. You'll also find a huge lunchtime variety in Trinidad's larger shopping malls, where **food courts** offer delicious curries, roti, Chinese staples, macaroni pie and lentil peas, potato or green-fig salad, Creole-style fish, chicken and the ubiqui-

TOP 5 STREET SNACKS

Corn soup Fortifying and delicious, great after a night out.

Doubles Delectable chickpea delights, best at breakfast time or post-party.

Gyros Wraps of meat, fish or falafel are ubiquitous to the street-food scene.

Pholouri Addictive doughballs with a spicy dipping sauce.

Pies Filled with potato, beef or fish, and dressed with Trini chutney.

tous pelau alongside burgers, grilled meats and sandwiches.

In **Tobago**, Crown Point has a decent spread of restaurants, from Italian pizza joints to seafood, Creole cooking, curry and roti. Away from the southwest, most restaurants are small-scale affairs serving strictly seafood and Creole cuisine, though hotels do hold some more upmarket places to eat. If you're here in the low season (mid-April to mid-Dec), bear in mind that many kitchens close at around 9pm, or even open up for bookings only, especially for dinner.

Breakfast

Breakfast is traditionally a hearty meal, designed to stand you in good stead for a hard day's work. Staples include spicy **fried fish**, **smoked herring** cooked up with onions and peppers (and sometimes egg), or **buljol**, a delectable blend of flaked saltfish with raw onions, tomatoes and sweet peppers, usually eaten with avocado and a couple of light, airy rolls called **hops**, or with **coconut bake**, a flat round bread made with grated coconut. It's ideally washed down with a steaming mug of sweet **chocolate tea**: fresh cocoa spiced up with nutmeg, cinnamon and bay leaf. The most popular breakfast on the go, however,

is **doubles** (see below): vendors do a brisk trade from as early as 5am.

Street food

T&T offers the best **street food** in the Caribbean, with everything from Indian specialities to gyro wraps, fried chicken and, of course, roti (see page 30); and as vendors are subject to stringent hygiene checks, eating on the hop doesn't constitute a health risk.

The most popular Indian snack is **doubles**, two pieces of soft, fried *bara* bread sandwiching a runny channa (chickpea) curry that's dressed with cucumber, pepper sauce and *kucheela* (green mango chutney), and usually sold in the mornings from streetside stalls noticeable for their long queues. **Aloo pies** (flattened fried doughballs filled with spiced potato and dressed with channa) are another popular snack, as are cheese, beef or fish versions. A little less substantial are the addictive **pholouri**, fried split-pea-flour doughballs served with tart and tasty tamarind curry sauce; **sahina**, a ground channa and dasheen leaf fritter; and **baiganee**, aubergine fried in a seasoned split-pea batter. Port of Spain's Savannah and most junctions along the Eastern Main Road are flanked by vendors selling small local **oysters**, served in a cup with a peppery, vinegary tomato sauce. Creole street delicacies include **corn soup**, a thick and satisfying split-pea broth with vegetables, chunks of sweetcorn and mini dumplings. **Accra** is a peppery saltfish fritter, while **bake and shark** (see below) is available far beyond its traditional home, Maracas Beach.

As well as chicken wings and burgers, bar snacks – known as **cutters** – served up in the nation's watering-holes – include **geera pork**, laced with hot

SHARK TALES

One of T&T's most popular street foods has long been **bake and shark**, slices of seasoned shark meat, served hot in a floaty fried bake, slathered in delicious chadon beni, tamarind and garlic sauces, and topped with fresh salad. The bake and shark capital of Trinidad is Maracas Beach, where scores of vendors compete with stalwart operator *Richard's* to draw in the queues. Delicious as shark and bake may be, however, you might want to **think twice** before tucking in. Sharks are increasingly rare in Caribbean waters, as they are globally. Trinidad and Tobago hold the dubious honour of being the sixth-largest exporter of shark fins in the world, while overfishing and the practice of landing juvenile sharks has pretty much decimated the **shark population** in local waters. Sharks play a vital role in the already fragile ecosystems of the Caribbean Sea, and the decrease in their numbers is having dire consequences for the region's reefs and its fish populations. For this reason, T&T's environmentalists advocate asking for more **sustainable fish** with your bake: flying fish, mahi-mahi, and carite are all sound choices.

TRINBAGO MENU READER

Blue food/provisions Tubers such as yam, dasheen, sweet potato, tannia and cassava, usually boiled and served as a carb side to a meal.
Bodi Local variety of string beans.
Bhaji Spinach.
Buljol Breakfast dish of saltfish, onion and sweet peppers.
Buss-up-shut Variety of roti skin, bashed up to look like a ripped shirt, and used to scoop up curry.
Calalloo Soupy side dish made with dasheen leaves, okra, pumpkin and coconut milk.
Choka Stewed tomatoes or aubergine, served with bready sada roti skins for breakfast.
Chow Unripe mango, pommecythere or other fruit, sliced and mixed with garlic, hot pepper and salt.
Doubles Streetside snack of fried breads with a dollop of curried chickpeas.
Melongene aubergine; also called baigan.
Pelau One-pot rice and chicken dish.
Pies Fried dough parcels filled with potato (aloo) beef and the like, split open and dressed with chutney.
Roti Wheat-based bread ("skins"), wrapped around curried seafood, meat and veg.

pepper and cumin: a unique local find. You might also find Lebanese-style **kibbies**, spiced meat of lentils wrapped in crushed bulgur wheat and fried.

Fast food

Though International fast-food chains – particularly *Subway, Pizza Hut, Burger King* and *McDonald's* – are part of the scenery, **local outlets** still manage to draw the crowds. chicken chains *Japs* and *Royal Castle* are the Trinbagonian *KFC* equivalent, using a tasty blend of spices and herbs in the batter and serving flying-fish sandwiches and veggie burgers. *Joe's Pizza* (Trinidad only) is another good option, and also delivers.

Creole cooking

In T&T culinary terms, **Creole** refers to African-style cooking which has picked up many other influences along the way. Often served with coleslaw and a slice of *zaboca* (avocado), **pelau** is a classically Creole chicken dish, utilizing the "browning down" tradition of caramelizing meat in burnt brown sugar. Rice, pigeon peas, pumpkin and seasoning are then added and cooked down in coconut milk to delicious effect.

Browning is also used to make traditional **Sunday lunch** of baked chicken, usually served with rice, stewed peas (aka pulses such as pigeon peas, lentils or kidney beans), with cheesy macaroni, potato pie or mayo-heavy pasta and green fig (green banana) salad. Another Creole staple is **callaloo**: chopped dasheen leaves cooked with okra, pumpkin, coconut milk and occasionally crab meat: a tasty,

pleasantly slimy mixture that's sometimes puréed as a soup. It's often served with **coocoo**, a kind of cornmeal polenta flavoured with okra. Two dishes not for the squeamish are the highly spiced local **black pudding**, and **souse**, pigs' or chickens' feet marinated in lime juice and peppers, and served cold. A classic accompaniment to main meals is **oil down**: vegetables (particularly breadfruit or cassava) stewed in coconut milk and flavoured with pig tail.

Despite the protests of environmentalists citing the decimation of local species, "**wild meat**" such as iguana, agouti, lappe, manicou, tattoo (armadillo) and quenk are considered a delicacy, and end up in the pot where available. A two-year hunting ban (2013–2015) saw numbers begin to stabilize, but wild meat was still caught and sold illicitly throughout the banned period, as it continues to be outside of the official Oct–Feb hunting season. Steer well clear.

Creole soups include **corn soup** (see page 28); **san coche**, a lentil soup cooked with pig tail; and **cow-heel** soup, thick with split peas and slowly cooked meat. **Fish broth** is a thin and delicious fortifying soup padded out with boiled green bananas and dumplings, while **pacro water** is similar but substitutes pacro (a mollusc known as chip-chip in Trinidad) for fish, and is touted as a strong aphrodisiac. Soups made from pumpkin, callaloo or pulses (red peas, black-eyed peas etc), often flavoured with pig tail, are also classic Creole creations.

Seafood is extremely popular and unfailingly good: from thick steaks of dense and delicious kingfish, grouper, tuna, cavalli, carite, barracuda and mahi-mahi/dolphin (the fish also known as

TOP 5 PLACES TO EAT

Caribbean Kitchen, Castara, Tobago.
See page 232
The Fish Pot, Pleasant Prospect, Tobago.
See page 217
Kariwak Village, Crown Point, Tobago.
See page 208
Sails, Chaguaramas, Trinidad. See page 102
Veni Mange, Port of Spain, Trinidad. See page 86

and mahi-mahi/dolphin (the fish also known as "dorado", not the mammal), to smaller fillets of "red fish": moonshine, snapper, parrotfish, flying fish and tilapia. (Note that of these, mahi-mahi, flying fish, carite and tilapia are the most sustainable choices.) Creole-style fish is usually fried or stewed in a coconut sauce or a peppery tomato-based marinade of onion, sweet and hot peppers and garlic, while **curry crab and dumpling** (small whole crabs cooked in a coconut curry sauce and served with boiled dumplings) is a marvellous Tobago speciality; you'll occasionally see curry conch, too. Local **lobster** is usually doused in a lemon, garlic or herb butter, or sometimes curried.

Indian cooking

Though the obvious staple of Indo-Trinidadian cooking is **curry**, the T&T version is somewhat different to that served in India, made with a blend of curry powder that's unique to the islands alongside fresh hot peppers. One of the most popular curry dishes is **duck**, which forms the centrepiece of the ever-popular Trini tradition of a "curry duck lime". Another mainstay is the vast array of **chutneys**, ranging from super-sweet to tart or peppery. Sweetly curried mango or *pomme cythere* on the seed, peppery **anchar** and **kucheela**, a hot mango pickle, are universally plopped into rotis, doubles and aloo pies.

Roti

The unofficial national dish, **roti** is a stretchy flat bread ("skin") used to wrap curried meat, vegetables or shrimp (and sometimes fish), a style of preparation that originated in Trinidad but is now popular across the Caribbean. There are several variations of **roti skins** including: basic **dhalpuri** (with seasoned split peas layered into the dough); **sada** (more like a flatbread, it's cooked on a hot griddle, usually in the early morning, and served with sauteed fresh tomato or aubergine "choka"); and **buss-up-shut**, a thin, tasty shredded skin that resembles a torn cloth shirt and is used to spoon up mouthfuls of curry sold in "snackboxes". **Paratha** or **dosti** is a plain roti skin.

Roti fillings range from curried chicken and beef to conch, goat and shrimp. Most vendors include meat on the bone – if you don't fancy sucking out the marrow as the locals do, ask for "boneless". Common **vegetarian** fillings (also used to complement the meats) are channa (curried chickpeas) and potato, sweet pumpkin, bodi (green beans) and *bhaji* (local spinach). In a restaurant, you may be offered a bowl of peppery lentil dhal as an accompaniment.

Good roti shops abound in the capital, but most locals agree that the best roti is to be found in the Indian heartlands of central or south Trinidad.

Fruit and vegetables

Local fruit and vegetables are plentiful and cheap, particularly if you buy from large markets. Some unusual local fruits include the super-sweet and extremely popular **sapodilla**, grey-brown and globular with gritty, sweet pulp, while cherry-sized **chenets** (also called guinep) have smooth green skin and a large seed with sweet, slightly acidic flesh. The knobbly green-and-brown skin of the **soursop** surrounds a delectable milky white pulp, often made into ice cream; its smaller cousin the **sweetsop** is less common. Look out also for the scrumptious **caimet**, a round, deep-purple fruit with seeds that form a star shape when the fruit is cut in half. The round **pomme cythere** (or "pomsitae"); golden apple/June plum in other islands) is sweet and yellow when ripe, but is often eaten green with salt and hot pepper as "**chow**" – as is the star-shaped **carambola** (five finger), pineapple and unripe mango.

Grown to huge proportions in T&T, **pawpaw** (papaya) is best eaten with a squeeze of fresh lime, while **bananas** (often called figs – look out for the tasty, tiny finger variety or young green bananas boiled and eaten as a savoury), **watermelon** and **pineapples** are all very common. **Citrus** is ever popular; you'll see lemons, limes and exceptionally sweet oranges and grapefruit, while **portugals** are easy-peel, thick-skinned mandarins.

Many varieties of **mango** grow profusely in rural areas, perfuming whole communities with the distinctive aroma of rotting fruit from April till August. The most popular (and expensive) type is the rosy, medium-sized Julie, while the long stringy mango is best avoided unless you have dental floss handy.

The most frequent vegetables seen on the Creole dinner plate are boiled **root vegetables** (known as **blue food** or **ground provisions**) such as yam as well as slightly denser tannia; chewy, purple-tinted dasheen; and softer, white-coloured eddoe and cassava; sweet potatoes; and boiled ripe **plantain**, the latter a larger, denser member of the banana family. Deliciously sweet when ripe, it's also fried and made into crisps. Dasheen leaves are cooked up with okra to make callaloo (see page 29). You'll also see aubergine (locally called melongene or baigan), **christophenes** – pear-shaped and light green with a bland, watery taste similar to marrow – green **bodi** string beans and **breadfruit**, which is green and thick-skinned with clothy white flesh that can be baked, boiled or fried.

Thanks to the **Indian influence**, pulses (referred to as peas) are widely used: look out for of split pea dhal; green lentils, split peas or pigeon peas cooked with pumpkin and coconut; and chickpeas (channa) mixed with potato and curried.

Desserts and sweets

Though there are plenty of fantastic local puddings, from nutmeg-laced cassava **pone** to the classic **black cake** – a ridiculously rich, rum-soaked Christmas speciality – most restaurant dessert menus concentrate on serving international staples. Home-made **ice cream** is ubiquitous and delicious, however, with flavours such as cherry-sorrel or barbadine sold everywhere from street stalls to supermarkets.

As for sweets, look out for **bene balls**, tooth-cracking globes of sesame seeds and sugar, and **coconut cake**, a slab of shredded coconut boiled in sugar syrup and pink food colouring. **Tamarind balls** take a little getting used to, combining the tart taste of tamarind with sugar and salt, as do **salt prunes** (seasoned, sweet-and-sour prunes rolled

in a dusty red colouring, often dropped into white rum) and **red mango**, which is green mango, well seasoned with spices and sugar and doused in bright red colouring. Other candies include **toolum**, a sticky ball of grated coconut, molasses and ginger, **pawpaw balls** (shredded green papaya boiled in sweet syrup and rolled in sugar) and gingery **fudge**, while there are hundreds of often sickly sugared and fried **Indian sweets**; kurma (sweet fried doughballs) are probably the most popular.

Fine local **chocolate** made in T&T from locally grown cocoa beans has seen a resurgence in recent years (see page 238), and is utterly delicious. As well as individual chocolates from the likes of Cocobel (see page 92) or Gina's Truffles (see page 238), head to *Adam's* (see page 88) or the Cocoa Pod in Port of Spain (see page 92), or Tobago Chocolate Delights (see page 227), to pick up chocolate produced by members of the Alliance of Rural Communities – from Brasso Seco's coffee-infused bars to Grande Riviere's delectable cinnamon - and organic bars, cocoa powder and gluten-free brownie and pancake mixes from Sun Eaters Organics (@facebook.com/suneatersorganics).

Drinking

Given T&T's capacity for consumption of beer, it's hardly surprising the national brews go down smoothly. The market leaders are **Carib**, a light, golden lager, and **Stag**, a little more robust and marketed as "a man's beer". Both taste best drunk very cold straight from the bottle (women are usually offered a straw), and both are available on draught. **Carib Pilsner Light** is a bearable if rather insipid lower-alcohol alternative. **Guinness** is brewed in Trinidad but, though bitter and refreshing, it bears little similarity to versions elsewhere. The sweeter Royal Extra or Mackeson **stouts** are excellent local alternatives. The ubiquitous Heineken and other international lagers are also widely available.

VEGETARIAN, VEGAN AND GLUTEN-FREE T&T

Trinbagonians are big meat-eaters, but **vegetarians** won't find it hard to get a good meal on either island. Veg rotis are ubiquitous, there are plenty of meat-free street food options, and an extra serving of stewed pulses ("peas") can always be added to a Creole meal for a protein fix. Tobago is thin on places catering solely to vegetarians, though *Kariwak Village* (see page 208) and *Shore Things* (see page 227) are good places to start, but there are richer pickings in Port of Spain: several great vegetarian restaurants – *Mother Nature* (see page 85), *Hardline Vegetarian* (see page 85) and *New Earth Organic* (see page 86) – plus lots of **vegan** and **dairy- or gluten-free** options at *Livet Gourmet* (see page 86) and *Zabouca Breads* (see page 87).

Rum

Produced in Laventille by the House of Angostura, T&T's dark (or "red") and white **rum** are downed with equal enthusiasm, the white tending to be less abrasively strong than the overproof brands of other islands; regular rums are 43 percent alcohol. The most popular brands are the clear **White Oak** and its dark counterparts **Black Label** and **Royal Oak**, all perfectly drinkable but best when mixed into a cocktail or with a chaser. Trinbagonian **rum punch** is delicious, using blended fruits, syrup, a sprinkle of ground nutmeg and, of course, a splash of the delectable **Angostura bitters** (see page 76), also a worthy addition to any mixed drink. At 75 percent alcohol, the eye-watering **Forres Park puncheon rum** is perhaps best avoided, though it does add a kick to a rum cocktail.

Of the more high-end **aged rums**, **Angostura Single Barrel** matures in oak casks for five years and is a decent sipping or mixing rum; the bourbon casks used for **Single Barrel Premium** produce an agreeably buttery rum, and there's a very smooth seven-year-old in the range, too. Moving up a notch, **Angostura 1919** is a premium 8-year aged rum in a distinctive square bottle; its 12-year-old counterpart, **Angostura 1824**, is heavy with molasses and is great drunk neat or over ice, as is the ultra-premium 15-year-old **Angostura 1787**. Look out, also, for the fantastic **El Dorado** aged rums, produced in Guyana but widely available in T&T. If you're in T&T around Christmas, you might be offered **poncha creme**, an eggnog boosted with plenty of rum.

Most bars also offer the usual range of fruity **cocktails**, from piña coladas to frozen margaritas.

Wine

Sweet and strong **home-made wines** – cashew, banana, aloes, hibiscus and so on – are excellent if you can get your hands on them; **imported wine** is widely available by bottle and, less expensively, by box: larger supermarkets carry standard selections of Pinot Grigio, Chardonnay and Sauvignon Blanc, as well as Cabernet, Merlot and the like, and a range of proseccos. Expect to pay a little more than you would at home, particularly if you order by the glass in a restaurant.

Soft drinks

Local soft drinks include the energy-boosting **Ginseng-Up**; delicious **Carib Shandy**, in sorrel and ginger varieties; **LLB**, a mix of lime, lemon and bitters that makes a good mixer for spirits; and **Bentley**, a refreshing bitter-lemon soda. The best thing for the

heat, however, is mineral-packed fresh **coconut water**, sold in water or jelly varieties. Vendors chop off the outer husk to expose a drinking hole (use a straw as the juice stains clothing), and then hack the nut in two so you can scoop out the delicious jelly. You can also buy bottles of fresh coconut water in supermarkets.

Made from boiled tree bark, cloves and aniseed, reddish-brown (sometimes yellow) **mauby** is a wonderfully bitter still drink. Other unusual options include tart, deep cerise **sorrel**, enjoyed at Christmas with a dash of rum, and **sea moss**, a white and glutinous preparation made from sea moss and milk, which is widely believed to enhance sexual performance; another stamina-inducing potions is the "bomb", a blended concoction of Guinness, nutmeg and condensed milk or a carton of Supligen energy drink. Cinnamon- and nutmeg-infused carrot juice and **peanut punch**, blended with condensed milk, are a meal in themselves, sold from punch stalls across the islands.

The media

Dipping into the local media is an excellent way to acclimatize yourself with the nation's cultural and political life. Outspoken columnists, scurrilous newspaper headlines and the local programming available on TV all offer a fascinating picture of Trini society – especially during Carnival, when local stations preview costumes, road march songs and fetes, and the papers hotly debate the merits of the year's calypsos.

Print and online

Trinidad's main **daily newspapers** are the *Trinidad Guardian* (Ⓦguardian.co.tt), a vaguely high-brow tome with a traditionally conservative attitude, the *Express* (Ⓦtrinidadexpress.com) and *Newsday* (Ⓦnewsday.co.tt); the latter two are picture-dominated with plenty of space for their sometimes outspoken columnists. All of the dailies have fat weekend editions with extended music, lifestyle and children's features. Tobago has a weekly paper, *Tobago Today* (Ⓦtobagotoday.co.tt), which concentrates on local sports, events and entertainment.

Sold at Piarco and Crown Point airports, supermarkets and book stores, **foreign magazines** – *Time*, *Newsweek*, *Cosmopolitan* and the like – are easy to find, but foreign newspapers – except for *USA Today*

– are practically nonexistent. Of the **local glossies**, lifestyle and culture magazine *Maco* (ⓦmacomag.com) is worth a look, while Carnival souvenir magazines provide a good insight into T&T's biggest festival; all are sold in pharmacies and supermarkets. Newspapers are sold at petrol stations, supermarkets, pharmacies and by street vendors.

As to **online resources**, collated stories featuring T&Ts most insightful and funny bloggers and commentators are posted at ⓦglobalvoicesonline.org (search for Trinidad and Tobago); there's also plenty of good stuff in the Air Caribbean inflight magazine, *Caribbean Beat* (ⓦcaribbean-beat.com), which is available in full online. Loop TT (ⓦlooptt.com) is a great web-based source of local news.

TV and radio

Of Trinidad and Tobago's several **TV stations**, the main players are CCNTV6, CNC3 and CNMG-TV, which screen daily **news bulletins** alongside American soaps, sitcoms, game shows and some educational and homegrown programmes. The main **local news** (with some international stories) is shown on TV6 and CNMG at 7pm and 10pm. **Cable TV** is universally available (and where it isn't, Direct TV satellites step in) showing a huge range of American channels and BBC World.

Radio is hugely popular, keeping the nation tapping its collective feet and serving as a source of information on upcoming events and parties. From November until Ash Wednesday, most stations are entirely devoted to soca and calypso (with a break for parang around Christmas time), but after Carnival the playlists switch to dancehall, reggae, R&B, hip-hop and international pop hits. Among the best stations for **contemporary Caribbean music** are Boom Champions 94.1 (ⓦboomchampionstt.com), Red 96.7 (ⓦred967fm.com) and Sweet 100 (ⓦsweet100fm.com), while numerous others

broadcast Indian pop and classical music, chutney and chat. Tobago's Radio Tambrin – 92.7FM – (ⓦtambrintobago.com) is an excellent way of keeping informed.

Festivals and public holidays

Trinidad and Tobago's public holidays embody the nation's cultural and ethnic diversity, acknowledging Hindu, Muslim, Baptist and Roman Catholic communities as well as trade unions and people of African and Indian descent; in 2017, T&T's indigenous population were also honoured by a one-off First Peoples holiday.

Every year there is a debate whether the Chinese should be given a day for Chinese New Year, and frequent discussion, too, as to whether the country has too many days off – but no politician is likely to risk offending a sector of the society by cancelling one.

For more on what's on, visit Discover T&T (ⓦdiscovertnt.com) and Ins and Out of T&T (ⓦinsandoutstt.com), which publish a regularly updated **events calendar** online and in their annual free magazines; Buzz TT (ⓦbuzz.tt) is another worthy online resource for events.

Festival calendar

JANUARY

Carnival season The festivities swing into action with the season's first fete, usually Soca in Moka in early Jan, and the fetes, calypso tents, steel pan competitions and general buzz build in intensity as the main days approach. See pages 34 and 260.

PUBLIC HOLIDAYS IN T&T

In addition to the dates below, note that the Monday and Tuesday of **Carnival** as well as Ash Wednesday are also observed as public holidays. When a public holiday falls on a Sunday, it is observed on the Monday, and when two holidays fall on the same date the following day is also given.

Jan 1 New Year's Day	**June 19** Labour Day
March 30 Spiritual Shouter Baptist Liberation Day	**Aug 1** Emancipation Day
	Aug 31 Independence Day
March/April Good Friday & Easter Monday	**Se4** Republic Day
May 30 Indian Arrival Day	**Oct/Nov** Divali
May/June Corpus Christi	**Dec 25** Christmas Day
May/June Eid ul Fitr	**Dec 26** Boxing Day

CARNIVAL CALENDAR

The dates of Carnival and its associated events shift around each year depending on the days of the main parade, which takes place on the last Monday and Tuesday before Lent; **upcoming Carnival dates** are as follows: Feb 12 & 13, 2018; March 4 & 5, 2019; Feb 24 & 25, 2020; Feb 15 & 16 2021. The National Carnival Commission website (⦿ ncctt.org) has a fairly up-to-date **calendar of events**; the list below represents the main events, which appear in **rough order of occurrence**; Carnival season traditionally begins on January 1.

Opening of Calypso Tents Calypsonians battle it out in the "tents" – regular buildings, these days – for a place in the Calypso Monarch finals. Longstanding tents include Calypso Revue, at the SWWTU Hall, Wrightson Road; and Kaiso House at the Queen's Park Savannah. Contact the Trinbago Unified Calypsonians Organization (☎ 623 9660, ⦿ tucott.com) for more information.

Panorama Steel pan bands play their composition of choice on the Savannah stage as they compete for the prestigious first prize. The prelims held at individual panyards are well worth checking out, but the semi-finals are the biggest deal, held on the Saturday two weeks before Carnival. The finals take place on Carnival Saturday.

National Chutney Soca Monarch The best of Trinidad's popular chutney performers compete for the annual crown at Skinner Park in San Fernando.

Kiddies' Carnival The children's costumes and characters rival those of the adults. There are three parades: the Red Cross Children's Carnival, held at the Savannah ten days before Carnival; the smaller St James Kiddies' Carnival on the following day; and the Junior Parade of the Bands from South Quay to the Queen's Park Savannah on Carnival Saturday.

Traditional/Individual Mas Held on the Sunday preceding Dimanche Gras, and the last Friday before Carnival Monday, with parades throughout the day and evening from South Quay to Adam Smith Square on Ariapita Avenue; this is the best place to see traditional Carnival characters such as Blue Devils, Dame Lorraine, Burrokeets, Fancy Sailors and Firemen. There are also traditional mas parades in St James (outside the Amphitheatre, Western Main Rd); check the press for dates and timings. The Carnival Monday blue devil mas in Paramin is also legendary.

International Soca Monarch "Fantastic Friday" (the Friday before Carnival) sees soca stars and up-and-coming acts sing for the prestigious International Soca Monarch and Groovy Soca Monarch titles in the National Stadium.

Canboulay Riot Re-Enactment Staged at Piccadilly Greens, downtown Port of Spain, this flambeaux-lit performance re-enacts the resistance against British colonial authorities of the early Carnival (aka Canboulay) in 1881.

Dimanche Gras The finals of the Calypso Monarch competition, staged at the Queen's Park Savannah on the Sunday before the main parades, see calypsonians go all-out with theatrical presentations of their compositions. The highlight of the show is the Kings and Queens Finals: the sheer size of the huge costumes on show, and the skill, sequins and special effects expended, make for a truly amazing display.

Jouvert (pronounced "joovay", from the French "jour ouvert", the break of day). Marking the beginning of the festivities, Jouvert is "dirty mas": raw, earthy and energetic. Wear as little as possible (no jewellery), join an organized band (see page 70) and expect to be covered in mud, paint, chocolate or even oil.

Carnival Monday Parade of the Bands Mas bands (see page 70) parade through the streets of Port of Spain (as well as smaller towns in Trinidad and in Scarborough, Tobago) from noon till dusk; most masqueraders don't wear their costumes on this day, instead getting creative with skimpy "Monday Wear".

Carnival Tuesday Parade of the Bands The full display of all the costumes. The route is the same as Carnival Monday; if you're not in a band, you can view the bands from anywhere along the parade route or the stands at the Queen's Park Savannah (for which you pay an entry fee), and the bleachers set up at the judging points at South Quay, Victoria Square on Park Street and Adam Smith Square on Ariapita Avenue; there's also seating at the Socadrome (see page 80). Starts 7am.

Ash Wednesday Cooldown parties at Maracas and Manzanilla have been scaled down in recent years; check the press for details of what's on, or follow the crowds and escape to Tobago.

Tobago Harvest Festivals Year-round. These Sunday community events are staged throughout the year in villages across Tobago. Each harvest kicks off with a church service and moves on to cookouts, music and general merry-making.

FEBRUARY

Carnival Feb/March. The nation's most famous festival, celebrated throughout Trinidad (and to a lesser degree, Tobago), with fetes, pan and calypso competitions, and culminating in two days of costumed street parades. See pages 34 and 260.

MARCH

Phagwah March/early April. Honours the Indian tradition of Holi, which celebrates the arrival of spring, and best experienced in central Trinidad. It's not a public holiday, but many Trinis of all backgrounds participate in the large-scale events at Aranguez Savannah, Tunapuna and Carlsen Field. See page 154.

Spiritual Shouter Baptist Liberation Day March 30. Public holiday in recognition of the African-based religion (see page 254) that suffered persecution in colonial Trinidad, with church services and small-scale processions.

Easter Weekend As well as attending church and baking hot cross buns, Trinidadians indulge in the "beating of the bobolee", which involves pummelling an effigy of Judas Iscariot or, more usually these days, any politician or public figure who's seen to deserve a good pounding. Kites are flown on Port of Spain's Savannah, with a competition for the biggest and best.

Goat Races March/April. Held at Mount Pleasant in Tobago on Easter Monday, with the main event at Buccoo the following day, Tobago's goat races are one of the highlights of T&T's festival calendar. See page 214.

APRIL

Bocas Lit Fest ⓦ bocaslitfest.com. Brilliant literary festival, with workshops, readings, film screenings, open-mic sessions and book-signings across Port of Spain, plus the presentation of the coveted Bocas Prize.

La Divina Pastora and Siparee Mai On the third Sunday after Easter in Siparia in southern Trinidad, La Divina Pastora sees a Black Virgin statue carried from Siparia's parish church in a procession through the town, followed by feasting and merrymaking. On the Thursday before Easter, Siparee Mai sees Hindu pilgrims pay their respects to the icon. See page 184

Point Fortin Borough Day Late April/early May
ⓦ pointfortinborough.com. More a series of events than a day, held over a couple of weeks: exhibitions, fetes and concerts which culminate in a Jouvert (see page 71), mas parade (including traditional characters) and pan on the streets, followed by Dragon Boat Festival the next day.

Tobago Jazz Experience ⓦ tobagojazzexperience.com. International and local artists performing at several venues across Tobago; headline acts have included Stevie Wonder, Randy Crawford, George Benson, Chaka Khan and Grace Jones alongside the likes of Erykah Badu, Lauryn Hill, Maxwell and Mary J. Blige.

MAY

Indian Arrival Day May 30 ⓦ ncictt.com. This public holiday commemorates the 1845 arrival of the first indentured Indian labourers in Trinidad, with re-enactments of the *Fatel Rosak* landing (the first ship that carried workers here) on several beaches, and cultural shows at the Divali Nagar site in Chaguanas.

Tobago International Game Fishing Tournament ⓦ tgft.com. Big boats go after big fish from Charlotteville.

Duanwu Jai ⓦ bit.ly/TTDBF. Trinidad's Chinese community stage a festival in Chaguaramas, with traditional dragons, dance, games performances and dragon-boat races. The date changes according to the lunar calendar.

JUNE

We Beat ⓦ bit.ly/WeBeatTT. Held in and around the Amphitheatre on Western Main Road in St James, Port of Spain, with concerts, parties and lots of steel pan.

Tobago Dragon Boat Festival ⓦ bit.ly/TTDBF. Held over two days in mid-June, with teams of rowers racing Chinese-style dragon boats off from Pigeon Point.

Labour Day June 19. A public holiday held in recognition of trade unions and workers. It is most publicly celebrated in Fyzabad in southern Trinidad, where the powerful Oil Workers' Union was established. See page 185.

Fishermen's Fetes June to August. Tobago's beaches serve as venues for a day and night of eating, drinking and partying, kicking off with events to celebrate St Peter's Day on June 29, though some communities hold their fetes in July and August. Main venues are in Lambeau, Castara and Man O'War Day in Charlotteville.

JULY

Tobago Heritage Festival ⓦ tobagoheritagefestival.com. Held in the last two weeks of July all over the island. Festivities include a Jouvert, old-time mas parade and calypso competition in Plymouth; the "Ole Time Wedding" procession in Moriah; Charlotteville's National Treasure Day, with everything from "dancing" of cocoa beans to heritage foods; and the Pembroke Salaka Feast, with traditional dance, singing and feasting in honour of islanders' ancestors.

AUGUST

Emancipation Day August 1 ⓦ emancipationtt.com. The 1834 abolition of slavery is commemorated with cultural events and a procession through Port of Spain with participants bedecked in African finery.

Great Race ⓦ bit.ly/TTPBA. Speedboats navigate the dangerous currents of the Dragon's Mouth in a race starting around 6am from the foreshore in Port of Spain, with the winners reaching Store Bay in Tobago a little over an hour later to the cheers of enthusiastic crowds, and racers in lesser classes arriving within an hour or so. The race is followed by much drinking and liming in and around Crown Point, and a "Great Fete" party at Pigeon Point after dark.

Pan on D'Avenue ⓦ bit.ly/PanAve. Held in late August on Ariapita Avenue in Port of Spain, with Trinidad's best pan bands playing their hearts out from 6.30pm onwards.

Santa Rosa Festival Ⓦ santarosafirstpeoples.org. Held in the last week of Aug at Arima in Trinidad. Celebrates the culture and tradition of indigenous Amerindians, with a parade through town led by the Carib King and Queen, ritual smoke and water ceremonies performed by shamans, and feasting on traditional foodstuffs such as cassava and street parties.

Independence Day August 31. Independence from Britain in 1962 is celebrated with flags and bunting on all public buildings, banks and institutions, fireworks at Queens's Park Savannah in Trinidad and Scarborough, Tobago, and a host of fetes and parties.

SEPTEMBER

Trinidad & Tobago Film Festival

Ⓦ trinidadandtobagofilmfestival.com. Held over two weeks, with films from all over the Caribbean, plus arthouse cinema from around the world, screened at MovieTowne Port of Spain, Chaguanas and Tobago.

OCTOBER

Divali Ⓦ ncictt.com. Festival in Oct or Nov honouring Mother Lakshmi, the Hindu goddess of light, via the lighting of *deya* candles throughout T&T. The National Council of Indian Culture stages nine days of shows, stalls and events.

Trinidad & Tobago Restaurant Week Ⓦ bit.ly/TTRestWeek. Held over ten days, with restaurants across both islands devising special set menus to showcase their cuisine, all at a 30 percent discounted rate.

Tobago Blue Food Festival Ⓦ visittobago.gov.tt. Bloody Bay is overtaken by this celebration of the starchy tubers – yam dasheen, eddoes and the like – which feature so heavily in Tobago cuisine, and which are cooked up in many imaginative and delicious ways: don't miss the dasheen ice cream.

NOVEMBER

Hosay This religious festival changes date every year according to the Islamic calendar. The biggest event takes place in the Port of Spain suburb of St James, though it is also celebrated in Curepe, Tunapuna, Couva and Cedros. See page 72.

DECEMBER

Parang season Ⓦ npatt.com. A tradition of nativity songs sung in Spanish with a mix of French patois dating from colonial days; performed by parang groups in bars, nightclubs and door to door, filling the streets with rich, haunting music. The parang season formally starts in late October.

Outdoor activities

A far cry from your average sun-sand-and-sea Caribbean destination, T&T offers plenty to do beyond the beach. The hugely rich natural environment affords many opportunities for birdwatching, hiking and freshwater swimming, either in rivers or in the pools below water-falls, **while offshore pursuits include an impressive range of watersports.**

Birdwatching

Trinidad and Tobago ranks among the world's top ten countries in terms of **bird species** per square kilometre, boasting a diversity unmatched in the Caribbean: some 485 species have been recorded, with around 250 known to breed. Migrant species from South America are most common between May and September, while birds from North America visit between October and March. The dry months (Jan–March/April) are traditionally the most popular time for birders to visit; during the wet season, however, birds grab whatever chance they can to feed between showers, so you'll still see a lot of activity.

The best place to start in Trinidad is the Northern Range at the acclaimed **Asa Wright Nature Centre** (Ⓦ asawright.org; see page 124); workers there assert that even on a relatively short visit you can see as many as 150 species. Other stops include the **Caroni Swamp** (see page 152), where you can take an afternoon boat tour to see the flocks of scarlet ibis, the national bird and most arresting of the 157 species that live in this swampland. The **Pointe-a-Pierre Wildfowl Trust** (see page 159) is an important waterfowl conservation centre nestling amid an industrial wasteland, with a successful breeding programme and the opportunity to see ibis up close.

The best **book** to bring is Richard ffrench's encyclopedic *A Guide to the Birds of Trinidad and Tobago*, which describes calls as well as plumage, habitats and behaviour; Helm Field Guides' *Birds of Trinidad and Tobago* is also useful. Online, visit Trinidad Birding (Ⓦ trinidadbirding.com). Plenty of tour companies and guides specialize in birding tours (see page 38). In addition to the areas covered above, **good places to go birdwatching** in Trinidad include the Aripo Savannas and Arena Dam, just south of Arima (see page 163); Mount St Benedict (see page 128); Brasso Seco, and anywhere along the Arima–Blanchisseuse Road (see page 120); Nariva Swamp on the east coast (see page 167); and Oropuche Lagoon in the southwest (see page 180). Note that permits are needed for some of these sites; guides (see page 38) can arrange these for you.

In Tobago, head for Little Tobago (or Bird of Paradise Island) on the windward coast (see page 241) to see sea birds in their natural environment; the Bon Accord Lagoon (see page 203), Adventure

TOP 5 WATERFALLS

Argyle, Tobago. Tobago's best waterfall, with several tiers and some nice swimming pools, and just a short walk from the coast road to boot. See page 238

Avocat, Trinidad. One of Trinidad's most accessible falls, with a 12m drop and a sizeable pool for swimming. See page 121

Guanapo Gorge, Trinidad. A 30m-high gorge carved out of the granite with numerous little falls along the way. See page 134

Paria, Trinidad. A couple of hours' walk along the coast from Blanchisseuse takes you to pristine Paria beach, with a pretty cascade just inland in which to wash off the salt. At the start of the trail, the Marianne River's Three Pools (see page 117) is more easily accessible. See page 119

Rio Seco, Trinidad. A forty-minute walk through stunning forest, Trinidad's most beautiful waterfall offers a deep emerald-green pool swathed by lush foliage. See page 138

Farm (see page 219) and the Grafton Caledonia Bird Sanctuary (see page 218) are also fine birdwatching sites. At the protected Tobago Forest Reserve (see page 234), there are plenty of well-trained guides to accompany you, and the Roxborough–Parlatuvier Road through the forest is always good for birding.

Hiking

Trinidad and Tobago are ideal for **hiking**, despite the heat – the best plan is to start early and cover plenty of distance before midday, or choose a hike that goes through forest. You don't have to be supremely fit for most trails, nor do you need special equipment. In Trinidad, there is excellent hiking to be had in the forests of the Northern Range, especially around Paria and Brasso Seco (see page 123); or the Chaguaramas hills. Of the numerous waterfall hikes, Guanapo Gorge (see page 134) is particularly spectacular. The best hiking in Tobago is in the Forest Reserve (see page 234).

Be very wary of setting out on a hike if rain is promised; flash floods can be deadly. **And don't hike alone**. In addition to incidents of robberies on remote trails, there is no one to provide assistance should you run into problems; experienced local hikers always set out with two or more people. Plenty of tour companies provide private hiking trips (see page 38), and the hundred-year-old **Trinidad and Tobago Field Naturalists' Club** (⦿ttfnc.org) offer eco-oriented field trips to sites of interest around the islands; visitors are welcome and fees are low. Their *Trail Guide* (see page 279) makes essential reading, describing fifty walks in minute detail. Another inexpensive option is to join a **local hiking group** on their regular weekend jaunts into rural areas: you assemble at around 7am, pay about TT$50 and set off. Groups can normally arrange transport for you if you don't

have your own (call ahead). Bear in mind, though, that group sizes can be large, which puts pressure on safety. If you hike with a large group, always stay close to lead walkers. Established outfits include Hikeseekers (⦿hikeseekers.com), Island Hikers (⦿islandhikers.com) and Hikers Inc (⦿hikersinc.com). You could also check out **hashing**, a kind of cross-country race (which can be done as a walk) with lots of beer and rum drinking; if you want to have a go, contact the Port of Spain Hash Harriers (⦿poshhh.org).

And be sure to abide by **hiking etiquette**: stick to paths and trails wherever possible, which avoids soil erosion and safeguards you from getting lost; bring all rubbish home with you, and bury used toilet paper; do not discard matches or cigarettes and make sure any fires are completely extinguished; and, don't collect plant or wildlife specimens.

In terms of equipment, **sturdy shoes** with good grip will suffice if you don't have boots, though trainers work as a last resort; and always wear socks to protect against blisters and ticks. If hiking along a river-course, stout sandals are your best bet. Wear long trousers or sports leggings to protect against nettles, razor grass and insects (tuck trousers into socks); a long-sleeved shirt may also be advisable. A **hat** is good protection against sun and rain, and a light **waterproof** is useful in rainy season. Jeans are best avoided as they quickly become uncomfortable if wet. A dip is very often on the agenda, so wear or bring **swimming gear**; a set of spare clothes and a pair of flip-flops left in your vehicle is a good idea for when you finish walking.

Diving and watersports

While **snorkelling** and **scuba diving** are popular on both islands, both are far better in **Tobago**, where

T&T'S BEACHES

Maracas is Trinidad's most popular beach thanks to excellent facilities and a swathe of fine yellow sand and cool, clear green water (though its botched-up "regeneration" means it's in a poor state at the time of writing); more stunning places to swim lie a few miles down the road at **Las Cuevas** and **Blanchisseuse**, though all are sometimes subject to rough seas and undertows. Away from the oil refineries, many parts of the south coast offer fabulous swimming as well, while the east coast boasts the fabulously scenic **Manzanilla** and **Mayaro**.

Most agree, though, that T&T's best beaches are in Tobago, where the water is calmer and tourist infrastructure more developed. The epitome of a Caribbean seashore, **Pigeon Point** is the queen of them all, with turquoise water, white sand and pretty palm-thatched gazebos, though it's rather marred by its overt commerciality. Nearby **Store Bay** is also lovely, while **Mount Irvine** offers perhaps the best swimming in the southwest, but the alluringly undeveloped **Castara**, **Parlatuvier**, **Englishman's Bay** and **Pirate's Bay** on the leeward side are far more stunning.

Bear in mind that undertows and strong currents make many of Trinidad's (and some of Tobago's) beaches risky. Yellow and red flags indicate safe areas; in their absence, don't swim until you've checked with someone local.

the water is clearer away from the sediment-heavy currents from the South American mainland. The best **dive sites** are centred around Speyside on the windward coast (see page 242), where you can see pristine reefs and a host of fish, including deep-water manta rays and the odd shark. Other top spots are offshore Charlotteville and the Sisters Rocks on the leeward side, as well as the Shallows or Flying Reef at Crown Point; Buccoo Reef remains popular, as the disintegrating coral sadly reveals. Everywhere, you'll see a dazzling variety of fish, from barracuda and grouper to angel, parrot, damsel and butterfly fish as well as spiny sea urchins and lobster nestled among the coral. Throughout the Guide, we have listed reputable dive operators, most of whom also rent snorkelling gear.

There's an excellent watersports outlet, Radical Sports (see page 205), at Pigeon Point Bay beach, and just down the coast, try Mount Irvine Bay Watersports (see page 205). In Trinidad, Chaguaramas is the main watersports area, where you can **kayak** and **stand-up paddleboard**, while there's also the option of **wakeboarding**, **waterskiing** and **wakesurfing** offshore of Port of Spain.

During the winter, big breakers – especially around Mount Irvine in Tobago and Toco in Trinidad – make ideal conditions for **surfing**. You can rent boards in Tobago, but in Trinidad you'll probably need to bring your own; check with the Surfing Association of Trinidad and Tobago (❶ surftt.org) for details and further contacts.

T&T also boasts excellent **sport fishing** at around US$4400 for a half day and US$700 for a full day – though not cheap, many boats accommodate up to six, and rods, tackle and bait are included. You're

pretty much guaranteed some excitement; main catches include marlin, sailfish, tuna and dolphin. Boats for charter are listed throughout the Guide wherever available, and if you want more information about sport fishing, contact the Trinidad and Tobago Game Fishing Association (Ⓦ ttgfa.com).

Tour operators in Trinidad and Tobago

Tour companies' offerings range from eco-oriented **hiking**, **birdwatching** trips and **kayaking** to more conventional **driving tours** of the islands' "highlights": the list below represents the very best of the bunch. We've specified whether each company is based in Trinidad or Tobago; most offer trips primarily in their home island, plus a few basic options in their sister isle. Note that you'll often get a reduced rate if you book in groups of four or more; some operators will not set out with less than four in any case. The prices for operators listed below are all per-person. If you're in Trinidad during the summer, you can join one of the "**Experience T&T**" tours (Ⓦ facebook.com/ExperienceTT) staged by the local tour operators association; geared toward locals, they're often at discounted rates.

Additional tour operators in Tobago are detailed on page 202.

TOUR OPERATORS

TRINIDAD

ARC Destinations Port of Spain ❶ 768 7613, Ⓦ bit.ly/ARCTnT. A fantastic roster of options (from TT$100; TT$300 with a meal included) from this co-operative group that supports T&T's community chocolate makers; Bean to Bar tours in both islands reveal the complete process of chocolate-making from cocoa harvesting, fermenting and drying to the production of bars and chocolate products, and can be combined with eco-attractions in the surrounding areas. Other options include a visit to Banwari Trace archeological site with local film-maker Tracy Assing to learn about Trinidad's First Peoples, and trips focused on endemic plants and their medicinal uses. Hikes, waterfalls and camping trips also available, as are several Port of Spain options (see page 79).

Avifauna Tours Port of Spain ☎ 633 5614 or ☎ 477 2650, Ⓦ rogernecklesphotography.com. Trini-English Roger Neckles is one of T&T's most respected wildlife photographers, and his tours – from Asa Wright to Nariva and Aripo Savannas, plus Tobago – are conducted in a comfy a/c SUV and are excellent for ornithologists, photographers and amateur birdwatchers alike. US$150.

Caribbean Discovery Tours Port of Spain ☎ 620 1989 or ☎ 339 1989, Ⓦ caribbeandiscoverytours.com. Entertaining, informative hikes plus safaris aboard a Land Rover, all with a birdwatching and animal-spotting slant. One of the best for Nariva, as well as Brasso Seco/Asa Wright and Northern Range waterfalls/hikes, nights in host homes and Paramin; and the only company to offer overnighting at remote Petit Iacarib (US$150). Central Trinidad options include Caroni Swamp, birdwatching and rare-plant spotting at Aripo Savannas, while as well as the usual Pitch Lake trip in south Trinidad there's an Icacos tour with visits to small-scale soap and coconut-oil makers, and wetland birdwatching. Day tours from US$100.

Ieri Nature Adventures Arima ☎ 667 5636 or ☎ 685 6206, Ⓔ ierinatureadventures@hotmail.com. Dynamic guide Ivan Charles is a former national road cyclist, and offers both relaxed road trips and more hardcore mountain biking, plus tours covering most of Trinidad's natural attractions, from expert hiking adventures to Northern Range peaks and waterfalls, Tamana caves, kayaking at Caroni Swamp and visits to turtle-nesting beaches (including a two-night camp on a nesting beach). All-inclusive full-day trips from US$80.

Indiversity Tours Port of Spain ☎ 743 1604, Ⓔ indiversity@gmail.com. As well as running a destination management company, owner Jalaludin Khan offers thoughtful historical and heritage tours that offer insight into cultural sights islandwide, especially Hindu temples, mosques and out-of-the-way places in the underexplored south. Hiking, birding, foodie and arts-based trips are also available. Full-day tours from US$80.

In-Joy Tours Port of Spain ☎ 633 4733 or ☎ 753 2775, Ⓦ injoytours.com. Great option for "down the islands", trips take in Gasparee caves plus swimming and relaxation at Chacachacare or Monos islands. Other possibilities include Trinidad's National Museum and Maracas Bay; cultural/panyard tours, Lopinot, Paramin, the Pitch Lake and other things south; and a day-trip to Tobago. Carnival packages available. Tours US$50–125.

Island Experiences Port of Spain ☎ 621 0407 or ☎ 756 9677, Ⓦ islandexperiencestt.com. Professionally run, small-group eco-cultural tours led by charming guides who provide an excellent insight into Trinidadian life. Great for city tours, mas camps and panyards at Carnival, and evening tours that provide a thorough grounding in the art of Port of Spain liming, including live calypso and steel pan, as well as bars and clubbing if the mood takes you. Island tours cover all the main attractions, from Asa Wright and Caroni kayaking/boat trips to the north coast (Maracas, Las Cuevas and Blanchisseuse), Angostura distillery, Pitch Lake and central Trinidad (Waterloo, Carapichaima, Felicity potteries and Chaguanas market). There's also a Paramin jeep tour and lots of options in the Bocas islands, from Gasparee caves to Chacachacare, as well as coastal cruises. German- and English-speaking guides available, and upcoming tour schedules are posted online, enabling you to join up with others if travelling solo. Tobago tours also available. Half-day and evening tours US$35–60, full-day US$75–105.

Paria Springs Tours Port of Spain ☎ 620 8240, Ⓦ pariasprings.com. Excellent and well-informed birdwatching and eco-tours with experienced naturalist, Courtenay "Bushman" Rooks, which are often more adventurous that the standard tour offerings. Options include birdwatching all over Trinidad, plus Northern Range waterfalls and hikes, Tamana bat caves, adventurous and soft mountain-bike excursions in Chaguaramas, Northern Range and Grande Riviere (with tuition if needed), as well as lovely kayak paddles "down the islands" and to Caroni Swamp. For adrenaline seekers, there's also wakeboarding, waterfall rappelling and rock climbing. From US$85.

TOBAGO

NG Nature Tours ☎ 660 5463 or ☎ 754 7881, Ⓦ newtongeorge.com. A fantastic birding guide, Newton George offers tours for both serious birdwatchers and those with just a passing interest, pointing out hard-to-see birds with the aid of a light pen. Trips cover the Forest Reserve, Little Tobago, Bon Accord Lagoon, Grafton Caledonia Bird Sanctuary and the Magdalena Grand wetlands, and there's also an all-inclusive Trinidad day-trip including Asa Wright and Caroni. Full-day tours US$75–95, Trinidad US$250.

Peter Cox Wildlife Tours ☎ 751 5822 or ☎ 294 3086, Ⓦ petercoxnaturetours.com. One of the top birding guides on Tobago, with Main Ridge walks that include a night-time option (great for seeing nocturnal creatures such as armadillos and owls) and trips tailored for children in which you explore forest rivers and pools home to wabeen and crayfish. All the birding hotspots are covered too, from Little Tobago to the Magdalena Grand wetlands, as are Argyle Falls and the Tobago Cocoa Estate, Scarborough market and Fort King George, round-the-island sightseeing and turtle-watching during the laying season. Full-day tours US$90–115.

Yes Tourism ☎ 357 0064, Ⓦ yestourism.com. A reliable all-round operator, offering sightseeing tours around Tobago: Caribbean coast, rainforest walks, Speyside glass-bottom boat to Little Tobago, Tobago Cocoa Estate etc plus waterfalls and shopping trips. Full-day tours US$75–99.

Sports

Sport is as much a national pastime as liming, and Trinbagonians are justifiably proud of their country's sporting achievements, in cricket, track and field – and football, since the Soca Warriors competed in the 2006 World Cup.

Cricket

Cricket is a national passion in T&T and the source of much debate; when the West Indies team is playing, radios everywhere are tuned in, regardless of the Windies' uninspiring performances of recent years. As long as you're not foolish enough to criticize legendary batsman Brian Lara, the "Prince of Port of Spain", mentioning cricket to any Trinbagonian is pretty much guaranteed to break the ice.

Big matches, from Tests to one-day events, take place at the **Queen's Park Oval** in Port of Spain, and are great fun even if you're not a cricket fan; soca blares in the intervals, plenty of cold Carib gets downed, and fans are animated to say the least. Tickets are available from the Queen's Park Cricket Club, 94 Tragarete Rd, Port of Spain (☎622 2295, ⓦqpcc.com); those that like to party as they watch head for the all-inclusive "Trini Posse" stand. Match schedules are advertised in the media; for further information, contact the Trinidad and Tobago Cricket Board (☎636 1577, ⓦttcb.co.tt).

Football

Football (soccer) is extremely popular in T&T, with fanatical support for the national team, the Soca Warriors (ⓦsocawarriors.net) heightened since their spirited performance at the 2006 World Cup in Germany. Major matches take place at the National Stadium on Wrightson Road, Port of Spain; for more information, contact the T&T Football Federation (☎623 9500, ⓦttffonline.com).

Other activities

T&T boasts some lovely **golf courses**, most with in-house caddies and clubs and carts for rent. In **Trinidad**, the best is St Andrew's in Moka, Maraval (☎629 2314, ⓦgolftrinidad.com), while the only public course is the nine-hole Chaguaramas Golf Course, Bellerand Road, Chaguaramas (☎225 4232, ext 310, ⓦchaguaramas.com). In **Tobago**, there's the pristine 18-hole course operated by the *Magdalena Grand* hotel (☎387 0288, ⓦmagdalenagrand.com) on the wind-blown Atlantic coast; and the eighteen palm-dotted holes attached to the *Mount Irvine* hotel (☎639 8871, ⓦmtirvine.com). All but the Chaguaramas course host professional and amateur tournaments. For more information, contact the Trinidad and Tobago Golf Association (☎629 7127, ⓦttgolfassociation.org).

Cycling is very popular; the Trinidad and Tobago Cycling Federation website (ⓦttcyclingfederation.

THE RULES OF CRICKET

The basic rules of **cricket** are by no means as complex as the official twenty-page rule book suggests. There are two teams of eleven players. A team wins by scoring more runs than the other team and dismissing the opposition; a team could score many more runs than the opposition, but (in a Test or other first-class match) still not win if the last two enemy batsmen doggedly stay "in", ensuring a draw. The match is divided into **innings**, when one team bats and the other team fields. One-day matches have one innings per team, Test matches have two.

The aim of the fielding side is to limit the runs scored and get the batsman "out". Two players from the batting side are on the pitch at any one time. The fielding side has a **bowler**, a **wicketkeeper** and nine **fielders**. Two umpires adjudicate whether a batsman is out (backed in international matches by a third off-field, with the benefit of technology). Each innings is divided into **overs**, consisting of six deliveries, after which the wicketkeeper changes ends, the bowler is changed and the fielders move positions.

The batsmen score **runs** either by running up and down from wicket to wicket (one length = one run), or by hitting the ball over the boundary rope, scoring four runs if it crosses the boundary having touched the ground, and six runs if it flies over. The most common ways for batsmen to be dismissed are by being **"bowled"**, where the bowler dislodges the bails of the wicket; by being **"run out"**, when one of the fielders dislodges the bails with the ball while the batsman is running; by being **caught** out, when one of the fielding side catches the ball after the batsman has hit it; or by **"LBW"** (leg before wicket), where the batsman blocks with his leg a delivery that would otherwise have hit the stumps.

These are the rudiments of a game whose beauty lies in its **skills and tactics**. The captain, for example, chooses which bowler (spin or fast) to play and where to position his fielders to counter the strengths of the batsman, the condition of the pitch and a dozen other variables. Cricket also has a poetry in its **esoteric language**, used to describe such things as fielding positions ("silly mid-off", "cover point", etc) and types of bowling delivery ("googly", "yorker" and so on).

org) has lots on competitive meets and leisure rides. Major **horse racing** meets take place at the Santa Rosa Race Track, Arima (ⓦarimaraceclub.com). Fitness freaks will find Trinidad well equipped with **gyms** (packed in the run-up to Carnival, so people look good in the skimpy costumes). **Tennis courts** are to be found at the *Hilton* hotel and Nelson Mandela Park (aka King George V Park) in Port of Spain and the *Mount Irvine* and *Magdalena Grand* hotels in Tobago.

Culture and etiquette

Despite the wild bacchanalia of Carnival, T&T is generally a friendly but conservative society. As a foreigner you will be treated politely and the same will be expected in return.

Outside the cities, it's usual to acknowledge people passing on the street with a nod of the head, "good day/afternoon/evening" or just "hello". Before starting any conversation, whether in a shop or asking for directions, local norm is to offer a **formal greeting** ("good morning" etc); the same goes when entering, say, a maxi or a public office. Everything is **slowed down** in T&T; people take longer to interact, to converse and to serve you in a shop or a diner. If you arrange to meet someone, be prepared to wait – being on time in T&T may well mean being 30–45 minutes after the time originally arranged, with no apology. Don't get frustrated; be flexible and tolerant and you will save yourself a lot of stress. Inevitably, though, if you follow suit and turn up late, you'll confront an irritated Trinbagonian who's timekeeping is impeccable.

Religious faith holds strong in T&T, and underpins almost all aspects of public and private life. Though you may see overtly sexual dancing and hear lewd lyrics, local people are still quite morally conservative; public drunkenness, for example, is very much frowned upon. Couples in T&T tend to be very undemonstrative in public, and the highly erotic-looking dancing ("wining") you'll see is usually between friends or couples. As a foreigner you may well be asked to dance by a stranger, but there's no necessity to demonstrate your wining skills unless you choose to – and twerking against several new acquaintances in one night will probably raise a few eyebrows. Note also that while local women may accept a dance with a stranger, she may just give him a "small

TIPPING

Private- and route-taxi drivers in Trinidad don't expect a **tip**, but in Tobago, where many make their living from tourists, a ten-percent tip is standard. Restaurants often add a service charge (usually ten percent) into the bill; if not, a tip of 10–15 percent is the norm. If you're staying in a hotel, you might consider leaving some dollars for the chambermaid.

wine", dancing for a minute so as to be polite but breaking off swiftly.

Of other social conventions, **beachwear** is restricted to the beach; nude and topless bathing is not allowed. Bear in mind also that **camouflage clothing** is illegal in T&T (a law passed following the 1990 coup in an attempt to prevent civilians from impersonating the military). The ban is most often enforced at airport arrivals halls, where offending items are confiscated, but camo (even a bikini or kids' hat) shouldn't be worn outdoors and is best left at home. Using obscene language in public is illegal and though the law is not often enforced, it is nevertheless important to be aware of it.

Finally, it is illegal to **smoke** in all enclosed public spaces in T&T– something adhered to rigidly.

Crime and personal safety

Despite the warnings on government travel advisories, most visits to Trinidad and Tobago are trouble-free – crime is far more of an issue for residents than it is for tourists. There have been incidents involving visitors in Tobago, but these are rare and as long as you choose secure accommodation and use your common sense – not walking alone on deserted beaches or exploring downtown areas by night – there's no reason to feel intimidated.

In Port of Spain, the communities east of Charlotte Street around the market are probably best left unexplored, while there is more **crime** – much of it violent – further east in the hillside suburb of Laventille and in nearby Morvant and Beetham than in any other part of the country; these are not places for the casual visitor. In Tobago, there have been **robberies** over the years, some of them violent, at villas and guesthouses; wherever you stay, make sure you lock up properly at night and don't sit on open verandas well into the wee hours.

If you use your common sense, and take the same precautions you would in any strange environment, you should find that the prospect of trouble is minimal wherever you are in T&T. **Avoid walking alone** or in small groups late at night or on deserted beaches and forest trails, keep flashy jewellery to a minimum (especially during Carnival), think twice before accepting lifts from strangers and don't go telling everyone where you're staying – or letting new acquaintances into your hotel room. Carry only as much cash as you need, get small notes when changing money so that you don't have to pull out wads of hundreds, and never leave belongings unattended on a beach or in a car. Store **valuables** in the safes that many hotels have in their guest rooms.

In rural areas, you have little to fear – doors are still sometimes left unlocked in the countryside – but as a foreigner you may be a target. If you're unlucky enough to be the victim of theft or other offences, report the incident immediately, as you'll need a police report to make any insurance claim. Local officers are generally happy to help, though things will take longer than you're used to.

Harassment

Proud to hail from a Caribbean nation that doesn't depend on holidaymakers for the bulk of its revenue, Trinidadians are far more likely to avoid tourists than hassle them; even in more touristy Tobago, **harassment** hasn't reached the proportions you encounter in more established Caribbean destinations. Many Tobagonians nonetheless make their living from foreign visitors; you'll be approached on the beach by vendors selling crafts or boat trips, but are rarely pushy if you're not interested.

Drugs

Visitors to the Caribbean often assume that all West Indians move around in a permanent haze of marijuana fumes. Though many islanders do of course smoke, this stereotype is hardly the reality.

Cannabis (weed, herb, ganja) is illegal to grow or possess in Trinidad and Tobago, and penalties are quite severe. Tourists caught in possession are likely to be deported without a moment's notice, and jail sentences and fines are frequently imposed; the excuse that "it's OK at home to carry a little marijuana for personal use" is not acceptable. Local people who smoke do so with caution, shutting windows and doors and lighting incense. Many visitors also choose to indulge, and if you do, bear in mind that in Tobago particularly you will need to be extremely discreet. Don't light up in the street, or in nightclubs and popular beaches, and never leave paraphernalia lying around your hotel room.

Marijuana is not the only illegal drug with a following; powder and, particularly, **crack cocaine** are common in T&T. Geographically well placed as a transshipment point from South America, both Trinidad and Tobago have been badly affected; narcotics police patrol stretches of coastline, and there are "crack blocks" in every large town. You are more likely to be offered the drug in Tobago, where some visitors' taste for cocaine has provided a lucrative market.

Finally, do not consider smuggling drugs in or out of the country under any circumstances; customs officers have seen all the methods of concealment before and the chances are that you will be caught and imprisoned.

Shopping

Trinidad and Tobago offer a wide variety of souvenirs and products to suit every budget, from woven palm hats to expensive jewellery in Port of Spain's malls. Local artists create fine woodcarvings, shell and bead jewellery, paintings and beaten-copper pieces, as well as lovely leather sandals. T&T also produces great music and has exceptionally talented writers – purchasing a few books and CDs will enable you to carry a little local culture back home. Chocolate, pepper sauce, rum and spices are also well worth stocking up on.

Port of Spain and San Fernando have Trinidad's widest variety of **shops**, but there's a lot less on offer in Tobago, where you should head for Gulf City Mall or central Scarborough; there are also shops and a couple of small-scale malls along Milford Road.

Prices are generally higher in Tobago than in Trinidad. For bargains, check out streetside vendors and small backstreet shops – souvenir shops, boutiques and malls have higher prices. Bargaining is conducted to a certain extent with street and beach vendors, but not in shops.

T&T's rich musical culture (see page 264) has spawned an astonishing variety of styles – steel pan, calypso, soca, rapso, chutney, reggae and parang – and produced many marvellous songs with strong lyrics and powerful rhythms. There are good **music stores** in Port of Spain (see page 92), while roadside vendors sell inexpensive pirate copies of popular reggae and soca tracks. In Tobago, try the stalls lining Wilson and Milford roads in Scarborough.

Book stores usually stock a good range of fiction and non-fiction by local writers, as well as books based in/about T&T; best shops are in Port of Spain (see page 92). Prices are often higher than you may be used to, though shelves stocked with local titles often turn up unheard-of gems that you might not find elsewhere.

Food and drink

T&T has some of the best-quality **cocoa** in the world, and **chocolate** made locally from Trinitario beans is a burgeoning industry in T&T (see page 238). In Port of Spain, you can buy exquisite chocolates from Cocobel's workshop (see page 92), while gourmet food shops like Port of Spain's Cocoa Pod (see page 92) and Tobago Chocolate Delights (see page 227) in Tobago sell bars by the best of the local producers (see page 238); Cocoa Pod also has a delicious range of chocolate spreads and a cracking cocoa liqueur. Note also that Machel Montano's M Store at Piarco Airport sells his own-brand chocolate, alongside merchandise related to the soca superstar's oeuvre. As well as chocolate, look out for **cocoa balls** – solid spheres or sticks of cocoa and spices, which you grate and boil up with milk and sugar to make traditional chocolate tea; many chocolate producers also sell a powdered version these days. Local **coffee**, which comes in a variety of flavours such as coconut and rum, can be bought in supermarkets and souvenir shops, or fresh from the roaster in Brasso Seco (see page 122).

Trinidad's famous Angostura Brewery (see page 76) produces a wide range of excellent **rum** (see page 32) as well as their ever-popular bitters, all readily available in shops throughout the islands. Both airports in Trinidad and Tobago have a selection of duty-free goods, though prices at Piarco in Trinidad are lower.

Arts and crafts

Locally made **arts**, **crafts** and unusual **souvenirs**, like carved calabashes, woven palm grasshoppers, shell jewellery and carved driftwood, are sold on or near the more popular beaches and in souvenir shops. Ornate carvings are also sold in art galleries and at individual stalls that occasionally appear on country roads. The road- and beach-side stalls are run by local craftspeople and artists who sell good-quality handmade goods at reasonable prices. You'll often see Rastafarians selling handmade leather sandals from stalls or on the street – try Port of Spain's Independence Square.

In **Tobago**, the widest variety is sold at the huts adjacent to Store Bay Beach, but you'll get better deals in Scarborough market and the stalls that line Milford and Wilson roads around the market square.

In order to protect local endangered animals, avoid buying products made from turtle shell, black coral, conch or bird feathers.

Travel essentials

Costs

Though no Caribbean island could be considered a budget place to visit, Trinidad and Tobago is undoubtedly one of the **cheapest Caribbean destinations** due to its strong oil and manufacturing-based economy. If you are prepared to take the least expensive accommodation, eat at budget cafés and street stalls and travel by public transport, you can get by on TT$500/US$75/£55/€62 a day. If, however, you opt for fancier accommodation and eat at restaurants, you will need at least TT$1000/US$150/£110/€124 a day. Renting a car is obviously an added expense, with rates starting at TT$300/US$45/£33/€37 per day.

Costs vary around T&T: Tobago – where the already-imported goods from Trinidad have to be imported all over again – is generally more costly than Trinidad. Accommodation is cheaper outside Port of Spain, San Fernando and Tobago's Crown Point area. Restaurants vary greatly in price: fine dining establishments charge TT$170/US$25/£18/€21 and up for a main course; the more basic restaurants, with plastic tables and buffet-style service, offer huge meals from around TT$50/US$8/£5/€6.

During **Carnival season**, accommodation rates are hiked (see page 27), as often are drinks, taxi fares and club covers. And then there are the Carnival fetes (parties), which start at about TT$200/

ALOE VERA

The thick, spiky stems of **aloe vera** grow profusely throughout T&T. A staple of local healing and skin care, the plant is a veritable cure-all – drunk as a purgative, used as a conditioning rinse and applied to cuts, grazes and burns to draw out infection. It's an excellent remedy for sunburn, heat rash and insect bites, and is even made into wine.

To extract fresh aloe gel from the stem, cut off a section and pare away the spiky edges. Slice in half and wipe the vaguely mauve gel onto the affected areas, scratching the surface to release more jelly as needed and being careful not to get it on clothing, since it leaves a stubborn purple stain.

US$30/£22/€25 for basic cooler parties (where you bring your own drinks) to TT$800/US$118/£88/€100 or more for a high-end all-inclusive event with food and top-drawer alcohol included.

The **minimum wage** in T&T is currently TT$15/US$2.22/£1.66/€1.87 an hour; you might want to bear this fact in mind when negotiating taxi fares to off-route destinations and prices for other goods and services.

Electricity

Currents run on 110 or 220 volts, 60 cycles. The current is often sluggish around peak times, particularly in Tobago, making everything run a little less efficiently than at home. **Plug pins** are flat two-pronged, sometimes with a third, round pin too. Many hotels have generators, as power outages are common. Unplug appliances when not using them, as power surges after shutdowns can damage electrical goods.

Health

There are few health risks in Trinidad and Tobago: the islands are **nonmalarial**, and the chlorinated **tap water** is safe to drink (though it doesn't taste great, and most locals filter and/or boil it before drinking). There are no mandatory **immunizations**, though you should ensure that you're up to date with polio and tetanus vaccines, and if you intend to arrive by ferry from Venezuela (or by plane from South/Central America, Haiti, Dominican Republic, Asia and Africa), you'll need a yellow fever vaccination certificate.

The most likely hazards are overexposure to the sun, too much rum and the inevitable minor stomach upsets that come with unfamiliar food and water. Heat and humidity make **cuts and grazes** slower to heal, so apply iodine or antiseptic spray/powder (cream just keeps a cut wet) and try to keep the wound dry. **Heat rashes** are caused by blocked sweat ducts; to avoid them wear loose cotton clothes, and to treat a rash take frequent cool showers without soap, dust skin with medicated talcum powder and don't use sunscreen or moisturizer. Always drink plenty of water (coconut water is especially rehydrating) and use a good-quality, high-factor sunscreen (plus, if possible, keep out of the sun between 11am and 3pm).

Trinidad and Tobago has the fourth highest incidence of **HIV and AIDS** in the Caribbean (around 1.5 percent prevalence), and cases of other sexually transmitted diseases like gonorrhoea and syphilis are also high. If you do have sex while away, always use a condom.

Animal and plant hazards

Mosquitoes and **sandflies** can be a real nuisance, particularly in the wet season (June–Dec). Sandflies in particular deliver an incredibly itchy and long-lasting bite and are at their most aggressive at sundown, especially around standing water. Cover your arms and legs at dusk and use plenty of strong insect repellent; Avon's Skin So Soft moisturizer is said to have miraculous anti-mosquito properties. Once you've been bitten, do not scratch or even touch the bites except to apply soothing creams – homeopathic pyrethrum is particularly good, as is a coating of fresh aloe vera gel (see above), or of antihistamine cream; Benadryl is the main brand available in T&T. Note that mosquitoes here do carry **dengue fever**, an unpleasant viral infection that lasts for a couple of weeks and can be serious in the very young or old; and in 2014, there was an outbreak of another flu-like mosquito-borne virus, **chikungunya**, which also has the unpleasant side-effect of long-lasting joint pain. Neither has a vaccine, so best protection is to avoid getting bitten in the first place.

Another problem in the forests are **chiggers**, tiny mites whose bite leaves a very itchy and long-lasting red bump with a tendency to get infected; apply antiseptic regularly to keep the bite clean. Likewise, stings from hornet-like **wasps** (known as jackspaniards) are nasty but fairly harmless, though **African-**

ized **bees** are now common throughout Trinidad and are aggressive if disturbed; do not wear strong perfume in the bush and follow guides' directions. Never kill a bee after having been stung, as this will cause it to emit a pheromone which attracts even more bees.

Though there are no deadly snakes in Tobago, Trinidad's forests harbour four venomous varieties (see page 273); the **fer-de-lance** and the **bushmaster** or **pit viper** (both known as *mapepire*, pronounced "mah-pee-pee"), and two species of brightly coloured **coral snake**. It's best to wear long trousers, shoes or boots and socks when walking in the bush, and obviously to refrain from investigating rock crevices with your bare hands. If you do encounter a snake, either give it a wide berth or, if necessary, move it gently out of the way with a long stick. In the event of a bite, keep calm; death from a snakebite is almost unheard of here, and your worst enemy is panic. Bandage the affected area tightly (if the bite is on a limb, tie a tourniquet above it), note down what the snake looked like, and seek medical help – all local hospitals have stocks of the relevant antidote.

Endowed with sharp teeth and a bit of an attitude if cornered, **barracuda** are best admired from a distance, as are **moray eels**. Don't stick your hand into rock crevices when diving or snorkelling, and never touch **coral**; quite apart from killing the organism with a caress, you'll probably come away with an unattractive, slow-healing rash. Another hazard you may well encounter are the many spiny **black sea urchins** that inhabit reefs and bays; if you tread on one, remove as much of the spine as possible, douse the area in vinegar (or urine) and see a doctor. Washing with vinegar is also the best way to treat **jellyfish** stings. Take care to avoid the long trailing tendrils of the purple Portuguese man-of-war, fairly common in the waters around Trinidad. Seek medical help if you've been stung, and don't touch dead ones washed up on the beach, as they remain harmful.

Take care to avoid poisonous **manchineel trees** – unremarkable-looking small trees with a wide, spreading crown of small, dark green leaves on long stalks, green flowers and tangerine-sized, apple-like green fruits. All parts of the tree are toxic – even the milky sap causes skin blister – so don't shelter underneath them during rain. They've been removed from popular beaches and signs put up where they've been allowed to remain, but they do grow along the coast in remote areas, and the fruits can wash up on other stretches of sand.

Medical services

The main **hospitals** in Trinidad are Port of Spain General (169 Charlotte St; ☎623 2951) and Mount Hope in St Augustine (Eastern Main Rd; ☎645 4673); there are also small hospitals in all the main towns, as well as the more efficient private establishment St Clair Medical Centre in Port of Spain (18 Elizabeth St; ☎628 1451, ⓦmedcorpltd.com). Tobago's Scarborough General Hospital is at Signal Hill (☎660 4744 or ☎639 4444), and has an A&E department. For an **ambulance**, call ☎811 or ☎990.

You won't have to pay for treatment at public hospitals, but will be charged a **fee** at Mount Hope and St Clair. Long waits and stretched facilities make it more sensible to plump for a private option, particularly as your insurance should cover costs. If you do find yourself in need of medical attention, remember that most insurance policies require you to pay up initially and retain the receipts.

Many pharmacies stock a modest range of herbal remedies and other **alternative medicines** Reputable alternative health practitioners include ex-surgeon Harry Ramnarine, based at 403 Rodney Rd, Chaguanas (☎665 8041, ⓦbit.ly/IshtaraTT). Rajesh Dharrie-Mahraj, 14 Murray St, Woodbrook, Port of Spain (☎624 2410) is an excellent osteopath.

Insurance

As Trinidad and Tobago's public health system is pretty basic, you'll want to seek private treatment should you fall ill, so it's essential that you take out **travel insurance** before entering the country.

A typical travel insurance **policy** (see page 46) provides cover for the loss of baggage, tickets and – up to a certain limit – cash or cheques, as well as cancellation or curtailment of your journey. Most of them exclude so-called dangerous sports. In Trinidad and Tobago this can mean scuba diving, windsurfing and (in some policies) hiking, though probably not kayaking; read small print carefully as coverage can vary wildly for similar premiums. Many policies can also be chopped and changed to exclude coverage you don't need.

Internet

Almost all accommodation options in T&T have **wi-fi** (usually free, and noted in our reviews with 🛜 throughout the Guide), while the *Rituals* coffee-shop chain offers wireless hotspots, as do many cafés and bars. There are a few **internet cafés** are scattered around the islands, though these are few and far between these days.

ROUGH GUIDES TRAVEL INSURANCE

Rough Guides has teamed up with **WorldNomads.com** to offer great travel insurance deals. Policies are available to residents of over 150 countries, with cover for a wide range of adventure sports, 24hr emergency assistance, high levels of medical and evacuation cover and a stream of travel safety information. Roughguides.com users can take advantage of their policies online 24/7, from anywhere in the world – even if you're already travelling. And since plans often change when you're on the road, you can extend your policy and even claim online. Roughguides.com users who buy travel insurance with WorldNomads.com can also leave a positive footprint and donate to a community development project. For more information, go to ⓦroughguides.com/travel-insurance.

Laundry

Most hotels provide a laundry service, albeit at extortionate rates in larger properties, while guesthouses often have a machine for guests' use. There is a coin-operated laundry in Crown Point, Tobago (see page 210).

LGBT+ travellers

Although T&T is less aggressively homophobic than many other Caribbean countries, "buggery" has remained a criminal offence since the colonial era, as has any same-sex intimacy (classed as "serious indecency"). However in April 2018, activist Jason Jones secured a landmark **legal** victory against these archaic laws (visit ⓦbit. ly/CaisoTT for more information), with a judge deeming them unconstitutional and so paving the way for them to be permanently repealed – much to the ire of religious groups. There is a creeping acceptance of the LGBT+ community in Trinidad (less so in Tobago), and Port of Spain has one or two LGBT+ bars, though the **scene** remains quite underground with events publicized by word of mouth. LGBT+ travellers are unlikely to suffer any direct prejudice – but, even so, public displays of affection are best avoided.

Maps

Various private entities produce free maps of both Trinidad and Tobago, showing main roads, beaches and tourist attractions, which are adequate for mainstream exploration, and are available in hotel lobbies and airport tourist booths. The *Discover Trinidad & Tobago* free booklet (see page 47) also carries decent island and city maps.

Reise Know-How publish a 1:150,000 map of Trinidad and Tobago, though like its competitors, it hasn't been recently updated. T&T's **Land and Surveys** Division produce a 1:150,000 road map of Trinidad and the 1:50,000 map of Tobago, and a detailed map of Port of Spain, but again these are outdated, and impossible to find outside of T&T, where they're sometimes stocked in the islands' bookshops.

Money

The local currency is the **Trinidad and Tobago dollar**. This is usually abbreviated to TT$, and is divided into one hundred cents. Coins start at 1 cent and range up through 5, 10 and 25 cents. Notes start at one dollar and in denominations of 5, 10, 20, 50 and 100. It's best to keep some of your cash in small denominations: supermarkets and bars can usually exchange TT$100, but taxis and street vendors often can't and should be paid with TT$50 or $TT20 notes.

At the time of writing, the **exchange rate** was US$1 to TT$6.74; £1 to TT$9.18 and €1 to TT$8. **Cambios** are few and far between (though there are some excellent FX Trader outlets in Trinidad; see page 90), but you can change cash in all banks for a small commission. Using a debit card in an **ATM** machine is a lot easier; ATMs are easy to find, and some dispense US dollars, which are also widely accepted locally. All major **credit and debit cards** are accepted in shops, petrol stations and many restaurants and hotels.

Opening hours

Shop opening hours are generally Monday to Friday 8am to 5.30pm and Saturday 8am to 5pm; malls are usually open from 10am until 8 or 9pm, while supermarkets open 8am–8pm daily. Opening times are often variable, depending on the individual shop and mood of the shopkeeper.

Banking hours vary slightly depending on the bank, but are usually Monday to Thursday 8am to 3pm, Friday 8am to 1pm and 3 to 5pm. Most banks in Trinidad's larger malls open 10am to 6pm with no break. **Post offices** are generally open Monday

CALLING HOME FROM ABROAD

To make an international call, dial the international access code (011 in Trinidad and Tobago), then the destination's country code, before the rest of the number. Note that the initial zero is omitted from the area code when dialling the UK, Ireland, Australia and New Zealand from abroad.
Australia + 61
New Zealand + 64
UK + 44
US and Canada + 1
Republic of Ireland + 353
South Africa + 27

to Friday from 7am to 5pm and Saturday from 8am to noon.

Phones

Local operators bmobile (Ⓦ bmobile.co.tt) and Digicel (Ⓦ digiceltt.com) offer **pre-paid SIM cards** with credit, sold at their own outlets or at phone shops and kiosks in malls, all of which are ubiquitous islandwide. Bmobile has a kiosk just past the immigration desks at Piarco, should you wish to get connected on arrival; in Tobago there are Digicel and bmobile outlets at Gulf City Mall in Lowlands. You'll need photo ID to buy a SIM, and should carry the handset you'll be using so that you can ensure it's not locked; note that bmobile switched to 4G in 2017, so older handsets may not work in T&T. Both companies usually have deals where you get a SIM, some credit and a basic phone for around TT$300; Digicel also sell time-specific (1, 3, 5, 10 and 30 days) bundles of talk and data credit. **Top-up talk credit** (added remotely when you buy, or by way of a card/paper receipt with a code that you punch into the phone) is widely available from shops, pharmacies and supermarkets, and from the odd machine. Calling rates are listed on the company websites, and are reasonable even for international calls.

The **area code** for Trinidad and Tobago is Ⓣ 868; local and international operator is Ⓣ 0, directory enquiries Ⓣ 6411. In Tobago, the Ⓣ 211 service can find business numbers for you and provide information on the island and its festivals.

Photography

It's important to always **ask permission** before taking someone's picture – many visitors don't, much to the ire of the market trader or fisherman who doesn't appreciate being snapped while going about a day's work. Be sensitive, also, around temples and mosques, where photography may not be allowed.

Post

The country's postal service, **TT Post** (Ⓦ ttpost.net), is inexpensive and fairly reliable. Outgoing and incoming post travels reasonably quickly (one to two weeks to Europe and the US, three to Australia). The closer you are to the capital, the sooner your letters will be delivered. Send valuable items by registered mail, TT Post courier or by an international courier; FedEx and DHL both have local offices.

Most towns and villages have a **post office**, post office locations are detailed on the website above. Post boxes on the street are small, red, quite rare and easily missed; many still bear the insignia of the British postal service, a remnant of the colonial era. **Stamps** are sold at post offices, pharmacies and small shops, and letters and postcards cost under TT$5 to anywhere in the world.

Time

Trinidad and Tobago is four hours behind Greenwich Mean Time (five during the summer months), and one hour ahead of Eastern Standard Time.

Tourist information

Official **tourist information** is pretty poor, with no useful tourist offices other than booths at the airport – T&T's tourist board, the TDC, was dissolved in 2017, and is slated to be replaced with separate entities for Trinidad and for Tobago. There was no official tourist-board website for Trinidad at the time of writing; check Ⓦ tourism.gov.tt for updates. The Tobago Division of Tourism site (Ⓦ visittobago.gov. tt) is worth checking out, with accommodation and tour operator listings, and a calendar of events. The radio and national press advertise upcoming events, especially during Carnival.

The fact-filled *Discover Trinidad & Tobago* (Ⓦ discovertnt.com) includes features on T&T's culture and attractions, plus hotel, restaurant and tour operator listings. The *Ins and Outs of Trinidad and Tobago* (Ⓦ insandoutstt.com) is a glossy annual publication which has sections on Carnival, shopping, art and craft, eco-tourism and business, along with accommodation, eating and nightlife listings for both islands; while *Créolé* (Wwww. créolé.com) has detailed reviews of restaurants in both islands. These publications are available at hotels, tourist offices and other places frequented by foreigners. Other **useful websites**, covering everything from accommodation and restaurants to panyard listings, include Wmytobago.info and the more Trinidad-oriented Wtntisland.com.

Travellers with disabilities

There is little infrastructure for those with **disabilities** in T&T. However, a small but growing number of hotels, guesthouses and villas have been made accessible; these are mentioned in the text. If you want to make local contacts, try Disabled Peoples' International (T624 6060, Wdpi.org), at 13a Wrightson Rd, Port of Spain.

If you use a wheelchair, note that getting around Port of Spain and other large towns can be problematic. There are large gullies at the sides of most streets, and few of them have chair-accessible slopes or ramps.

Travelling with children

Travelling with children is pretty hassle-free in T&T. Almost all local hotels are have designated family rooms, and can provide cots for babies; many also provide babysitting services. **Nappies**/wipes etc (local brands and Pampers/Huggies), **formula** and jarred baby food are widely available in supermarkets (with a wider selection in Trinidad than Tobago); pharmacies also stock **accessories** such as bottles, car-window sunscreens etc – Trinidad's SuperPharm chain are particularly good.

The main **risks** to children are insect bites (use repellent liberally, cover legs before dusk; and apply a dry antiseptic spray on any picked bites) and over-exposure to the sun: days on the beach call for rash vests with long sleeves and a hat if possible. Apply sunscreen (never less than factor 50) before you leave for the day, to give it a chance to sink in, and re-apply regularly. Many **beaches** in Trinidad (and some in Tobago) can be risky for swimming, so it's best to keep a close eye on children when in the sea; even locals' favourite Maracas has a strong undertow. Tobago's Store Bay, Pigeon Point and Canoe Bay are the calmest, but Macqueripe in Trinidad can be quite benign too.

In terms of keeping kids amused, the beach is usually the best bet; **playgrounds** are few and far between (and unusable in the heat of the day in any case). In Port of Spain, there is a decent public play area at Nelson Mandela Park (aka King George V Park) on St Clair Avenue in St Clair. As well as the Five Islands Park in Chaguaramas, the capital also has two decent **soft play** options: IJump, in Newtown at 177 Tragarete Rd (Wed & Sat 10am–6pm, Fri & Sun 11am–4pm; T313 9319, Wbit.ly/IJumpTT); and the slightly more expensive Jungle Jam, 20 Hamilton Holder St, Woodbrook (Tues–Sun 11am–6pm; T225 5002, Wjungle-jamtt.com). Tobago has no specific child-friendly attractions.

Finally, it's worth noting that while children are loved and indulged in T&T, **attitudes towards child-rearing** can be quite traditional, of the "seen and not heard" variety – tantrums in public or backtalking to adults will raise a few eyebrows, especially if these are not immediately quashed by the parent (spanking still remains a common disciplinary method in Trinidad and Tobago). As a mark of respect, Trinbagonian children often call all adults "uncle" or "auntie"; encouraging your children to follow suit will be happily received.

Weddings

Couples can **marry** in Trinidad and Tobago as soon as three days after their arrival. Many hotels offer sumptuous honeymoon suites, and Tobago Weddings (T639 4347, Wtobagoweddings.com) will make necessary arrangements. You will need passports, airline tickets, and if either you or your soon-to-be spouse is divorced or widowed, the decree absolute or death certificate, along with proof of name change if it differs on the document.

Women travellers

Like other Caribbean countries, T&T has a predominantly **macho culture**. It's customary here to be friendly to strangers, acknowledge passers-by and even make small talk; perhaps as an extension of this, verbal comments or innuendo directed at passing women are commonplace. You'll probably be expected to be flattered by such "sweet talk", and to be fair comments are often humorous and amusing – though sometimes very direct and perhaps somewhat lewd. Foreign women may get more of this attention, which is usually unthreatening and best dealt with either via total insouciance or a witty comeback.

Be prepared to meet surprised reactions if you're a woman **travelling alone**, as doing so (or even venturing out unescorted after dark) is not at all common in T&T. Also be aware that as in other islands, the ritual of foreigners visiting Tobago to hook up with local men for no-strings sex is so entrenched that solo female travellers may well be approached by men with this in mind – unsurprisingly, given many foreigners fly in with just this in mind. If sex is not on your agenda, simply say no and mean it.

Port of Spain and the western tip

1 Port of Spain and the western tip

Spread over a peninsula that extends towards Venezuela and divides the Gulf of Paria from the Caribbean Sea, Trinidad's northwestern tip comprises the island's most urbanized area. The main focus of the region is Port of Spain, the country's capital and its commercial and cultural centre, which sits between the forested foothills of the Northern Range mountains and the choppy waters of the gulf. Home to nearly a third of Trinidad's population, as well as many immigrants from Venezuela and other islands in the region, it's a city that buzzes with metropolitan verve, a thriving place that serves as the hub of the southern Caribbean. Although exciting in any season, with a brilliant nightlife and arts scene, the best time to be here is during the weeks leading up to Carnival, when there are nightly fetes and panyards as well as the biggest Jouvert celebrations in Trinidad and, of course, the kaleidoscope of the Parade of the Bands.

Beyond the city's western suburbs, the coastal road heads toward **Chaguaramas**, Port of Spain's playground, where Tucker Valley is crisscrossed by a network of forest trails, and the sheltered cove of **Macqueripe** offers excellent swimming. Contrastingly, the southern Chaguaramas coast is all business – though its marinas and commercial boatyards are interspersed with some appealing waterside bars and restaurants. The further west you go, the more wild and undeveloped the terrain becomes. Beyond Chaguaramas, the western tip crumbles into a series of rocky islands separated by rough, swirling channels known as the **Bocas del Dragon** – the Dragon's Mouth. Though the islands – the most accessible and developed of which is **Gaspar Grande**, the most isolated and atmospheric being **Chacachacare** – lie just a short distance offshore, they are completely free of motorized traffic. In the eighteenth century, they were a refuge for whalers, smugglers and pirates; today, they're the preserve of yachting enthusiasts, fishermen and anyone in search of tranquillity.

Port of Spain and its suburbs have a wide range of **accommodation** to suit all budgets. Whether you're visiting the city for Carnival or plan to explore other parts of Trinidad, you will almost certainly end up staying here at some point. Indeed, it's entirely feasible to base yourself in Port of Spain and visit the rest of Trinidad on day-trips, either by renting a car or using the public transport network that radiates out from the City Gate bus and maxi terminus.

Port of Spain

PORT OF SPAIN occupies a crucial place in T&T's national psyche. It's the hub of the republic's booming economy, the home of government and the crucible of

Highlights

❶ Queen's Park Savannah at dusk As the heat lifts, people gravitate here to walk, drink a coconut water or sample some street food. See page 63

❷ Carnival With panyards and fetes, Jouvert and the main parade, Port of Spain is the epicentre of Trini Carnival. See pages 71, 74 and 80

❸ Foodie Port of Spain From a roti to an *arepa* or some fine Italian food, the capital's wonderful dining scene offers a wealth of variety. See page 84

❹ Avenue lime Work your way along Ariapita Avenue's succession of fantastic bars and clubs. See page 88

❺ Cocoa delights Sample delectable chocolate creations at Cocobel and the Cocoa Pod, or take a cocoa themed city tour. See pages 92 and 79

❻ Chaguaramas Whether a walk in Tucker Valley, a swim at Macqueripe or a meal at a seaside restaurant, Chaguaramas is a lovely foil to the hectic capital. See page 94

❼ Going "down the islands" Just a short boat ride from the mainland, the beautifully rugged Bocas offer sandy beaches, clear waters and plenty of peace. See page 102

HIGHLIGHTS ARE MARKED ON THE MAP ON PAGE 54

PORT OF SPAIN AND THE WESTERN TIP

HIGHLIGHTS
1. Queen's Park Savannah at dusk
2. Carnival
3. Foodie Port of Spain
4. Avenue lime
5. Cocoa delights
6. Chaguaramas
7. Going "down the islands"

Trinidad's rich **cultural life**, with legions of mas camps and panyards, art galleries and theatres. It was here that Carnival was first established in Trinidad, and – in the suburb of Laventille – that the steel pan was invented.

Spreading back from the Gulf of Paria and enclosed by crumpled green hills, Port of Spain has a dynamic, sophisticated feel that's markedly different from the rest of the country. City dwellers and the weekday influx of workers who pour in from the East–West Corridor commuter belt jostle for space in and around its compact centre, which displays a schizophrenic mix of the old and the new, with street traders selling cinnamon sticks or mauby bark in front of shopping malls bursting with international chains, and glinting high-rises overlooking impoverished squatter communities. The mishmash of architectural styles makes for an ugly first impression, especially **downtown**, with its traffic-choked streets and dusty commercial buildings. But there are many fine nineteenth-century buildings here, from dignified churches and state offices to quaint "gingerbread" houses, named for their decorative wooden fretwork. Tree-shaded squares break up the downtown grid and grandiose mansions of colonial planters overlook the large open space of the **Queen's Park Savannah**, which was created by enlightened town planners in the early nineteenth century and now affords the city some much-needed breathing room.

Stretching along the flat coastal plains to the west and bordering the western side of the Savannah, the districts of **Woodbrook**, **St James**, **Newtown** and **St Clair** are very much part of the city. Bars and restaurants line the after-dark hotspots of Ariapita Avenue and the Western Main Road, and costumes are created here at **mas camps** during the months preceding **Carnival**, when the city's volatile mix of style, hedonism, creativity and *joie de vivre* explodes onto the streets. Spreading north and east into the Northern Range foothills, **St Ann's**, **Cascade**, **Belmont** and **Laventille** are mostly residential, though the last has a rather grim reputation for violent crime. North of the Savannah, leafy **Maraval** has some great places to eat, and is also the place to hop in a jeep taxi up to the friendly farming community of **Paramin** for heady city views and some welcome respite from the heat and bustle.

Brief history

Port of Spain became Trinidad's capital almost by accident. In 1757, a series of pirate attacks on the then-capital St Joseph left the residence of the new **Spanish governor**, Don Pedro de la Moneda, uninhabitable, prompting him to move the seat of government to the more convenient location of Puerto de España (a port of Spain). Though the town consisted of no more than two streets with a few hundred residents and was built on swampy, flood-prone ground, it did have the great advantage of a fine natural **harbour**, and was quickly made the permanent capital.

The colonial era

As French Catholics flooded into Trinidad in the 1780s, Port of Spain's **economy** boomed and the city spread. Land was reclaimed from the sea, and streets were built over the surrounding mangrove swamps and woods. The last Spanish governor, **José Maria Chacón**, greatly facilitated this expansion when, in 1787, he diverted the St Ann's River to the outskirts of the town, along the foot of Laventille Hill, alleviating the floods that had often troubled central Port of Spain. Chacón was less effective, however, when it came to defending the city against the **British**, who invaded and took over the island in 1797. In 1808, a devastating fire led the British governor, **Sir Ralph Woodford**, to make a number of civic improvements, establishing the Queen's Park Savannah and developing Woodford Square. Learning from Spanish mistakes, the British also improved the city's defences by building Fort George and Fort Picton.

Emancipation and beyond

After **emancipation** in 1834, freed slaves left plantations to find work in the capital, settling in the hills to the east of the city where they established the suburbs

1

Maraval (1km) St Ann's (1km) Cascade

Trinidad Theatre Workshop
Wildflower Park
Stollmeyer's Castle
ST CLAIR
Whitehall
Archbishop's House
JACKSON SQUARE
Roomor
Mille Fleurs
Hayes Court
HAYES ST
Queen's Royal College

Emperor Valley Zoo
The Hollows
Botanical Gardens

CIRCULAR ROAD

Queen's Hall

Queen's Park Savannah

Peschier Cemetery

ST CLAIR AVE
SWEET BRIAR RD
Canadian High Commission
ALCAZAR ST
RUST ST
NEWTOWN

QUEEN'S PARK WEST
US Embassy
MARLI STREET
All Saints Anglican Church
Boissiere House
WARNER STREET

Grand Stand & North Stand

Street food stalls

QUEEN'S PARK WEST
George Brown House
ALBION ST
Knowsley Building
NAPA
Memorial Park
National Museum & Art Gallery

ROBERTS ST
Silver Stars Panyard
WOODBROOK
Desperadoes Panyard
BADEN POWELL ST
FRENCH ST
ARIAPITA AVE
Lapeyrouse Cemetery
METHUEN'S ST
MCDONALD
PHILIPPS STREET

KEATE ST
GORDON ST
NEW ST
LORD HARRIS SQUARE
OXFORD ST

Renegades Panyard

Caribbean Court of Justice
Immigration Office
Rosary Roman Catholic Church
GREEN CORNER
PARK ST

N

VICTORIA SQUARE
DUKE STREET WEST
SYDNEY ST
Police Station
CHARLES STREET
SACKVILLE STREET
LONDON STREET
DOCK ROAD

Hall of Justice
City Hall
KNOX ST
Old Public Library
WOODFORD SQUARE
HART ST
NALIS
Old Fire Station
Holy Trinity Cathedral

Trinidad All Stars Panyard
PRINCE STREET

Central Police Station & Police Museum
Red House

Government Campus Plaza
Cruise Ship Complex
King's Wharf
Waterfront Complex
Gulf of Paria
Water Taxi Terminal

Brian Lara Statue
Central Bank
INDEPENDENCE SQUARE NORTH
BRIAN LARA PROMENADE
INDEPENDENCE SQUARE SOUTH
Nicholas Tower
Arthur Cipriani statue
SOUTH QUAY
Fort San Andrés

Cathedral of the Immaculate Conception
City Gate

CENTRAL PORT OF SPAIN

BEETHAM HIGHWAY
Tobago Ferry Terminal
Queen's Wharf
Lighthouse

Scarborough, Tobago Churchill Roosevelt & Uriah Butler highways & Piarco Airport (24km)

0   250
metres

EATING
Breakfast Shed	16
Buzo Osteria Italiana	4
D'Bocas	14
Dopson's	3
Häagen-Dazs Café	5
Hardline Vegetarian	12
Kava	1
La Cantina	11
Living Water	9
Lola's	7
Mother Nature	13
Shiann's Food Palace	10
Town	6
Trotters	1
Waterfront/Sushi Bar	15
Zabouca Breads	8

DRINKING & NIGHTLIFE
51°	2
Kaiso Blues Café	1

SHOPPING
101 Art Gallery	1
Cocoa Pod	2
Metropolitan Book Suppliers	4
Samaroo's	3

ACCOMMODATION
Alicia's Palace	1
Caribbean Tourist Villa	8
Forty Winks	4
Hyatt Regency	11
Inn at 87	7
Johnson's	7
Kapok	2
La Calypso	5
Pearl's	9
Radisson Trinidad	10
Villa de Rose	6

of Laventille and Belmont. With a growing population of workers, traders and entrepreneurs, Port of Spain sprawled outwards into the old plantations of Maraval and St Ann's. Indian immigrants brought to Trinidad under indentured labour schemes settled in St James, while the population was further swelled by migrants from China, Portugal, Venezuela and Syria. The descendants of these groups, and those of the French and Spanish communities, compose the cosmopolitan mix of peoples and cultures that make Port of Spain unique today.

As the nation's capital, Port of Spain was naturally the focus for both the **political turmoil** and the **growing prosperity** that marked the country's history during the twentieth century. From the water riots of 1903, through the independence movement of the 1950s down to the bloody 1990 coup attempt, Woodford Square has been an arena of political strife. The dredging of the city's **deep-water harbour** in the 1930s made Port of Spain the leading port of the southern Caribbean, while the discovery of offshore oil in the 1970s funded the construction of the **financial district**, dominated by the imposing twin towers of the Central Bank.

Port of Spain today

Thanks to the expansionist dreams of former People's National Party prime minister Patrick Manning, Port of Spain's skyline now bristles with **high-rise blocks**, from sleek Nicholas Tower to the rash of government buildings on Wrightson Road. The buoyant consumerism of the last twenty years or so has seen **lavish developments** springing up all over the city, from American-style luxury malls and exclusive gated communities to the futuristic National Academy for the Performing Arts on the Savannah and the slick new waterside promenade around the *Hyatt Regency* hotel. And though civic spending contracted in the wake of the 2008 global economic collapse, Port of Spain has endured, with its prettiest public squares restored again to vibrant meeting places and its outlying districts electrified by a slew of new restaurants and bars.

Downtown Port of Spain

Dating back to the 1780s, **downtown** Port of Spain is the city's oldest district, and in places it still looks the part, though the colonial-era buildings on the backstreets are fast giving way to a rash of recent development. Constantly reinventing itself in a frenzy of modernization, this is the capital's shopping and financial centre. Within the compact grid of streets surrounding broad **Independence Square/Brian Lara Promenade** and bustling **Frederick Street**, shops jostle for space with old Spanish warehouses, coffee exporters' offices, finance houses and the paraphernalia of the **docks**, while the thoroughfares are jammed with traffic, pedestrians and pavement vendors.

PORT OF SPAIN ORIENTATION

Port of Spain's compact **downtown area** is based on a grid system, and is easy to explore on foot, with everything in walking distance of **Independence Square/Brian Lara Promenade**, one block north of City Gate, the main transport terminal. There are four main roads leading out of the central downtown area: **Wrightson Road** skirts the southern edge of the city, becoming the Audrey Jeffers Highway as it heads west past the suburbs of Diego Martin and Westmoorings, and out towards Chaguaramas. **Tragarete Road** and parallel **Ariapita Avenue** run from uptown Park Street through Woodbrook before joining, respectively, the **Western Main Road** into St James and the highway at the MovieTowne complex.

The green expanse of the Queen's Park Savannah serves as a boundary between downtown and the rest of the city. From its northwest corner, **Saddle Road** leads to Maraval and eventually Maracas Beach, and is the access point for Paramin. From the northeast corner of the Savannah, **St Ann's Road** takes you to St Ann's and Cascade, while minor roads on the Savannah's western edge thread into the businesslike districts of Newtown and St Clair.

1

Independence Square/Brian Lara Promenade

Set on two parallel streets, **Independence Square/Brian Lara Promenade** is divided by a shady paved area (the promenade) dotted with benches and concrete chess tables; it's a popular after-work liming spot, with street food vendors doing a brisk trade; the square is also home to what's said to be the most profitable *KFC* in the world, on the corner of Broadway. The throngs of people here inevitably attract a fair number of beggars (particularly around the cathedral), who patrol the promenade and tend to latch onto foreigners – keep your wits about you.

The cumbersome title is a result of frequent **name changes** in recent decades. Until independence, it was Marine Square, in honour of the fact that this land was reclaimed from the sea in 1816. It was rechristened Independence Square in 1962, and its central section was later renamed to honour Trinidad's most famous cricketer, Brian Lara. A bronze statue of the "Prince of Port of Spain" stands in the middle of the Promenade at the western end of the square, which is overlooked here by the sleek blue-and-silver **Nicholas Tower**, and the twin towers of the **Central Bank of Trinidad and Tobago**, completed in 1985 and brutally 1980s in style. The slew of high-rises overlooking the other side of the Promenade make up the new **Government Campus Plaza**, built to accommodate various government ministries from Legal Affairs to Customs and Excise. Towards its eastern end, Independence Square intersects with Nelson Street, which runs through one of Port of Spain's rougher areas and isn't a great place to wander, tempting as the crumbling colonial-era buildings may look.

Arthur Cipriani statue

In the centre of Independence Square, at the junction with Frederick Street, the **Arthur Cipriani statue** commemorates a former Port of Spain mayor who campaigned energetically for compulsory education for all and self-government for the island – the only legislator of his day to defend workers' rights. He died in 1945 and is buried in the Lapeyrouse Cemetery in Woodbrook (see page 69).

Cathedral of the Immaculate Conception
Independence Square

At the eastern end of the square, the Promenade is taken up with the imposing Roman Catholic **Cathedral of the Immaculate Conception**, a legacy of Governor Woodford's post-fire reconstruction, and looking spiffy following a TT$65 million restoration. Completed in 1836, the twin-towered Gothic construction took sixteen years to build; its ironwork frame was shipped from England, while the limestone wall blocks were quarried in Laventille. Sixteen **stained-glass windows** were added in the 1980s, depicting T&T's many ethnic groups, and are the highlight of the interior.

The Promenade ends just east of the cathedral at diminutive **Columbus Square**, named after the colourful statue of the Spanish "discoverer" and today a very run-down spot that serves as a base for homeless people.

Charlotte Street

Striking north off Independence Square one block west of the Cathedral of the Immaculate Conception, **Charlotte Street** is lined with fabric shops, general stores and umbrella-shaded street stalls selling everything from fruit and vegetables to leather sandals, sneakers, clothes and homewares. It's a vibrant place for a wander, thick with the aromas drifting out from roti shops and the incense burned by stallholders, and ringing out with the reggae and soca played by music vendors and the parping of horns as cars squeeze through the narrow stretch of tarmac not taken up by commerce. It's also the best place to pick up a bargain in Port of Spain, whether you're on the lookout for souvenirs or spices – though do keep your wits about you.

King's Wharf

The city's southern edge is dominated by the gritty industrial area surrounding the docks, sliced through by Wrightson Road and overlooked by the chimneys of the Powergen electricity plant and the silos of the National Four Mills factory. With its vast warehouses and jagged skyline of cranes, gantries and mounds of containers, **King's Wharf** is the hub of Trinidad's booming import-export trade. Everything from bananas to cars passes through this hectic port, with most of the action taking place in the early hours when it's still relatively cool. Dredged in the 1930s, the deep-water harbour allowed Port of Spain to accommodate deep-draught ships, boosting Trinidad's economy and consolidating the city's position as the most important southern Caribbean port.

Waterfront Complex

The only let-up in Wrightson Road's rows of warehouses and industrial buildings is at the western end of Independence Square, where the **Waterfront Complex** has opened up the Gulf of Paria to pedestrians. A promenade runs along the seafront past the high-rise *Hyatt Regency* hotel and along to the cruise ship pier, and is a popular spot for an evening stroll. Adjacent to the *Hyatt* building, Tower D is the temporary home of Trinidad's **parliament** during ongoing restoration of the Red House, its entrance on Wrightson Road flanked by **mural sculpture panels**. Designed by mas-maker Brian McFarlane, these depict the different peoples of Trinidad and Tobago alongside sporting and economic achievements, as well as the country's motto: "together we aspire, together we achieve".

The *Hyatt*'s oceanside restaurant and bar (see page 85) is a lovely option for a drink or a meal, with the *Breakfast Shed* (see page 85) a less expensive alternative.

South Quay

One block south of Independence Square, the parallel **South Quay** is a wide commercial street dominated by **City Gate**, a grand Victorian stone building that served as Port of Spain's train station until the line from here to Arima/San Fernando was shut down in 1968. It remains Trinidad's main transportation hub, with PTSC buses and maxi taxis arriving from and departing to all parts of the country. It's also the site of the main downtown **judging point** during Carnival, when the rows of bleachers offer a great view of the bands as they pass.

Just west of City Gate, across Broadway, the unassuming cream-painted **Fort San Andrés** was built by the Spanish as the island's only defence against British invasion. The curved wall behind, with rusting cannons embedded, is all that survives of the original 5m-high perimeter, now mostly buried thanks to successive land reclamation projects. When the fort was constructed in 1787, the sea lapped against its ramparts; today it's a good couple of hundred metres inland. The British added a second storey to the original structure, and used it as a customs house and reading room, as well as a processing facility for some 65,000 African slaves and 30,000 Indian indentured workers entering Trinidad. After serving as a desultory city museum for some years, it's currently closed pending restoration.

The lighthouse

Wrightson Rd

Presiding over Wrightson Road south of Fort San Andrés, Port of Spain's **lighthouse** was built in 1842 at what was then the end of St Vincent Jetty. Some 19.5m high, the handsome hexagonal structure has since been marooned inland by reclamation; it stands in the middle of a traffic island, and the busy highway that thunders constantly past has skewed it five degrees from the vertical. Local insurance company Beacon took over its maintenance in 2017, treating it to a fresh new blue-and-white paint job and installing solar-powered lights in the lantern room at the top.

1

BEYOND THE LIGHTHOUSE

East of Port of Spain's lighthouse, the rusting corrugated-iron roofs and crumbling buildings that make up **Sea Lots** provide a stark contrast to the sleek glass and concrete of the waterfront high-rises. Condemned by many as a hotbed of crime, this impoverished community is hemmed in by the oily Gulf of Paria to one side and the highway to another; wall murals facing the highway commemorate the lives of Sea Lots resident Haydee Paul and her two children, tragically killed in a traffic accident in 2013. Beyond Sea Lots, the highway runs east toward **Beetham**, site of the country's main rubbish landfill and, on the inland side of the road, the notoriously rough residential community that has grown up around the dump, its boundaries marked by piles of scrap metal reclaimed by locals who make a living picking through the waste. Some 875 tonnes of rubbish find their way to the Beetham every day, and regular fires at the dump smother Sea Lots and Beetham in clouds of toxic smoke; residents here have some of the highest instances of respiratory disease in the country. Though the dump has reached its official capacity, plans to have it cleared and rehabilitated have yet to be realized, despite the continued efforts of local environmental campaigners who point out that the Beetham sits above the El Socorro aquifer, Trinidad's main source of groundwater, into which it's leaching a toxic chemical soup.

Frederick Street

Frederick Street is Port of Spain's main shopping drag, at its busiest between Independence Square and Park Street. Like much of the downtown area, Frederick Street has assumed a modern face in recent years, with many shops accommodated in multi-storeyed, air-conditioned malls complete with food courts; sadly, the mall hoardings obscure most of the intricate iron balconies that front the few remaining original buildings. The stalls on the corner of Frederick and Queen streets are all that's left of the **People's Mall** (or Drag Mall), which was destroyed in a 2005 fire; the maze of tiny shops selling hand-painted T-shirts, incense and Rasta craft are good for a browse.

Woodford Square

Boundaried by Knox and Hart streets to the north and south, the pretty, tree-shaded **Woodford Square** (named after the British governor who had it built in the early nineteenth century) holds a picturesque colonial-era bandstand and an elegant cast-iron fountain supported by statues of mermaids and mermen, which dates back to 1866. The square's main claim to fame, however, is as a centre of **political activism**. In 1903, it was the scene of a protest meeting against the introduction of new water rates, which quickly got out of hand – in the ensuing riots, the original Red House was burned to the ground. The square's reputation as a political cockpit really got going in 1956 with the establishment of the "**University of Woodford Square**". This was the brainchild of **Eric Williams** – historian, father of the national independence movement and first prime minister of the country – who delivered hugely popular weekly public lectures here on the issues of the day. In the 1970s, the square became a focal point for the Black Power movement, which renamed it the "people's parliament"; in April 1970, some 30,000 people converged here for the funeral of Basil Davis, a young activist shot dead by the police during a Black Power protest.

A Trinidadian version of Speaker's Corner, Woodford Square is still a centre of political discussion. On the eastern side of the square a blackboard lists the topic for discussion each day; these **debates** typically take place at a rather unsociable 7am and anyone can join in, provided that they can get a word in edgeways – it's not a platform for the fainthearted or soft-spoken.

Knox Street

The buildings flanking Woodford Square are a mishmash of architectural styles. On Knox Street, which forms the northeast border of the square, the oldest and most attractive building is the former **Public Library**, a large brick and stone structure built in 1901 and sporting a beautiful arcaded second storey. It's incongruously sandwiched between two brutally functional slabs of glass and concrete: the concrete pile to the east, on the corner of Frederick Street, is the 1961 **City Hall**, home to Port of Spain's council and the mayor's office; while westward, on the corner of Abercromby Street, is the plain **Hall of Justice**, built in 1979 and home to the Supreme Court of Trinidad and Tobago.

Red House

Abercromby St • Ⓦ ttparliament.org

Taking up half of a block between St Vincent and Abercromby streets, and bordered to the north and south by Knox and Hart streets, the imposing Neo-Renaissance **Red House** is actually more a faded, peeling terracotta; though you'll have to crane your neck to see any of it, as it's been under renovation since 1999, covered with a crude metal roof, swathed in scaffolding and enclosed by high construction-zone fences.

The Red House inherited its popular name from an earlier building on the site, which was painted bright red to celebrate Queen Victoria's diamond jubilee in 1897. The present structure, completed four years after its predecessor was burnt down in the 1903 water riots, was itself attacked in the **1990 coup** (see page 62), and bullet holes still scar the stonework; outside the front entrance on Abercromby Street, an eternal flame commemorates the seven government and security personnel who died during the coup. Though the Red House has long served as the official seat of Trinidad and Tobago's parliament, sessions have been shifted over to the Waterfront Complex (see page 59) during the current repair works. The TT$5 billion works were put on temporary hold in 2013 while archeologists investigated skeletal human remains and Amerindian artefacts, thought to date from between 430 AD and 1390 and found during excavations of the building's foundations. The somewhat optimistic estimate for the reopening of the Red House is mid-2018.

Holy Trinity Cathedral

Hart St • No set hours • ☏ 623 7271, Ⓦ bit.ly/HTCTT

Holy Trinity Cathedral was another of Governor Woodford's many initiatives to improve Port of Spain's public spaces. The original idea was to build it in the middle of the square itself, and work was already underway when the governor bowed to popular protest and moved it to its present site. Completed in 1818, the elegant stone structure is built along Gothic lines, with a large clock tower. The cool, shady interior boasts a mahogany hammerbeam roof, made in England and modelled on London's Westminster Hall. A life-size effigy of Governor Woodford lies on his tomb by the south wall; the plaques nearby commemorate various other colonial dignitaries. It's worth taking a stroll around the pretty gardens to see the stonework **labyrinth** at the side of the building.

NALIS

Cnr Hart and Abercromby streets • Mon–Fri 8.30am–6pm, Sat 8.30am–4pm • ☏ 623 6962, Ⓦ nalis.gov.tt

On the southwest side of Woodford Square, the modern **NALIS**, Trinidad and Tobago's national library, was built to resemble a beached cruise ship – something that's particularly obvious when it's lit up at night. The main hall inside, with its *Rituals* coffeeshop and wi-fi, is a good place to take a break from the heat, and there are often small exhibitions centred on local history and culture. The **amphitheatre** outside is used to stage plays and workshops; check the website to see what's on.

Next door, and part of the library complex, the **Old Fire Station** is a handsome cut-stone construction, built in 1896 and sporting a modern pink-and-grey paint job. It's now used to stage talks, events and the odd temporary art exhibition (check boards put up outside or in NALIS), and serves as one of the main venues for the annual Bocas literary festival (see page 35).

1

THE 1990 COUP

At 6.30pm on July 27, 1990, radical Islamic fundamentalist **Yasin Abu Bakr** interrupted programming of the state-run TTT TV company to announce that he had captured the station offices and overthrown the government of Trinidad and Tobago in a **coup d'état**. Thirty minutes earlier, members of his **Jamaat-al-Muslimeen** group had stormed the Red House and taken several government ministers hostage, including then-prime minister A.N.R. Robinson, while the old police headquarters around the corner on Sackville Street had been firebombed and all but destroyed. Looting took the capital by storm, and a **state of emergency** was called, requiring all citizens to remain indoors after dark. In total some 26 people were killed during the coup attempt, and millions of dollars' worth of damage were done to downtown Port of Spain.

THE AFTERMATH OF THE COUP

With little public support, and with food rations running low (the Muslimeen hadn't prepared for a drawn-out standoff), the rebels **surrendered** to the troops surrounding the Red House on August 1, after a six-day siege – though only after negotiating an **amnesty agreement** which guaranteed that perpetrators of the coup would not be arrested for their activities. Nonetheless, Bakr and 113 other Jamaat members were immediately taken into custody, and remained in jail for two years while the courts debated the validity of an amnesty which, it was argued, had been granted only as a means of preventing the hostages from being killed. The Jamaat members were eventually freed after a ruling by the UK Privy Council that the amnesty was invalid, but that it would be against due process to have them re-arrested and tried for the offences committed during the coup.

As well as relying on the army to support the revolt, the Jamaat had hoped to capitalize on public discontent with the harsh fiscal policies of the time (satirized by the calypsonian Sparrow in his song *Capitalism Gone Mad*). Yet however little love they may have had for the government, few Trinbagonians were willing to support its violent overthrow by an armed group of religious extremists. Many found it hard to believe that such events could take place in their stable, democratic, party-loving country, and though reflections of the coup tend to be understandably sober today, many people also tell stories of the inevitable "**curfew parties**".

THE JAMAAT TODAY

Nearly thirty years on, the coup remains a contentious and much-talked-about issue. The Jamaat-al-Muslimeen (🔟 bit.ly/JamaatTT) is still active in T&T: their **headquarters** at 1 Mucurapo Rd on the outskirts of Woodbrook hold a school and a mosque (one of five dotted around the country), and membership – estimated at around 7000 nationally – continues to rise, despite allegations of links with shady dealings, from murders and drug smuggling to terrorism. It's alleged, too, that politicians haven't been shy in co-opting the Muslimeen's intimidating reputation for their own ends, with Patrick Manning's PNM government widely thought to have provided covert financial backing in return for their support (and strong-arming of votes in communities such as Laventille) during the 2002 election campaign. The Jamaat, meanwhile, remain unrepentant in their stance on the coup, arguing that it had its roots in state harassment of their group, which had been involved in many run-ins with the authorities prior to 1990 over a land dispute at Mucurapo and the killing of one of its members by the police.

THE COMMISSION OF ENQUIRY

In 2010, Kamla Persad-Bissessar's People's Partnership government convened a **Commission of Enquiry** into the coup. Despite the fact that Abu Bakr refused to give evidence (and was taken to court as a result), some 100 witnesses did participate in the seventeen hearings, including A.N.R. Robinson, former PM Basdeo Panday and one-time Jamaat activist Jamaal Shabazz, who participated in the takeover of the TTT offices. The Commission finally delivered its report in March 2014, citing numerous recommendations concerning national security, but for many the report was something of a damp squib, offering too little too late; and the issues surrounding the events of July 1990 remain shrouded in mystery and suspicion.

Central Police Station

Cnr Sackville and St Vincent streets • Museum Tues–Fri 9am–3pm • Free • ☎ 624 6722, ⓦ nmag.gov.tt

1

Though it might look like a church, with its variegated brickwork and arched windows, the elegant Gothic-style stone building on the corner of Sackville and St Vincent streets is a renovated version of the **Central Police Station**, which was pretty much destroyed in the 1990 coup (see page 62). The upper floor holds a small **museum** centred around T&T's police service. Highlights include an old warrant book from 1941, in which the offences detailed include "fraudulent conversing" and "larceny of a fountain pen"; and a duty book from the same era which includes a complaint by one Monica Darlington of Delaford, who dropped into the station to report that "Mrs Blackman and her daughter Viva are always annoying her" – a far cry from the news that makes the headlines these days. Equally fascinating is a Criminal Register from 1882, with each page devoted to the crimes of the unhappy suspect in the photo at the top. The stairwell up to the gallery is bedecked with tributes to former Commissioners of Police alongside pictures of the Red House ablaze during the 1903 water riots, while the veranda outside the museum room gives a good perspective onto the Red House.

Opposite the Central Police Station, on the other side of Sackville Street, is the **police administrative building**, which displays Trinidad and Tobago's police force emblem, a hummingbird and a police badge inside a Star of David, the latter the symbol not of a Jewish connection but of Governor Picton's patron saint.

Rosary Roman Catholic Church

Cnr Henry and Park streets

Built between 1892 and 1910, the dignified Gothic Revival **Rosary Roman Catholic Church** is the most impressive of the city's three main churches, though its imposing towers and ornate stonework are hemmed in by buildings on all sides. You're in luck if you find it open, for the spacious interior is an oasis of peace in this hectic part of the city, and the old **stained glass**, with its finely detailed biblical scenes, is the most beautiful in Port of Spain. Unfortunately the effect is somewhat spoilt by the fluorescent lighting, peeling paint and general dilapidation.

Around the Savannah

Marking the division between downtown and the city's upper reaches, the **Queen's Park Savannah** is Port of Spain's largest open space, and a great place to take a gentle walk and admire the capital's prettier side. Fringing the edge of the Savannah are the **National Museum**, a passable **zoo** and the beautiful **Botanical Gardens**, while the palatial mansions of the **Magnificent Seven**, built by the colonial plantocracy, provide some architectural distraction.

Queen's Park Savannah

Despite the traffic that whizzes clockwise around the 3.7-km perimeter road, the **Queen's Park Savannah** is a surprisingly restful spot, crisscrossed by paths and shaded by the spreading branches of some lovely trees, from huge samaans and fragrant carobs to the pink and yellow pouis that burst into spectacular bloom at the start of the rainy season and carpet the ground to beautiful effect as the petals fall.

Originally part of a sugar-cane estate, the Savannah was bought by Governor Woodford in 1817 and subsequently developed into a city park. The terms of the sale decreed that no permanent structures would be erected on the land, but though the Savannah has remained its original size, tarmac and Carnival-related buildings are slowly encroaching onto the grass in the southern portion. The largest of these are the semi-permanent Grand Stand and North Stand; each year, the stage constructed between these two spectator stands serves as the centrepiece for the **Carnival celebrations**, from the Panorama steel pan competition and Dimanche Gras show to

1

the epicentre of the Parade of the Bands. The only other construction on the Savannah is the walled **Peschier Cemetery** right in the middle, the burial ground of the original French Creole owners and closed to the public. Otherwise, it's just wide-open spaces, though at the northwest corner, the dips and depressions of the **Hollows** sunken garden, with its fishponds and pathways, are popular with kids.

Pretty much deserted during the hot daylight hours, the Savannah comes to life in the cool of the afternoon, with football games and cricket matches on the grass, walkers and joggers exercising along the boundary path, and the jelly-coconut vendors doing a roaring trade from the ornate vans parked up on the western boundary. During the windy months of March and April, the Savannah is also a favourite spot for flying **kites**; visit at this time and you'll usually be able to buy one of the brilliant home-made Mad Bulls, T&T's kite of choice, sold by a roving craftsman. Over on the southern paved area, meanwhile, stalls set up as the light fades and do a roaring trade in **street food** snacks (see page 84) such as pholouri, corn soup, roasted corn and barbecue chicken; if you're feeling adventurous, try the oysters doused in peppery tomato sauce, dispensed from a stall opposite the Knowsley Building (see page 65) on Queen's Park West.

National Academy for the Performing Arts (NAPA)

Queen's Park West • ☎ 625 4224, ⓦ bit.ly/NAPAtt

Occupying a block of Queen's Park West between Frederick Street and Chancery Lane, the futuristic **National Academy for the Performing Arts** glowers over the Savannah grass, its arcs of glass and steel looking somewhat incongruous against its colonial-era neighbours. The design was said to be based on the national flower, the chaconia, though this isn't immediately obvious from ground level. Built at a cost of some TT$500 million by Patrick Manning's PNM government, and opened in 2009, the controversial centre has been lambasted as a white elephant thanks to its shoddy construction. It has numerous fundamental design flaws as a performance space, from an analogue (rather than digital) sound and light system to a backstage loading area so small that even a steel drum can't fit through. To compound all of this, no maintenance programme was put in place after its construction, and by 2014, parts of the building were deemed unsafe and closed down by health and safety inspectors. Nonetheless, repairs were carried out and at the time of writing NAPA was being used to stage a range of events, from concerts and theatre performances to film screenings and craft markets.

National Museum and Art Gallery

Cnr Frederick and Keate streets • Tues–Sat 10am–6pm, Sun 2–6pm • Free • ☎ 623 5941, ⓦ nmag.gov.tt

Just south of the Savannah and overshadowed by the NAPA building, the German Renaissance-style Royal Victoria Institute was built in 1892 to commemorate Queen Victoria's diamond jubilee, and today holds the **National Museum and Art Gallery**. The museum's collection is extensive, covering everything from early **Amerindian history** to the technology of the **oil industry**. Although some of the displays are very much twentieth century in style, with plenty of yellowing typed labels rather than interactive verve, they provide an essential overview of Trinidad and Tobago's history. The star of the show is undoubtedly the **art gallery** upstairs, with a rotated collection of works by local artists.

The ground floor

The first rooms are taken up with the **geological history** of the islands, with racks of locally found specimens including some enormous quartz crystals. There's also plenty on the **colonial era** and beyond, including pictures of the long-defunct tram and trolleybus networks, a re-creation of a 1940s **barrack yard** and yellowing photos of Port of Spain through the ages, including shots of the devastation wreaked by the 1808 fire. Local industry, from coconuts and cocoa to sugar, rum and oil, are also covered, and around the back, there's a nice little exhibit on the Shouter Baptist faith, with examples of items used for prayer, and a gallery detailing T&T's sporting achievements sponsored – with no hint of irony – by the local tobacco company, WITCO. Another room on the ground floor is used for temporary exhibitions, while some portions are closed off pending refurbishment of the displays on Carnival.

The upper level

The upper level of the National Museum is mostly given over to **Trinbagonian art**, either pieces from the museum's collection or temporary exhibitions by local artists. The works change frequently, but you'll usually see pieces by big local names such as Leroy Clarke, Shastri Maharaj, Carlisle Chang and Boscoe Holder; on the stairwells, check out the Robert Fraser's wooden reliefs of the Savannah's Magnificent Seven buildings. Elsewhere, there's a room exploring T&T's **natural history**, with stuffed birds and animals, pickled snakes and desiccated spiders and insects, while the **Settlement Gallery** is dedicated to the islands' original Amerindian inhabitants, with heaps of pottery, a re-creation of a burial midden and a dugout canoe, as well as exhibitions on the Spanish, British and French eras. There's also a room filled with lithographs of old Port of Spain and bucolic scenes of rural Trinidad by nineteenth-century painter **Michel Cazabon**, a French Creole man who became Trinidad's first internationally known artist, though it's often locked; you may be able to access it if you ask staff.

Queen's Park West

Travelling clockwise around the Savannah from Frederick Street on **Queen's Park West**, you'll come across numerous examples of the gingerbread buildings by Glaswegian architect George Brown, who mass-produced this distinctive fretted woodwork and used it extensively in his designs. Dating from 1904, the ornately decorated **Knowsley Building** at the corner of Chancery Lane resembles a child's fantasy doll's house; the black-and-white **George Brown House** at the corner of Victoria Avenue is somewhat plainer, though still graced by a great deal of refined fretwork. Just up from the junction with Cipriani Boulevard, **Boissiere House** is fondly called the "Gingerbread House" by locals, and you'd be hard pushed to find a better example of the style. Having been treated to a sensitive restoration, it's a splendidly whimsical concoction of fretted wooden finials and bargeboards, with stained glass depicting meandering strawberry vines and pagoda-like roofs.

The Magnificent Seven

Overlooking the northwest corner of the Savannah along **Maraval Road**, the magical realist parade of buildings known as the **Magnificent Seven** is the result of the competing egos of rival plantation owners, each of whom tried to outdo his neighbours in the grandeur of their construction. Employing assorted European architectural styles infused with a tropical slant, the buildings were constructed in 1904 (except Hayes Court, which dates from 1910), but though three remain in regular use, some of the others have fallen into a sad state of disrepair. None are open to the public; they are best admired from the Savannah perimeter path.

Queen's Royal College

Working south to north along Maraval Road, the first of the Magnificent Seven is the handsomely restored **Queen's Royal College**, Trinidad's most prestigious school, whose former pupils include the authors V.S. and Shiva Naipaul and the country's first prime minister, Eric Williams. Built in a German Renaissance style and topped with a clock tower, its arcaded balconies and cream-and-ochre stucco offset the blue limestone cornerstones.

Hayes Court

Across Hayes Street from QRC, **Hayes Court** is a grand mansion fusing French and British architectural influences, designed by George Brown and sporting his characteristic cast-iron pillars and railings along the lower veranda. Built as the residence of Trinidad's Anglican bishop (and named after the second incumbent, Bishop Thomas Hayes), it is still in use by the Diocese today.

Mille Fleurs

Next to Hayes Court, **Mille Fleurs** is another of George Brown's elaborate gingerbread houses, originally built for Dr Henrique Prada, a well-to-do doctor who went on to serve as the city's mayor between 1914 and 1917. Now state-owned and unoccupied, it's in a terrible condition, much to the despair of conservationists, who lay wreaths of flowers at its gates each April to draw attention to its plight. Restoration is under discussion, and an awning has been erected over the roof to protect it from the elements, but some say that the damage is irreparable and the building will have to be demolished.

Roomor

Commissioned by estate owner Lucien Ambard, **Roomor** is a florid exercise in French Baroque, slathered with Italian marble and tiles from France, its columns, galleries, towers and pinnacles decorated with elaborate ironwork. The only one of the Magnificent Seven that remains a private residence, its original name was the Ambard House; its current moniker is a combination of the surnames of Timothy Roodal, who bought it in 1940, and that of his granddaughter Dr Yvette Morgan, the current owner.

Archbishop's House

Crossing Flood Street from Roomor, you'll come to the official home of Port of Spain's Roman Catholic archbishop, **Archbishop's House**. A weighty, Neo-Romanesque pile of Irish marble and red granite, capped by a copper roof, it's perhaps the least visually interesting of the Magnificent Seven, though is at least well maintained.

Whitehall

The next house along is **Whitehall**, a Venetian-style palazzo whose gleaming white paintwork gives it the air of a freshly iced birthday cake. Originally the home of cocoa estate owner Joseph Leon Agostini, the building has had a somewhat chequered history. It was commandeered by the US military during World War II, after which it became a cultural centre, a library and then a broadcasting unit. In 1954 it was sold to the government and served as the Office of the Prime Minister until 2009; it's currently vacant and, like its neighbours, in dire need of restoration.

Stollmeyer's Castle

The most outlandish structure of the seven, Killarney – more popularly known as **Stollmeyer's Castle** – stands at the northern end of Maraval Road just before it veers east into Circular Road. A fairy-tale castle of brick and limestone, bristling with turrets and spires, it was built for a German plantation owner named Stollmeyer by the Scottish architect Robert Giles, who modelled it on Queen Victoria's residence at Balmoral. Architectural historian John Newel Lewis perfectly captured Killarney's delicious absurdity when he wrote: "A German built a bit of an untypical Scottish castle in Trinidad and called it by an Irish name. He must have been by that time a Trinidadian, because only Trinidadians do these things". The Stollmeyer family sold the castle to the government in 1979, after which it entered rapid decline; at the time of writing, however, the first phase of its restoration had been completed and, from the outside at least, was looking pretty good.

Trinidad Theatre Workshop

6 Newbold St • ☎ 624 8502, ⓦ ttheatreworkshop.wixsite.com/website02

Recently moved from its longtime home in Belmont, the **Trinidad Theatre Workshop** established a theatrical tradition in Trinidad, made acting a recognized profession and launched the careers of many of the Caribbean's most famous thespians. It was founded in 1959 by poet, playwright and Nobel Laureate **Derek Walcott** (1930–2017), who spent much of his life in Trinidad, alongside his brother Roderick and luminaries of the local arts scene such as dancer Beryl McBurnie. The TTW enjoyed its heyday in the 1960s and 1970s with stagings of now classic plays such as Walcott's *The Joker of Seville, Ti-Jean and his Brothers* and *Dream on Monkey Mountain*. Walcott was awarded the 1992 Nobel Prize for Literature, which inspired a renaissance of sorts, though the TTW is a quiet place these days, staging regular workshops and the occasional production.

Lady Chancellor Road

The Savannah's northern edge is lined by Circular Road. Just past the Hollows, there's a signposted turn-off to **Lady Chancellor Road**, a precipitous meander of switchback turns that winds its way up the hillside past some palatial homes. A popular spot for afternoon walkers and joggers, Chancellor affords some lovely **views** over the Savannah and across the city skyline.

Emperor Valley Zoo

Circular Rd • Daily 9am–6pm, last tickets sold at 5.30pm • TT$30, children TT$15 • ⓦ zstt.org

First opened in 1952, the **Emperor Valley Zoo**'s original design wasn't particularly animal-friendly, with tiny cages predominating, but efforts are being made to move with the times by way of an ongoing enhancement programme, constrained somewhat by the small proportions of the complex. Though there are still many small cages that don't seem to offer much quality of life for their inhabitants, the new enclosures are a big improvement. The zoo remains a magnet for local kids, with balloon- and novelty-sellers aplenty at the entrance; it also offers the chance to see local species that you're unlikely to spot in the wild. Close to the entrance is an **otter** enclosure with an underwater viewing area, while the upper reaches of the zoo hold enclosures for **giraffes** and **tigers**. Other residents include **brocket deer, zebra, collared peccary** (known locally as **quenk**), **capybara, lions** (fed daily at 2.30pm), a large selection of **monkeys** (including a cage of native howlers behind the reptile house), aquarium **fish** and **snakes**. There are also **tarantulas** and one of Trinidad's improbably large **giant centipedes**, as well as **ocelots, spectacled caiman** and numerous **birds**, including parrots, flamingos, toucans and scarlet ibis.

Botanical Gardens

Circular Rd • Daily 6am–6pm • Free • ☎ 622 1221, ⓦ bit.ly/BGPoS

The lovely **Botanical Gardens** were established in 1818 by Governor Woodford and the botanist David Lockhart, making this collection of 700-odd trees one of the oldest in the western hemisphere. Paths loop around the lawns and up the bamboo-smothered hillsides, and a small **cemetery** in the middle contains the crumbling gravestones of many of the island's governors, including Solomon Hochoy. It's a lovely spot for a wander, often deserted during the heat of the day but livelier in the late afternoon, when joggers, walkers and families take to the paths and lawns.

Adjacent to the gardens are the manicured lawns that front the **President's House**, a beautiful fretworked structure built in 1876 as the residence of the island's British governors, but now hunkered under a protective metal roof following the collapse of the west wing in 2010. Restoration is said to be imminent.

1

Lady Young Road

Past the Botanical Gardens, a roundabout at the edge of the Savannah has exits for the residential districts of St Ann's and Cascade, and for **Lady Young Road**, a steep and twisting route up past the *Hilton* hotel and into the hills; a **viewing point** some ten minutes' drive from the Savannah affords excellent views over the city and of the container ships queuing up in the Gulf of Paria. Stalls sell Trini sweets, snacks and souvenirs.

Beyond the Lookout, Lady Young swings through **Morvant**, a close-knit but impoverished community that's sadly known for its high crime rate, much of it thanks to gang violence and drug wars.

■ ACCOMMODATION		● EATING		Veni Mange	13	■ DRINKING & NIGHTLIFE		More Vino	7
Ana's Place	4	Adam's Bagels	1	ZaZou Kitchen	4	#63 Lounge	15	Paprika	6
Courtyard by		Aioli	2			All Out Sports		Pub House	12
Marriott	7	Chaud Café	5			Bar and Grill	3	Residence	1
Culture Crossroads		El Pecos	10	● SHOPPING		Brooklyn Bar	8	Smokey and	
Inn	1	Hakka	7	Cocobel	5	Coco Lounge	14	Bunty Avenue	10
Fabienne's	3	House of Sakura	3	Crosby's	2	Drink Lounge	4	Stumblin' on	
Gingerbread House	6	Irie Bites	12	Medulla Art Gallery	5	Frankie's	11	the Avenue	18
Inna Citi Place	2	Livet Gourmet	11	Rainy Days	1	Hog & Whistle	9	Tequila Twist	13
Melbourne Inn	8	More Sushi	8	Samaroo's	6	Island Beer		Tzar	17
Sam's	5	New Earth Organic	9	Tulip Productions	4	Chill & Grill	2	Vas Lounge	8
		Patraj	6	Y Art Gallery	3	La Habana	16		

Newtown and St Clair

Spreading back southwest of the Savannah and bordered to the south by busy Tragarete Road lie the neighbouring districts of St Clair and Newtown, an upscale mix of commerce and residential streets. A network of narrow streets between Maraval Road and Queen's Park West, **Newtown** holds some pretty colonial-era buildings, most housing offices these days, but no sights per se; however, with its decent accommodation options and burgeoning restaurant scene, it makes a good base from which to explore the city.

West of Maraval Road, the leafy backstreets of **St Clair** are home to the country's well-to-do as well as most of the country's diplomatic missions. An exclusive enclave of lavish houses protected by high walls, barking guard dogs and sophisticated security systems, St Clair holds some handsome and well-kept colonial-era mansions. The area is also home to the **Harts mas camp** at 5 Alcazar Street, run by the same family since 1959 (see page 80). Famous for their skimpy feathers-and-beads designs, Harts were the first to market themselves as a "fun" band and have been at the forefront of the development of bikini mas.

Queen's Park Oval

Tragarete Rd • **Grounds** Daily 8am–4pm; ask the security guard at the gate to let you in • **Museum** Appointment only ☎ 753 2775 • TT$60 • **Matches** Seats in the stands cost around TT$135 depending on the level of the match taking place, or you can pay TT$300–450 for an all-inclusive ticket to the Trini Posse stand (food and drink included; ⓦ bit.ly/TriniPosse) • Box office Information ☎ 622 2295, ⓦ qpcc.com

On the southern border of St Clair stands the **Queen's Park Oval**, originally built in 1896 and still Trinidad's premier **cricket ground**, hosting national and international matches in season (Feb–April), as well as doubling as an occasional concert venue at Carnival time. Even if you're not a cricket fan, attending a match here is a unique and enjoyable experience; the game is a national obsession in Trinidad, and matches are followed with a passion. The atmosphere is rowdy but good-natured, with fans draped in the national flag and music blaring from sound systems after every over and wicket. Cricket fans might also want to check out the Oval's **Cricket Heritage Museum**; highlights include a bat signed by the 1950s West Indies team that won the region's first Test against England at Lord's, and a whole section dedicated to the legendary Brian Lara, including the bats he used to hit his record-breaking innings of 375, 400 and 501.

Woodbrook

Immediately west of the downtown area, and demarked by Colville Street to the east and the Maraval River to the west, the elegant old district of **Woodbrook** was established in the early twentieth century on land that once formed part of a sugar estate owned by the Siegert family, creators of Trinidad's famous Angostura bitters (see page 76). Many of the streets here – Carlos, Luis and Siegert – bear their names, and you'll still see plenty of the houses built by the original middle-class inhabitants, with wonderful fretworked bargeboards and delicate balustrades and finials. Running straight through the centre of Woodbrook is the wide boulevard of **Ariapita Avenue**, the capital's primary liming and dining location, lined with bars and restaurants and a lively place to be most nights of the week. The Avenue is also one of the busiest parts of town during Carnival, with a judging point at Adam Smith Square, and stalls and crowds lining the tarmac. Woodbrook's backstreets, meanwhile, hold a healthy sprinkling of mas camps where the Carnival bands have their bases, as well as a host of inexpensive guesthouses.

Lapeyrouse Cemetery

Philipps St • Daily 6am–6pm

At Woodbrook's eastern edge is the entrance to the **Lapeyrouse Cemetery**, a walled burial ground dating back to 1813. Victorian tombs adorned with Gothic spires and

PLAYING MAS

The headquarters of Carnival costume bands (see page 80), **mas camps** are scattered throughout Port of Spain, with the majority in Woodbrook. Traditionally, these are the workshops in which Carnival costumes are made, with troops of mas-makers (many unpaid volunteers) labouring away to get the designs finished in time for the big day amid a sea of wire, sequins, feathers and glue-guns. Mas camps have long provided a focus for the Trinidadian arts community, with many a painter, actor, dancer or writer pitching in to make mas, but these days costumes are increasingly produced in the Far East and shipped over to be assembled here. With fewer and fewer costumes made on site, mas camps instead serve as a showroom for the designs, where potential masqueraders can get a close-up view of the various sections that make up a band; they're also the place where revellers **register to play mas** and, often, collect their costumes (though the larger bands often distribute at bigger venues such as the National Stadium or *Hilton* hotel).

THEMES AND COSTUMES

Every year, each band chooses a **theme** to portray during Carnival, anything from the loosely whimsical – "Birds of a Feather" – to a historical period. The band is then divided into different named **sections**, each with its own costume linked to the theme, and with a designated position within the band during the street parades (note that masqueraders can wander through the band when on the road, but must stay with their section at judging points). Anyone with the inclination and the money to pay for the costume can register with a band to "play mas". In recent years, **costumes** have increasingly catered to the desire to wear as little as possible, including thongs and Brazil-style cage-bras for women; most female costumes, though, consist of a decorated bikini top and belt, plus bikini pants/boy shorts, a headpiece and accessories for the arms and legs; male costumes are less elaborate, usually board shorts, a small headpiece and some kind of sash around the chest. If skimpy "pretty mas" doesn't appeal, you could play sailor mas with a steel band such as All Stars, or opt for a smaller outfit such as Cat in Bag, which makes more individualistic and elaborate costumes (see page 80).

It's usual not to wear your full costume on Carnival Monday, instead saving it for the main Tuesday parade. The all-inclusive bands used to give out T-shirts and shorts to their masqueraders, who'd add a few simple embellishments, but today, **Monday wear** is a whole industry, with revellers creating their own elaborate costumes or going to specialist Monday-wear designers. You might also want to give a thought to **footwear**; while trainers are perfectly acceptable (colour co-ordinated with your costume, of course), most serious masqueraders play mas in decorated long boots. Again, there are a host of outfits that will decorate your footwear for you, though you can buy some bling from a Carnival store (see page 91) and do it yourself.

REGISTERING WITH A BAND

To play mas, you must first **register** with a mas band; you can do this online at the band websites (see page 80) or, if you're in Trinidad ahead of Carnival, go directly to the mas camp and try your luck. All-inclusive packages with the big bands, including costume, and food and drink on both parade days, cost anything from TT$5000 for a basic "Backline" costume to TT$10,000 upwards for a "Frontline" or "Individual" extravaganza; smaller bands are cheaper. Note also that if you wish to play in premium bands such as Tribe, Fantasy or Bliss, you'll need to check the Trinidad Carnival Diary website (see page 80) in early summer to find out when bands are launching and when registration begins; most are fully booked within a few days, while the hot costumes of the year are snapped up in a matter of hours. Bear in mind, too, that as the popular bands offer priority registration to previous masqueraders, you may not be able to get a costume however early you visit the website.

If you arrive in Trinidad late or decide you want to play mas at the last minute, you could try the costume classifieds at Ⓦfineahban.com, though many sellers hike up prices to ridiculous levels if demand is high. Most bands also sell uncollected costumes on the Sunday before the main parade; contact the mas camps to check availability.

Contact details and more information on individual mas and Jouvert bands appear in our Carnival listings section (see page 80).

angels are eerily framed against the lush, tropical backdrop, while strands of ivy trail over the graves. The Siegert family are buried here, as are the labour leader Arthur Cipriani, the calypsonian Melody, and Charlie King, the policeman killed in the Butler Riots in the 1930s (see page 185). The names on the gravestones provide clues to the diverse origins of Port of Spain's inhabitants – Chinese, Spanish, African, Indian and European – and the inscriptions reflect its varied religious affiliations: Catholics, Anglicans, Baptists and many other denominations are represented. The cemetery's newer residents, the vagrants who sleep in the more dilapidated tombs, have been a talking point for years, often provoking press articles about the problem of homelessness.

St James

West of Woodbrook, the grittier district of **St James** is a cosmopolitan place, known as the "city that never sleeps" thanks to the string of bars and street-food stalls along the Western Main Road. The area of today's St James was the first place that the British set foot on Trinidadian soil; landing in 1797, they are said to have found the courage required to capture Port of Spain in the rum produced at what was then the Peru sugar-cane estate. After emancipation, the area was settled by **Indian** indentured labourers, and the names they gave to their streets – Calcutta, Delhi, Madras – bear witness to their homesickness. Today, the estate is long-gone, but rum remains central to the life of the area by way of the street-front bars and slightly seedy clubs that line the Western Main Road, best visited after dark when music blares and stalls serve food late into the night for queues of hungry limers. St James' Indian population has also stayed very visible, with a smattering of mosques and puja flags in many front gardens along the residential backstreets. The area is also notable as the focus of the annual Muslim **Hosay** processions (see page 72).

Roxy Roundabout

Signifying the division between Woodbrook and St James, the **Roxy Roundabout** takes its name from the adjacent **Roxy Building**, originally built as a cinema and with a ritzy classical-modern colonnade; it now houses a branch of *Pizza Hut*. On the other side of the road is a weatherbeaten concrete statue in tribute to the grandmaster of calypso, the late **Lord Kitchener**, by Pat Chu Foon. The entrance to St James itself is marked by the bridge over the Maraval River, spanned by an ornate green and pink iron archway bearing the area's name and decorated with shells and with eight Hindu-style domes. Overhanging it all are the high-rise blocks of One Woodbrook Place, an exclusive gated community with its own shops, restaurants and cinema.

JOUVERT

Carnival officially starts with **Jouvert** ("joo-vay"), an anarchic and raunchy early-hours orgy of pure, unadulterated bacchanalia, with generous coatings of mud, chocolate, oil or body paint – and libations of local rum, of course – helping you lose all inhibitions and slide through the streets in an anonymous mass of dirty, drunken, happy humanity. You can just head out onto the streets of Woodbrook and St James and get stuck in, but given Jouvert's wild overtones it's a much better idea to join an organized **Jouvert band** and play "dirty mas". A fee of US$50–100 will get you a basic costume and all the mud, body paint or liquid chocolate you desire, as well as security (an excellent idea, as Jouvert can be rowdy). Many bands are all-inclusive, meaning you get drinks and snacks on the road, and breakfast afterwards; some also offer a hose-down at the end of it all. New bands appear each year, so listen to radio adverts or check the press and ⓦtrinidadcarnivaldiary.com for details; our Carnival listings section (see page 80) includes some of the most popular and long-standing bands.

HOSAY

The Islamic festival of **Hosay**, commemorating the martyrdom of Mohammad's grandsons Hussein and Hassan during the jihad (Holy War) in Persia, has been celebrated by Shi'a Muslims in Trinidad since the first Indians arrived in 1845. Though the Hosay procession may look like something resembling Carnival, with loud music and lots of colour, it's actually quite a serious affair, and in recent years participants have taken great pains to restore the occasion's solemnity. Alcohol is actively discouraged, but spectators are welcome to watch the proceedings from the side of the street – if you're in Trinidad during Hosay, it's well worth seeing. Hosay is celebrated in Curepe, Tunapuna, Couva and Cedros, but the best place to catch it is undoubtedly St James. Trinis of all religions come here to view the parades, which are held over four days (dates change according to the Islamic calendar; see ⓦbestoftrinidad.com/culture.html).

THE BUILD-UP

In the weeks leading up to Hosay, craftsmen spend many hours building **tadjahs**, ornate tombs resembling miniature mosques made from bamboo, coloured paper and richly embellished cloth that are carried in procession. There are only five families who build the structures each year, four based in St James and one in Cocorite, a little further west. Families have to be approved by a local committee, and strict rules apply – builders are required to fast during daylight hours and refrain from alcohol and sexual activity for the duration. *Tadjahs* cost many thousands of dollars to produce, and families strive to outdo each other in making the most spectacular and the largest: many are 4m or so high.

THE FESTIVAL NIGHTS

For participants, Hosay is a ten-day affair, with the first **six days** taken up with fasting, prayers and the building of *tadjahs*. On the **seventh day**, the first procession is **flag night**, when devotees walk through the streets with multicoloured flags representing the beginning of the battle of Kerbala, in which the brothers lost their lives.

On the **eighth night**, called **Small Hosay**, petite *tadjahs* are carried slowly through the streets to the throbbing, hypnotic drumbeats of **tassa groups**, percussion bands of six or more players. Carrying their drums on straps around the neck, *tassa* drummers use thin, flexible sticks to beat out standardized rhythmic patterns (*taals*) as directed by the cutter, or lead drummer, who also ignites the drumming with rapid-fire and very loud improvisations known as "shots". *Tassa* drums are traditionally made from goatskin, which needs to be tightened by being heated up, producing a better, more high-pitched sound – you'll still sometimes see the shredded-paper fires at the side of the road used to warm up the drums, though these are becoming less common as goatskin is replaced by synthetic skins. All ensembles include a large, double-ended *dhol* bass drum, and hand-held cymbals called *jhal*. Hosay sees lots of competition between the individual *tassa* groups, with drumming reaching a frenetic crescendo as they pass each other on the parade.

The **ninth night**, Big Hosay, is the most spectacular. Huge, exquisite *tadjahs* are paraded through the streets, with Hussein and Hassan represented by a pair of sickle moons (one green, one red) mounted on the shoulders of dancers. At midnight there is the ritual "kissing of the moons", as the dancers symbolically re-enact a brotherly embrace, and the *tassa* and parade continues well into the early hours.

From around 10am on the **tenth day**, known as **Ashura**, there's a final, spectacular parade of the moons and the *tadjahs*; *tassa* drummers are again out in force and the resplendent *tadjahs* glitter in the sunlight. Before sunset, the *tadjahs* are then sacrificed to the sea amid much prayer and solemnity (this last stage is observed by participants only).

Western Main Road

Running through the centre of St James, **Western Main Road** (WMR) is a broad thoroughfare lined with shops, bars and takeaways. Street vendors sell vegetables, incense and household goods on corners during the day, while at night there's a food, punch or home-made ice-cream stall every couple of metres. Halfway down the road, **St James Market** fills the air with the smell of fresh fish and meat in the early mornings.

& Fondes Amandes Community Reforestation Project (1.5km)

EASTERN SUBURBS

1

0   500
metres

■ ACCOMMODATION
Alicia's House	1
Heritage Inn	4
Hilton Trinidad	5
L'Orchidée	3
Normandie	2
Thanna's Place	6

● SHOPPING
Akilah's Jewellery	1
Paper Based	2
The Shop	3

■ DRINKING & NIGHTLIFE
B3	1

● EATING
Apsara	4
Chaud	2
Ciao Café	1
Tamnak Thai	3

ST ANN'S
SYDENHAM AVE
ST ANN'S ROAD
St Ann's River
EAST HILL
CASCADE AVENUE
Cascade River
CASCADE ROAD
CASCADE
St ANN'S AVE
NOOK AVE
COBLENTZ GARDENS
COBLENTZ AVE
FIRST AVE
LADY YOUNG ROAD
SEE "CENTRAL PORT OF SPAIN" MAP
Queen's Hall
CIRCULAR ROAD
BELMONT VALLEY ROAD
LAYAN HILL
Viewpoint
Queen's Park Savannah
CADIZ ROAD
MEYER ST
BELMONT
BELMONT CIRCULAR ROAD
ST FRANCOIS VALLEY ROAD
ERTHIG ROAD
NORFOLK ST
PELHAM ST
QUEEN'S PARK E
JERNINGHAM AVENUE
ST BARB ROAD
QUEEN'S PARK WEST
Memorial Park
NAPA
KEATE STREET
National Museum & Art Gallery
GORDON STREET
NEW STREET
LORD HARRIS SQUARE
OXFORD ST
Renegades Panyard
St ANN'S River
OBSERVATORY ST
PEMBROKE ST
FREDERICK STREET
ST VINCENT STREET
Immigration Office
PARK STREET
Caribbean Court of Justice
Rosary Roman Catholic Church
LAVENTILLE ROAD
Fort Chacon
Desperadoes Panyard
Our Lady of Laventille Shrine
Central Police Station & Police Museum
Hall of Justice
Old Public Library
City Hall
DUKE STREET
Trinidad All Stars Panyard
WOODFORD SQUARE
NALIS
Holy Trinity Cathedral
PRINCE STREET
CHARLOTTE ST
PICCADILLY STREET
NELSON STREET
LAVENTILLE
Fort Picton
Old Fire Station
ABERCROMBY ST
CHACON ST
Arthur Cipriani statue
QUEEN ST
INDEPENDENCE SQUARE
Nicholas Tower
Central Bank
Cathedral of the Immaculate Conception
John John Towers
SOUTH QUAY
Fort San Andrés
Lighthouse
City Gate
EASTERN MAIN ROAD
PICTON ROAD
Central Market
Gulf of Paria
BEETHAM HIGHWAY
SEA LOTS
Piarco Airport

Ariyapi (3km); Eastern Main Road (5km- & Angostura Distillery (5km)

Eastern Main Road & Angostura Distillery (1.5km)

1

VISITING PANYARDS

The best way to hear **steel pan** is live, in the open air – listening to its rich chiming harmonies drifting on the wind on a warm starry night is a spine-tingling experience. Throughout the year Port of Spain hosts events in which pan features prominently, but in the run-up to Carnival, it's well worth taking a tour around the city's **panyards**, where the musicians gather most nights to practise their compositions for the Panorama competition (see page 268). Visitors are welcome (crowds get quite sizeable as the big day approaches), and there's always a bar and somewhere to sit and take in the music – though bear in mind that you may hear a section of a song being practised over and over again rather than the whole thing. Panyards are also open at other times, though the scene isn't as animated.

If you don't have a car or want to get a better insight into pan, one of the best ways to visit the yards is to take an evening **tour** with Island Experiences (☎621 0407 or ☎781 6235, ⓦislandexperiencestt.com; US$45); these are best in Carnival season, though bands do practise throughout the year. Details of Port of Spain's better-known **panyards** appear in our Carnival listings section (see page 80); Phase II, Invaders, Silver Stars, Renegades and All Stars usually draw the biggest crowds. For full listings of the country's pan bands, visit ⓦpantrinbago.co.tt.

Fort George

Fort George Rd • Daily 10am–6pm • Free • Taxis leave sporadically from the corner of Western Main Rd and Bourne's Rd

Perched on a hilltop above St James, ten minutes' drive north of the Western Main Road, **Fort George** affords some spectacular views of Port of Spain and beyond into Caroni and the Central Plains, as well as west along the coast to the Bocas. The route up passes through some slightly dodgy areas, so it's best not to walk. The fort was built in 1804 to defend the island against the French Caribbean fleet during the Napoleonic Wars, though it never saw any action; the original cannons still point out to sea.

Stone defensive walls surround the wooden **signal station** designed by an exiled West African prince, Kofi Nti, who came to Trinidad after becoming a Ward of the British courts following the Ashanti War of 1872; he's described on the information boards as a "quiet, unassuming man with a great interest in stamp collecting". The station itself was used to signal between here and the other post stations along the coast, and the bare interior displays an ornate, armoured wooden chest from Marseilles, thought to have been brought here to store valuables. Though the fort's lock-up looks secure enough – check out the window bars made from rifle barrels – the only thing it ever guarded were the valuables of Port of Spain's merchants, who carted their treasures up here whenever the threat of insurrection loomed.

The **grounds** are dotted with picnic tables, and make a popular spot to come and get a little respite from the city, with a constant cooling breeze.

Belmont

A maze of narrow lanes flanking the eastern side of the Queen's Park Savannah, **Belmont** is one of the most densely populated areas of Port of Spain. It was the city's first suburb, settled in the early nineteenth century by Africans who had escaped slavery on other Caribbean islands, and many original wooden houses survive from this era, proudly displaying their characteristic ornate gingerbread fretwork. After emancipation, freed slaves from Trinidad and a number of peoples from West Africa also settled here. In 1868, the tribal chieftain of the **Rada community** – a religious group from the French protectorate of Dahomey – bought land in the area to establish a settlement. Representatives from the Mandingo, Ibo, Yoruba and Krumen tribes also came to live here, and Belmont became an established African settlement. The community was well organized and close-knit, ensuring the survival of African traditions such as the Orisha religion (see page 254), which still has many followers here. Belmont was also the birthplace of **Stokely Carmichael** (1941–1998),

DESPERADOES

Many of T&T's great calypsonians hail from Laventille, but the area is more closely associated with Trinidad's national instrument, the **steel pan**, which was invented here by local son Winston "Spree" Simon (see page 268). Laventille is also home to one of Trinidad's oldest and most esteemed steel bands, **Desperadoes**, established by pan legend Rudolph Charles in the 1940s and later led jointly with fellow Laventille luminary Bertie Marshall. Desperadoes (first known as the Dead End Kids) quickly notched up a deadly reputation, thanks both to the skill of their pannists and the quick fists of the "bad johns" that made up their numbers. With eleven Panorama wins to their credit (the last in 2016), Despers today attract a crowd of die-hard supporters who make performances an exciting prospect. However, the uneasy notion of venturing up to the panyard just off the main Laventille Road has led Despers to set up a temporary base just off the Savannah in the run-up to Carnival, on Victoria Avenue.

founder of the **Black Power** movement and one of its vocal activists during the 1970s. Carmichael migrated to Harlem, New York, aged 11, and his civil rights work is today commemorated by a plaque outside his former home at 54 Oxford Street, now a community education centre.

At Carnival time, the community centre just off the Savannah on Jerningham Avenue is also worth a visit, as it hosts what's known as **Five Nights**, a brilliant reggae jam staged by the Twelve Tribes Rasta sect and a great antidote to the frenetic menu of soca, soca and more soca.

Laventille

Elwyn Francis tours ⏱ 3hr; TT$125 per person, plus $US150 for transport • ☎ 627 3377 or ☎ 356 5118

Tumbling down the hillside that borders Port of Spain to the east, **Laventville** was established by freed slaves who settled here in the 1840s – right "on the eyebrow of the enemy", as the Trinidadian novelist Earl Lovelace rather beautifully put it. Eulogized by the late Nobel laureate **Derek Walcott** in his poem *Laventille*, this is one of city's most impoverished and crime-ridden areas, and remains a volatile place, riven by drug- and gang-related violence and forever used as a political football by politicians keen to swing the African vote. The birthplace of the steel pan, Laventille's winding lanes are lined with a dense mishmash of buildings which sit on steep and twisting streets in defiance of gravity. Due to the unpredictability of the area, it's not a place for a casual wander; if you do want to get a flavour of Laventille it's best to go on a **walking tour** with local Elwyn Francis who also works as a tour guide for the Chaguaramas Development Authority and is well placed to gauge if it's a good time to visit; violent flare-ups sometimes make it best avoided.

Our Lady of Laventille Shrine

Upper Picton Rd

Laventille Hill is crowned by **Our Lady of Laventille Shrine**, an imposing landmark that's visible from all over Port of Spain. Atop the 16m belfry of this white stone church stands a statue of the Virgin Mary, a gift from France in 1876 and still a pilgrimage site on the Feast of the Assumption. Look closely and you can also pick out the Martello Tower at **Fort Picton**, just up from the church, built by the notorious British governor of the same name in the late 1790s, and now an outpost of the Trinidad Defence Force.

Angostura Distillery

Cnr Eastern Main Rd and Trinity Ave • Tours Mon–Fri 9.30am & 1.30pm; 2hr 15min • US$10/person • ☎ 623 1841, ⓦ angostura.com • From downtown Port of Spain, head along the Eastern Main Rd from South Quay; a more scenic alternative from the Savannah is to follow Lady Young Rd to the Morvant junction and turn right onto the Eastern Main Rd; the distillery entrance is on the left

1

THE ANGOSTURA SAGA

As T&T's sole producer of rum, **Angostura Distillers** hold a special place in the hearts of local limers. Trinbagonians stick by Angostura with a nationalistic zeal, declaring its rum the best in the world and adding a dash of its **aromatic bitters** to everything from drinks to marinades, soups and puddings, as well as swearing by the mixture as a cure for almost any ailment.

Angostura was founded by **J.G.B. Siegert**, a German surgeon who left his homeland to join Simón Bolívar in the fight for Venezuelan independence from Spain. Alarmed at the debilitating stomach ailments that plagued Bolívar's troops, Siegert began experimenting with South American herbs and spices to concoct a remedy. He succeeded in 1824, creating the secret blend of botanicals that still make up the bitters today, and named his tonic after the Venezuelan town where Bolívar's movement was based.

Popularized by sailors who brought wind of its curative powers to England, the mixture was first exported six years later, and demand increased rapidly. Production was shifted to the more economically and politically stable Trinidad, and the George Street plant soon dominated the small town of Port of Spain. After Siegert died in 1870, the company was taken over by his sons. The founder's great-grandson Robert Siegert, who took the helm in 1928, steered Angostura to loftier heights, establishing the Caribbean's most modern distillery in 1949 and exporting Trinidad's beloved product all over the world.

As the company became more valuable, so foreign investors began to make increasingly generous takeover bids. By now, however, Angostura had become so entrenched in the psyche (and the economy) of Trinidad that the government stepped in, taking control of the company in the mid-1950s and returning it to Siegert Holdings, who offered cut-price shares to employees and affirmed Angostura as the "**people's distiller**". Despite its bitters being voted the world's worst-displayed product by the British Advertising Council in 1995 (the packaging has changed little since 1824, with a paper label extending over the main body of the bottle to flap over the neck), Angostura has gone from strength to strength, buying out other local distillers, establishing a sprawling factory on the outskirts of Laventille and winning scores of awards; no fewer than seven monarchs, including Britain's Queen Elizabeth II, have given bitters the royal stamp.

The company continues to take its traditions seriously, and the **secret recipe** for bitters remains cloaked in mystery. No one knows the entire recipe; instead, five individuals memorize a specific part of the mix, and these five are not allowed to enter the blending room (or even travel) together. After mixing the ingredients, each sends their part of the blend down a chute to the same percolating container that's been used since the company began trading in Trinidad, where the herbs and spices are "shampooed" in alcohol for twenty hours before fermentation and bottling.

Though Laventille proper isn't a place for casual sightseeing, it is worth making the trek out to its outskirts, where the rows of old warehouses between the highway and the Eastern Main Road hold the massive complex of the **Angostura Distillers**, producers of T&T's famous **bitters**. They also make **rums**, from Black Label and White Oak to Forres Park puncheon and the premium Single Barrel and 1919 brands. Tours of the rum factory cover the history of the company as well as a look around the bottling plant, distillery and bitters production area; you'll also see the 700-plus specimens of the Barcant Butterfly Collection, and get to sample the rums. Tours are only available to groups of ten or more; call to see if it's possible to fit in with existing bookings.

St Ann's and Cascade

From the northeast corner of the Queen's Park Savannah, St Ann's Road heads past **Queen's Hall**, a favourite venue for pre-Carnival calypso revues, drama, dance and fashion shows. The leafy suburb of **St Ann's** melts almost seamlessly into the equally well-to-do **Cascade** to the east, both residential districts that offer little in the way of sightseeing.

Fondes Amandes Community Reforestation Project (FACRP)

Fondes Amandes Rd • Daily, no set hours • Guided walks US$10–30, by appointment only • ☎ 689 7794 or ☎ 750 1716, ⓦ facrp1.webs. com or ⓦ bit.ly/FACRP • From the Savannah, it's around 10min by car: take St Ann's Rd, and then turn left and follow Fondes Amandes Rd to its end

It's well worth heading to the far reaches of St Ann's to seek out the brilliant **Fondes Amandes Community Reforestation Project** which, as the name suggests, has been doing marvellous work replanting the denuded St Ann's hillsides and creating "fire paths" to stop seasonal bush fires in their tracks. Some 80,000 tree seedlings have already been planted, and the project's land is laced with easy hiking trails that afford lovely views of the city; there's also an organic nursery garden. **Guided walks** are run, during which you can learn more about the project's work, and relax afterwards with a natural juice made with fruits from the trees that now flourish on the hillside. Staff can also lead walks to the higher reaches of the St Ann's River, which has lovely **pools** for swimming.

Maraval

Surrounded by lush green hills, **Maraval** lies at the base of the Northern Range some 5km north of central Port of Spain. What was once a small village on the outskirts of the capital has now mushroomed into an upmarket residential suburb, with a sprinkling of hotels and guesthouses. Past the open-plan Ellerslie Plaza Shopping Centre, Maraval's main thoroughfare (and the route to Maracas Beach) is **Saddle Road**, lined with shops and houses; just up from the Junction with Long Circular Road, the Shoppes of Maraval and adjacent Royal Palm Plaza include a supermarket, pharmacy and several fast-food restaurants.

North of Saddle Road, you'll pass the turn-off for the expansive, well-kept **St Andrew's Golf Course** in Moka (see page 79). Beyond St Andrew's, Saddle Road takes a scenic route over the hills, providing good views of the forested slopes of the Maraval Valley and eventually arriving – after many steep inclines and hairpin bends – at Maracas on the north coast.

ARRIVAL AND DEPARTURE   PORT OF SPAIN

BY PLANE

Domestic and international flights arrive and depart from Piarco International Airport (☎ 669 4866, ⓦ tntairports. com), 24km east of Port of Spain via the Churchill Roosevelt Hwy. The small tourist information office (daily 8am–11pm; ☎ 669 5196) to the right of arrivals can provide you with maps and basic information. Just after you clear immigration there is a bureau de change (daily 24hr), and a bmobile outlet selling local SIM cards and mobile phones. The main concourse in between the arrivals and departure areas has ATMs and fast-food outlets; there's also a local food court adjacent to arrivals; turn left as you exit. There are several hotels nearby.

Airlines American Airlines ☎ 821 6000; British Airways ☎ 669 2630; Caribbean Airlines ☎ 625 7200; LIAT ☎ 1888 844 5428.

Airport taxis and transfers Official airport taxis, which wait outside the main entrance, will take you to Port of Spain for US$45 (40min, or 1–2hr during the 6–9am & 4–6pm rush hours). Prices to all destinations are listed on a board in the arrivals hall; drivers will accept US and local currency. Note that between 10pm and 6am fares to and from the airport increase by fifty percent. If you fancy

a gentler introduction to Port of Spain than a taxi ride, with lots of local info thrown in to prime your trip, get in touch with Island Experiences (☎ 621 0407 or ☎ 781 6235, ⓦ islandexperiencestt.com), whose drivers charge around US$5 more than regular taxis.

Route taxis and maxis into town If travelling very light, a dirt-cheap option is to take a shared route taxi to Arouca Junction on the Eastern Main Rd, from where you can catch an eastbound red-band maxi taxi to downtown Port of Spain's City Gate (see page 78). However, route taxis don't come into the airport concourse – you'll have to walk for ten minutes to the main road, where taxis pass at regular intervals; and don't expect to be able to stow large cases.

Buses into town A PTSC bus runs between Piarco and Port of Spain's City Gate terminal fifteen times a day, departing from Piarco's main entrance (10min walk from arrivals) at 6.30am, and then hourly at 15min past the hour until 8.15pm; and City Gate at 5.45am, 6.30am and then at 5min past the hour until 7.05pm.

BY CAR

Car rental There are several booths located to the left of the arrivals area within the concourse.

1

Driving into Port of Spain The only route into the city is the Churchill Roosevelt Hwy, which heads directly into Port of Spain, becoming Wrightson Rd as you pass Independence Square. The right-hand turn-off onto Colville St, next to the Powergen plant, is convenient for many of Port of Spain's accommodation options. For Woodbrook's Ariapita Ave, take the first left off Colville; to reach the Savannah and the turn-offs for Newtown, Maraval, St Ann's and Cascade, go straight across Tragarete Rd at the end of Colville, and onto Cipriani Blvd.

BY FERRY

Ferries from Tobago (see page 225) arrive and depart at the Port of Spain terminal on Wrightson Rd, opposite Independence Square (☎ 625 4906, ⊛ https://ttitferry.com); sailing time is around 4hr. The journey between Trinidad and Tobago can be rough; take seasickness tablets, and try to find a seat in the middle of the ferry. One-way tickets cost TT$50/person (half-price for kids), and are available online. There's no official private taxi rank at the ferry terminal, but you should be able to find a driver easily; alternatively head over to the rank on Independence Square (see page 79).

BY BUS AND MAXI TAXI

All buses and maxi taxis arrive and depart at the busy City Gate terminal on South Quay, at the heart of downtown Port of Spain one block south of Independence Square, and in walking distance of the departure points for maxis and route taxis to elsewhere in the city (see below).

BY WATER TAXI

Water taxis between Port of Spain and San Fernando (45min; TT$15) arrive and depart from the Water Taxi Terminal (☎ 624 5137, ⊛ nidco.co.tt) on Wrightson Rd, between the Ferry Terminal and the *Breakfast Shed*, adjacent to Independence Square.

GETTING AROUND

During the day, Port of Spain and its environs are served by plenty of **buses**, **maxis** and **route taxis**, though traffic jams are terrible during the rush hours (roughly 6–9am & 4–6pm). Route taxis – and to a lesser extent maxis – also operate throughout the night on the more popular routes (including Maraval), albeit a lot less frequently than during the day. As they're subject to change and cost very little, we haven't quoted exact **fares** for public transport. Most route or maxi taxi drivers are unlikely to try and rip you off, but the best plan is to ask around, watch what other passengers pay, or just offer up a TT$10/20 note and hold out your hand for change (looking, of course, as though you know exactly what you should be getting back).

BY BUS

City buses PTSC (Public Transport Service Corporation ☎ 623 2262, ⊛ ptsc.co.tt) buses provide a fast, a/c means of travelling around the city, though services are not as frequent as you might hope. All buses start from City Gate, and fares are TT$2.50; tickets need to be purchased before you board from outlets in the terminus. The website carries detailed route maps and schedules, and lists fares. Most services start at around 6am, and end at 9 or 10pm.

USEFUL BUS ROUTES

To central Port of Spain (City Gate special): City Gate, Abercromby St, New St, Frederick St, Queen's Park Savannah, Belmont.

To Chaguaramas Same as Diego Martin route, but once on Audrey Jeffers Hwy the bus continues on through St James along the Western Main Rd, passing West Mall, West Moorings, Glencoe, Carenage and Chaguaramas, ending at the *Chaquacabana* hotel (5am–10pm).

To Diego Martin Wrightson Rd, Ariapita Ave, Mucurapo Rd, Audrey Jeffers Hwy, Diego Martin Hwy.

BY MAXI TAXI

Maxi taxis operating in Port of Spain and the western tip have yellow bands along the side of the vehicle. Routes are set although some drivers may be willing to make off-route drops, and if a maxi is empty, the driver may vary the route in the hope of picking up some passengers. Note that many drivers now won't accept passengers not travelling the full (or most of) the route in what's called a "short drop"; if you need to go only partway, take a route taxi. For further information call the maxi rank on South Quay (☎ 625 4053). Port of Spain maxis depart from the fenced-off area between City Gate and Wrightson Rd, and from three main stops listed below.

MAXI RANKS

To Carenage and Chaguaramas (via Wrightson Rd) Departures from the junction of South Quay and St Vincent St.

To Carenage and Chaguaramas (via Ariapita Ave in Woodbrook) Departures from Green Corner (cnr St Vincent and Park streets).

To Maraval via St James Departures from the corner of Charlotte and Park streets, opposite the petrol station.

BY ROUTE TAXI

As for maxis, all off-route drops in route taxis depend on the driver's goodwill. Signposted starting points for city routes are dotted around downtown Port of Spain. Note that route taxis are the best option for heading downtown; the one-way system can be confusing and parking is a nightmare.

1

ROUTES AND TAXI STANDS

To Belmont Cnr of Charlotte St and Queen St.

To Chaguaramas Cnr of South Quay and Chacon St.

To Diego Martin/Petit Valley Cnr of Abercromby St and South Quay. Route ends at Diego Martin waterwheel via Four Roads and Diego Martin Main Rd. After 6pm Diego Martin taxis can be found near the Arthur Cipriani statue on Brian Lara Promenade.

To Laventille Cnr of Nelson St and Prince St.

To Maraval/Paramin Cnr of Duke St and Charlotte St. Route ends at Maraval village/beginning of Paramin.

To St Ann's Hart St, on the side adjacent to the Holy Trinity Anglican Cathedral. Route ends at Bishop Anstey School.

To St James/Tragarete Rd Hart St, on the side adjacent to Woodford Square. From around 7pm to 5am St James/ Tragarete Rd taxis can be found on Independence Square, at Henry St.

To Wrightson Rd/Long Circular Rd Cnr of Chacon St and South Quay. After 6pm Wrightson Rd/Long Circular Rd route starts from near the Arthur Cipriani statue on Brian Lara Promenade.

BY PRIVATE TAXI

Officially sporting "H" plates, and usually with a/c, private taxis are as expensive as cabs in New York or London. They're not hailed on the street, but ordered by phone or by going to their ranks, usually outside larger hotels such as the *Hilton* and *Kapok* or on Independence Square. Uber are now operation in Port of Spain and its surrounds; visit

w uber.com/cities for an update on service coverage and fare estimates.

Taxi firms Reputable firms include Phone-a-Taxi (☎ 628 TAXI), Kalloos (☎ 622 9073) and Ice House Taxi Service on the north side of Independence Square (☎ 627 6984), or Independence Square Taxi Service, Independence Square, at Frederick St (☎ 625 3032).

BY CAR

As the downtown streets are choked with traffic and the one-way systems can seem confusing at first, cars are not the best way to explore the downtown area; it's better to park on the outskirts, or take a route taxi/maxi, and proceed on foot.

Parking If you do drive in Port of Spain, always use an official car park, as vehicles illegally parked are routinely "wrecked" as it's called here, and towed to either the lot between MovieTowne and the port, or across the road from the Central Market, just off the highway to the east of town. There's a multi-storey car park downtown on Richmond St, and a host of small, privately run car parks where you'll pay a small fee to leave your vehicle. It is possible to park on the streets, but seek local advice, pay attention to signs and road markings, and never park adjacent to a fire hydrant.

Car rental Alamo ☎ 826 689, w alamo.com; Avis ☎ 669 0905, w avistrinidad.com; Econo Cars ☎ 622 8072, w econocarrentalstt.com; Europcar ☎ 621 2159, w europcar.co.tt; Kalloo's ☎ 622 9073, w kalloos.com.

INFORMATION

Tourist information Trinidad's tourist board, the TDC, was in the process of being dissolved at the time of writing, pending setup of separate entities for Trinidad and Tobago. In the meantime, you should be able to pick up brochures and free

magazines at the Ministry of Tourism office in Tower C of the Waterfront Complex on Wrightson Rd in downtown Port of Spain (Mon–Fri 8am–4.30pm; ☎ 624 1403, w tourism.gov.tt). There's a basic information office at Piarco airport (see page 77).

TOURS AND ACTIVITIES

City tours If you want to see Port of Spain from an insider's perspective, it's well worth joining one of the excellent city tours offered by Island Experiences (☎ 621 0407 or ☎ 781 6235, w islandexperiencestt.com), from daytime sightseeing in Port of Spain, Chaguaramas and the Bocas islands to evening excursions taking in practice sessions at panyards and live calypso (half-day and evening tours from US$45, full-day from US$80). New operator ARC Destinations (☎ 768 7613, w bit.ly/ARCTnT) offers some unique options based around local chocolate production, including a condensed Bean to Bar trip taking in the city's cocoa hotspots, from shops to chocolatiers, plus historical walking tours, foodie outings and (at Carnival time) visits to mas camps and Jouvert bands that daub their revellers with cocoa (from TT$255).

Outdoor activities Chaguaramas holds the bulk of the outdoor activities, from kayaking (see page 101) to zip lining (see page 100) and hiking (see page 96). Liquid

Adrenaline, based at C3 Marina, 199 Western Main Rd, just past the Peake's service station in Cocorite (☎ 779 6647, w liquidadrenalin.com), offers a range of watersports in the Gulf waters just off Westmoorings, from waterskiing, wakeboarding, wakesurfing and wakeskating (all US$40) to SUP-boarding (US$30) and dolphin-boarding, where you're boosted above the water by an underfoot jetpack (US$100); all activities include tuition.

Golf St Andrew's Golf Course's picturesque 18 holes nestle under the foothills of the Northern Range (St Andrew's Wynd, Moka; daily 6am–7pm; ☎ 629 0066, w golftrinidad. com). Nine holes cost TT$180–325, 18 holes TT$300–545. To reach it, follow Saddle Rd past Morne Coco Rd, and carry straight on along Perseverance Rd; turn right onto Moka Main Rd, and left onto St Andrew's Wynd.

1

CARNIVAL IN PORT OF SPAIN

Port of Spain is the epicentre of Trinidad's **Carnival**, home to the Panorama steel band competition (see page 268), the calypso tents (see page 34) and most of the mas camps (see page 80) of the bands that make up the main **costume parade** and the pre-festival **Jouvert** (see page 71). And as well as enjoying the pre-Carnival fetes and panyards, anyone can be a part of the main event and **play mas** (see page 70), simply by signing up with the bands below. You can also **watch the parade** from anywhere along the route, or take a seat in the stands at the Queen's Park Savannah or the smaller stages at Adam Smith Square and Piccadilly Greens, on Piccadilly Street. The more exclusive bikini bands also parade at the so-called **Socadrome** (Ⓦbit.ly/Socadrome) at the Jean Pierre stadium in Woodbrook, which also has seating.

CARNIVAL ACCOMMODATION

The run-up to Carnival is easily the busiest time of year in Port of Spain, and if you intend to stay anywhere in the city during this time it's essential to book well in advance. Regular Carnival goers reserve their **accommodation** for the following year on Ash Wednesday, and it's a good idea to book very early if you have your heart set on a particular place – or area, with downtown, Woodbrook, Newtown and St Clair being the most convenient for the parade route. As well as trying the places listed in this book, it's a good idea to check options on Airbnb (see page 26); also, rooms in private houses are advertised, sometimes at very reasonable rates, in the classified sections of newspapers (also available online; see page 32). Carnival **accommodation prices**, which can be more than double normal rates, usually apply from the Wednesday or Friday preceding Carnival through to Ash Wednesday. The majority of hotels and guesthouses insist on five- to eight-night **minimum stays**, which you'll have to pay for even if you don't stay there the whole period. Note that the prices listed in this book are non-Carnival rates.

CARNIVAL WEBSITES

Fineahban Ⓦfineahban.com. A lifesaver if you're scrabbling to play mas last minute, with costumes for sale and swap, as well as Carnival accommodation and some fete info. The site Ⓦmycarnivalbands.com is an alternative for swaps and sales.

National Carnival Commission Ⓦncctt.org. Info on the history of Carnival, plus parade routes, band listings and an official calendar of events.

Trini Jungle Juice Ⓦtrinijunglejuice.com. Fete pics and reviews and events info.

Trini Scene Ⓦtriniscene.com. Much-visited for its shots of patrons at parties around T&T, but also good for listings and live streaming of fetes around Carnival time.

Trinidad Carnival Diary Ⓦtrinidadcarnivaldiary.com. The go-to place for Carnival information, from essential advice for "Carnival Virgins" to the lowdown on Monday wear, boots and tights and on companies that buy fete tickets and deliver them to your hotel, via summer band launches and the subsequent dissection of costumes and on-the-road reviews. Links to all the bands and relevant websites, too.

MAS BANDS

The list below represents a selection of the best-known large and medium **mas bands** in Port of Spain: new bands surface each year, but you can find online listings at several of the websites above and at Ⓦtntisland.com/mas.html, which also lists smaller (and usually cheaper) outfits; all bands offer costume sneak peaks and updates on Facebook and Instagram. Note also that the **McFarlane** mas band (loved by some, disparaged by others as a derivative substitute for Peter Minshall) brings out a band every few years: visit Ⓦbit.ly/McFMas for updates. For creative mas with a frisson of political comment, you could check out the small **Cat in Bag** outfit (❶628 7508, Ⓦbit.ly/CiBMas), while a more sedate alternative to bikini mas is a sailor band, such as the huge one organized by the **Trinidad All Stars** steel pan band (❶627 2127, Ⓦbit.ly/TTAllStars); revellers provide their own drinks and costumes (variations of flared white trousers, tailored liveried jacket and peaked cap – all available locally). Don't forget to bring your talcum powder, flung into the air as a traditional part of sailor mas – as the saying goes "Yuh can't play mas and 'fraid powder"!

Bliss 18 Rosalino St, Woodbrook ❶625 6800, Ⓦbliss carnival.com. The "exclusive" offshoot of the mighty Tribe, and just as popular.

D Krewe 36–38 Dundonald St, Port of Spain ❶623 9296, Ⓦdkrewecarnival.com. Bikini mas, but slightly less high-octane than Passion or Fantasy (so you might

even be able to get a costume).

Fantasy 6 Alberto St, Woodbrook ❶221 4966, Ⓦmy carnivalfantasy.com. The preserve of the young and the beautiful, this is one of the apex "It" bands – so costumes go fast.

Harts 5 Alcazar St, St Clair ❶622 8038, Ⓦharts

carnival.com. The band of choice for Trinidad's white middle classes, young and old, and the originator of the feathers-and-beads style that predominates today. Sells out fast.

K2K Alliance 22 Oleander Row, Victoria Gdns, Diego Martin ⓦ767 9655, ⓦk2k-carnival.com. Combining mas with runway-style high fashion, K2K's elaborate and intricate costumes are mini works of art.

Legacy 88 Roberts St, Woodbrook ☎622 7466, ⓦlegacycarnival.com. Inexpensive and a little bit old-school, with no surprises in the feathers and bikinis on parade, but a bit more inclusive and forgiving of different body shapes and sizes, and good for more mature masqueraders.

The Lost Tribe 59 Alberto St, Woodbrook ☎350 6219, ⓦlosttribecarnival.com. Offshoot of Tribe, dedicated to bringing real creative mas back to the large bands. Costumes are seriously gorgeous and in high demand.

Mardi Gras 3 Cipriani Blvd, Newtown 488 0062, ⓦbit. ly/MGrasTT. A party-hard, inexpensive option, offering drinks, food and basic bikini/board shorts costume for a little over TT$1000.

Passion 3 Rosalino St, Woodbrook ☎235 3603, ⓦpassioncarnival.com. Frontline-heavy, lavish costumes, gym toned bodies and a young crowd make this one of Carnival's premium options.

Ronnie and Caro Cnr Anna and Warren streets, Woodbrook ☎628 4521, ⓦronnieandcaro.com. Great costumes and more of a family vibe than the large bikini bands; easier to get a costume, too.

Showtime 51 French St, Woodbrook ☎621 0001, ⓦshowtimetrinidad.com. Fun all-inclusive band that's a lot more affordable than some of the heavyweight names.

Tribe 20 Rosalino St, Woodbrook ☎625 6800, ⓦcarnivaltribe.com. The naughty child of the once-mighty Poison, Tribe has long been the apex of bikini mas in Trinidad, though it's got some stiff competition from new bands these days. Get a costume early, or forget it.

Trini Revellers 35 Gallus St, Woodbrook ☎628 7275, ⓦtrinirevellersmas.com. With less focus on the perfect gym-honed body and costumes that tend to display a bit less flesh than the it-crowd large bands, Revellers are a Carnival stalwart.

YUMA 12 Alcazar St, St Clair ☎628 1919, ⓦyumavibe. com. YUMA (Young Upwardly Mobile Adults) is a high-end band with suitably ornate costumes and emphasis on customer service. Hit the gym before you sign up (and do so in person, as there's no online registration).

JOUVERT BANDS

The list below covers **jouvert bands** that have stayed the course for several years; new ones pop up each year, so keep an eye on carnival websites or listen to the radio once in T&T to keep abreast of what's new.

3canal 33 Murray St, Woodbrook ☎622 1001, ⓦ3canal. com. Since their first Jouvert band, Jocks-Tuh-Pose, in 1997, 3canal have won a huge following, especially among Trinidad's arts intelligentsia. This is a simply brilliant Jouvert experience, for once not all-inclusive: all you get is a T-shirt, a bandana and endless joy.

Chocolate City 42 Baden-Powell St, Woodbrook ☎704 9999, ⓦbit.ly/ChocCityTT. A well-established and well-organized outfit whose USP is coating its patrons in liquid chocolate.

Clay Jouvert 2 Warren St, Woodbrook ☎316 2266, ⓦclayjouvert.com. Relatively new to the Jouvert scene but with a huge and loyal following. Pre-parade lime is followed by a great time on the road: rhythm section, trucks playing old-school soca and current hits, ample drinks, plenty of clay and paint and a cool-down session.

Dirty Dozen 16 Hayes St, St Clair ☎756 8829, ⓦdirty dozenjouvert.com. Mud, paint and powder, plus all-inclusive food and drinks and tight security.

Nasty Devils 66 Ariapita Ave, Woodbrook ☎686 2789, ⓦbit.ly/NDevils. Glowing horns for women, good music and a cooldown zone and water-truck washdown at the end.

WeLoveJouvert 67 Petra St, Woodbrook ☎472 5050, ⓦwelovejouvert.com. A full Jouvert package, with a pre-party from 2am near the stadium, an all-inclusive on-the-road experience with paint and water, and an after-party cooldown.

PANYARDS

All Stars 46 Duke St, Port of Spain ⓦbit.ly/AllStarsTT.

Desperadoes Upper Laventille Rd, East Dry River, Laventille; Carnival season: 2–4 Victoria Ave, cnr Cadiz and Queen's Park East; ⓦbit.ly/Despers.

Invaders 147 Tragarete Rd, opposite the Queen's Park Oval, Woodbrook ⓦinvaders-tt.com.

Phase II Pan Groove 15 Hamilton St, off Damian St, Woodbrook ⓦbit.ly/Phase2TT.

Renegades 138 Charlotte St, Port of Spain ⓦbit.ly/ RenegadesTT.

Silver Stars 56 Tragarete Rd, Newtown ⓦbit.ly/ SilverStarsTT.

Starlift Mucurapo Rd, St James.

1

ACCOMMODATION

The **accommodation** options in Port of Spain are plentiful and varied, from inexpensive guesthouses to business-oriented chain hotels, with some nice boutique-type places in between. Staying **downtown** is convenient for shops, services and sightseeing, but it's quiet after dark here and there isn't much choice. **Woodbrook** is the best option, with the lion's share of the guesthouses, good public transport links and plenty of restaurants and bars – and if you stay at the eastern end of the suburb, the downtown area is only ten minutes' walk away. A short walk from the Savannah, **Newtown** and **St Clair** are less vibrant (and quieter), with a sprinkling of reasonably priced options, while there are a few lovely places on the outskirts of residential **St Ann's** and **Cascade**.

DOWNTOWN AND THE WATERFRONT

Hyatt Regency 1 Wrightson Rd ☎ 623 2222, ⓦ trinidad. regency.hyatt.com; map p.56. This glinting tower on the waterfront is Trinidad's most upmarket hotel; facilities run from a gorgeous rooftop infinity pool overlooking the Gulf of Paria to a state-of-the-art spa, gym, excellent waterside restaurant/bar and a sushi bar (see page 85). The rooms are anonymously chic, with bamboo floors, flatscreen TVs and handsome city views, and there's a huge private car park. 🛜 US$209

Pearl's 3–4 Victoria Square East ☎ 625 2158, ⓔ peter henry64@yahoo.com; map p.56. A rambling old colonial house with a veranda overlooking picturesque Victoria Square, this is the cheapest place in downtown Port of Spain, and rates are reasonable even for Carnival. The rooms are very basic, with standing fan and a sink; bathrooms are shared and there's a communal kitchen and TV room, but it's a great first stopoff with plenty of travellers passing through. Friendly, helpful hosts, and perfectly situated for Carnival and downtown sightseeing. 🛜 US$44

Radisson Trinidad 1017 Wrightson Rd ☎ 625 3366, ⓦ radisson.com; map p.56. Glitzy, rather faceless corporate hotel, treated to a full refurb since it became part of the Radisson chain. Facilities are all you'd expect: pool, two restaurants, bar, gym, business centre, shops and a large car park. All rooms have excellent views of the city, and come well equipped. 🛜 US$129

WOODBROOK AND ST JAMES

Ana's Place 5 Ana St, Woodbrook ☎ 627 2563, ⓦ anas-place.com; map p.68. Small but perfectly formed, in the heart of the action off Ariapita Ave. There's a one-bed apartment with kitchen, and an en-suite double room with kitchenette; both are beautifully maintained by the owner (who lives on-site in a separate building), with bright decor, cable TV and a/c. Great rates, too. 🛜 Doubles US$45, apartment US$60

Caribbean Tourist Villa 7 Methuen St, Woodbrook ☎ 627 5423, ⓦ caribbeantouristvilla.com; map p.56. A great position on the downtown fringes of Woodbrook, though the rooms are dark and rather dated; all are clean and tidy, and have a/c, cable TV and fridge; there's also a small pool, though you pay extra to use this as well as the communal kitchen and laundry facilities. 🛜 US$65

Courtyard by Marriott Invader's Bay, Audrey Jeffers Hwy, Woodbrook ☎ 627 5555, ⓦ marriott.com; map p.68. Within walking distance of MovieTowne and a favoured choice of business travellers, so rates are reduced on weekends. Rooms have all the amenities you'd expect of an international chain, and there's a pool, restaurant and bar. Neat, tidy and friendly if a little soulless. 🛜 US$131

★ **Culture Crossroads Inn** Cnr Bengal and Delhi streets, St James ☎ 622 8788, ⓦ culturecrossroadstt. com; map p.68. Great little boutique inn with the finish of an upmarket hotel, and supremely friendly and helpful staff/owners. Each named after one of Trinidad's mas-men, calypsonians and steel pan bands, the attractive, modern rooms is finished with loving detail and equipped with all the necessary extras, as well as fridge, cable TV and a/c; some are equipped for people with disabilities. Security is super-tight. Breakfast available. 🛜 US$105

Fabienne's 15 Belle Smythe St, Woodbrook ☎ 622 2773, ⓔ fabiennes1961@hotmail.com; map p.68. Set in the owner's house, just steps from Ariapita Ave, and offering just two plain and somewhat dated en-suite rooms with fridge, fan and a/c; main draw here is the fantastic location. There's a communal lounge with cable TV, laundry facilities, and breakfast is available. 🛜 US$65

★ **Gingerbread House** 8 Carlos St, Woodbrook ☎ 627 8170, ⓦ trinidadgingerbreadhouse.com; map p.68. Beautifully maintained gingerbread house with a wraparound veranda and quirky, chic modern touches courtesy of the architect owner. There are three lovely rooms in the main house, and another two in a separate building with its own patio; all are en suite with a/c, fridge and cable TV, and there's a rather unique plunge pool out back. Fantastic value for the quality of accommodation; book well ahead. Two-night minimum stay at weekends, when the rate goes up by US$10/night. 🛜 US$70

Inna Citi Place 15 Gaston Johnson St, Woodbrook ☎ 622 0415, ⓦ bit.ly/InnaCity; map p.68. In a great location close to Ariapita Ave, this is a friendly and very secure place offering clean, bright rooms, all with fan, a/c and cable TV, plus a communal kitchen and use of laundry facilities. Full breakfast included. 🛜 US$65

Johnson's 16 Buller St, Woodbrook ☎ 628 7553, ⓔ johnsonsbandb@hotmail.com; map p.56. Friendly, helpful hosts and spotless, well-maintained rooms with fans and cable TV; a/c rooms with fridge cost a bit more

(US$65), and the cheaper ones share bathrooms. Guests have use of a kitchen and lounge. Good value, and in walking distance of both Ariapita Ave and downtown Port of Spain; full breakfast is included in all rates. 📶 <u>US$55</u>

La Calypso 46 French St, Woodbrook ☎ 622 4077, 🌐 aliciaspalace.com; map p.56. A decent little bolt-hole, in a convenient location between the Avenue and Tragarete Rd, with well-kept if dark rooms, the cheapest with a fan and separate bathroom. More expensive options (US$49–58) are en suite with a/c, kettle and microwave. There's a breezy chill-out area on the roof. <u>US$41</u>

Melbourne Inn 7 French St, Woodbrook ☎ 623 4006, 📧 melbourneinn@hotmail.com; map p.68. A slightly dilapidated air, but a great location for Carnival and perhaps the cheapest rooms in Woodbrook. The budget option is a basic economy room, with fan and shared bathroom; there are also fan-only rooms, some en suite (US$50–55), and larger a/c, en-suite rooms with fridge and cable TV (US$55–70). There's a sundeck and a large communal veranda, and breakfast is available. 📶 <u>US$40</u>

Sam's 5 Alberto St, Woodbrook ☎ 627 4865, 🌐 samsguesthousett.com; map p.68. On the lower stretch of Alberto St, this friendly place has a homely lounge downstairs and rooms off a main corridor upstairs, where there's also a breezy communal balcony. Rooms are appealing, modern and clean, with a/c, fan, fridge and cable TV; the brightest overlook the balcony. 📶 <u>US$75</u>

THE SAVANNAH, ST ANN'S, CASCADE AND BELMONT

Alicia's House 7 Coblentz Gardens, St Ann's ☎ 623 2802, 🌐 aliciashouse.com; map p.73. All the rooms at this busy little hotel on a quiet road close to the Savannah have a/c, fridge and cable TV; larger ones cost a bit more (US$75–100). There's a swimming pool, sundeck and jacuzzi on site. Meals are available, and breakfast is included. 📶 <u>US$65</u>

Alicia's Palace 1 ¾ Mile Post, Lady Chancellor Rd ☎ 624 8553, 🌐 aliciaspalace.com; map p.56. Gorgeous location on this scenic road, with cool breezes and a bird's-eye view of Port of Spain and down the coast to Caroni – rooms 98 and 105 have the best vistas (US$95). All rooms are en suite, with a/c, cable TV and fridge, there's a pool and the veranda restaurant is beautifully situated overlooking the valley. Shuttle service down into town, and breakfast included in the rates. 📶 <u>US$78</u>

⭐ **Heritage Inn** 7 Coblentz Ave, Cascade ☎ 621 5663, 🌐 heritageinntrinidad.com; map p.73. Great location in an expansive old house, beautifully restored and with some of its original wooden floors, this is an excellent getaway from the city, with a large pool in flowered gardens. Appealing, spacious and tastefully decorated, the rooms all have fridge, a/c and cable TV; economy ones

share bathrooms, loft and standard rooms are en suite (US$132/US$143). Breakfast included. 📶 <u>US$110</u>

Hilton Trinidad Lady Young Rd, St Ann's ☎ 624 3211, 🌐 trinidad.hilton.com; map p.73. "Upside down" hotel built down the side of a hill, with the reception at the top and the floors numbered downwards from 1 to 11. Each room has a balcony with excellent views over Port of Spain and the hotel's landscaped garden, plus all the usual *Hilton* amenities. Facilities include restaurants and bars, tennis courts, a sauna and fitness centre, and a newly refurbished pool. 📶 <u>US$139</u>

Kapok 16–18 Cotton Hill ☎ 622 5765, 🌐 kapokhotel. com; map p.56. Elegant, stylish hotel decorated with handsome artwork, and in a great position for Carnival just off Saddle Rd north of the Savannah. Rooms are spacious and with all the amenities you'd expect; studios and suites with kitchen facilities (US$214) are also available. Good restaurant (see page 85), wine and coffee bar, swimming pool, gym and sundeck on site, and breakfast is included. 📶 <u>US$159</u>

L'Orchidée 3 Coblentz Gardens, St Ann's ☎ 621 0618, 🌐 trinidadhosthomes.com; map p.73. Tucked away on a side street off the Savannah, this is an inviting little hotel fitted out to a very high standard, with twelve bright, modern rooms themed around different orchids, plus a pretty outside terrace and excellent service from the very professional staff. Popular with business travellers, with a full breakfast included. 📶 <u>US$120</u>

⭐ **Normandie** 10 Nook Ave, St Ann's ☎ 624 1181, 🌐 normandiett.com; map p.73. On a quiet cul-de-sac just a 5min walk from the Queen's Park Savannah, this is one of the city's more atmospheric large hotels, with a lively feel provided by the annual Carnival concerts and by the on-site boutiques, café and popular restaurant (see page 85). Most rooms have wooden floorboards (the refurbished ones are tiled), a/c, cable TV, iron and board, hairdryer and en-suite bathroom, and there's a lovely pool. Continental breakfast included. 📶 <u>US$143</u>

Thanna's Place 27 Erthig Rd, Belmont ☎ 225 6582, 🌐 thannas.com; map p.73. Tucked away off the Savannah in residential Belmont but in walking distance of transport options and the Carnival parade, this is a businesslike place with bright, compact a/c rooms, with shared bathroom, a fridge and cable TV; en-suite rooms cost US$10 more. The rates are a little high considering the location but the hosts are extremely friendly and helpful, and there's a pretty little outdoor area. Breakfast included. 📶 <u>US$75</u>

NEWTON AND ST CLAIR

Forty Winks 24 Warner St, Newton ☎ 622 0484, 🌐 fortywinkstt.com; map p.56. Great little guesthouse aimed at the business traveller who doesn't want to stay at a typical business hotel. The en-suite rooms are on the

1

smallish side, but all come with a/c and cable TV. The house is brightly decorated and has an outdoor patio, rooftop terrace and kitchen for guests' use. Breakfast included. 📶 US$105.50

★**Inn at 87** 87 Woodford St, Newtown ☎622 4343, ⓦinnat87.com; map p.56. Set in a restored former printery dating from the 1930s, and boasting pretty exterior fretwork, beautiful high ceilings and original wooden floors in its communal lounge, this is an atmospheric place, very friendly and professionally run. Though compact, rooms are comfortable and welcoming, with fresh, clean decor and a/c, cable TV and fridge; some

sleep four (US$121). Full breakfast available, and free tea and coffee all day. 📶 US$109

Villa de Rose 3a Borde St ☎625 2513, ⓦvilladerosett. net; map p.56. Great for those of an independent bent, with appealing double rooms with shared lounge and kitchen, and four cheerful, well equipped one-bed apartments with full kitchen/living area. Both have cable TV, a/c and bedroom fan, and there's access to a washer/dryer. Nice and secure, in an excellent location for Carnival and the surrounding restaurants/bars and the rates are some of the best in town. Off-street parking available. 📶 Doubles US$65, apartments US$75

EATING

Port of Spain's **restaurant** scene is booming, with everything from high-class establishments serving fancy nouvelle Caribbean cuisine to more casual places cooking up excellent local food and takeaway diners offering good budget eats. There are endless options along **Ariapita Avenue** in Woodbrook, a cluster of high-end places on the terrace of the **One Woodbrook Place** complex between St James and Woodbrook, and in the residential streets of **Newtown**. At the back of the **MovieTowne complex** opposite the stadium on Audrey Jeffers Highway, **Fiesta Plaza** has several restaurants, from a *Ruby Tuesdays* to sushi, seafood and Brazilian-style *churrascaria*, most of which have tables in the central courtyard as well as inside; all have a chain-restaurant feel and it's a somewhat sanitized scene, but can still be fun. If you have your own car, it's also well worth driving out to **Chaguaramas**, which has a few great places to dine right on the water (see page 101). Note that many of the fancier restaurants offer prix fixe lunch menus or buffets, which can work out surprisingly good value for the quality and quantity of food. Many restaurants also double up as good places for a **drink**, and we've highlighted the best options in the reviews below.

STREET FOOD AND TAKEAWAY

With its great tradition of street food, Port of Spain offers plenty of tantalizing alternatives to a sit-down meal. **Doubles** (see page 28) are sold from streetside carts from as early as 6am, and many of the most popular vendors run out by lunchtime. Everyone has their personal favourite, but you'll always see long queues at the George and George's X stalls on Carlos Street in Woodbrook (outside *Brooklyn Bar* and *Coco Lounge*, respectively); you can also find several vendors outside the main entrance to Long Circular Mall, and along Western Main Road in St James, and there's a late-night doubles vendor at the corner of Cipriani Blvd and Tragarete Rd. St James also holds the lion's share of the many stalls that set up in the city as the sun goes down, cooking up **roti**, **aloo pies**, **corn soup**, **bake and shark**, **geera pork**, **pholouri** and the like, as well as delicious fresh **juice**, punches and home-made **ice cream**. Equally popular are the avenue of stalls on a paved area of the Queen's Park Savannah opposite the National Academy for the Performing Arts.

Gyros (flatbread wraps filled with chicken, lamb, shrimp, fish or falafel) are also found at all the city's street food spots in ever-increasing numbers, while the adventurous might want to sample the local **oysters** slurped down with peppery tomato sauce from stalls around the Savannah on Queen's Park West and Maraval Road.

FOOD COURTS AND TAKEAWAYS

For something more substantial, there are legions of hole-in-the-wall places offering inexpensive local lunches, while the **food courts** in all of the shopping malls are also good for a quick bite of something Chinese, Creole or Indian from around TT$50.

There are also **fast-food** outlets all over town, from excellent local fried-chicken outfits such as *Japs* (on Western Main Rd, St James) or the ubiquitous *Royal Castle* to *KFC*, *McDonald's* and *Pizza Hut*. There's a concentration of outlets along Independence Square, and you'll find *Dominos* pizza and *Subway* sandwiches along Ariapita Avenue, near the corner of Carlos Street. There are also a host of options in the MovieTowne complex, off the highway in Woodbrook opposite the Stadium, and in the Shoppes of Maraval complex at the start of Saddle Road in Maraval.

DOWNTOWN

★ **Breakfast Shed** Wrightson Rd, opposite Independence Square; map p.56. Established in 1936 to provide workers' meals, this breezy open-sided "shed" with communal tables overlooking the Gulf of Paria is filled with outlets selling excellent local food, from buljol or smoked herring breakfasts to fish broth, stewed chicken and all the usual Trini sides. Lunches start at around TT$50; head for the stall with the longest queue, as quality varies. There's also a fresh juice booth. Daily 6.30am–4pm.

D'Bocas 68 Independence Square ✆ 627 3474, ⊛ dbocas. com; map p.56. Reliable, inexpensive Creole food: you pick what you want from the array of cooked dishes on display and pay by weight (TT$40/lb). Also a popular spot for a drink (though foreigners are a definite rarity), with a lovely veranda overlooking the square and a dancefloor inside. Mon–Fri 9.30am–late.

★ **Hardline Vegetarian** 34 Park St ✆ 623 9560; map p.56. Adorned with piles of fresh fruit and vegetables, this justifiably popular lunchtime diner serves up delicious, healthy vegetarian meals – steamed veg, soya stew, marinated dumplings (from TT$40) – as well as fruit salads and refreshing blended fruit juices (from TT$20). A stall outside sells more snacky food, from pholouri to corn soup. Mon–Fri 6am–5.30pm.

Living Water 109 Frederick St ✆ 623 6570; map p.56. The a/c canteen of this Catholic charitable organization offers delicious, inexpensive meals, and channels profits into its good works. The menu changes daily: breakfasts range from buljol and bake to eggs (TT$17–20), while lunches always include meat, fish and vegetarian options (including veggie gravy); you pay by weight, at TT$40/lb, and all packaging is sustainable. Mon–Fri 7–9am & 10.30am–2pm, Sat 9.30–11am.

Mother Nature Cnr of St Vincent and Park streets ✆ 623 3300; map p.56. Inexpensive vegetarian meals and salads (from TT$35), wholewheat roti and Jamaican patties, and smoothies and juices freshly made in front of you using a variety of fruits and energy supplements. The buffet-style a/c café is small with limited seating. Mon–Sat 6am–3pm.

Waterfront/Sushi Bar Hyatt Regency, 1 Wrightson Rd ✆ 821 6550, ⊛ trinidad.regency.hyatt.com; map p.56. *The Waterfront* restaurant combines a lovely setting by the Gulf of Paria with reliable food cooked with sustainable and local ingredients. Lunches run from soup and salad (around TT$70) to burgers (TT$90–140), pastas and meat or fish mains (TT$120–190), while dinner mains (TT$140–370) include grilled meat and fish, Thai seafood curry and jerk pork with a coffee glaze and papaya chutney. The adjacent *Sushi Bar* serves some of the freshest sushi in town (rolls TT$50–90, sashimi TT$80–170), and the terrace bar is a cool spot for a cocktail. ☎ Waterfront Mon–Sat 11.30am–2.30pm & 6.30–10pm, Sun 12.30–2pm &

6.30–10pm; Sushi Bar Mon–Thurs & Sat 5–10pm, Fri 1–10pm.

THE SAVANNAH AND ST ANN'S

Apsara 13 Queen's Park East ✆ 623 7659, ⊛ apsaratt. com; map p.73. Traditional North Indian cuisine, from tandooris to tikka masala, served in very plush a/c surroundings; the Hyderabad masala (TT$150) is sublime. Lots of vegetarian choices and delicious desserts, and the weekday lunch buffet (TT$150) is good value. Daily 11am–3pm & 6–11pm, closed Sun eve.

★ **Chaud** 6 Nook Ave, St Ann's ✆ 621 2002, ⊛ bit.ly/ ChaudTT; map p.73. Relocated to a quiet setting in St Ann's, this super-swanky place is run by one of Trinidad's most celebrated chefs and promises seriously good food, with starters (TT$95–125) such as tandoori-spiced octopus or seared scallops with crispy pork belly and dinner mains (TT$195–395) like butter-poached lobster with vanilla-bean orzo or slow-cooked beef cheek with kale and parsnip purée. The weekday three-course prix-fixe lunch (TT$295 including wine and coffee/tea) is a great way to sample the menu, and changes daily. Daily 11am–3pm & 6–10.30pm.

★ **Ciao Café** Normandie Hotel, 10 Nook Ave, St Ann's ✆ 624 1181, ⊛ bit.ly/CiaoPoS; map p.73. A great place for a salad or burger lunch (around TT$50), but best for a romantic dinner, with tables outdoors on a fairy-lit terrace just a short way from the Savannah. Good wine, attentive service and a reliable menu of Caribbean and Italian food, from starters of stuffed mushrooms or juicy coconut shrimp (TT$45–95) to mains such as fish with white wine and capers, baked lamb and chicken in a tomato-cream sauce (TT$75–225). There's also a tasty brunch spread on Sundays (8am–1pm; TT$185). ☎ Daily 11.30am–3pm & 6–10.30pm.

Häagen-Dazs Café 2 Queen's Park West ✆ 627 5892, ⊛ hdcafett.com; map p.56. Unsurprisingly, given the climate, ice cream is big business in T&T, and this is a lovely spot for a cone (from TT$22), sundae, milkshake, coffee or a cake/pastry, set in a glass-fronted fretworked building overlooking the Savannah with a terrace at the front. Wine, beer and cocktails also on offer. ☎ Mon–Thurs & Sun 11am–11pm, Fri & Sat 10am–midnight.

Kava Kapok Hotel, 16–18 Cotton Hill ✆ 622 5283, ⊛ bit.ly/KavaTT; map p.56. Excellent hotel restaurant, with handsome minimalist decor and a menu centred around brick-oven pizzas topped with such things as goat's cheese, caramelized onions and capers, or prosciutto and rocket (from TT$105); there are also burgers (from TT$70) and more substantial mains (from TT$150) such as herb-crusted red snapper or aubergine parmigiana (TT$90). Also a great spot for a drink, with excellent cocktails and regular special deals. ☎ Mon 3–11pm, Tues–Thurs 11.30am–11pm, Fri & Sat 11.30am–midnight.

1

Tamnak Thai 13 Queen's Park East ☎625 0647, ⊕tamnakthaitt.com; map p.73. Elegantly decorated in rich Thai style, this smart restaurant has indoor and outdoor sections, and the food is excellent and authentic, from starters of *tom yum* soup (TT$65) or satay chicken skewers (TT$55) to green curry (TT$135 with chicken), sautéed beef (TT$140) or steamed fish with salt plums, ginger and Chinese mushrooms (TT$175), plus the usual stir-fries and rice dishes. Good weekday lunch buffet (TT$150). Daily 11am–3pm & 6–11pm, closed Sun eve.

WOODBROOK

Chaud Café Damian St ☎628 9845, ⊕bit.ly/ChaudCafe; map p.68. Occupying the corner of the One Woodbrook Place development, this is a good spot for a quality salad (niçoise, coronation lamb, Mediterranean), braised beef sandwich or fish tacos (TT$75–150), or more elaborate dishes such as duck confit with lentils and wilted greens (TT$95) or honey-mustard glazed mahi-mahi (TT$160). After dark you can also enjoy a glass of wine on the terrace with the Woodbrook lights twinkling below; there are plenty of lovely small plates such as Thai salmon sliders or Mexican grilled corn (TT$60–125) to go with your drinks. ⊛ Mon–Thurs 11am–11pm, Fri & Sat 11am–midnight.

El Pecos 84 Ariapita Ave ☎622 9713; map p.68. Basic, inexpensive Creole food: veg rice, lentil peas, macaroni pie, plus jerk and rotisserie chicken, fried fish and salads. You serve yourself and pay according to weight (TT$40/lb), and there are a few tables for dining in. One of several branches throughout Trinidad. Mon–Sat 11am–10pm.

Hakka 4 Taylor St ☎622 0004, ⊕hakkarestaurant.com; map p.68. Chinese cuisine with an Indian flavour, served up in a handsome a/c dining room decked out in subtle shades of orange and brown. Menu highlights include starters of chilli paneer kofta or pepper-and-salt shrimp and calamari; spicy Konjee crispy chicken; and Hong Kong pork with ginger and red chilli paste. Reasonable prices (dishes from TT$63) and reliable food. Mon–Thurs 11am–11pm, Fri & Sat 11am–midnight, Sun 11am–10pm.

★ **House of Sakura** 22 Mucurapo Rd ☎271 8644, ⊕sakuraartstt.com; map p.68. Just west of the Avenue, this tiny diner offers up really delicious sushi at affordable prices: signature rolls (TT$68–80) include the Volcano, with tuna and salmon skin; and the Smoke Bomb, with smoked salmon, cream cheese, cucumber, crab salad and sriracha. Mains from the fusion section (from TT$70) include ramen bowls, teriyaki chicken and crispy firecracker fish. You can pre-order online too. Tues–Thurs 11am–9.30pm, Fri 11am–10.30pm, Sat 2–10.30pm, Sun 10am–4pm.

Irie Bites 71 Ariapita Ave ☎622 7364, ⊕iriebitesjerk.com; map p.68. Jamaican jerk shack serving some of the tastiest and best-value meals in the city. Nicely seasoned and cooked over pimento wood, the generous combos of jerk chicken, pork and fish (from TT$48) are served with side dishes such as green fig salad, sautéed breadfruit/cassava or bhaji rice. Ackee and saltfish available on Saturdays. Delivery available. ⊛ Mon–Thurs & Sat 11am–9pm, Fri 10am–10pm, Sun 10am–2pm.

★ **Livet Gourmet** 80 Ariapita Ave ☎674 5015, ⊕bit.ly/LivetTT; map p.68. The wonderful *Livet* offers a fresh take on buffet food (you pay by weight; TT$40/lb). The emphasis is on healthy eating (labelling shows nutritional values and what's gluten- or dairy-free), but that's not to say that the food is all unseasoned brown rice and quinoa: choose from a daily changing menu of delicious fish, seafood, meat or veggie proteins alongside lasagne and delectable sides such as cassava gratin, stew peas, callaloo, ground provisions, baked cinnamon plantain, plus a daily soup, curry/roti options, salad from the lovely salad bar and baked sweet treats; they even have gluten-free doubles and macaroni pie. Sustainable packaging, and a few tables inside and out on the veranda. Mon–Thurs 7am–7pm, Fri & Sat 7am–9pm, Sun 7am–4pm.

More Sushi 23 O'Connor St ☎622 8466, ⊕morevino.com; map p.68. This excellent wine bar offers great sushi and sashimi, reasonably priced and always super-fresh, including rolls (TT$78–118), such as the Scorpion Pepper and Maracas, with a local twist. Other mains (from TT$100) include Japanese katsu curries, chicken teriyaki and pad Thai, plus Alfredo pasta and a lovely crab dip starter (TT$138). Mon 11am–9.30pm, Tues–Thurs 11am–10.30pm, Fri & Sat 11am–11.30pm, Sun 5–9.30pm.

New Earth Organic 80 Roberts St ☎381 3785, ⊕bit.ly/NeoTT; map p.68. Tiny little organic store and café offering fresh fruit and veg and reasonably priced vegetarian lunches, cooked with whatever fresh produce is in stock; check the daily menu online and pre-order. Look out also for baked goods such as banana muffins or spelt bread. Always delicious and a great place to meet people. Tues–Sat 6am–2pm.

★ **Veni Mange** 67 Ariapita Ave ☎624 4597, ⊕venimange.com; map p.68. Set on the first floor of a greenery-swathed building and decorated with Caribbean artwork, *Veni* is a Port of Spain institution, as good a liming spot as it is a place to eat. The food is a happy blend of local staples with an international twist; menus change daily, but you might get such delights as Creole stewed pork with melongene and dumplings or grilled mahi-mahi with tamarind sauce (mains TT$95–138). There's always a good veggie option, such as tofu and pineapple kebabs in a chilli sauce (TT$95), as well as hearty salads and excellent puddings. Inexpensive lunch combos (TT$40–55) also available for takeaway. Mon–Fri 11.30am–3pm, plus Wed–Fri 7–10pm.

ZaZou Kitchen One Woodbrook Place, Damian St ☎750 2083, ⊛bit.ly/ZazouTT; map p.68. New bistro offering a delicious, beautifully presented blend of French, Asian and Caribbean cuisine. Starters (TT$55–95) include parsley-butter escargot, roasted carrot salad with crispy quinoa and confit tomatoes, or Thai-style pork sausages with steamed buns; there are also excellent burgers and bowls of veggie soba noodles, Thai shrimp curry or pork ramen (TT$105–145), and mains of Moroccan-spiced lamb shank, soy-miso salmon or flat-iron steak with roasted polenta. Home-made ice cream and sorbet, or the likes of Trinitario cocoa chocolate mousse and apple tart for dessert. Great cocktails, too, and open late for liming Fri & Sat. Tues 5–10pm, Wed & Thurs 11am–3pm & 5–10pm, Fri 11am–3pm & 5–11.30pm, Sat 11.30am–10.30pm.

TRAGARETE ROAD, NEWTOWN AND ST CLAIR

★**Buzo Osteria Italiana** 6a Warner St, Newtown ☎222 2896, ⊛buzorestaurant.com; map p.56. Simply the best Italian food in T&T, served with style and humour in a very chic dining room within a lovely old cut-stone building. All the standards of Italian cuisine are on offer, from antipasti (TT$49–129) and home-made pasta such as squid-ink tagiatelle with seafood (TT$89–109) to perfect pizza with all the classic toppings (TT$79–110). Main dish (TT$119–259) highlights include grouper with fresh tomato sauce, capers and olives; chicken with Marsala and mushrooms; and meatballs. The cocktails and wine list are fantastic, and there's a separate bar with an outdoor area for drinks and snacks. Book ahead. Mon–Sat 11.30am–11pm.

★**Dopson's** 28 Maraval Rd, Newtown ☎628 6141; map p.56. This brilliant takeaway sells some of the city's best roti: beautifully stretchy dhalpuri skins (or buss-up-shut) and excellent fillings, from shrimp to conch or goat, plus the usual veg, chicken and beef and a mean curry mango; rotis from TT$30. Expect queues. Mon–Fri 6.45am–5.30pm, Sat 8am–5.30pm.

La Cantina 12 Victoria Ave ☎627 4992, ⊛lacantina pizzeria.com; map p.56. Decent Italian place, with a lovely setting in an airy colonial-era building. Baked in a wood-fired oven, the thin-crust pizzas (TT$99–149) are reliably delicious, with the range of forty encompassing all the classic combinations, while mains (TT$150–200) include rack of lamb and a seafood platter; kids' menu, too, plus rather un-Italian platters of ribs, chicken and spicy calamari to go with drinks. Mon–Thurs 11.30am–11pm, Fri & Sat 11.30am–midnight, Sun 5pm–midnight.

★**Lola's** 82 Tragarete Rd, Newtown ☎345 5439, ⊛bit.ly/LolasTT; map p.56. Compact restaurant that's a great option for breakfast (T$15–35), with everything from coconut bake/sada roti with choka, black pudding, buljol or corned beef to egg and bacon/sausage combos, pancakes and pies. Lunch runs from excellent sandwiches

(beef burger, chicken, Cajun shrimp, fish and chargrilled veg, all with home-made remoulade or aioli), salads (try the roasted beetroot with cheese, walnuts and chickpeas) and more substantial offerings (TT$38–60) such as grilled fish, shrimp or chicken with sides of kale cornbread, cheddar and chive mash, mung-bean noodles or roast baby potatoes. Friendly service, and sustainable packaging for takeaways. Local delivery available. Mon–Thurs 7am–3.30pm, Fri 7am–4.30pm, Sat 8am–4.30pm.

Patraj 161 Tragarete Rd ☎221 9592; map p.68. Hailed by many Trinis as the capital's best roti shop. Consistently good food, from the delicious morning sada roti with tomato choka to the usual array of skins and fillings for lunch and early dinner. Rotis from TT$30. Mon–Sat 8am–5pm.

Shiann's Food Palace 62 Tragarete Rd, Newtown ☎304 5004; map p.56. Longstanding roti place, with sada and tomato/aubergine choka or buljol and bake for breakfast, plus a lunchtime Creole buffet (chicken, stewed peas, callaloo, mac pie, salad, etc) as well as excellent wrapped rotis and buss up shut snackboxes with a wide array of curry veg and meat. Inexpensive and tasty. Mon–Sat 8am–3pm.

Town 51 Cipriani Blvd, Newtown ☎627 8696, ⊛towntt.com; map p.56. Tucked underneath *51°* nightclub, with tables out on a deck and inside, this is a somewhat upmarket place for a drinking and dining, popular with a well-dressed, mature crowd. As well as pasta (lobster or spinach ravioli, creamy mushroom penne; TT$75–155) there are burgers (TT$65–90), steaks (TT$185–215) and a long menu of Chinese dishes, from Szechuan beef to pork char sui (TT$114–150). It's also a popular place for a drink, with good cocktails. Mon–Thurs 11am–10pm, Fri & Sat 11am–11pm.

Trotters Cnr Maraval and Sweet Briar roads, St Clair ☎627 8768, ⊛trotters.net; map p.56. Cavernous bar and restaurant that's a popular place to watch big sporting events. The wide-ranging menu covers everything from pork or chicken dumplings (TT$69) to popcorn shrimp (TT$84) starters to excellent burgers (TT$89–95), huge salads with fish, seafood and meat (TT$99–149), American-style pizza (including a tandoori chicken version; TT$93), coconut shrimp, fried chicken, pasta and steaks (TT$88–299), and a kids' menu. 🛜 Mon–Thurs & Sun 10am–midnight, Fri & Sat 10am–2am.

Zabouca Breads 73 Tragarete Rd ☎628 1656, ⊛zaboucabreads.com; map p.56. Cool little artisan bakery, with a daily changing roster of delicious bread (around TT$60), from sourdough to sunflower rye, jalapeno cornbread, herb and olive braided loaf and cinnamon-raisin bread. Other treats include scones (blueberry cornmeal; chocolate hazelnut; coconut ginger; TT$15), plus a host of gluten-free options (TT$20–70), and pizzas made to order (TT$50). Mon–Fri 9am–6pm, Sat 9am–3pm.

1

MARAVAL

★ **Adam's Bagels** 15a Saddle Rd ☎ 622 2435, ⓦ adamsbagels.com; map p.68. Busy deli selling all kinds of goodies, from fresh bread, bagels and cakes to chocolates, savoury snacks (try the veg or beef kibbies) to baba ganoush and delicious pastelles in fish, chicken, beef and lentil varieties. There are also tables in the a/c rear section where you can order barista coffees and excellent filled bagels, sandwiches, soups, salads, kebabs, burgers and wraps, all made with care using good quality ingredients; breakfasts (TT$20–50) are great too, with plenty of local choices alongside the eggs and bacon. Mains around TT$60. ☎ Mon–Sat 7am–6.30pm.

★ **Aioli** Ellerslie Plaza, Saddle Rd ☎ 222 4654, ⓦ aioli trinidad.com; map p.68. This is an absolute gem in the otherwise uninspiring surrounds of a small shopping plaza, with handsome modern decor and a mouthwatering Mediterranean/fusion menu of beautifully presented food. Highlights include the starter of bone marrow and escargot (TT$95); truffle lobster pasta (TT$295); Thai duck breast with pak choi and edamame (TT$295); or pork loin with sweet potato and coffee anise jus (TT$180). There's also a Friday tapas menu (TT$55–180), a three-course Wednesday dinner deal (TT$300), and great cocktails. Mon–Fri 11am–11.30pm, Sat 6–11pm.

DRINKING AND NIGHTLIFE

Trinidadians wouldn't dream of restricting their **partying** to Carnival time – anything from a public holiday to the end of a workday is cause for celebration. Port of Spain is an excellent place to enjoy a night on the town at any time of the year, and you can find something going on every night of the week, especially along Ariapita Avenue. Upcoming parties and special events are advertised on the radio, in the print versions of local newspapers and the events section of ⓦ buzz.tt. Most places come alive after 8pm and are busiest at weekends, with bars often deluged on Fridays for the customary after-work lime – though Wednesdays and Sundays can also see decent crowds. Published **opening hours** are often a bit hazy; if there's a crowd, places will stay open later; similarly, on a quiet night you may find doors closed early or not open at all.

Bars and club-bars Port of Spain's western suburbs are packed with bars, from intimate places with funky modernist decor and a good wine list to pumping spaces where people go to dance as much to drink. Most host busy after-work limes on a Friday afternoon, with drinks promotions, and many have a happy hour or drinks promotions on the weekends. Several places blur the lines between bar and club, with a dancefloor and DJs pumping out soca, dancehall and pop hits; for some of these, you might pay a cover charge of TT$40–150; at the higher end expect some drinks to be included. If you fancy a drink in more relaxed surroundings, head out to Chaguaramas, where there is a string of lovely places by the sea (see page 101).

Clubs As so many of Port of Spain's bars are places to dance, there are surprisingly few dedicated club venues; note, though, that arts venues such as Big Black Box (see page 90) occasionally stage some excellent parties. The two clubs listed here (*Tzar* and *51˚*) adhere to strict dress codes; although foreigners can usually get away with more than locals, bear in mind that men may be turned away if wearing sneakers, shorts or hats, while women should wear heels or strappy sandals (flip-flops are not deemed appropriate). Cover charges start at around TT$60, or TT$100 with some drinks included, and women often get in free.

WOODBROOK

#63 Lounge 63 Ariapita Ave ⓦ bit.ly/63Lounge; map p.68. Newish, super-neon-lit bar, raised a little off the Avenue in a spot that seems to change its name with each

season. Big-game sports on the TVs, weekend DJs and lots of special deals on drinks; occasional live music, too. Mon & Sun 6pm–late, Tues–Sat 3pm–late.

★ **Brooklyn Bar** Cnr Roberts and Carlos streets ☎ 238 7185, ⓦ bit.ly/BrooklynTT; map p.68. This casual, laidback place is a post-makeover rum bar, its traditional Woodbrook building having been painted over with murals. Beers are inexpensive and always "beastly" cold, and the good-natured crowd spills out onto the pavements for the busy Friday night after-work lime. A great place to start your night. Daily 9am–1am.

Coco Lounge 35 Carlos St, cnr Ariapita Ave ☎ 296 6210, ⓦ bit.ly/CocoTT; map p.68. Popular with a well-dressed crown of pretty young (and not so young) things who come to lime on the raised balcony or dance in the indoor a/c lounge. Regular special events and drinks promotions. TT$40–60 cover charge after 9pm Thurs–Sun. Mon–Wed 11am–midnight, Thurs 11am–3am, Fri 11am–5am, Sat 11am–5am, Sun 9–11pm.

★ **Drink Lounge** 63 Rosalino St, cnr Roberts and Warren streets ☎ 223 7243, ⓦ bit.ly/DrinkTT; map p.68. Cosy and friendly wine bar, popular with an arty crowd and offering a great wine list, excellent cocktails and good food, too, including breakfast. Nicely detached from the Avenue so offering a quieter place to drink and talk. Tues–Thurs 7am–11pm, Fri & Sat 7am–2am.

Frankie's 68 Ariapita Ave ☎ 622 6609, ⓦ bit.ly/ FrankiesTT; map p.68. Perpetually busy Avenue hangout, with a fenced-off area outside that's always packed with crowds of drinkers enjoying inexpensive beers and cocktails, and simple barbecue and Indian food.

Especially busy on Friday evenings. Daily 6am–late, kitchen closes 9pm.

Hog & Whistle Cnr De Verteuil St and Ariapita Ave ☎ bit.ly/HogWhistle; map p.68. Casual, laid-back spot for a drink, tucked underneath a tiny shopping plaza at the quiet end of the Avenue and with a few tables out front. Lots of deals on drinks, and occasional special events too. Daily 11am–late.

Island Beer Chill & Grill One Woodbrook Place, Damian St ☎235 2337, ☎bit.ly/IBeerChill; map p.68. Sports bar and pub, with some 120 beers from all over the world, including 24 on draught and many ales and bitters as well as lagers; cider, too. Major sports events on the 15ft screen, and DJs at the weekends. There's an in-house smoker churning out smoked ribs, brisket and the like alongside burgers and more substantial meals. Mon–Thurs 3pm–midnight, Fri 11am–1am, Sat 11am–midnight, Sun 3–11pm.

La Habana 61 Ariapita Ave ☎625 7393; map p.68. This friendly bar with a Latin flavour opens onto the street, and the mixed Venezuelan/local crowd spills out over the pavement and onto the tarmac. DJs play Latin, soca and techno on the dancefloor inside, and there are regular drinks promotions and special events. Mon–Sat 4pm–late.

More Vino 23 O'Connor St, cnr Ariapita Ave ☎622 8466, ☎morevino.com; map p.68. Popular with a mixed crowd of young and old, this is a relatively quiet spot for a glass of wine or a cocktail, either on the decked area outside or the a/c indoor bar. Great service, excellent food (see page 86), regular drinks promotions and good music that's kept at a conversation-friendly level. Mon 11am–9.30pm, Tues–Thurs 11am–10.30pm, Fri & Sat 11am–11.30pm, Sun 5–9.30pm.

★ **Pub House** 73 Ariapita Ave ☎684 6873, ☎bit.ly/PubHouseTT; map p.68. Friendly, busy spot that draws a laidback crowd. By day/early evening, it's good for a game of darts or to watch sporting events in the big screens; later on, DJs take over and the dancefloor fills up. There's also a fairly spacious terrace outside. Bar snacks available. Daily 11am–3am.

Residence One Woodbrook Place, Damian St ☎235 3566, ☎bit.ly/ResidenceTT; map p.68. At the back of the One Woodbrook complex, this rather upmarket place (dress code in effect) stages good Latin parties on Thursdays as well as the usual soca/dancehall playlist from DJs on other nights. An interesting menu of Peruvian food, too. Tues–Thurs 5pm–midnight, Fri & Sat 5pm–late.

Smokey and Bunty Avenue 76 Ana St, cnr Ariapita Ave ☎bit.ly/SBAveTT; map p.68. A Port of Spain institution, moved from its original St James location following a catastrophic fire. The Avenue setting doesn't have the seamy St James vibe, but it remains a popular late liming spot, with cold, cold beers and tables on the terrace outside. Mon–Sat 11pm–3am, Sun 10pm–midnight.

Stumblin' on the Avenue 42 Ariapita Ave, Woodbrook ☎223 5017, ☎bit.ly/stumblinTT; map p.68. Unpretentious club-bar, with a dancefloor opening out onto a streetside terrace, great music (soca, reggae, hip-hop etc) and a friendly, laidback crowd of all ages packing out the place till the wee hours. Drinks are reasonably priced and entry is often free. Wed, Fri & Sat 4pm–3am, Thurs 5pm–2am.

Tequila Twist 58a Ariapita Ave ☎bit.ly/TwistTT; map p.68. Small but very loud, and perhaps a bit more rough around the edges than its neighbours, with regular drinks promotions. Daily 11am–late.

Tzar 33 Carlos St, cnr Ariapita Ave ☎704 7031, ☎bit.ly/TzarTT; map p.68. Ariapita Avenue's only full-blown club, housed in a black box of a building and attracting a young crowd. Dress your best – and to be sure of getting in, secure a place on the guest list via the hotline numbers on the FB page (though visitors will often be let in without being listed). Tues–Sun 10pm–5am.

NEWTOWN, ST CLAIR AND ST ANN'S

51° 51 Cipriani Blvd, Newtown ☎627 0051, ☎51degrees.biz; map p.56. One of Trinidad's most popular clubs, attracting a mixed, uptownish party crowd and with a wide music policy, mostly dancehall, soca and hip-hop, with some dance and "alternative" thrown in too. To be assured entry at weekends, arrive before 10pm, or call/email to get on the guest list in advance. The main party nights are Friday and Saturday, but there's also karaoke on a Thursday. Thurs–Sat 9pm–late.

All Out Sports Bar and Grill 1st Floor, Queen's Park Oval, 94 Tragarete Rd, St Clair; map p.68. Slightly upmarket sports bar, popular with a mature and moneyed crowd: great for catching big games on the nine plasma screens and as a post-match haunt. English beers, good food such as wings, pizza, calamari and the like, and an outdoor terrace. ☎ Daily 11am–midnight, Fri till 1am.

★ **B3** Normandie complex, Nook Ave, St Ann's 680 0825, ☎bit.ly/B3PoS; map p.73. This fantastic shop-cum-wine bar is a great find if you're after a really good glass of wine or a quality beer, with just a few tables out front. There are racks of bottles from all the main producing regions, with knowledgeable staff on hand to help you choose, as well as a great selection of proseccos and champagnes (including half-bottles). Many are available by the glass; if you take a whole bottle and don't drink it all, you can have it corked and kept till your next visit. There are also craft beers from the UK, Belgium, France and Germany, and a great selection of rums, whiskeys and other spirits. Check the FB page for details of wine and food pairing events, and Sunday brunches. Mon–Thurs 10am–7pm, Fri & Sat 10am–11pm, Sun 10am–4pm.

Kaiso Blues Café 85 Woodford St, Newtown ☎477 2262, ⓦbit.ly/KaisoBlues; map p.56. Genial, friendly place to catch a live music performance, with everything from calypso to jazz, blues, reggae, afrobeats and R&B, plus other events such as comedy shows or poetry/open mic nights. Cover charge (around TT$60) for some events, most starting 7.30–8pm. Wed–Sun 6.30pm–late.

★ **Paprika** 15 Rust St, St Clair ☎789 8917, ⓦbit.ly/ PaprikaTT; map p.68. With opulent decor that ranges between a Moroccan souk and a Parisian bordello, this is a perennially popular party spot for a somewhat upmarket, mixed-age crowd, who quaff champagne and premium cocktails and dance the night away to an eclectic playlist that might run from Machel Montano to Madonna. Tables inside and out, and a good wine list too. Thurs 6pm–3am, Fri & Sat 6pm–4am.

★ **Vas Lounge** 16 Rust St, St Clair ☎235 3224, ⓦbit. ly/VasLounge; map p.68. Right opposite *Paprika* and drawing a slightly more mixed (but equally dressed up) crowd, *Vas* offers up a similar menu of drinking and dancing, with modern, minimalist decor, a large dancefloor inside and a roomy terrace out front. Food available, too. Wed–Sat 6pm–4am, Sun 8pm–2am.

ENTERTAINMENT

Aside from partying, Trinidad has some interesting arts possibilities, from exhibitions at the city's galleries (see page 92) to performance-based work at spaces such as Alice Yard or Big Black Box. **Theatre** is also popular diversion, with a hugely varied set of productions staged at Queen's Hall, alongside the odd play at the Trinidad Theatre Workshop (see page 67) or Little Carib Theatre. As well as staging their brilliant annual Carnival show, rapso band 3canal (ⓦ3canal.com) sometimes produce a summer show; check their website for details. MovieTowne is by far the most popular place to see a film; less mainstream **cinema** is showcased during the Trinidad & Tobago Film Festival and the European Film Festival, staged in September and May (see page 36) respectively.

THEATRE AND THE ARTS

★ **Alice Yard** 80 Roberts St, Woodbrook ⓦbit.ly/ AliceYard. The backyard of the former family home of a local architect, Alice Yard is an eclectic arts space curated by artists and writers which stages a wonderful range of events, from visual arts to poetry readings and workshops.

★ **Big Black Box** 33 Murray St. Woodbrook ☎623 7411, ⓦbit.ly/bbbTT. Performance space created by rapso group 3canal, with regular performances from them as well as productions featuring a wealth of other local talent. Also regular parties in the run up to Carnival season and the intermittent Bass Yard event, the only place in T&T to hear quality underground dance music.

Central Bank Auditorium Twin Towers financial complex, Independence Square South ☎623 0845, ⓦcentral-bank.org.tt. Set in the bowels of the Bank's Brutalist towers, this modern theatre features productions by well-known Trinidad theatre companies – usually comedies. Entrance through Eric Williams Plaza.

Little Carib Theatre White St, cnr Roberts St, Woodbrook ☎622 4644, ⓦbit.ly/LittleCarib. Opened in 1948 and recently refurbished, this intimate and historic theatre concentrates on plays and shows highlighting local talent and culture.

Queen's Hall 1–3 St Ann's Rd, St Ann's ☎624 1284, ⓦqueenshalltt.com. This is the largest theatre in Trinidad, featuring drama, dance, music and fashion shows, as well as calypso concerts in Carnival season; it's also the regular venue for 3canal's renowned pre-Carnival show – definitely one to look out for.

Under the Trees Normandie Hotel, 10 Nook Ave, St Ann's ☎624 1181, ⓦnormandiett.com. Around Carnival time, catch atmospheric evening performances under the stars in the grounds of the *Normandie* hotel, showcasing local artists doing everything from calypso to stand-up comedy and choral concerts.

CINEMA

Digicel IMAX One Woodbrook Place, Damian St, Woodbrook ☎299 4629, ⓦimax.tt. One of the few IMAX cinemas in the Caribbean, with a single screen showing 3D movies for adults and children.

MovieTowne Audrey Jeffers Hwy ☎627 8277, ⓦmovietowne.com. Port of Spain's cinema scene hinges around the ten screens at the fiercely a/c complex opposite the Hasely Crawford Stadium; expect all the latest blockbusters.

SHOPPING

Downtown Port of Spain's main shopping area is around **Frederick Street** and **Charlotte Street**, where you can buy everything from make-up to market goods. More upmarket shopping (though less local colour) is to be had at the a/c **West Mall** in Westmoorings and **Long Circular Mall** in St James, both of which have international clothing store chains as well as local retailers. There are **supermarkets** at West Mall, Long Circular Mall, Saddle Road in Maraval, just off St Ann's Road in Cascade and French Street in Woodbrook.

FETING CARNIVAL

With Christmas over and done with, the New Year in Trinidad means one thing for dedicated Carnivalists: **fetes**. Staged by everyone from the local water company to the T&T army, alongside endless private promoters, these huge outdoor parties get everyone in the Carnival mood and set you up for a great experience on the road. There are hundreds to choose from, all with a very different flavour and character, ranging from rawer events such as Army Fete to laidback cooler parties where you bring your own drinks, and top-end all-inclusive parties staged in gorgeous rural surroundings, with premium drinks and food. The roster of events changes each year, with new ones popping up and established parties fading away; check online and listen to the radio (most local stations are available online; see page 33).

At **cooler fetes** most people arrive primed with a cooler stocked full of drinks and ice, but there's always a bar too. Note also that not all of the fetes are night-time affairs: many of the more upmarket events take place in the afternoon and run on into the evening, giving you time to hit a night-time fete too, if you have the stamina. Most evening fetes don't get going until around 11pm, and the best acts perform in the early hours, so don't arrive too early. **Breakfast fetes**, which start in the wee hours and end at lunchtime, are another Carnival staple.

WHAT TO WEAR AND TAKE

As feting is a frenetic and extremely sweaty business, it pays to **dress appropriately**. For women, a pretty top (usually a vest – you'll get very hot when dancing) with shorts or jeans is *de rigueur*, while a rag to wave and wipe your brow with is also essential – you'll often find promotional rags stamped with logos given away on the night. High-end all-inclusive fetes, however, are a very different kettle of fish, with patrons dressing to impress and heels aplenty for the women.

In terms of **security**, pickpocketing is fairly common at the more hardcore events and at shows such as Soca Monarch – thieves often work in teams, with one person dancing with the unsuspecting victim while another slides a hand into a pocket to remove cash or valuables. Be aware of this, and don't carry much cash with you; expensive jewellery or watches, and a wallet full of credit cards, are also best left at your hotel.

TICKETS AND PRICES

Many of Carnival websites (see page 80) carry fete schedules, with details of dates, prices and ticket outlets. You can buy **tickets** from music stores such as Crosby's (see page 92) as well as selected outlets in Port of Spain's malls; listen to the radio or check online for details. If you don't buy ahead, you can invariably get a ticket outside the venue from a tout (or scalper, as they're known here); most ask a lot more than face value, but you can usually negotiate a deal, especially if you're buying a few tickets. Note, however, that you'll have to know a committee member to be able to attend some of the most prestigious events, such as Sunny Side Up. Ticket Federation (W ticketfederation.com) is a useful service that will secure fete tickets for you. Fete **prices** range enormously, and seem to rise alarmingly each year; the average for the large, more hardcore fetes is TT$275, while the high-end all-inclusives, with premium drinks and food, range from TT$750 to TT$1000; for the most exclusive parties, rates get a little bonkers: Lime at the *Hyatt* hotel cost US$300–400 in 2018. Many of the mid-range fetes sell both general admission and VIP tickets; the latter usually include some drinks and allow you to get close to the stage without mixing in the melee of the main crowd – worth considering if you're new to feting or want slightly superior facilities.

CARNIVAL SUPPLIES

Samaroo's 11–13 Abercromby St ☎ 624 8431; First Floor, Fiesta Plaza, MovieTowne ☎ 625 6834; W samaroosgroup.com; map p.56 and p.68. The original purveyor of feathers, sequins, glue-guns and the like, with everything you need to make your own costume or adapt the one you buy. Downtown Mon–Fri 8.30am–5pm, Sat 8.20am–2pm; MovieTowne Mon–Thurs 11am–7pm, Fri & Sat 10am–7pm.

Tulip Productions 76 Ariapita Ave, Woodbrook ☎ 627 2230, W tulipproduction.com; map p.68. As well as a great range of Carnival paraphernalia including ready-decorated bras, Tulip have party supplies and fancy-dress costumes. Mon–Fri 8am–4.30pm, Sat 9am–1pm.

1

BOOKSHOPS

Metropolitan Book Suppliers Capital Plaza, 11–13 Frederick St ☏623 3462; map p.56. In the basement of this little mall, Metropolitan has an excellent range of books on T&T's history and culture as well as Caribbean fiction. Mon–Fri 8.30am–4pm, Sat 9am–1pm.

★ **Paper Based** Normandie Hotel, Nook Ave, St Ann's ☏625 3197, ⓦpaperbased.org; map p.73. Fantastic little bookshop, conveniently located just off the Savannah and with a great array of carefully chosen fiction and non-fiction from the Caribbean and beyond; DVDs of local films, too. Regular readings and book launches, and a great website with discussion of the titles on sale. Mon–Fri 10am–6pm, Sat 10am–4pm.

CHOCOLATE

★ **Cocoa Pod** 23 Gordon St ☏326 1952, ⓦbit.ly/CocoaPod; map p.56. Fabulous shop dedicated to everything cocoa, with some eighty cocoa-based products on sale, from delicious "Not Too Sweet" spreads that mix chocolate with everything from peanuts to sorrel, tahini, guava and mango; plus wonderful cocoa pepper sauce, maté tea made from cocoa pod shells, grateable cocoa tea balls and drinking chocolate, a memorable cocoa liqueur, and home-made treats such as chocolate bene balls and rum balls. There's also soap, lip balm, body cream and, of course, the best of the locally made chocolate bars. Unmissable. Mon–Fri 10.30am–6pm, Sat 11am–2pm.

★ **Cocobel** 37 Fitt St, Woodbrook ☏622 1196, ⓦbit.ly/Cocobel; map p.68. Cocobel's handmade chocolates are as beautiful as they are delicious, each a little work of art courtesy of architect-turned-chocolatier Isabel Brash, who also designed the building in which Cocobel is based. Trinidad fine-flavour cocoa is combined with local ingredients to create such delights as Mermaid's Kiss (pineapple and chadon beni under dark chocolate, with local salt crystals) or Basil Wild (dark ganache with Paramin mint); there are also chocolate-covered cocoa and coffee beans, bars and flavoured chocolate sticks. Call ahead to arrange a tasting session; and don't miss Fresh Baked Fridays, when cocoa forms the main ingredient of fabulous cakes and pastries. Mon–Fri 10.30am–6pm, Sat 11am–2pm.

CRAFTS

Akilah's Jewellery Fondes Amandes Community Reforestation Project, Fondes Amandes Rd, St Ann's ☏689 7794 or ☏750 1716, ⓦbit.ly/Akilahs; map p.73. Made by the woman behind this fantastic community project (see page 77), this beautiful natural jewellery is crafted from local seeds, pods and nuts, and is completely unique. Daily, no set hours.

Rainy Days 60 Ellerslie Plaza, Maraval ☏622 5597; map p.68. The best place in town for locally made crafts and souvenirs, with everything from miniature wooden rum shops to hand-painted postcard-sized watercolours, batiks, DVDs and CDs. Daily 10am–5pm.

★ **The Shop** Normandie Hotel, Nook Ave, St Ann's ☏625 8732, ⓦbit.ly/ShopTnT; map p.73. Lovely selection of local goods, from jams, chutney and chocolate to clothes (look out for the fabulous pieces by Sew Lisa Designs), jewellery and, of course, rum. Mon–Fri 10am–6pm, Sat 10am–4pm.

MUSIC

Crosby's 54 Western Main Rd, St James ☏622 7644; map p.68. All you could ask for in the way of soca, plus reggae and other Caribbean music. Mon–Fri 9am–6pm, Sat 9am–1.30pm.

GALLERIES

101 Art Gallery 84 Woodford St, Newtown ☏628 4081, ⓦ101artgallery.com; map p.56. Regular exhibitions by well-known local artists including Peter Sheppard, Martin Superville and Geoffrey Holder.

Medulla Art Gallery 37 Fitt St, Woodbrook ☏622 1196, ⓦbit.ly/MedullaTT; map p.68. Thought-provoking exhibitions from upcoming and established artists from Edward Bowen and Bunty O'Conner to Justin de Verteuil and Richard Mark Rawlins.

Y Art Gallery 26 Taylor St, Woodbrook ☏628 4186, ⓦbit.ly/YArtTT; map p.68. Swish gallery that represents some prestigious local artists, from Christopher Cozier to Jackie Hinkson, LeRoy Clarke and Peter Shim, as well as younger names such as Che Lovelace and jewellery maker Janice Derrick.

DIRECTORY

Banks Numerous branches (all with ATMs) on Independence Square downtown; Republic Bank also has branches in West Mall and Long Circular Mall, and Ariapita Ave (cnr of Murray St) in Woodbrook. Scotiabank is at Ellerslie Plaza in Maraval and Western Main Rd (cnr of Bengal St) in St James. You'll get a better rate of exchange at FX Trader, with locations at the branches of Excellent Stores on the corner of Frederick St and Independence Square (Mon–Thurs 8.30am–5pm, Fri 9am–6pm, Sat 8.30am–2.30pm) and on the corner of Frederick and Park streets (Mon–Thurs 8am–5pm, Fri 8am–5.30pm, Sat 9am–2pm), and next to Mario's in City Gate bus station (Mon–Fri 8am–5pm, Sat 8am–2pm).

Embassies and high commissions British High Commission, 19 St Clair Ave, St Clair (☏350 0444, ⓦukintt.fco.gov.uk/en); Canadian High Commission, 3–3a Sweet Briar Rd, St Clair (☏622 6232, ⓦtrinidadandtobago.gc.ca); US Embassy, 15 Queen's Park West (☏622 6371, ⓦtt.usembassy.gov).

Hospital The main public hospital is Port of Spain General,

169 Charlotte St (☎623 2951); waiting times can be long and facilities basic. The private St Clair Medical Centre, 18 Elizabeth St, St Clair (☎628 1451, ⊛medcorpltd.com) is a good private hospital with an A&E department. For an ambulance, dial ☎811 or ☎990.

Pharmacies SuperPharm, 1 Columbus Circle, West Mall complex, Westmoorings (☎633 1663), and Royal Palm Plaza, Maraval (☎622 6025); both open Mon–Sat 7.30am–11pm, Sun 8.30am–11pm.

Police Report crimes at the Central Police Station, St Vincent St, at Hart St ☎625 1261 or ☎625 2684. In an emergency, dial ☎999.

Post office TT Post has several branches, including: 23 Chacon St (Mon–Fri 7am–5pm, Sat 9am–2pm); City Gate, South Quay (Mon–Fri 7am–6pm, Sat 8am–1pm); 177 Tragarete Rd, next to Roxy roundabout, Woodbrook (Mon–Fri 7am–5pm, Sat 8am–noon).

Swimming pool The *Hilton Trinidad* (see page 83) allows non-guests to swim in their newly refurbished pool for a daily fee of around TT$100.

Paramin

Occupying the rolling hills above Port of Spain's Maraval district and spreading back towards the north coast, the charming hillside community of **PARAMIN** seems a million miles from the hustle of the city streets below. The area is known as the "herb basket of Trinidad" thanks to its many farmers, who have carved terraced plots into the precipitous peaks to grow the thyme (French and Spanish) and mint, as well as celery and spring onions (here known as chives), used to make up the tied bundles sold in shops and markets throughout T&T, and blended into bottles of the green seasoning which flavours Trinbago cooking. The local population is descended from French Creoles who came to Trinidad in the colonial era, as well as Venezuelans who arrived in the nineteenth century to plant cocoa, and the close-knit but friendly community maintains many of its traditions, most famously in its **parang** bands, who travel from house to house during the Christmas season, singing nativity songs in a mix of French and Spanish. The Monday before Christmas, Paramin hosts a **parang festival** at the soccer field at the lower end of town, while on the afternoon of Carnival Monday, the town is overtaken by troupes of **blue devils**: traditional Carnival characters impersonating imps from hell, who dance through the streets demanding money from onlookers and daubing them with a little of their trademark blue – it's the most anarchic display of Blue Devil mas you'll see anywhere in the country.

Paramin has few specific sights, but the neatly tended hillsides of seasoning plants and the green-swathed mountains are superbly scenic and often clad in mist; on clear days, there are lovely views down to the sea, while the fresh, clean air is fragrant and noticeably cooler than down on the flats. For the best of the **views**, head up to the mobile phone masts on Saut d'Eau Road.

Our Lady of Guadalupe Church

At the lower end of Paramin, on a terrace overlooking the Maraval Valley, the beautiful **Our Lady of Guadalupe Church** looks more like a conservatory than a place of worship, with its green roof and plant-lined windows; each year on the Sunday before Carnival, a Mass is conducted here entirely in the French Creole patois that's still spoken by Paramin elders.

ARRIVAL AND DEPARTURE   **PARAMIN**

By jeep Paramin's insanely steep, switchbacking roads are out of the question for those who don't know the area and are driving a regular car. The most sensible way to reach it is to take one of the jeeps which run between Paramin and the base of Morne Coco Rd; to get to the departure point, take the turn-off onto Morne Coco Rd from Saddle Rd in Maraval opposite the church and next to the petrol station; after some 200m, the road forks; jeeps depart from the start of the right-hand fork. Fares depend upon how far you're going, but won't be more than TT$10 for short drops.

By organized tour Caribbean Discovery Tours (☎624 7281, ⊛caribbeandiscoverytours.com) and Island Experiences (☎621 0407 or ☎756 9677, ⊛island experiencestt.com) offer 4WD tours of Paramin, which

1

include a visit to a seasoning farm and a stopoff at the gorgeous North Deck, a viewing platform overlooking Saut d'Eau island on the north coast. For a more local flavour,

Portia Brown (☎629 0441 or ☎779 629 4848), driver of the Paramin jeep "General" and a resident of the area, conducts informal excursions; prices are negotiable.

EATING AND DRINKING

Kool Breeze Bar Saut d'Eau Rd, Paramin. A rum shop with a view, this is a friendly and a fantastic place to drink

a cold beer or a glass of rum and enjoy the breeze. Daily, no set hours.

Chaguaramas

West of Port of Spain, the Audrey Jeffers Highway runs parallel to the coast, swooshing past turnoffs to the suburbs of Diego Martin, Petit Valley and Westmoorings, the latter home to the plush West Mall shopping centre, beyond which the tarmac narrows into the **Western Main Road**. This cuts through upscale Glencoe and less salubrious Carenage en route to the narrow peninsula of **Chaguaramas** (pronounced "sha-ger-*rah*-mus"), Port of Spain's playground. Chaguaramas' south coast is taken up with waterside restaurants and marinas where yachts hole up during the hurricane season or dry-dock for maintenance work, as well as the hulking hangars built by the US Army in the 1940s, when the area was leased as a military base. Inland, the impenetrable forested hills have remained virtually untouched, and are home to red howler and capuchin monkeys, armadillos, ocelots and anteaters. The hills are cut through by the lush surrounds of **Tucker Valley**, with hiking and mountain-biking trails and a golf course, while on the north coast the delightful **Macqueripe Beach** is the best place to swim in the Port of Spain environs, with cool green waters and some handsome landscaping.

Though the Americans are long gone, Chaguaramas retains a military flavour: the final section of the coast road is blocked to civilian traffic and the peninsula beyond here is the exclusive preserve of the military, with the Trinidad and Tobago Regiment headquarters at Teteron Bay the Coast Guard at nearby Staubles Bay; you'll often see trainee coastguards or soldiers on parade or tramping through the Tucker Valley bush on exercises. The area's administrators, the **Chaguaramas Development Authority** (CDA), have made efforts in recent years to beautify the coast, lining Williams Bay with a boardwalk and, just behind, constructing other leisure facilities that were unfinished at the time of writing. Just up from here at Chagville Beach, the new **Five Islands Water and Amusement Park** occupies a prime piece of seafront – to the vexation of some locals, who can no longer swim and lime at the beach here.

Brief history
The name Chaguaramas, derived from the Amerindian word for the palms that once lined this coast, is the only remnant of the area's indigenous population. The protected natural harbours here provided the **Spanish** with a hiding place for their ships when the **British** invaded in 1797, though when it became clear that defeat was inevitable, the ships were scuttled. The harbour at Williams Bay was also the reason the **US military** wanted Chaguaramas as its Caribbean naval base during World War II, and they leased the peninsula from the British in 1940 in return for fifty used destroyers.

American occupation
Though initially greeted with a warm welcome, the American soldiers quickly became unpopular. Many Trinidadians resented the US occupation of the beaches and countryside most easily accessible from the capital, not to mention the social effect of having so many young American soldiers living in the region. The GIs outnumbered the local men, who couldn't compete with the Americans' ostentatious wealth, and the resentment this generated was immortalized by Lord Invader in his famous calypso *Rum and Coca-Cola*:

Rum and Coca-Cola,
Go down to Point Cumana,
Both mother and daughter,
Working for the Yankee Dollar

(Ironically, a bastardized version of the song saw the Andrews Sisters spend ten weeks at the top of the US billboard charts in 1945, much to the disgust of Invader, who successfully sued for copyright infringement.)

The situation in Chaguaramas was not improved by the Americans' attitude towards **race**. A 1945 edition of *Life* magazine reported that "US soldiers confused by the mix of colour lines would keep a brown paper bag at the doorway to their parties. Anyone whose skin was lighter than the bag was considered white (and allowed entry)." With

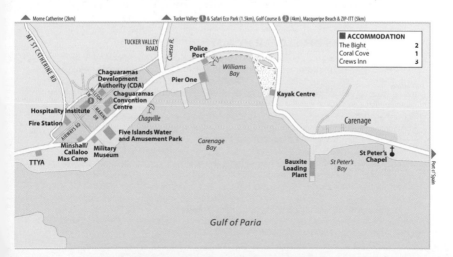

1

the growth of the **independence movement**, Chaguaramas became a focus of conflict between the British colonial government and the local population, and in April 1960 thousands of local residents marched through the rain to campaign for the return of Chaguaramas. Their goal was achieved the following February, when the area was given back to Trinidad and the Americans departed.

Chaguaramas today

Chaguaramas has long been a place of recreation for Trinidadians, and with this in mind the government declared the region a **national park** in 1961, though the protected status that this should afford to the area's wildlife and rainforest is negligible, as there have long been plans to develop the area, many of which have been shouted down by environmentalists. The built-up part of Chaguaramas, lining the Western Main Road to the west of Williams Bay, was promoted as the seat of the future Caribbean parliament in the 1950s, but these plans were thwarted by the collapse of the West Indian Federation in 1962. Subsequently, the **Chaguaramas Development Authority** (CDA) was established to maintain the nature reserve and encourage leisure-oriented businesses. In 1999, Chaguaramas served as the venue for the Miss Universe competition, and the resulting beautification saw an upgrade in the CDA's hotel and cavernous conference facilities. These days, though, the long-floundering hotel serves as a police training centre and there's a bit of a ghost-town feel away from the marinas.

Western Main Road

There's only one way in and out of Chaguaramas: the **Western Main Road**. Narrow, twisting and often congested, it's something of a stumbling block in plans to expand the area's leisure facilities. Quite apart from the environmental concerns of development in a national park, detractors argue that there's little point in building endless new attractions if no-one can easily access them. Driving from Port of Spain, traffic starts to build as you approach **GLENCOE**, where there's a mini shopping mall with a supermarket, fast-food outlets and a bank. Beyond here, there are some lovely vistas out over the Gulf of Paria to the so-called **Five Islands**, of which the largest, **Nelson**, was used as a processing point and quarantine for Indian indentured workers and later as a prison.

Rum shops, roti places and fish market line the road at **CARENAGE**, which takes its name from the time when ships were taken here to be careened by Spanish colonists. After the British took the island in 1797, Carenage reverted to a fishing village and

---

CHAGUARAMAS DEVELOPMENT AUTHORITY (CDA)

Based in the orange-painted building behind the Chaguaramas Convention Centre on Airways Road, the **Chaguaramas Development Authority** offer excellent and educational **tours** (Mon–Fri 8am–4pm; tours TT$40–85; ☎634 4227 or ☎225 4232, ⊛chaguaramas.com) led by experienced and knowledgeable guides, into the **Chaguaramas National Park**, most of which pass through the lush vegetation, rivers and cultivated forest of the Tucker Valley. Though a minimum group size of ten is specified for tours, this is sometimes waived; equally, you may be able to join with existing bookings, many of which are with local schools.

Perhaps the best **hike** is to **Covigne River** (4hr), a moderately challenging walk along a riverbed, which includes a beautiful section of twisting gorge and a rope-aided climb up a waterfall to an emerald bathing pool surrounded by rainforest. On the way back, you can pick your own nutmeg at an abandoned plantation and bathe in a spring. The CDA also provide guides for the **Golf Course to Macqueripe** trail (3hr) – a fairly strenuous hike that affords lovely views over Tucker Valley, the north coast and over to Venezuela – as well as the walk to the top of **Morne Catherine** (2hr) and the **Edith Falls** trail (2hr). The rates above cover transport from the CDA office to the start of the hike and back, though not to and from Chaguaramas. Bring your own water and snacks on all trips.

sank into a century-and-a-half-long torpor, but its character changed drastically with the arrival of the US military base in 1941, when all the western tip's residents were forcibly relocated here. The village soon acquired a seedy reputation as a place where American soldiers went to have fun and find local women, and there are still a couple of flophouses around advertising rooms for rent by the hour. Today, it retains a somewhat salty air.

Williams Bay
Western Main Rd

Carenage is capped by a looming bauxite loading plant that juts into the sea, beyond which the Western Main Road makes an almighty bend as it swings into **Williams Bay**, a wide cove enclosed by a forested outcrop to the west, and with a narrow beach overhung by a paved boardwalk, popular with beachgoers by day and strolling families in the evenings. Local bathers descend en masse at weekends, bringing coolers packed with food and drink and making a day of it, but the water isn't particularly inviting, its brownish waves tinted with petrol rainbows from the heavy traffic of container ships in the Gulf of Paria. Better to rent a **kayak** from the Kayak Centre (see page 101).

Phase II of the Williams Bay boardwalk opened in 2014, with a circle of covered gazebos which locals rent for cookouts, and an artificial **lake**, all overshadowed at the time of writing by fences enclosing a construction site slated to hold a children's playground, climbing walls and other leisure facilities; it's anyone's guess as to when these will be completed.

Five Islands Water and Amusement Park
Chagville Beach, Western Main Rd • Mon–Thurs 10am–10pm, Fri–Sun 10am–midnight • Admission prices according to height: 48 inches and above TT$200, 36–47 inches TT$150, under 36 inches free • ☎ 612 7275, ⓦ fiveislandswaterpark.com

Despite its pebble-strewn scrap of sand and muddy waters, breezy **Chagville Beach** was once a popular spot for locals to swim and lime; today, however, the majority of its length is taken up with the **Five Islands Water and Amusement Park**, a slick new family attraction with an indoor soft play area with trampolines, an overhead rope course, designated toddler play area and gaming machines; and an outdoor section with motorized go-karts, a surf machine, (plastic-covered) ice rink and the "Dragonfly" fairground ride. It's not much fun in the searing heat of the day, but it's a good option for those with kids in the cool of the late afternoon. Construction of an adjacent **waterpark** and seaside boardwalk were underway at the time of writing, slated for completion in late 2018.

Chaguaramas Military History and Aerospace Museum
Western Main Rd • Tues–Sun 9am–5pm • TT$50, children TT$30 • ☎ 634 3491 or ☎ 634 2992, ⓦ bit.ly/MilitaryTT

Squeezed between the Five Islands park and the Coast Guard's training ground and heliport, the **Chaguaramas Military History and Aerospace Museum** is hard to miss thanks to the collection of military hardware on the forecourt, including a monumental 88-ton, US Army LARC (Lighter, Amphibious, Resupply Cargo) vessel, a rusting tank and a battered ex-BWIA jet, which had to be dismantled into nineteen pieces to transport it along the winding route from Piarco. A stone-built castle facade, complete with drawbridge and battlements, has been constructed in front of the entrance to the main building; inside, wedged between some smaller pieces of military equipment, exhibits chronicle the military history of T&T from 1498 to the present, as well as touching on wider world militaria and history. Although the presentation can be somewhat haphazard, it's an absorbing and occasionally touching array, worth a glimpse if only because it so sharply counteracts the usual beaches-and-palms image of the Caribbean. Highlights include a re-creation of a **World War II trench** and a German machine-gun bunker, complete

1

with battle sounds and flashing lights simulating explosions, as well as photos and explanatory panels illuminating the extensive (and often overlooked) role of local soldiers in international warfare. Look out also for displays on pirates, the Trinidadian police and various local skirmishes, with detailed drawings of the Battle of Scarborough Bay in Tobago and the British takeover of Trinidad; newspaper photographs from the **1990 coup** provide a glimpse of the turmoil in Trinidad during the six-day siege.

Toward the western tip

West of the Military Museum, the Western Main Road runs parallel to the coast all the way to its road-end at the barriers for the military base. There are pretty ocean views in

---

PETER MINSHALL AND THE CALLALOO COMPANY

Awarded an Emmy for his costume design work on the 2002 Winter Olympics opening ceremony, and the Chaconia Medal (the country's second-highest honour) in 1987 for his services to the nation, **Peter Minshall** is a legend in the annals of Trinidad Carnival. One of the nation's most admired mas designers, he is known for his unique interpretation of traditional Carnival characters, innovative production techniques, and for the strong sense of theatre within his mas presentations.

Born in Guyana and raised in Trinidad, Minshall studied theatre design at the Central School of Art and Design in London. He designed his first Carnival band for London's Notting Hill Carnival in 1975, and returned to Trinidad soon afterwards to bring out **Paradise Lost**, the first of his many acclaimed presentations. Formed in 1991 and at its height comprising many of Trinidad's most talented actors, dancers and artists, Minshall's **Callaloo Company** functioned as a production company, mas factory and performance group. Based in an American-era hanger on the Western Main Road in Chaguaramas, this close-knit and loyal crew took its name from Trinidad's national dish, whose various ingredients reflect the country's ethnic mix ("all ah we is one" was the company's philosophy), and used everything from leaves to bottle tops and lengths of fibreglass to create the amazing costumes that won many a **Band of the Year title** during the glory years of the late 1980s and 1990s.

Unlike many Carnival costumes, which are thrown away on Ash Wednesday, dusty Minshall creations still decorate houses throughout Trinidad. While most contemporary mas presentations tend to concentrate on escapist, fantasy themes with minimal costumes, Minshall's lavish and detailed works dealt with spiritual and political issues: the environment, the interconnectedness of humanity, the transience of life. Many of his best-known pieces were more like kinetic sculptures than costumes in the traditional sense: figures (a butterfly, a mechanical crab, a huge stick-figure couple) with moving limbs and fluttering wings. In emphasizing the aspect of Carnival that allows people to escape their own identity by playing a role, Minshall continued the tradition of Carnival as **theatre for all**: "In most countries," he has often remarked, "people pay to see others perform. However in Trinidad, people pay to perform".

Sadly, however, Minshall's dissatisfaction with the bikinis and good-time carelessness that make "pretty mas", alongside the general lack of regard for the creative traditions of Carnival, saw him take a step back from mas-making. He produced his last large-scale mas, Picoplat, in 2002, and in 2006 brought out an AIDS-themed band, the Sacred Heart, which saw the return of some of his most popular King and Queen costumes in the form of Son of Saga Boy and Miss Universe, a tribute to the seminal Tan Tan and Saga Boy designs from his 1990 mas, Tantana. In 2014, he designed a small Monday-only band, Miss Miles (A Band on Corruption), and in 2016 his mesmerizing Carnival king mas Dying Swan: Ras Nijinsky in Drag as Pavlova saw Jhawhan Thomas transformed into a moko jumbie ballerina, complete with sculpted feet *en pointe*. The 2017 and 2018 carnivals saw him create sailor bands alongside Exodus steel band – 2018's Eyes of God (🌐bit.ly/Minshall) was particularly spectacular – but it remains to be see whether a full-blown Minshall mas will again cross the Savannah stage.

between the marinas and warehouses, especially attractive around the seashore known as **Small Boats**, just before the turnoff to the Crews Inn complex of hotel, marina and restaurants, with yachts bobbing in the emerald green waters of a calm bay, and lovely views back to the Port of Spain skyline.

Just before the road ends, the **Chaquacabana** complex (☎634 4319, ⓦchaquacabana. com), which has remained semi-completed for a number of years, makes for a nice place to spend a day by the sea; day-visitors can lounge by the oceanside pool (TT$87.50/day), and there's a restaurant.

Tucker Valley

Accessed via the Tucker Valley Road, which cuts north from the Western Main Road roughly opposite the Pier One marina, **Tucker Valley** is the highlight of Chaguaramas, a gorgeous swathe of thick forest, most of which is undeveloped and laced with hiking trails; there are also a couple of low-key attractions. You'll need your own transport to travel the length of the Tucker Valley Road to **Macqueripe Beach**, or up to the **golf course** – truly beautiful drives, with pastures and fields dotted with enormous, bromeliad-smothered samaan trees to each side, gently rising to meet forested peaks. If you want to stop, the most convenient spot is **Samaan Park**, a grassy area shaded by huge trees to the right of the road, with picnic tables and a car park.

Mount Pleasant village
Tucker Valley Rd

Not far from the Western Main Road junction, the haphazard group of gravestones and the dilapidated St Chad's church on the right of Tucker Valley Road are pretty much all that's left of **Mount Pleasant** village. During the colonial era, when this fertile valley was planted with citrus, cocoa and coffee as part of the Tucker Estate, Mount Pleasant was a thriving settlement, home to many estate workers and their families; today, the derelict remaining buildings barely stand. Among the plain gravestones you can pick out the rather grand tomb of Amelia Tripp, daughter of the estate's English owner, William Sanger Tucker.

U-Pick
Tucker Valley Rd • Thurs–Sat 7am–2pm, Sun 7am–noon • Free, tractor tour TT$40 • ☎ 271 2681, ⓦ bit.ly/UPickTT

Well signposted from the main road and set over fifty acres of prime Tucker Valley land, **U-Pick** is a novelty in Trinidad, offering you the chance to pick your own veg straight from the field; crops vary seasonally, but there are usually local staples such as melongene (aubergine), sweetcorn, tomatoes, okra, carrots and the like, all of which is also available to buy at the farm shop, alongside U-Pick's own honey. Around Halloween, you can pick and carve pumpkins, and the tractor tours are fun for kids. The café (see page 102) is a great place to pick up a picnic breakfast en route to Macqueripe.

Safari Eco Park
Tucker Valley Rd • Daily 9am–5pm, last entry 4.15pm • TT$40, children aged 4–12 TT$30 • Guided tours 9.30am, 12.30pm & 2.30pm; TT$100, children TT$60 • ☎ 733 8920, ⓦ bit.ly/SafariTT • There's usually a zebra-print jeep parked at the Tucker Valley Rd turnoff, which is the first right after U-Pick

Trinidad's version of a petting zoo, the **Safari Eco Park** is an anomalous addition to Tucker Valley, its fenced-off enclave home to enclosures of domestic animals such as ponies and rabbits alongside local agouti, quenk (collared peccary), monkeys and birds, plus camels, zebra, llamas, a lone (and lonely-looking) kangaroo and a cougar, again alone in an enclosure which looks tiny but is labelled as far exceeding the recommended square footage for its species. You can buy feed at the entrance, and there are handwash stations dotted around.

1

Bamboo Cathedral

No set hours • Free • The entrance is a signposted right-hand turnoff from Tucker Valley Rd, just before Macqueripe Beach

The **Bamboo Cathedral** is a whimsical but apt name for the tunnel of bamboo that encloses a section of road, the thick foliage allowing shafts of green-tinged sunlight to filter through. It's a scene that inspired renowned Trinidadian artist and national hero **Michel Cazabon**, who included the cathedral in the many paintings he did of the Tucker Valley in the nineteenth century. Today, it's a popular spot for locals out for a bit of exercise.

Tracking station

Past the Bamboo Cathedral, the path into the interior snakes upwards towards the rusting bulk of the **tracking station** at the top of a ridge. This huge dish was erected by the US military in the 1950s to track nuclear missiles, though its main claim to fame is less sinister. The dish's technology soon became redundant, and the radar scanner was converted into a radio transmitter in 1960; on August 12 of the same year it was used to transmit the first radio signal to be bounced off a satellite – the signal was received at Floyd Air Force Base in New York. The station was used to develop the technique until 1972, when it was abandoned. The tracking station stands on a nine-acre plateau with gorgeous views of Tucker Valley, the north coast and of Venezuela. On the way down, keep an eye (or an ear) out for the wide variety of **birds** and troops of **howler monkeys** that inhabit the area.

Macqueripe Beach

Tucker Valley Rd • Lifeguards daily 10am–6pm • Car park daily 9am–6pm • Cars TT$20, pedestrians free • Changing facilities TT$1

Tucker Valley Road ends at the Chaguaramas peninsula's north coast and the picturesque cove of **Macqueripe Beach**. From the car park, where there's a snack bar selling soft drinks and, at the weekends, corn soup and snacks, wooden-fenced steps switchback down an attractively landscaped hillside to a concrete deck. The slip of beach below is pretty small, and the deck's wall detracts somewhat from the beauty of the surrounding wooded hillside, but it's still a gorgeous spot, with stunning sunsets and a distant view of Venezuela's Paria Peninsula. The sea on this side of the peninsula is unpolluted and wonderful for swimming (and even a spot of snorkelling if you have your own gear), and though the beach can get crowded at weekends, you'll often find it deserted during the week. Keep in mind that strong currents make it unwise to swim out too far.

ZIP-ITT Adventure

Tues–Fri 10am–4pm, Sat & Sun 10am–4.30pm • Adult lines TT$150, children's course TT$85 for 2hr • ☎ 303 7755, ⓦ zipitt.net • Shoes with covered toes are required

Accessed from a platform behind the path down to Macqueripe Beach, **ZIPP-ITT Adventure** offers seven zip lines and five net bridges which allow you to get up into the forest canopy and swoop across the Macqueripe Bay, getting some fantastic views of the Chaguaramas coastline and a bit of an adrenaline rush. To the right of the access road into Macqueripe car park, there's also a **children's zip line** and **play park**; essentially wooden climbing frames linked by ropewalks; lots of fun for little ones.

Bellerande Road

The first major left turn from Tucker Valley Road takes you onto pretty **Bellerande Road**, overhung by thick forest on either side. About half way along on the left is **Bellerande Park**, a children's playground with a basic jungle gym, "human sized" chequers board, toilets and picnic tables. It's also the start of the so-called "**Chag 10**", an exercise trail around the valley with ten designated points where signboards detail various different exercises.

Edith Falls

Bellerande Rd • You can walk alone, or with the CDA or a tour company (see page 38) • TT$20 fee for golf course car park

Accessed via a marked trail on the left side of the road just before the practice range of the Chaguaramas Golf Course, **Edith Falls** is reachable via an easy forty-minute (1.5km) walk past stands of towering bamboo interspersed with fishtail palms and rubber trees seeping black sap; blue morpho butterflies are common, and if you're lucky, you'll hear the distinctive roar of the valley's troops of howler monkeys. At the end of the trail, you scramble up a few boulders to reach the waterfall itself. Water seeps through the steep craggy rockface, sending showers tumbling 180m into the shallow pool below (not deep enough for swimming). The falls slow to a trickle in dry season (Nov–June).

From the golf course, you can also follow a 2.5km-long **hiking trail** up through the forest and over the ridge to Macqueripe Beach, with gorgeous views of the north coast at several points.

Chaguaramas Golf Course

Bellerande Rd • Daily 6am–6pm • TT$126 for nine holes, TT$253 for eighteen holes, lessons, cart and basic club rental also available • ☎ 225 4232 ext 310, ⓦ chaguaramas.com

Bellerande Road ends at the **Chaguaramas Golf Course**, built on a former tonka-bean plantation by American servicemen during World War II, its smooth hillocks of even green providing a pretty contrast to the surrounding forest. There's a breezy bar in the **clubhouse**, where you can get a drink and, at weekends, a local meal (see page 102).

ARRIVAL AND GETTING AROUND

CHAGUARAMAS

By car A rental car (see page 79) is by far the most convenient way to get to and around Chaguaramas, particularly Tucker Valley (where there's no public transport).

By bus and maxi taxi Regular PTSC buses and maxis run from Port of Spain along the length of the Western Main Road in Chaguaramas, stopping at all points in between.

TOURS AND ACTIVITIES

Kayaking In a signposted building in the concrete lot on the eastern side of Williams Bay, the Kayak Centre (daily 6am–6pm; ☎ 633 7871 or ☎ 680 6244, ⓦ bit.ly/KayakTT) has single and two-person kayaks and stand-up paddleboards; fees are TT$40–60/hr at weekends, TT$10 less on weekdays. You can also contact Courtenay Rooks at

Paria Springs Tours (☎ 620 8240, ⓦ pariasprings.com) for more adventurous guided kayak tours around the bay and even out to the Bocas islands (see page 102).

Mountain biking Courtenay Rooks offers excellent guided rides along off-road trails in Tucker Valley; US$55–105 depending upon route and duration, bike included.

ACCOMMODATION

The Bight Peake's Marina, Western Main Rd ☎ 634 4427, ⓦ peakeyachts.com; map p.94. Ten smart rooms in Peake's marina west of town, used mainly by visiting yachties. In a lovely position right over the edge of the water, rooms are tastefully furnished and have a/c, cable TV, fridge and tea/coffee-making facilities. 🛜 **US$85**

Coral Cove Coral Cove Marina, Western Main Rd ☎ 634 2040, ⓦ coralcovemarina.com; map p.94. Rather uninspired but efficient and friendly hotel. Rooms are on the expensive side but clean and modern, with a/c, cable

TV and kitchenette, and there's a small pool on site. 🛜 **US$75**

Crews Inn Point Gourde ☎ 634 4000, ⓦ crewsinn. com; map p.94. Overlooking the busy marina, this is the smartest place to stay in Chaguaramas, and the only resort-like place, with high-end prices to match. Recently refurbished in a clean, minimalist style, the rooms have all the amenities you'd expect, as well as kitchenette and balconies overlooking the sea, and there's a restaurant, bar, gym and a lovely pool. Rates include buffet breakfast. 🛜 **US$240**

EATING

Port of Spain's lack of waterside dining is more than made up for in Chaguaramas. The marinas along the Western Main Road hold plenty of open-air **restaurants**, some quite low-key, others fairly upmarket; most also double up as a good place for a **drink**. Chaguaramas is also a place to **party**, with venues such as *Anchorage*, *02* and *Pier One* opening up for huge outdoor fetes (see page 91) throughout the year, with Carnival season a particularly busy time.

1

Café Feel-Oh Coral Cove Marina, Western Main Rd ☎ 634 2323, ⊛ cafefeeloh.com; map p.94. Facing the road, with a cool, dark a/c interior and a couple of tables outside, this is a convenient stopoff right in the middle of Chaguaramas, with inexpensive breakfasts of sada roti or eggs (TT$20–40) plus fish sandwiches, fresh fish and pasta dishes (from TT$50) during the rest of the day. Mon–Sat 7.30am–11pm, Sun 10am–10pm.

Caffè del Mare Crews Inn Marina, Point Gourde Rd ☎ 634 3484; map p.94. Swish coffee shop, in pole position at the front of the marina, with tables inside and on a deck overlooking the water. Breakfast runs from filled brioche buns to waffles (TT$30–49), plus the full range of coffees; lunch options (TT$29–85) include filled bagels/ panini, soup (try the filling she-crab), a lovely smoked-salmon salad and deli treats such as quiches, pastries, cakes and Häagen-Dazs ice cream too. Mon–Thurs 8am–6pm, Fri–Sun 8am–8pm.

★ **Clubhouse** Chaguaramas Golf Course, Bellerande Rd ☎ 225 4232, ext 310; map p.94. On a covered deck overlooking the smooth greens and forested surrounding hills, this is a picturesque spot for a rum or a beer and, at weekends only, a meal: breakfasts of bacon and eggs or coconut bake with saltfish or smoked herring (TT$30), plus cowheel soup on Saturdays (TT$40), and Trini-style Sunday lunch (baked chicken, macaroni pie, stewed peas etc; TT$55). Bar daily 8am–10pm, restaurant Sat & Sun 8am–2pm.

Hilltop Cnr Airways Rd and Hilltop Lane ☎ 634 2144, ⊛ bit.ly/HilltopTT; map p.94. Trinidad's Hospitality and Tourism Institute opens up to the paying public each weekend, with students going all-out to provide high-end food and service. The Saturday dinner and Sunday lunch offers five courses and a glass of wine for TT$195, kicking off with an appetizer, soup and a choice of three mains (such as seared mahi-mahi with peppercorn sauce, pork loin in a red wine compote or roast aubergine with smoked mozzarella, pesto and tomato fondue); you can also get just a main for TT$70. Occasionally opens for weekday lunch, too (mains TT$50–160); check online. Sat 6.30–8.30pm, Sun noon–2pm.

Lighthouse Crews Inn Marina, Point Gourde Rd ☎ 634 4384, ⊛ crewsinn.com; map p.94. Attractive open-air restaurant and bar overlooking the marina, underneath a red-and-white-striped mock lighthouse, serving tasty international-style food, from catch of the day and rack of lamb to grilled steaks, seafood and lobster (TT$89–375).

alongside frothy cocktails and good desserts. During the week there are lunch specials (TT$99), plus a three-course set dinner (TT$299); Sunday brunch (6.30–10am) is TT$199 (children under 11 eat free). Daily 7am–11pm.

★ **Sails** Power Boats Marina, Western Main Rd ☎ 634 1712, ⊛ bit.ly/SailsTT; map p.94. Great little bar and restaurant patronized by a casual crowd of yachties and locals, with tables by the water and in an indoor bar area with a pool table. The Mon–Fri lunch special (meat or fish with a couple of sides; TT$50) changes daily, and there are also burgers and sandwiches (TT$50–104). Otherwise, starters (TT$ 75–99) include crab backs, geera pork and coconut shrimp, and the wide range of mains (TT$135–250) encompasses lasagne, herbed catch of the day with garlic butter, fish pie, shrimp meatballs, lamb or pork chops and chicken dishes, as well as veggie pastas and pies, while Sunday evenings feature a barbecue. There's usually a genial drinking crowd to lime with after you eat. Mon–Thurs 11am–11pm, Fri 11am–midnight, Sat 8am–midnight, Sun 8am–11pm.

U-Pick Tucker Valley Rd ☎ 271 2681, ⊛ bit.ly/UPickTT; map p.94. Stop by on your way to Macqueripe or Tucker Valley's hiking trails to pick up an inexpensive breakfast or brunch: sada roti or fried bake with tomato/melongene choka or saltfish buljol (TT$15–20), plus eggs or omelettes (TT$30–45). Thurs–Sat 7am–2pm, Sun 7am–noon.

Wheel House Pub Tropical Marine, Western Main Rd ☎ 634 2339; map p.94. At the back of a tiny marina just past Crews Inn, this is a cool little spot for drink or a local meal, with shaded waterside tables overlooking the bobbing boats and a pool table in the a/c interior. The restaurant cooks up simple, tasty plates of grilled lamb, pork, chicken, shrimp or fish served with local sides; burgers and baby-back ribs in the evening, too. Lunch TT$45–55, dinner TT$60–160. Daily 10am–11pm.

Zanzibar by the Sea Peake's Marina, Western Main Rd ☎ 634 3346, ⊛ zanzibartt.com; map p.94. Offshoot of the MovieTowne original, with a similarly buzzy atmosphere, serving a massively varied menu that runs from burritos to burgers (TT$69–99), grilled meat and fish or pasta dishes (TT$105–188), plus steaks and seafood (TT$199–299). Good lunchtime specials (TT$70), from boneless chicken in a coconut, rum and cilantro sauce to pan-seared garlic fish with cassava and salad, plus a long list of cocktails. Mon–Thurs & Sun 7am–11pm, Fri & Sat 8am–midnight.

The Bocas

When Trinidadians refer to **THE BOCAS**, they talk of going "down the islands" in tones of wistful longing. These rocky islets are separated from the mainland, and from one another, by the **Bocas del Dragon (Dragon's Mouth)**, a series of channels connecting the Gulf of Paria with the Caribbean. The name is appropriate, for the coastlines here are jagged and rocky, and the sea hides treacherous currents and undertows that can make even the short journey to the nearest island, Gaspar Grande, a rough ride. Dolphins frequent the waters here, so keep your eyes peeled; if you're lucky, you may even see a leatherback turtle or a pilot whale.

The islands had a thriving **whaling industry** in the eighteenth century, with whaling stations on **Gaspar Grande**, **Monos** and **Chacachacare**. Today the Bocas are sparsely inhabited, lacking any roads, with dense forest covering the interiors and holiday homes, accessible only by boat, scattered along the coasts. For Trinis the islands have always been a popular weekend getaway from the mainland, when yachts drop anchor in the bays for an afternoon of eating, drinking and swimming, and there are several operators offering boat trips to the islands as well as to the **Gasparee Caves** at Gaspar Grande. Apart from one intermittently functioning resort on Gaspar Grande, there are no hotels, guesthouses, restaurants or bars, and away from popular mooring points such as Scotland Bay (actually on the mainland), the atmosphere is so still that it can verge on the uncanny – especially on deserted Chacachacare, with its abandoned leper colony and accompanying ghostly legends.

Carrera

The first island you pass when heading down the Bocas chain from Chaguaramas marinas is the small and rocky **Carrera**, a prison island that's Trinidad's equivalent to Alcatraz; seven convicts have braved the strong currents and shark-infested waters to swim to the mainland, but only three made it, and all were recaptured within a couple of weeks. The prison was established in 1876, and inmates still do hard labour as they serve out their sentences. Conditions are said to be pretty terrible, and the prison has long been slated to close, perhaps to be redeveloped as a tourist attraction.

Gaspar Grande and Gasparee Caves

The CDA manage the caves, and their tours (TT$140; see page 96) are the cheapest way to visit; however their ten-person minimum group size means it's much better to go with a tour company such as Island Experiences or In Joy (see page 105)

Just fifteen minutes by boat from the mainland, **Gaspar Grande** (also known as **Gasparee**) is the most accessible of the islands. The eerie **Gasparee Caves** at Point Baleine – "Whale Point", so named for its former role as a whaling station – were once used by pirates to hide their booty; these days, the only thing that glitters are the walls and the huge, green-tinged stalactites and stalagmites. It's also an excellent place to observe the **fruit bats** which inhabit the caves, and the many local species of bird that congregate outside them.

An impressive, cathedral-like cavern some 35m deep, the cave is a weirdly beautiful place, silent but for the chirping fruit bats and dripping water. Reflected sunlight causes calcium crystals in the rocks to sparkle, and a deep, clear, marvellously turquoise tidal pool reflects the colours and shapes of the stalactites and stalagmites. The water changes daily with the tides, and looks very inviting, though swimming isn't allowed (most tours stop off at a secluded bay on the way back to the mainland instead). Past Gasparee's pool, there's a short path to the back of the cave, where you can gaze up at roosting bats and pick out the rock formations that have been given apt nicknames such as "The Lovers", "Buddha" and the "Virgin Mary".

Scotland Bay

Though actually part of the mainland, **Scotland Bay** is always considered as being "down the islands", since it can only be reached by boat. Right at the end of the peninsula, it's an idyllic small cove blessed with soft sand and calm waters that offer opportunities for snorkelling. Spreading back from the shore is some gorgeous primary forest that provides a habitat for howler monkeys and a rich array of birds and plants.

1

Monos

Scotland Bay looks out across the swirling waters of the Boca de Monos to the island of **Monos**, whose densely wooded interior once supported a large colony of howler monkeys – the island's name is Spanish for apes – but these are now confined to the mainland. There's a passable stretch of **beach** here, reminiscent of Macqueripe; follow the path from the main marina.

Beyond the sheer western ramparts of Monos and another fierce *boca* lies the privately owned and seldom-visited island of **Huevos**.

Chacachacare

Island Experiences or In Joy (see page 105) offer guided visits to the island (around US$100)

Utterly peaceful **Chacachacare** (*sha*-ka-sha-*karr*-eee) is the largest island of the Bocas and, at an hour's boat ride from the mainland, also the farthest-flung. It has none of the well-to-do holiday homes found on the other islands, and the mountainous interior is covered in dense forest. There is just one useable road, leading from the jetty to the lighthouse; the others, which serviced the now-abandoned **leper colony**, have long been overgrown, and only tracks remain.

Chacachacare's name may derive from *chac-chac*, the Amerindian word for cotton, which grows profusely here, or might also have something to do with the chattering of the monkeys once found in droves on the island. Remains dated to around 100–400 AD suggest that Chacachacare was once inhabited by Amerindians. Under Spanish rule it became a cotton plantation, and subsequently a whaling station was established. It developed into a popular health and holiday resort with Trinis from the mainland until, to their consternation, the leper colony was established in 1887. The Dominican nuns ran the colony like a prison, and conditions provoked strikes among the patients to gain such rights as male–female fraternization. The last thirty patients left in 1984, and all that remains are the decaying wooden houses, the infirmary, the nuns' quarters and the chapel, all poking through the foliage to the right as you approach the island from the mainland.

Exploring the island

You're free to explore the structures of Chacachacare's former leper colony, but as they're all derelict, you should watch your step. Also on this stretch are a string of lovely **beaches**, with pale sand and shallow, calm, crystal-clear water; these see some traffic at weekends, but are often deserted during the week.

Chacachacare is now uninhabited except for its wildlife (look out for unusually large iguanas) and the two men who work the small, white **lighthouse**, built in 1885. On the southwest of the island is **La Tinta Bay**; the name, meaning "ink" in Spanish, alludes to the black sand of its beaches. Once a favourite place for smugglers, today this coarse-grained beach is deserted save for the refuse washed up by the tide, and the odd iguana and scavenging hawk. Nearby is the **Salt Pond**, a marsh-fringed sulphurous lake that provides the perfect habitat for unusual trees such as the campecho, known locally as the **bread and cheese tree** on account of its textured fruit with a cheesy taste. The lake's bathwater-warm waters offer some interesting swimming, with the high salt content allowing you to float with ease.

Note that the odd **manchineel** tree also grows on the island's beaches. Its beautiful yellow flowers hide the fact that it produces a toxic fruit, used by the Amerindians to make poisoned arrows. Avoid contact with any part of this tree: its sap causes painful blisters (see page 45).

TOURS

It is possible to charter a fishing pirogue to get you out to the Bocas from the **Island Property Owners' Association marina**, on the Western Main Rd just before the road ends (call the marina's guard booth; ☎ 634 4331), but boat captains are known for overcharging and as a first-time visitor it's much better to go on an organized **day-trip**, which will ensure you get to see the best spots and give you some history along the way.

In Joy tours ☏ 633 4733 or ☏ 753 2775, ⊛ injoytours. com. Excellent trips covering all the islands and taking in Scotland Bay, Gasparee Cave and swimming and relaxation at beaches on Monos or Chacachacare, all accompanied by commentary on the islands' history. Tours US$75–125.

Island Experiences ☏ 621 0407 or ☏ 781 6235, ⊛ islandexperiencestt.com. Great tours for groups of four-plus people aboard a comfortable yacht, taking in all the islands plus Gasparee Caves, and with enthusiastic and charming guides. SUP and sunset dinner cruises also available. Tours US$75–105.

ACCOMMODATION AND EATING

Staying on one of the Bocas offers a lovely getaway from Port of Spain, with great swimming and snorkelling on your doorstep. Most **holiday homes** are privately owned, but a few are let out to visitors (search on Airbnb or look in the classifieds section of the local papers), and there's one **hotel** on Gaspar Grande, which also has a restaurant. All owners will be able to organize a boat out to the islands, usually an open fishing pirogue from the Island Property Owners' Association marina (see page 104). If booking a villa stay on one of the Bocas, you'll need to bring **groceries** and **supplies** with you; stock up in Glencoe.

Gasparee Island Vacation Resort Gaspar Grande ☏ 672 6549, ⊛ bit.ly/Gasparls. Recently refurbished, these smart a/c studios and one-bedroom villas built on a hillside overlooking the waters of Bombshell Bay have a lounge and a kitchenette. There's a restaurant, bar, swimming pool, tennis court and mini-mart on the property, and a good sandy beach just below. Studio US$148, villa US$266

The Island Villa Gaspar Grande ☏ 625 6841, ⊛ trinidadgingerbreadhouse.com. Owned by the family behind the lovely *Gingerbread House* in Woodbrook (see page 82), this is a gorgeous villa, with four bedrooms (sleeping 14 altogether), two recreation rooms, full kitchen and a veranda overlooking the sea. Steps lead down to the water, which offers safe swimming. Two-night minimum stay. Villa US$289

Northern Trinidad

MARACAS BAY

Northern Trinidad

2

The north of Trinidad is dominated by the rainforested mountains of the Northern Range, which form a rugged spine that rises up dramatically from the coastline to over 900m at the peaks of El Cerro del Aripo and El Tucuche. The region is also lined with Trinidad's most stunning beaches, of which Maracas Bay and Las Cuevas are the prime destinations for sun, sand and swimming. Beyond is the glorious, laidback seashore of Blanchisseuse, from where the road dissolves into undeveloped coastline. A narrow road winds through the mountains south of the village, providing an opportunity to see some of the island's prolific birdlife at Asa Wright Nature Centre and the idyllic village of Brasso Seco.

Occupying the stretch of land south of the jungle-smothered mountains is one of Trinidad's most densely populated areas, a string of urban communities known collectively as the **East–West Corridor**, spreading back from either side of the traffic-choked Eastern Main Road and bordered to the south by the Churchill Roosevelt Highway. Though you'll see plenty of temples, mosques and Hindu prayer flags around **Tunapuna**, Indian culture is far less visible here than in the south: Creole cooking reigns supreme and the soundtrack that blares from shops, bars and maxis is soca and Jamaican dancehall rather than chutney. Of the individual communities, **St Joseph** is the most absorbing, named by the Spanish as the island's first capital, with a historic church and barracks. Slightly further east, **St Augustine** is dominated from the hills above by the stunning **Mount St Benedict Monastery**, home to a lovely guesthouse that's one of the most attractive of the low-key and little-used accommodation options across the region. The East–West Corridor also offers access to a host of interior mountain attractions: numerous spectacular waterfalls and opportunities for river swimming are to be found in the **Maracas and Caura valleys**, at **Lopinot** and, especially, from the **Heights of Guanapo Road**, the starting point of several fantastic Northern Range **hikes**.

East of **Arima**, home base of Trinidad's First Peoples community, the shops and houses that line the Eastern Main Road peter out. The last town of note is workaday Valencia, beyond which the road narrows as it snakes toward Trinidad's **northeastern tip**. A wild and rugged peninsula, this **Toco coast** juts some 20km into the Atlantic Ocean, and is one of Trinidad's best-kept secrets. Between March and August **leatherback turtles** clamber up onto wave-battered sandy beaches at **Matura** and **Grande Riviere** to lay their eggs, backed by spectacular scenery.

Many of the places along the East–West Corridor, as well as Maracas and Las Cuevas beaches, are best seen on day-trips from Port of Spain; however, Blanchisseuse has a smattering of **accommodation** options, and if you plan on making the long drive up to Grande Riviere, you'll almost certainly want to stay a night or two before heading back.

LEATHERBACK TURTLE, GRANDE RIVIERE

Highlights

❶ North Coast Road Switchback through the lush Northern Range jungle and enjoy the rugged coastline between Maracas and Blanchisseuse. See page 113

❷ Beach lime Trinidad's northern beaches offer the island's best swimming; Maracas and Las Cuevas are the prime spots. See pages 113 and 115

❸ Waterfalls From Avocat to Paria, Salybia to the Mermaid Pool, the north offers fabulous freshwater swimming. See pages 121, 119, 137 and 138

❹ Brasso Seco A low-key ecotourism destination in the heart of the mountains, Brasso is a must for hikers, birdwatchers and relaxation seekers. See page 121

❺ Mount St Benedict Monastery Stunning views over the central plains and a historic guesthouse provide soothing respite from the East–West Corridor below. See page 128

❻ Café Mariposa, Lopinot Enjoy a wonderful Spanish Creole meal in this verdant and beguiling mountain valley. See page 131

❼ Grande Riviere With rainforest hikes, river swims, great places to stay and a rugged golden-sand beach where hundreds of turtles lay eggs each night during the spring, Grande Riviere is simply unique. See page 141

HIGHLIGHTS ARE MARKED ON THE MAP ON PAGE 110

GETTING AROUND   **NORTHERN TRINIDAD**

By car As is the case everywhere in Trinidad, a car is the most convenient way to see the sights in the north, particularly far-flung spots such as Blanchisseuse, Asa Wright, Toco and Grande Riviere. There are plenty of rental companies in Port of Spain (see page 79).

By public transport The north is fairly well served by public transport – taxis and maxis travel along the East–West Corridor 24 hours a day via the fast-track Priority Bus Route and along the Eastern Main Rd, and also serve the communities inland of the EMR; most rural areas are also covered, but long waits are common. As with everywhere in Trinidad, relying on public transport can be a little time-consuming; to get to places off the EMR such as Lopinot, for example, you'd need to take a maxi or route taxi from Port of Spain, change to a Lopinot route taxi at the junction of the valley road on the EMR, and then do the same on the way back, probably with a wait at each of the stages.

By organized tour Most tour companies (see page 38) include the top northern sights – the north coast, Asa Wright/Brasso Seco, Mt St Benedict, Yerettê – in their itineraries.

Santa Cruz Valley

Beyond the grand residences of Maraval at the northern fringe of Port of Spain, buildings give way to abundant rainforest and the road climbs through a succession of hairpin bends to a T-junction. Marked by two stone pillars put up by American servicemen during construction of the road, the left-hand turn is the North Coast Road (see page 113); continuing straight ahead, Saddle Road squeezes through a narrow gorge of solid rock before meandering downhill through the pastoral **Santa Cruz Valley**, a very scenic half-hour jaunt past cattle pastures and farmland south towards the urban bedlam of San Juan (see page 126).

The valley's cocoa groves and plant nurseries – punctuated by residential communities – are overhung by towering samaan trees and impressive clumps of bamboo, mango, sapodilla and banana, though a thriving nearby **quarry** has gouged messy yellow scars into the hillsides. Cricket legend **Brian Lara** spent his childhood in **Cantaro Village**, about 3km along the road, which has a friendly, suburban feel, its lively main street lined with roti restaurants and rum bars. At the back of the village is a cricket stadium built in Lara's honour, with a placard outlining his remarkable Test world records.

2

Green Market

Pole 213, Saddle Rd, nr Cutucapano Rd, Upper Santa Cruz • Sat 6am–1pm, Sun 7am–noon • Car park TT$2 • ☎ 221 9116, Ⓦ greenmarketsantacruz.com

Hunkered under the green, jungle-clad hills of Santa Cruz, the **Green Market** is a fantastic initiative, offering the chance to buy local craft and produce, and sample

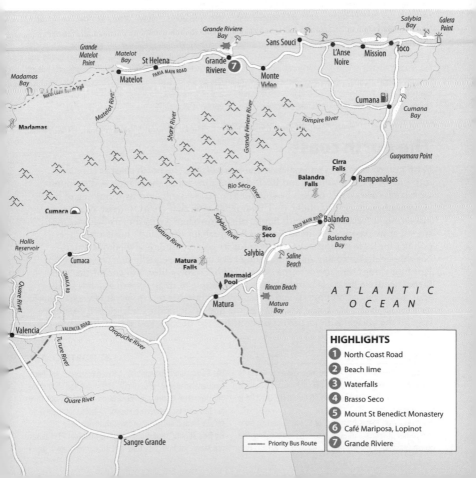

HIGHLIGHTS

1. North Coast Road
2. Beach lime
3. Waterfalls
4. Brasso Seco
5. Mount St Benedict Monastery
6. Café Mariposa, Lopinot
7. Grande Riviere

– – – – Priority Bus Route

2

quality food and drink. The market's beautiful setting is reason to visit in itself, with naturalistic landscaping, bird feeders busy with hummingbirds, plenty of tables and benches and a kids' playground. Locals flock to the stalls heaped with fresh produce (much of it organic), from dasheen bush and ground provisions to tropical fruit and North Coast fish, while up on the top level, open-sided thatch-roof booths house vendors selling traditional cocoa tea (just the thing if you arrive in the early morning), as well as local breakfast delicacies such as smoked herring or saltfish buljol with coconut bake, plus cakes, pastries, Venezuelan street food, home-made wine and fantastic unsweetened juices (try the tamarind or pomme cythere). You can also explore a re-created cocoa house and nature trails, and peruse displays of handmade wooden bowls, soaps, jewellery, mirrors, clothes and other high-quality, unusual craft items.

ACCOMMODATION AND EATING   SANTA CRUZ VALLEY

Chocolate Bar Café ☎ 237 9351, ⓦ bit.ly/CBarTT. Nestled by a river in the green surrounds of the Santa Cruz Valley, this is a popular breakfast and brunch spot (book ahead at weekends). There's less of a focus on chocolate than the name suggests, though you can get excellent cocoa tea and house-made bars. Otherwise, highlights are fried or coconut bake with veggie-laced buljol, smoked herring or sautéed aubergine/spinach (TT$25), plus pancakes, bagels, omelettes, panini, salads, burgers (TT$30–60); coffee, smoothies and gooey cakes, too. Seating is inside or on a pleasant grassy terrace. It can be a little tricky to find; coming from Port of Spain, turn right off the main road onto a small bridge over stream just before an orange-painted fruit/fish stall; the café is on the

immediate right (car park opposite). Mon–Sat 8am–8pm, Sun 8am–6pm.

★ **Waterville Estate** ☎ 676 7057 or ☎ 396 6165, ⓦ watervilleestate.com. Santa Cruz is home to a very attractive accommodation option, which is ideal for visits to both capital and country. Owned by a very welcoming Irish-Trinidadian family, there are two comfortable, attractive studio rooms with verandas, set amid abundant fruit trees with birds flitting about. Hiking trails are nearby (Maracas Bay is under 2hr walk), and further hiking and birdwatching is available at their sister property *Mount Brasso Estate* (see page 122). Rates include breakfast and pick-up from the airport or Port of Spain; all-inclusive option available. **US$65**

The north coast

With gorgeous beaches and quiet, somnolent villages, the **north coast** is Trinidad's top spot for a bit of sun, sea and R&R. Its coastline offers the island's best swimming, with cool, clear waters backed by coves of fine yellow sand, and its sprinkling of hotels and guesthouses create a uniquely Trini holiday vibe that's hard to resist. Many people just swing in for a day-trip, with hordes of city-dwellers navigating its first snaking stretch at weekends en route to **Maracas Bay**, perhaps the island's busiest beach, as popular for its shark and bake outlets as for its golden sands and vigorous waters. Neighbouring **Tyrico Bay** and shimmering **Las Cuevas** are equally fine places to swim. Past here things slow down to the sleepy pace of country life, with end-of-the-road **Blanchisseuse** a great place to kick back for a couple of days. As well as a few small-scale accommodation options and several rugged beaches to explore, it offers freshwater swimming in the Marianne River and prime **hiking** along the undeveloped coastline beyond the village, with its perfect coconut-littered beaches and **waterfalls** such as the one at **Paria Bay**.

GETTING AROUND   THE NORTH COAST

By car As ever, a car is by far the most convenient way to explore the north coast, given the infrequency of public transport. The only petrol station on the North Coast Rd is at Maracas.

By maxi taxi Maxis from Port of Spain (departing from the corner of Prince and George streets) run all along the North Coast Rd to Blanchisseuse, stopping at Maracas Bay,

Las Cuevas and all points in between; services are fairly frequent on weekdays until mid-afternoon, and one or two ply the route in the evening and on Saturdays, but they are few and far between on Sundays. Note that there is no service from Blanchisseuse onwards to Arima.

By bus Slightly slower but marginally cheaper PTSC buses run Mon–Sat from City Gate at 4.30am, 9am and 1.30pm

THE MAGNETIC ROAD TO MARACAS BAY

A small stretch of apparently ordinary tarmac between La Vache and Maracas Bay has an unusual claim to fame. According to local folklore, this is the **"magnetic road"**, where vehicles roll up an incline in defiance of gravity – and it's easily experienced. Stop just before the North Coast Road begins its descent to Maracas Bay; as the cliffs to the right recede, revealing the Northern Range, the road ahead appears to have a definite upward incline. On stopping your vehicle, putting the gears in neutral and releasing the handbrake, you'd assume that the car would obey gravity and roll backwards; in fact you move forward in what feels like the "wrong" direction. Although this marvel is nothing more than an optical illusion, more romantic locals insist that it's the work of God, obeah, or a bizarre magnetic field.

2

and 5pm, returning roughly two and a half hours later from Blanchisseuse, and stopping at all points in between.

By organized tour The north coast is a staple on most Trinidad tour itineraries; all of the island's tour companies (see page 38) offer trips to Maracas, Las Cuevas and beyond, as well as Avocat Falls, Asa Wright and the like. Island Experiences also offers a Maracas beach shuttle.

North Coast Road

Squeezed in between the Caribbean Sea and the Northern Range, with fleeting views of glittering, island-studded ocean to one side and cliffs smothered with tangled jungle on the other, the **North Coast Road** is one of Trinidad's most spectacular drives. It was laid by the US Army in 1944 as a recompense for their use of the Chaguaramas peninsula, which deprived residents of sea bathing at Macqueripe and other bays. Bois cano trees drop claw-like leaves onto the tarmac and mineral springs pour down into roadside gullies; the water is chilled, delicious and safe to drink, and many locals stop off to fill up bottles or take a freshwater shower. Be warned that at weekends, the road between Port of Spain and Maracas can get quite busy, and is prone to frequent landslides during the rainy season.

As the road climbs up into the hills north of Maraval, the first of many spectacular panoramas stretches over the Maraval Valley to the tiny spice and parang centre of Paramin and down into the outskirts of Port of Spain. Cliffs and jungle close in beyond here (with glimpses of Santa Cruz to the right), and a few kilometres further reveals a gorgeous coastal prospect: the ocean far below dotted with rocky islets. The largest of these is **Saut d'Eau**, a 100,000 square-metre breeding colony for brown pelicans, chestnut-collared swift and the rufous-necked wood rail.

La Vache Scenic Area

The North Coast Road is punctuated by fruit stalls and refreshment huts with dramatic sea views, the air noticeably cooling as you climb to **La Vache Scenic Area**, a car park and viewing platform at the highest point on the North Coast Road. The views of the unravelling coastline are marvellous, with the white sand of Maracas just visible beyond the first headland, and vendors sell souvenirs, cold drinks and snacks such as salt prunes and mango chow to the weekend hordes on their way to the beach.

Maracas Bay

Lifeguards on duty daily 10am–6pm • Car park TT$10 • Changing rooms/toilets daily 10am–6pm, TT$2 • Beach loungers TT$20, umbrellas TT$60

Some 45 minutes' drive from Port of Spain, the North Coast Road plunges down to **Maracas Bay**, a ravishing, generous curve of fine, off-white sand bordered by groves of skinny-stemmed palm trees and with a stunning mountainous backdrop. Easily the most popular beach on the island, Maracas is an institution: thousands make the traditional Sunday pilgrimage to show off their newest swimwear, frolic in the water, sunbathe and network. During the week, it's much quieter, and perhaps all the more enjoyable for it. Longstanding **upgrade works** do mar the scene somewhat, however. A refurb of its facilities was first approved in 2009, but changes of government have seen development initiatives come and go, and led to years of delays. A newly expanded car park, bathrooms/changing rooms and food-vendor huts have been completed, but a large-scale sewerage/water treatment plant was still underway.

Past the roundabout at the western end of the bay, the North Coast Road passes over the Maracas Bay River and onto the **beach** itself, a gorgeous wide swathe with wave-whipped emerald-green waters that make for an exhilarating swim. Be wary of tides and undercurrents, as they're often dangerously strong; stick to the areas between red and yellow flags where **lifeguards** stand by, whistling furiously at anyone who goes too far out.

Maracas Bay Village

The left-hand turn-off from the North Coast Road at the western end of Maracas Bay leads down to **MARACAS BAY VILLAGE**, a fishing hamlet whose catch – fresh carite, cavalli and shark – is in demand throughout the north. Here you'll find a couple of rum bars, a grocery and post office, alongside lots of beached pirogues, drying nets and a pretty cream-and-blue church next door to the *Maracas Bay Hotel*. The village is also home to a profusion of scavenging dogs and few bathers; most people stick to the main beach to avoid the odd fishy entrail.

ACCOMMODATION AND EATING   MARACAS BAY

Accommodation in the area is limited to one hotel, though the odd budget room is available to rent in the village; ask around. When it comes to **eating**, bake and shark is the Maracas Bay mainstay: two fried breads (the bake) with seasoned fried shark, dressed at a buffet with all manner of condiments from tamarind, chadon beni, garlic and pepper sauces as well as coleslaw, salad and fresh pineapple. You'll find it for around TT$35 from multiple takeaway outlets, some of which also serve the more sustainable kingfish and bake (from TT$46), as well as aloo, beef and fish pies (from TT$12), pholouri and roti. Cold **beers** and **soft drinks** are available at all the stalls. Note that at the time of writing, owing to ongoing works, the bake and shark vendors were housed in temporary structures on the beach itself.

Asha's Offering more variety than most of the Maracas food vendors: as well as bake and shark, there's fried chicken, burgers (including veggie versions), hot-dogs and fried bake with shrimp, salmon, kingfish and flying fish (TT$40–60), plus fries and pies, ice cream and coffee. Daily 8am–7pm.

Maracas Bay Hotel ☎ 669 1914, ⊛ maracasbay.com. Bland yet reliable place at the west end of the bay, this is the only place to stay on Maracas, offering decent if plain rooms with en-suite bathroom, a/c, and sea-facing porches; ask for one in the refurbished east wing. The hotel's *Bandanya* restaurant serves breakfast, lunch and dinner, and the food is basic but good: fish sandwich and fries at TT$75, grilled fish or chicken with sides at TT$140/110. There's a small bar on site. Continental breakfast included. U̲S̲$̲8̲0̲

Richard's The eternally popular *Richard's* always has the longest lines of all the Maracas bake and shark vendors, and the quick turnover means the sandwiches, dressings and condiments are always super-fresh. If you're concerned about sustainability, plump for kingfish, carite or cheese instead of shark. Daily 8am–7pm.

Uncle Sam's This bar and grocery store at the eastern end of the bay is the most popular drinking location on the beach – sound systems pump reggae and soca and draw large, spirited crowds, and the bake and shark is eternally popular, too. Tues–Sun 8am–late.

Tyrico Bay

Lifeguards on duty daily 10am–6pm

Hidden from Maracas Bay by a steep headland, **Tyrico Bay** is about a kilometre east around a small headland. Popular with the Indian community who flock here for weekend picnics and family beach-cricket tournaments, the bay is roughly half the size of Maracas with slightly less in the way of wave action, making it a better choice if you are travelling with children. There's also a small lagoon on the west side of the beach for very safe paddling. Luxuriant, fine yellow sand and a gentle shelf add to the feeling of calm, and there are no food and drink vendors. The only buildings are the lifeguard towers and portable toilets, and you can drive right down to the sand.

Las Cuevas

Lifeguards on duty daily 10am–6pm • Changing rooms/toilets daily 10am–6pm, TT$2 • Las Cuevas Eco-Friendly Association ☎ 309 0113, ⓦ bit.ly/LCEFA • Las Cuevas is a 10min drive east of Maracas Bay, and an easy day-trip from Port of Spain

East of Maracas, after an inland curve that provides impressive views of the jagged double apex of Mount El Tucuche, Trinidad's second highest mountain, the North Coast Road turns back to the sea at **Las Cuevas**, one of the north coast's longest beaches. Named by the Spanish after the caves that riddle both the seabed and the rocks to the west end of the bay, Las Cuevas boasts a wide, clean and unadorned swathe of whitish sand, fringed by coconut palms and invitingly calm emerald waters that provide better swimming than Maracas. It's also a great place for beachcombing, especially along the seldom-visited western reaches, littered with shells and stones. The beach is surrounded by headlands, which enclose the bay in a tight horseshoe and provide protection from the wind and a relatively gentle surf. During the week it's often deserted, although the fishing community is still very active, but weekends see the sand dotted with family groups who make a day of it, bringing coolers packed with food and drink and beach umbrellas to provide much-needed shade. Keep in mind, though, that the legendary **sandfly** population, a particular problem in the late afternoon or after rain, can make for unpleasant sunbathing – take repellent and cover up as the day wears on.

There's a large (free) car park above the bay, as well as changing rooms, showers, toilets and a first aid room. Lifeguards patrol and put out yellow and red flags to mark safe bathing spots, and it's not a good idea to swim outside of these areas. The calmest waters are to the eastern side of the bay. The beach is also a nesting site for **leatherbacks** and other turtle species (see page 142), most of which lay at the wilder western end; the Las Cuevas Eco-Friendly Association leads night-time trips to see them during the season (March–Aug), as well as offering tours in the area.

ACCOMMODATION AND EATING   LAS CUEVAS

Las Cuevas Beach Lodge ☎ 669 6945, ⓦ lascuevas beachlodge.com. Precariously balanced on a ridge above the beach, this is the only place to stay in Las Cuevas, and it's a decent option. Rooms range quite a bit in size, and only the larger studio apartments get the full benefit of the view, but all are clean and bright, with a/c, plus fridge and microwave in the apartments. Rates include breakfast. The wooden terrace bar and restaurant (daily 7.30am–10pm) offers fantastic views, and serves simple lunches and dinners such as local fish (TT$75), chicken

(TT$65) and shrimp (TT$160) – curried, stewed, fried or grilled – curried conch (TT$65), steaks (TT$100–390) and other meaty treats such as baby-back ribs, pulled pork and lamb kebabs (TT$55–70); burgers and fries on offer too. 🛜 Doubles US$80, apartments US$113

McLean's This bar overlooking the bay at the edge of the car park is a favourite with local fishermen, serving budget-priced Creole breakfasts and fish-and-chip lunches (around TT$60) alongside soft drinks, beer and rum. Daily 6am–5pm.

One Hundred Steps Beach

Mitchell Trace, North Coast Rd • The beach is about a 15min drive from Las Cuevas, just before the village of La Filette

Secluded **One Hundred Steps Beach** is named for the seemingly endless concrete steps that wind down the cliffs – though be warned that landslides have made navigating them a little dangerous. To get to the steps, turn down Mitchell's Trace, a dirt track opposite the larger Rincon Trace, which strikes inland from the North Coast Road a couple of kilometres east of Las Cuevas. Ideal for a secluded swim and popular with local fishermen, this curve of soft, greyish sand is backed by almond trees and a few **manchineels**, which should be treated with caution (see page 45). Be careful of strong tides here, even on apparently calm days, as there's no one to help if you encounter problems. It's best visited in a group.

Rincon Falls

Hike Seekers ☎ 399 1135, ⓦ hikeseekers.com

Inland of One Hundred Steps Beach, Rincon Trace is also the route to spectacular **Rincon Falls**, the largest in Trinidad, a good two-and-a-half-hour uphill trek through the bush. Nestled on the side of El Tucuche, the falls tumble over 30m of rocks before cascading into a large pool safe for bathing. You'll need a guide to find it; Laurence "Snakeman" Pierre at Hike Seekers knows the area intimately.

La Filette

East of Chupara Point, with its improbably suburban row of bright yellow holiday villas, the North Coast Road narrows and becomes increasingly potholed before entering the fishing village of **LA FILETTE**, a pretty cluster of neat houses and blooming front gardens straddled over two hillocks about 5km from Las Cuevas. A rum bar and cookshop on the western outskirts is good for watching the world go by with a "beastly" cold beer, or for gossiping with the fishermen about the rumoured contraband landing spots on this part of the coast.

Yarra

A few kilometres east of La Filette, a series of narrow bridges force traffic to slow down before the road passes through a teak plantation, after which you enter **YARRA**, a rather quiet hamlet. Look out for a grassy turn-off towards the sea, the only one not leading to a house; this goes to **Yarra Beach**, another perfect, wide and deserted seashore. A Yarra River tributary runs down to the sea here, and is sometimes deep enough for you to whitewater bodysurf right into the ocean. As always on this coast, be sensible if you enter the water, as the beach is known for dangerous riptides and strong currents.

Blanchisseuse and around

A five-minute drive east of Yarra and the last village before the North Coast Road trails off into the bush, **BLANCHISSEUSE** (pronounced "*blaan*-she-shers"), is a popular holiday retreat for Trinidadians. The village's name (French for "washerwoman") suggests it got its moniker from the time when all laundry was done in the many rivers and streams hereabouts. With a population of around three thousand and spanning over 3km of road, Blanchisseuse today isn't exactly a hamlet, and the clutch of flashy holiday homes on the western outskirts are testament to its popularity. Even so it's still pretty quiet; the atmosphere is relaxed and friendly, and most visitors are weekend day-trippers from Port of Spain. The few overseas tourists that do visit this Caribbean gem divide their time between the four marvellous sandy **beaches**, make the hike to gorgeous **Paria Bay** and Falls, or walk through the rainforest for river swimming at nearby **Three Pools**, or **Avocat Falls** on the Arima–Blanchisseuse Road.

Like most on this coastline, the beaches at Blanchisseuse are ruggedly beautiful, though they do have a reputation for **treacherous waters**, particularly between October and February when breakers crash onto the sand and surfers come into their element; get local advice before taking the plunge.

Lower Blanchisseuse

Lower Blanchisseuse to the west is the older portion of the village, a lengthy and attractive assortment of weather-beaten board houses and crumbling tapia buildings wreathed by rambling bougainvillea and neat croton hedges. Steep cliffs plunge down to the ocean, while breaks in the palms or almond trees reveal white-tipped waves below. The small village atmosphere is reinforced by a couple of rum bars, a fishermen's cooperative, the attractive arched windows and blue porticoes of the Georgian-style

police station, and a boxy, single-spired Catholic **church** overlooking the sea, complete with three bells housed in an outdoor tower.

Lower Blanchisseuse beaches
Opposite the police station, and marked by a broken sign, an easy flight of stone steps lead down to a marvellous and secluded bathing **beach**, with 100m of soft greyish sand, headlands offering protection, and almond and sea grape trees tangling down the cliffs. The fishermen's beach – 50m back down the road next to the cooperative – is a better place to lime than swim, as it has a measly pebble shore.

There's another beach just off the Paria Main Road to the west of the lower village, right before the old stone bridge, where a track leads down to the sea and a swath of wide sand, surrounded by cliffs at both ends. There's a tiny parking area but the beach is usually deserted, save for the odd surfer.

L'Anse Martin
Popular with sun-bronzed surfers, **L'Anse Martin** has been locally renamed in their honour as Surfer's Beach; its true name is seldom used, though it is marked as such on the sign. There is an almost imperceptible shelf here that makes for excellent waves, while craggy rocks border each end and the forest drips down onto the sand. The beach is accessed via a walkway opposite the dilapidated sign for the long-gone *Surf's Country Inn*.

Upper Blanchisseuse
Upper Blanchisseuse begins after the Paria Main Road loops inland to meet the improbably large intersection with the Arima–Blanchisseuse Road. This is the main residential area, with a couple of tiny general stores and pastel-painted homes clustered by the roadside, and streets trailing uphill into the area known as "Paradise". Towards the eastern end of the village are the community centre and sports field, while past here the road goes down to sea level and runs parallel to **Marianne Beach**.

Marianne Beach
Car park TT$15 • Beach facilities TT$10 • Kayak rental TT$30 per 30min; contact Eric Blackman on ☎ 759 9514
The longest and most popular beach in Blanchisseuse, **Marianne** is a breathtaking seashore, its yellow sand battered by crashing waves – the perfect place to watch the moon rising over the headlands from the east, ideally on an evening when **leatherback turtles** are to be found laying their eggs (March–Aug; see page 142).

At the eastern end the clear water of the Marianne River is partially dammed by the ever-shifting sands into a **lagoon** – an inviting place to swim when the water is flowing out to the sea. Locals tend to congregate here for an after-work bathe or cricket match, and fishermen paddle canoes in search of freshwater salmon. There are rudimentary showers and toilets at the sandy car park and house ambitiously named the *Marianne Beach Resort*, which occasionally has a bar selling drinks and snacks; otherwise the *Cocos Hut* restaurant (see page 118) lies just above the beach (separated from it by a grove of trees).

Marianne River and Three Pools
Three Pools tours TT$150/person, contact Eric Blackman on ☎ 759 9514, ✉ kayakeric@gmail.com
East of Marianne beach, the North Coast Road runs alongside the **Marianne River** and terminates at the water's edge, adjacent to a rusting suspension bridge and its ugly modern replacement. Over the bridge, an unpaved road continues past more luxury villas before becoming a rutted bench trail eastwards to Paria Bay (see page 119). Originating at Brasso Seco (see page 121), the river tumbles downhill, carving deep swimming pools and waterfalls along the way, and offers good **birdwatching** – green woodpeckers, yellow orioles and silvered antbirds are commonly seen – as well as a

2

lovely watery trek south along the riverbed to **Three Pools**, forty minutes or so from the mouth of the Marianne. Most people hire a guide in the village to lead the way, but it's a fairly straightforward route you can follow independently; the easiest way is to follow the riverbed, splashing through sometimes deep water and swimming, though a path does lead along the river's western bank, crossing to the east about halfway (any "No Entry" signs are universally ignored). Overhung by vines, ferns and huge buttress-rooted trees, it's a gorgeous and easy wade, and the stunning Three Pools easily surpass any of the other swimming spots along the way.

The first of the three, 12m across, is the least impressive, with a natural **water-slide** of sorts, through a narrow channel in the rock. Passing over the grey rock, you'll find the second pool, so deep that it's difficult to touch the bottom, with another gushing channel creating a **natural jacuzzi**. The third pool is the smallest but also the most impressive, overhung by tall cliffs, with rock carved into bizarre folds and small caves you can swim into and climb up to see the waterfall above. To go beyond this point to the spectacular Avocat Falls (see page 121), you'll need a guide; best option is the jovial Eric Blackman, owner of *Northern Sea View Villa*.

ARRIVAL AND DEPARTURE   BLANCHISSEUSE

By public transport Maxis and route taxis can drop you in either Lower or Upper Blanchisseuse; go for Upper if you want to head to the beach or the Marianne River.

ACCOMMODATION AND EATING

Blanchisseuse is a lovely place to really get away from it all for a few days, staying in one of the three local **guesthouses**, but you may find eating something of a challenge unless you cook for yourself. There are a couple of cookshops in the village, though these open only sporadically; ask at your guesthouse if you want to arrange for regular meals from one of them. If you plan to **self-cater** you'll need to stock up before arriving here; there's very little in the way of groceries on offer in Blanchisseuse itself, other than a tiny bar and general store in the lower village, and a smaller roadside store on the main road in Upper Blanchisseuse.

Cocos Hut ☎ 669 2964. The only restaurant in Blanchisseuse, set in a converted cocoa-drying house at the roadside opposite *Laguna Mar* hotel, and often the only place in town selling hot food, with decent fish, chicken, beef or pork lunches and dinners (TT$70–150). The bar is great for a drink, its end-of-the-road location providing a sense of cosy isolation, though as the owner is getting on these days, opening hours can be sporadic. Daily 8am–9pm.

Laguna Mar ☎ 669 2964, ⓦ lagunamar.com. Set in a very quiet spot on the inland side of the road just above Marianne Beach and opposite its restaurant, *Cocos Hut*, the basic rooms here are in blocks of six with a lovely communal balcony. Each has two double beds, fan and bathroom; the upstairs rooms are noticeably breezier. US$80

Northern Sea View Villa ☎ 759 9514, ⓔ kayakeric@ gmail.com. These spotlessly clean apartments offer few luxuries, but have a great location opposite Marianne Beach, a plunge pool in the front garden and an extremely friendly owner, Eric Blackman. Each has two bedrooms and sleeps four (you can pay a bit less to have just one room rather than a whole apartment) with fans, a/c, satellite TV, full kitchen, spacious veranda and living room, and there's a homely feel with crafts dotted around. Rates include breakfast. ⓦ US$80

★ **Second Spring** Lamp Post 191, Paria Main Rd ☎ 669 3909 or ☎ 379 5562, ⓦ secondspringtnt.com. Really lovely small guesthouse near the beach at the western end of the lower village, with three attractive, tastefully decorated studios and a smart private two-room cottage right on the clifftop (not suitable for small children). Each has fans, mosquito nets, a veranda and a kitchenette, sea views and walls hung with lovely local art. Offering spectacular coastal views, the grounds are lovingly tended by the friendly French/Trini owners, and there's a splendid deck overlooking the water, with steps down to the sea. A perfect place to get away from it all. Breakfast and other meals available. ⓦ Studios US$70, cottage US$120

North coast bench trail

East of Blanchisseuse, the North Coast Road gives way to undeveloped coastline, with the next piece of tarmac some 30km to the east at Matelot (see page 144). In between, you'll find some impressive **hiking** along a beautiful **bench trail** – the local name for the old donkey tracks cut in the late nineteenth century to transport goods and service the then thriving cocoa estates. Well-trodden, the trail dips and climbs through the remnants of abandoned estates and secondary forest, with the sea swinging spectacularly in and out of view. Despite periodic government proposals to construct a road along this stretch of the coast, the area remains a sanctuary for bird and animal life. Many of the beaches are prime laying spots for the giant **leatherback turtle** during the March–August season (see page 142), and the birdwatching is superb; as well as rich pickings for nature lovers there's also fine fishing for pompano, tarpon, jackfish and ancho.

Though few attempt it, you can hike the bench trail all the way from Blanchisseuse to Matelot, but only the fittest can hope to complete the journey in a day. Most make the trip in two stages, camping on a beach along the way. Though it is easy to follow, it's not a good idea to walk the trail alone past Paria Bay; there have been reports of drug-smuggler landings at deserted bays. Saturdays, Sundays and public holidays are prime times for local hiking groups to take to the bush. Make sure you start your hike with a full bottle of **water**; you can fill up from streams along the way.

2

GETTING AROUND	**NORTH COAST BENCH TRAIL**

By organized tour Caribbean Discovery Tours (☎ 620 1989 or ☎ 339 1989, ⊛ caribbeandiscoverytours.com), organize excellent packages in this area, hiking or by boat, and overnighting at Petit Tacaribe (see page 120). For hiking, also try Courtenay "Bushman" Rooks of Paria Springs, who has been instrumental in clearing and maintaining the bench trail (☎ 620 8240, ⊛ pariasprings.com), while Eric Blackman in Blanchisseuse (☎ 759 9514, ⊜ kayakeric@

gmail.com) is great for shorter forays along the trail. Carl Fitzjames (☎ 669 6054, ⊜ carlfitzjames@hotmail.com), who lives up in Brasso Seco, is your best bet if you want to hike down to the bench trail from the Northern Range.
By boat Local fishermen in Blanchisseuse will take you along the coastline parallel to the bench trail by boat, which costs around TT$200/person each way to/from Paria Bay. Ask around or at your guesthouse.

Marianne to Paria Bay

The moderately challenging round trip trek to **Paria Bay** is the most common hike from Blanchisseuse. You can do each way in two hours at a good pace, though most take a picnic and make a day of it, stopping to eat and swim at Paria. Past the Blanchisseuse bridge over the Marianne River, the track passes beach homes for the first couple of kilometres, before dipping down to a stream and entering the forest. The trail can get a little muddy in the rainy season, but nothing can detract from the marvellous scenery: look out for massive termite nests and a splendid specimen of the weird **cannonball tree**, with its heavily perfumed rotund pink flowers, twisted branches and trunk supporting 15cm-wide "cannonballs". There is a constant accompaniment of birdsong, though the soothing calls are often shattered by the raucous shriek of parrots.

Passing a number of stunning coves along the way, you finally emerge onto the beach at **Paria Bay** – an idyllic, completely undeveloped 1.5km of fine, coconut-littered golden sand with a backdrop of thick jungle; at its western end, a natural rock arch makes for a fine photo opportunity. Swimming is fairly safe, with the exception of October to January/February when currents become more intense. **Leatherback turtles** (see page 142) come here in good numbers to lay their eggs between March and August, the eggs hatching from June to September.

Paria waterfall

If you've walked as far as Paria Bay, it's well worth pressing on for another fifteen minutes to the secluded **waterfall** for a freshwater bathe. Three-quarters of the way up Paria beach, a track to the waterfall heads inland. Some ten minutes along, you reach a fork: the right turn heads up to Paria Point and eventually to Brasso Seco village (see page 121), while the left one meets the Paria River a few minutes later. Head upstream for five minutes to arrive at the waterfall, where cold spring water crashes down the 5m cascade into a deep grotto 10m across, perfect for a dip. Blue morpho

2

PETIT TACARIBE

Petit Tacaribe is the most unusual place to stay in Trinidad, a magical and secluded spot comprised of three cedar-framed bamboo *cabañas* and a cooking shed overlooking the bay (c/o Stephen Broadbridge ☎620 1989 or ☎339 1989, ⓦcaribbeandiscoverytours.com; US$150). Rates are per person, per night and cover transport to Blanchisseuse, boat trip to Petit Tacaribe and great meals made with fresh produce (though you should bring any extras – beer, rum, chocolate and so on), plus excursions into the forest. The boat from Blanchisseuse takes about half an hour; six people and their baggage can cram in, but you can always hike if you're feeling hardy, with the boat bringing just your bags.

---

butterflies flit about for the first few months of the year, and you're unlikely to see another soul on the entire route.

Paria Bay to Matelot

Past Paria Bay, the bench trail is less well travelled and a little more overgrown. After ten minutes' walk, you pass through attractive **Murphy Bay**, and it takes around an hour and a half to reach **Petit Tacaribe bay** (see above), with **Grand Tacaribe**, over the Trou Bouilli-Riz Point headland, a further half an hour. Both have marvellous sandy beaches and plentiful fruit trees such as mammee apple and mango. From here, it's a five- to six-hour jungle walk onward to civilization at Matelot. Gorgeous **Madamas Bay** is reached after around an hour and a half: it's a curve of deserted off-white sand with a river lagoon at one end, almost rivalling Paria in beauty. Half an hour inland from the beach is another splendid cataract, **Madamas waterfall**, though you'll need a guide to find it, as well as the **Madamas Gorge** (see page 123) even further into the interior.

The Arima–Blanchisseuse Road

The **Arima–Blanchisseuse Road** cuts through the middle of the steamy Northern Range forest, climbing high into misty, breeze-cooled peaks. Between them, **Brasso Seco** village is an excellent starting point for exploring the **hiking trails** and **waterfalls** that course through the mountains. A little closer to civilization you descend to the **Asa Wright Nature Centre**, one of the Caribbean's finest birdwatching sites. Though easily driveable in a regular car, the sharply winding, potholed and generally ill-kept road can be challenging, but the payoff is tremendous. Light filtering through the overhanging canopies of mahogany, teak, poui, cedar and immortelle colours the tunnel-like road green, and every available surface is smothered in plant life: mosses, ferns and lichens cover rocks and tree trunks already laden with massive wild pine bromeliads, and vines and monkey's ladder lianas trail down to the tarmac. During the regular rain showers, mists descend over the road.

Closer to **Arima**, the road dips downhill, rounding spectacular corners and passing hillsides cleared for christophene cultivation supported on rough trellises (the pear-shaped, pale green fruits are commonly used in Chinese cooking), and former cocoa estates left to grow wild. As the jungle thins out and a few sporadic buildings appear, look out for the numerous Hindu prayer flags fluttering in the breeze and tiny do-it-yourself temples on the eastern side of the road.

GETTING AROUND THE ARIMA–BLANCHISSEUSE ROAD

By car Though the odd route taxi plies between Brasso Seco and Arima, services are so infrequent that there is no feasible public transport along the Arima–Blanchisseuse Rd; the only sensible way to travel is in your own car.

By organized tour If you don't fancy driving yourself through the mountains, an organized tour can be a great way to see the area; all of Trinidad's operators (see page 38) do trips to Asa Wright, Brasso Seco and Avocat Falls.

Avocat Falls

Eric Blackman in Blanchisseuse (see page 117) is a good option for an impromptu Avocat visit from Blanchisseuse; all the main tour companies also offer trips; for something more adventurous, try rappelling the falls with Paria Springs Tours (see page 39)

Wet and humid, the first portion of road up into the Northern Range from Blanchisseuse is a succession of leaf-covered hairpin bends, climbing gently up from the coast, with quarter-miles marked by roadside posts (though many have crumbled). Just before the twenty-and-a-quarter-mile marker (around 5km from Blanchisseuse), look out for a neat grove of pommerac trees to the left; here, a track leads past a few dwellings towards **Avocat Falls**. After a ten-minute walk, you turn left along the banks of a shallow riverbed for fifteen minutes until you reach a watery junction. Wade upstream a few minutes until you arrive at a steep bank, haul yourself up with the aid of tree roots and straight in front of you is a stunning 12m cascade with a deep swimming pool.

Morne La Croix

A short way south of Avocat, the mountain road climbs a steep hill before entering the picturesque hamlet of **MORNE LA CROIX**, where most of the inhabitants still speak French Creole as well as Trini English. A tiny general store and bar is the only place for limited food and drink here, but the main attractions are the impressive views and superb **birdlife** wherever you stop. Just beyond the town, look for a hedge of purple-flowered vervain, a favourite haunt of yellow-breasted ruby-topaz hummingbirds and the red-crested tufted coquette, and also for the metre-long, teardrop-shaped nests of the crested oropendola, whose manic calls can be heard echoing across the peaks. As the road climbs ever higher, a **lookout point** adjacent to the Andrew's Trace dirt track – at 600m – provides chilly breezes and sweeping views through a break in the forest, with the sea just visible; above you can often see hawks coasting on thermal updraughts.

Brasso Seco

Tucked away at the end of a well-signposted turn-off from the Arima–Blanchisseuse Road, a good up-and-down 7km from Morne La Croix or Asa Wright, **BRASSO SECO** is a naturalist's dream. Translating as "dry branch" in reference to an arm of the Paria River which only ever gets wet in heavy rainy seasons, the village is populated by people of mixed Amerindian, Spanish and African descent (and clearly recognizable as such; some of the elders still speak Spanish); known as "**cocoa panyols**", many are descended from people who moved to Trinidad from Venezuela in the nineteenth century to work on the burgeoning cocoa and coffee estates. Hunkered under the dramatic 941m peak of El Cerro del Aripo to the south, Brasso is charming, languorous and picturesque. Converted cocoa sheds and still-occupied tapia houses intermingle with more modern concrete homes, a couple of rum shop-cum-parlours, a church, school and community centre. Children play cricket in the middle of the road, young men lime outside the rec club and everyone has time to greet each other.

Brasso is also a great place for visitors to get a real flavour of mountain life via the marvellous **community tourism** initiative developed by the village residents; as well as being one of the island's best bases for **hiking** (see page 123) thanks to its proximity to both mountains and coastline, at least five **waterfalls** and numerous river pools, the Tourism Action Committee here offer the chance to see traditional methods of cocoa processing and coffee roasting, as well as tours of their chocolate-making facility. As for **birdwatching**, the diversity of species seen here often exceeds that of the island's well-known birding centres; scientists from a variety of universities have made this their base for studying rarely seen species and leking sites (communal display sites where males show off their prowess to potential mates). Red-legged honeycreepers, bearded

2

bellbirds, tufted coquette hummingbirds, all types of parrot, green and red macaws, the black-faced ant-thrush and the endangered piping guan are all to be found, among innumerable others.

If you're in Trinidad in early November, try to get up to Brasso Seco for their annual village **festival**, which celebrates local culture, indigenous and otherwise, by way of dancing, parang and plenty of amazing local food and drink, from wine and cocoa to pastelles and smoked meat. There are also plenty of games to keep kids amused; visit ⓦ bit.ly/BrassoSeco for more info.

Brasso Seco Visitor Facility
Madamas Rd · ☎ 718 8605 or ☎ 493 4358, ⓦ brassosecoparia.com

Signs on the outskirts of the village alert you to the **Brasso Seco Visitor Facility**, HQ of the local community association, Brasso Seco Tourism Action Committee. It's best to call ahead and arrange a visit (see page 123), but there's often someone out on the open deck processing coffee or cocoa. Inside are a few displays on the mountain environment, as well as a selection of fantastic locally made products to buy: organic coffee, cocoa-tea balls, cocoa nibs, pepper sauce and roucou (a bright orange cooking sauce made from achiote seeds). Perhaps the best thing to take away, though, is a bar of **chocolate** made by the Brasso Seco Chocolate Company with single-origin beans from the village estate; try the dreamy mocha or espresso varieties flavoured with local coffee.

Manchuria Estate
Tours available via the Tourism Action Committee ☎ 718 8605, ⓦ brassosecoparia.com

Reachable via a bumpy forest track just off the main road through the village, **Manchuria Estate** is an agro-tourism project run by the Tourism Action Committee, and is well worth a visit if you'd like to learn a little more about traditional ways of life in the mountains, or just soak up the scenery and take a swim in a crystal-clear river. Planted with cocoa and coffee, the estate's fifteen acres are being slowly rehabilitated as an organic plantation, and in a newly constructed **cocoa house** by the side of the river, you can see (season permitting) the whole cacao production process, from fermenting the beans to drying, roasting, shelling and grinding; coffee processing is a similar business, though without the fermentation stage.

ARRIVAL AND DEPARTURE   BRASSO SECO

By public transport PTSC buses (ⓦ ptsc.co.tt) run from Arima at 5am and 8am. Infrequent route taxis also make the trip.

By organized tour or transfer Brasso's Tourism Action Committee and some accommodation options (like *Mount Brasso Estate*) organize airport transfers or transport from elsewhere. Caribbean Discovery Tours (see page 119) also offer tours to and around Brasso.

ACCOMMODATION

It's worth staying a few days in Brasso Seco to fully appreciate the tranquillity of the valley; the choice is slim, but in addition to the places listed below, it's worth contacting the Tourism Action Committee about **private homes** to rent. Wherever you stay, check in advance whom you can hire to **cook** for you, or stock up well from supermarkets in advance (you may be able to buy chicken, fruit and vegetables locally).

★ **Mount Brasso Estate** c/o O'Farrell, Maraval ☎ 676 7057 or ☎ 396 6165, ⓦ watervilleestate.com. The sister property of an estate in Santa Cruz (see page 112), located at one of the highest driveable points in Trinidad, on the lower slopes of El Cerro del Aripo but just a 10min drive from Brasso Seco. The seventeen-acre grounds contain a converted cocoa-drying shed equipped with eight bunks and a full kitchen; you cook your own meals or arrange for someone to cater for you via the Brasso Visitor Facility.

There's also a walkway down to a natural swimming pool, and a wonderful thatched outdoor kitchen/dining area; cocoa, coffee, citrus, soursop, orchids and bois cano trees are scattered throughout, and the rich forest surrounds are a birder's paradise. The owners can arrange transport from Port of Spain. Bunks US$40

★ **Pacheco's Host Home** ☎ 669 6139 or ☎ 669 3781, ✉ pachecoagustina@gmail.com. In the heart of the village, the Pacheco family are a Brasso institution, the sisters

BRASSO SECO TOURS AND HIKES

Brasso is a wonderful place from which to head out into the hills on a **hike**, with endless possibilities in and around the village, from short strolls to adventurous, demanding treks – a few routes are summarized below, all of which promise excellent **birdwatching**. It's also well worth arranging one of the **community tours**, which cover local industries such as coffee, cocoa and chocolate production. First point of contact for arranging all hikes and visits are the **Tourism Action Committee** (☎ 718 8605, ⓦ brassosecoparia.com); options are detailed on their website.

VILLAGE TOURS

Booking a community tour is a wonderful way to get a flavour of Brasso Seco. Conducted by members of the village Action Committee, trips start off at the **visitor facility** (see page 122), where you can see traditional methods of roasting and hulling coffee beans, and perhaps ice-cream making or baking in the old-time clay oven. You then stroll around the village to the community centre, where an icily air-conditioned room serves as headquarters for the **Brasso Seco Chocolate Company** (☎ 705 9842 or ☎ 493 4358, ⓦ bit.ly/BrassoChoc), an Alliance of Rural Communities member (see page 38) which produces the fabulous bars on sale in the visitor centre. Makers will show you the various processes of chocolate production – conching, tempering – as well as giving you the lowdown on the social history of cocoa cultivation in the area and the science behind the process; samples are on offer, too. If you want to get the full picture of the journey from bean to bar, you can take a drive down to the Action Committee's cocoa processing house at **Manchuria Estate** (see page 122).

Minimum group size for village tours is usually five, but the Action Committee may be able to accommodate two or three people; call and ask. Prices vary depending on what you want to do, and whether you want to eat, but a village tour with a meal averages around TT$300 per person.

HIKING

Given the thick forest that surrounds Brasso Seco, you'll need a **guide** to go hiking from here. Several members of the Tourism Action Committee act as guides; one of the best is **Carl "Wang" Fitzjames**, who lives right in Brasso on Madamas Road (wooden house at last light pole on left; ☎ 669 6054 or ☎ 486 6059, ⓔ carlfitzjames@hotmail.com; hikes US$20–100), and has exhaustive knowledge of birds, leking sites and medicinal plants. He also has a campsite halfway to Tacaribe on the north coast for overnight stays.

Moderate hikes include to **Double River Falls** (3–4hr round trip; also easy by mountain bike), which follows a track through cocoa and coffee plantations, with wonderful views and good birding. There's a brief ascent through lush jungle to the 8m falls and swimming pool. The slightly larger **Madamas Falls** (6–7hr round trip) are a further 90min on the same trail, which is good for butterflies and birds. **Sobo Falls** (4hr round trip) are an impressive three-tier cataract deep in the forest, while the trek to stunning **Paria Bay and waterfall** (7–8hr round trip; see page 119) follows a relatively well-worn path along the Paria River.

If you want something more demanding, **El Cerro del Aripo** (7–9hr round trip) is the most challenging climb on the island, involving steep and rocky stretches, thick elfin forest, sights of golden tree frogs, but limited views. **Morne Bleu** peak is reached en route, and is ideal for serious birders. The route to the spectacular deserted **Petit and Grand Tacaribe bays** (see page 120; 8–9hr one way, or overnight with a bush or beach camp) is along a forest ridge and river; from here you could hike onwards along the coast or back to Brasso Seco, or else organize a boat to Blanchisseuse or Matelot. **Madamas Gorge** (3-day round trip) is a stunning cliff-lined river with rock pools and falls you swim/walk through; this could also be extended to finish at the coast, while **Macajuel Pond** (6hr round trip) is a dense-forest hike with steep climbs to a deep pond and waterfall for swimming.

having run the local school prior to retirement, and their brother presiding over the village shop. There are currently three rooms in a separate building to the family home, with a central lounge, a kitchen and shared bathroom; all are simple but sparklingly clean, with fans and mosquito nets. Rooms in a new, modern building were under construction at the time of writing. Rates are per-person and include a big breakfast; lunch and dinner available. � 🛜 US$50

2

EATING AND DRINKING

There are no **restaurants** in Brasso Seco, but you can sample some delicious local cuisine at one of the village's host homes and at the visitor facility (see page 122); you'll need to give a days' notice for both. The local speciality is delicious "Buccaneer" **smoked meat**, cooked very slowly on a construction of wood, leaves and grass called a branca, and a staple of the village's November festival (see page 122); if you're here for a few days, the Tourism Action Committee should be able to arrange to have someone make it for you. Otherwise, there are two small **stores** in Brasso Seco, one right at the start of the village (also a bar) and the other on the hill above the Pacheco home; there's also a larger **bar** on the road between the visitor facility and community centre.

★ **Pacheco's** ☎ 669 6139 or ☎ 669 3781. Home-cooked lunch (from TT$75) at the Pachecos' dining table is a highlight of a visit to Brasso Seco, and might consist of deliciously seasoned chicken with rice, ground provisions and salad, perhaps with pastelles thrown in at Christmas time, and always washed down with fresh fruit juice from the garden. Finish off with a cup of cocoa tea on the veranda, overlooking the garden and the hills beyond, as the hummingbirds flit between the flowers. No set hours; call a day in advance to book.

Asa Wright Nature Centre

90-minute tours daily 10.30am & 1.30pm; US$10 • ☎ 667 4655, ⓦ asawright.org

Internationally famous for its birdwatching, the 1500-acre **Asa Wright Nature Centre** was originally a coffee, citrus and cocoa plantation. In 1947 it was bought by Dr Newcome Wright and his Icelandic wife, Asa. Both were keen naturalists and birdwatchers, and when the New York Zoological Society set up the Simla Tropical Research Station on neighbouring land, the couple began to accommodate visiting researchers. After her husband died, Mrs Wright sold the land on the condition it remained a **conservation area**. A non-profit-making trust was set up in 1967, which established a nature centre for naturalists and birdwatchers, a first in the Caribbean. Simla donated its land and research station to the centre in 1970, and though tropical research is still undertaken here, Asa Wright is mainly visited these days as one of the most popular **birdwatching retreats** in the Caribbean. Resident guests tend to be middle-aged to retired North American or British bird fanatics, enthusiastically compiling checklists of the day's sightings over sunset rum punches. You can also visit as a half-day trip, watching birds from the veranda, taking a **tour** of the grounds and having lunch or afternoon tea. Between January and April (Mon–Fri), tours from docked **cruise ships** often crowd the centre from mid-morning to mid-afternoon; if you're not staying here but still wish to do some birdwatching during these times, arrive before 10am to avoid the rush.

The great house and veranda

Asa Wright revolves around a tapia **great house**, a maze of polished mahogany floors, stately heirlooms and antique furniture. At 360m above sea level, the views of the Arima valley rainforest are spectacular, and with Mrs Wright having begun feeding birds here in the 1950s, the **veranda** now attracts up to forty species per day, including dazzlingly colourful, thumb-sized hummingbirds, green- and red-legged honeycreepers, blue-grey tanagers, white-bearded or golden-headed manakins and many precocious bananaquits. Matte lizards and agoutis clear up the scraps below, three species of tarantula are easily seen at night around the drive, and the surrounding trees glitter with the bright feathers of nesting and roosting birds: rufous-tailed jacamars, toucans, mot-mots, woodpeckers, trogons, yellow orioles and the yellow-tailed crested oropendola. The multitude of creatures attracts daily crowds of birdwatchers, the low murmur of voices broken by the excited squeals of an unusual sighting (noted in a log book), or by the click of paparazzi-style cameras.

The grounds

A network of well-marked **trails** thread through the grounds, which non-resident visitors can only access on one of the expertly conducted **tours**. These take in manakin leks and allow you to see some of the more reclusive forest birds that don't frequent the veranda. Those staying here for more than three nights get a tour of **Dunston Cave**, which houses the world's most accessible colony of **oilbirds**; but everyone can take a dip in the centre's lovely **natural swimming pool**. Coffee is still grown and processed on site in the traditional method; you can see the production process and purchase bags of fresh beans in the small on-site shop.

ARRIVAL AND INFORMATION   ASA WRIGHT NATURE CENTRE

By organized tour Most people visit Asa Wright as part of an organized tour; all the operators run trips in the area (see page 38).

2

ACCOMMODATION AND EATING

Asa Wright Lodge ☎ 667 4655, ⊛ asawright.org. Asa Wright has 24 comfortable (though not luxurious) rooms in a number of lodges. All have large, screened verandas, private bathroom and two double beds; rates include all meals, afternoon tea, and tours of the grounds conducted in early mornings before day visitors arrive. Staying up here, right in the middle of the rainforest, is a unique experience, and the lodge offers a pleasant old-world charm. You can also book birding tours to all of Trinidad (and Tobago's) top sites. If you don't stay, it's well worth coinciding your visit to enjoy the excellent buffet lunch (daily noon–1pm; TT$140 Mon–Sat, TT$200 Sun); sandwiches are available on the veranda for a little less (daily 11am–4pm). Room rates are much reduced in the summer. 📶 **US$215**

The East–West Corridor

Spreading south from the flanks of the Northern Range, the **East–West Corridor** is a sprawling conurbation between Trinidad's east and west coasts, its numerous communities so close together it's hard to tell where one tails off and another begins. The corridor's whole length is traversed by three separate roads running parallel: the first, the traffic-clogged **Eastern Main Road** (EMR) is lined with shops, businesses, restaurants and rum bars for almost its entire distance; public transport avoids the crush by taking the second road, the **Priority Bus Route** – a fast-track thoroughfare just south of the EMR, built on now-obsolete train tracks. The third is the multi-lane **Churchill Roosevelt Highway**, a kilometre or so to the south, which has encouraged major development in the form of three large shopping malls, signposted along its route, and is also the access road for Piarco International Airport.

Frenetic, hot and dusty as it is, the East–West Corridor does have sights worth seeing. The EMR is the gateway to the old Spanish capital of **St Joseph**, where elegant colonial edifices sit incongruously with a more recent rash of concrete. The **Mount St Benedict Monastery** dominates the hillside eastwards, providing panoramic views of the Caroni Plains, superlative **birdwatching**, and restful surroundings for afternoon tea. Heading north into the mountains, a series of access roads to **Maracas**, **Caura**, **Lopinot** and **Guanapo** lead to off-the-beaten-path waterfalls, river swimming and hiking. And the grinding pace of traffic along the EMR itself at least allows you to absorb the commercial chaos outside of the capital. The road buzzes with life – shoppers dodging delivery trucks throng the pavements and vendors fill the air with the sweet aroma of street food.

In terms of **accommodation**, much of the area can be visited on day-trips from the capital, though there is a stand-out guesthouse at Mount St Benedict and a couple of options in **Arima** that are conveniently close to the airport and other sights such as the Asa Wright Nature Centre and mountain waterfalls.

GETTING AROUND   THE EAST–WEST CORRIDOR

By car As waiting times for public transport can be very long – maxis and route taxis are seriously oversubscribed at rush hours – a car is by far the most convenient way to get around. As traffic on the EMR can be pretty bad, it's often quicker to take the highway for most of the way, and then just turn off onto the EMR when you near your destination.

2

Make sure that you do not, under any circumstances, drive onto the Priority Bus Route (reserved for buses, maxis and licensed taxis only) when crossing between the EMR and the highway; private drivers on the PBR will be fined if caught. It's not always signposted, though the lack of regular traffic and the constant procession of whizzing maxis make it easy to pick out.

By route taxi and maxi The EMR is well served by both maxis and route taxis, and services into mountain communities arrive and depart from the EMR at the appropriate junction; just ask locals where to catch one. From Port of Spain, some maxis use the Priority Bus Route for express journeys between the capital and their destination.

San Juan

East of Port of Spain and its nondescript suburb, **Barataria**, commercial **SAN JUAN** (pronounced "sah-wah") is focused around a bustling junction known as the "**croisee**" ("kway-zay"), named when French Creole was the main local vernacular and marked by the Scotiabank clock tower. It's a scene of agreeable, organized pandemonium; doubles vendors, fruit stalls and racks of sportswear line the streets while fleets of taxis honk endlessly. The croisee is equally lively after dark, when the flambeaux of oyster salesmen throw up whiffs of pitch oil and "power punch" milkshake vendors provide party-goers with sustenance. North from the croisee, the Saddle Road to Santa Cruz and the north coast begins. South of San Juan, between the EMR and the highway, are the **El Socorro** and **Aranguez** districts, the latter dominated by the **Aranguez Savannah**, a main venue for the annual **Phagwah** celebrations in March.

EATING AND DRINKING   SAN JUAN

Sylvie's 4 Back Chain St, San Juan ☎ 221 1277, ⊚ bit. ly/SylvieTT. If you're hungry, forgo the host of eateries on the EMR and head for San Juan's Back Chain St (behind the bus route), where *Sylvie's* is considered by many to serve the finest roti (from TT$30) in the East–West Corridor

(though some bestow this honour to *Patraj* or *Ali's*, on the same street). The curry shrimp here is simply delicious, and breakfast sada with chokas equally good. Mon–Fri 6.30am–5.30pm, Sat 8.30am–5.30pm.

St Joseph

Old meets new at **ST JOSEPH**, Trinidad's oldest European town and first official capital. On the right is the elaborate **Mohammed Al Jinnah Memorial Mosque**, resplendent with a crescent- and star-topped main dome flanked by six smaller domes and two minarets (there's not much to see inside, but drop by the caretaker's house behind the mosque if you want to take a look). The main streets, however, are on St Joseph Hill just to the north, lined with genteel colonial French and Spanish architecture jostling with newer concrete structures.

Brief history

In 1592, Lieutenant Domingo de Vera founded a town on the site of an Amerindian settlement. Christening it **San José de Oruna**, de Vera built a church, a prison-cum-police barracks (the rebuilt remains of which are to be found directly opposite the mosque), a governor's residence and a *cabildo* (town hall). In 1595 **Sir Walter Raleigh** attacked San José, burning down the church and the barracks, though by 1606 both were rebuilt, only to be destroyed by the **Dutch** in 1637 and ransacked by **Caribs** in 1640. During the eighteenth century, San José prospered as a **plantation town**, but in 1766 was hit by a devastating **earthquake**. It never really recovered, and eighteen years later the last Spanish governor relocated the capital to Port of Spain. The town's troubles weren't over yet, however; in 1837, a detachment of the British West Indian Regiment stationed here **mutinied**. Led by a Yoruba ex-slave known as **Daaga**, the soldiers were protesting against the apprenticeship system that kept freed Africans in a state of semi-slavery. They set fire to the barracks and fought for several days before being overwhelmed. In the aftermath, forty Africans lay dead, and Daaga and two of his comrades were executed by firing squad.

St Joseph's Catholic Church
Abercromby St

From St Joseph's mosque and police station on the EMR, Abercromby Street strikes uphill, meeting **St Joseph's Catholic Church** after a couple of hundred metres. Sacked three times, the structure has undergone many changes since it was first consecrated in 1593, and today's Gothic stone and red-brick style dates back to 1815. Impressed by the religious devotion of the townspeople who clubbed together to fund the first stages of construction, British Governor Sir Ralph Woodford donated £2000 and laid the foundation stone. Inside, beautiful **stained-glass** windows depict the Holy Family, St John and St Andrew; the ornate Italian marble **high altar** was imported from Dublin in 1912. The graveyard behind contains headstones with inscriptions in French, English and Spanish; the oldest tombstone in the island, a weathered slab known as the **tombstone of the pirate**, is marked with a skull and crossbones and the date 1682, but no one knows the identity of the buccaneer interred beneath.

Further up Abercromby Street and framed by elegantly fretworked colonial houses, **George Earl Park** was the old Spanish town square, used for evening promenades, military parades and as a burial ground.

Maracas–St Joseph Valley

Cutting inland from the EMR at St Joseph, Abercromby Street becomes **Maracas Royal Road** less than a kilometre from the EMR, crossing the grand First River Bridge and winding north into the lush **Maracas–St Joseph Valley**. **Maracas** itself is a tiny place with a post office and the steepled church of St Michael, the houses separated by clumps of fluffy bamboo and neat provision grounds. A few kilometres further on, the Maracas Royal Road ends at **Loango Village**, at a T-junction with the bumpy tarmac of San Pedro Road. There is easy access to **bathing pools** along the Maracas River here, the deepest usually filled with swimmers from the village. The riverbed is scattered with sparkling bronze sedimentary rocks, which fed rumours of **gold** deposits in the early twentieth century.

Yerettê
88 Valley View, Maracas–St Joseph • Tours by appointment only, at 8am, 11.30am & 3pm • US$25 with light breakfast, light lunch or afternoon tea, US$35 with full breakfast, US$45 with full lunch • ☎ 663 2623, ⓦ yerettett.com • Most tour companies include Yerettê in their itineraries, but if you're driving yourself, the owners will send comprehensive directions to get there from Maracas Royal Rd; Valley View is about 5km into the valley from the EMR

Set in a private home overlooking the Maracas valley, **Yerettê** is a popular visitor attraction, allowing you to get a magical, close-up view of the many **hummingbirds** found in Trinidad. Some fourteen species are regular visitors, drinking delicately from the hundreds of nectar feeders dotted around the terrace and flowered gardens, and making acrobatic dives and swoops through the air as they perform complicated courtship rituals or defend their territory with surprising aggression. Most common are the metallic emerald-and magenta-tailed copper-rumped hummingbirds, but (depending upon the season) you may also see the spectacular flame-tailed ruby-topaz and the equally colourful tufted coquette, the second-smallest bird in the world. Visits are chaperoned by Yerettê's knowledgeable owner, Theo Ferguson, who provides some background on these fascinating little birds as well as taking you through a slide show that details each hummingbird species seen at Yerettê. You're also able to browse a gallery of exquisitely detailed photographs (all of which are available to buy) as well as hummingbird-themed craft items, and the visit includes a delicious breakfast, lunch or afternoon tea.

Note that all visits must be booked in advance, usually a week ahead at least, as Yerettê is very oversubscribed and does not operate regular hours.

2

> ### HIKES FROM MARACAS–ST JOSEPH
>
> The Maracas–St Joseph Valley is the starting point for a couple of adventurous **hikes**. From the Maracas River bathing pools you can hike over the mountains to **Maracas Bay**, a stiff three-hour trek along an old fisherman's trail, or – if you've got the stamina – climb 936m **El Tucuche** (variously pronounced "*tuh-cutchee*" or "*too-koosh*"), Trinidad's second-highest mountain. It's an eight-hour round trip, with a section of the trail bordered by a tree-covered, 300m cliff, but you'll be rewarded by epiphyte-laden montane as well as high-altitude, mist-drenched elfin forests. If you're lucky, you'll see **red howler monkeys**, though you're unlikely to catch a glimpse of the **golden tree frog**, Trinidad's only endemic animal which lives in the waterlogged leaves of wild pine bromeliads.
>
> A **guide** is essential for both of these walks – try Paria Springs, Caribbean Discovery Tours or Ieri Nature Adventures (see page 39).

Maracas Valley Waterfall

No set hours • Free • About 8km from the EMR, turn right from the Maracas Royal Rd onto the signposted Waterfall Rd and park at the end of the road. Route taxis run from Curepe junction between 7am and 6pm; most drivers will go off-route to Waterfall Rd for an extra fee

It's well worth heading deep into Maracas–St Joseph Valley to see the **Maracas Valley Waterfall**, which crashes magnificently down 90m of sheer rock. The signposted route is simple and easy to follow independently from Waterfall Road. After twenty minutes of uphill walking along a wide track lined by groves of tall balata trees, a path strikes off right to three tiers of mini-waterfalls with two swimmable, ice-cold **pools**. Signs warning "no candles" are puzzling until you near the **main falls** twenty minutes further; here you'll see clusters of candles or pools of wax on the rocks, left by followers of the Hindu, Spiritual Baptist and Orisha religions, who regard the waterfall as a sacred place.

Curepe and St Augustine

CUREPE is a hub for **transport** all over the island: route taxis and maxis go from here to Port of Spain, east along the EMR as well as south to San Fernando and into the mountains of the Northern Range – though if you're heading to Lopinot, you should change at Arouca further east. There's little to stimulate the imagination in Curepe, save for locally famous doubles vendor *Sauce*, south of the bus terminus; people drive all the way from Port of Spain just for a Curepe doubles fix.

Curepe merges imperceptibly into **St Augustine**, a wealthier residential area north of the EMR, while just south the Priority Bus Route mounts a cut-stone flyover under which a road takes you to the **University of the West Indies St Augustine Campus**. Usually referred to by its acronym, UWI also has branches in Jamaica and Barbados. The campus was formerly a sugar plantation, and the great house now serves as the principal's home. The students are a cosmopolitan mix from across the Caribbean, and the campus offers numerous **fast-food** outlets and the especially comfy *Rituals* coffee shop.

Mount St Benedict

St John's Rd • The access road is signposted from the EMR between St Augustine and Tunapuna; route taxis leave from opposite the Scotiabank on the corner every few minutes

Towering over St Augustine with phenomenal views to the south of Trinidad coast to coast is the **Mount St Benedict Monastery**. An eye-catching network of white-walled, red-roofed buildings dominating the hillside, the monastery was established in 1912 by Benedictine monks fleeing religious persecution in Brazil. The first of its kind in the Caribbean, the monastery initially consisted of nothing more than a mud-walled, thatch-roofed *ajoupa* at the peak of Mount Tabor; additional buildings were added over the years including, in 1918, a gorgeous burnt-orange central tapia house, now slowly crumbling. With a boxy steeple tower forming the tallest portion of the complex, at 243m above sea level, the imposing church was consecrated as an **abbey** in 1947. In keeping with their motto "ora et labora" (prayers and work), the ten (now ageing) resident monks maintain an estate of coffee, cocoa, citrus and planted forest, as well as producing delicious yoghurt for domestic use and commercial sale. Mount St Benedict houses the Caribbean's main regional training college for priests, the **St John Vianney and the Uganda Martyrs Seminary**, which is also UWI's theology faculty. Nearby **St Bede's Vocational School** is also run by the monks, who teach local youngsters practical skills such as machining, welding, plumbing and carpentry. Though firmly a centre of Catholic study and worship, the site nonetheless remains inclusively Trinidadian, with Spiritual Baptists and Hindus undertaking pilgrimages here at different times of the year.

For a panoramic view of Trinidad that surpasses even the vistas at the monastery, take the **Alben Ride** trail just before the final monastery buildings and climb the fire tower, built to give warning of blazes in the plantations below.

Pax Guest House

🕿 662 4084, 🌐 paxguesthouse.com

Constructed in 1916 to fulfil the Benedictine tradition of welcoming travellers, and sitting pretty just below the Mount St Benedict Monastery complex, **Pax** is the oldest guesthouse in Trinidad and remains a popular retreat for Trinidadians and visitors. A favourite haunt of American soldiers based in Trinidad during World War II, today the guesthouse caters for birders, nature lovers and anyone in need of tranquillity, and is well worth a visit for a meal or a drink even if you're not staying here. At 800 feet above sea level, it's cooled by mountain breezes and offers lovely views of the plains below, and its creaking wooden floors and antique furniture offer a glimpse into a Trinidad long ago replaced by concrete and commercialism.

Pax has a long reputation as a specialist **birdwatching centre**. Manager Gerard Ramsawak organizes **tours** through the grounds, home to a huge array of birds; the elevation means that raptors – hawks, vultures, kites and falcons – are common, as are woodpeckers, parrots and thirteen of the island's sixteen species of hummingbird (you can hand-feed a hummingbird from the terrace). Five **trails** (30min–2hr) weave through jungle and secondary forest of Caribbean pine: a beautifully illustrated trail guide is available from the guesthouse. Gerard is also an expert on the monastery and its history, and can conduct tours of some parts of the building, such as the small **observatory**.

ACCOMMODATION, EATING AND ENTERTAINMENT   THE EAST–WEST CORRIDOR

★ **Pax Guest House** Mount St Benedict Rd 🕿 662 4084, 🌐 paxguesthouse.com. *Pax* exudes a feeling of calm and serenity that many find addictive; you'll even come across business visitors in search of a homely, friendly atmosphere. In keeping with their monastic history, the rooms are simple and fitted with solid wooden furniture, some of which are made by the monks; all are cooled by a/c and fans, and some share bathrooms. Rates include breakfast and a complimentary glass of rum punch, while after the dinner gong echoes through the corridors at 7.30pm a superb three-course Caribbean meal is served, on the candlelit terrace facing the rainforests of the Northern Range. There's also a lovely afternoon tea (daily 3–5.30pm; US$10); lunch and dinner (US$15/25) are also available by reservation. 📶 **US$95**, en suite **US$120**

Trevor's Edge 1 St John's Rd 🕿 685 1001, 🌐 bit.ly/ TrevEdge. Vaguely alternative bar just off the EMR on the road to *Pax*, popular with UWI students and hosting a wide variety of events, from arthouse film screenings to poetry and spoken-word nights, Latin dancing (every Sun) karaoke and live music, including parang in the run-up to Christmas. Daily 10am–late.

Caura Valley

Towards the eastern end of **Tunapuna**, a bustling conurbation with a lively fruit and veg market, the Caura Royal Road turns north to the **Caura Valley** – one of the most popular **picnic spots** on the East–West Corridor. Carved by the serpentine Tacarigua River, the valley was nearly turned into a reservoir in the 1940s: the inhabitants – many mixed Amerindian and Spanish – were relocated to Lopinot and even Brasso Seco, but the proposed **dam** was thwarted by the sandy soil and never built.

About 6km up the **Caura Royal Road** from the EMR is a right turn that will take you to a well-used **swimming spot**. Picnic tables line the bamboo-fringed riverbanks, and at weekends cooking fires smoulder and the shallow water is crowded with families enjoying a dip – though it does often look murky in the dry season. Past the picnic spots, high walls of bamboo form an intermittent tunnel over the road, opening up to reveal small-scale farms and homes at **La Veronica** hamlet. As the Caura Royal Road emerges onto the Tacarigua riverbanks, the water deepens and picnicking is more secluded – the road is eventually terminated by a river tributary. The drive back to the EMR affords some spectacular views of the central plains that are easily missed on the way up.

Lopinot

Ten kilometres from the EMR, via a winding road lined with lush forest studded with Caribbean pines, **LOPINOT** is a pretty hamlet with a remote feel, clustered around a sports field and the neat flowerbeds of a former cocoa estate that has been transformed into a beautiful recreation spot.

The valley was first settled by one Charles Josef, **Compte de Lopinot**, a planter who fled Haiti following Toussaint L'Ouverture's 1791 revolution. He arrived in 1800 with his wife and a hundred slaves, and it's not difficult to see why he chose to settle in this absurdly abundant alluvial valley surrounded by high, protective mountains. Lopinot's cocoa thrived, allowing him to build a tapia estate house, a prison and slave quarters and to amass a small fortune before his death in 1819. The Compte is buried alongside his wife by the Arouca River, which runs through the valley, and local legend has it that on stormy full moon nights his ghost rides through the estate on a white horse. A photograph taken in 1981, and on display in the great house, claims to show exactly that.

Today, Lopinot is a great place to **picnic** or to take a gentle **hike** into the surrounding forest. The community's annual **Fiesta de Lopinot** (ⓦbit.ly/LopFest), with parang and Spanish-style food such as pastelles, takes place in early December, and is well worth checking out, as is the **Cocoa Innovations** festival, staged at *Café Mariposa* (see page 131) just after Carnival, a fantastic celebration of cooking with cocoa with lots of samples of savoury and sweet delights.

The great house and picnic ground
Daily 6am–6pm • Free

The modest restored **great house** now has a glassed-over section showing the original mud walls, and the surrounding gardens are meticulously maintained, linked to the road by a quaint wooden bridge with a roof smothered with wild pine bromeliads. The grounds contain a cocoa-drying house and a dirt oven, while picnic tables shaded by several enormous samaan trees make an ideal spot for relaxation and a bit of birdwatching; look out for the white-shouldered tanager, bare-eyed thrush and violaceous euphonia. The beauty of the valley somewhat belies its rather violent history of enslavement – something that is not addressed at all in the saccharine info-boards dotted around the place, or in the small **museum** inside the house, dedicated to the culture of the local community. Of Spanish, African and Amerindian descent, they were relocated here when the Caura dam was proposed, and Lopinot has since spawned some of Trinidad's finest parang players. Each Christmas, a band of roving players still serenades each household, and a number of parang bars in the valley hold regular events from September to Christmas.

The rest of the valley

The boxy, cut-stone **La Veronica Roman Catholic church** near the playing field was originally built in Caura in 1897, but was taken piece by piece from the neighbouring valley during the Caura evacuation and reassembled here.

Beyond, lichen-smothered cocoa trees line the road, and a downhill turn-off leads to the **La Pastora** chapel and shrine, one of many on the island with the title. This dedication to the Virgin of Shepherds stems from Capuchin monks who established several missions on the island during the late seventeenth century, instilling devotion to La Pastora in their Amerindian converts. Carved in the 1940s, the plain white shrine inside the chapel depicts the Virgin Mary, and is said to have been chipped directly from the mountain.

Buildings thin out heading north, and the road eventually forks; a left down San Francisco Road brings you to a series of deep, swimmable **pools** on the river.

ARRIVAL AND ACTIVITIES   LOPINOT

By car There's a clearly signposted junction to get onto Lopinot Rd at Arouca on the EMR; the road forks at one point, and the sign pointing to the right-hand turn is partially obscured by a tree, so keep your eyes peeled.

Tours A community initiative, Lopinot Countrystyle Community Tourism (☎ 721 0616 or ☎ 744 7309, ✆ bit.ly/Lopinot) offers several trips in the village, including a Bean to Bar chocolate tour (US$12) and a Taste Lopinot option where you help make and then sample local delicacies in five different local homes (US$50). Lopinot Countrystyle Community Tourism

also offer some good hiking (trips US$9–15), with gorgeous hilltop views and two caves in which you can see greater spearnosed bats; birdwatching tours (US$15) are also excellent. The staff at *Café Mariposa* conduct guided walks of their organic gardens, planted with medicinal plants and herbs, as well as walks up the Mariposa mountain (from US$30); they also coordinate the Hot Trinbago Cocoa Trail tours (see page 238), with trips to several of Trinidad's cocoa estates.

Fishing *Mariposa* offer fishing in their tilapia pond; you can have your catch cooked up for you in the café.

ACCOMMODATION AND EATING

★ **Café Mariposa** 58 Village Settlement, Lopinot ☎ 669 8647 or ☎ 684 9358, ✉ mariposalopinot.com or ✆ bit.ly/mariposaTT. Signposted opposite the village school, and with tables on a veranda overlooking the gardens, this is a fantastic place to sample Spanish Creole cooking, from tortillas to pastelles, plus fish, chicken and vegetarian dishes, all cooked lovingly with imagination using homegrown organic veg and herbs. Cocoa is employed in a variety of delicious ways, from seasoned rice to cocoa-crusted lamb

and sublime cocoa-avocado ice cream, and all the chutneys and sauces are made from scratch; the fresh juices are truly memorable, too. Handmade chocolate is also available to buy, and gluten- or dairy-free meals are on the menu. Mains TT$200–250, or there's a four-course cocoa-inspired set meal on Sat (TT$600 for two); book ahead for all meals. Four appealing fan-cooled wood-panelled rooms are available for rent, with en-suite bathrooms and balconies looking out over the hillside; rates include breakfast. <u>US$89</u>

Arima

Named "Naparima" by its original indigenous inhabitants, **ARIMA** is the third largest town in Trinidad, and can be a somewhat confusing prospect for drivers as the EMR departs from its ruler-straight course and gets swiftly swallowed up in a one-way system through the urban clamour of shops, banks and wandering pedestrians; it's far easier to park up on the outskirts and soak up the hustle and bustle on foot. The town's main landmarks are the **Arima Dial**, featuring a four-faced timepiece presented to the townspeople by then-mayor John Francis Wallen in 1898, while on **Hollis Avenue** the line of local street vendors stops at a small park with a statue of venerated calypsonian **Lord Kitchener**, who was born and brought up here and is buried in the **Santa Rosa Cemetery** on King Street, as attested by a small roadside plaque. The main purpose to come Arima, however, is to get some insight into the culture and contribution of the town's **First Peoples community** (see page 133), who are honoured by another statue on Hollis Avenue, a gorgeous gold figure of **Hyarima**, a *cacique* (chief) who led Trinidad's First Peoples in many revolts against the Spanish.

Cleaver Woods Amerindian Museum

Eastern Main Rd, D'Abadie • Daily 6am–6pm • Free • ☎ 645 1203

Just west of Arima, as you enter the fringes of Arima at the diminutive village of **D'Abadie**, the EMR runs through **Cleaver Woods** where, hunkered in the midst of bois cano, balata and crappo trees and cocorite palms is a signposted **Amerindian Museum**, housed in a thatch-roof *ajoupa* hut. Its displays are interesting, if somewhat neglected, and include a model indigenous village, pottery, hunting traps, bows and arrows and equipment used to process cassava, which was farmed by Amerindians and formed a major part of their diet.

ARRIVAL AND DEPARTURE
ARIMA

By car Situated roughly equidistant between Trinidad's west and east coasts, Arima is the last main town on the EMR before Valencia; there are several access points from the Churchill Roosevelt Highway, the easiest being the O'Meara Rd turnoff, which takes you onto Hollis Ave via Railway Rd.

By route taxi Route taxis to Sangre Grande and Valencia leave from near the Arima Dial, and taxis to Port of Spain can be caught on Broadway.

By maxi taxi Maxis are the most constant service for Port of Spain, arriving and departing from the junction of St Joseph and Green streets, though bear in mind there

Calvary Hill (500m), Asa Wright (18km), Brasso Seco (28km) & Blanchisseuse (39km)

ARIMA

● **EATING**
O'Meara Doubles — 1

■ **ACCOMMODATION**
Chateaux Guillaumme — 1

PAUL MITCHELL STREET
LONGDEN STREET
Santa Rosa First Peoples Community Centre
DE GANNES STREET
QUEEN STREET
ST JOSEPH STREET
CHURCH STREET
Santa Rosa Catholic Church
Cemetery
KING STREET
SANCHEZ STREET
PRINCE STREET
COLUMBUS STREET
Arima Old Road
WOODFORD STREET
SORZANA STREET
Cinema
RAGLAN STREET
BROADWAY
Port of Spain Taxi Stand
Arima Dial
Sange Grande & Valencia Maxi Stand
Port of Spain Maxi Stand
Al's Plaza
Police Station
Sangre Grande & Valencia Taxi Stand
GUANAPO STREET
EMR & Valencia (6km)
GREEN STREET
EMR West Maxi Stand
Anglican Church
ROSE STREET
FARFAN STREET
MAURICE STREET
EMR & Valencia (6km)
EMR & Port of Spain (28km)
Port of Spain Bus Stop
DEVONISH STREET
HOLLIS AVENUE
Lord Kitchener Statue
Market
Bus Station
ARIMA VELODROME
0 — 100 metres
Hyarima Statue
& Road from Churchill Roosevelt Highway (one-way system)
Churchill Roosevelt Hwy & Port of Spain (29km)

THE FIRST PEOPLES OF ARIMA

Arima has a far deeper history than its commercial facade would suggest, as it's the stronghold of Trinidad's **First Peoples** (Amerindian/Carib) community, many of whom live around the crucifix-strewn **Calvary Hill**, a precipitous thoroughfare that overlooks the town from the north and connects to the Arima–Blanchisseuse Road. Many are distant relatives of the Carinepogoto tribe who once inhabited the Northern Range, and family names such as Boneo, Campo, Calderon, Castillo, Hernandez, Martinez and Peña are common. The **Santa Rosa First Peoples Community Association** (☎ 664 1897, ⓦ santarosafirstpeoples.org) was formed in 1974 to look after the interests of people with Amerindian ancestry, and in recent years has become ever more prominent in its efforts to have the contribution of Trinidad's indigenous peoples celebrated and recognized; in 2017, this was finally honoured by way of a one-off **public holiday**, which saw Arima erupt with a week of celebrations around the big day, October 14. The only organized Amerindian group in the country, the First Peoples Community is led by a Chief (currently Ricardo Bharath Hernandez), alongside prominent elders such as the Shaman or *Pyai* (Cristo Adonis) and Queen (currently Jennifer Cassar), and is based in a **community centre** at 7 Paul Mitchell St, behind the cemetery, some three blocks west of the Santa Rosa RC church. It's well worth getting in touch in advance to arrange a **tour** of the centre (prices dependent on group size and duration), which has displays on indigenous culture and traditions; guides from the community will regale you with the history of Trinidad's First Peoples, alongside their plans to build a replica Amerindian village and living museum on lands granted by the government on the Arima–Blanchisseuse Road. You can also to buy beautiful craft items such as woven baskets and carved calabashes. There are also displays on First Peoples heritage at the Cleaver Woods museum, just outside Arima (see page 132).

FIRST PEOPLES FESTIVALS

The main festival in the First Peoples calendar is the **Feast of Santa Rosa de Lima**, held over the last weekend of August. The oldest continuously celebrated event in Trinidad, having been inaugurated in 1786, it's also the only one in the island that honours the first canonized Roman Catholic saint of the "New World". Following a morning of church services, the community's King and Queen lead a parade in which a white-gowned statue of Santa Rosa is paraded through the streets, the procession bedecked with white, yellow, pink and red roses. Rum flows, and traditional Amerindian foods such as pastelles and cassava bread are eaten. The origins of the festival are somewhat murky, but in true fairy-tale style, community elders relate that three Amerindian hunters chanced upon a young girl lying in the woods, and brought her back to Calvary Hill. She disappeared three times, only to be returned to the community. A local priest told the hunters that this was no normal child but the spirit of Santa Rosa, and that they should make an image of her while she was still with them, for if she vanished again, her physical body would never again be seen. They made the statue, and the girl duly disappeared, leaving only a crown of roses where she had first been discovered. Ever since, Santa Rosa has been the patron saint of Arima's First Peoples community.

---

are separate lines for the express bus route and the much slower EMR journey. Maxis for Sangre Grande, Manzanilla, Toco and Mayaro leave from the corner of Raglan St and Broadway.

ACCOMMODATION

Arima makes a strategic base for trips into the mountains, or as a more characterful alternative to the airport hotels if you want to stay close to Piarco.

Chateaux Guillaumme 3 Rawle Circular ☎ 667 6670, ⓦ caribsurf.net/cguillaumme; map p.132. Close to the town centre, and set in a large building with an attractive garden, the four rooms here have tiled floors and either double or twin beds, each with a/c, private bathroom and TV. Owners Joan and Matthew are extremely welcoming, offer excellent island-wide tours, a full Carnival package, and also arrange discount car rental. Rates include a good Trini breakfast and airport pick-up if staying three nights. 📶 US$65

2

EATING

There are many low-key self-service Trini stalls clustered around the central streets offering great breakfasts, Chinese food, roti and pelau at rock-bottom prices.

O'Meara Doubles O'Meara Rd; map p.132. Just off the highway, on a piece of open land immediately to the right as you make the O'Meara turning from the Churchill Roosevelt Highway, the doubles stores here serve up some of the very best snacks in Trinidad. Both places are good, but the white-topped stall fries their bara breads on demand, and tops the doubles (around TT$6) with exemplary channa and kucheela; they also have truly memorable sahina. Simply delicious. Stalls close when the food runs out, usually by noon. Mon–Sat from 6am.

Heights of Guanapo Road

The Churchill Roosevelt Highway comes to an abrupt end east of Arima, with barely signposted turns north to the EMR, which itself switches abruptly from commercial thoroughfare to rural road, bordered by farmland and an impenetrable wall of forest pierced by a few country lanes leading to some marvellous natural attractions. Just after the EMR meets a road heading northwards to join the Arima–Blanchisseuse Road, a turn-off marked "WASA Guanapo Waterworks" brings you to the **Heights of Guanapo Road**, which runs along the Guanapo River for 3km before petering out into a country lane, often churned up by logging vehicles and best accessed by 4WD. The logging activity in the area is kept pretty low-key and the area remains a peaceful and beautiful hikers' paradise, for which you'll need the help of a knowledgeable **guide** (see below). The main attractions of the area are the breathtaking **Guanapo Gorge**, and the **La Laja** and **Sombasson waterfalls**, two of the most impressive on the island. With effort, you can see both the falls and the gorge in a day, but you'll need to be pretty fit.

Guanapo Gorge

About an hour's walk from the Heights of Guanapo Road, **Guanapo Gorge** is a narrow deep-water channel whose vine-wreathed walls of smooth grey rock tower 15–30m above the water. Dark and cool even on a hot sunny day, the gorge runs for some 400m; exploring it – wading and swimming all the way – can be quite hard work. Though you can start the trek from the southern (downstream) end, it is more exciting to begin upstream, where a large boulder blocking the river has created a small waterfall. From here, you enter the gorge by simply jumping into the deep pool and swimming a few metres before your feet meet the riverbed. Water levels vary according to the time of year – there is a risk of flash floods in rainy season (making the gorge best avoided if it's raining), but you shouldn't have to swim further than 25m for most of the year. The tiny **Tumbason River** threads through rocks to meet the Guanapo at the southern end of the gorge; a 45-minute walk upstream meets another small waterfall with a deep **pool**.

NORTHERN RANGE HIKING GUIDES

A **good guide** is essential if you intend to go hiking in the Northern Range; trails to places such as **Guanapo Gorge** (see above), **La Laja** and **Sombasson waterfalls** (see page 135) and **Aripo Caves** (see page 135) are unmarked and impossible to follow without local knowledge. Apart from being able to tell the difference between a harmless rainbow boa and a venomous mapepire snake (both of which are rarely seen, in case you're worried), a guide will also be able to enrich your hike with background on the fauna and flora of the forests. Full details of tour companies in Trinidad are given in Basics (see page 38); most will be able to drive you up to Asa Wright and Brasso Seco, but Paria Springs, Caribbean Discovery Tours and Ieri Nature Adventures specialize in Northern Range hiking, as do groups such as Hikeseekers and Island Hikers (see page 37).

La Laja and Sombasson waterfalls

The La Laja and Sombasson **waterfalls** are hidden deep in the folds of the Northern Range – a long, difficult, though exciting hike through abandoned cocoa plantations and forests of bois cano, sandbuck, nutmeg, balata and silk cotton. The trail dips and climbs constantly, and even though frequent use by hunters has kept the majority of the trails passable, your guide will no doubt need to blaze a path in the last stages. The first of the falls, **La Laja** is the smaller at about 20m high, with a couple of good pools below; the water is kept icy cold by the overhanging cliffs and dense foliage. Above La Laja you're in virgin forest, and the trek to **Sombasson Falls** is harder, but the three-tiered 50m cascade with deep pools is well worth the effort.

2

Aripo Road and around

Lonely fields line the EMR for a couple of kilometres east of Heights of Guanapo Road before it meets the potholed, nondescript-looking **Aripo Road**, which meanders northwards uphill for 14km into the mountains, following a valley cut by the Aripo River. The road's upper reaches are pretty and pass through some quiet rural communities. Guides (see page 134) are essential to explore the area.

Aripo Caves

Even though they're weather-beaten and battered, you can still make out the Forestry Division signs along the road which point the way to the **Aripo Caves**, Trinidad's largest system of caverns, deep into the Northern Range off Aripo Road; guides will take care of the permissions required to enter the area, a scientific reserve. The fairly taxing two- to three-hour trek through undisturbed forest, with plenty of hills and gullies to navigate, is best undertaken in the dry season (Jan–March), when the three rivers that cross the path usually slow to a trickle; if it's been raining, you'll have to wade them. In the rainy season, you'll also have to get wet to enter the caves, as a stream courses straight into the mouth – the going can be slippery. Nearing the entrance to the caves, you get the occasional view of the Central Plains below, and you'll start to hear the unearthly rasping shriek of one of the island's few colonies of **oilbirds** (see page 274). The **mouth** is large and dramatic, with a rather fusty mist rising constantly. Water drips from the limestone roof, and every surface is covered with fruit stones and guano. With a good torch you can navigate the rocks and go fairly deep inside, but the oilbirds' cries near an ear-splitting pitch; the Amerindians named them "Guacharo", meaning "the one who wails and mourns". If you want to go deeper, you'll need rope, a compass and caving experience.

El Cerro del Aripo

The Aripo forests are richly populated by Trinidad's **mammals**, and hunters make regular forays after agouti, armadillo, wild pig and manicou. If you're really lucky, you might catch sight of an ocelot on the flanks of the 941m **El Cerro del Aripo**, the island's highest mountain. The peak is covered with prehistoric-looking elfin (cloud) forest: short, scrubby and smothered with lichen, mosses and epiphytic growth. It's a tough full-day hike from the top of the Aripo Road, but as the temperature at the peak is ten degrees lower than in the lowlands, you don't have to worry about the heat. Note that this hike can also be undertaken from Brasso Seco (see page 123).

The northeast tip

The wild and rugged coastline of Trinidad's **northeast tip** feels more remote than anywhere else in the region; it takes close to four hours to drive from Port of Spain to **Matelot**, where the paved road ends. Cut off from most of the island by the dense

2

rainforest of the Northern Range, the region seems suspended in a time warp; people and houses are few and far between and an air of hypnotic quiet pervades. The villages strung along the coast are close-knit and spirited communities, making their own entertainment at **rum shops**, country parties and fishermen's fetes. **Farming** and **fishing** are the mainstays of the economy, with tiny roadside stalls offering fruit and vegetables, plus shark oil, saltfish, honey and sea moss.

The Toco Main Road loops northeast from Sangre Grande to **Matelot**, beyond which untamed bush and unreachable rocky coves entice you to scramble down the cliffs. While a number of fantastic **waterfalls** lie inland, the region's coastline is most famous for the **leatherback turtles**, which lumber up onto the sand here to lay eggs between March and August, their tiny shuffling hatchlings emerging between June and September. **Matura** and **Grande Riviere** are the most well-known places for guided night-time turtle-watching. Grande Riviere has the advantage of a good choice of **accommodation**, though its distance from Port of Spain means some visitors opt for Matura, enabling them to do some turtle-watching and return home the same night. Most people take a few days to visit this region, however, in order to fully appreciate its awe-inspiring coastline of weather-beaten cliffs and golden beaches, with **surfers** riding the breakers.

GETTING AROUND   THE NORTHEAST TIP

By car If you're driving from Port of Spain, take the Churchill Roosevelt Hwy until its end, turn left at the sign for Valencia, and then right onto the quiet portion of the Eastern Main Rd to Valencia itself. Follow the road straight through the town, keeping straight at a Y-junction on the main commercial street onto the Valencia Rd. After another 20min or so, you reach a T-junction; turning right takes you to Sangre Grande, left to Matura, Toco and, ultimately, Grande Riviere and Matelot. From Sangre Grande, driving time to Grande Riviere is about 2hr. The northeast tip's only petrol station is in Cumana (Mon–Sat 8.30am–6pm, Sun 8.30am–noon).

By transfer Given the long and winding journey, you might prefer to arrange a transfer with your hotel if heading for Grande Riviere; you'll pay around US$130 for up to four people.

By public transport Sangre Grande, in central Trinidad, is the region's main transport hub; most public transport to Toco starts here, though you may be able to pick up a route taxi in Arima or Valencia. PTSC buses (ⓦptsc.co.tt) and maxis leave from central Sangre Grande and run all along the north coast, from Matura to Matelot twice a day, in the early morning and evening; route taxis run with the same frequency, though are marginally more expensive.

Valencia

The small town of **VALENCIA** sits about 8km east along the EMR from Arima, a bustling centre with shops, bars, restaurants, the last petrol station until Cumana, and plenty of street vendors selling everything from jelly coconuts to doubles and pholouri. At the eastern end of the main drag, the EMR swings right toward Sangre Grande; driving straight takes you onto the **Valencia Road**. A short way north of Valencia, via the Quare Road, the **Hollis Reservoir** lies like a sea in the middle of the forest, and is a serene spot for birdwatching if you visit early in the morning; as you need a permit, it's best to go with an established tour company (see page 38), which will be able to secure one for you. Slightly further east along Valencia Road is the well-signposted North Oropouche River recreational facility – a rather grand name for picnic tables by the river. There's a good **hike** 6km upriver from here – the North Oropouche gouges its way through the rock and jungle, opening up a series of deep pools suitable for diving, the route finishing at the **Cumaca caves**, where colonies of **oilbirds** and bats are easily viewed – though you'll need a guide to explore (see page 134).

Matura

Some 19km east along the Toco Main Road from Valencia, the elongated town of **MATURA** consists of a police station, school, health centre, a handful of grocery stores and residential houses slung along a mile of tarmac. Other than stopping for a drink, the main reason to spend any time in the area is for the **beach**, a windswept, 4km stretch of fine yellow sand strewn with coconut husks and flotsam and jetsam washed up by the fearsome waves; it's best known for its seasonal turtle-watching possibilities (see below). Alternatively, you can **hike** inland for a freshwater swim in the lovely Mermaid Pool (see below).

Rincon Beach

There are two entrances to **Rincon Beach**, both marked by Forestry Division signs; the first a potholed tarmac and gravel road from the centre of Matura, and the other reached from the far side of town down a dirt track, and signposted. Though local people often take a dip, it's not a place for the uninitiated to swim, as the currents are extremely powerful. The beach is a protected area and a permit and guide are required to enter between March and August, due to the presence of Matura's real attraction: the **leatherback turtles** which haul themselves onto the sand to lay eggs.

2

Mermaid Pool

You should be able to find the pool independently, but guides are available locally from Nature Seekers (see below), who charge TT$100 for a 2hr trip

A short, easy hike inland of Matura, the **Mermaid Pool** rivals Rio Seco (see page 138) as the northeast's best place for a freshwater swim. Starting from Thomas Trace, just next to Matura's police station, the trail runs through the forest along the Matura River, passing mini waterfalls and gorges. After fifteen minutes the waters deepen into a magnificent, jungle-wreathed pool – especially beautiful on a sunny day, with the water lit up in a deep emerald green and dapples of sunlight filtered through the surrounding forest.

Salybia

North of Matura, the Toco Main Road meets the east coast for the first time. The view is often obscured by a thick cover of bush, though you do catch sight of some stunning

---

NATURE SEEKERS AND TURTLE-WATCHING AT MATURA

With a well-signed headquarters on the main road in the centre of Matura, **Nature Seekers** (☎668 7337 or ☎319 0172, ☏natureseekers.org) was established in 1990 by local stakeholders on a mission to educate locals and visitors on the importance of conservation – particularly of the turtles that nest of Matura's beaches, at a time when indiscriminate poaching was the main threat to turtle numbers here. Today, group members have turned into activists, organizing beach clean-ups and reforestation projects and promoting environmental awareness. They also patrol the beach day and night during the laying season, moving nests from at-risk areas and thus saving hundreds of turtles every year.

Nature Seekers is something of a social enterprise, too, teaching local people how to make lovely jewellery fashioned from recycled glass and other oddments found on the beach. It's available to buy at their Matura base, and visitors can have a go at making the pieces themselves (TT$100). They also offer **accommodation** in the village at *Suzan's Guest House* (☎398 3038; TT$450), where rooms have a/c and private bathroom.

NATURE SEEKERS TOURS

Nature Seekers' members also make a living as tour guides. During the nesting season (March–Aug), they offer **turtle-watching tours** (2hr 30min; US$25) that allow you to view the amazing laying process. You can also get involved in turtle conservation and **research**, helping beach patrols to weigh (2hr 30min) or tag nesting females (4hr); both experiences cost US$41.

Other tour options are **hikes** (3–4hr; US$60) to the Mermaid Pool (see above) and Rio Seco waterfall (see page 138), a **nature walk** into the Matura Forest (2hr; TT100), and **kayaking** on the serene Salybia River (2hr; TT100), with guides giving insight into the birds, plants, animals and history of the area.

small, wave-battered coves. On the other side of the road the bush conceals recent quarries that scar the landscape for a short stretch, before you arrive in the tiny village of **SALYBIA** 4km further on, with its roadside vendors selling home-made ice cream and pholouri. Across the road, the grand *Playa del Este* and adjacent *Salybia Nature Resort* (see below) hotels seem incongruously upmarket in this otherwise quiet area; both offer day passes if you want to stop by to swim and have lunch.

Saline Beach

Lifeguard on duty Sat & Sun 10.30am–3.30pm

The small rugged beach in front of the *Salybia Resort* is not safe for swimming, though a great option nearby is **Saline Beach**, a short downhill stretch just to the west, across a large concrete bridge over the Rio Seco. Just before the bridge a turn-off leads down to the sands, a popular chill-out spot at weekends when families come to bathe and picnic. For less crowded swimming, a small lagoon at the point where the river meets the sea is ideal for children. At weekends, a stall on the approach road sells snacks and drinks.

Rio Seco waterfall

The walk to the falls takes about 1hr, and the trail is easy to follow independently; however most of Trinidad's tour companies (see page 38) offer hikes to the falls, as do Nature Seekers (see page 137; TT$100), just down the road in Matura

Known locally as Salybia Falls, **Rio Seco waterfall** is easily one of the country's most spectacular cascades. From a signposted turn from the Toco Main Road opposite Saline Beach, you can drive ten minutes up a paved road and park by the caretaker's house on the left, just before the tarmac ends – the house is marked by a couple of green-painted benches and a sign giving information on the Matura Forest. Past the house, the path is easy to follow, with battered signposts at the few junctions. After twenty minutes' walk, it reaches the river, and you can scramble down to the water to bathe in one of the many deep swimming pools. Continuing on, after crossing a river tributary and meandering through some gorgeous mature forest, the trail enters its final steep stretch, and you get a good prospect of the waterfall and its wide pool of turquoise water. The waterfall itself tumbles some 8m down the rocks, with plenty of handholds and a rope for an easy climb up and a dive from the top, while the break in the canopy above the pool means that it's bathed in sunshine most of the day.

ACCOMMODATION AND EATING   SALYBIA

Playa del Este ☎ 691 2632, ⌨ playadelesteresort.com. Slightly less upmarket than its similar neighbour, this offers a waterfall pool and a plunge pool, plus a huge oceanfront terrace that's often employed to host weddings. The spacious if slightly dated rooms come with all amenities, and there's a restaurant, bar and full spa. Rates include breakfast, lunch and dinner for two people. Day-passes are TT$199 with a buffet lunch. 🛜 US$193

Salybia Nature Resort ☎ 691 3211, ⌨ salybia-nature-resort.com. Panoramic views, an oceanfront infinity pool with waterfall and swim-up bar, and clean, bright rooms; the more expensive suites (US$205) have the added bonus of a sea-facing jacuzzi. The on-site restaurant offers good-quality cuisine: dinner options (from TT$225) might be shrimp in pepper sauce or stuffed aubergine. Rates include breakfast. Day passes, including bar snacks and use of the pool, are TT$200. 🛜 US$115

Balandra and Rampanalgas

The Toco Main Road rejoins the coast at **BALANDRA**, a pretty fishing community with a popular **beach**, the entrance to which is at the western end of the village, marked by a small sign. You should be able to find a space in the car park unless you visit at a weekend, when cars line the path to the road. Backed by the fishing village and fringed by palm trees and Indian almonds, the beach is wide and inviting, with clean yellow sand and moderate waves. Most of the weekend crowds swim by the sheltered walled area past the car park, though swimming is safe along the whole length of the beach.

Balandra flows imperceptibly into **RAMPANALGAS**, which trails into the hills on the landward side of the road. It's a friendly sort of place – the local hot spots are *D'Arthur's* hotel and the neighbouring bar/cookshop.

Balandra Pools and Cirra Falls

A short trek inland of Balandra brings you to some lovely deep swimming spots known as **Balandra Pools** and **Cirra Falls**. From a backroad, which strikes off the Toco Main Road just past the sign announcing the village, a trail leads inland, crossing a stream and winding uphill. You pass a rather grand wooden house on the right and after a ten-minute walk come to a river, where crazy paving leads to the cascade. The waterfall is small but attractive, with a deep, greenery-wreathed pool and a tree stump as a diving board. You can climb up the bank to the top of the falls, where there's another, smaller cascade.

2

EATING AND DRINKING

BALANDRA AND RAMPANALGAS

D'Arthur's ☎ 670 4384 or ☎ 727 3585, ⌨ darthurshotel. com. A great little ten-room hotel, with smart, bright rooms of varying sizes, all with a/c and satellite TV; there's also a communal area with kitchenette and supremely friendly staff. Breakfast included. ☎ **US$89**

★ **Jenny's Country Kitchen/Kay's Pot** ☎ 351 0234. Run from the same building by separate members of the same family, this is a fantastic place to try proper Trini

country cooking, from bowls of rich, thick cowheel soup to curry crab and dumplin', pelau or fish with macaroni pie, callaloo and provisions at lunchtime (TT$40–70), to traditional breakfasts of sada roti and tomato choka or coconut bake with saltfish buljol. Grab a drink from the bar at the back of the building and go early as food runs out by around 1pm. Daily 6am–2pm.

Guayamara Point and Cumana

Some 3km north of Rampanalgas the Toco Main Road goes uphill to **Guayamara Point**, a jut in the headland whose wooden benches are perfect for a picnic or to admire fantastic views stretching south to Matura and Manzanilla. Just beyond, there's a lively stretch of open shoreline that invites a stop to drink in the sea breezes and sink your toes in the sand; the rough waters make swimming inadvisable.

The next village, another 4km north, is **CUMANA**, once the focal point for missionary work in the area, and still one of the larger communities in the north, with constant traffic at its petrol station, bars and a couple of mom-and-pop places where you might be able to grab a local meal. Cumana Depot Road leads off from the main road to a short swathe of **beach** protected by offshore reefs.

Toco

A few kilometres north of Cumana, **TOCO** is the largest community along this stretch of coast, an attractive, quiet fishing village with a distinctly antiquated air, its many ancient gingerbread houses slowly succumbing to the elements. This proud, close-knit place has one of the largest concentrations of Baptists in the Caribbean, which helped inspire one of its sons, the revered Trinidadian writer Earl Lovelace, to write *The Wine of Astonishment*, a novel about Baptist persecution under colonial rule (see "Books", page 277). Though most residents make their money from fishing or farming, much family land has been sold off to developers tempted by high real-estate prices for a proposed (but so far not delivered) ferry terminal here to serve Tobago, a mere 20km away and easily visible on clear days. Though the port idea has been discussed for some years, the project hit the headlines again in early 2018, when the PNM goverment announced a new consultation on the matter and a pledge to have a functional port open by 2021.

Toco enjoyed an earlier brief spell in the (local) limelight in 2012, when the whopping 84.58m throw by local lad **Keshorn Walcott** earned him the gold medal for javelin at the London Olympics – the first black male athlete to do so. Just 19 when he competed in London, Walcott was also the youngest ever Olympic javelin champion.

2

A placard on the Toco Main Road, just past the turn-off from the Valencia Road, celebrates his achievement.

Toco Folk Museum

Daily 8am–3.30pm or ring to make appointment • TT$5 adults, TT$3 children • ☎ 670 2554 • To get here, take Galera Rd (the right-hand turn from the main road as you enter town); the museum is housed in the Toco Secondary School

Started as a school project, the small **Toco Folk Museum** houses a diverse collection, from Amerindian artefacts and traditional Carnival costumes to antique bottles and household items, including a gramophone and some rare 78rpm calypso records, which can be played if requested. Natural history specimens range from local shells and snakeskins to huge beetles, a dried sunfish and many fish and animal bones, including dolphin skulls and a blackfin shark's jaw. The curators, mainly schoolteachers, are an excellent source of local history.

Toco beach

Past Toco Secondary School, Galera Road continues to a passable **beach**, a double horseshoe of brown and yellow sand, its calm waters protected by an offshore reef. It's a popular weekend spot for a cook-out among locals, who drive pick-ups loaded with food and drink right up to the shoreline. Fried fish, soft drinks and local sweets are sold from a couple of stalls; bear in mind, though, that the portable toilets are often closed due to lack of water.

Galera Point

Galera Road meanders onward past Toco beach to **Galera Point**, Trinidad's extreme eastern tip and site of the **Galera lighthouse**, officially renamed in 2012 in Keshorn Walcott's honour. A stocky tower built in 1897, the lighthouse flashes its red beacon over a treacherous stretch of sea known to fishermen as the "graveyard". Below the lighthouse is a windblown, rocky bluff – known as Fishing Rock – pounded by crashing waves that send up mists of salty spray; a blowhole under the rocks gives off occasional moans, and the point where the royal blue Caribbean Sea meets the murky, pastel blue Atlantic Ocean is easily visible out to sea. Local people maintain that Galera Point is haunted, with tales of car doors slamming when there is no car, and ghostly wails in the still of the night. The tales spring from an incident that occurred during a 1699 **rebellion** at a Spanish *encomienda* in San Rafael, in which Amerindians killed three Capuchin monks. Incensed, Spanish forces pursued the culprits to Galera, where they leapt off the cliffs to their deaths rather than be killed by the slave-masters.

ACCOMMODATION AND EATING   **TOCO**

Toco has a wonderfully remote **accommodation** option, great for a few days' retreat or just to hang out at the pool and have lunch. It doesn't have any dedicated **restaurants**, though there are a couple of bars on the main road that occasionally do a barbecue and serve basic food, and a sometimes open cookshop at the start of the Galera Rd. If you're planning to stay here, it's best to bring groceries with you, as little is available locally.

★ **Almond Park Estate** Hamburg Crown Trace ☎ 670 2580 or ☎ 681 2037, ⊛ jammevbeachresorts.com. Owned by Soca superstar Machel Montano and managed by his charming father Monty, who lives on site, this is a lovely retreat, just a 5min drive from Toco's beach in its own valley planted with hundreds of fruit trees (follow the signs for Hamburg Hollows to get here). Accommodation varies hugely from basic rooms with TV and shared kitchen to slightly pricier "standard" doubles (US$90), and more luxurious, spacious and modern rooms in the new block with satellite TV, microwave and fridge (US$110); there's also a larger apartment which sleeps 5–6 (US$180), as well as two self-contained two-bedroom cabins (US$150), one with a jacuzzi on its deck, the other (on the other side of the valley) with a lovely outdoor shower and plenty of privacy; all units have a/c. Another, even more remote cabin retreat is under construction. There's a large pool overlooking the valley, outdoor cooking facilities and a hammock-strewn veranda; a day-pass with use of a room is about TT$100. Fantastic meals available (breakfast TT$40, lunch and dinner TT$60); non-guests need to give advance notice. 📶 Basic double US$75

Mission and L'Anse Noir

West of Toco, the coast road (now the **Paria Main Road**) runs close to the cliffs and makes for a beautiful – if occasionally heart-stopping – drive. At the residential community of **Mission**, Mervyn Dillon Street honours the locally born West Indies cricketer, while further west the tiny village of **L'Anse Noire** has a small but safe beach. Beach house rentals are advertised by weatherworn roadside signs.

Sans Souci

There are several relatively safe beaches at **Sans Souci**, all boasting waves large enough to make this the island's **surfing** capital and a regular venue for competitions – as well as for egg-laying leatherbacks in season. From here you can see Tobago on a clear day (or its lights at night). Past the bay, Paria Main Road winds inland through impossibly lush rainforest, which lets up only at tiny **Monte Video** village, notable for the cold beers on sale at its lone bar.

Grande Riviere

With a spectacularly rugged curve of wave-whipped beach, capped by jungle-covered hills to each side and with a wide, clear river offering calm freshwater swimming, **GRANDE RIVIERE** is a truly beguiling place, far enough from Port of Spain to feel deliciously remote, but with a sprinkling of appealing places to stay and eat and a welcoming community-based approach to visitors, as many of whom are Trinidadians as foreign. Nicknamed "beyond God's back", this close-knit village owes much of its popularity with visitors to the **leatherback turtles** (see page 142) that lay their eggs in the coarse sand here; with some 500 females lumbering up on to the beach each night at the peak of the season, Grande Riviere is one of the most important leatherback nesting sites in the world, and certainly the one with the highest density of turtles visiting to lay. After the beautiful *Mt Plaisir Estate* hotel (see page 143) opened up right on the beach in the 1990s, a host of local residents and international entrepreneurs established other **guesthouses** and places to eat, but the end-of-the-road location has kept development low-key and the village remains unspoilt and idyllic. Interaction between visitors and local people has little of the money-oriented duplicity of resorts elsewhere, and local people tend to be genuinely welcoming to visitors.

There's plenty to do in Grande Riviere even if you don't visit during turtle season. Most people divide their time between the beach and river and the interior, where there are hosts of **waterfalls** and **river walks** as well as excellent **birdwatching** – this is one of the few places in Trinidad where you may be able to see the rare **piping guan** or pawi, distantly related to the cocrico of Tobago but a far finer specimen, with dark plumage splattered with white on the wings, a fanned tail, iridescent blue throat and a white crest at the top of its head.

Grande Riviere beach

To get to the beach, take the side road off the main road through the village, signposted for the *Mt Plaisir* hotel

Named after the wide, fast-flowing river that originates deep in the Northern Range and runs down to the sea at the eastern end of town, Grande Riviere boasts a superlative **beach**, a gentle curve of coarse sand with a few unobtrusive buildings. Tall headlands border the sand to the east, where you can take a freshwater bath in the river, while a good kilometre away the western end is sealed by rocky outcrops. Strong waves provide an invigorating swim (and can make swimming inadvisable between Nov and Jan), kicking up a spray that gives the cove a misty look, and give **leatherback turtles** the extra push they need to haul themselves up the sand at laying time; hawksbill and Olive Ridley turtles also nest here, though in far smaller numbers. As in Matura, note

2

LEATHERBACK TURTLES

Weighing up to 700kg and measuring up to a metre across, **leatherback turtles** have undergone few evolutionary alterations in their 150-million-year history. Named for the soft, leathery texture of their ridged, blue-grey carapace (more like a skin than a shell, which bleeds if cut), leatherbacks spend most of the year in cool temperate waters gorging on jellyfish. During the **egg-laying season** (roughly March–Aug), females swim thousands of miles, returning to the beach on which they hatched to lay their own eggs in the sand, a fascinating and somewhat moving process that usually takes place under the cover of night. Choosing a spot above the waterline, the turtle excavates a metre-deep egg chamber with her muscular back flippers, her body heaving with the effort and her eyes dripping mucous "tears" to protect against flying grains of sand. Once the hole is complete, she enters a trance-like state as she lays around a hundred soft-skinned white eggs, approximately the same size as a chicken's. After filling in the nest and compacting the sand, the turtles may make several decoy nests with their powerful front flippers to confuse predators. The process over, they lumber exhaustedly back to the water.

Leatherbacks can return to the same beach up to ten times per season – a necessary repetition, as only sixty percent of all eggs laid will mature into hatchlings (many are dug up by dogs or vultures) and only one or two eggs from each clutch will become fully grown turtles. **Hatchlings** emerge from the sand about sixty days later and make a moon-guided dash for the sea; if they're lucky, they'll escape being eaten by predators.

TURTLE-WATCHING

The best spots for **turtle-watching** are Grande Riviere and Matura in Trinidad (see pages 141 and 137), and Stonehaven and Turtle beaches in Tobago (see pages 216 and 218). Turtles also nest on many other beaches in both islands, from Paria to Pirate's Bay, but only the places listed above offer organized trips with trained guides. If you do want to go turtle-watching (or if you happen upon a laying turtle by chance), it's important to ensure that your presence doesn't disturb the laying process. Guides use infra-red lights when close to turtles, and it's best to avoid using torches anywhere on laying beaches; flash photography is a no-no – and bear in mind that in places such as Grande Riviere, many turtles lay in the early morning or even in full sunshine, allowing to photograph the event non-invasively. On laying beaches it's best to walk close to the shoreline so as to avoid compacting the sand and damaging nests, and of course never discard plastic bags on the beach, as many turtles die after eating them, mistaking them for jellyfish. Though they're rarely seen these days, souvenirs made from turtle-shells are illegal and are obviously not something you should consider buying.

that the beach is a protected area in the March–August laying season, and you'll need a permit to enter (see page 143). During this time, the sand is littered with the shells of empty eggs, some discarded by recent hatchlings, others dug up by turtles themselves as they create their own nests – the high density of turtles that visit Grande Riviere means that it's almost impossible for the leatherbacks to find a virgin space as the season wears on. If you're here late in the season, you'll also be able to see **hatchlings** emerging from nests and making a break for the sea. Those that emerge during the day are placed in boxes and released en masse around sunset, a beautiful and touching sight. Behind the beach, towards the centre, the GRNTGA (see page 143) have also set up sandboxes into which they transfer eggs from nests made too close to the waterline (and thus liable to flood), or laid by less common visitors such as hawksbills.

The liveliest part of the beach centres around the *Mt Plaisir* and *Grande Almandier* hotels, whose **bars** are favourite liming spots, and a lovely stall on the beach sells fine calabash art and locally made jewellery.

Grande Riviere Chocolate Company

Visitor information Centre • No set hours; call to arrange a tour • ☎ 493 4358

A part of the renaissance of all things cocoa in Trinidad (see page 238), the **Grande Riviere Chocolate Company** was established in 2016 under the auspices of the Alliance of Rural Communities umbrella group (see page 38). Based in the GRNTGA visitor centre and staffed mostly by the group's members, the company uses beans from a small-scale local supplier (who also ferments and dries the raw cocoa) to produce a delicious sixty-percent bars, one a plain dark chocolate, the other a very special cinnamon variety laced with locally grown spice; both are available to buy, as is cocoa powder. You can call ahead to arrange a **chocolate-making demonstration** (TT$100) here at the visitor centre; longer excursions include a walk through a local cocoa estate and a full lowdown on cocoa processing from bean to bar, plus a local meal (TT$300).

2

ACCOMMODATION

GRANDE RIVIERE

★ **Acajou Hotel** Paria Main Rd ☎ 670 3771, �ⓦ acajou trinidad.com. Six luxurious and well-ventilated hardwood cabins in a lush garden setting at the side of the river; a path winds 50m through trees to the beach. Each comes with ceiling fan, mosquito net, sundeck with hammock and a four-poster bed; two are family cabins (US$220) with a ceiling platform for children. There's a good restaurant on site (see page 144), and continental breakfast is included. Rates increase by about US$35/night during turtle season. ⓦ **US$130**

Le Grande Almandier Grand Riviere beach ☎ 670 1013, ⓦ legrandealmandier.com. Comfortable, pleasant rooms in an attractive and friendly hotel, situated off a large sea-facing sundeck right on the beach; rooms have a fan, a/c, cable TV, en-suite bathroom and small veranda (corner room #8 has the best views). There are also suites sleeping 4–6 (US$267–333) and, next door, self-contained two-bedroom villas (US$267). The beachfront bar/restaurant

(see page 144) is usually lively too. Hotel rates include full breakfast. ⓦ **US$167**

McHaven Cnr Bristol and Thomas streets ☎ 670 1014 or ☎ 304 6122, ⓔ ingridw6@yahoo.com. This yellow guesthouse perched on the hillside (take the road uphill opposite the beach turn-off) provides clean, homely rooms sleeping up to five, with a/c, fans, mosquito nets, satellite TV and en-suite bathroom. Fantastically friendly owner Ingrid is a font of local information, her husband Eric is "Roots" of the local band Roots and Branches, and their children are all GRNTGA tour guides. Guests can use the open-air kitchen and meals are available. Rates include breakfast. ⓦ **US$80**

★ **Mt Plaisir Estate** Grande Riviere beach ☎ 670 1868 or ☎ 670 2217, ⓦ mtplaisir.com. Grande Riviere's original hotel, and still the best. Right on the beach, this easy-going, eco-friendly place oozes rustic class rather than straightforward luxury; en-suite rooms are filled

---

GRANDE RIVIERE TURTLE-WATCHING AND TOURS

Most guides in the village work through the **Grande Riviere Nature Tour Guide Association** (GRNTGA), housed in a **Visitor Information Centre** (turtle season daily 7pm–2am, rest of the year 8am–1pm; ☎ 469 1288, ⓦ bit.ly/GRNTGA), set back from the road to the beach adjacent to *Mt Plaisir Estate* hotel. During the turtle-nesting season (March 1–August 31), the GRNTGA offer excellent **turtle-watching tours** (US$16 including permit); you go to the Information Centre on the evening you want to tour, pay your fee and collect your permit, and a guide will come and get you at your hotel when there are turtles on the beach; if you're not staying in town you can wait at the Information Centre. Group sizes vary, but are always kept pretty small, and guides provide an informed commentary on both the laying process and on the turtles themselves, as well as explaining the tagging programme being conducted in Grande Riviere. You can also ask for a personalized individual tour if you prefer; costs depend on group size. A tip for your guide at the end of any tour is appreciated.

GRNTGA also offer other trips, such as wonderful forest **hikes** (TT$200–300) from the abandoned cocoa and coffee plantations at its fringes and to the primary forest further inland. These encompass river swimming and exploration of the Alan River gorge and Homard Waterfall, as well as the bench trail from Matelot to Blanchisseuse. **Boat trips** (from TT$600/day) are also a fantastic way to explore the local coastline, head out to Tacaribe or Paria beach and waterfall, or do a little fishing; you're in an open pirogue, so wear a hat and plenty of sunscreen. Lifejackets are available. Grande Riviere's **birdwatching** is also sublime, with endless species (including the rare piping guan, or pawi) frequenting the area; GRNTGA have established a covered hide on land nearby, and also lead birding trips into the forest; GRNTGA member Nicholas (ⓔ nicocalexander@gmail. com) offers a 3hr birding trip for TT$240.

with locally made furniture, much of it refurbished antique pieces, while beautiful paintings hang on the walls and surfaces are decorated with driftwood sculptures. Those upstairs are more luxurious (US$185), with a lovely veranda overlooking the beach, while downstairs rooms are right on the sand; there are also two lofts sleeping six (US$225). All have a/c, fans and mosquito nets, and the on-site restaurant (see below) offers wonderful food. 🛜 (some areas only). US$165

EATING AND DRINKING

For evening **dining**, you're restricted to the hotels along the beach, which offer excellent food but (thanks to the village's remoteness) are all quite expensive; as well as *Maria's* there are a couple of snackshops on the main road, though opening hours vary. Basic groceries are available from the rum shop on the main street and a small supermarket opposite. **Nightlife** is nonexistent here save for the odd party at *McHaven* hotel's bar area, where the village band, Roots and Branches, perform most Sundays and the dancing goes on into the night. The hotel bars also offer cocktails and drinks, but things tend to close up shop pretty early here. The annual **fishermen's fete**, on the last weekend of June, is a raucous affair, with much music, dancing and drinking.

Le Grande Almandier Grand Riviere beach ☎ 670 2294, ⊕ legrandealmandier.com. A reliable place to eat, dishing up burgers, chicken and fish with fries (TT$65–125) plus sandwiches (TT$45) and more elaborate meat and fish mains (from TT$150). Dinner options (TT$160–250) include chicken in a white wine and mushroom sauce, braised lamb in a red wine sauce and fish with a garlic sauce. The bar is usually a lively spot for a drink. Daily 7.30am–9pm.

Lime Inn Acajou Hotel, Paria Main Rd ☎ 670 3771, ⊕ acajoutrinidad.com. A lovely setting on an open wooden terrace by the river's edge, with starters such as Greek salad, shrimp balls or gazpacho (TT$65–90), plus pizzas, bake and shark (TT$70/105) and mains (TT$145–180) from fish with lemongrass butter or coconut and lime sauce to various chicken option (curried, BBQ or bacon-wrapped breast filled with gorgonzola), roast duck or pork in a tamarind sauce. Good desserts, too. Daily 7.30–10am, 12.30–2pm & 6–8pm.

Maria's Paria Main Rd 353 4163. Inexpensive, tasty chicken and fish lunches with local sides (TT$35–45), plus evening offerings of pholouri, and chicken or fish with fries. Tues, Fri & Sat 11.30am-2pm & 5.30–8pm.

★ **Ylang Ylang** Mt Plaisir Estate, Grande Riviere beach ☎ 670 8381 or ☎ 670 2217, ⊕ mtplaisir.com. A lovely beachside setting, and delicious food made with fresh, often organic ingredients. Try the coconut bake with buljol or tomato/aubergine choka for breakfast (eggs, bacon and pancakes also available; TT$45–95). Otherwise, starters range from salads, fishcakes and calamari (TT$55–65); mains (TT$80–225) include pasta with pesto or bolognaise sauce; home-made ravioli; chicken with wine, capers and herbs; or a lovely array of seafood – fish comes roasted or stewed in coconut or with a white wine and cream sauce, shrimp with ginger and garlic, and there's roast lamb and steaks, too. Daily 8–10.30am, 12.30–2.30pm & 6.30–8.30pm.

Shark River

Of the many plank-lined bridges that pepper the Paria Main Road past Grande Riviere, the one crossing **Shark River** is the largest. A popular swimming spot, the river has a couple of deep **pools** from the sea all the way upstream; during holiday weekends, campers pitch tents along its banks. Walking upriver makes a great excursion, though you have to clamber over some mighty rocks to reach the best pools. You'll probably need a guide, perhaps from the GRNTGA (see page 143), to negotiate several tributaries and the occasional swing off into the bush.

Matelot

There's not much to keep you in the hamlet of **MATELOT**, the last settlement on the Paria Main Road before the tarmac ends and wild and undeveloped bench trail to Paria and ultimately Blanchisseuse, 19km to the west, begins (see page 118). A track leads down to the fishermen's beach, houses meander up the hillsides, while swimming is possible in the **Matelot River** – follow the main road to the left and bear right. The adjacent football field sees plenty of action at dusk, and in one corner a large TDC sign points the way to the **Madamas River Nature Walk**, the start of the bench trail. Locals have formed the Pawi Sports Culture & Eco Club, a group of **tour**

guides (see below) who can take you along the coast and into the forest inland of Matelot, which is crisscrossed by hunters' trails; one of the best treks is the half-day hike to 3m **Matelot Waterfall**, with its wide, deep pool. Like their counterparts in Matura, Pawi members are part of the monitoring and protection programme for leatherback turtles.

ACTIVITIES   MATELOT

Hiking guides Contact Renwick "Pawi Boy" Roberts (☎ 702 0789), or ask for him around in the village, to arrange guided walks into the surrounding forest (from TT$300).

2

Central Trinidad

SCARLET IBIS, CARONI SWAMP

Central Trinidad

Central Trinidad encompasses a fantastic variety of landscapes. Alongside the brash commercial centre of Chaguanas, the largest conurbation in the Central region, the industrialized west coast holds unexpected natural oases such as the Caroni Swamp, home of the strikingly crimson scarlet ibis – T&T's national bird – while to the south the peaceful pools of Pointe-a-Pierre Wildfowl Trust boast an unlikely location within a huge oil refinery.

In the middle of the island, the flatlands of the **Caroni Plains** are dotted with the somnolent villages that characterize this overwhelmingly rural region, formerly dominated by sugar-cane cultivation and where many still make their living from the land. The plains rise gently to the wooded **Central Range** and **Montserrat Hills** to the south, and are bordered to the east by the remarkable **Aripo Savannas**, a beautiful protected area and a prime birdwatching spot. There's more excellent birdwatching along the banks of the **Caroni Arena** reservoir and the **Navet Dam**, while the **Tamana caves** make for an awesome spectacle at dusk, when millions of bats fly out to feed. To the northeast of the region, the hectic market centre of **Sangre Grande** is the gateway to the east coast, where the road runs parallel to the sea for some 46km and offers a spectacular drive past the stunning **Manzanilla Beach**, where the **Cocal** avenue of palms forms a coastal barrier that protects the starkly beautiful **Nariva Swamp**, and on to drowsy **Mayaro**, a popular local getaway with another spectacular undeveloped beach.

Central Trinidad's population is mostly descended from the Indian indentured labourers who arrived in Trinidad during the 1840s following the abolition of slavery, and today this heritage is very much in evidence. Hindu shrines and prayer flags adorn front gardens and ornate temples are ten-a-penny, but the **Waterloo Temple**, sitting on the brown waters of the Gulf of Paria south of Chaguanas, is particularly stunning, as is the towering **Hanuman Murti** statue at the nearby **Sri Dattatreya temple**. Both are given some context by the nearby **Indian Caribbean Museum** at Carapichaima, which provides a fascinating insight into Indo-Trinidadian history and culture. And if you visit during the Divali celebrations (see page 36), you can see some of the country's most intricate and spectacular *deya* creations, which light up the community of **Felicity**.

Accommodation in untouristy "Central" is minimal; there are a few options on the west coast geared towards business travellers, but this isn't a particularly enticing place to stay, and it's far better to base yourself in Port of Spain or San Fernando and see the area on day-trips. The only exception is Mayaro on the east coast, where a string of beach houses and hotels offer the opportunity of some Trini-style beach time. As for **eating**, there are innumerable hole-in-the wall places selling delicious roti and Creole food, while doubles and other Indian snacks are also easy to find, as are fast-food joints, Chinese takeaways and, of course, **rum shops**.

The west coast

Trinidad's **west coast** is as far as many visitors venture into the centre of the island, heading down to the **Caroni Swamp** for a boat tour in search of scarlet ibis, and perhaps

Highlights

1 Caroni Swamp Take a lazy boat trip through this maze of mangroves to see the flocks of scarlet ibis that swoop in en masse to roost each evening. See page 152

2 Carapichaima Waterloo Temple in the Sea, the gigantic statue of monkey-god Hanuman and the Indian Caribbean Museum provide an impressive insight into Trinidad's Indian culture See page 155

3 Sunrise at Aripo Savannas Take in a dramatic light show through moriche palm trees and a fantastic range of birdlife at this most atmospheric of Trinidadian landscapes. See page 163

4 Mount Tamana bat caves Walk up through cocoa groves to witness the awesome exodus of over a million bats as they leave their daytime roost by twilight to search for food. See page 164

5 The Cocal Where else in the touristy Caribbean could you find an unbroken 24km of sand flanked by nothing more obtrusive than coconut trees swaying in the breeze? See page 166

6 Nariva Swamp A kayak is the ideal way to explore this important wetland area, where a freshwater ecosystem supports a vast array of wildlife. See page 167

7 Mayaro A world away from the sanitized Caribbean seashore, Mayaro offers beachtime Trini-style: football on the sand, cookouts and endless swathes of golden sand. See page 168

HIGHLIGHTS ARE MARKED ON THE MAP ON PAGE 150

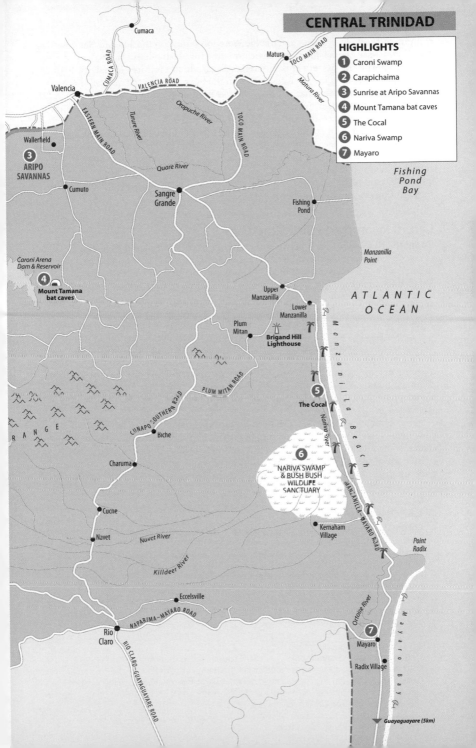

CENTRAL TRINIDAD

HIGHLIGHTS

1. Caroni Swamp
2. Carapichaima
3. Sunrise at Aripo Savannas
4. Mount Tamana bat caves
5. The Cocal
6. Nariva Swamp
7. Mayaro

Cumaca

Matura

CUMACA ROAD

TOCO MAIN ROAD

Matura River

Valencia

VALENCIA ROAD

Oropuche River

TOCO MAIN ROAD

Turure River

EASTERN MAIN ROAD

Wallerfield

3
ARIPO SAVANNAS

Quare River

Cumuto

Sangre Grande

Fishing Pond

Fishing Pond Bay

Caroni Arena Dam & Reservoir

4
Mount Tamana bat caves

Manzanilla Point

Upper Manzanilla

ATLANTIC OCEAN

Lower Manzanilla

Plum Mitan

Brigand Hill Lighthouse

 O R A N G E

PLUM MITAN ROAD

CUNAPO SOUTHERN ROAD

Biche

5
The Cocal

Nariva River

Manzanilla Beach

Charuma

6
NARIVA SWAMP & BUSH BUSH WILDLIFE SANCTUARY

Cucne

Navet

Nuvet River

Kernaham Village

MANZANILLA–MAYARO ROAD

Point Radix

Killdeer River

Eccelsville

Rio Claro

NAPARIMA–MAYARO ROAD

Ortoise River

7
Mayaro

Mayaro Bay

RIO CLARO–GUAYAGUAYARE ROAD

Radix Village

▼ Guayaguayare (5km)

stopping off for a look at the remarkable **Waterloo Temple in the Sea** and **Hanuman Murti** statue at Carapichaima. But there are some interesting lesser-known attractions, from the family-run **pottery** at Edinburgh village, which produces industrial quantities of the *deya* lights used in Divali festivities, to the busy and vibrant market at the sprawling town of **Chaguanas**, perhaps the most visitor-friendly place on the island to check out all matter of tropical fruit and veg. The area is also pretty easy-access in terms of **transport**, with turn-offs from the Uriah Butler and Solomon Hochoy highways to all of the small villages and settlements, and plenty of maxis from Port of Spain to Chaguanas, from where route taxis depart for all points in the area. The precursor to the highway, and a slower if more interesting route, the **Southern Main Road** (SMR) runs parallel to (but quite a way east of) the Uriah Butler Highway from Curepe, but crosses over onto the western side of the highway at Chaguanas and continues south through **Couva** and **Pointe-a-Pierre**.

Caroni Swamp and Bird Sanctuary

Bordering the Gulf of Paria between the mouths of the Caroni and Madame Espagnole rivers, **Caroni Swamp and Bird Sanctuary** is one of Trinidad's most popular attractions, situated a few kilometres south of the East–West Corridor, and accessed via the Uriah Butler Highway. As well as serving as a roosting spot for flocks of elegant and spectacularly red **scarlet ibis**, T&T's national bird, these forty square kilometres of tidal lagoons, marshland and mangrove forest are home to 157 species of birds, while caimans, snakes, opossums, racoons and silky anteaters live in the water and mangrove canopy. Rich in fish and oysters, the swamp is also a spawning ground for massive tarpon and groupers (the largest caught here weighed 250lb). It was designated a protected wildlife area in 1953, but industrial waste pollution remains a problem, and poaching is an ongoing issue; its flock of **flamingos** have been all but decimated, and the scarlet ibis is targeted by hunters, despite the protestations of local environmentalists. Nonetheless, it remains a beguiling and beautiful place, and is well worth a visit.

Most people visit Caroni for a **motorboat tour** (see below) of the swamp; two companies offer trips aboard open pirogues that chug slowly through a maze of channels into the mangroves. These have an otherworldly appearance: some have twisted aerial roots growing downwards into the water, while others have roots that grow upwards, emerging from the murky depths like stalagmites. Guides point out

---

CARONI TOURS

Caroni boat tours leave daily at 4pm from the assembly point in the car park and last two and half hours; advance booking is advisable (though not essential), and you should get there by 3.40pm. Of the two operators, **Nanan's** (☎645 1305 or ☎681 8274, ⊛nananecotours.com; boat tour US$10, double-kayak tour US$40) is the larger, a professional outfit whose numerous boats often carry up to thirty people; **Madoo's** (☎664 0458 or ☎769 0787, ⊛bit.ly/Madoo; boat tour US$15, double-kayak tour US$50) offer more personalized trips, with smaller groups, and are better for serious birders; they also offer guided kayak trips. Whichever operator you choose, try to sit at the front of the boat to avoid engine noise and fumes, and always douse yourself in plenty of repellent before you board as mosquitoes here are rapacious. It's also a good idea to bring binoculars or a powerful zoom lens, as it's not possible to get close to the roosting spots without disturbing the ibis.

Another option for **kayak tours** – and **SUP tours** – is Paria Springs (3hr; US$115; ☎620 8240, ⊛pariasprings.com); trips include round-trip transport from Port of Spain, instruction on kayak/SUP techniques, and the paddle at dusk through a narrow channel to the roosting site, from where a boat collects you and motors you back to base. You'll get wet so bring a change of clothes and waterproof bags for cameras/phones.

birds, plants and animals of interest – you'll usually see snakes and common wetland birds such as egrets and blue herons – but the main attraction are the scarlet ibis, which roost on mangrove islands in the middle of open lagoons far into the swamp. Once the boat engines shudder to a halt, a spectacular scene unfolds as thousands of birds flock in, gradually turning their preferred clump of trees a vibrant red. This intense plumage owes its pigment to carotene, derived from the bird's main prey – shrimp, worms and fiddler and tree-climbing crabs. In April and May, breeding pairs construct flat, open nests in the mangroves; once laid, their eggs incubate for just under a month before all-black hatchlings emerge – it takes up to three years for their diet to replace the dark feathers with a brilliant crimson.

The noise from the boat engines and the large group sizes can take away from the beauty of the swamp, however, so an excellent alternative to the conventional trip are the **kayak** or **SUP tours** (see page 152), which enable you to glide silently through the channels at a slower pace, increasing your chances of seeing more animal- and bird life.

ARRIVAL AND DEPARTURE CARONI SWAMP AND BIRD SANCTUARY **3**

By car Driving to the swamp from Port of Spain, it's best to leave at around 2.30pm to catch the 4pm tour, as rush-hour traffic can be terrible. From the Churchill Roosevelt Hwy, you turn off to the south via the flyover onto the Uriah Butler Hwy, and then take the first exit with a bridge over the highway (there was no signpost at the time of writing); cross the highway and follow the signs to the large car park.

By taxi and organized tour A taxi to and from Port of Spain will cost around TT$400 including waiting time. All Trinidad's tour operators (see page 38) can take you to Caroni, often as the final stop on a day-long tour. Nanan's (see page 152) also offer transfers from Port of Spain (US$45 for 2 people, including boat tour).

Chaguanas

The sprawling settlement of **CHAGUANAS** is one of the island's oldest and largest towns. Ranged around the junction of Chaguanas Main Road and the old Southern Main Road, **central Chaguanas** is a busy amalgam of shops and streetside stalls ranged around three large malls: Mid Centre, the slightly dilapidated Centre Pointe and Centre City. All are great places to find bargains in shoes and clothes, including imports direct from India.

Taking its name from its original inhabitants (the Chaguanes Amerindian tribe), Chaguanas was pretty much a one-horse town until Indian indentured labourers came in the 1840s to work on nearby sugar and cocoa estates. By the 1880s Chaguanas had become the most important **market town** in central Trinidad, connected to Port of Spain by rail lines and steamer ships. As the sugar industry declined in the early twentieth century, many Indians moved into professions such as journalism and law, creating the middle-class intelligentsia from which **V.S. Naipaul** emerged and which served as the milieu for some of his early novels. Though the trains and steamers are long gone, the construction of the Uriah Butler and Solomon Hochoy highways has ensured that the town remains well connected to the rest of the island, while the 1970s **oil boom** gave Chaguanas a new lease of life; conveniently located near the oil-rich south, it has developed into a shopping centre for those who prefer not to travel all the way into Port of Spain. The swanky Lange Park suburb, alongside out-of-town shopping mall Price Plaza, attests to the area's continuing prosperity.

The markets

Occupying the narrow alleys stretching back from the southern end of Chaguanas Main Road, the big, old-fashioned **market** is highly absorbing: the pavements are chock-a-block with wooden stalls selling dirt-cheap clothes, ornaments and accessories, while the giant **produce market**, in an industrial-style hangar bedecked with bright red

3

PHAGWAH

A joyous celebration of the new year and the arrival of spring, the Hindu Holi festival – known in the Caribbean as **Phagwah** (pronounced "pag-wah") – is held around the first full moon in March to mark the end of the Hindu calendar's twelfth month (Phagun). Upbeat and lighthearted – to the horror of more traditional Hindus, who consider this attitude *adharamic* (anti-religious) – Phagwah celebrations are massive outdoor gatherings that represent a symbolic triumph of light over darkness and happiness over suffering. In Indian religious mythology, the festival commemorates the death of Holika, the sister of evil king Hiranyakashyapu, who repeatedly tried to murder his son Prahalad because of the latter's insistence on worshipping Vishnu as the only God. Immune to flames, Holika carried Prahalad into a fire, but the gods ensured that she burned to death; her brother was later slain by Vishnu. Holika's conflagration is re-enacted the night before the main festivities, when sins amassed in the previous year are ceremonially consumed by the flames of large bonfires.

The main festivities revolve around traditions such as the singing of devotional folk songs called **chowtals**, sung in a mix of English and Hindi and composed specifically for Phagwah to tell the story of the festival, normally accompanied by goatskin *dholak* drums and brass cymbals called *ghanj*. Local businesses sponsor *chowtal* competitions in the weeks preceding Phagwah, and the winners perform on the day itself. The principal focus of the festival, though, is the **throwing of colours** – intense dyes of various hues, including the fuchsia-pink *abir*, are strewn about as powder or mixed with water and squirted from a plastic bottle renamed a *pichakaaree*; participants wear white to make the most of the ensuing glorious mess. As the festivities wear on, classical Indian dancers display their movements and chutney soca fuels the more risqué dancing. Games add to the fun; adults participate in **makhan chor**, where teams form a human pyramid in order to grab a suspended flag; and children compete in roti-eating contests in which skins are strung through the middle and tied in a line to be eaten with no hands allowed.

PHAGWA PRACTICALITIES

Celebrations tend to begin around 1pm and are held all over Trinidad; foreigners should expect to get very dirty as they're extra special targets for dye throwing. In the north, **Aranguez Savannah**, off the Eastern Main Road, is particularly lively. At **Chaguanas**, the car park of the National Council of Indian Culture is a popular location, as is the Kendra Phagwah Festival in an open space on Ragoonan Road, off Longdenville Old Road. Bear in mind none are widely publicized – to find the exact date, you'll have to scan the community events listings in the newspapers, contact a tour guide, or ask around.

wrought-iron arches, is a feast for the eyes, with wizened stallholders presiding over stands groaning under the weight of plantain, dasheen, peppers, ground provisions and artfully arranged piles of fruit. Main trading days are Friday to Sunday, when the markets and the entire central area buzz with activity.

Lion House

Chaguanas Main Rd · Closed to the public · ⓦ thelionhouse.com

West along Chaguanas Main Road from the market, the stocky, arch-fronted **Lion House** was the birthplace and childhood home of Trinidad's most celebrated writer, **V.S. Naipaul**, who was awarded the Nobel Prize for Literature in 2002. A fine example of classic North Indian architecture, with the eponymous lions adorning stout columns supporting its grand arcade, it was built in 1926 by the Pundit Capildeo, and became the residence of the Naipaul family when the writer's father Seepersad married Capildeo's daughter. Naipaul's 1961 novel *A House for Mr Biswas* describes growing up here surrounded by his stepmother's wealthy, religious and domineering family. Still owned by the Capildeo family, the Lion House is not open to the public, and sadly it's in a bad state of repair these days.

ARRIVAL AND DEPARTURE   **CHAGUANAS**

By public transport From Port of Spain, Chaguanas maxis depart from City Gate and drop off next to the Mid Centre Mall, as do route taxis, which depart from Broadway, Port of Spain. PTSC buses stop next to *KFC* near the Uriah Butler Hwy. Maxis and route taxis to the rest of the west coast depart from the transportation stands at the Mid Centre Mall.

By organized tour Maze-like Chaguanas is an easy place to get lost in, and is best visited as part of a tour; Island Experiences (☎ 621 0407 or ☎ 781 6235, ⓦ islandexperiencestt.com) include the markets in their all-day island tour.

EATING AND ENTERTAINMENT

There's no real reason to stay in Chaguanas but there is plenty of fantastic Indian food available from the legions of **roti shops** and **doubles stalls** all over town; the malls also have air-conditioned restaurants serving Creole and Chinese food. The upmarket **Price Plaza** shopping mall, just off the highway a little way out of town, has international chain stores alongside American-style restaurants and fast-food joints, and a MovieTowne **cinema** (☎ 627 8277, ⓦ movietowne.com).

Felicity

A couple of kilometres south of Chaguanas centre, on the western side of the highway, the Southern Main Road (known here as the Felicity Main Road) is bordered to the west by acre upon acre of arable fields, some still used for the cultivation of sugar cane. The roadside village of **FELICITY** is home to a predominantly Indian community, with many homes fronted by mini shrines and forests of colourful prayer flags. Come **Divali**, Felicity residents are particularly lavish with their decorations, and this is one of the best places in Trinidad to take a look at the beautiful displays, most of which are in front gardens or open lots just off the main road, along Pierre Road and Cancadee Road. Complicated bamboo structures are fashioned to hold some 100,000 *deyas* (pottery bowls filled with oil and a wick to light), and fairy lights are strung up above the streets, which give off an incredible glow in the evening. There are also tassa drummers, Indian dancers and fireworks, as well as loads of delicious food to sample. Since traffic slows to a standstill during Divali, it's best to park closer to Chaguanas and walk to Felicity (about fifteen minutes).

Edinburgh

Right at the side of the SMR in otherwise unremarkable **EDINBURGH VILLAGE**, look out for the ornate, white-painted **Edinburgh Temple** on the western side of the road, its walls, arches and turrets richly embellished with plaster reliefs and with a colourful shrine to Kali outside. Interfaith services are conducted each Sunday in the richly decorated **interior**, with its brightly painted plaster statues of the Hindu deities.

Radika's pottery

Southern Main Rd, Edinburgh Village • Mon–Sat 10am–5pm • Tours TT$20 • ☎ 789 4079

The area around Felicity and Edinburgh village has long been known for its **potteries**, which alongside vases and plant-pots churn out the tiny *deyas* each Divali: clay bowls which are filled with oil and a wick, used to light up beautiful bamboo sculptures during the festivities. One of the oldest operators is **Radika's**, where you can browse the goods in the main shop and take a tour of the pottery works in the back. The clay is kneaded by foot to remove stones and lumps, then hand-rolled or shaped on a wheel before being fired in a huge wood-fuelled kiln.

Carapichaima

The collective name for the cluster of villages on and around the SMR south of Edinburgh, **CARAPICHAIMA**, like its neighbours, is home to a large Indian population, whose forefathers settled here to work on the vast sugar estates that once covered the area. This was once prime **sugar territory**, first planted with fields of swaying sugar cane when the land was owned by the Tate & Lyle sugar producers, but since the state-owned Caroni sugar company closed down in 2003, the industry has gone into decline and the fields turned over to other crops. Today, Carapichaima is wholeheartedly Trinidadian melange: along the central **Waterloo Main Road**, the Church of Zion and Presbyterian school sit side by side with a healthy quota of rum shops, while Hindu prayer flags flutter next to trees strung with blue plastic bottles that traditionally ward off *maljo*, or bad luck. Nowhere else is the creative potential of Trinidad's cosmopolitan cultural mix more clearly visible than at Carapichaima's **Carnival** celebrations, where the length of the main road is lit up with lanterns each night, and a masquerade of traditional carnival characters such as robbers, jab jabs and jamettes (see page 262), combined with Indian drumming and costume, draws hundreds of visitors – this and other aspects of Indian culture are covered at the excellent **Indian Caribbean Museum**.

As well as the museum, Carapichaima is home to two of Trinidad's most spectacular Hindu sites, the ornate **Sri Dattatreya Temple**, with its towering **Hanuman statue**, and the unique **Waterloo Temple in the Sea**, while the coastline here offers excellent **birdwatching**, with both Waterloo and nearby Brick Field good places to see skimmers, wattled jacanas, long-winged harriers, ospreys, neotropic cormorants, plovers, ruddy turnstones and the striking red-breasted blackbird. Courtenay "Bushman" Rooks of Paria Springs Tours (see page 39) organizes regular birding tours in the area.

Sri Dattatreya Temple and the Hanuman Murti

Orange Field • Temple daily 9am–noon & 5–7pm • Free • No photography in the temple; donation accepted for taking photos of outdoor statuary • Modest dress is required (no uncovered shoulders or above-knee skirts or shorts), and shoes need to be left outside • ☎ 673 5328, ⓦ sridattatreyayogacentrett.com • The centre is 200m up from the junction of the Orange Field and Waterloo roads

Dotted with stunning devotional statuary, the spectacular **Sri Dattatreya** complex is easily one of Trinidad's highlights and a spiritual centre for Hindus islandwide.

INDO-TRINIDADIAN RELIGIONS

T&T's largest religious denomination after Catholicism, **Hinduism** was brought to Trinidad in the nineteenth century by indentured Indian workers, whose wide-ranging geographical and social origins reflected the huge differences in religious practice and status in India. As they settled into their new life in the Caribbean, Indo-Trinidadians created a hybrid Hinduism that's unique to the island. One of the main differences to India is the lack of a **caste system** in T&T. The strong friendships forged during the passage over – which gave rise to the term *jihaji bhai* ("ship brother") – transcended differences in social status, and many new-found friends chose to settle together and work the same plantations. Slowly, the caste system was eroded; only the priestly Brahmin caste, whose pundits officiate at religious rites, has survived in Trinidad.

Rituals have also been modified. Prayers for blessing – **puja** – are lengthy processes in India, each with a specific meaning and directed towards a particular deity, but in Trinidad, several *puja* are often combined, with multiple deities involved. At sacred places such as Waterloo, you'll often see the scattered remains of articles required for *puja* – incense, flowers, pictures (*murtis*) of the deity to be honoured – while the smell of the oils, herbs, spices and ghee offered to the gods hangs heavy in the air; bamboo poles topped with a **jhandi** (prayer flag) in the colours of the relevant deity are also essential to *puja*, and you'll see clusters of them at *puja* sites island-wide as well as fluttering in the gardens of Hindu households.

Though you'd hardly believe it judging by the proliferation of grandiose mosques, **Islam** actually has a smaller worship base, with just six percent of the population practising Muslims. For the most part, Islamic religious practice has changed little since arriving in T&T, save for the festival of **Hosay** (see page 72), which has grown from a rather sombre ceremony to a Carnivalesque affair, much to the distress of the devout.

From the enormous car park, you pass by a gilded statue of a camel-like beast before entering the complex proper. To the left, towering over the whole complex – and the entire area – is Sri Dattatreya's majestic, 26m-high **Hanuman Murti**, the largest representation of the Hindu monkey god outside of India. Consecrated in June 2003, the statue was a gift from the temple's spiritual leader, Ganapathi Sachchidananda Swami. Its workmanship rivals anything to be found in Asia, with beautifully detailed, colourful relief work courtesy of twenty expert craftsmen sent over from India by the Swami.

Past the *murti*, there's a smaller Hanuman under a richly embellished, open-sided shrine topped by a frothing gold roof, beyond which is the salmon-pink **temple** itself. Both the largest in Trinidad and the only one in the ornate, single-storey Dravidian South Indian style, it was built in 2003, again by craftsmen from Tamil Nadu in India, and is a popular venue for weddings as well as a place of worship. The entrance is flanked by two elegant blue-and-gold elephants and, at the main doors, a pair of female dancers, and its interior is awash with superb and brightly coloured bas-reliefs of Hindu deities, and features four shrines topped by crown-like *vimana*. Visitors are welcome to look around. The complex is also home to a **yoga centre**, with classes each Wednesday evening.

Indian Caribbean Museum

Waterloo Main Rd • Wed–Sun 10am–5pm • Free • ☎ 673 7007, ⓦ icmtt.org

Waterloo Village is home to the **Indian Caribbean Museum**, the only permanent exhibition of its kind in the region. Put together with extensive research from both local and expatriate sources, it's a thoughtful and absorbing collection that documents the Indian experience in Trinidad across Hindu, Muslim and Christian religions, something that often gets overlooked in a society whose culture can be dominated by the calypso, soca and steel pan of the Afro-Trinidadian population. Exhibits include letters and photographs of early **Indian arrivals** on the island and models of the ships that brought the first immigrants, while sugar is a running theme throughout, with agricultural tools and photos documenting rural life and indentureship, and information on the phasing out of **sugar cane** attesting to the psychological importance of the crop to Indo-Trinidadians. Traditional clothing, paintings and musical instruments are all well represented, as are marijuana pipes – cannabis was originally brought to the Caribbean by Indians, and according to many Hindus it was only outlawed when rum factories were built, so as to promote consumption of the new drug of choice.

Religious festivals and icons form a sizeable part of the collection, from displays on Divali and Phagwah to tassa drums and photos of early *tadjas* from the Muslim Hosay commemoration (see page 72), as well as a translation of the Bible into Hindi by nineteenth-century Presbyterian missionaries. The construction of Hindu schools from the 1950s onwards holds particular significance, as this is seen as the point at which Hindus began to be accepted into Trinidadian society. The museum's knowledgeable curator is often on hand to answer any questions about the exhibits or wider issues.

Waterloo Temple in the Sea

Waterloo Main Rd • Daily 6am–6pm, though these times depend on when the caretaker arrives • Donation accepted • ☎ 681 4435, ⓦ templeinthesea.wordpress.com

Waterloo Main Road meanders towards the sea, overlooked to the left by a row of swaying royal palm trees planted during the heyday of the sugar era. Intermingled with the concrete buildings that line the road are a few remaining some pretty wooden buildings; on the right-hand side, look out for the former train station, once a stop on the Port of Spain–San Fernando line. Just before you meet the sea, the old Anglican cemetery on the left includes a plot reserved for Muslim burials, and just beyond this, a car park and information board (and, through a hedge, traditional Hindu cremation pyres at the water's edge) mark the site of the unfailingly impressive **Waterloo Temple**. A gleaming white onion-shaped dome, it sits at the end of a concrete causeway surrounded by the Gulf of Paria at high tide, and at low tide by extensive mud flats. It's a stunning setting, inordinately peaceful and spiritual, the shoreline littered with broken coconut shells and fruits left by Hindus during *puja* ceremonies, and legions of flags (*jhandi*) – representing prayers and offerings – flapping in the breeze.

The octagonal temple – used by the local Hindu community for weddings and *puja* – covers an area of over 100 square metres, with coloured-glass windows that enable you to see the brightly painted stone and marble gods inside. Anyone can enter the temple, provided they remove their shoes first, though it's often locked up; caretakers may open up for you if you ask. The **causeway**, meanwhile, is a good vantage point from which to view the **birds**, including terns, gulls, whimbrels and skimmers, that feed in the mud flats throughout the year.

Back at the car park, there's also a life-size statue of **Sewdass Sadhu**, an Indian labourer whose zeal and persistence enabled the temple to be built. Sadhu constructed a temple on the shore here in 1947, on land owned by the state sugar monopoly Caroni, but the government bulldozed the structure five years later, and sent him to jail for fourteen days. He then decided to rebuild his temple in the sea, where no permission was required, and struggled single-handedly for the next 25 years, using a bicycle to carry the foundation rocks out into the water and placing barrels full of concrete on the sea floor at low tide. Help finally came in 1995, when the 150th anniversary of the arrival of Indians in Trinidad inspired the government to declare the temple an Unemployment Relief Project. With labourers paid by the state to rebuild the structure, the causeway was added and the temple swiftly completed.

ARRIVAL AND DEPARTURE   CARAPICHAIMA

By car Carapichaima is most easily accessed from the Freeport exit of the Solomon Hochoy Hwy: head west crossing the Southern Main Rd at St Mary's village (look for the *KFC*); at the next junction, turn right onto Orange Field Rd for the Sri Dattatreya Temple and left for the museum and Waterloo Temple.

By public transport You can take a route taxi from the Mid Centre Mall in Chaguanas to St Mary's Junction on the Southern Main Rd just beyond the Orange Field Rd turn-off, where you pick up another taxi to the junction of Orange Field and Waterloo Main roads. Route taxis ply the lengthy Waterloo Main Rd from Orange Field to Waterloo Temple.

Point Lisas

South of Carapichaima, the SMR enters Trinidad's industrial heartland, with the coast lined by a series of small communities interspersed with oil refineries and petrochemical plants. The liveliest settlement in the area is **Couva**, with a few lovely gingerbread houses surviving among the concrete, and several places to eat and drink lined up along the road. Just south of Couva, a roundabout marks the turn-off to the massive **Point Lisas Industrial Complex**, whose belching chimneys are visible from miles around. The complex was built during the oil boom years of the 1970s to produce liquefied natural gas, steel and fertilizers (it has the unfortunate distinction of being the largest exporter of fertilizer in the world), but, industrial as it is, Point Lisas still has its wildlife. Every year between December and June, thousands of **blue crabs** make the hazardous journey across the main road from the swampland beside the complex to lay eggs in the sea; given the road traffic here, many don't make it, leaving a crunchy trail of broken shells on the tarmac. Just by the turn-off for Point Lisas, **Atlantic Plaza** offers air-conditioned respite from the heat in the form of a *Rituals* coffee shop and food court.

Pointe-a-Pierre Wildfowl Trust

Petrotrin Oil Refinery, Pointe-a-Pierre • Mon–Fri 9am–5pm, Sat & Sun 10am–5pm; tours 9.30am & 1.30pm • TT$20 • ☎ 658 4200, ext 2512, ⓦ papwildfowltrust.org • From Port of Spain or San Fernando, leave the Solomon Hochoy Hwy at the Gasparillo–Pointe-a-Pierre exit and follow the signs west through the Petrotrin Oil Refinery; otherwise the turning is signposted from the SMR

Perhaps the most unlikely bird sanctuary in Trinidad, the remarkable **Pointe-a-Pierre Wildfowl Trust** is a series of greenery-swathed pools right in the midst of the huge Petrotrin Oil Refinery at Pointe-a-Pierre, just north of San Fernando. The reserve came into being in 1966, when a hunter who worked at the refinery realized that wildfowl stocks were diminishing, and set aside an area within the complex to breed the birds. In time it became an established reserve, supported financially by the Canadian and British governments as well as by Shell – though barely at all by Petrotrin itself. Today, the reserve's attractively landscaped grounds surround two lakes filled with lotus and water lilies and bordered by wooden walkways. Many **rare bird species** can be seen here, including wild Muscovy duck, red-billed whistling duck, white-cheeked pintail and red-capped cardinal. Notwithstanding the fact that some of the rarer birds, including scarlet ibis, are caged within an aviary to allow breeding programmes to continue, the reserve doesn't feel at all like a zoo. Indeed, the ibis breeding programme has been something of a landmark project, particularly as some of the released birds have chosen to stay on the site, allowing visitors their only opportunity in Trinidad to see wild scarlet ibis up close; at Caroni Swamp, home of the scarlet ibis (see page 152), you're usually some distance from the ibis roosting trees.

The **learning centre** at the entrance has photographic displays of the reserve's flora and fauna, plus a small collection of shells and insect specimens alongside Amerindian artefacts, with an informative account of the culture and belief systems of Trinidad's original inhabitants. The trust's guides are vastly knowledgeable not only about the birdlife, but also the medicinal qualities of Trinidad's indigenous plants, and though you can explore the reserve independently, you'll get a lot more from your visit if you arrange for a tour. The best time to visit is before 11am or after 3pm, as many birds hide in the shade during the hottest part of the day; it's also well worth visiting on a Thursday or Sunday to coincide your visit with a meal at the excellent on-site restaurant, *Freebird* (see below).

EATING
POINT-A-PIERRE WILDFOWL TRUST

★ **Freebird** 2 Petrea Rd, Petrotrin Complex ☎ 658 5322, ⓦ bit.ly/freebirdTT. On a greenery-wreathed veranda just steps from the Wildfowl Trust lakes, this great new fine-dining restaurant offers wonderful food, much of it made with vegetables grown in the on-site kitchen garden, and all beautifully and delicately presented. The seasonally inspired Sunday brunch spread (TT$275) might include smoked-fish buljol on cassava hash with charred peppers and eggs, or roasted squash frittata with pumpkin leaves, goat's cheese and chimichurri, plus sweet treats such as brioche French toast with Cointreau mascarpone, strawberry butter and banana brulée. Thursday afternoon tea (TT$195) runs from beef tenderloin with horseradish aioli and rocket pesto on foccacia to pumpkin, creamed kale and gruyère tart, plus memorable mango-ginger panna cotta or chocolate hazelnut petit fours. All visits must be pre-booked before 4pm on the day you want to eat, and there are plans to offer dinner in the future. Thurs 3–6pm, Sun 11am–4pm.

The interior

Despite the beauty of its rolling countryside, **the interior** holds few specific draws for visitors; in fact, perhaps the best way to get a feel for the area is simply to get happily lost in its maze of rural roads, stopping off for a drink or an Indian snack at one of the innumerable small bars and food stalls in the villages. As **maxis** and **taxis** take long, circular routes to the villages, this is a difficult area to explore without your own vehicle, though the absence of road signs can be frustrating; asking for directions is usually your best bet for finding the right road.

Montserrat Hills

East of the Solomon Hochoy Highway, the **Montserrat Hills** are the most picturesque part of the **Central Range**, a rolling landscape which shelters huge cocoa estates and the **Navet Dam and Reservoir**, as well as some of Trinidad's sleepiest villages, accessed via winding roads with rickety wooden bridges. The nineteenth-century English novelist Charles Kingsley, who visited in 1870, described the panorama from the top of Montserrat as "the most vast and most lovely which I have ever seen". Most of the villages have little specific to recommend them apart from the odd picturesque colonial house and a great deal of rural charm, though there are a few gentle attractions on which to hinge a visit.

San Antonio Cocoa Estate

619 Couva Main Rd, around 7km east of the Solomon Hochoy Hwy • 1hr guided tours Wed & Sat 10am–noon, must be arranged in advance on ☎ 679 9515 or ☎ 377 7780, ✉ m_deverteuil@hotmail.com • TT$50 • Take the Gran Couva exit from the Solomon Hochoy Hwy and follow the road past Gran Couva for about 20min

The 250-acre **San Antonio Cocoa Estate** is a working cocoa plantation, in operation since the colonial era. Its beautifully weathered processing facility allows you a fascinating glimpse into the workings of this end of the cocoa industry, from the planting and picking of the pods through to the drying process in sheds with sliding roofs, and the storing of the beans for export. It's best to go between November and June, when the bulk of the crop is processed. Trinidad produces "fine flavour" cocoa beans, some of the best in the world, and traditionally the bulk of the processed cocoa has been exported to the US and Europe; these days, though, San Antonio is at the forefront of the local revolution in cocoa production and chocolate-making. The processing station is the base of the **Montserrat Cocoa Farmers Co-Operative Society** (☎341 9330, ⓦmontserratcocoa. com), a collective of local farmers who bring their beans here to be fermented and dried. Certified for their sustainable agricultural practices by the Rainforest Alliance in 2016, the co-op have also secured a Certificate of Geographical Indication for their beans (similar to the AOC classification for French wines), a testament to the unique flavour of the cocoa grown here – as evidenced by the delicious bars sold at the estate office (containing 50–80 percent cocoa); you can also by coco tea balls, soaps and cocoa butter.

La Vega Estate

76 Gran Couva Main Rd • **Estate** Daily 9am–5pm; free if you've come to shop, gardens TT$25, guided tour TT$40 • Fishing TT$30 • Paddleboating TT$40 for 30min • **Pools** Daily 10am–5pm • Adults TT$100, kids TT$75, under 2s free • ☎ 679 9522, ⓦ lavegaestate.com • Take the Gran Couva exit from the Solomon Hochoy Hwy and follow the road past Gran Couva for about 25min

A thriving commercial plant nursery and nature retreat, the **La Vega Estate** is nestled in the hills about 10km east of the Solomon Hochoy Highway, between Gran Couva and Flanagin Town. A large swathe of the estate is devoted to exquisitely **landscaped gardens**, with nature trails that you can explore independently or on a guided tour; there are also ponds for fishing and paddleboating (public holidays only), as well as picnic tables in sheltered bamboo groves, bromeliad and Japanese gardens, a meditation space and a children's play area. At weekends, you can usually buy delicious ice cream made with estate fruits, in flavours such as silk fig, barbadine and carambola, while fresh fruit and veg grown on site are always available.

The estate's newest addition is two inviting **swimming pools**, overlooked by lush greenery and equipped with loungers, changing rooms, snack bar and gazebos – a lovely place to spend the day.

Knolly's Tunnel

John William Trace • Daily, no set hours • Free • The tunnel is about 40min by car from the Solomon Hochoy Hwy; take the Gran Couva exit and follow the brown signposts

East of the Montserrat Hills, past the tiny village of Tabaquite, there are lovely views of the central range from the main Tabaquite Road. It's worth turning off along John

William Trace to peer into the dark, dripping reaches of **Knolly's Tunnel**, an abandoned railway tunnel on the long-lost line between Cunupia and Tabaquite, which is named after the colonial governor who opened it in 1898. You can walk or drive right through the 180m tunnel, home to a sizeable colony of bats, and the surrounding hillside has been prettily landscaped, with a couple of shady picnic areas.

Navet Dam and Reservoir

Tabaquite Rd • Daily 8am–6pm • Take the Gasparillo exit from Solomon Hochoy Hwy and follow Tabaquite Rd, which runs along the southern slopes of the Montserrat Hills to the dam

With only the minuscule hamlet of Brasso Venado nearby, the towering **Navet Dam** is an isolated place and an excellent spot for birdwatching, with plenty of waterfowl scooting around on the reservoir's intricate network of inlets and coves. As with visits to Caroni Arena, you need a **permit** to enter the area, best arranged via a company such as Caribbean Discovery Tours or Paria Springs Tours (see page 39).

3

Piparo

Piparo is a 20min drive from the Solomon Hochoy Hwy (take the Gasparillo exit, follow the main road and take a left turn at Williamsville)

Set in beautiful low-lying hills south of Montserrat, about 10km from both Tortuga and Tabaquite, **PIPARO** has the dubious distinction of having suffered one of the Trinidad's largest **mud volcano** eruptions in 1997, which saw mud spewed 200m into the air, covering 2.5 square kilometres and displacing three hundred residents. Half of the village cemetery remains buried under the (now solidified) mud "lake", which has two small oozing mounds at its centre that occasionally spatter out small eruptions of mud. Piparo is also infamous as the former home of notorious drug lord, **Dole Chadee** (see page 162), whose 1994 arrest drew attention both to the significance of cocaine as part of the island's economy, and to the extent of his Piparo estate, close to the volcano site, where behind 4.5m razor-wired walls an extensive mansion (and Hindu temple) attest to the extravagance of the cocaine don's lifestyle. The rest of his land, just north of the village, was seized by the government and has been turned into a rehabilitation centre for drug users and the homeless.

Triveni Mandir

Tours by arrangement only • Donation appreciated • ☎ 784 9808, ⌨ trivenimandir.com • Turn off the Solomon Hochoy Hwy at the Gasparillo exit

Set among the canefields of south-central Trinidad, in the fantastically named community of Hard Bargain, the remarkably large **Triveni Mandir** owes its existence to the vision and devotion of local furniture-seller-cum-Hindu teacher Shri Ramoonsingh, who spent his entire life savings on the temple's construction. It's wonderfully detailed, with huge elephant sculptures outside and solid marble figurines of Shiva, Ganesh and Lakshmi set in recesses in the walls both inside and out, while stained-glass windows and ornate paintings on the inside walls add to the atmosphere. Shri Ramoonsingh died before the temple was completed, but a small plaque at the front of the building dedicates the mandir to him.

Caroni Plains

Running roughly parallel to the Uriah Butler Highway, the old **Southern Main Road** south from Curepe, on the Churchill Roosevelt Highway, is little more than a parochial thoroughfare these days as it potters through one small community after another surrounded on all sides by the **Caroni Plains**. Trinidad's original sugar heartland, the

3

THE RISE AND FALL OF DOLE CHADEE

Widely claimed to have been Trinidad's most influential and successful drug lord, **Dole Chadee**'s story reads something like a rags-to-riches tale worthy of the Colombian cartels. Born Nankissoon Boodram in 1952 to a poor Indo-Trinidadian family in Curepe, Chadee went from mason to cocaine empire-builder, and was a charitable community godfather who skillfully avoided arrest until his eventual downfall, which was shrouded in unanswered questions and political intrigue.

At the peak of his reign, Chadee owned a large estate guarded by gun-wielding henchmen at the village of **Piparo**; he had his own ornate no-expense-spared Hindu temple, owned racehorses, a fleet of flashy cars (despite not having a driving licence), as well as shopping centres and petrol stations as far afield as Princes Town and San Fernando. Chadee employed a large contingent of the Piparo community and was intent on looking after the village's welfare, offering money for food and electricity at difficult times, as well as funds for sporting events and other community activities. His group remained seemingly untouchable (he's even said to have bought a car from former prime minister, Patrick Manning), despite showing a ruthless side which saw witnesses to alleged crimes poisoned, killed or have their jaws shot off, and families intimidated or murdered.

Chadee was never tried as a narco-trafficker, however. Despite US authorities' suspicions that he, along with partner **"Shortman" Beharry**, were heading the eastern Caribbean's leading cocaine cartel, in league with Cali of Colombia, it was for a dual **murder charge** that he and eight accomplices were eventually arrested in 1994. They were found guilty and sentenced to death by hanging in 1996. A lengthy appeal process ensued: Chadee and the other accused maintained they had no involvement in the murder and were the victims of a witch-hunt for drug traffickers by a range of conspirators. The authorities disagreed, and in 1999, all nine went to the **gallows**.

Though Chadee and his cohorts were clearly no angels, there are inconsistencies over their ultimate demise: regardless of their guilt in the murder charge, the group apparently leapfrogged a long line of murderers waiting on death row; jurors on the case were said to have been cobbled together without due process; and Amnesty International points to the failure of political officials to disclose evidence. Chadee certainly served a purpose as a **media tool**: the war on drugs was seen to be visibly waged, despite the fact that Trinidad continued to be flooded with cocaine. Chadee's downfall is also alleged to have been orchestrated by rival Syrian operators with political clout in both T&T's main parties, who didn't like the fact that Chadee's gang were "independent players" operating at the risk side of the business rather than in the cartel they were purported to be part of; certainly, the moneyed side of cocaine trading in Trinidad remains wholeheartedly intertwined with legitimate businesses.

region is home to many Indo-Trinidadians, whose ancestors settled here as indentured workers (see page 252). The complete restructuring of the sugar industry during the 1990s and the eventual closure of the state-owned Caroni Sugar Company in 2003 has forced farmers to diversify, however, planting rice, pigeon peas and cassava in the former canefields. Some 5km south of Curepe, **Caroni village** was founded around the old Caroni Sugar Factory, though this and the rum distillery closed in 2003; you can still sample local rum in any number of rum shops along the road, however. Set in a former train station, the *Railway Bar* is especially distinctive.

South of Caroni, the SMR becomes increasingly urban as you pass through **Warrenville**, home to a particularly attractive mosque, which merges imperceptibly into **Cunupia**, itself morphing into a suburb of Chaguanas. The route displays a fascinating combination of old and new Trinidad, with mandirs and mosques interspersed with evangelical churches, while extravagant signboards shout out the wares of the small shops and mom-and-pop restaurants that line the road, many of the latter selling excellent **Indian fast food**.

Aripo Savannas

Ⓦ bit.ly/AripoSav • Entry permits are required for Aripo Savannas, best arranged through a tour company such as Paria Springs or Caribbean Discovery Tours (see page 39), which offer birding trips to the area

Northeast of the Caroni Plains and right at the end of the Churchill Roosevelt Highway (though there are plans for the highway to be extended), stone pillars at the edge of the tarmac mark the entrance to the former American airbase at **Wallerfield**. The hangars, barrack blocks and control rooms are long gone, though the old runway is still used for drag-racing meets. The main draw in the area, however, is the 18-square-kilometre **Aripo Savanna Scientific Reserve**, Trinidad's last remaining portion of savanna land, which was given protected status in 1934 and designated an Environmentally Sensitive Area in 2007. In 1871, author Charles Kingsley wrote that the area "filled me with more admiration than anything I have seen in the island", and it's still a startlingly beautiful place – vast, eerie and empty despite its proximity to the Northern Range and the clamour of the East–West Corridor. The emptiness is deceiving, however: comprised of open savanna, marsh forest and palm forest, the latter dominated by stands of beautiful moriche palms, the area's sensitive ecosystems provide a home to some 260 species of **birds** and 457 documented species of **flora**, many of which are rarely (if ever) seen elsewhere on the island. Among the plants are parasitic vines, wild calabash, ground orchids and the endemic carnivorous sundew plant, while Savanna hawks, red-bellied macaws and fork-tailed palm swifts (among innumerable others) are more easily spotted here than elsewhere on Trinidad. The best time to visit Aripo is at dawn, when you will be rewarded with a spectacular aspect of the palms glowing in the light, along with the birds' enchanting early morning chorus.

Despite the savanna's ecological worth, a huge swathe of wetland forest adjacent to the southern boundary of one of Aripo's savannas was **cleared** in January 2018 as part of the first phase of an **extension of the highway** to Sangre Grande and, ultimately, Manzanilla. A court case brought by NGO Fishermen and Friends of the Sea (Ⓦ ffostt. com) secured an injunction that halted the works almost as soon as they'd started, thanks to procedural anomalies concerning the way clearance was granted for the project, but given the poor track record of successive governments when considering environmental concerns over new highway projects, it seems likely that the cessation will only be temporary.

Talparo Road

Signposted from the Churchill Roosevelt Highway, **Talparo Road** runs south through serene rainforest where you'll rarely meet another car. As you pass the tiny settlements of Brazil and Talparo, the foothills of the **Central Range** appear, cloaked in luxuriant vegetation: thickets of bamboo jostle with papaya, mango, banana, cashew and breadfruit trees. The blooms of the golden poui dominate in April, while from December to March magnificent immortelle trees blaze a fiery red.

Caroni Arena Dam and Reservoir

Permits are required to access the dam, best arranged through a birding guide such as Courtenay "Bushman" Rooks of Paria Springs Tours (see page 39), who offers a marvellous birding tour here

Reaching 40.85m at its highest elevation, the **Caroni Arena Dam** is Trinidad and Tobago's largest, while the **Reservoir** covers 6.8 square kilometres. Caroni is a haven for **birds** and **animals**. Parrots, hawks and white egrets are frequent visitors to the area while blue emperor butterflies flutter among the reeds by the water's edge, caimans lurk in the swamps bordering the reservoir and red howler and capuchin monkeys, toucans and tree porcupines inhabit the surrounding forest.

★ **Hacienda Jacana** Talparo ☎ 498 7597, ⓦ hacienda jacana.com. A tranquil and charming place to stay, a short drive southwest of the Caroni Arena Dam and Reservoir nestled amid trees on a riverbank. The smart wood-panelled one- and two-bedroom cottages (the latter US$265), with full kitchen, are furnished with locally made teak fittings and have a veranda overlooking a small lake where you can go fishing and kayaking; there's also a pool and plenty of birdlife in the lush surrounds. Meals (breakfast US$15, lunch and dinner US$30) are available. 🛜 <u>US$185</u>

Mount Tamana bat caves

The distinctive, flat-topped **Mount Tamana** is the highest in the Central Range, at 308m, and its porous limestone core holds a series of lengthy **cave systems** which provide the perfect home for huge colonies of **bats**; eleven of Trinidad's 67 bat species are found here, and this is one of the largest colonies in the region. The gentle thirty-minute walk up Tamana's slopes is pleasant enough, threading through shady groves of lichen-covered cocoa trees and under giant silk cotton trees, with the occasional eye-popping view over the Caroni Plains. However, the real draw here are the bats, which make a spectacular exit en masse at **dusk** to feed. It's best to arrive around 3pm, in order to have enough time to walk up to the top of the hill and admire the spectacular views over the forested slopes of the Central Range, and descend to the caves before the sun goes down. It's worth making the easy descent into the first of the caves to peek at the ceiling – almost every inch is covered with roosting bats (though be warned that copious bat guano coats the walls and floor; Paria Springs tours equip visitors with protective rubber gloves). As dusk approaches, the first stragglers make their way out, and as the darkness thickens, the trickle becomes a stream as about a million and a half bats shoot past like furry, flapping balls, their sonar clicking away as they avoid flying into you.

By organized tour Bang in the centre of Trinidad, Tamana is most easily reached from Sangre Grande (see page 165) via the Cunupo Rd. From there, it's a winding journey along heavily potholed minor roads, but as most of the route isn't signposted, and there's no easy way to find the path to the caves unless you know it, it's nigh-on impossible to visit Tamana independently. Caribbean Discovery Tours, Paria Springs Tours, Limeland Tours (see page 168) and Ieri Nature Adventures (see page 39) all offer trips.

The east coast

South of **Sangre Grande**, the largest town on this side of the island and a transportation hub of considerable commercial vigour, Trinidad's **east coast** is dominated by the **Cocal**, 24km of unbroken sand lined by swaying coconut palms, that begins at **Manzanilla** and stretches south to Point Radix. Beyond here the beach continues at **Mayaro**, long a popular holiday resort with Trinidadians but almost entirely undiscovered by foreign visitors. The Manzanilla–Mayaro Road runs the length of the east coast down to Galeota Point and **Guayaguayare**, fringed inland by the pristine rainforest and – behind the Cocal – the mangrove-smothered wetlands of **Nariva Swamp**, a primary breeding ground and habitat for all manner of rare animals and birds, including manatees and monkeys.

By public transport Manzanilla route taxis leave from the Republic Bank in Sangre Grande; if you're headed on to Mayaro, you need to wait by *Hotel Carries on the Bay* in Manzanilla. Taxis are few and far between and waits can be long. There is also a bus service between Sangre Grande and Manzanilla/Mayaro.

By car As taxis between Sangre Grande and Manzanilla are fairly infrequent, the only practical way to explore the east coast is by car.

Sangre Grande

A thriving little market town slung along the Eastern Main Road, **SANGRE GRANDE** ("big blood", after a long-forgotten battle between Amerindians and the incoming Spanish) – pronounced "sandy grandy" but usually just called "grandy" – is a bustling transportation hub for the whole east coast from Toco to Mayaro, and the only place in the region with a bank or ATM. Residents of surrounding villages crowd the pavements every Friday to deposit wages, shop at the market stalls, take a fast-food fix and drink the night away at the many **rum shops**. Most visitors pass through en route to the east coast, or stop off to change taxis, but it makes an agreeable place for a wander.

ARRIVAL AND DEPARTURE   SANGRE GRANDE

By bus Buses arrive and depart from the square behind *Royal Castle* in the middle of the main drag; ask around to find the correct queue. There are early morning services to Manzanilla (5am, 6.30am, 8am & 9.30am) and to Mayaro (4.30am & 8.30am), returning straight back to

Sangre Grande.
By route taxi Manzanilla and Mayaro taxis leave from the main street, just past the police station next to the Republic Bank on the eastern side of town.

Brigand Hill Lighthouse

Daily 8am–5pm • Free • The lighthouse is about 5km inland of Manzanilla Beach by road: heading from Sangre Grande on the EMR, you come to a T-Junction; turn right (left heads down to the beach), then after 5min or so there's a small signposted (and steep) turn-off for the lighthouse to the left

Sitting pretty on a hilltop above Manzanilla is **Brigand Hill Lighthouse**, whose sweeping views down the east coast offer a great perspective over the whole area. Built in 1958, this stubby white-painted lighthouse is one of only three in Trinidad. You can't enter the building itself, but guards at the gate will usually let you in to climb the steep twenty-odd iron stairs that run up the outside of the building. The platform at the top affords a magnificent view stretching from Toco in the north to Galeota Point in the south, taking in the Caroni Plains and the flatlands of Nariva Swamp. Red **howler monkeys** inhabit the trees around the lighthouse; the troop passes close by each evening at around 5.30pm.

Manzanilla Beach

Manzanilla–Mayaro Rd • Lifeguards daily 10am–6pm • Changing facilities TT$1 • There's a free car park at the northern end of the beach

Southeast of Sangre Grande, the Eastern Main Road cuts a picturesque and winding 8km route towards the Atlantic coast; underground waterflows regularly cause subsidence, so if you're driving, take things slowly on these very bumpy roads. The EMR ends at a T-junction with Plum Mitan Road; take the left turn through somnolent **MANZANILLA** village, with its fruit stalls and rum bars, to reach the wonderful expanse of **Manzanilla Beach**. Windswept and exposed, and stretching for some 24km down to the headland that separates it from Mayaro, this wide span of fine, brownish sand is often all but deserted during the week, but becomes a popular swimming spot at the weekends (though the murky water isn't particularly enticing), when locals descend with car boots full of food and drink. Take care while swimming, as the undercurrents can be dangerous, and bear in mind that the jellyfish-like Portuguese man-of-war is occasionally found in the waters here; ask local advice.

If you don't fancy a sea swim here, take the track that leads from the main road next to the *Carrie's on the Bay* hotel (which now rents rooms strictly on an hourly basis and isn't a viable base); 100m or so down, the otherwise careworn *Coconut Cove* hotel has a nice pool, which non-guests can use for a TT$50 daily fee.

Manzanilla only has one viable **accommodation** option, though *Dougie's* bar in the village has a couple of budget rooms –if you're after sun and sand, head down to Mayaro. **Eating** options are equally limited: the café-bar at the beach facility offers inexpensive local lunches, though opening hours are sporadic, and there are a couple of small bars and snack shops just up from the beach in Manzanilla village. The friendly stall opposite the beach entrance sells soft drinks, snacks and cold jelly coconuts.

D'Hammerhead Beach Bar Manzanilla–Mayaro Rd ☏ 691 0034. On the main road as it meets the sea just as you enter Manzanilla, this is a basic beer joint offering cold Carib and Stag; simple meals such as barbecue chicken and pork with fries and salad (from TT\$30) are occasionally available. Daily 10am–late.

Limeland House Old Plum Rd, Manzanilla ☏ 668 1356 or ☏ 798 5750, ⊛ limeland-tours.com. Located a few hundred metres along a bumpy road inland from *Dougie's* bar, just up from the beach, these two smart self-contained apartments are the best option in the village. Each has two bedrooms with double and twin beds and a/c, plus kitchen and bathroom. Friendly English-Trini host Kayman Sagar is a knowledgeable tour guide (see page 168) and mine of local information. ⊛ US\$120

The Cocal

Many of the coconuts piled up at Trinidad's innumerable street stalls come from Manzanilla, grown in the waving groves of palms known collectively as the **Cocal**. Lining both sides of the Manzanilla–Mayaro Road for the full length of unspoilt, wave-pounded Manzanilla beach, the Cocal makes for an awe-inspiring drive: the graceful, leaning palms dance in the sea breezes, clumps of wild anthurium lilies put on a pretty show at ground level and the wetlands of Nariva Swamp open up the sky inland. There are no hotels or restaurants anywhere along the road (the only buildings are private holidays homes), but roadside stalls sell the shellfish known as chip-chip, freshly caught crabs, black conch, fish and watermelons, and there are plenty of places where you can stop to take in the gorgeous surrounds.

Three-quarters of the way along, the road crosses the **Nariva River**, worth a stop for a lovely view of the mangroves along the banks; the waters are a popular swimming spot come the weekend, when cars line the roadside and chutney music blares out over the smooth sands. Nearing Mayaro (see page 168), the road runs past a coconut processing plant, surrounded by huge mounds of discarded husks. Between 5.30 and 6pm every night the air around here is raucous with the calls of the **red-chested macaws** that come to roost in the trees (binocular-toting birdwatchers often mark the spot), while the surrounding swampland is a good place to see southern lapwings and the rare red-breasted tanager. The ponds in this area are full of **cascadura**, a small brown fresh-water fish – a type of armoured catfish, with a tough skeletal covering. It's said that if you eat these rather chewy fish (invariably served curried), you'll return to end your days in Trinidad.

COCONUTS

Grown on estates throughout eastern Trinidad and the southwest peninsula, **coconuts** are in constant demand on account of their sheer versatility. Depending on when they are harvested, they can be a source of oil, soap or animal feed, while their fibrous husks are used as a potting material for plants. Green nuts are full of sweet **water**, a popular drink sold fresh from the fruit from many an old Bedford van around the country. As the nut matures, much of the liquid is replaced by an equally delicious edible white **jelly**. A few weeks later, the jelly solidifies into firm white flesh, which can be grated, dried and roasted in cooking. Later still, a bread-like substance grows in the centre of the fruit; if caught at the right time, it makes a tasty snack. Soon afterwards it develops into a sprout, from which a new tree will grow. Depending on the type, a tree will take five to ten years to mature and live for many years after that, producing nuts all year round.

NARIVA'S WILDLIFE AND ECOLOGY

Nariva's swamps are home to a herd of **manatees**, or sea cows, impossibly endearing elephantine mammals whose peculiar appearance once fuelled rumours of mermaids lurking in the brackish depths. Very seldom seen, manatees grow up to 4m in length, weigh over 600kg, and feed on water hyacinth, moss and water lilies, and are in danger of local extinction: in the 1970s hundreds of manatees inhabited Nariva's swampland, but their numbers are now down to around forty as a result of increased human activity in the area, notably fishermen's nets. Equally hard to spot are **freshwater turtles**, though the swamp is an excellent place to view **caimans**, **red howler monkeys** (whose rather alarming, otherworldly roars reverberate around the forest), white-fronted **capuchin monkeys** (which have been known to shower human intruders with a hail of twigs), **opossums**, **porcupines** and three-toed and silky **anteaters**. Snakes include **macajuel boa constrictors** and non-venomous, greenish-brown, black-spotted **anacondas**, which can grow up to 9m long and are the heaviest reptiles in the world. Reputedly washed here from South America on the current of the Orinoco River, they're rarely seen despite their impressive size, and there have been no known attacks on humans in Trinidad.

The swamp has many impressive **trees**, including the island's largest sandbox, with its vicious-looking spiked trunk, plenty of cannonball trees (locally known as jumbie calabash), whose heavy fruits grow directly from the trunk, and towering silk cotton, with beautiful buttressed roots spreading out from the bottom of the trunk. The canopies and the flatlands also harbour a wide variety of birds, from **savanna hawks** to **dicksissels**, **orange-winged** and **yellow-capped Amazon parrots**, and blue-gold and red-bellied **macaws**.

3

Nariva Swamp

One of Trinidad's most significant wildlife areas, the **Nariva Swamp** covers fifteen square kilometres behind the coconut estates along the coast south of Manzanilla. The area is made up of agricultural land (rice and watermelons are the main crops), as well as reed-fringed marshes and, between the Mayaro–Manzanilla Road and the swamp itself, mangrove thickets. Deep in the southwestern corner lies the 16 square kilometres of **Bush Bush Wildlife Sanctuary** (often referred to as an island but actually a peninsula standing around 3m higher than the surrounding land), bordered by palmiste and moriche palms and covered in hardwood forest; it was designated a protected sanctuary in 1968. A unique freshwater ecosystem, Nariva harbours large concentrations of rare **wildlife**, with some 45 species of mammals, 39 species of reptiles and 204 species of birds. It's also home to 92 species of mosquito, so remember to bring your insect repellent.

The 1996 **Ramsar Convention** – to which Trinidad and Tobago is a signatory – designated the swamp a "Wetland of International Importance", placing a legal obligation on the government to protect and maintain the area. Reconciling human needs with the demands of conservation hasn't been easy, however. Many locals still hunt for both sport and sale, while illegal rice farming has destroyed much of the swamp's northern end. The government has expelled the major rice farmers, but small-scale cultivation continues. In addition, **bush fires**, often deliberately set to clear land, have ravaged almost half the territory; as a result, access is often prohibited during the dry season.

Kernaham Village

Nariva is hard to explore in any real depth independently, but if you're just passing by, it's worth taking a stroll along the signposted Kernaham Trace, which swings in from the Manzanilla–Mayaro Road to **KERNAHAM VILLAGE**, a widely dispersed collection of picturesque board houses, mostly on stilts, that are home to a friendly, overwhelmingly Indian community of farmers and fishermen. It's a beautiful scene, with the flatlands opening up huge expanses of open sky. Kernaham has a bar which occasionally serves food, as well as a building for worship that accommodates the community's Hindus,

Muslims and Christians; it's marked with a moon and stars design on the outside, and a peek through the wall reveals icons (in picture form) of all three religions, illustrating Trinidad's strong tradition of cultural and religious acceptance.

INFORMATION AND TOURS

NARIVA SWAMP

Organized tours If you want to visit Bush Bush and Nariva, a guide is essential; prices average US$100. Both Paria Springs and Caribbean Discovery Tours (see page 39) offer a marvellous walk through Bush Bush, with a kayaking/dinghy trip if water levels permit and an Indian lunch cooked by residents of Kernaham Village. Kayman Sagar of Limeland Tours (☎ 668 1356 or ☎ 798 5750, ⓦ limeland-tours.com), based in Manzanilla village, visits the swamp regularly; his 5hr tours include kayaking and a Bush Bush walk, and he's an expert on Nariva's flora and fauna.

Mayaro and around

Some 24km south of the Manzanilla Beach facilities, the coast road heads inland at Point Radix, crossing over the Ortoire River and passing the local market, where stalls sell fresh fish, lobsters and strings of wriggling crabs. **MAYARO** itself has grown out of two old French villages, Pierreville and Plaisance, and is still marked as such on some maps. **Pierreville**, on the Mayaro–Guayaguayare Road, is the business end of town, a neat nexus of fast-food outlets, shops and small businesses. A side road cuts east to the village's seaside quarter, **Plaisance**, a lovely place with a thoroughly relaxing atmosphere whose greatest attraction is its **beach**. A gentle, coconut-tree-lined curve of clean, soft brown sand, the beach is one of the most popular bathing spots on Mayaro Bay, along with **Queen's Beach** a couple of kilometres further south (to get to the latter, take signposted Church Road from the Mayaro–Guayaguayare Road); both spots only see crowds at the weekends. Lifeguards keep a watch on bathers, but there are no public changing rooms, toilets or other facilities on this or any other part of the bay, though some of the Queen's Beach resorts have restaurants, and non-guests can buy a day pass to use the pools/sundeck at the *Queen's Beach Resort* TT$150; see below). Note that the sea in this area has **strong currents**, so exercise caution.

Past Queen's Beach, the road swings past pasturelands and, with increasing frequency, luxurious houses built by the oil companies for their managers and workers; BP even have an entire compound, a fenced-off affair reminiscent of a 1950s holiday camp.

ACCOMMODATION AND EATING

MAYARO AND AROUND

As well as the places listed below, Mayaro holds a number of private houses rented out as **holiday homes**, advertised on Airbnb and in the classified sections of the local papers and perfect if you're travelling in a group and want to make a weekend of it. Trini holidaymakers tend to do their own cooking, often barbecuing on the beach, and most hotels have rooms with kitchens; stock up on supplies before you arrive, as the supermarkets along the Mayaro–Guayagayare Rd and in Mayaro Village aren't up to much. In terms of **restaurants**, *The Ranch* is the standout option, but there are several fast-food outlets, from *Subway* to *KFC*, in the village centre, as well as rum shops and places selling Creole food and roti lining the Mayaro–Guayaguayare Rd.

Queen's Beach Resort Church Rd, Radix Village ☎ 630 5532, ⓦ queensbeachresort.com. The largest of the beachside properties, and the only one that feels like a proper resort hotel, this is a friendly place with a personal touch. The large en-suite rooms have a/c, TV and kitchenette, though lack a sea view; on site are two pools (one indoor, with an adjacent hot tub and sauna), beachside decks, two restaurants (*Chip Chip* for casual dining, *Three Palms* for more elaborate meals) and a lively bar. Rates include breakfast. ☎ US$154

★ **The Ranch** Mayaro–Guayaguayare Rd ☎ 223 6798, ⓦ bit.ly/RanchMayaro. Professionally run place with tables in a cool a/c interior and a plant-wreathed patio garden outside, great for ice-cold beers and for a spot of lunch and dinner, from light bites (around TT$50) like bake and shark, fish broth, crab and dumplin' or burgers, to more substantial options (TT$55–260) from curry duck and steaks to shrimp, lobster and fish dishes; highlight is a delicious whole snapper, perfectly seasoned and served with local sides. Sports games on the plasma TV, pool tables, karaoke on Fridays and occasional live music. Daily 10.30am–midnight, lunch Wed–Sun only.

Splash by R.A.S.H. Resort Church Rd, Radix Village ☎ 630 7274 or ☎ 386 5803, ⓦ bit.ly/RashMayaro. A collection of brightly painted one- to four-bedroom self-contained apartments with a/c, full kitchens, cable TV and balcony; the cheapest have no ocean view. Note that linen is provided, but towels are not. There's a covered, hammock-slung gazebo for barbecues and chilling out, recliners for relaxing on the beach, and a pool and jacuzzi on site. 🛜 <u>US$60</u>

Galeota Point and Guayaguayare

The southeastern tip of Trinidad, **Galeota Point** (see map, page 150) is strictly the domain of American oil companies, with oil storage tanks dotted along the roadside and several rigs offshore. The point itself is the private reserve of Amoco. Two kilometres past Galeota Point, the road swings onto the south coast at **GUAYAGUAYARE**, a quiet fishing village with a flotilla of pirogues bobbing in the bay, which holds the distinction of having been the place where oil was first discovered on the island in 1819; the village blossomed in the early twentieth century when the petroleum industry really got going. Unless you are here in connection with the oil business, however, it's a quiet and uneventful place, with the action centred around the roadside *Sea Wall Beach and Boat Club* bar.

3

San Fernando and the south

PITCH LAKE, LA BREA

San Fernando and the south

Geographically, Trinidad's south presents a mirror image of the north: a long littoral extending west beyond the main body of the island, with the low ridge of the forested Trinity Hills rising up from the southeast coast. In the Gulf of Paria, where the southwest peninsula crooks a finger towards Venezuela, Trinidad's second city, precipitous San Fernando, sits at the base of its oddly shaped landmark hill, while to the south, the vast reserves of asphalt at the Pitch Lake represent the only organized attraction in these parts.

That's as far as the comparison goes, however. **San Fernando** is a booming business town, but beyond its city limits lies Trinidad's most sparsely populated region. Although many southerners still earn a living from agriculture and fishing, the economy here is hinged around **oil**, pumped both from offshore rigs and the 1600-odd pumping jacks scattered all over the countryside, many in large expanses of forest which, aside from the pumps, remain largely undeveloped. The coast, meanwhile, is similarly untouched, with picturesque **Cedros** and **Icacos**, and the remote fishing village of **Moruga**, seeing few visitors, despite offering gorgeous scenery and lovely yellow-sand **beaches**, best visited during the dry season (December to May) when the sea and sand are clear; during the rainy months, rivers wash mud and a fair bit of rubbish into the sea.

Though the south isn't traditional tourist territory, you'll find that hospitality is second to none here, with locals often keen to show visitors what Trini life is like away from the capital. The lack of tourism is a mixed blessing, though: there are no crowds but also few facilities for visitors. Outside of San Fernando, **accommodation** is practically nonexistent, but given the somnolent nature of the south, and its relatively compact area, you're best off staying in San Fernando anyway, exploring by way of day-trips and returning in the evenings to take advantage of the city's bars and restaurants. Given that Port of Spain is only an hour's drive from San Fernando, it's also more than possible to see the south from the capital if you're based there, too.

GETTING AROUND
SAN FERNANDO AND THE THE SOUTH

By car A car is easily the most convenient way to get around the south. In and around the Pitch Lake, roads can often be quite rough thanks to the bitumen seeping up to the surface; drive slowly and defensively.

By public transport San Fernando is the transport hub for south and central Trinidad, with buses, maxis and route taxis going direct to the major towns, as well as some farther flung destinations such as Erin and Cedros. As ever, waiting times can be long and public transport isn't a practical way to explore the region.

San Fernando

Nestled against the base of its eponymous flat-top hill, **SAN FERNANDO** boasts a striking setting, and despite its status as T&T's industrial capital, the city has a beguilingly old-fashioned, laidback charm. With sloping streets reminiscent of a miniature, low-key San Francisco, its warren of steep, winding lanes offer pretty sea

VIEW FROM SAN FERNANDO HILL

Highlights

❶ San Fernando Trinidad's second city boasts a host of handsome gingerbread buildings and some great restaurants, bars and clubs in which to dine and lime. See page 172

❷ Heritage tours Explore the history of Trinidad's First Peoples at Banwari Trace, or get a flavour of Merikin culture on a tour around the Company Villages. See pages 180 and 186

❸ Pitch Lake This fascinating geological wonder is the largest natural deposit of pitch in the world. See page 181

❹ Icacos and the far southwest One of the island's most stunning landscapes: quiet,

undulating roads bordered by coconut plantations and wetlands, and some wild, undeveloped beaches. See page 183

❺ Indian food at Debe Arrive in the village at dusk for the best street food on the island, from great doubles to *saheena* and sugary traditional sweets. See page 184

❻ Moruga Isolated but still accessible, and with a lovely beach, this quiet and deeply religious fishing village has a unique atmosphere all its own. See page 187

HIGHLIGHTS ARE MARKED ON THE MAP ON PAGE 174

views, while many weather-beaten gingerbread buildings have survived the rapid industrial development of recent years.

San Fernando – often just "Sando" to locals – has always maintained an independent spirit. An oil city first and foremost, it sees many business visitors but few sightseers, and tourists are basically left to figure it out independently – though the friendly and hospitable residents make it a pleasurable place to get a flavour of Trini life. And in recent years, the burgeoning wealth from the natural gas and oil industries have helped to push up demand for quality entertainment, with a slew of high-class **bars**, **restaurants** and **clubs** alongside many more grassroots options for dining, drinking and partying.

Bordered by the Gulf of Paria on one side and the rocky, wooded outcrop of **San Fernando Hill** on the other, the city's compact centre is easily negotiated on foot, with most of the historical sights, shops and transport stands located on and around **Harris Promenade**, a broad, elegant boulevard running west from the main junction and focal point, **Library Corner**.

Brief history

Having served as a sacred spot for Amerindian tribes, San Fernando's first European arrival was **Sir Walter Raleigh**, who put to shore here during a voyage in 1595 – he was unimpressed and sailed on. **Capuchin priests** established a mission in 1687, but the settlement only began to flourish after 1784, when French plantation owners attracted by the Cedula (see page 250) were allocated land here and established the first estates; in the same year, Spanish governor José Maria Chacón named the settlement San Fernando de Naparima in honour of King Carlos III's new son. By 1797, when the British captured the island, San Fernando had more than a thousand inhabitants, twenty sugar mills and eight rum distilleries. Surrounded by fertile agricultural land, the town continued to grow, and by 1811 the population had trebled; by the middle of the century, it was the hub of southern Trinidad, a busy trading centre for the region's planters, with a regular coastal steamer to Port of Spain – the overland route took three days of rough riding

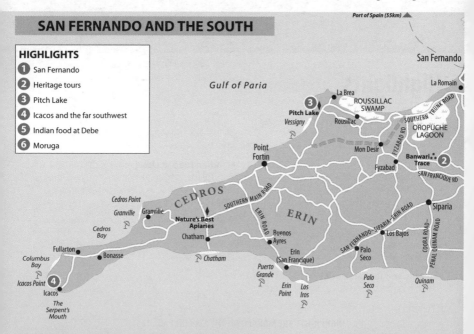

SAN FERNANDO AND THE SOUTH

HIGHLIGHTS

1 San Fernando
2 Heritage tours
3 Pitch Lake
4 Icacos and the far southwest
5 Indian food at Debe
6 Moruga

through forests and swamps. The arrival of the **railway** in 1882 led to another population increase, and by the late 1880s San Fernando had been thoroughly modernized. Suburbs grew as the plantations disappeared – the result of falling sugar prices in the 1920s – and the town was soon dominated by the expanding **oil industry**. Designated a city in 1988, San Fernando continued to expand through the early 1990s, bringing the northern city limits up to the oil refinery at Point-a-Pierre and increasing its population by around 10,000 (it's around 50,000 today), with many inhabitants moving out to the chocolate-box housing developments on the eastern outskirts of town.

San Fernando Hill

Circular Courts Rd • Daily 9am–6pm • Free • The signposted road to the summit is off Circular Rd next to *Soong's Great Wall* restaurant

At 200m high, **San Fernando Hill** overshadows the city centre, and has long been a sacred place for **Amerindian** tribes from the South American mainland, who made annual pilgrimages to the site from 6500 BC up to the early 1900s. According to legend, the hill is the final resting place of Haburi the Hero and his mother, who stopped here on their flight from the Frog Woman in the Orinoco Delta in Venezuela; on reaching Trinidad, however, they were turned into "Anaparima", the original Amerindian name for the hill. Half flattened, with steep protruding points, it owes its modern-day profile to years of gravel mining, which lopped off a third of its original height. Protests by locals saw quarrying put to a stop and the hill declared a national park in 1980.

The summit has been landscaped, with shaded picnic tables, a children's playground, café, public toilets and several lookouts from which to enjoy the **views**; there's a telescope mounted on the open balcony of the new visitor centre. The panorama includes the city and the exclusive St Joseph Village suburb, the Gulf of Paria and the flaming chimneys at Point a Pierre and Point Lisas, and the ever-growing suburbs and agricultural plain of the interior. Also prominent is the controversial **Brian Lara Stadium**, adjacent to the highway at Tarouba. Supposed to have been completed in 2007 for the Cricket World Cup, the complex became a huge white elephant, shrouded in accusations of corruption that led to an investigation by a Commission of Enquiry into UDeCOTT, the state company responsible for its construction. It finally opened in 2017.

Harris Promenade

The centre of San Fernando's civic life and the location of several attractive colonial-era buildings, **Harris Promenade** stretches from the long 1950s-style facade of **San Fernando General Hospital** to Library Corner in the east. Its shady paved centre is dotted with benches and tables, and has an ornate Victorian bandstand and **statues** of Mahatma Gandhi and Jamaican black rights activist Marcus Garvey. At the southwestern end, the distinctive yellow-stone building with its curving arched windows is the city's **police station**; half of it remains roofless after a fire in 2009. Across the road, the grand Neoclassical **City Hall** from 1930 dominates the western end of the promenade, though it faces stiff competition

SAN FERNANDO

Port of Spain
Marabella, Point-a-Pierre & Port of Spain

0 — 250 metres

King's Wharf
Transport Terminal
Fish Market
Water Taxi Terminal
Chancery Lane Market
Bus and taxi stand
San Fernando General Hospital
Naparima Bowl
City Hall
Church of Our Lady of Perpetual Help RC
Carnegie Free Library
San Fernando Hill (200m)
Police Station
Paradise Cemetery
Carib House
Skiffle Bunch Panyard
Fonclair Panyard
Southern Academy for Performing Arts
Skinner Park
Cross Crossing shopping
Gulf City Mall
Cipero River
Gulf of Paria

PLEASANTVILLE

● EATING	
Amin's	5
Atherly's	3
More Vino More Sushi	6
Mother Nature	1
Parlour Royale	2
Rising Star	4

■ ACCOMMODATION	
Paria Suites	3
Royal Hotel	2
Tradewinds Hotel	1

■ DRINKING & NIGHTLIFE	
The Rig	2
Space La Nouba	1

Penal & Siparia

from the Catholic **Church of Our Lady of Perpetual Help** one block to the east, a huge white modern building with a tall clock tower that can be seen from most places in the city.

The promenade's two roads converge in front of the **Carnegie Free Library**, an ornate terracotta pile built in 1919 and financed – like many others the world over – by the Scottish philanthropist Andrew Carnegie. Behind the library, the promenade is home to a beautifully restored **steam train**, now resplendent in the original red and green livery of the Trinidad Government Railway. The oldest surviving steam locomotive in Trinidad, engine no.11 dates from 1894 and was built by Kitson and Co in Leeds, UK; in 1918 was converted to enable it to burn locally available oil rather than coal. Though no.11 wasn't the engine that pulled the final train (it was consigned to the "railway graveyard in St Joseph in 1965), it is here to commemorate the last run of the rail line from Port of Spain to San Fernando in 1968: people packed the carriages, hanging out of the windows to be part of this historic occasion, which was subsequently immortalized by Lord Kitchener's famous calypso *Last Train to San Fernando*. Just east of the library, the chaotic junction of seven roads is known as **Library Corner**, with its modern clock tower.

Coffee Street

South of San Fernando Hill, **Coffee Street**, takes its name from the coffee plantations that once thrived here. "The Coffee", as it's familiarly known, was the original home of many of the south's **steel bands**, including the highly acclaimed **Fonclaire**, now located on Dottin Street, one block south of Coffee Street. Opposite the Southern Food Basket supermarket on Coffee Street is the panyard of the **Skiffle Bunch**, a regular participant in the Panorama Finals at Carnival time. Just past the panyard, on the corner of Cipero Street, a statue of a lone pannist attests to the importance of T&T's national instrument to the area. The Coffee is particularly lively during the run-up to Carnival, when Skiffle Bunch practice sessions ring out into the street.

High Street, Happy Corner and King's Wharf

High Street is San Fernando's main shopping drag, where street vendors hawk everything from plastic trinkets to leopardskin underwear on the pavement in front of the stores. At its western end, as High Street doglegs into Queen Street, the sea comes into view. This area, ironically known as **Happy Corner**, is the most run-down in the city, but a few colonial buildings, including *Hotel Happy Corner* bar with its pretty balcony overlooking the junction of Queen and King streets, provide some architectural interest, while the patrons of the local rum shops add a touch of raffish zest. Happy Corner gives onto **King's Wharf**, a scruffy tarmac dock fronting a small harbour where fishing boats bob up and down on the swell; the adjacent **fish market** stands next to the **Water Taxi Terminal**.

Lady Hales Avenue

Lady Hales Avenues skirts the coast then veers east through the southern part of the city (where it runs parallel with the Rienzi-Kirton Highway), close to two of San Fernando's **shopping malls**, the enormous Gulf City and Cross Crossing, with their food courts and scores of international shops. Lady Hales is also home to the **Southern Academy for Performing Arts** (SAPA), the sister building to the one on the Queen's Park Savannah in Port of Spain, and without its northern counterpart's infrastructural problems; it's regularly used for concerts and other events. Just past SAPA, **Skinner Park** cricket ground serves as a venue for regular concerts and fetes as well as sporting events.

ARRIVAL AND DEPARTURE | **SAN FERNANDO**

By car There are several exits signposted for San Fernando from the Solomon Hochoy Hwy; for the centre of town, take the Naparima-Mayaro Rd exit, cross over the San Fernando bypass, and follow Royal Rd, which later becomes Coffee St and then Harris Promenade. Parking can be an issue right in the centre, as can congestion; you may find spaces in the sideroads off the main streets, or look out for private car parks dotted around town, which charge a small fee.

By water taxi Services to and from Port of Spain arrive and depart from the Water Taxi Terminal (☎624 5137, ⓦnidco.co.tt) at King's Wharf, just past Happy Corner. Schedules do change, but at the time of writing were Mon–Fri only, departing Port of Spain at 6.40am, 7.15am, 2pm, 3.30pm, 4.30pm and 5.30pm, and San Fernando at

5.30am, 6am, 6.30am, 7.50am, 8am and 3.10pm. Journey time is about 1hr and tickets cost TT$15.

By public transport A large lot between the Chancery Lane Market and the San Fernando General Hospital serves as the main transport stand for buses, maxis and route taxis heading to and from all destinations in the south of the country. PTSC (☎652 3705, ⓦptsc.co.tt) runs an express bus service between Port of Spain (Mon–Sat from 5am to 8.20pm) and San Fernando (Mon–Sat from 4.30am to 7.40pm); journey time is 1hr 20min, and services depart every 15–20min.

GETTING AROUND

By car Given the city's sprawling layout and its numerous hills, you'll need a car or public transport to get around if heading away from the centre. Car rental is available from Southern (☎653 2424, ⓦexecuservice.co.tt) or Alamo (☎657 8521, ⓦalamo.com).

By route taxi Route taxis ply the streets around the clock; almost all routes originate at – or at least pass through – Library Corner, but be sure to ask the driver where he's

going before getting in. From next to the *KFC* in Library Corner, "round the road" taxis follow a loop around the city centre, circling San Fernando Hill; this is also the departure point for taxis to the Cross Crossing and Gulf City shopping malls.

By private taxi Two local private taxi firms are Mattadeen's Taxicab Service (☎658 4973) and St Anthony's Taxicab Co-Operative (☎648 3941). Uber also operate in the city.

ACCOMMODATION

Given the lack of tourist infrastructure and the expense accounts of business travellers, the city is woefully short on accommodation at the cheaper end of the spectrum. Be aware that the *Hotel Tokyo*, right in the city centre on St James St, and *Villa Capri* in Marabella just north of San Fernando, are both brothels.

Paria Suites Southern Main Rd, La Romaine ☎697 1442, ⓦpariasuites.com; map p.176. Overlooking the Gulf of Paria a few kilometres southwest of San Fernando, but easily reached on any maxi or taxi going to La Brea, Point Fortin, Fyzabad or Siparia, this is a smart option, slightly less business oriented than the places in town. Rooms come with a/c, private bathrooms and cable TV, while an on-site swimming pool, restaurant and busy bar provide welcome entertainment. 🛜 US$125

Royal Hotel 46–54 Royal Rd ☎652 4881, ⓦroyal hoteltt.com; map p.176. As central a location as you're going to get in San Fernando, a 15min walk from Library Corner. Comfortable, bright rooms have a/c, cable TV, phone, fridge and en-suite bathrooms. There's a breezy

open-air restaurant on site, as well as a pleasant, reasonably large swimming pool and a fitness centre. Rates include continental breakfast. 🛜 US$115

Tradewinds Hotel 38 London St, St Joseph Village ☎652 9463, ⓦtradewindshotel.com; map p.176. The best-equipped hotel in the south, occupying a pleasant – albeit not very central – location on a breezy hill in quiet St Joseph Village, a 10min drive from the centre. The most appealing rooms are in the renovated and ultramodern building next to the swimming pool, bar and restaurant, all with a/c, cable TV, fridge, microwave oven, minibar, kettle and nice bathrooms. There's a large gym and jacuzzi, and a good buffet breakfast is included in the rates, as is a shuttle to Piarco airport. 🛜 US$170

EATING

Grabbing a quick fix of roti, chow mein or fried chicken is hardly a problem in San Fernando, where numerous fast-food outlets line the streets. There's an especially high concentration of informal places for weekday lunches or early dinners along High St, Cipero St and the Coffee, while the food courts at San Fernando's malls offer a variety to suit most tastes. If you're after some evening street food, check the stalls that set up on Lady Hales Ave opposite Skinner Park, serving corn soup, doubles and the like.

Amin's 10 Cipero St ☎652 5108; map p.176. Reckoned by many to be the city's best roti shop, with all the usual fillings and long queues forming at lunchtime. Food tends to run out by 2 or 3pm, so go early. Rotis from TT$25. Mon–Sat 7am–5pm.

★ **Atherly's** 34 Sutton St ☎652 7373, ⓦbit.ly/Atherlys;

map p.176. *Atherly's* offers inexpensive, reliable Creole and Indian food, including local breakfasts (around TT$25) and lunch specials (from TT$60). Good for a drink in the evenings, when a DJ plays a nice selection of calypso, reggae and old hits (Wed–Sun), and there's a happy hour on Friday evenings. Mon & Tues 6am–4pm, Wed–Sun 6am–1am.

4

★ **More Vino More Sushi** 33 Scott St ☎223 8466, ⓦmorevino.com; map p.176. The sister establishment of the enduringly popular Ariapita Ave sushi restaurant-cum-wine bar, the southern version is just as good, with a wide variety of rolls and sashimi (from TT$78), plus mains (around TT$80) such as katsu curry, pad Thai and pastas Alfredo. Great wine list and cocktails, and a lively liming spot, with hookah pipes available. Mon–Wed 11am–midnight, Thurs–Sat 11am–1am.

Mother Nature 58 St James St ☎313 0777; map p.176. This shop and café is known for its good range of inexpensive natural juices and vegetarian snacks, alongside "miracle" vitamin supplements. Provides a good break from the downtown Sando mayhem. Lunch from around TT$40. Mon–Sat 6am–3pm.

Parlour Royale 38 Royal Rd 222 1090; map p.176.

Lovely little café that's great for light lunch or tea, with all the offerings (from TT$40) beautifully laid out in a very stylish plant-filled vintage-chic interior. Savoury highlights might include chicken-and-mushroom or potato-and-cheese galettes, salami croissants and chicken sandwiches, while street treats run from raspberry cream-cheese Danishes to chocolate and salted caramel cake. Cocobel chocolates, too. Wed–Fri 11.30am–6pm, Sat 11.30am–4pm.

Rising Star M. Rampersad Building, Hilda Lazzari Terrace ☎685 9539, ⓦrisingstartt.com; map p.176. Busy place, serving a huge menu of reasonably priced Chinese food (around TT$50 per half-portion) including good veggie options, as well as steaks and grilled chicken and fish (TT$90–120), while the bar area makes a good liming spot, with regular live music. You can puff away on hookah pipes, too. Daily 10am–late.

DRINKING AND NIGHTLIFE

The city's numerous friendly rum shops remain the evening location of choice for the majority of locals – ideal to sink a few beers and partake in some drunken conversation. There are also some lively bars, and several of the restaurants listed above are good for a drink.

The Rig Southern Trunk Rd, La Romaine ☎653 9129; map p.176. Just on the outskirts of the city, about 2km southwest of the centre opposite Gulf City Mall, this is a busy, popular bar with regular live music and a buzzing atmosphere. Food also available, and there are regular drinks promotions. Mon–Sat 11am–3am, Sun 4pm–3am.

Space La Nouba Southern Trunk Rd, La Romaine ☎697 1165, ⓦspacetrinidad.com; map p.176. A few buildings down from *The Rig*, this purpose-built round building with a Star Trek-style interior is an ever-busy spot, with regular drinks-inclusive nights and a changing music selection each week. Cover around TT$100. Wed, Fri & Sat 10pm–4am.

ENTERTAINMENT

In addition to the places below, San Fernando also has several cinemas, each catering to distinctly different tastes, and a number of places to catch live music.

Naparima Bowl 19 Paradise Pasture ☎652 2526, ⓦnaparimabowl.com. A worthy venue for live music year-round.

Skinner Park Rienzi-Kirton Hwy ☎657 7168. At the southern edge of the city, Skinner Park hosts Carnival fetes

and concerts; entrance tickets vary.

Southern Academy for the Performing Arts Cnr Rienzi-Kirton Hwy and Todd St ☎657 4380, ⓦbit.ly/SapaTT. Two large theatres used for concerts and plays.

DIRECTORY

Banks and exchange facilities First Citizens, cnr High St and Penitence St; Republic, 92–94 Cipero St; Scotiabank, cnr Cipero St and Rushworth St. All have ATMs.

Hospital San Fernando General, Independence Ave (☎652 3581).

Pharmacy SuperPharm, Gulf City Mall, Southern Trunk Rd

(Mon–Sat 9am–10.30pm, Sun 9am–9pm; ☎653 9934).

Police The main police station is at the western end of Harris Promenade (☎652 3206).

Post office Carlton Centre, St James St. Mon–Fri 7am–5pm, Sat 8am–2pm.

The southwest peninsula

Often referred to as the "deep south", Trinidad's **southwest peninsula** has it fair share of gritty industrial development, though its sleepy rural backwaters are worthy of exploration. Beyond the oil towns of **Point Fortin**, **Siparia** and **Fyzabad** you can drive down via pretty **Erin** through teak plantations to quiet **Quinam** beach, where the soft brown sand is backed by red-earth cliffs and lapped by calm seas – an escapist's fantasy and usually deserted apart from the odd fisherman. Heading along the Southern Main Road down to Trinidad's extreme southwest tip takes you through seaside **Cedros** and the vast coconut plantations around **Columbus Bay** to **Icacos Point**, with its rugged fishing beach and pretty wetlands. The atmosphere in this part of Trinidad is irresistibly low-key – and this tranquillity, along with the scenery, is its main draw.

Despite its proximity to industrial San Fernando, and its threatened status thanks to the ongoing construction of a highway between San Fernando and Point Fortin, the mangrove swampland of the **Oropuche Lagoon** remains a wildlife haven, teeming with tropical birds. Close by, the **Banwari Trace Archeological Site** has yielded the Caribbean's oldest Amerindian relics, and is a fascinating place to visit by guided tour. A better-known tourist attraction is the unique **Pitch Lake** at **La Brea**, while as for culinary exploration, look no further than the delicious roti shops and street-food stalls of **Debe**, one of Trinidad's most wholeheartedly Indian settlements.

Oropuche Lagoon

Spreading back from the Southern Main Road some 6km south of San Fernando, the little-visited tidal mangrove swamps of the **Oropuche Lagoon** are an excellent place to view **butterflies** as well as **birds** such as egrets, black-bellied whistling duck, American bittern, ringed kingfish, white-headed marsh tyrant, pygmy kingfisher, spotted toddy flycatcher and a variety of herons. Paria Springs Tours (see page 39) includes the Oropuche Lagoon on its excellent West Coast Wetlands and Icacos **birding tours**, tending to go to the inland areas of the swamp at dusk.

Banwari Trace Archeological Site

Ⓦ bit.ly/BanwariNT • Indigenous History Tours TT$225; ☎ 768 7613, Ⓦ bit.ly/ARCTnT

Southeast of the Oropuche Lagoon, just off the San Francique Rd, the **Banwari Trace Archeological Site** is perhaps the most significant in the country for people of Amerindian descent as the place where, in 1969, archeologists uncovered the 5000-year-old remains of **Banwari Man** (see page 250). Subsequent carbon dating revealed that the remains (and the site) represent the oldest human settlement in the Caribbean. Banwari is a protected heritage site, and you need a permit to enter; best plan is to arrange an **Indigenous History Tour** with First Peoples film-maker and artist Tracy Assing, who offers an expert insight into Amerindian Trinidad past and present, and will guide you around the site.

Rousillac

West of Oropuche, **ROUSILLAC** is best known for the landmark **roadside pepper sauce** stall at the community's southwestern end. Run by the Thomas family for decades, the stacks of sauces – brightly coloured fine pepper, tamarind and chadon beni, alongside lime pepper, the fiery "mother-in-law" and mango chutneys – are impossible to miss and makes a great photo opportunity as well as a chance to take home a truly authentic taste of Trinidad.

La Brea

Taking its name from the Spanish word for "pitch", the community of **LA BREA** (also called Union Village) is usually bypassed by those en route to the **Pitch Lake**. One of the first two oil wells in the world was drilled here in 1857 by the American Merrimac Oil Company, but even with the omnipresent pumping jacks and despite the fact that the lake has been commercially exploited since the early twentieth century, this is one of Trinidad's more impoverished communities today. Spreading back from the main road towards the sea, La Brea's many colonial-era buildings are well worth a look: the grand old police station and courthouse right at the water's edge are particularly impressive, as is the old rum shop at the village's centre (if it hasn't been pulled down by the time you visit, like so many old buildings in Trinidad), which makes for an atmospheric stopoff for a quick drink.

Vessigny Beach

3km south of La Brea • Lifeguards daily 10am–6pm • Changing rooms TT$1

The wide brown sands and shallow waters of **Vessigny Beach** are popular with Trinis at weekends. There are changing rooms, a snack bar and kayaks for rent, but it's not especially appealing for swimming as a river discharges muddy water into the bay here. Nonetheless, the bar makes for a scenic place to refresh yourself en route to the Pitch Lake.

Pitch Lake

Southern Main Rd, 1.5km south of La Brea • Daily 9am–5pm • Tours TT$50 • ☎ 651 1232

Just south of La Brea, the **Pitch Lake** is touted by some Trinis as the eighth wonder of the world. It may not look particularly impressive from a distance, bearing a remarkable resemblance to a flooded car park (albeit one ringed with cashew trees and bird of paradise flowers), but this 40,000-square-metre site is the largest deposit of pitch in the world, and it's well worth taking a **guided tour** of the lake to learn more about its intriguing complexities.

Although there's nothing stopping you from exploring the lake on your own, a tour is pretty much essential for safety – some parts of the lake are not firm enough to walk on, with soft patches difficult for the uninitiated to recognize; guides will also provide some illuminating commentary, and make sure you don't leave with your shoes covered in tar (it's virtually impossible to remove if caught on clothing). Official guides, identifiable by their orange T&T-monogrammed shirts, are available via the museum (see page 182), the complex on your left as you approach the lake. On arrival you'll probably be approached by unofficial guides, too, who will usually negotiate on tour prices. Based at the yellow snack shop on the left as you enter the lake, they charge a little less but may not offer as full or informed a tour.

4

PITCH PERFECT

La Brea's **Pitch Lake** was formed some five to six million years ago, when asphaltic oil flowed into a huge mud volcano here and slowly developed into pitch. Some 180 tonnes are now extracted each day, to be refined into asphalt and used to pave roads the world over. The depth of the lake is estimated at 75m and the level of pitch rises naturally after each excavation – calculations suggest that there's enough to last four or five centuries, though the surface is several metres lower than it was when excavation began in 1867.

Amerindians believed that the lake was created to punish an Amerindian tribe that killed and ate the sacred hummingbird, and were swallowed up in its depths. **Sir Walter Raleigh** was the first European "discoverer", happening upon the lake in 1595, and using the pitch to caulk his ships, while colonial governor Sir Ralph Woodford used it to pave over the capital's dirt roads in 1815, making Port of Spain the first city in the world with asphalt streets. Control of pitch excavation remained in British hands until 1978, when it was taken over by the T&T government.

The Pitch Lake is not the only place hereabouts that asphalt swells from the earth: local **roads** are often excruciatingly bumpy thanks to upward pressure from the underground volcanic eruptions that replenish the lake, while many a front garden or driveway hereabouts is paved with lumpy local pitch.

The gooey, tar-like "**mother of the lake**" takes up some 25 percent of the total surface. Guides will explain the lake's history (see page 181) and its various geological features, and use a stick to scoop up some of the soft tar, which feeds the pitch, but is in itself useless for making asphalt. Dotted with reeds and water lilies and frequented by wading birds, the pretty pools around the edges of the lake are popular spots for locals to take an evening dip, as their sulphur-rich waters are said to be good for mosquito bites and skin conditions. Lake tours also include a look around the small **museum**, with info boards covering the lake's history, from Amerindian legends to commercial pitch extraction.

Point Fortin

The south's industrial flavour continues at the oil town of **POINT FORTIN**. Its tennis courts, golf course and old country club were built for expat managers by Shell (former owners of the refinery here), while the suburbs are characterized by sprawling houses with high walls and barking dogs. Point Fortin offers very little to visitors unless you happen to have a personal interest in the oil industry, and only comes to life after 4pm, when workers come out to lime in the **bars** and hang around the main junction. By far the best time to visit is for the annual **Borough Day** celebrations at the beginning of May: two weeks of Carnival-style revelry and music and dance competitions, including a raucous Jouvert morning and a two-day procession: see ⓦpointfortinborough.com for more.

ACCOMMODATION   POINT FORTIN

4

South Western Court 16 Cap-de-Ville Main Rd ☏ 648 0075, ⓦ swc-hotel.com. Useful for Borough Day or as an alternative southern base to Sando, this is a fifteen-room business-oriented place with large dining and conference facilities, and bright a/c rooms with cable TV, some with balconies. It's obliquely opposite the market. In the unlikely event that the rooms here are full, ask about the nearby sister property, *Clifton Hill Manor*. ☏ US$173

Cedros

The catch-all name for the extreme tip of the southwest peninsula, **Cedros** was first settled by Spaniards, whose influence lingered longer in this isolated region than in the rest of the island; despite an influx of Indian indentured labourers, Spanish was still widely spoken until the 1880s, almost a century after the British had captured Trinidad. During the nineteenth-century heyday of the sugar estates, Cedros was a bustling place, with twice the current population and no fewer than seven rum distilleries. These are long-gone, however, and Cedros **village** is a fairly sleepy place today, its network of residential streets spreading back from a seafront promenade. In the middle of the bay is a concrete jetty, kept busy by local fishermen and the many Venezuelans who make the nine-mile pirogue journey from the mainland to Trinidad to shop, checking in at the village's tiny customs post before heading in to San Fernando's malls.

Nature's Best

Off the Southern Main Rd, just outside Cedros • No set hours • Call to arrange a visit ☏ 690 2061 or ☏ 330 5462

Nature's Best is one of three apiaries in the area, and manufactures beeswax, royal jelly and a couple of skin- and haircare products. You can view the production process and buy some products at source at the home of apiary owner Chunilal Roopnarine, a font of information on bee-keeping in Trinidad.

Cedros beaches

Every bay in Cedros seems to have a picture-postcard **beach**, where the idyllic setting more than compensates for the total lack of facilities. At **Chatham**, a left turn runs about 6km to the south coast, where there's a picturesque and deserted beach of sand and red rocks. The beach at **Granville** is so far off the beaten track – 5.5km from the

Southern Main Road through the village of the same name, about halfway between Point Fortin and Icacos Point – that it's often completely deserted.

Columbus Bay

Some 2km from the roadside village of **Fullarton** is lovely **Columbus Bay**, a long stretch of flotsam-dotted beach lined with the coconut palms of the huge San Rafael Estate, one of the most extensive in Trinidad. The eye-popping **views** extend down to the South American mainland, and looking southwest it's difficult to tell where Trinidad ends and Venezuela begins. It's a view that's changed little from the one that greeted the eponymous explorer when he stopped here after landing at Moruga in 1498 (see page 188); just offshore lie the three **Sisters Rocks**, while the eastern end of the bay is capped by the brown sandstone Los Gallos Point, its cliffs eroded into intricate formations by the tides. Columbus Bay attracts small crowds of bathers at weekends, and there are basic facilities available, including a (sporadically open) bathroom/changing room and a snack shop.

Icacos Point

Southwest of Columbus Bay, the views become ever more spectacular as the road winds through the coconut plantation and along a causeway that runs right through some beautiful **wetlands**, with acres of marsh and limpid pools home to a huge variety of birds – look out for **scarlet ibis**, which roost here at dusk. Past the wetlands, the road winds down to the sleepy little village of **Icacos** ("eye-*car*-cus"), a tiny place that nonetheless has a mosque, church and Hindu temple. Turn right when you arrive at the village and walk for about twenty minutes along a track bordered by coconut trees to reach **Icacos Point**, Trinidad's extreme southwest tip. It's a faraway spot, with the vague outline of the Venezuelan coast 11km away across the **Serpent's Mouth**, whose swirling waters don't deter the drug smugglers who use the area's beaches to bring in Colombian cocaine via Venezuela, eventually destined for the American mainland. Nine kilometres west out to sea, the craggy silhouette of **Soldado Rock** marks the division between Venezuelan and Trinidadian territorial waters, and is a major breeding site for frigate birds, grey breasted martins and brown pelicans, and a nesting site for sooty tern and brown noddy.

Erin

Blessed with many pretty villages and little-visited beaches, the area east of Cedros and south of Point Fortin and La Brea is known as **Erin**. Driving from the Cedros side, tiny **Buenos Ayres** is especially attractive, with beautifully dilapidated colonial houses and a couple of good rum shops. **Erin village** (San Francique on many maps) is equally easy on the eye, with old board houses set in flowering gardens and fishing boats bobbing in the bay – this is one of Trinidad's most important fishing villages. During the fishing season (June–Dec), **Puerto Grande** beach buzzes with activity, as fishermen land their catch and weigh it on large old-fashioned scales at the shoreline, discussing prices in discreet tones, while nets are mended or laid out to dry on the sand. It's a fascinating scene, though things are a lot quieter out of season, when the boats move to Moruga to follow the fish.

Erin's beaches

The Erin area has some attractive secluded bathing spots off the San Fernando–Siparia–Erin Road (usually shortened to the SS–Erin Road). Some 2km east of Puerto Grande via a signposted turn-off, the pretty cove of **Los Iros** offers calm, clean waters and a small snack parlour and bar; at weekends, whole families descend with Sunday lunch loaded into pots, containers and coolers. Eight kilometres east of Erin village, there's another marvellous beach at **Palo Seco Bay**; turn onto Beach Road by the YKC & Son supermarket in Palo Seco village, park at the Petrotrin beach club, and walk for fifteen minutes along a dirt road to reach the driftwood-scattered 4km beach.

Debe

On the southern outskirts of San Fernando at **La Romaine**, a left turn by *Paria Suites* hotel brings you onto the SS–Erin Road, which threads through the wholeheartedly Indian communities of the island's oil belt. Note, however, that at the time of writing the junction was being worked on as part of a new highway extension, and the road layout may well change once the highway link road is constructed. Heralded by a riot of clashing shop signs that wouldn't look out of place in Delhi or Kolkata, the first town of any size is **DEBE**, credited for the invention of **doubles**, Trinidad's most popular street food (see page 28). Doubles are sold at the roadside daily from 6am, and as the afternoon cools down, vendors also set up stalls selling a huge variety of fantastic **Indian snacks**, from pholouri to the less widely available *baigani* (sliced aubergine in batter), *saheena* (split-pea and dasheen-leaf fritters) and *katchourie*, fried fingers of ground channa and spices; sweets include *kurma* doughballs, milk and ginger *barfi*, and *jalebi*, a sticky neon orange curl of fried batter. Debe and its neighbour, **PENAL**, are both known for their lively **Divali celebrations**, when the streets are lit up at nights and Indian dancers and *tassa* drummers provide the entertainment.

Fun Splash Water Park

M2 Ring Rd, north of Debe • Daily 10am–6pm • Adults TT$70, children TT$30 • ☏ 647 0350, ⍵ bit.ly/FunSplashTT

The excellent **Fun Splash Water Park** offers a welcome chance to cool off, with pools (one is for adults only) and eleven water-slides for adults and kids, plus kayaking and pedal boats; there are picnic areas and snack shops on site, plus a sizeable car park, and you can bring your own coolers.

Siparia

Penal slides imperceptibly into **SIPARIA**, though the main street here retains a few attractive **colonial houses** alongside the concrete storefronts. As well as poking around the central produce market, it's worth peeking into the **La Divina Pastora Catholic church** (follow the road that branches off the Southern Main Road opposite Republic Bank) to see the **Black Virgin**, a small statue of the Virgin Mary which is carried through the streets as the centrepiece of the annual La Divina Pastora festival (see below).

Quinam Beach

Lifeguards daily 10am–6pm

South of Siparia, the Coora Road/Penal–Quinam Road (turn off the SS–Erin Road just before *KFC* and follow the signs) swings past pumping jacks and through teak plantations to **Quinam Beach**, the south coast's most popular swimming spot, with a wide swathe of sand at low tide overlooked by crumbling cliffs studded with Baptist,

---

LA DIVINA PASTORA AND SIPAREE MAI

Held on the second Sunday after Easter since the early twentieth century, Siparia's **Festival of La Divina Pastora** holds a special place in Trinidad's religious calendar as the only day of the year on which Hindus worship at a Catholic church. The celebrations are centred around the **Black Virgin** statue, which is decked out in new clothes, carried in procession through the streets to the beat of *tassa* drums, and showered with offerings of gold bracelets, flowers, sweets, fruit, oil and money. The festival is one big street party, with the whole town coming out to celebrate, and culminates in a blow-out feast. Though the statue's origins are hazy, she's said to have been responsible for many miracles, while Spiritual Baptists accredit her with mystical powers. Hindus associate her with the goddess Kali, the destroyer of sorrow, and call her **Siparee Mai** or Mother of Siparia. Before the festival, special barbers set up along the main street to give Hindu children their first haircut, with the locks then being presented as offerings to the statue in the hope of ensuring good luck in the year ahead.

URIAH BUTLER

Trinidad's foremost trade union activist, **Tubal Uriah "Buzz" Butler** was a Grenadian who came to work in Trinidad's oilfields in 1921. After an industrial accident in 1929 left him unfit for oil work, he joined the Moravian Baptist church and became a preacher, developing the rousing oratorical skills that characterized his political career. Disillusioned with Cipriani's Trinidad Workingmen's Association (see page 255) after it failed to support an oilworkers' strike in 1935, he established the **British Empire Workers** (BEW) to further the "heroic struggle for British justice for British Blacks in a British colony".

The BEW campaigned for better pay and working conditions in the oilfields, where many of the managers were white South Africans who had instituted an apartheid-type regime. Among the workers' many grievances were low wages, long working hours and the frequency of industrial accidents, for which there was no compensation. Workers were liable to be dismissed on the spot and, once sacked, a blackballing system made it impossible for them to find work elsewhere.

DISSENT, PROTEST AND IMPRISONMENT

In June 1937 strikers started a **sit-in** at the Forest Reserve oilfield. The police broke up the protest, and in response the strikers set fire to two wells in the Apex oilfield. When the police arrived at Fyzabad to arrest Butler on a charge of agitation, they found him addressing a large crowd; as they attempted to serve the warrant, a **riot** broke out. One plain-clothes officer, the deeply unpopular **Charlie King**, fled into a nearby shop, found himself trapped, and jumped from an upstairs window, breaking his leg; the furious crowd burned him alive, and when his colleagues tried to retrieve his body, a British police officer was shot dead. A 1938 calypso caught the popular mood: "Everybody's rejoicing, How they burned Charlie King, Everybody was glad, Nobody was sad, When they beat him and they burned him, In Fyzabad."

Strikes spread like wildfire and became increasingly violent, with a mounting death toll on both sides. Butler, in hiding after the riot, was soon discovered and sentenced to two years in prison. Nonetheless, the strikes won important concessions: public workers were granted an eight-hour day and a higher minimum wage, while trade unions were given official recognition (though the police continued to harass union officials). On his release in 1939, Butler was given a hero's welcome, but during his imprisonment the BEW had changed, adopting a more mainstream position, and he was soon expelled. In September 1939 Butler was once again incarcerated for sedition, and remained behind bars till the end of World War II.

BUTLER'S LATER YEARS

Butler continued to be politically active after his release in 1945, campaigning in the national elections, but though his party won the largest block of seats in 1950, he was outflanked by the rise of Eric Williams' nationalist politics (see page 256), and his star faded. In remembrance of his role in defending workers' rights, the Princess Margaret Highway linking north and south Trinidad was renamed in his honour in the 1960s. In 1971 the government awarded him the **Trinity Cross** – the highest honour in the land – and June 19, the day of the riots, was declared a public holiday, celebrated in Fyzabad with a parade through the streets. Butler died in February 1977, and is buried in Fyzabad's cemetery.

Muslim and Hindu prayer flags and devotional figurines. There are several thatch-roofed barbecue pits close to the car park, but unless you're here at the weekend, when vendors sell snacks and drinks, you'll need to bring your own refreshment.

Fyzabad

North of Siparia, the Siparia–Fyzabad Road strikes north towards the coast; some 5km along, the rather raggle-taggle **FYZABAD** was named by Indian indentured workers after the Uttar Pradesh district where most of them hailed from. After oil was discovered here in 1917, the town became the centre of the emergent labour movement, while the original Indo-Trinidadian Presbyterian community were quickly outnumbered by migrants from Grenada and St Vincent who came to work on the oilfields, and whose descendants make up the majority of the town's population today.

The compact commercial centre clusters around Charlie King Junction, overlooked by the Oil Workers' Trade Union Hall (OWTU) and a statue of the workers' leader **Uriah Butler** (see page 185) in his black suit and bowler hat. Come **Labour Day** (June 19), the street here is blocked to traffic to make way for a street party with a political undercurrent, with fiery speeches and the inevitable calypso and soca blasting from speakers.

The southern central region

South-central Trinidad is one of the most impenetrable parts of the island. Running from the west to the east coast through rolling plains of sugar cane, and linking the region's two main towns, **Princes Town** and **Rio Claro**, the Naparima–Mayaro Road is the only transport artery. South of the tarmac, wild forest predominates. There are few passable roads, signs are almost nonexistent and trying to follow a map is a lesson in frustration – you'll need to ask for directions if driving yourself. Moruga Road is the only decent thoroughfare through this wilderness, running down to the isolated fishing village of **Moruga**.

GETTING AROUND

By car Though south-central Trinidad is covered by maxis and route taxis, renting a car is the best way to get around, unless you're happy to endure long waits and lots of changes. **By maxi and route taxi** Maxis and taxis are frequent along the Naparima–Mayaro Rd from Princes Town to Rio Claro. You can also get a maxi or taxi to Moruga from Princes Town. The maxi stand in Princes Town is in the Nipdec Car Park on the main drag just east of the market.

Princes Town

East of San Fernando, beyond the blackened chimneys of the old **St Madeleine Sugar Factory** – now closed but still a rather incongruous sight in the midst of rolling fields and lines of palm trees – **PRINCES TOWN** is a mishmash of new buildings in every imaginable style (check out the colourful murals and reliefs of Hindu gods and the Statue of Liberty on the walls of the **Tyre Warehouse** store), alongside more sober structures such as the grand mosque on the east side of the centre, with its copper dome and steel-plated minarets. Originally called Mission de Savanna Grande, Princes Town was renamed following a visit in 1880 by British princes George (who later became King George V) and Albert Victor, who planted two poui trees in the grounds of the spiffily refurbished St Stephen's Church, one of which is still standing.

The Company Villages

Merikin Heritage Foundation tours US$60, including transport from Port of Spain; lunch TT$65 • ☎ 689 7794, ✆ bit.ly/Merikin

On the outskirts of Princes Town, the tiny **Company Villages** are a legacy of black American soldiers (and former slaves) who fought for the British in the War of 1812 in return for the promise of land; after the British defeat, they were allocated lots in Trinidad, and became known as **Merikins**. Landing here in 1816, the soldiers managed to establish successful plantations in what had been uncharted jungle, earning themselves the reputation of pioneers, but their complaints about the condition of the land went unheard; British governor Ralph Woodford not only wanted to open up the southern interior, but had a vested interest in keeping radical black soldiers isolated from potentially rebellious slaves elsewhere on the island.

The **Fifth Company** and **Sixth Company** villages retain their original names, but these days First Company is known as **New Grant**, Third Company as **Indian Walk** and Fourth Company as **Hard Bargain**; there is no village called Second Company – this unit is thought to have been lost at sea on the voyage to Trinidad. Save for a few signboards dotted around the villages detailing the basics of Merikin history, there's little for the casual visitor to differentiate the Company Villages from any other settlements in the area, so it's well worth getting in touch with the **Merikin Heritage Foundation** before you visit. Their tour provides the lowdown on Merikin history and culture, taking in all the Company Villages as well as significant sites such as the grave of the legendary Merikin elder, Orisha devotee and healer Papa Neezer; there's also a demonstration of stickfighting, and Merikin drumming and storytelling. You can opt for a traditional lunch, too.

As you navigate the Company Villages, look out for a large **Hanuman Murti** statue along the Naparima–Mayaro Road (no. 419); it's similar to the giant structure at Carapichaima (see page 156) but a lot smaller – its roadside sign has been amended to read that it's the "Second Largest Hanuman Murti in the Caribbean".

Devil's Woodyard

To drive to Devil's Woodyard, turn down the signposted Hindustan Rd, 4.5km past Indian Walk off the Naparima–Mayaro Rd; by public transport take a maxi from San Fernando to Princes Town, change here and get another from the main stand direct to Devil's Woodyard

Named after an 1852 eruption which scattered the planks of surrounding houses like matchsticks, the **Devil's Woodyard** mud volcanoes attract a regular procession of Trinidadian visitors. For many years, the site consisted of a series of rather underwhelming small hillocks, around 1m high, with grey mud bubbling lazily to the surface from small vents. This all changed in February 2018, when three major eruptions, spurting some 5m high, threw up the equivalent of some 174,500 barrels of mud; the resulting mudflow covered over 11,000 square metres, left angry cracks in the surrounding lawns and paths, and took out a few trees at the site's perimeter. Luckily, no one was injured, and the volcanoes had since remained quiet at the time of writing.

Amerindians are said to have believed that mud volcanoes were passages between this world and another below, and that the explosions were the devil coming out to shake the earth; the recent activity here no doubt lent a bit of current credence to the modern cautionary tale told to children, that at midnight a smartly dressed devil is said to dance on the volcano, and if you're awake to see it you vanish forever. The reality is of course less dramatic, but if you're curious to see a mud volcano this is the most accessible site, with picnic tables, toilets and a bar.

Moruga

South of Princes Town, the Moruga Road threads through untamed forest for 21km before meeting the sea at **MORUGA**, a pretty and very remote village that seems to have changed little since it was settled by black American soldiers after the War of 1812 (see page 252). The bright colours of the old board houses have weathered to pastel shades, but colourful fishing boats still lie on the seashore and fishermen while away their spare hours liming outside the shops-cum-bars on the main road. The seafront Catholic church dominates both the physical surroundings and the life of the villagers.

MUD VOLCANOES

Though marked on many maps and promoted as something of a tourist attraction, south Trinidad's many **mud volcanoes** are largely inaccessible – unless you like chopping through dense forest – and in most cases it's not worth the effort. The volcanoes are small mounds mostly less than a metre high that seep grey sulphuric mud, which is believed to be good for skin conditions.

The volcanoes can appear anywhere: in the middle of the bush, in people's back gardens and by the road. They are usually ignored, though those who live near them do so at their peril, for they have a tendency to explode every few years. The most recent and damaging explosion was in **Piparo** in central Trinidad in 1997 (see page 161), though the sizeable eruption at **Devil's Woodyard** (see above) caused a stir in early 2018.

This is a place of strong but heterodox beliefs: Morugans may avow allegiance to Catholicism, to the Spiritual Baptist faith or to Rastafari, but many believe in aspects of all (alongside a sprinkling of obeah; see page 251) and, perhaps thanks to the area's isolation, a palpably religious, well-nigh superstitious, atmosphere pervades.

Moruga's beaches

Moruga's main street, **Grand Chemin**, ends at the yellow sands of **Columbus Beach**, a pretty swathe of sand backed with impressive rocky outcrops, and named after Christopher Columbus, who briefly landed nearby in 1498 (see below). Also on the beach is a 4.5m-high statue of **St Peter**, erected by the St Vincent Ferrer Society, a Catholic community group which is led here by the energetic Eric Lewis, a community activist known as the Prince of Moruga (see page 189).

Turn off Grand Chemin at the police station and a road winds past Moruga's cemetery to another small bay, where Columbus is commemorated by a **statue** sculpted by Lewis. Carry on past the statue to reach Moruga's best swimming beach, an often deserted spot with fine brown sands and calm waters.

Moruga Museum

40 Grand Chemin, Moruga • Mon–Fri 8am–4pm, Sat 9am–5pm • TT$20 • ☎ 355 8318, Ⓦ morugamuseum1.wordpress.com

Founded and curated by Eric Lewis, the **Moruga Museum** holds some 800 artefacts, from fossils and shells to housewares, clothing, bottles and Amerindian ceramics, as well as displays centred on Catholicism in Trinidad and the Merikin peoples who

4

COLUMBUS IN TRINIDAD

Christopher Columbus had nearly run out of drinking water when, on July 31, 1498, he sighted the three peaks of the Trinity Hills, which are said to have inspired him to name the island Trinidad. He landed near present-day **Moruga**, where he gathered fresh water from the river. His crew reported seeing fishing implements that had clearly been abandoned in haste, and realized that they had arrived in a region that was already well populated. In fact, there were some 35,000 **Amerindians** (from the Arawak, Shebaio, Nepoio, Carinepagoto and Yao peoples) then living on the island that they called "Ieri", the land of the hummingbird.

Columbus sailed west and encountered the island's residents the next day while anchored off Icacos Point. Twenty-four Amerindians armed with bows and arrows set off in a large canoe to investigate the foreign ship; upon sighting them, Columbus ordered a drum to be played and the sailors to dance, believing the indigenous population would be entertained by this spectacle. However, the Amerindians mistook this for aggression and rained arrows on the Spaniards; as the latter returned fire, the Amerindians fled. That night, Columbus had little sleep as strong currents here tossed the ship, rocking it so violently that the anchor broke. Bewildered and fearful, Columbus swiftly sailed on, though not before bestowing the name "Serpent's Mouth" for the treacherous waters between Trinidad and Venezuela.

MORUGA'S COLUMBUS DAY

Moruga's Columbus connection has long been celebrated at the village's annual **Columbus Festival**, held on August 1, a holiday replaced elsewhere in Trinidad by Emancipation Day, which commemorates the abolition of slavery. Controversially, festival organizers here hold the view that without Columbus, the majority of Trinidadians would not have the benefit of living on the island, or of the Catholic faith; detractors of course point to the irony of celebrating European colonization of the Caribbean, which led to the slaughter and eradication of the First Peoples on so many islands. Nonetheless, Morugans defend their right to mark all aspects of their community's history, and though the event has now been renamed **Moruga Heritage Day**, it still sees boats decorated as fifteenth-century galleons and locals playing the part of Columbus and the Amerindians, the latter greeting the explorer armed with bows and arrows – not exactly an accurate account, but an entertaining spectacle nonetheless. Accompanying the re-enactment are stalls, music performances and plenty of local food and drink, as well as pirogue races in the bay.

MORUGA TOURS

Eric and Katherine Lewis, aka the Prince and Princess of Moruga, have developed several **tours** in and around the village (from TT$50 per person). Most include a guided visit to the Moruga Museum, the Columbus statue and Moruga's beautiful old **"spring bridge"**, the last of Trinidad's colonial-era suspension bridges still in operation (though a modern road bridge has been built alongside). From here, you can take a **boat tour** in an open pirogue down the mangrove-swathed river and out along the coast. The cocoa industry in Moruga, like many other places in Trinidad, is undergoing something of a revival, and there's also a **cocoa tour**, with a visit to old cocoa estate house where you can taste chocolate (with 75, 60 and 50 percent cocoa, plus honey and coconut varieties) made with local beans supplied by the Moruga Cocoa Co-operative, as well as venturing out for a walk around local cocoa plantations. **Hikes** in the local area are also available.

settled in the Company Villages (see page 186). Guided tours of the museum are usually available, as are trips into the surrounding area (see above); and locally made chocolate, cocoa balls, tamarind and pepper sauces (the latter featuring the legendarily hot Moruga scorpion pepper) are available to buy.

Rio Claro

Located on the Naparima–Mayaro Road some 24km east of Princes Town, **RIO CLARO** is the region's administrative hub, and a busy place compared with its surroundings – though that's not saying much in this somnolent corner of the island. The town enjoyed a period of prosperity between 1914 and 1965, when it was connected to Trinidad's major cities by the railway, but has been in a long decline ever since the trains stopped running, as young people abandon agricultural work for more profitable jobs in the oilfields and the cities. Rio Claro's connections with its Spanish heritage emerges towards Christmas, as the town's famous **parang** singers (see box, page 265) come out to entertain the clientele of the local bars and clubs. There's little to occupy you at other times, though on the western outskirts, the grand wedding-cake-pink and ice-blue **Catholic church** and **Hindu temple**, which has a stepped dome and gold and blue trimmings, are worth a look.

Trinity Hills Wildlife Sanctuary

Caribbean Discovery Tours (see page 39) offer full-day excursions, while Jalaludin Khan of Indiversity Tours (see page 39) and Eric Lewis in Moruga (see above) can also advise on trips and set you up with a local guide

Some 65 square kilometres of evergreen forest running down to the sea east of the Rio Claro–Guayaguayare Road, the **Trinity Hills Wildlife Sanctuary** encompasses the Trinity Hills and Mount Derrick, the tallest peak in the south at 314m. The hills form a watershed that's vital to the nation's water supply, and was declared a protected reserve in 1900. The many **rivers**, **streams** and **waterfalls** are excellent for bathing, while the lush forests of carat, redwood, cooperhoop and bois pois trees shelter animals such as lappe, agouti, quenk, tatoo and red howler monkeys, as well as rarely seen ocelots, capuchin monkeys, buck deer, armadillos and opossums. The wide variety of birdlife includes the mountain quail dove, while deep caves harbour many species of bats. A 45-minute hike from the road is a **mud volcano** and lake known as **Lagoon Bouffe**, at 100m wide one of Trinidad's largest.

Information on the reserve is hard to find due to its remoteness and the paucity of visitors. If you don't visit via an organized tour, you could drive or mountain-bike along the Moruga–Guayaguayare Road (also known as Edward Trace), an exceptionally pretty route which loops through thick virgin forest; you'll rarely see another soul the entire 35km. To avoid any problems at the oilfield gateposts, it's wise to get a free permit from Petrotrin, who have a number of pipelines running through the reserve.

Tobago

ENGLISHMAN'S BAY

5 Tobago

An elongated oval just 41km by 14km, Tobago manages a surprising diversity within her craggy coastal fringes. Rich in natural allure, from deserted palm-lined beaches and lively coral reefs to a wealth of lush rainforest, and with plenty of tourist infrastructure in its southwest corner, the island offers something for every taste. Tobago's greatest appeal, however, is its relatively unspoilt feel. Although tourism has definitely taken root here, development has so far been fairly low-key compared to many other Caribbean islands. There are few all-inclusive resorts and none of the high-rise hotels that have blighted many other tropical paradises – and the hustler mentality that exists on more touristy islands is less intense here.

A place where locals and tourists tend to co-exist in an easy equilibrium, with everyone frequenting the same beaches, bars and nightclubs, Tobago's overall vibe is overwhelmingly laidback and relaxing. Moreover, celebrations such as the Easter **goat races** are attended by more Tobagonians than tourists, and local culture is honoured at the annual **Heritage Festival** each August. The uniquely friendly mentality here is best expressed at the year-round **Harvest Festivals**, where entire villages open their doors to passing revellers.

Tobago is breathtakingly beautiful; heavy industry is confined to Trinidad, so the beaches here are clean and the landscape left largely to its own devices. The flat coral and limestone plateau of the **southwest tip** is the island's most heavily developed region, with the majority of hotels, bars and restaurants as well as the best – albeit most commercialized – beaches such as **Pigeon Point** and **Store Bay**. There are also quieter stretches of sand along this stretch of coast, where glass-bottom boats head for **Buccoo Reef**, palms sway over the **Mount Irvine** golf course, and hotels around **Plymouth** run night excursions to watch giant **turtles** laying eggs on the beach. Strong currents in this area provide some excellent **surfing** possibilities, with the rough seas between November and February (the height of the tourist season) producing big breakers at Mount Irvine Beach.

But Tobago isn't just sun, sand, surf and the tourist dollar. The commercial clamour of the southwest tip is kept in check by the capital, **Scarborough**, a lively, picturesque port town tumbling down a fort-topped hillside. Pummelled by the dark-green, wave-whipped Atlantic, the island's rugged **windward** (south) **coast** is lined with appealing fishing villages; **Speyside** and **Charlotteville** in the remote eastern reaches have **coral reefs** as ornate as you'll find anywhere in the Caribbean and **scuba diving** is a burgeoning industry. Tobago is an excellent and inexpensive place to learn to dive, and there's plenty of challenging drift diving for the more experienced, while the many

Highlights

❶ Get active Take a horse ride through Buccoo Bay, a stand-up paddle in Bon Accord Lagoon, a bike ride across the interior or a round of golf at either of Tobago's two beautiful courses. See pages 202 and 205

❷ Coastal cruise Hop onto a boat and cruise along Tobago's ravishing Caribbean coast, with stops for snorkelling at some of the island's best reefs and a barbecue lunch on a deserted beach. See page 202

❸ Creole lunch at Store Bay Fresh fish, "blue food" and curry crab and dumpling, the delectable staples of Tobagonian cooking are served up at a row of booths by the sea. See page 209

❹ Sunday School Dance your cares away every Sunday at this big, brash open-air party in Buccoo. See page 212

❺ Castara This picturesque fishing village has embraced tourism without being consumed by it, and boasts two fantastic beaches. See page 229

❻ Tobago Forest Reserve The oldest protected rainforest in the western hemisphere makes a sublime location for hiking or birdwatching. See page 234

❼ Pirate's Bay This secluded Charlotteville beach offers excellent swimming and snorkelling in an idyllic setting. See page 245

HIGHLIGHTS ARE MARKED ON THE MAP ON PAGE 194

5

fringing reefs within swimming distance of the beaches make for fantastic **snorkelling**. Coral sands and glassy Caribbean waters along the **leeward** (north) **coast** provide some of Tobago's finest beaches; some, like **Englishman's Bay**, are regularly deserted, while at **Parlatuvier** and **Bloody** bays, you'll share the sand with local fishermen. **Castara**, meanwhile, holds the only real tourist infrastructure along Tobago's Caribbean coast, with a host of guesthouses and places to enjoy the excellent fresh fish meals.

The landscape of the eastern interior rises steeply into the hillocks and rolling bluffs that make up the central **Main Ridge**. These mountains shelter the **Tobago**

TOBAGO

0   2
kilometres

N

CARIBBEAN SEA

Englishman's Bay

Castara Bay — Castara — **5**

King Peter's Bay — Mount Dillon — **Mount Dillon Lookout**

Runnemede

Culloden — Golden Lane — Moriah

Arnos Vale Bay — **2** — Arnos Vale — Les Coteaux

Mason Hall

Great Courland Bay (Turtle Beach) — Plymouth — **Craig Hall**

Black Rock

Stonehaven (Grafton) Bay — **Grafton Caledonia Bird Sanctuary**

Rocky Point — Pleasant Prospect — Orange Hill — Mount St George

Mt Irvine Bay — Bethel

Booby Point — **4** — **1** — **Kimme Museum** — Patience Hill — **Fort King George** — French Fort — **Dwight Yorke Stadium**

Buccoo Reef & Nylon Pool — **Mt Irvine** — Orange Hill — **SCARBOROUGH**

No Man's Land — Buccoo Bay — Buccoo — Signal Hill — Rockly Bay — Bacolet — Hillsborough Bay

Pigeon Point — **1** — Bon Accord Lagoon — Lambeau — Bacolet Bay — Minister Point

Bon Accord — Canaan — Little Rockly Bay — Bacolet Point — Minister Bay

Store Bay — **3** — MILFORD ROAD

A.N.R. Robinson International Airport — **1**

Sandy Point — Canoe Bay — **LOWLANDS**

Forest Reserve – the oldest protected rainforest in the western hemisphere – an abundant tangle of mist-shrouded greenery dripping down to fabulous coastlines, often with neither building nor road to interrupt the flow. Ornithologists and naturalists flock in for the **bird-** and **animal** life that flourishes here; David Attenborough filmed parts of his celebrated *Trials of Life* series at **Little Tobago**, a solitary sea-bird sanctuary off the coast of Speyside. For slightly less committed nature-lovers, the island's forested interior offers plenty of opportunities for birdwatching or a splash in the icy **waterfalls**.

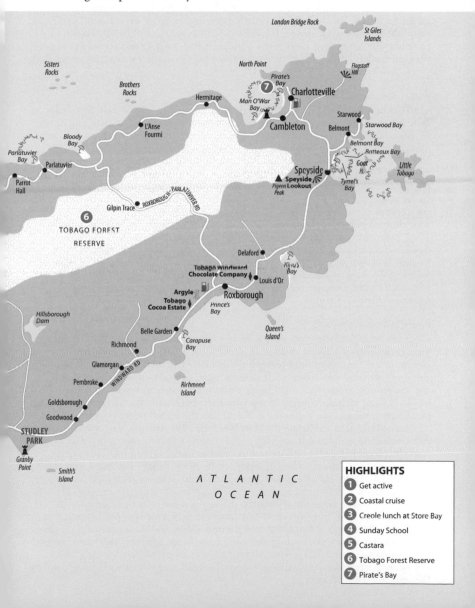

London Bridge Rock

St Giles
Islands

Sisters
Rocks

North Point

Flagstaff
Hill

Brothers
Rocks

Pirate's
Bay

7

Hermitage

Man O'War
Bay

Charlotteville

L'Anse
Fourmi

Cambleton

Starwood

Belmont

Starwood Bay

Bloody
Bay

Belmont Bay

Parlatuvier
Bay

Parlatuvier

Batteaux Bay

Goat
Is.

Little
Tobago

Parrot
Hall

ROXBOROUGH–PARLATUVIER RD

Speyside

Speyside
Lookout

Pigeon
Peak

Tyrrel's
Bay

Gilpin Trace

6

TOBAGO FOREST
RESERVE

Delaford

King's
Bay

Tobago Windward
Chocolate Company

Louis d'Or

Hillsborough
Dam

**Argyle
Tobago
Cocoa Estate**

Roxborough

Prince's
Bay

Belle Garden

Carapuse
Bay

Queen's
Island

Richmond

WINDWARD RD

Glamorgan

Pembroke

Richmond
Island

Goldsborough

Goodwood

STUDLEY
PARK

Granby
Point

Smith's
Island

A T L A N T I C
O C E A N

HIGHLIGHTS

1 Get active
2 Coastal cruise
3 Creole lunch at Store Bay
4 Sunday School
5 Castara
6 Tobago Forest Reserve
7 Pirate's Bay

5 Brief history

Tobago has long been a hotly contested property. The original **First Peoples** population fiercely defended the paradisiacal island that they called Tavaco (the name is derived from their word for tobacco) against other Amerindian tribes, and thwarted European colonization throughout the late 1500s and early 1600s. English sailors staked Britain's claim in 1580, tacking a flag to a tree trunk during a water stop en route to Brazil, and in 1641 England's King Charles I presented Tobago to his godson James, the Duke of Courland (a state of the Grand Duchy of Lithuania, now in Latvia). A group of **Latvians** arrived a year later, but their settlement at Plymouth suffered constant attacks from the Amerindians, and in 1658 was taken by the Dutch, who called it Nieuw Vlissingen; the same year, they were joined by 500 **French** colonists who established a separate settlement called Three Rivers. Twenty years later, the Courlanders left for good, and in the following years, the Amerindian population slowly petered out.

Pirates and plantations

Over the next hundred years, the belligerent shenanigans of the Dutch, British and French turned the coasts of Tobago into a **war zone**, with the island changing hands 31 times before 1814. Forts sprang up at every vantage point, and Tobago descended into turmoil, plundered by **pirates** and officially declared a no-man's land in 1702. In 1762, the British sent a powerful fleet, taking possession of the island with swift precision. Sustained by the promise of stability that came with firm British control, **plantation culture** began in earnest. The British were ousted by the French in 1781, but retook control of Tobago in 1793 – but both powers were equally efficient in their efforts to transform the island into a sugar, cotton and indigo factory. Africans were shipped in to work as **slaves**, with around 3000 toiling on the plantations by 1772 under the brutal control of less than three hundred Europeans. The economy flourished and, by 1777, the island's eighty or so estates had exported 1.5 million pounds of cotton, as well as vast quantities of rum, indigo and sugar. The numerical might of the slave population led to many bloody **uprisings**, with planters doling out amputations and death by burning and hanging to the those that stood up to the inhuman plantation regime.

Emancipation and beyond

Once the **Act of Emancipation** was passed in 1834, most of Tobago's African population took to the interior to plant small-scale farms, while others established coastal fishing communities. Some continued to work the estates as free men and women, but when Britain removed its protective tariffs on sugar sales, Tobago's unmechanized industry was unable to compete with other, more efficient producers. A severe hurricane in 1847, along with the collapse of the West India Bank (which underwrote the plantations), marked the beginning of the end for the island's sugar estates.

In the aftermath of the **Belmanna Riots** (see page 239), Tobago's Legislative Council relinquished its tenuous rule, and the island became a Crown colony in 1877. Having reaped all it could from the island and its sugar industry, Britain had little further need for this troublesome, ailing dependency. In 1899, Tobago was made a ward of Trinidad, effectively becoming the bigger island's poor relation with little control over her own destiny.

With the **collapse of the sugar industry**, the islanders fell back upon other crops, planting the acres of limes, coconuts and cocoa that still remain in patches today. Boosted by the arrival of **free Africans** in the mid-1800s, the black population clubbed together to farm the land, tending their food crops in the efficient "**Len-Hand**" system of shared labour that is still celebrated during Harvest Festivals. By the early 1900s Tobago was exporting fruit and vegetables to Trinidad, and was granted a single seat on the legislative council in 1927.

Tobago today

In 1963, **Hurricane Flora** (see page 236) razed whole villages and laid waste to most of the island's crops; the ensuing restructuring programme saw the first tentative steps towards developing a tourist industry. By 1980, the island had her sovereignty partially restored when the **Tobago House of Assembly** (THA) was reconvened, but it had authority only over the island's more mundane affairs while the main decisions were still made in Trinidad. Although Tobago now has a stronger profile in the republic's affairs, the local populace still resentfully perceives itself as looked down on by bigger Trinidad.

In terms of the economy, though visitor arrivals are well down on the heyday years of the 1990s, **tourism** remains the island's main earner. Development projects abound along some of the island's most pristine and lovely stretches of coast, such as the proposed *Sandals* mega-hotel at Buccoo/Bon Accord Lagoon. It remains to be seen whether all this construction will erode the very things that attract tourists to Tobago in the first place.

ARRIVAL AND DEPARTURE   TOBAGO

BY PLANE

A.N.R. Robinson International Airport International and domestic flights (see page 25) land at this airy complex, small enough to feel overwhelmed by the arrival of a single jet. The little row of shops opposite the terminal building includes a tourist office (see page 204), a newsagent selling mobile phone top-ups and two restaurants.

Airport taxis The hotels in Crown Point are mostly within walking distance of the airport, though it's of course easier to take a taxi than lug your case in the tropical heat; licensed taxi drivers meet each flight. There is a taxi price list in the arrivals lounge, just before the exit doors, to which all licensed taxi drivers conform; note that fares increase by ten percent after 10pm. If you're on a budget, you can cross the street and haggle with the sometimes-cheaper unlicensed drivers or catch a route taxi or bus (see page 197) going to Scarborough.

BY FERRY

The ferry from Port of Spain (see page 78) docks at Scarborough (see page 225); taxis wait outside the main terminal where foot passengers alight.

GETTING AROUND

Given Tobago's small size, **public transport** can be a useful option for short journeys, particularly in the southwest, with plenty of route taxis, maxis (with blue bands in Tobago) and buses plying the main roads. In remote corners of Tobago, and on Sundays throughout the island, waiting times can be long. All public transport to outlying spots such as Castara, Charlotteville or Speyside departs from Scarborough (see page 225); bear in mind that it's best to get an early start, since many of the services to outlying towns and villages leave early in the morning, with a significant lull during the middle part of the day. **Renting a car** is by far the easiest way to explore the island, even if just for a whirlwind one-day round trip.

BY BUS

Services and information The cheapest way to get around is Tobago's public bus system, run by the Public Transport Service Company (PTSC; ☎639 2293, ⓦptsc. co.tt). Information on specific bus routes has been given under the relevant headings in this chapter.

Tickets and fares Fares range between TT$2 and TT$8. All tickets must be pre-purchased as drivers will not accept cash; they are available from the shops opposite the airport complex, the bus station in Scarborough or from bars and mini-marts throughout the island.

BY ROUTE TAXI

Legions of route taxis ply the western portion of the island; travelling between Crown Point, Buccoo, Mount Irvine or Plymouth simply involves standing on the correct side of the road for your destination, sticking out your hand and asking the taxi driver where they're heading. Traffic is lighter along the windward and leeward sides of the island, but even here you should find something going in your direction if you're patient.

BY TAXI

As well as using taxis for short journeys, you can hire one for a full or half-day (around US$25/hr, or US$80–100 for a full day) to explore the island; you can concentrate on the scenery not the road, and you'll get a commentary on the island along the way. Taxi drivers congregate at the airport; you can also call the Tobago Owner Drivers' Association (☎639 2692) or Tobago Taxi Cab Co-Operative (☎639 2659). Of individual drivers, try Vernon Abraham (☎639 4475) or Liz Lezama (☎639 2309).

5

DRIVING TIMES

While the roads around Scarborough can be busy during peak times, approximate driving times are:

Crown Point to Scarborough – 15min   Plymouth to Bloody Bay – 1hr
Roxborough to Speyside – 30min   Scarborough to Castara – 45min
Speyside to Charlotteville – 10min   Bloody Bay to Roxborough – 45min
Scarborough to Plymouth – 20min   Crown Point to Castara – 1hr

---

BY CAR AND BIKE

There are **petrol stations** along Milford Rd in Bon Accord, in Scarborough, on the Claude Noel Hwy at the junction with Orange Hill Rd, Plymouth, Carnbee (take the first right from Shirvan Rd or the turn-off from the highway marked for Auchenskeoch), Roxborough and Charlotteville. Opening hours are generally Mon–Sat 7am–8pm and Sun 7am–noon; the Milford Rd station opens 24hr. The **speed limit** is 30mph/50kmph throughout the island, even on the highway.

Car rental Most of the international car rental firms – as well as the local operators with two or three vehicles to rent – are clustered around the airport. Rates are around US$50/day for a car or jeep. Local operators tend to be cheaper than their international counterparts, but the smaller the company the less likely you are to be offered 24-hour

assistance and adequate coverage in case of an accident: some of the most reliable local firms include KCNN (☎682 2888, ⓦtobagocarhire.com), Sheppy's (☎639 1543, ⓦtobagocarrental.com) and the Tobago franchise of Sixt (☎780 2886, ⓦsixt.com), while Yes Tourism (☎357 0064, ⓦyes-tourism.com) acts as a broker for several operators.

Bike and scooter rental Car rental firms occasionally rent motorbikes and scooters (around US$30/day). Be especially careful to check the condition of your bike and helmet before you ride away, as some are less than perfect. Bicycles (around US$10/day) are good for short hops, though the daytime heat is intense and riding on the roads can feel a bit precarious. Mountain biking tour companies (see page 203) can rent bikes, as can Easy Goers, on Airport Rd in Crown Point (☎681 8025 or ☎787 0685, ⓦeasygoersbikes.com).

Crown Point and around

Tobago's flat, low-lying southwest tip is the island's most heavily developed, accessible and populated region, with the **Crown Point** area around the airport home to the vast majority of its hotels, restaurants and bars, as well as its most popular beaches – **Store Bay** is just a couple of minutes on foot from the airport, and **Pigeon Point** ten minutes further. The terrain between the two is jam-packed with all the familiar tourist trappings – craft stalls, restaurants, bars and endless hotels – and many people never make it any further into the island. This highly commercialized hotchpotch sometimes lacks aesthetic charm, but the concentration of facilities and activities offers practical convenience as well as Tobago's most energetic vibe.

Directly east of Crown Point, Airport Road serves as a rough boundary line between Crown Point and **Bon Accord**, distinguishable only by its preponderance of residential streets threading towards the lovely Bon Accord wetlands. Airport Road leads into ruler-straight **Milford Road**, bisecting the southwest tip, and the main thoroughfare through the southwest. Trucks, cars and route taxis fly past a roadside lined with shops, fruit stalls and houses, and the whole stretch is the busiest you'll find away from Scarborough. Milford merges into the Claude Noel Highway just before the sign for the pretty **Canoe Bay beach**. Running parallel to Milford Road, **Store Bay Local Road** is a quieter affair but still home to a fair few accommodation and eating options.

Store Bay Beach

Lifeguards on duty daily 10am–6pm • Changing facilities daily 10am–5.45pm; entry $5, lockers TT$10/day

Just a two-minute walk from the airport, **Store Bay Beach** is Crown Point's best place to swim. Named after early Dutch settler Jan Stoer, this is some of the most popular sand in Tobago, and deservedly so – it's close to the main hotels, has tasty and inexpensive local food and is a great place to buy crafts from the many huts behind the beach. Store

5

Bay offers up a lively scene: holidaymakers (many of them from Trinidad) consume vast quantities of curry crab and dumpling and keep the beach-chair operators busy, while glass-bottom boats (see below) load and offload groups of visitors in the bay.

Though fairly small and hemmed in by the *Coco Reef* hotel (see page 206) and the rocks, the beach's fine, off-white sand is excellent; lifeguards patrol the area flagged off for safe bathing, and there are loungers and umbrella available to rent. With a gentle shelf and crystal-clear water, a calm Store Bay is a good choice for adults and children – though be careful on rougher days, when waves get pretty big. Store Bay is the finishing point for the Great Race powerboat contest each August (see page 210), as well as a venue for open-air parties around Easter weekend, and the bars opposite are a popular liming spot, particularly during and after sunset.

Opposite the beach there are a couple of bars blasting reggae and soca, an ice-cream kiosk and the row of shacks housing the irresistible **cookshops** where most people purchase their lunch (see page 209).

Fort Milford

Store Bay Local Rd • No set hours • Free

West of Airport Road, Store Bay Local Road runs past the small dead-end road that leads to Store Bay Beach, and threads around the headland to hotel-filled Sandy Point

---

BUCCOO REEF AND NYLON POOL

Covering around 12 square kilometres of Caribbean seabed between Pigeon Point and Buccoo Bay, **Buccoo Reef** is Tobago's largest and most heavily visited collection of corals, from hard stag and elkhorn varieties to waving purple sea fans and peach-coloured fire coral, patrolled by the brilliantly coloured trigger, butterfly, surgeon and parrot fish which thrive here. To the south of the reef is **Nylon Pool**, a gleaming coralline sandbar forming an appealing metre-deep swimming pool smack in the middle of the sea. It's said to have been named by Princess Margaret during her stay in the 1950s; she supposedly remarked that the water was as clear as her nylon stockings.

Sadly, however, human interference has taken a devastating toll on Buccoo Reef. In addition coral bleaching caused by warming sea temperatures worldwide, carelessly placed anchors and thoughtless removal of coral souvenirs – not to mention the inevitable pollution – mean that many parts have been terribly **damaged**, and bear more resemblance to a coral graveyard than a living reef. Buccoo also took a pounding during the years when boat operators handed out plastic shoes to allow visitors to walk on the reef as a part of the glass-bottom boat tour. Large sections have died off completely, leaving white skeletons in their wake, while overfishing has reduced the fish and crustacean populations, and poorly aimed spear guns have ripped chunks from the coral. The situation became so bad that Buccoo was declared a **protected national park** in 1973, but with scant resources to enforce the law the legal status meant little and the damage continued practically unabated. Today, glass-bottom boat operators are more conscientious, no longer promoting reef walks and anchoring at designated buoys, as well as warning visitors that touching or removing reef matter and shells is illegal. The **Buccoo Reef Trust** (☎ 635 2000, ⓦ buccooreeftrust.org.tt), meanwhile, is a local NGO working to help preserve the reef and educate boat operators and fishermen about sustainable practices. You can do your bit by standing on the seabed only and refusing to buy any coral trinkets.

Despite the damage, there's still plenty to see at Buccoo, particularly at outlying areas such as Coral Gardens. You'll have no difficulty in finding a **glass-bottom boat** to take you; most leave from Store Bay (see page 198) and, to a lesser degree, Buccoo and Pigeon Point. Two- to three-hour trips with **snorkelling** and a stop at the Nylon Pool included cost around TT$120, and usually leave at about 11am and 2pm; touts approach potential customers on all the main beaches. The tours are often fairly raucous, accompanied by loud music on the way home, but offer a good glimpse of the coral as well as a pretty perspective back over Tobago's southwest coastline and hilly interior.

5

and the ruined **Fort Milford** stockade. The fort, of gun-slitted coral stone, was built by the British in 1777, and briefly appropriated by the French during their 1781–93 occupation of Tobago. Of the six cannons that remain, five are British and one French. Surrounded by well-kept gardens that make a quiet, shady chill-out spot, the fort gives a panoramic perspective over Store Bay Beach and Milford Bay right up to Pigeon Point.

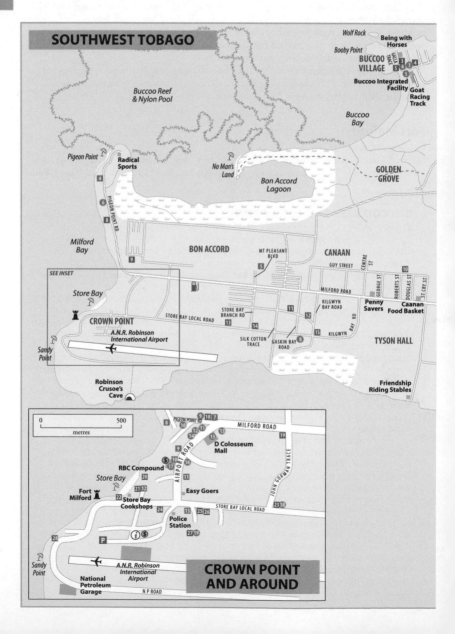

SOUTHWEST TOBAGO

Wolf Rock
Being with Horses
Booby Point
BUCCOO VILLAGE
Buccoo Integrated Facility
Goat Racing Track

Buccoo Reef & Nylon Pool

Buccoo Bay

Pigeon Point
Radical Sports
No Man's Land
Bon Accord Lagoon
GOLDEN GROVE

Milford Bay
BON ACCORD
MT PLEASANT BLVD
CANAAN
GUY STREET
MILFORD ROAD
Penny Savers
Caanan Food Basket

SEE INSET
Store Bay
CROWN POINT
A.N.R. Robinson International Airport
Sandy Point
STORE BAY LOCAL ROAD
STORE BAY BRANCH RD
KILGWYN BAY ROAD
SILK COTTON TRACE
GASKIN BAY ROAD
KILGWYN
TYSON HALL

Robinson Crusoe's Cave
Friendship Riding Stables

0   500
metres

PIGEON POINT RD
MILFORD ROAD
D Colosseum Mall
RBC Compound
Store Bay
Fort Milford
Store Bay Cookshops
Easy Goers
AIRPORT ROAD
JOHN GORMAN TRACE
STORE BAY LOCAL ROAD
Police Station
Sandy Point
National Petroleum Garage
A.N.R. Robinson International Airport
N P ROAD

CROWN POINT AND AROUND

Sandy Point Beach

Store Bay Local Rd

South of Fort Milford, Store Bay Local Road swings left before meeting the fences of the airport runway, encircled by narrow NP Road. Obscured by trees and shrubs, pretty and often deserted **Sandy Point Beach** is easy to miss; take the first dirt road off NP into the bush (just opposite the end of the tarmac) and you'll emerge onto a

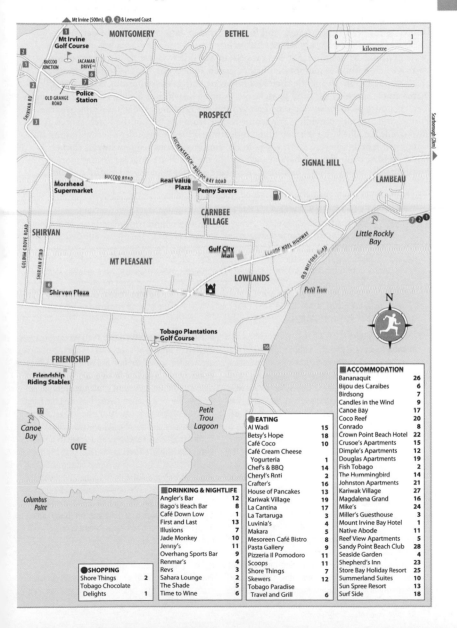

ACCOMMODATION

Bananaquit	26
Bijou des Caraibes	6
Birdsong	7
Candles in the Wind	9
Canoe Bay	17
Coco Reef	20
Conrado	8
Crown Point Beach Hotel	22
Crusoe's Apartments	15
Dimple's Apartments	12
Douglas Apartments	19
Fish Tobago	2
The Hummingbird	14
Johnston Apartments	21
Kariwak Village	27
Magdalena Grand	16
Mike's	24
Miller's Guesthouse	3
Mount Irvine Bay Hotel	1
Native Abode	11
Reef View Apartments	5
Sandy Point Beach Club	28
Seaside Garden	4
Shepherd's Inn	23
Store Bay Holiday Resort	25
Summerland Suites	10
Sun Spree Resort	13
Surf Side	18

EATING

Al Wadi	15
Betsy's Hope	18
Café Coco	10
Café Cream Cheese Yogurteria	1
Chef's & BBQ	14
Cheryl's Roti	2
Crafter's	16
House of Pancakes	13
Kariwak Village	19
La Cantina	17
La Tartaruga	3
Luvinia's	4
Makara	5
Mesoreen Café Bistro	8
Pasta Gallery	9
Pizzeria Il Pomodoro	11
Scoops	11
Shore Things	7
Skewers	12
Tobago Paradise Travel and Grill	6

DRINKING & NIGHTLIFE

Angler's Bar	12
Bago's Beach Bar	8
Café Down Low	1
First and Last	13
Illusions	7
Jade Monkey	10
Jenny's	11
Overhang Sports Bar	9
Renmar's	4
Revs	3
Sahara Lounge	2
The Shade	5
Time to Wine	6

SHOPPING

Shore Things	2
Tobago Chocolate Delights	1

5

picturesque and completely undeveloped strip of fine white sand and translucent sea bordered by sea grapes and palms. Currents can be strong here, however, so it's a spot for paddling rather than swimming.

Pigeon Point

Pigeon Point Rd · Daily 8am–5.30pm · TT$20, children TT$10 · Beach loungers TT$30 · ☎ 639 0601, ⓦ pigeonpoint.tt · Pigeon Point Rd is off Milford Rd opposite D Colosseum Mall

Lauded as the island's best beach, and for good reason, **Pigeon Point** is the definitive Caribbean seashore: powdery white sand, calm turquoise sea and a backdrop of swaying palms. Its swimming area is capped on one side by a headland and the other by a weathered wooden pier topped with a thatch-roofed hut – easily Tobago's most photographed spot. The gentle shelf and tame currents make swimming benign, and there's ample space on the sand to stake out your niche without feeling cramped – though it can get busy on a cruise-ship day. East around the headland, the wind whips over the Bon Accord Lagoon, providing a welcome respite from the heat of the beach as well as ideal conditions for kite-boarding and windsurfing – there's an outlet offering lessons and equipment rental (see page 205). Close to the entrance, shops sell beachwear, clothes and souvenirs, while the two **bars** at each end of the beach are popular liming spots at sundown; like Sandy Point, the sunset views here are magnificent. A handful of **food**

ORGANIZED TOURS AND ACTIVITIES

Tobago is replete with tour companies offering **round-the-island trips** to all the main hotspots, as well as **birdwatching**, **waterfall swimming** and excursions to the weekly **Sunday School** party, while a **boat ride** is one of the best ways to appreciate the island's gorgeous coastline. Several operators work the waters, and trips usually include lunch, **snorkelling** at little-visited coves, and an open bar; half-day, or sunset and moonlight dinner trips are also available. Note that the prices given below are for adults; all companies offer reduced rates for children.

In addition, there are also several guides who specialize in the **Forest Reserve** (see page 235). Aside from **watersports** (see page 205), other activities on offer include **mountain-biking**, **golf**, **yoga** and **horseriding**.

ISLAND TOURS

Alibaba Tours ☎ 635 1017 or ☎ 686 7957, ⓦ alibaba-tours.com. Excellent all-round operator, based in Castara, offering the standard rainforest and sightseeing island trips, which can be tailored to include whatever you want to see. Also boat trips with snorkelling, fun-fishing and a beach barbecue. Half-day trips from US$70, full day including lunch US$80–100.

Hans Tours ☎ 759 2880 or 361 8486, ⓦ hanstours tobago.com. Reliable, professional operator offering the full raft of tour options, from birdwatching at Adventure Farm to boat trips and an all-day island excursion; trips to Little Tobago, turtle-watching, a sunset cruise and a visit to Sunday School are also available. US$40–90.

Harris' Jungle Tours ☎ 639 0513 or ☎ 759 0170, ⓦ harris-jungle-tours.com. Genial former lifeguard Harris McDonald is a lovely guide for all the Tobago sights, and conducts full- and half-day rainforest and birdwatching trips, and an exciting night-time rainforest walk. Also offers Sunday School trips, Little Tobago, waterfalls and an all-island excursion. Tours US$65–100.

BIRDING AND WILDLIFE TOURS

NG Nature Tours ☎ 660 5463 or ☎ 754 7881, ⓦ newton george.com. One of the best birding guides in Tobago, Newton George is excellent for serious birders and novices alike, his light-pen (sensitively) employed to help you pick out even the most reclusive species. Trips cover the Forest Reserve, Little Tobago, Bon Accord Lagoon, Grafton Caledonia Bird Sanctuary and the Magdalena Grand wetlands, and Trinidad excursions are available. Full-day tours US$75–95.

Peter Cox Wildlife Tours ☎ 751 5822 or ☎ 294 3086, ⓦ petercoxnaturetours.com. A great birding guide, and also good for turtle-watching (see page 219) during the laying season, plus night-time rainforest walks (perfect for seeing nocturnal creatures such as armadillos and owls) and trips tailored for children in which you explore forest rivers and pools home to wabeen and crayfish. Full-day tours from US$90.

BOAT TRIPS

Frankie's Tours ☎ 681 3717 or ☎ 394 4553, ⓦ frankie tours.com. One of the largest of the boat-tour operators,

outlets sell inexpensive snacks; if you want something more substantial, head to the indoor restaurant at the Bon Accord end of the beach selling Creole lunches.

Picturesque as it is, Pigeon Point is not without **controversy**. It was the first beach on Tobago (and still the only one) to charge an entry fee, much to the consternation of locals and the fishermen whose right to walk and fish freely from the shore has been curtailed. Equally, many bemoan the water quality, thanks to runoff from the area's many hotels, and lack of water circulation following constriction of groynes.

Bon Accord Lagoon

East of Crown Point, Milford Road slips imperceptibly into the **BON ACCORD** district, a mostly residential area whose main point of interest is the **Bon Accord Lagoon**, a sweeping oval of mangrove swamp and reef-sheltered, shallow water which forms one of the island's most important fish nurseries. Though the marine life has been adversely affected by runoff from a nearby sewage treatment plant, the lagoon's sea-grass beds remain a sanctuary for conch, snails, shrimp, oysters, crab, urchins and sponges.

Most of the land skirting the swamp is **privately owned.** You can get pretty close by turning down Golden Grove Road, the turn-off for which lies a couple of kilometres east along Milford Road, and taking the first dirt track you come to – passing the crumbling remains of a windmill and cocoa drying house, once part of the Bon Accord

with a base at Mount Irvine Beach car park and a varied selection of cruises aboard small boats with covered areas for shade (full-day US$95), plus fishing, hiking and sightseeing tours.

Picante ☎ 620 4750 or ☎ 369 8814, ⓦ yachtpleasures. com. The only sailing charter in Tobago – a catamaran with sunbathing nets over the hulls and an inside area. A full-day trip with lunch and snorkelling costs US$100, or a Nylon Pool cruise US$80, with sunset and overnight options.

Pops Tours ☎ 738 8226 or ☎ 383 2384, ⓦ popstours tobago.com. Based in Buccoo, this friendly, well-run and locally owned outfit offeris a full-day boat tour with beach barbecue (US$90), plus a half-day snorkelling trip (US$75); there's also game fishing for tuna, wahoo, marlin and the like (US$400 for up to 4 people) and fun-fishing trips (US$75). All boats have a covered area.

MOUNTAIN BIKE TOURS
Mountain Biking Tobago ☎ 639 9709 or ☎ 681 5695, ⓦ mountainbikingtobago.com. A wide roster of tours (from US$50) for both beginners and serious riders.
Tobago Mountain Bike Tours ☎ 332 5872, ⓦ tobago mountainbike.com. Offers everything from an easy no-hills cycle around the Bon Accord Lagoon to an extreme downhill ride from Moriah. Tours from US$50.

HORSERIDING
★ **Being with Horses** Buccoo ☎ 639 0953, ⓦ being-with-horses.com. This wonderful operation (see page 212) takes a refreshingly holistic attitude to riding, using

bitless bridles and bareback pads rather than saddles. Rides include a trip around the Buccoo headland with a chance to swim your mount across the bay (US$100), and there's also therapeutic riding for people with disabilities.
Friendship Riding Stables Canaan ☎ 660 8563, ⓦ friendshipridingstables.com. Beach rides (1hr 30min) through mangroves and onto the beach (from TT$350), as well as lessons and gentle rides for small children.

GOLF
Mount Irvine ☎ 639 8871, ⓦ mtirvine.com. The oldest course on Tobago, and very pretty, with its par-72 18 holes (9 holes US$30, 18 holes US$48, club rental US$25) set on undulating greens, lined with palm trees and overlooked by luxury villas.
Tobago Plantations Golf Club ☎ 387 0288, ⓦ magdalenagrand.com. Opened in 2001, this is a par-72, 18-hole course overlooking the ocean (9 holes US$60, 18 holes US$90, plus US$62.50 for club rental; lessons US$90/hr).

THERAPIES, TREATMENTS AND YOGA
Kariwak Village Crown Point ☎ 639 8442, ⓦ kariwak. com. Yoga and t'ai chi (classes US$10) in a gorgeous thatch-roofed open-sided ajoupa, surrounded by tinkling waterfalls and flowering plants, plus a wide range of alternative therapies and treatments (around US$60), including Ayurvedic, Thai, hot stone and aromatherapy massages, plus shiatsu and acupuncture in the Holistic Treatment Centre.

5

sugar estate. The road becomes extremely bumpy after the small bridge, and is best attempted with 4WD in the wet season. You can also drive right down to the water by taking Gaskin Bay Road, a wide paved turn-off to the left from Milford just before the housing scheme. A better way to see the lagoon is on a boat tour (see page 202) that includes a barbecue at a deserted sandy spit on the lagoon's north side known as **No Man's Land**, an idyllic place to swim; you can also explore the lagoon's bioluminescent waters by night on a kayak or SUP tour (see page 205).

Sadly, though, this pristine scene may soon be the thing of the past, with the area extending east from No Man's Land around the headland to Buccoo Bay (properly known as the Buccoo Estate) slated as the site for a 750-room **all-inclusive Sandals hotel**, built at government expense but managed by Sandals in the same vein as Trinidad's *Hyatt* and *Hilton* complexes and Tobago's *Magdalena Grand*. The project has been championed by PNM Prime Minister Keith Rowley as a means of injecting marketing might into Tobago's ailing tourism sector, but environmentalists point to the fact that constructing a mega-hotel on a sensitive mangrove wetland is likely to be an ecological disaster, while other detractors cite the indifferent contribution of all-inclusives to the wider economy elsewhere in the Caribbean. Nonetheless, the project looked to have been given the green light at the time of writing.

Canaan

East of Bon Accord, residential **CANAAN** was given its rather odd name by Moravian missionaries. The area was once carved up into individual sugar plantations, and away from the main road there are still large tracts of undeveloped land where cattle graze or coconut trees sway heavy with nuts. These days, though, Canaan is a place to stock up on provisions, with the island's largest supermarket, Penny Savers, right on Milford Road (see page 207), and a host of excellent fruit and veg stores as well as plenty of small-scale rum shops and cookshops in which to sink a few beers or pick up a local-style meal.

Canoe Bay

Daily 9am–5pm • TT$15

East of the junction with Shirvan Road, the route to Buccoo (see page 211), Milford Road's commercial activity tails off; just beyond here, a turn-off to the right is signposted for **Canoe Bay**, a pretty and quiet **beach** that was once the site of a large Amerindian settlement; the English named it after the Indian pirogues moored here. Today, the beautifully landscaped bay is an appealingly peaceful place to spend the day. The main area boasts lawns, thatched gazebos, picnic tables and a secluded beach of clean yellow sand (slightly marred by some sea-grass beds), with a view that stretches right down to Crown Point. It's an excellent place to come if you're travelling with children, since the sheltered water makes for safe swimming and the large grassy areas are perfect for ball games. There's also a bar serving drinks.

| ARRIVAL AND INFORMATION | CROWN POINT AND AROUND |

By bus An hourly shuttle service operates between A.N.R. Robinson airport in Crown Point (there's a stop just outside the main complex; see page 197) and the island's main depot on Sangster Hill Rd in Scarborough; buses leave at roughly half past the hour from Crown Point and on the hour from Scarborough between 5am and 9pm.

Tourist information The tourist office is housed in the last shop on the left of the row opposite the airport arrivals (daily 6am–10pm; ☎ 639 0509). Staff can provide very basic advice on accommodation, transport and activities, and have free maps of Tobago and copies of tourist-oriented flyers and magazines.

ACCOMMODATION

The sheer amount of accommodation in the **Crown Point** area makes choosing a place to stay mind-boggling. Space is at a premium here, with many hotels and guesthouses built back-to-back with little individuality and scant regard

5

WATERSPORTS AND FISHING IN SOUTHWEST TOBAGO

The southwest is the best place for watersports, with a large variety of outlets and operators. **Jet-skis** have gained in popularity, and you can rent them from operators working the sands at Store Bay Beach and Pigeon Point for around US$40 per half-hour. Many also rent snorkel equipment for around US$10 per day (though if you plan on **snorkelling** a lot, it's best to bring or buy your own); leeward coast boat trips (see page 202) always include snorkelling, and there's also one specialist snorkelling charter company. Though the best dive sites (see page 242) in Tobago are outside the Crown Point area, many of the island's **scuba diving** operators are located here. We've listed some of the reliable operators below, all of which are members of the Association of Tobago Dive Operators (ⓦtobagoscubadiving.com), also a good source of general information on diving the island's waters. If you're interested in diving with a conservation bent, head up to Charlotteville, where a couple of dive operators are dedicated to marine research (see page 246). Other Otherwise, there are several options for **kayaking**, **windsurfing** and **stand-up paddleboarding**. And during the season (Oct–March), there's excellent **surfing** at Mount Irvine Beach – early morning often sees twenty to thirty surfers riding the waves (see page 215).

As for **fishing**, rich pickings of marlin, sailfish, tuna and dolphin are caught year-round. Chartering a sport fishing boat is exciting but expensive; a speedy boat accommodating up to six and equipped with rods, tackle and bait will cost in excess of US$450/half-day, US$900 for a full day; some operators also offer inshore spinning and fly-fishing from a small boat (around US$70/hr or US$200 half-day). Reliable options are listed below; Pops Tours and Alibaba (see page 202) also offer fun-fishing trips for less serious anglers.

WINDSURFING, KITEBOARDING AND KAYAKING

Mount Irvine Bay Watersports Mount Irvine beach ☎771 9997, ⓦbit.ly/MIWater. Overlooking the sand between Mount Irvine's hotel and main beaches, this is a professional, locally owned kayaking outfit, offering double, quad and glass-bottom kayaks (TT$60/150/80 per hr), plus SUP boards (TT$120/hr) – a lovely way to explore the bay here. Kayak instruction comes with rental, as do lifejackets.

Radical Sports Pigeon Point beach ☎631 5150 or ☎728 5483, ⓦradicalsportstobago.com. Right on the beach, around the headland from the main swimming area, Radical are perfectly placed to take advantage of the coastal breezes sweeping across the bay. Their mainstays are kite-boarding (1hr private lesson US$95; rig rental 2hr US$77, full day US$105), windsurfing (equipment rental US$45/hr or US$83/day, 1hr lesson US$70), kayaking (US$22/hr) and sailing on a Hobie Cat (1hr rental US$50, 1hr lesson US$65).

SNORKELLING AND PADDLEBOARD TOURS

Stand-Up Paddle Tobago Pigeon Point beach ☎681 4741, ⓦstanduppaddletobago.com. Based at Radical Sports on Pigeon Point beach, this popular outfit offers 1hr SUP lessons and a range of paddleboarding

tours around the southwest coast (all US$60); you can also drive along the Caribbean coast to explore little-visited rivers and beaches by board (US$120). The best option, though, is the fantastic night time tour through the Bon Accord Lagoon to see bioluminescence caused by blooming phytoplankton (6.30–9pm; US$60).

Zoe Snorkelling Charters Pigeon Point beach ☎681 4741, ⓦsnorkeltobago.com. Another arm of the Radical Sports outfit, offering snorkelling charters aboard a covered speedboat with a water-level swim platform to allow easy entrance and exit from the water. The 4hr tour (US$80) picks out the best snorkelling spots on Buccoo Reef's Coral Gardens.

SCUBA DIVING

Frontier Divers Sandy Point Beach Club, Crown Point ☎631 8138, ⓦtobagofrontierdivers.com.

R & Sea Diving Company Shepherd's Inn, Store Bay Local Rd, Bon Accord ☎639 8120, ⓦrseadivers.com.

Undersea Tobago Coco Reef, Crown Point ☎631 2626, ⓦunderseatobago.com.

FISHING

Grand Slam ☎639 9961 or ☎683 1958, ⓦbit.ly/GSlamTT.

Hardplay ☎639 7108 or ☎682 3474, ⓦhardplay.net.

for aesthetics. On the other hand, the high competition keeps prices fairly low, and the absence of ugly high-rise developments makes things feel much less crowded than they actually are. You're also in walking distance of the busiest beaches, restaurants and bars, and can often stroll straight from the airport tarmac to your room. Hotels bordering the

5

runway get some aircraft noise, though there are too few flights for this to be a problem. **Bon Accord**, meanwhile, holds a few quieter options, as does **Store Bay Local Rd**.

GUESTHOUSES AND APARTMENTS

Bananaquit Store Bay Local Rd, Bon Accord ☎ 639 9733 or ☎ 368 3539, ⓦ bananaquit.com; map p.200. Set around a shaded grassy courtyard, these eclectic studios and apartments have plenty of character, with rattan furnishings and kitchenettes or full kitchen. There's also a ground-floor budget "backpackers" room (US$60). All have a/c, fan and cable TV. ☎ US$67

Candles in the Wind 145 Anthony Charles Crescent, Bon Accord ☎ 631 5335, ⓦ candlesinthewind.biz; map p.200. This very friendly hotel in a quiet, mainly residential part of Bon Accord contains eight en-suite rooms with cable TV and a/c; there's also an attic dorm with bunk beds for those on a budget. There are two fully equipped shared kitchens and laundry facilities on site. ☎($) Dorms US$25, doubles US$65

Canoe Bay Cove Estate ☎ 631 0367, ⓦ canoett.com; map p.200. Right on the beach and in spacious grounds, this beautifully secluded place has amenable, plain apartments with a/c, TV, balcony and kitchenette; there's also a heart-shaped pool. It's an ideal spot for families needing some peace and quiet, though you'll need a car. ☎ US$65

Crusoe's Apartments Store Bay Local Rd, Bon Accord ☎ 639 7789, ✉ crusoesholidayapartments@gmail.com; map p.200. Spacious self-contained one- and two-bedroom apartments (the latter US$96), cheerfully decorated in blue and orange with a/c, cable TV and fully equipped kitchen; there's also a pool at the centre of the complex and ample parking. Friendly and very good value. ☎ US$65

★ **Dimple's Apartments** Store Bay Branch Rd, Bon Accord ☎ 660 8156 or ☎ 786 8134, ⓦ dimples-apartments.com; map p.200. Just back from Store Bay Local Rd, and run by a friendly and knowledgeable English/Tobagonian couple, this is a real bargain, with spotless, comfortable one-bedroom a/c apartments with a full kitchen/living room and a porch. A new development of self-contained apartments with a pool was under construction at the time of writing. ☎ US$45

Douglas Apartments John Gorman Trace, at Milford Rd, Bon Accord ☎ 639 7723, ⓦ douglastobago.com; map p.200. Sparkling clean, spacious one- and two-bedroom apartments, each with a lounge, full kitchen, patio, a/c and TV – the three loft rooms sleeping five are especially nice. Pool and a friendly family atmosphere. Car rental is available on site. ☎ US$85

Johnston Apartments Store Bay Connector Rd, Crown Point ☎ 639 8915, ⓦ johnstonapartments.com; map p.200. Right above Store Bay and sharing the pool and restaurant of its larger neighbour, *Crown Point Beach Hotel*, these one- to three-bedroom apartments are huge

(there's also one that sleeps ten; US$320) and come with fully equipped kitchen, living room, a/c and cable TV – and immediate access to the sand and sea. ☎ (variable). US$125

Mike's Store Bay Local Rd, Crown Point ☎ 620 8280 or 778 4990; map p.200. Excellent value and a 2min walk from the airport, this busy, locally owned place has spacious, clean and inviting one-, two- and three-bedroom apartments with a/c, ceiling fan, cable TV and full kitchen. There's a mini-mart on site. ☎ US$60

Native Abode 13 Fourth St, Bon Accord ☎ 631 1285, ⓦ nativeabode.com; map p.200. Just off Gaskin Bay Rd (itself off Store Bay Local Rd), and boasting a quiet location among residential streets. The owner's garden has plenty of fruit trees which guests can pick from, and the a/c rooms with kitchenette are attractively decorated in a modern, swish style. Rates include breakfast. ☎ US$140

Sandy Point Beach Club Store Bay Local Rd, Crown Point ☎ 639 0820, ⓦ sandypointbeachclub.com; map p.200. Overlooking the sea at the western extreme of Store Bay Local Rd, this is a well-run place with studios (which sleep four) and one-bedroom apartments (sleeping up to six; US$170); all have a/c, kitchen and TV. Facilities include a restaurant, pool, outdoor hot tubs, tennis court, kids' playground and a beach bar. Daily shuttle to local beaches. ☎ Studio US$130

Store Bay Holiday Resort Store Bay Local Rd, Crown Point ☎ 639 8810, ⓦ bit.ly/StoreBayHol; map p.200. Likeable place in an excellent location close to Store Bay, with friendly staff, a pool and a range of modern, appealing studios, plus standard and deluxe rooms (the latter US$102/$126) with a/c, TV and fully equipped kitchenettes. ☎ Studios US$80

Sun Spree Resort Store Bay Local Rd, Bon Accord ☎ 631 5196, ⓦ sunspreeresortltd.com; map p.200. Great little place spreading back from the road with a pool, restaurant and bar and spacious, modern rooms with a/c, cable TV, fridge and safe; some suites, too (US$110). Close to the beaches and restaurants but still nice and quiet, and very friendly staff. ☎ (pool only). US$65

Surf Side Pigeon Point Rd, Crown Point ☎ 639 9702, ⓦ bit.ly/SurfSide; map p.200. Crown Point old-timer, popular with visiting Trinis and offering basic but clean studios and deluxe apartments (the latter US$60) in a one-storey block with a small pool out front. Not very atmospheric but inexpensive and in an excellent location. ☎ US$48

HOTELS

Coco Reef Airport Rd, Crown Point ☎ 639 8571, ⓦ cocoreef.com; map p.200. This peach-painted enclave is Crown Point's largest hotel and the most resort-like in Crown

SUPERMARKETS IN TOBAGO

If you're staying in self-catering accommodation and plan cooking for yourself, bear in mind that supermarkets outside of southwest Tobago sell only the most basic items. Even if you're staying in Castara or further afield, it's best to stock up here on your way from the airport. The best all-round supermarket is **Penny Savers** (Mon–Sat 8am–8.30pm, Sun 8am–1pm), on Milford Road at the Canaan end; it's competitively priced, relatively well stocked and has lots of imported foods. There's another branch in Carnbee, on the Auchenskeoch–Buccoo Bay Road, and one on Wilson Road in Scarborough. **Morshead Supermarket** on Buccoo Road, off Shirvan Road (Mon–Fri 8am–6pm, Sat 8am–7pm, Sun 8am–noon) sells a wealth of imported goods, including cold meats and cheeses, plus some local delights such as Tobago Cocoa Estate Chocolate, though prices are high. For fruit and veg, head to the **Canaan Food Basket** on Milford Rd (usually daily 9am–8pm).

Point, with high perimeter walls enclosing the grounds and a man-made white-sand beach. Two restaurants, two bars, spa, tennis courts, pool, watersports and 135 pastel-coloured rooms, suites and villas (the latter from US$648), all with all the usual mod cons. Rates include breakfast and (non-motorized) watersports; all-inclusive plans are available. 🛜 US$328

Conrado Pigeon Point Rd, Crown Point ☎ 639 0145, ⓦ conradotobago.com; map p.200. The closest you can stay to Pigeon Point and one of the relatively few hotels in Tobago next to the beach – you can almost feel the ocean spray from the expansive balconies that come with the more expensive sea-view rooms (US$115). The rooms are modestly proportioned, but come with en-suite bathrooms, a/c, fridge and cable TV. Good breakfasts (included) and an on-site restaurant/bar right by the sand. 🛜 US$105

Crown Point Beach Hotel Store Bay Local Rd, Crown Point ☎ 639 8781, ⓦ crownpointbeachhotel.com; map p.200. Expansive hotel on the westerly side of Store Bay Beach. The modern, comfortable studios all have sea-facing views, as do the more private cabanas (US$137) dotting the garden. Both have kitchenette, a/c, cable TV and small patio/balcony, and there's a pool, restaurant and tennis courts on site. Usually busy with a Trinidadian/European crowd. 🛜 Studios US$127

The Hummingbird 128 Store Bay Local Rd, Bon Accord ☎ 635 0241, ⓦ hummingbirdtobago.com; map p.200. This intimate, family-run hotel has ten spotless en-suite rooms named after tropical flowers – all have a/c, fridge and cable TV, and suites (US$100) have a kitchenette, too. They're set around a pool, with a restaurant and bar on an adjacent terrace. The likeable Anglo-Trinidadian owners are a useful source of information. 🛜 US$60

★ **Kariwak Village** Store Bay Local Rd, Crown Point ☎ 639 8442, ⓦ kariwak.com; map p.200. A jewel in the middle of this bustling area: yoga classes in the lush gardens, excellent, friendly staff and peaceful atmosphere give a real feeling of holistic retreat (see page 203). The thatch-roofed cabanas are split in two and furnished using local wood crafted on the premises; each has a/c. There's also the option of larger and more luxurious garden rooms, and facilities include an ozonated pool, outdoor waterfall-fed jacuzzi, and a fabulous restaurant/bar (see page 208). Rates include an excellent breakfast. 🛜 US$222

Magdalena Grand Tobago Plantations, Lowlands ☎ 660 8503, ⓦ magdalenagrand.com; map p.200. Overlooking the ocean behind the Tobago Plantations Golf Course, which it now maintains, this is currently the largest hotel on the island, with extensive facilities that include three pools, a sauna, spa, fitness centre, tennis courts and a kids' playground, nature trails through the wetlands surrounding the course, and several restaurants and bars. The private beach isn't Tobago's best, though you do get constant breezes via the Atlantic winds that blast the coastline here. 🛜 US$235

Shepherd's Inn Store Bay Local Rd, Crown Point ☎ 639 1543, ⓦ shepherdsinntobago.com; map p.200. Formerly the *Toucan Inn* and now with new owners, this welcoming hotel is a little removed from the area's bustle, but still within easy walking distance of the action. Decked out with wooden fittings, the spacious garden rooms (US$120) and smaller (and slightly cheaper) poolside cabanas all have a/c, tea- and coffee-making equipment and a porch area, and there's a restaurant on site. Rates include breakfast. 🛜 US$100

★ **Summerland Suites** Roberts St, Bon Accord ☎ 631 5053, ⓦ summerlandsuites.info; map p.200. Tucked away on a quiet street (though close to the *Shade* nightclub, so expect some noise come weekend evenings), this is a lovely place to stay, with an inviting pool overhung by towering saaman trees and a row of well-maintained, appealing one- and two-bedroom apartments with kitchen, living room and a porch. Friendly, helpful staff, too. 🛜 US$80

EATING

Crown Point has eating options for all tastes and budgets, mostly within easy walking distance of the area's hotels and guesthouses. For inexpensive gyro wraps, doubles and barbecue, look for roadside stalls around the Pigeon Point Rd

5

junction and along Store Bay Local Rd. **D Colosseum Mall**, at the corner of Airport and Milford roads, has a *Rituals/Pizza Boys* and a host of takeaway places, from Jamaican to Italian, and there's a branch of the *Royal Castle* fried chicken joint just down Airport Rd adjacent to *Chef's BBQ*.

Al Wadi D Colosseum Mall, Milford Rd, Crown Point ☎ 639 8694; map p.200. Great Middle Eastern grill, with combos (TT$50–70) such as chicken skewers, lamb chops, shrimp or fish served with two sides (garlic/parsley potatoes, Arabic rice, fattoush or tabbouleh); veggie options include falafel, hummus, baba ganoush and the like. Take away or eat outside at the mall's food court tables. Daily 11am–11pm.

Betsy's Hope Shepherd's Inn, Store Bay Local Rd, Crown Point ☎ 639 1543, ⊚ shepherdsinntobago.com; map p.200. With tables on an open-sided deck, this hotel restaurant is a reliable option, serving up burgers (from TT$75) and chicken dishes alongside catch of the day, lamb chops, baby-back ribs and steaks (mains TT$130–190). There's local-style and international breakfast, too, and live calypso shows on Sat nights (8–10pm). Daily 7.30am–11.30pm.

Café Coco Just off Pigeon Point Rd, Crown Point ☎ 639 0996; map p.200. Part of the *Coco Reef* hotel, with its dining area strewn with fairy lights and greenery, this is a romantic spot perfect for a quiet dinner. The food can be a little passionless, but it's all pretty decent: grilled or blackened fish, garlic shrimp, rack of lamb, Chinese-style pork chops and Cuban-style beef (mains TT$120–150), plus lobster and steak (TT$200–300), pasta and pizzas (TT$50–120) and a kids' menu. Good service. Daily 5.30–9.30pm.

Chef's & BBQ Airport Rd, Crown Point ☎ 631 3000; map p.200. This is a great option for a cheap takeaway (though there are a couple of tables out front), selling barbecued chicken and pigtail or grilled fish, plus local staples such as pigeon peas, macaroni pie, callaloo and salads. You pay by weight; a meal should cost about TT$50. Saltfish and bake breakfasts are also well executed. Mon–Thurs & Sun 10am–10.30pm, Fri & Sat 10am–midnight.

Crafter's Airport Rd, Crown Point ☎ 714 2955, ⊚ bit. ly/CraftersTT; map p.200. Newish spot right in the heart of Crown Point, with tables on a deck outside and a meat-heavy menu featuring dishes such as pork loin in a whisky sauce, fish in lemon butter, grilled rack of lamb with mint sauce, plus ribs and steaks (mains TT$150–220). Lots of burgers (TT$80–120, including salmon and shrimp options, and a kids' menu too. Excellent service, and a nice option for a drink, too. Mon, Wed, Thurs & Sun noon–11pm, Fri & Sat noon–midnight.

House of Pancakes Milford Rd, Crown Point ☎ 639 9866; map p.200. Tucked away just off Milford Rd adjacent to D Colosseum Mall and opposite the Pigeon Point Rd, this Tobago old-timer is still one of the best spots in the west for breakfast (TT$35–55), cooking up succulent omelettes, buljol and coconut bake, eggs and bacon and, of course, delicious pancakes. Daily 7.30am–noon.

★ **Kariwak Village** Store Bay Local Rd, Crown Point ☎ 639 8442, ⊚ kariwak.com; map p.200. Homegrown vegetables and herbs, inventive slants on local staples and a relaxing setting make this hotel restaurant one of the best places to eat in Tobago. Breakfast (from TT$30) might be saltfish buljol with coconut bake or a herb omelette, while at lunch you can get sandwiches and salads, from shrimp to Tobagonian goat's cheese (TT$80–90). Dinner menus are set (three courses TT$185–230), usually with a meat, fish or vegetarian option, and everything is supremely fresh, succulently cooked and completely delicious. Tables are set in the main dining room or quieter thatched gazebos. Accompanied by live music, the Fri and Sat night buffets (TT$230) are particularly worth checking out. Great service and vegan food available. Daily 7am–10pm.

★ **La Cantina** RBC compound, Airport Rd, Crown Point ☎ 639 8242, ⊚ lacantinapizzeria.com; map p.200. Bustling little place serving truly excellent pizzas (TT$105–170) baked in a wood-fired oven. The forty different toppings range from Capricciosa (tomato, mozzarella, prosciutto, mushroom, artichokes and anchovies) to Greca (mozzarella, feta, tomato), and there are also artful salads and specials, plus excellent cocktails and wines (including Prosecco). No bookings so you may have to wait for a table, but takeaway available. Mon & Thurs–Sat noon–9.45pm, Tues & Wed noon–2.45pm & 6–9.45pm, Sun 6–9.45pm.

★ **Mesoreen Café Bistro** Store Bay Local Rd, Bon Accord ☎ 639 8726, ⊚ bit.ly/Mesoreen; map p.200. This locally owned place is a great addition to the Crown Point dining scene, with truly friendly service, candle-lit tables under a thatched roof and great food, mixing Tobago favourites with international dishes. Starter highlights (TT$25–50) include shark and bake fritters or curried pumpkin soup, while mains (TT$110–160) run from herbed chicken breast in peppercorn sauce to lamb in guava sauce, beef in an onion gravy and grilled fish in white wine sauce; also tasty veggie lasagne, tofu noodles or vegetable curry (all TT$60). Kids' menu too. Tues–Sun noon–11pm.

★ **Pasta Gallery** Pigeon Point Rd, Crown Point ☎ 727 8200, ⊚ pastagallery.net; map p.200. Great little pasta joint, with tables outside on the patio and in the indoor art-bedecked dining room, serving reliable pasta dishes (TT$75–100) such as fettuccine with shrimp, spaghetti with mixed seafood, pesto linguine, beef lasagne and spaghetti carbonara. Great service and decent wine. Gluten-free pasta available, as is takeaway. Mon & Tues 6.30–10pm, Thurs & Fri noon–2pm & 6–10pm, Sat 6.30–10pm.

5

STORE BAY DINING

An essential part of any visit to Tobago is a plate of crab and dumpling, macaroni pie with callaloo, or fresh fish with provisions from one of the row of **food huts** facing Store Bay Beach. This strip of cookshops (from right to left there's *Miss Jean's*, *Miss Trim's*, *Miss Joycie's*, *Alma's*, *Sylvia's* and *Miss Esmie's*) offer tasty, inexpensive local cuisine, and the covered sea-facing gazebo with seating and tables is an attractive place to sit, eat and watch the world go by. Prices and food vary little from stall to stall: bake with fish or eggs, buljol and smoked herring for **breakfast**; while for **lunch**, there's goat, beef, chicken or vegetable roti, stewed beef or chicken, conch or crab and dumpling, pelau, vegetable rice, stewed lentils, macaroni pie, callaloo and ground provisions. Most stalls also make **juices** such as mauby or grapefruit, and perhaps peanut or sea-moss punch. All are open daily from around 8.30am to 8.30pm, but the flow of custom dictates business hours.

Pizzeria Il Pomodoro Airport Rd, Crown Point ☎280 7754; map p.200. Tucked into the row of restaurants at the corner of Airport and Pigeon Point roads, this is a great place to grab a quick bite, with pizza by the slice (TT$15–30) – you can order whole ones too – as well as excellent calzone, focaccia and salads. Mon, Tues & Sun noon–10pm, Fri & Sat noon–11pm.

Scoops Cnr Pigeon Point and Milford roads, Crown Point ☎631 2233; map p.200. An essential Crown Point stopoff, with a huge selection of ice-cream flavours (local and international brands; scoops from TT$30) as well as milkshakes, gooey cakes and slushies. Daily 1.30–11.30pm.

Skewers Airport Rd, Crown Point ☎631 8964; map p.200. Permanently busy (and tiny) Middle Eastern place with just a couple of tables, serving mostly takeaway orders of grilled chicken, shrimp or fish, plus steak, usually served as a combo with one side order (TT$45–80), as well as gyros with beef, chicken, fish or shrimp (TT$35–50) and home-made, well-spiced falafel (combo TT$40), tabbouleh, baba ganoush, fattoush and hummus (portions TT$20–30). Daily 10am–10pm.

★ **Tobago Paradise Travel and Grill** Pigeon Point Rd, Crown Point ☎344 1703 or ☎344 1703; map p.200. Tiny little seafood shack in an unbeatable location, with tables on a deck right on the beach. The speciality is lobster (TT$180–450), grilled with a garlic-butter sauce, but you can also get fresh grilled or fried fish, all with simple sides of salad, rice or fries; there's no alcohol, but you can bring your own. Unmissable. Lunch available if you pre-book. Daily 5.30–10pm.

DRINKING AND NIGHTLIFE

Crown Point is the centre of Tobago's nightlife scene, with a string of **bars** along the stretch of Airport Rd between the Store Bay and Pigeon Point turn-offs; the only **club**, *The Shade*, is a little way up Milford Rd in Bon Accord.

Angler's Bar Store Bay Beach, Crown Point (no phone); map p.200. Facing the sea at Store Bay, this is a good spot to sink a few beers as the sun sets, accompanied by blasting dancehall and soca. Daily 9am–10pm.

★ **Bago's Beach Bar** Pigeon Point Rd, Crown Point ☎384 2460; map p.200. Popular beach bar in a quiet spot next to a pretty stretch of sand on the way to Pigeon Point. Cold beers, cocktails and occasional karaoke – there's no better place to have a few drinks while watching the sun set than here. Happy hour 5.30–7pm. Daily 6pm–midnight.

First and Last Store Bay Local Rd, Crown Point (no phone); map p.200. Just off Airport Rd, on the first stretch of Store Bay Local Rd, this classic Tobago rum shop puts out the speakers on weekend evenings to pump gentle reggae into the streets – and the beers are truly "beastly" cold. Daily 11am–late.

Illusions Pigeon Point Rd, Crown Point ☎639 7876; map p.200. With an outdoor bar area pumping high-octane soca into the street, and an a/c indoor section with pool tables and room to dance, this is usually a lively spot, with occasional live entertainment. Daily 10am–6am.

Jade Monkey Airport Rd, Crown Point ☎631 0044, ⊕ bit.ly/JadeBago; map p.200. Open-air bar (with an attached casino), with lots of booths under thatch-roofed gazebos, attracting a mixed clientele. With music from DJs in the evenings, this is one of the liveliest spots in the area for a few drinks. Live music on Thurs and special events throughout the year. Daily 11am–late.

Jenny's Airport Rd, Crown Point ☎778 6663; map p.200. On a raised deck right at the roadside, Jenny's is a busy spot for a drink, with pumping music and friendly vibes; great for people-watching. Mon–Sat 6pm–late.

Overhang Sports Bar Airport Rd, Crown Point ☎639 8929; map p.200. With a raised veranda that's ideal for people-watching and a chilly a/c interior with a dancefloor, this genial place offers karaoke, sports games on the big-screen TVs and lots of drinks specials throughout the week. DJ Thurs, Fri & Sat evening, plus a menu of burgers and bar snacks. Tues–Sun 6pm–late.

Renmar's Pigeon Point Beach, Crown Point ☎631

5

TOBAGO FESTIVALS

Though Carnival in Trinidad tends to take precedence in the T&T festival calendar (see page 33), Tobago more than holds its own in terms of celebrations, and even if your visit doesn't coincide with some of the bigger events, there's almost always a beach party or fete to liven things up. Of the annual events, the **Tobago Heritage Festival** (Ⓦtobagoheritagefestival. com), held in the last two weeks of July, celebrates the island's culture from music and dance to folk traditions and food; events include the marvellous "Old Time Wedding" parade in Moriah, a "National Treasures" day in Charlotteville, storytelling in Les Coteaux, an old-time mas parade in Plymouth and the colourful Salaka Feast in Pembroke. In mid-August the **Great Race** sees a flotilla of high-powered speedboats compete to be the first to cross the waters between the two islands, with spectators gathering at Store Bay to see the winning boats, and plenty of general partying all weekend. The annual round of **fishermen's festivals** celebrate patron of the trade, St Peter, by way of friendly beach parties at Castara, Charlotteville and other coastal villages in June: vats of pacro water (shellfish soup) simmer and stacks of speakers (as well as plenty of rum and beer) get everyone in the mood for dancing. For something gentler, you might check out the **Harvest Festivals** held in the island's villages throughout the year. With a friendly, community vibe, they feature plenty of folk singing and dancing, and heaps of "blue food" such as dasheen and tannia. In October, the huge **Blue Food Festival** at Bloody Bay is entirely dedicated to imaginative ways of preparing these provisions, from ice cream to jam. Though more low-key than it used to be, April's **Tobago Jazz Experience** usually attracts some big-name acts; 2017 saw Grace Jones, Shabba Ranks and Wyclef Jean take to the Pigeon Point stage alongside a host of great local artists.

8768; map p.200. Right on the famed sands of Pigeon Point – the drinks are a little overpriced but the sunsets are magical and the setting lovely. Daily 9am–8pm.

★ **The Shade** Mt Pleasant Blvd, Bon Accord ☎639 9651, Ⓦbit.ly/BagoShade; map p.200. Just off Milford Rd, a few minutes' walk from Crown Point, this is Tobago's biggest and best nightclub. Beneath a large, open-sided building, the dancefloor is invariably packed with both locals and tourists, but only from around midnight onwards. Cover charge Fri & Sat. Wed–Sat 8pm–late.

SHOPPING

Shopping is not one of the southwest's – or Tobago's – strong points. You can pick up souvenirs from the craft market at Store Bay Beach, though the selection at **Shore Things** (see page 227) is better quality. The concrete conglomeration of the **Gulf City Mall** at Lowlands off Claude Noel Hwy has a toyshop (which also sells kids' pool inflatables, armbands and so on) and various clothing stores. **Penny Savers** is the island's best supermarket (see page 207).

DIRECTORY

Banks and exchange There's a bureau de change upstairs in the airport terminal, and a branch of Republic Bank (Mon–Thurs 8am–3pm, Fri 8am–1pm & 3–5pm) with an ATM in the shops opposite the arrivals area. Other ATMs in the area are located at the RBC bank on Airport Rd, just past the turn-off to Store Bay, and at Penny Savers supermarket on Milford Rd and in Canaan. There are also several banks in Scarborough.

Cinema Past the Tobago Plantations golf course, Lowlands' Gulf City Mall holds the modern MovieTowne cinema (Claude Noel Hwy; ☎ 631 1843, Ⓦmovietowne. com), screening Hollywood hits. The a/c is icy, so bring something warm.

Hospitals and medical care The Scarborough General Hospital (☎660 4744) is just off the Claude Noel Hwy at Signal Hill, and has an A&E department. For an ambulance, call ☎ 990. If you need a doctor, try Dr Sonia Telfer (☎772 5770).

Laundry The Clothes Wash Café, in the RBC Bank compound on Airport Rd (daily 8am–8pm; ☎639 0007), have self-service machines, and will also wash and fold for you.

Pharmacies Late-opening pharmacies include Dove Drugs, in the Real Value Plaza on Auchenskeoch–Buccoo Bay Rd, Carnbee, which runs from Claude Noel Hwy to Shirvan Rd (Mon–Sat 8am–7pm, Sun and public hols 9am–noon; ☎639 2976). In Scarborough, there's Scarborough Drugs, opposite *KFC* on the corner of Carrington St and Wilson Rd (Mon–Sat 8am–8pm, Sun and public hols 8am–noon; ☎639 4161).

The northwest coast

Just before Milford Road widens into the highway, the left-hand turn-off of **Shirvan Road** is the route to Tobago's **northwest coast**, home to **Buccoo Bay** and its famous **reef**, the golf course and surfing beach at **Mount Irvine** and, ultimately, **Stonehaven Bay**, **Turtle Beach** and the neat town of **Plymouth**, from which the Arnos Vale Road threads along the Caribbean coastline through **Arnos Vale** and the pretty hilltop villages of **Golden Lane** and **Les Coteaux**. Within easy driving distance of the beaches, restaurants and nightlife of Crown Point, but with a much more laidback and sometimes upmarket feel, this is a great area in which to base yourself, with plenty of lovely, less high-octane beaches and a smattering of great places to eat and drink.

Shirvan Road

North of the shopping plaza at the corner of Milford Road, the first stretch of **Shirvan Road** is bordered to the left by a plantation of towering coconut palms and to the right by thick hedges masking what was once Shirvan Park **horse racing track**. A fire in 1985 put a permanent stop to horse racing in Tobago and part of the site is now a residential development. Continuing north, Shirvan Road passes turn-offs to quietly residential **Mount Pleasant** and **Carnbee** (the latter has a couple of supermarkets; see page 207), while a cluster of tourist-oriented signposts mark the next crossroads, **Buccoo Junction**. Here, route taxis running between Scarborough and the north coast pick up and drop off passengers, so you'll often see beckoning hands if you're driving. The right turn at the crossroads is Auchenskeoch (pronounced "or-kins-styor") Buccoo Bay Road – take the first left from this road and you'll climb into the residential portion of **Mount Irvine**, with its lavish villas and fantastic views down over Buccoo Reef; carry straight on and you head through residential Carnbee to meet the highway.

A little further up Shirvan Road and you're at the outskirts of tiny **Bethel**, a precipitously situated and completely charming rural village that affords more wonderful views of Lowlands and the Buccoo coast. From Bethel, Orange Hill Road eventually meets Claude Noel Highway a couple of kilometres west of Scarborough.

Buccoo

The seaward turn off from Shirvan Road at Buccoo Junction runs past a small supermarket and into **BUCCOO** village, built on a promontory overlooking the calm and beautiful bay that shares its name. Fishing remains a major industry here – the day's catch is cleaned and sold next to the beach when the boats return in the late afternoon – but this close-knit community is best known for the weekly **Sunday School** (see page 212) shenanigans and for the annual Easter **goat races** (see page 214). The latter are now held at a smart purpose-built track and pavilion behind the new **Buccoo Integrated Facility**, a rather incongruously large concrete complex just back from the beach which encompasses a dancefloor used for Sunday School, an upstairs seafood restaurant, craft vendors' booths, a rather desultory tourist information kiosk and a big car park.

The **beach** immediately in front is primarily the preserve of fishermen and not really a place to swim, but the undeveloped, palm-lined western fringe of the bay is gorgeous, with clean water and plenty of shells and coral fragments to collect; this is also where the marvellous **Being With Horses** stables offer rides through the shallows. Trees and mangroves separate the beach from the Bon Accord wetlands, and if you walk right to the end of the sands and clamber into the bush (keep an eye out for toxic manchineel trees (see page 45), you can explore the remains of the house that Britain's Princess Margaret stayed in during a Tobago sojourn in the late 1950s.

5

SUNDAY SCHOOL

A Tobago institution, **Sunday School** is most definitely not for the pious. This outdoor party is the highlight of the week's nightlife, with swarms of people, food stalls and cars taking over Buccoo village. The action begins at around 8pm, when the **Buccooneers Steel Orchestra** play pan (sometimes at the beach facility, or otherwise at the *Captain's Sand Bar* just up the hill on the main road) for a couple of hours while the crowds sample food or browse the craft stalls; there's also traditional dancing and drumming at *Hendrix* bar, opposite the beach facility, which also plays more sedate "back in times" music as the night wears on. The crowd begins to thicken at around 10pm, when the **sound system** starts up in the beach facility; music policy is Jamaican dancehall and soca, and the dancefloor is invariably jumping as experienced winers (see "Glossary," page 280) display their skills, foreigners let loose or take a wining lesson, and the gigolos (and tourists) scout for a partner – Sunday School is well known as a kind of pick-up joint, so it's the ideal place to watch the intricate mating dance of thrill-seeking foreigners and hard-working local lotharios. Sunday School is not just for the young – locals and tourists of all ages come here to chill out and many tour guides offer Sunday School trips for about US$20. Note that parking can be difficult as the night wears on, so try to arrive early.

Though it's a friendly vibe, Sunday School is a place where you should be more mindful than usual of the risk of **theft**. Leave valuables and other items you can't afford to lose at the hotel, avoid getting so drunk that you become a sitting duck for opportunistic robbers and, if driving, try to park in busy, well-lit places, since muggings have been known to take place as revellers return to their cars at the end of the evening.

Being with Horses

14 Galla Trace, Buccoo • Trail ride and swim US$100, Magical Park TT$100; by appointment only: book well in advance • ☎ 639 0953, ⓦ being-with-horses.com

Quite unlike any equestrian establishment you may have experienced before, **Being with Horses** is a holistic stable, run with love by Lennon and Veronika La Fortune from their rainbow-painted base just back from Buccoo's beach. The herd, as the horses here are called, are ridden with bitless bridles and bareback pads, and as well as offering wonderful trail rides and sea swims, they provide therapeutic riding for children with disabilities as part of the **Healing with Horses** offshoot, which also runs holiday camps for children and provides occupational therapy and the like for clients. 2017 saw the opening of the **Magical Park** play area, just up Galla Trace from the main complex, with sensory play equipment alongside the usual swings, slide and trampoline; users get a chance to meet some of the horses, and it's a lovely way for younger children to spend a morning or afternoon.

ACCOMMODATION   BUCCOO

Close to the lovely beaches at Mount Irvine and Stonehaven, and the restaurants and bars of Pleasant Prospect, Buccoo is a great place to **stay**, with several inexpensive options just back from the beach.

★ **Fish Tobago** 26a Buccoo Point ☎ 309 0062, ⓦ fishtobago.com; map p.200. Set back from the main street to the right as you enter Buccoo, this is a popular guesthouse, well run and a good place to meet fellow visitors. The brightly painted rooms are all well appointed with kitchenette/living area and a separate a/c bedroom with en-suite bathroom; some are larger than others (and prices vary accordingly). There's also a one-bedroom apartment (US$100), and a dorm with shared kitchen. ☎ Dorms US$20, doubles US$50

★ **Miller's Guesthouse** Miller St ☎ 660 8371 or ☎ 772 5609, ⓦ millersguesthouse.com; map p.200. Lovely guesthouse in a prime spot overlooking Buccoo

Bay. The rooms (sleeping two or three) are basic yet bright, comfortable and immaculately maintained, with private bathroom, sink and fan. Dorm beds are available, and there's also a one-bedroom apartment with kitchen (US$85) and great views. All rooms have fridge, a/c and cable TV, and there's an attractive communal area plus a shared kitchen. ☎ Dorms US$30, doubles US$65

Reef View Apartments Miller St ☎ 660 7264 or ☎ 373 0904, ⓦ reefviewapts.com; map p.200. In a fantastic hilltop position overlooking Buccoo Bay, this locally run place is a great option. One-bed apartments have two double beds, living room and a fully equipped kitchen, as well as lovely sea views from the private porch; there are

also two-bedroom apartments downstairs (US$133). All are spotless, with a/c and cable TV. 🛜 **US$60**
Seaside Garden 29 Buccoo Point ☎ 639 0682, 🌐 tobago-guesthouse.com; map p.200. A great bargain, within walking distance of the action in the centre of Buccoo,

and offering clean, simple and inviting room (some smaller than others) with a/c and en-suite bathrooms, plus a shared kitchen and sundeck. The upstairs apartment with living area and fully equipped kitchen (US$100) has lovely bay views. 🛜 **US$45**

EATING

Buccoo is well served with great places to eat, and aside from the restaurants, vendors set up elaborate **food stalls** around the beach facility each Sunday to cater to Sunday School patrons, serving anything from barbecued fish or chicken with all the trimmings to lobster; ask about pricing in advance, as they can be surprisingly expensive. There are also a host of little cookshops along the main road offering inexpensive fish, chicken and roti lunches.

La Tartaruga Buccoo Village ☎ 639 0940; map p.200. Owned and run by a mercurial Italian émigré, with tables indoors or on an open-air patio, *La Tartaruga* features top-class Italian cuisine: lovely starters (TT$35–125) include fish carpaccio, parmesan eggplant or antipasti; there's also a range of home-made pasta (gnocchi in gorgonzola sauce, sage ravioli, beef and mushroom cannelloni; TT$75–145) or specialities such as grilled lobster, shrimp and fish (TT$85–345). Desserts – Drambuie crème caramel, home-made Italian ice cream – are equally memorable. The food is reasonably priced given the quality, but dipping into the extensive wine selection will increase your bill considerably. Mon–Sat 6.30–10pm.

★ **Luvinia's** Buccoo Point, Buccoo ☎ 631 1266, 🌐 bit. ly/Luvinias; map p.200. In a fantastic setting on a terrace overlooking the sea (and reachable via Miller St or by walking along the seafront), the location is as enjoyable as the food, with sea breezes and a perfect sunset view best enjoyed with a rum punch in hand. The menu is dominated by seafood and includes shrimp salad and calamari at

lunchtime (mains TT$65–75); dinner highlights (mains TT$140–320) include jumbo tequila shrimp or "Mexicano" fish in a jalapeno and white wine reduction, plus excellent lamb chops, lobster and steaks. Breakfast (TT$40–70) is also available; try the huevos rancheros: eggs with red beans, ham, fried plantain and garlic bread. Tues–Sun 8am–10pm.

★ **Makara** Buccoo Integrated Facility, Buccoo Main Rd ☎ 340 9547, 🌐 makaratobago.com; map p.200. Fabulous fine-dining restaurant on a covered deck overlooking the bay, perfect for a special meal out. Service is excellent and the modern Caribbean cuisine is executed with flair and an eye for presentation: starters (TT$45–95) run from mini crab and dumplings to fish tacos, while mains (TT$185–275) include spiced braised pork belly with prawns and callaloo; blackened fish in a coconut sauce; or rack of lamb with moussaka and a tomato and cardamom jus; "Meatless" meatballs are a tasty vegetarian option. A great option for a proper cocktail, too. Daily except Tues 11.30am–10pm.

DRINKING AND NIGHTLIFE

Buccoo is a great place for a **drink** overlooking the bay as the sun sinks behind Pigeon Point, and there's a newish **nightlife** option on Shirvan Road. It's also the venue for the weekly Sunday School party shenanigans (see page 212).

Café Down Low Buccoo Main Rd 475 0240; map p.200. Named for its location just below the main road, this locally owned bar and grill is an appealing and friendly place for a drink, with an open-air section enhanced by a waterfall and hummingbird feeders, and a busy bar area with sports games screened on TV. Ice-cold beers, inexpensive cocktails and simple meals of grilled fish, chicken or ribs for around TT$45, plus hearty soups on Sat. Tues–Sun noon–11pm.
Revs 196 Shirvan Rd ☎ 789 9620, 🌐 bit.ly/RevsBar; map p.200. Indoor/outdoor bar right on Shirvan Rd, with various deck areas and an indoor section with a/c and screens showing sports. It gets busy come the weekend with a more mature crowd who come to drink and dance; Fri is the best night. Bar food available. Tues–Thurs 5pm–midnight, Fri 5pm–3am, Sat & Sun 5pm–1am.
Sahara Lounge Buccoo Town Centre Mall, Shirvan

Rd ☎ 282 5272, 🌐 bit.ly/SaharaTT; map p.200. The location might be rather prosaic, on the first floor of a shopping mall overlooking Shirvan Rd, but this is a fun spot for some serious partying, more popular with locals than visitors. The indoor dancefloor area is usually packed, with DJs playing soca, dancehall and the odd pop tune, and patrons spill out onto the balcony to get a breather. Entry is TT$80 on Fri with free drinks, or TT$40 (women), TT$60 (men) on Sat. Fri & Sat 10pm–5am.
Time to Wine Shirvan Plaza, Shirvan Rd 🌐 639 7212, 🌐 bit.ly/WineBago; map p.200. Tucked away in the Shirvan Plaza mini-mall, this is a quiet spot for a glass of good wine, as well as one of the best places in Tobago to buy a bottle or two, with wines from all around the world. Craft beers too, and a great rum selection. Mon–Sat 10am–10pm, Sun 10am–6pm.

5

GOAT RACES

Easter weekend in Tobago is an unofficial national holiday when hotels are filled to the brim and the island erupts with festivities. A succession of open-air parties and well-attended harvest feasts culminate on Easter Tuesday at the **Buccoo goat races**, a tradition since 1925. Though attempting to race one of the world's most belligerent animals may seem a little ridiculous to the uninitiated, these tournaments are taken very seriously by aficionados, who study the form (and character) of the sleekly groomed animals and place bets on their favourites. Raised separately from the run-of-the-mill roadside grazer, and considerably larger, racing goats undergo a rigorous training routine and return to the tracks year after year. Prize specimens live out their days as stud goats to breed more potential champions.

The preliminary round at the Mount Pleasant Family Fun Day on Easter Monday gives everyone a chance to see which goat is running best, but the main event is at Buccoo on the Tuesday. Food vendors and craft stalls line the streets and a carnival atmosphere builds as fast as the crowds, who are kept entertained by dancing and drumming in between stakes. Smartly attired in white shorts and coloured vests, the jockeys limber up by the side of the tracks, a necessary exercise, as their ability to keep up with their goat (and keep hold of it) over the 150m race has more influence on their success or failure than the capabilities of the goat itself: animals are raced at the end of a rope, and kept on course via taps from a long switch. Once the jockeys manage to manoeuvre their malignant charges into starting position, the actual races are a joy to watch. With wild-eyed stares, the goats tear haphazardly down the track, often taking a diagonal course that trips up competitors and runners alike, to the delight of the spectators. The best of the bunch battle for supremacy in the final "Champ of Champs" race, while "Champion Jockey", "Champion Trainer" and "Most Outstanding Goat" prizes are also presented.

Once all the races are over on Tuesday, the final **all-night party** swings into action, and the dancing continues until dawn.

Mount Irvine

The swaying palms and shaven greens of Tobago's original **golf course** herald the outskirts of **MOUNT IRVINE**, the next village along the coast north of Buccoo, a scattered community of luxury villas around the golf course that's centred around its gorgeous main beach, home to Tobago's surfing scene and one of the nicest spots in the southwest to spend a day by the sea. Beyond the golf course, the hitherto hidden Caribbean Sea coast swings spectacularly back into view; yachts bob on the waves and craggy volcanic rock formations bordering Booby Point make an arresting backdrop to the west. There's a lovely section of undeveloped beach known as **Grange** or Mount Irvine Wall behind a low concrete bulwark just past the golf course; it's very popular with locals who often sit chatting in the emerald-green water.

Mount Irvine Beach

Lifeguards daily 10am–6pm • Changing facilities TT$1

North of Grange Beach and around the next bend of Shirvan Road is **Mount Irvine Beach**, a busy slip of fine yellow sand surrounded by covered gazebos for picnicking and the ubiquitous palms and sea grape trees. The showers and changing facilities are adequate, and there's a bar/restaurant doling out cold drinks and simple fish-and-chips lunches. During the summer months, the sea here is calm enough to make exploration of the ornate offshore **reef** a joy, and the clear, greenish waters offer excellent swimming year-round. However, Mount Irvine is at its liveliest between December and March, when it becomes one of the island's best **surfing** beaches, with huge breakers crashing in and a cool surfers' scene on the sand, a world away from the packaged postcard-Caribbean feel of Pigeon Point; it's known to its devotees as the "Office". Note that the water here is initially shallow and there's a reef directly offshore, so surf fins can be badly damaged and no protective footwear is allowed (this is to protect the reef from over-eager surfers jumping in and damaging the coral).

Mount Irvine hotel beach

Bar and restaurant daily 10am–5pm.

Just to the south of the public area, past where fishermen sell their daily catch, the semi-private section of beach maintained by the *Mount Irvine Bay Hotel* offers even better swimming and excellent snorkelling, though it's perhaps less atmospheric, and parking is limited. Non-guests are welcome to swim; recliners are available to rent, and there's a restaurant serving lunch and drinks.

Back Bay

Around the headland that caps the eastern end of Mount Irvine Beach, **Back Bay** is a much quieter swathe of sand. To get there, take the dirt track toward the sea off from the main road opposite Gleneagles Drive; you have to scramble down a bank to get to the sand. Gorgeous and completely undeveloped, with several very photogenic rocky outcrops, Back Bay is a secluded spot. As currents can be dangerous, however, it's best to stick to paddling or bodysurfing in the shallows – and as the beach is quite remote and robberies have occurred, you're well advised to visit in a group.

ACTIVITIES   MOUNT IRVINE

Mount Irvine is known for its **surfing** possibilities, but it's also a good spot for some **kayaking**, with rentals from the Mount Irvine Bay Watersports outlet (see page 205), right on the beach overlooking the hotel section, which also has beach-fun toys like a floating sunbathing net. **Golf** is available at the Mount Irvine Hotel course (see page 203).

Surfing Boards (around US$20/hr) can usually be rented at Mount Irvine Beach; ask around. George Charles (☏ 294 6509, 🌐 surf-tobago.com/george) has been offering surfing classes here for some years, and is one of the best choices should you want to learn to surf; he charges US$50/hr for lessons and offers board rental (US$20/hr).

ACCOMMODATION

★ **Bijou des Caraïbes** 3 Jacamar Drive, Mount Irvine ☏ 639 9586 or ☏ 734 7303, 🌐 bijou-des-caraibes.com; map p.200. In a quiet residential setting above Mount Irvine, this is a peaceful little hideaway, set in flower-filled gardens with a good-sized pool. The studios and one- or two-bedroom apartments, with a/c bedrooms and kitchenette, are clean and functional (but not luxurious), ideal if you want a degree of independence. The helpful owner is a mine of information on Tobago. ☏ Studios US$65, one-bedroom apartment US$80

★ **Birdsong** ☏ 498 6959, 🌐 vrbo.com/187521; map p.200. Just above Mount Irvine at Grange, this lovely villa is a beautiful and peaceful place to stay. Set in gardens planted with fruit trees, it has three bedrooms, an open balcony area with dining table and lounge chairs, full kitchen, a secluded pool surrounded by greenery, and really reasonable rates which cover up to four people. US$150

★ **Mount Irvine Bay Hotel** ☏ 639 8871, 🌐 mtirvine. com; map p.200. The grand old lady of Tobago hotels, this sprawling property with a golf course above Mount Irvine bay has recently been given a handsome refurb and is looking great. Facilities are fantastic – tennis courts, spa, huge pool, excellent restaurant and several bars – while rooms are bright, fresh and spacious; the cottages (US$288) in the garden area are particularly appealing, and all are just steps away from Mount Irvine beach. US$158

VILLAS

Though **villas** are conventionally seen as luxury accommodation – and most of the newer villas are aimed at the wealthier traveller – they can work out to be quite cost-effective if you're travelling in a large group. There is a particular concentration of properties around the Mount Irvine golf course, and east along the coast toward Plymouth. Unfortunately, due to their sometimes isolated locations and the lack of round-the-clock security, villas have been targeted by burglars, so it's wise to check security before you book and ensure you lock up at night.

To find a villa, you can go through an agency such as **Villas of Tobago** (☏ 639 9600, 🌐 villasoftobago.com), a well-established and professional operation with an excellent range of properties for all budgets. The **My Tobago** website lists a good selection of villas at 🌐 mytobago.info/tobago-villas1.htm, and there are also lots of possibilities via 🌐 **airbnb.com** and 🌐 **vrbo.com**.

EATING

Café Cream Cheese Yogurteria Orange Hill Nature Ranch, Union Trace 660 7761, ⓦ goatdairy-tobago. com; map p.200. Nestled in the hills above Mount Irvine (follow Orange Hill Rd past the *Mount Irvine Hotel*), and with a flower-wreathed outdoor dining area set around the buildings of a former sugar factory, this is a pretty place to sample home-made goodies (TT$25–35), baked by the German emigrée owner using milk from her herd of goats; try the cheesecake or banana chocolate cake, or the fresh

goat's milk yogurt or smoothies. Delicious coffee, herb tea and fresh fruit juices, too. Daily 11am–6pm.

Cheryl's Roti Mount Irvine Beach ☎ 321 4619; map p.200. From her roadside gazebo above the beach car park, Cheryl cooks up excellent rotis (from TT$30), either veggie (with channa and potato, pumpkin and bodi beans) or all the veg with chicken, fish (Fri only) or beef (Sat only). Go early or call ahead, as food is often sold out by noon. Mon–Sat 10am–2pm.

Kimme Museum

Kimme Drive • Sun 10am–2pm, appointments taken for other days • TT$20 • ☎ 639 0257, ⓦ luisekimme.com • Take the right turn just past the Mount Irvine golf course then follow the signposts

Nestled in the hills behind the beach along Orange Hill Road is the **Kimme Museum**, the private gallery of German sculptor Luise Kimme, who settled in Tobago in 1979 and lived here until her death in 2013. Her eerily beguiling wood sculptures are still dotted around the surrounds of her quirky, mural-decorated turreted home, the "Fairyhaus". Though much of the collection has been shipped to Germany, what remains is stunning: 3m-high figures carved from whole trunks of oak depict the subtlest nuances of Tobagonian dancing, while Kimme's interpretations of local folklore characters such as the Soucouyant (see page 253) are powerful. In her latter years, Kimme spent long periods in Cuba learning the art of lost-wax casting; you can admire the results of these studies in a room full of her intricate bronze sculptures. There's also a room downstairs full of the more abstract but equally beautiful work of Kimme's Cuban mentor **Dunieski Lora Pileta**, whose pieces combine found objects with more classical sculpture, and who is usually on hand to conduct tours of the house.

Stonehaven Bay

Past Mount Irvine, Shirvan Road becomes Grafton Road. Marked by a flurry of signs advertising villas and hotels, Old Stonehaven Road (once the main coast road) turns off to the left and runs along almost the whole length of **Stonehaven Bay**, also known as Grafton Beach. A glorious, wide swathe with coarse sand that attracts turtles, which lay their eggs here in the March–August season, the beach offers some great swimming, and is deliciously uncommercialized. The presence of two large hotels overlooking the sand detract little from the beauty of the scene, particularly pretty at late afternoon as the sun sinks behind the black volcanic rocks that punctuate the seashore.

ACCOMMODATION

STONEHAVEN BAY

Grafton Beach Resort/Le Grand Courlan Stonehaven Bay Rd ☎ 639 9667, ⓦ graftontobago.com and ⓦ legrand tobago.com. Side by side and overlooking Stonehaven Bay, these garishly painted twin hotels limp along despite years of under-occupation, seemingly kept going by great package deals organized in conjunction with airlines from the UK. The *Courlan* side is adults-only, while the *Grafton* is family-friendly. They share a restaurant (see page 217) and pool, and both have loungers down on the beach. There's a tennis court, spa and gym on site, and rooms have all the usual amenities. Rates include breakfast. ⓦ **US$148**

★ **Plantation Beach Villas** Stonehaven Bay Rd ☎ 639 9377, ⓦ plantationbeachvillas.com. Set in lush gardens,

with gingerbread fretwork and wraparound verandas overlooking the sea, these gorgeous three-bedroom villas are one of the most appealing accommodation options in Tobago. Each is beautifully designed; out on the deck, recliners and a dining table allow you to eat and relax al fresco, while inside the decor is stylishly simple, with rocking chairs, solid wooden furniture, and everything you need for a perfect stay, from a gas-fired barbecue to a well-equipped kitchen, washing machine and dryer and a decent music system. There's a bar and communal pool, the sea is steps away from your villa and the staff are efficient and supremely friendly. ⓦ **US$313**

Seahorse Inn Stonehaven Bay Rd ☎ 639 0686, ⓦ sea horseinntobago.com. Small hotel right on a turtle-nesting beach offering four comfortable rooms with appealing quirks like arched windows and teak floors. Rooms come with a/c, ceiling fan, en-suite bathroom, cable TV and patios with great sea views. There's a good restaurant on site (see below) and evening entertainment during high season. Rates include continental breakfast. US$140

The Villas at Stonehaven Grafton Estate, Black Rock ☏ 639 0361, ⓦstonehavenvillas.com. Fourteen huge and very expensive three- and four-bedroom villas fitted with mahogany, marble and granite and every conceivable luxury: four-poster beds, private infinity pool and stunning views over Stonehaven Bay. The secure complex includes a clubhouse with bar and open-air restaurant. US$468

EATING AND DRINKING

★ **Seahorse Inn** Stonehaven Bay Rd ☏ 639 0686, ⓦseahorseinntobago.com. The perfect place for a romantic dinner with the sound of the waves crashing below, offering an imaginative and deservedly expensive menu. Well-executed appetizers such Creole crab cakes or seared scallop risotto (TT$65–85), are followed up with excellent mains (TT$155–350), from curried shrimp to blackened grouper and lobster Thermidor, steaks, rack of lamb or pan-roasted duck in a pineapple glaze. Good desserts, one of the best wine lists in Tobago, and English beers, too. Happy hour 5.30–6.30pm. Daily noon–3.30pm & 6.30–10pm.

Waves Beach Bar Stonehaven Bay Rd ☏ 639 0191, ⓦwavestobago.com. Handsomely refurbished, the beachside restaurant of the *Grafton/Grand Courlan* hotels is a lively little spot, set on a deck overlooking the water. It's great for both lunch and dinner: lunchtimes (mains TT$54–96) promise salads, burgers, fish/shrimp tacos, grilled chicken or beef panini and pulled pork buns, while in the evening (mains TT$165–220) there's fish with mango cilantro salsa, white wine or garlic butter, plus steaks, ribs, rack of lamb and pork chops, and a range of pasta dishes. A pleasant spot for a drink, too. Daily 10am–6pm.

Pleasant Prospect

Opposite the southern end of Old Stonehaven Road, and looping off the main road in a crescent, the main street of **PLEASANT PROSPECT** offers a smattering of restaurants and bars kept busy by Mount Irvine surfers, as well as people using the ATM, supermarket, fruit and veg stall and the *Pizza Boys* takeaway joint. The area comes into its own after dark, when music wafts from the bars, limers hang out in the street and diners drift in and out of the restaurants.

ACCOMMODATION AND EATING   PLEASANT PROSPECT

★ **The Fish Pot** Pleasant Prospect Main St ☏ 635 1728. Brilliant restaurant/bar with a blackboard menu dominated by seafood. Starters (TT$35–45) might range from crab cakes to rum liver pâté, jerk fish with plantain or goat's cheese salad, while mains (lunch from 11$60, dinner TT$160–185) are determined by whatever the fishermen bring in super-fresh that day, grilled or pan-fried in clever combinations of spices and fresh herbs, and with delicious sides; you can also get steaks and home-made burgers. The raised deck overlooking Pleasant Prospect is great for watching the world go by. Mon–Sat 11am–3pm, & 7–10pm.

Joanne's Pleasant Prospect Main St. From her little wooden kiosk outside Pleasant Prospect's supermarket, Joanne cooks up tasty, inexpensive local takeaway food (from TT$40), with a daily-changing menu that always includes fish, chicken and perhaps beef or curry goat, plus sides from callaloo to stewed peas and green salad. Excellent soup on Sat, and home-made cake daily. Mon–Sat 6.30–9pm.

Legger's Bar Grafton Rd ☏ 277 2777. Across the road from *Pizza Boys* and perched on a cliff top overlooking Stonehaven Bay, this unpretentious rum bar is a picturesque spot for a drink, especially during the sunset hours when

the view over the ocean comes into its own; there's a daily happy hour from 4–8pm. They also do excellent Creole breakfasts of smoked herring/saltfish buljol with coconut bake and the like (6–10am; from TT$20), BBQ fish, pork and chicken on Fri and fabulous Tobago-style Sunday lunch (baked chicken/fish, mac pie, callaloo etc; from TT$60), all of which you can eat here or take away. Call ahead for weekday lunch/dinner. Daily 6am–late.

Moon Over Water Pleasant Prospect Main St ☏ 709 9896, ⓦmoon-over-water.com. This cool little bar, pumping mellow reggae out over the lower end of the crescent, makes a nice place to chill out over a beer or shoot some pool. Regular special events and drinks promotions. Daily noon–late.

Two Seasons Guest House Pleasant Prospect Main St ☏ 639 1056 or ☏ 792 9329, ⓦtwoseasonstobago. com. Directly above the *Fish Pot* restaurant, with a lovely balcony overlooking the village and distant sea views, this is a great spot for meeting other travellers, and the price is fantastic for the location, just a couple of minutes' walk from Stonehaven Bay and 5min from Mount Irvine. The basic but decent rooms have fan and mosquito nets, and there's a shared kitchen. ☎ US$30

5

Grafton Caledonia Bird Sanctuary

Grafton Rd • Daylight hours; feeding time 8am & 4pm • Free, but donation welcome

North of Pleasant Prospect, a sun-bleached sign on the right of Grafton Road marks the entrance to the **Grafton Caledonia Bird Sanctuary**. Now somewhat run-down, the sanctuary was founded by the late owner of the surrounding estate, Eleanor Alefounder, who began feeding hungry local birds following the devastation wreaked by Hurricane Flora in 1963 (see page 236). Today, mot-mots, cocricos, bananaquits and practically every other feathered specimen found on the island are fed here, many of which will peck right out of your hand. There are extensive trails through the property which make for excellent, easy and scenic **hiking**.

Black Rock

Northeast of Pleasant Prospect, the main road narrows as it swings through **BLACK ROCK**, a somnolent little village with a couple of nice rum bars and a sprinkling of grocery stores. On the western outskirts of town, where Old Stonehaven Road loops back up from the sea, is a signpost for **Fort Bennett** (daily 9am–6pm; free), once the site of a stockade built by English mercenary Lieutenant Robert Bennett in 1680. During the plantation era, the fort was expanded by British troops, who built a brick oven to heat up the metal used to make cannonballs and placed two cannons here to defend the bay against US privateers during the American War of Independence. These days, though, it's more like a park, with paved paths looping through the site to benches and a couple of gazebos perfectly placed to enjoy the views. These stretch over Stonehaven Bay and down to the Pigeon Point headland to the west, and over Turtle Beach to Plymouth to the east – spectacular in both directions, particularly at sunset.

Turtle Beach

North of Black Rock, the coast road swings around a blind bend before entering a straight stretch. Trees mask lovely **Turtle Beach** (officially Great Courland Bay), a picturesque kilometre of coarse yellow sand flecked with the occasional swathe of volcanic grey; there are several dirt tracks from which to enter the bay from the road. The water shelves steeply from the beach and the waves are large, making for exhilarating swimming, while a river at the western end can sometimes be nice for a freshwater dip, but it's often no more than a trickle in the dry season. Jealously guarding pole position in the centre of the bay (only guests are allowed to use the thatched sunshades), the low-rise *Turtle Beach* all-inclusive hotel dominates the sand, and the presence of its guests has generated an ideal captive market for vendors selling sarongs and crafts or touting an aloe massage.

Plymouth

Roughly a kilometre north of Turtle Beach, Grafton Road meets a junction: going straight will put you on Plymouth Road to Scarborough, while to the left, a narrow bridge over the Courland River brings you to the outskirts of **PLYMOUTH**. Tobago's first European community, Plymouth was settled by a group of roving Latvians, usually referred to as Courlanders, then by the Dutch and finally by the British. Today, it's a quiet little town, predominantly residential, with neat houses lining the grid-patterned streets and a handful of very low-key historical sights. Life in Plymouth centres around *TJ's Grocery & Bar* at the junction of Shelbourne and Halifax streets; it's also the only place on the Caribbean coast with a **petrol station** (Mon–Sat 7am–9pm, Sun 7am–noon), so it's a good idea to fill your tank here if you're driving on up the leeward coast.

> ## TURTLE-WATCHING IN TOBAGO
>
> Turtle Beach acquired its colloquial title on account of the **leatherback turtles** (see page 142) that lay eggs here in the dark of night; like hawksbill and green turtles they also lay on many neighbouring beaches. The main laying season runs between March and August, and six weeks after the eggs are laid, hatchlings make a dash for the sea – both equally moving sights. All of the hotels along this stretch organize a turtle watch during the laying and hatching seasons, but if you're not staying in the area, contact a local tour company (see page 202) or locally run charity **Save Our Sea Turtles** (☎ 328 7351, ⓦ sos-tobago.org), which do free lectures on turtle nesting during the season and can direct you to specialized guides; their website has plenty of detailed information on the species in local waters.

Mystery tombstone

Shelbourne St; turn left at TJ's and continue about 200m down

Well signposted and sitting alone on a concrete platform on the inland side of Shelburne Street, the so-called **mystery tombstone** is an enigmatic reminder of Tobago's history of slavery. The double grave of a child and her 23-year-old mother, Betty Stiven, the "mystery" is the eighteenth-century inscription on the stone slab: "What was remarkable of her; she was a mother without knowing it, and a wife without letting her husband know it, except by her kind indulgences to him." Betty is said to have been an African slave and lover of Dutch planter Alex Stiven, and the general hypothesis has two strands: either she gave birth to Stiven's child and he took charge of it, raising it as his but not acknowledging Betty as the mother, giving her "freedom" to carry on as his lover and making her a "mother without knowing it"; or the affair between Alex and Betty was illicit and scandalous but passionate, carried out in secret to save the face of a white man. When she died giving birth to his child, he was overcome with grief and left this cryptic message in commemoration of their love.

Great Courland Bay Monument

A few metres before the mystery tombstone, a road opposite leads down to the stark concrete blocks of the **Great Courland Bay Monument**, put up in 1976 (and very much a product of its era) in testament to the "bold, enterprising and industrious" Latvians who colonized the area and lent their name to the bay.

Fort James

Carrying straight on past the mystery tombstone (head through the gates to the sports ground and follow the road around the headland) brings you to **Fort James**, the oldest stockade in Tobago, dating from 1650 and named after the Duke of Courland (see page 196). The solid coral-stone structure and four cannons that remain today are a British legacy, added in 1811, and there's an excellent view of Turtle Beach from the lawns in front.

Adventure Farm and Nature Reserve

Arnos Vale Rd • Daily 9am–6pm • US$10 • ☎ 639 2839, ⓦ adventure-ecovillas.com

On the eastern outskirts of Plymouth, on the Arnos Vale Road, a sign directs you to the turn-off for the **Adventure Farm and Nature Reserve**, a twelve-acre working organic estate planted with grapefruit, oranges, mangoes, bananas, papaya and guavas, as well as a huge range of mature tropical trees including towering samaans bedecked with epiphytic bromeliads and orchids. The woodlands attract an array of animals and birds, from matte lizards, morrocoy (tortoises), rabbits and agouti to mot-mots, green herons and cocricos, and there are a couple of marked trails down from the main house through the estate, past a man-made waterfall that splashes down into a fishpond. Up at the main house, sugar-water feeders on the covered porch attract a multitude of **hummingbirds**, from the common copper-rumped variety to the gorgeous

5

little rubytopaz, and you can sit and watch the antics of these surprisingly aggressive little birds at close quarters. A host of other birds regularly appear to feed in the late afternoon, summoned by the ringing of an antique ship's bell.

ACCOMMODATION   PLYMOUTH

★ **Adventure Eco Villas** Arnos Vale Rd ☎ 639 2839, ⊛ adventure-ecovillas.com. An oasis for birdwatchers, and for anyone seeking a little nature and serenity, these two lovely villas are built out of Guyanese greenheart wood and perched over a tree-filled valley in the Adventure Farm and Nature Reserve, with a large shared deck area. Both have a kitchen, a/c, cable TV and screened windows, and a living room with floor-to-ceiling louvres on one side that can open onto the trees. A cheaper apartment in the main house is also available (US$85). Villas US$140

Changrela Cocrico Inn North St, at Commissioner ☎ 639 2961, ⊛ changrela.com. This comfortable, charming and friendly place has a restaurant, pool and quiet location in

residential backstreets. There's quite a range of accommodation, including large rooms used for visiting groups, but the nicest options are on the top floor – clean and simple with cable TV and a small balcony; some have a kitchenette, others a full kitchen. Meals are available. ☞ US$40

Tropical Pleasure River Rd ☎ 660 2222, ✉ admin@ tropicalpleasure.net. This multi-storied orange-painted block on your left as you enter Plymouth, overlooking lawns planted with mature trees, offers sixteen beautifully maintained and very spacious rooms, all with a/c, cable TV, kitchenette and balcony or patio. Usually very quiet, it's reasonably priced and a good base from which to explore the area. ☞ US$66

Arnos Vale

Arnos Vale Road meanders northeast through the greenery towards **Arnos Vale**, one of the few former sugar plantations to keep its land, part of which is taken up with a now-closed resort hotel. **Arnos Vale Beach** is very pretty (though the crumbling hotel buildings behind add a *Marie Celeste* air) and the snorkelling just offshore is some of the island's best. However, its secluded nature and lack of security mean that robberies have occurred here, so unless you're in a big group it's best visited as part of a boat trip; many day-cruises (see page 202) stop here for snorkelling.

ACCOMMODATION   ARNOS VALE

★ **Top O' Tobago** Arnos Vale Estate ☎ 639 3166 or ☎ 687 0121, ⊛ topotobago.com. Perched above Arnos Vale Bay and cooled by constant breezes, this is a unique and beguiling place with great hill and sea views and plenty of birdlife. Stylishly decorated with great attention to detail, the main two-bedroom house sleeps up to six and

has a large sitting room, two bathrooms, fully equipped kitchen, patio, flat-screen TV, stereo, and washer and dryer. Smaller cabanas are equally appealing, with a king-size bed and two sofabeds, kitchen and private patio; and all have use of the pool. Free airport pick-up, and wonderful personalized service. Cabana US$150, house US$300

Golden Lane and Les Coteaux

Northeast of Arnos Vale, the main coast road heads into the hills and through **Golden Lane** and **Les Coteaux**, tiny but attractive villages that have some associations with local superstitions. Rumours of witchery and potions abound, and Golden Lane is said to hold the grave of a witch known as Gang Gang Sara, who flew here from Africa and married a local man – the community hosts spooky story sessions during the Heritage Festival celebrations. Beyond Les Coteaux, the Arnos Vale Road meets the Northside Road (see page 228) in a T-junction; turn right to reach Scarborough, and left to carry on up the leeward coast toward Castara.

Scarborough

Tobago's raucous, hot and dusty capital, precipitous **SCARBOROUGH** is a surprisingly appealing place, its houses and roads spilling higgledy-piggledy down a hillside, with the Atlantic providing a magnificent backdrop for **Fort King George** which perches at the top of the hill. The island's administrative centre and its main **port**, Scarborough is a flourishing town, brimming with a brisk vibrancy. Devoid of any touristy pretensions, its street corners buzz with liming locals, while pavement stalls are perused by shoppers and the bars spill out onto the streets. Away from the bustle, the shady suburb of **Bacolet** is home to some upmarket hotels and the secluded Bacolet Bay Beach – in former times the playground of many a rich and famous visitor to Tobago.

Though the largest town on the island, Scarborough is still pretty tiny, with most of the commercial action spreading back up from the port and along the precipitous Main Street. The heat, traffic and steep climbs can make it a bit tiring to explore, but the cool breezes and views from the port and the elevated parts of town offer respite.

Brief history

The **Dutch** were the first Europeans to settle what became one of Tobago's most hotly contested pieces of land. They navigated the treacherous harbour rocks in 1654, and constructed a fort and a few buildings, naming it **Lampsinsburgh**. Around the same time, a group of Courlanders (Latvians) were building up their stronghold on the opposite coast at Plymouth (see page 218). In 1658, the Dutch captured Plymouth – an act that led to the destruction of their own settlement when, in 1666, a British fleet came to the aid of the Latvians and blew Lampsinsburgh to smithereens.

The **British** officially won the island in 1672, but didn't maintain a presence, allowing the Dutch to return and build Lampsinsburgh into a more substantial settlement, with houses, a single street and a church, as well as warehouses and wharves at the harbour and a new fort. However, during the French assault of 1677, the newly improved **fortifications** proved to be the undoing of the Dutch; a French cannonball hit the fort's ammunition dump, and the resulting fireball destroyed the structure and killed all 250 occupants. Though still commemorated in the current name Dutch Fort Road, there's nothing left today of that original settlement.

The British bestowed the name **Scarborough** when they regained control of Tobago in 1762, establishing the House of Assembly here and constructing Fort King George. The **French** returned to take control, after a bloody and prolonged fight, in 1781. Scarborough was renamed Port Louis, while Fort King George – with finishing touches

5

added by French soldiers – became **Fort Castries**. The town ricocheted between the British and French until Tobago was finally ceded to the British in 1814.

Central Scarborough

Central Scarborough constitutes the area around the market and the port and is where you'll find most of the action, with shoppers, office workers, taxi drivers and street vendors giving the place a hectic feel. Entering from the Claude Noel Highway via car-choked Wilson Road, a left following the one-way traffic system onto Darrel Spring Road and then a right down Gardenside Street will take you past the back of **NIB Mall** to the right, and the Botanical Gardens (and a car park) to the left.

Scarborough Public Market

Wilson Rd • Mon–Sat 6am–4pm

Behind the NIB Mall is the capital's **market**. Main trading days are Friday and Saturday, though throughout the week vendors sell every tropical fruit and vegetable imaginable. The indoor meat section is an odoriferous melange of goat, beef, lamb, mutton and chicken, while fish on ice gleam at the back section, where stallholders attract customers by blowing on a **conch shell**. It's a friendly and absorbing scene, great for bargains and a chat with the stallholders, who can explain how to cook any unfamiliar produce. If you're after souvenirs such as knitted Rasta hats, sandals and woodcarvings, or cheap CDs and DVDs, check out the stalls lining busy Wilson Road and the western side of NIB Mall.

Botanical Gardens

Greenside St • Daily, daylight hours • Free • There are entrances on Gardenside St, Northside Rd (south of the highway) and from a signposted layby on the Claude Noel Hwy

A soothing oasis after the heat-retaining concrete and traffic fumes of downtown Scarborough, the **Botanical Gardens** are laid over eighteen acres of what were once the Dal Fair and Rockly Vale sugar plantations. Today, the broad sweeps of lawn interspersed with planted beds and shade trees could pass for an English park, were it not for the garish crimson of towering African tulips, flamboyant trees and the yellow and pink cascades of the poui trees. The gardens remain a firm favourite for wedding photos, but generally they're pretty much deserted. There are no guided **tours** as such, but the gardeners on site will usually answer questions. The gardens are at their most magical during the Christmas season, when almost the entire space is lit up by a beautiful array of coloured lights.

The waterfront

Though some older buildings remain in Scarborough's steep heights, most of the **waterfront** is relatively new. Souped up in 1990 by the addition of a deep-water cruise-ship pier, the harbour area is dominated by the modern **ferry terminal**. As well as the ticket office, the complex holds a few shops and Scarborough's main post office. The circular wooden buildings on Milford Road's seafront **esplanade** sell snacks, ice cream, cold beers and souvenirs, and the main open-air gazebo is often used to host concerts and special events; otherwise, it's a nice shady spot in which to enjoy the sea breeze.

Upper Scarborough

Comprising the hilly streets on the eastern side of the town, **Upper Scarborough** is a busy area with plenty of shops and banks, but gets steadily quieter the higher you climb. Proceeding east from the ferry terminal along Carrington Street, you soon reach a junction known as **King's Well**, originally the site of the town's main watercourse. A sharp left here takes you out of town along Northside Road and the edge of the

5

Botanical Gardens, while the sharp right is Castries Street, the route to precipitous **Main Street**, the principal shopping thoroughfare. Between the two, steeply inclining **Burnett Street** is one of Scarborough's best places for knick-knack **shopping** – anything from T-shirts to lingerie.

James Park and the Courthouse

As Burnett Street reaches a plateau, you enter **James Park**, a small walled square decorated with a bronze by Luise Kimme (see page 216) of A.P.T. James, a former Minister of Tobago Affairs. The park is bordered to the east by the imposing old **courthouse**, which has housed the administrative offices of the Tobago House of Assembly since the judiciary were shifted to their current Bacolet Street base in the late 1980s. Built between 1821 and 1825, the cut-stone structure was considered one of the finest examples of Georgian architecture in the Caribbean on completion. Subsequent alterations have, unfortunately, smothered the original brickwork with white paint and removed the pillars, rendering it a shadow of its former glory.

Bacolet Street

One block northeast of James Park, on the other side of the bustling shop-and-office-lined Main Street, **Bacolet Street** leads to the fire station, the main police station (and only jail) and the short **Gun Bridge**, sporting railings made from rifle barrels and stone walls embellished with four cannons, two at either end, taken from Fort King George – a commemoration of the town's historical discord. A few metres past the bridge is handsome **St Andrew's Anglican Church**, originally built in 1819 but razed by Hurricane Flora in 1963 and reconstructed a year later. The fire and police stations are opposite and behind the church respectively. Further south down Bacolet Street, the buildings thin out as you enter the quiet and attractive Bacolet suburbs (see page 224).

Fort King George

Fort St • Parking is available, adjacent to the museum and main fort

Forking off Main Street, Fort Street twists its way up a steep hill past the imposing Methodist Church and some attractive but dishevelled colonial architecture on its way to one of the most prominent sights in town, **Fort King George**, a precipitous fifteen-minute walk. The complex is the largest fortification in Tobago, built by the British in 1777 and initially composed of some thirty buildings, but reduced to around ten by an 1847 hurricane. It was occupied by French troops between 1781 and 1793, who built the solid stone perimeter walls. Inspired by the French Revolution, the soldiers **mutinied** in 1790, imprisoning their officers and razing the town below. There are signs dotted around the complex giving some background to the buildings, and you can also get a **guided tour** from one of the THA personnel in the Tourism division, to the left of the car park at the top of the fort area.

As you approach, the first of the fort's buildings is a ruined red-brick **prison**; it hasn't undergone the restoration of the main buildings, and time and the elements have opened its tiny, dingy cells to shafts of sunlight. Around the next bend, past the closed-up **Tobago County Hospital**, its 1930s buildings slowly crumbling since the opening of the Signal Hill complex in 2012, is the start of the fort complex proper. The first building on the left is the dome-shaped cover of an old **well**, built in 1926 to service the hospital. Over the road from the well, a path leads below the main complex to a landscaped **park**, lush with poui trees and colourful planted beds. Benches are perfectly placed for soaking up marvellous views of Scarborough and the Orange Hill district. In the shade of a massive, buttressed silk cotton tree is the (usually locked) **powder magazine**, a sturdy structure built to house stocks of ammunition and gunpowder.

5

At the top level of the complex, some 140m above sea level, the **Officer's Mess** is the fort's largest building, now housing the Tobago Museum. Beyond the Mess, a series of cannons point through cut-stone walls and out to sea; the walls afford spectacular views of Bacolet Bay, Minister Point and the rugged interior to the east, and Rockly Bay and the north coast of Trinidad to the west. Behind the Mess is the **lighthouse**, a squat structure transferred from Galera Point in Trinidad in 1958; the Fresnel lens beams 50km out to sea and sweeps spectacularly over the Scarborough suburbs.

Tobago Museum
Mon–Fri 9am–4.30pm, closed public hols · TT$10 · ☎ 639 3970

Laid out in the cool confines of the refurbished Officer's Mess, the **Tobago Museum** has a small but fascinating collection of idiosyncratic artefacts, with displays on everything from Amerindian society to life in the nineteenth century. There's an extensive collection of pre-Columbian axe-heads, chisels, cooking ware and talismans, known as *adornos*, found at Amerindian sites across the island, as well as three 800-year-old skeletons unearthed at Amerindian burial sites. Racks of shells and fossils give way to relics from the colonial era, from military ephemera to coins and notes and some rather chilling logs detailing names and "condition" of the slaves sold to the island's various estates. Look out also for satirical prints depicting the exploits of "Johnny Newcome in Love in the West Indies", and a copy of the second edition of the *Pleasant Prospect of the Famous and Fertile Island of Tobago* by John Poyntz, the pamphlet which local legend claims Daniel Defoe used as the inspiration for the setting of *Robinson Crusoe* (see below). Bric-a-brac from the early twentieth century includes a plate commemorating the inauguration of Eric Williams as Trinidad and Tobago's first prime minister.

Bacolet

As Bacolet Street eases east out of Scarborough along the coast past Sandy Hall and Fairfield Complex – the main administrative base of the Tobago House of Assembly as well as the Tobago Hall of Justice court and the island's main cemetery – the roadside homes become noticeably grander. Though **Bacolet** suffered a lull when its eponymous

---

ROBINSON CRUSOE'S ISLE?

"The Life and Strange Surprising Adventures of Robinson Crusoe of York, Mariner
Who lived eight and twenty Years all alone, on an uninhabited Island on the coast of America, near the mouth of the Great River of Oroonoque
Having been Cast on Shore by shipwreck, wherein all the Men perished but himself."

Thus reads the introductory blurb to the first edition of Daniel Defoe's **Robinson Crusoe**, dated April 25, 1719 and the oft-cited rationale behind the claim that Tobago was the setting for Defoe's story. In the book, the fabled island was situated, like Tobago, off the coast of (South) America near the mouth of the Orinoco River. In the late seventeenth century, the then sovereign Duke of Courland commissioned an Englishman, John Poyntz, to develop the island. Poyntz wrote a pamphlet praising Tobago's beauty and natural riches as well as giving a physical description of the island. Believers argue that Defoe got hold of the document and used it as the basis for his novel.

However, this clashes with the accepted notion that Defoe based the book on the experience of Alexander Selkirk, a crew member on the ship of English explorer and pirate William Dampier. During a voyage in the Pacific Ocean, Selkirk quarrelled with another crew member and, rather than continue in his company, volunteered to be put ashore at the tiny island of Juan Fernandez, off the coast of Chile. He spent four years alone there before Dampier rescued him. After Selkirk's return to England in 1711, his story became well known through various pamphlets, on which Defoe's novel was almost certainly based.

street was replaced by Claude Noel Highway as the main route to the windward coast, this is still a suburb of choice for Tobago's elite.

The area enjoyed a heady prestige during the late 1950s and early 1960s, when Rita Hayworth and Robert Mitchum stayed at the *Blue Haven* hotel (see page 226) while filming *Fire Down Below*, and the **Beatles** frolicked on Bacolet Bay Beach, which local lore also has as one of the settings for Walt Disney's *Swiss Family Robinson* (though the principal beach location was further along the windward coast at Richmond Bay). The *Blue Haven* was once part of Tobago's battlements – a cannon still stands on the hotel's grounds – and the bay itself was the site of many sea battles. The hotels tried to cordon off the sand in the 1960s but Dr Eric Williams – the premier who once declared that he had no intention of ruling "a nation of waiters and bellhops" – intervened to keep the beach public. South of the beach, the houses thin out as Bacolet Street swings left to meet with the highway and the traffic on its way along the windward coast (see page 236).

Bacolet Bay Beach

The best reason to linger here is the crescent-shaped **Bacolet Bay Beach**, a tranquil spot mostly visited by guests from the nearby hotels, with its yellow sand shaded by palms and Indian almond trees. A protective coral reef ensures good swimming despite the location on the Atlantic side of the island – but be aware of the occasional dangerous undercurrents and rough seas in winter. From the road, concrete steps lead down the cliff side to the sand, where the *Blue Haven* hotel's beach bar serves up drinks and snacks.

West of Scarborough: Old Milford Road

Old Milford Rd doesn't run directly into Milford Rd, as there's a short section of unpaved coastline between the two; to get onto Old Milford Rd from Scarborough, follow Milford Rd, which becomes Orange Hill Rd as it swings away from the sea and uphill, take the first left onto Milford Rd Extension and carry straight on past the Shaw Park Cultural Complex

West of Scarborough, **Old Milford Road** was the main thoroughfare through the southwest before the construction of the highway, which it connects to opposite the Gulf City Mall shopping mall at Lowlands. Now little more than a backroad, Old Milford cuts a winding and scenic route along the coast, with lovely views of the wind-whipped Atlantic peeking between the palms and houses, and salt spray crashing onto the tarmac thanks to the constant ocean breeze. Around halfway along, the venerable *Shore Things* (see page 227) offers meals and drinks, and some of the best craft available in Tobago.

There's an "official" beach facility by the side of the road at **Little Rockly Bay**, which was used as a site for horse racing before the construction of Shirvan racetrack, but the ruggedness of the coastline, the strong undercurrents and murky waters mean it's not a great place to swim. At low tide, the wide swathe of compacted yellow-brown sand makes for a fabulous beach walk, however, while the constant wind makes this one of Tobago's top spots for kiteboarding and windsurfing (see page 205). The most scenic part of the beach is adjacent to the **Petit Trou** car park, with its grove of swaying palm trees. Locals often park up here to eat lunch or just enjoy the breeze.

ARRIVAL AND DEPARTURE   SCARBOROUGH

By car Most people enter Scarborough via the Wilson Rd turn-off from Claude Noel Hwy and follow the one-way system towards the wharves bordering Carrington St; you can also turn down Orange Hill Rd (turn by the large petrol station) from the highway and, on the other side of town, via Northside Rd. Free parking is available at the wharf car park on the corner of Carrington and Castries streets, in the NIB Mall car park off Gardenside St (strictly speaking for shoppers only) and in the huge lot off Gardenside St.

By ferry Ferries between Trinidad and Tobago arrive and depart from the main waterfront opposite Independence Square (☎639 2417 or ☎639 4906, ⊕https://ttitferry.com; see page 25). You can buy tickets for same-day sailings at the ferry terminal, and online in advance. Fares are TT$50/person (half-price for kids), plus $150 for a

5

car. Bear in mind that the long journey (4–5hr) between Trinidad and Tobago can be rough; take seasickness tablets, and try to find a seat in the middle of the ferry. Taxis line up at the rank directly outside the terminal building.

By bus The PTSC bus depot (☎639 2293, ⌨ptsc.co.tt) is located a 5min walk from the centre on Sangster Hill Rd. Buses to all corners of the island run six days a week between roughly 4.30am and 8pm; remember to purchase your tickets before boarding.

Destinations Black Rock (Mon–Sat 15 daily); Buccoo (Mon–Sat 5 daily); Charlotteville (Mon–Sat 4 daily); Crown Point (Mon–Sat 15 daily); L'Anse Fourmi, via Castara (Mon–Sat 4 daily); Mason Hall (Mon–Sat 5 daily); Plymouth, via Arnos Vale (Mon–Sat 15 daily); Roxborough (Mon–Sat 4 daily).

By route taxi Scarborough is the departure point for route taxis serving the whole of Tobago, though finding where to catch your ride can be confusing, and departure

points do change; ask around for advice. For Crown Point, Bon Accord, Mount Irvine, Buccoo, Carnbee, Bethel, Mount Pleasant, Plymouth, Black Rock and Lambeau go to the "west end" taxi stand directly outside the ferry terminal. There are two lanes: the one nearest the terminal is for Crown Point and places along Milford Rd; the outside lane is for all other destinations. An alternative departure point for Plymouth, Black Rock and Mount Pleasant is on Wilson Rd opposite *KFC*, at the junction with Carrington St. This is also where you'll find taxis running the Northside Rd to Castara and Parlatuvier. If you have no luck here, walk up Wilson Rd to Penny Savers supermarket, where you can find transport to Mason Hall; it's easier to get taxis going further up Northside Rd from there. Taxis to Speyside and Charlotteville leave from Republic Bank on Main St and sometimes from St James Park.

By maxi taxi Maxis to Charlotteville leave a few times a day from next to James Park on Ross St.

ACCOMMODATION

Though Scarborough and the Bacolet suburbs were popular in the 1950s and 1960s, during the early years of Tobagonian tourism, they've now been eclipsed by Crown Point. Some high-end **hotels** remain in Bacolet, while inexpensive options can be found in both Bacolet and Scarborough; the latter are especially convenient if you're catching an early ferry.

SCARBOROUGH

★**Fort Cottage** Calder Hall Rd ☎680 1517, ⌨bit. ly/FortBago; map p.221. Beautifully restored shingle-walled old house in upper Scarborough, with wooden floors, high ceilings and lovely views down over town. It has two a/c bedrooms, a daybed and hammocks on the porch, and bags of atmosphere thanks to thoughtful decor and handsome antique furnishings. Discounts available for longer stays. 🛜 US$60

Hope Cottage Calder Hall Rd ☎639 2179, ✉hcgh tobago@hotmail.com; map p.221. Once the residence of Tobago's British governor (who was buried in the back garden in 1876), this is one of the island's oldest guesthouses, having opened its doors in 1940; it's showing its age a bit nowadays, but a great bargain nonetheless, with friendly, helpful owners, and a peaceful location in a hilly part of town close to Fort King George. Rooms are basic, some with shared bathroom, and there's a large communal kitchen. 🛜 US$40

Mill's Guesthouse Young St ☎639 2193, ✉cristalj@ hotmail.com; map p.221. The two spotless rooms of this pretty blue guesthouse set high on a hillside are pleasant and well maintained; both have a/c, fridge and cable TV, and one has bunk beds and serves as a dorm or family room. A well-equipped communal kitchen, reasonable rates, and great views over Scarborough (and 🛜) from the balcony out front. Dorm US$30, double US$45

Sandy's Guesthouse 5 Robinson St ☎639 2737; map p.221. Run by the owners of the *Blue Crab* restaurant just below (see page 227), this appealing little guesthouse

has three large, spotless rooms with a/c, TV and fridge; rates include breakfast, and there's a hillside-facing shared patio area outside. 🛜 US$80

BACOLET

Bacolet Beach Club Bacolet Bay ☎639 3551, ⌨bacoletbeachclub.com; map p.221. Chic boutique hotel, with an inviting infinity pool and a small, effectively private beach. Rooms and suites are decked out in a quirky vintage-meets-modern style, and all have a/c, flat-screen TV/DVD player and balcony. A cute little bridge leads to the excellent on-site restaurant; rates include breakfast. 🛜 US$206

Blue Haven Bacolet Bay ☎660 7400, ⌨bluehaven hotel.com; map p.221. This historic hotel was originally an outpost of Fort King George and retains its stunning panoramic views of the bay it once protected. The stylish rooms have four-poster beds, wooden floors, a/c, TV, minibar, spacious bathrooms and balconies overlooking stunning Bacolet Bay, and there's a swimming pool with ornamental waterfall, mini-gym, spa and tennis court, plus restaurant and a beach bar. 🛜 US$238

Half Moon Blue 73 Bacolet St ☎639 3551, ⌨half moonblue.com; map p.221. Comfortable en-suite rooms decorated in an unusual mixture of traditional and modern styles, with a/c, fan, fridge, TV and great views of Bacolet Bay from private balconies; there's also access to a small beach and the *Bacolet Beach Club's* infinity pool; rates include breakfast. 🛜 US$150

5

EATING

Scarborough's **dining scene** offers everything from low-cost diners to upmarket restaurants; in between, there are some excellent and unusual options, too. Fast-food outlets abound: *KFC* on the corner of Wilson Rd and Carrington St, *Royal Castle* on Wilson Rd and *Chef's* on Carrington St.

Blue Crab Cnr Robinson and Main streets, Scarborough ☎639 2737, ⬤tobagobluecrab.com; map p.221. Popular with an office crowd, this busy, friendly restaurant is a great place to sample traditional Creole cuisine, with tables in an a/c dining room and on a shady terrace with sea views. The lunch menu (mains TT$65) changes according to whatever's fresh in the market that day, but always includes fresh fish with sides such as cassava salad, bhaji (spinach) rice and fried plantain; great unsweetened juices too. Dinner (soup, salad, main and coffee; from TT$200) is by reservation only. Tues–Fri 11am–3pm.

Café Havana Bacolet Bay, Bacolet ☎639 2357, ⬤cafehavana.org; map p.221. Set in an airy split-level building, all white paint and wooden floors, with a menu that ranges from Cuban to Asian and Creole food: fish sandwiches, salads and burgers at lunchtime (TT$54–101), and a dinner menu that includes chicken satay (TT$67), scallops in beurre blanc or curry shrimp (both TT$181) or pork chops in a mustard and tarragon sauce (TT$174). It's also good for a drink, with excellent cocktails including proper mojitos; happy "hour" is 3–7pm. Daily 7.30–10am, noon–3pm & 6pm–late.

Oasis Salad Bar Unit D15, Scarborough Esplanade 660 7475, ⬤bit.ly/Oasisqt; map p.221. Nice little option for a healthy lunch, in a pleasant location right

on Scarborough's waterfront. There's a range of signature salads – three-bean, raw rainbow, Greek; all from TT$45 – plus fish, shrimp, chicken or veggie wraps (from TT$40), and delicious fresh fruit smoothies (from TT$30). Mon–Thurs 11am–4pm, Fri 11am–6pm.

Salsa Kitchen 8 Pump Mill Rd, Scarborough ☎639 1522; map p.221. A lovely place, a 5min drive from central Scarborough, set on a plant-wreathed veranda, best after dark when the fairy lights twinkle but also nice and shady at lunchtime. The fabulous Venezuelan-style tapas dishes (from TT$80) are cooked to order and might include lamb with tamarind and tomato choka; chadon beni marinated fish; minted pork; kebab skewers with tamarind or peanut sauce; and goat's cheese and mozzarella with onion and olive confit – perfect for sharing. Reasonably priced and very popular; reservations essential. Tues–Sun 6–10pm.

★**Shore Things** Old Milford Rd, Lambeau ☎635 1072, ⬤bit.ly/ShoreBago; map p.200. Beautifully situated among the greenery right on the cliffside, and cooled by delightful Atlantic winds, this is a lovely little café offering a menu of home-made pizza, burgers, salads, quiche and daily lunch specials from baked chicken with all the trimmings to soup or pelau (from TT$65), served on the veranda or waterside terrace. Juices, coffee, cakes and pastries are also excellent. Mon–Fri 11am–6pm.

DRINKING

There are plenty of **rum shops** along Carrington St and Wilson Rd, very much a locals' preserve but worth checking out, especially on Friday evenings when everybody celebrates the end of the working week.

Bar Code Milford Rd, Scarborough ☎635 2633, ⬤bar codetobago.com; map p.221. Scarborough's liveliest bar, complete with big-screen TV for watching sports and pool tables, the breezy outside deck has lovely sea

views, too. Regular party nights at weekends, and popular karaoke on Thurs. Tues & Wed 11am–2am, Thurs 11am–4am, Fri & Sat 11am–3am, Sun 6pm–2am.

SHOPPING

★**Shore Things** Old Milford Rd, Lambeau ☎635 1072, ⬤bit.ly/ShoreBago; map p.200. This excellent café also houses a wonderful shop, stocked with all manner of books, paintings, postcards and greeting cards, artworks, craft pieces and foodie treats – all of which are made in Trinidad & Tobago. Mon–Fri 11am–6pm.

Tobago Chocolate Delights Old Milford Rd, Lambeau ☎370 1907 or ☎738 6922, ⬤bit.ly/BagoChoc; map

p.200. Next door to the *Shore Things* café and shop, this locally owned and run enterprise makes and sells delicious chocolates made with Tobago cocoa beans and combined with local ingredients such as sorrel, rum, mango and hot pepper, alongside bars and other cocoa products from some of the best Trinidad producers. Also stocks jars of passion fruit curd, sorrel jelly and the like. Mon–Fri 11am–6pm.

DIRECTORY

Banks Scarborough has several banks: Republic Bank and Scotiabank on Carrington St opposite the wharf, Royal and

Republic on Main St and First Citizens in the NIB Mall. All have ATMs; there is also one at the ferry terminal.

5

Petrol stations There are two petrol stations on Milford Rd; the one at the corner of Claude Noel Hwy opens 24hr.
Post office The post office (Mon–Fri 7.30am–6pm, Sat 9am–1pm) is at the waterfront next to the ferry terminal.

Tourist information The office of the Tobago House of Assembly Division of Tourism is close to the bus station at 12 Sangster Hill (Mon–Fri 8am–4pm; ☎ 639 2125, ⓦ visit tobago.gov.tt), but is not really geared up for drop-in visitors.

The leeward coast

Northeast of Plymouth, the dramatic and sparsely populated **leeward coast** feels more wonderfully remote than any other part of the island; here, the claim that Tobago is not just paradise, but the capital of paradise, begins to ring true, lapped by the Caribbean Sea and drenched in tropical greenery. Tourism development is most evident at the lovely coastal village of **Castara**; elsewhere, ravishing beaches such as **Englishman's Bay**, **Parlatuvier** and **Bloody Bay** are much the same as they were decades ago. Locals still make a living off the land and sea: clusters of bobbing pirogues in every bay and seine nets drying in the sun reveal the importance of **fishing** to this area, and you'll often see machete-wielding fellows trudging the route to small-scale plantations or meandering along with a pack of hunting dogs.

Although you might assume the most direct way to the leeward coast would be the coastal Arnos Vale Road from Plymouth, this is actually the slowest route, due to its twists and turns; a better (if less scenic) bet is to take the **Northside Road** up from Scarborough, which meets the coast just before **Moriah**.

GETTING AROUND   **THE LEEWARD COAST**

By car The vast majority of visitors explore the leeward coast by car, and the Arnos Vale Rd and Northside Rd, though narrow and winding, are in fairly good condition. Keep your eyes peeled for loose cattle left to graze by the roadside, and sound your horn at blind corners.

By public transport This part of the island is among the least travelled by public transport. Buses from Scarborough run to L'Anse Fourmi a few times a day (see page 234), but maxis and route taxis often only go as far as Mason Hall or Moriah, so be prepared for vehicle changes and longer waits than elsewhere.

Northside Road from Scarborough

Less than a kilometre east of Scarborough on the Claude Noel Highway, the well-signposted **Northside Road** strikes right across the middle of Tobago and connects the windward with the leeward coast. Barely 50m along it, a right-hand turn by a bridge takes you up a narrow, near-perpendicular road to **French Fort**, the site of a Gallic garrison in the 1780s. It's now home to towering radio transmitters and satellite pylons and the only hint of its history is a plaque nestled in the trees. The journey up to the fort is definitely worthwhile, though, for its panoramic **views** of Scarborough, Fort King George, Rockly Bay and Lowlands, the northern coast around Plymouth and Arnos Vale, and the southeast as far as Granby Point. Past French Fort turn-off, the Northside Road swings past the clipped hedges flanking the **President's House** (closed to the public), and continues its snaking climb uphill.

Mason Hall

About halfway between the coasts lies the residential community of **Mason Hall**. The village itself contains little to detain you, but the marvellous **waterfall** hidden on its outskirts is worth seeking out. To find it, look for the roadside WASA sign for the Craig Hall water intake. Half an hour's walk from the road along the Sandy River will bring you to **Craig Hall Falls**, one of the island's tallest at about 50m. Taking the Craig Hall route leads you to the top of the main cascade, where there's another, smaller waterfall with a pool deep enough to jump into without touching the bottom. Several of the island's tour operators (see page 202) offer guided walks to the falls.

Moriah

Reachable both from the Northside Road and the Arnos Vale Road (from the latter, take a left at the only T-junction), the village of **MORIAH** is a picturesque settlement teetering at the top of steep hills, which plummet straight into a valley from the road. The views from here are superlative, with terraces on the surrounding hills supporting crops of pigeon peas and ground provisions, and Baptist prayer flags fluttering in the breeze. Moriah is best known for the **"Old Time" wedding procession** during the summer Heritage Festival, which sees the narrow main road lined with crowds to see the "grooms" adorned in formal black suits and top hats escort their elaborately costumed brides along the street to "walk the wedding" and perform the traditional brush-back dance.

Runnemede and Mount Dillon

Northeast of Moriah, Northside Road winds back toward the coast, providing breathtaking views as you pass through the tiny community of **RUNNEMEDE**. Look out for a truly monumental **silk cotton** tree at the roadside; its buttressed roots are said to be haunted by jumbies (ghosts). For one of the best vistas around, turn right at the signposted fork just after Runnemede to **Mount Dillon Lookout**, where benches are set up to admire the unravelling coastline and, on a clear day, as far as the island of Grenada.

ACCOMMODATION AND EATING   RUNNEMEDE AND MOUNT DILLON

★ **Cuffie River Nature Retreat** Runnemede ☎ 660 0505, ⓦ cuffie-river.com. Very popular with British birding groups, this is a peaceful family-run forest hideaway on the site of an old sugar plantation with large, airy and comfortable en-suite rooms; tours and hikes into the forest are offered to guests and non-guests. The elevated swimming pool is the perfect place from which to enjoy the surrounds. *Cuffie River* is also the best place to eat in the area, its atmospheric restaurant serving delicious, nutritious lunches (three courses US$30 lunch, US$50 dinner; book ahead), freshly prepared with local ingredients as you look out across the trees from the veranda. 📶 **US$200**

Castara

A picturesque fishing village, with terrific beaches and a laidback vibe that have made it increasingly popular with visitors, **CASTARA** is the busiest "resort" on this coastline – though don't expect anything as packaged and touristy as Crown Point. Although the number of guesthouses has grown exponentially in recent years, Castara's remote location has saved it from being eaten up by resort hotels, and there's an appealingly harmonious balance between visitors and locals. Fishing remains the main earner, and the beach is one of the best places to participate in the pulling of a **seine net**, still in constant use by the posse of local fishermen (who have been treated to an incongruously large new fishermen's facility, overhanging the centre of the main beach). The village abandons its languid air each August, when the beach is packed with revellers attending the **Castara Fishermen's Fete**, one of Tobago's biggest; the drinking, dancing, eating and swimming start at about noon and continue until well after dark.

To get your bearings before you enter the village proper from the west, pull up in the layby to the left just before the Northside Road makes its final steep descent – there's a postcard-perfect **view** of the village and the main **Big Bay** beach, separated from the smaller **Little Bay** (also known as Heavenly Bay) by a rocky outcrop, and all framed by the lush green tips of the rainforest.

Castara village and waterfall

Straddling the Northside Road, the main body of the village consists of a post office and a few weather-beaten rum shops interspersed with homes. A bridge on the southern side of town crosses the **Castara River**; a ten-minute walk southeast along

5

the riverbed brings you to a small **waterfall** with a fairly deep swimming pool below. Crossing the playing field behind the bridge cuts the walking time, and the pool is popular among local lads cooling off after a game of football; these frenetic, foul-filled tournaments take place in the late afternoon, and often attract a small crowd of spectators.

Big Bay

Lifeguards daily 10am–6pm • Changing facilities 10am–6pm, TT$1 • Sun-lounger rental available at the western end for TT$20

Castara's main beach, **Big Bay**, is a generous swathe of coarse yellow sand divided by the Castara River. If there hasn't been rain (which can turn the ocean a little murky), the water is a joy – crystal clear, relatively calm owing to the protection of the surrounding forested headlands, and patrolled most days by a couple of rays that drift up and down close to the shore. Flotillas of seagull-infested pirogues bob out to sea, birds swoop overhead and there's always activity around the hulking new Fishermen's Co-Op building, where the day's catch is weighed, scaled and sold. The beach is also one of the best places in Tobago to watch (and lend a hand) as fishermen pull in their **seine nets**. Just behind the beach, by the bridge over the river, delicious bread, cake and pastries are baked in a traditional **clay oven** each Wednesday and Saturday; go in the morning to order and come back after lunch to collect.

Little Bay

To get here from Big Bay, head northeast out of the village, passing the turn-off for *Castara Cottage* and taking the next left, Depot Rd; if you're walking, look for the small track linking Second Bay and Depot roads just before *Blue Mango*

Separated from Big Bay by an outcrop of rocks, the smaller beach to the north of Big Bay is **Little Bay**, also known as Heavenly Bay, and a quiet spot despite the profusion of guesthouses that now overlook the sand. The waters are often calmer than at Big Bay, and there's excellent **snorkelling** to be had on the reef that stretches around the headland from here; expect to see stingrays and perhaps the odd turtle. There are no changing facilities at Little Bay, although there is a lively beach bar/restaurant (see page 232).

ARRIVAL AND DEPARTURE   CASTARA

By car You can drive right on to Big Bay via Castara Bay Rd in the middle of the village, signposted for Castara Bay; there's a car park of sorts at the end of the road, and more space to park on the other side of the bridge over the Castara River. There's also the dead-end Second Bay Rd down to the eastern end of the beach (best not attempted in a car), and the steep but driveable Depot Rd just past this turn-off, which heads down to Little Bay. Many accommodation options offer pick-ups from the airport, sometimes included in the accommodation rate.

Car rental Porridge (see page 231) is a reliable option for car rental, as is Taylor's in Little Bay (☎354 5743, ⓦ taylorstobagoautorental.com).

5

TOURS

Tours Alibaba Tours (see box, page 202) is based in Castara, and runs excellent boat and land tours from the village. Of the other enterprising locals who offer trips, best is the ever-pleasant and very professional Derrick Lopez, aka Porridge (☎766 3656 or ☎787 0992), a one-man whirlwind who does pretty much any island tour (full-day tours US$100/couple). Porridge's son also offers boat tours aboard the well-equipped *Sonarise*, with fishing, snorkelling, drinks and a beach barbecue (TT$450/person), and a sunset cruise (TT$150), as does the affable Loady from Country Wave Tours (☎363 7678), whose trips are a little cheaper.

ACCOMMODATION

Castara is the only village along this section of coast where you'll find a choice of **places to stay**, many of them ranged around Big or Little bays and set in charming wooden cottages with lovely views. New places spring up all the time, so if the place you've set your heart on is booked up, it's well worth contacting the local community group, **Castara Tourism Development Association** (☎710 6588, ⓦbit.ly/castara) to ask about alternatives. The majority of rooms here include some kind of cooking facilities; if you plan on making a lot of meals yourself, you'd be well advised to stock up on provisions in Crown Point, as the shops here sell only the most basic of items.

BIG BAY AND CASTARA VILLAGE

Blue Mango Second Bay Rd ☎737 7298 or ☎317 4621, ⓦblue-mango.com; map p.230. Castara old-timer; the three Sweet Point apartments have great bay views, cool breezes, kitchens, fans, mosquito nets and plenty of privacy, while "Sea Steps" cottage (US$125) has indoor and outdoor showers and a sundeck overhanging the water; all are showing their age, however. There are also a couple of less appealing options set back from the sea. ☞ US$70

Carpe Diem Castara Village ☎639 3135, in UK ☎01932 848831, ⓦwww.castara.net; map p.230. Two fresh and airy apartments below the owner's gorgeous wood-built home, set on the hill and affording lovely views over both bays. Equipped with netted bed, fan, full kitchen and large bathrooms, the spotless studios downstairs are nicely styled and very inviting, while the self-contained two-bedroom apartment upstairs (US$250), with its huge veranda, is rented when the owners aren't in residence. ☞ US$95

Castara Bliss Castara Village ☎352 5727, ⓦcastara blissapartments.com; map p.230. Set back from the main road in a lofty position overlooking the football field and the sea, these neat, appealing self-contained studio apartments are really well maintained, with a/c, standing fans, cable TV, kitchenettes, nets over the beds, hot and cold water and cool sea breezes on the veranda. Friendly, helpful owner, and excellent rates. ☞ US$65

★**Castara Cottage** Second Bay Rd ☎757 1044, in UK ☎07525 724 201, ⓦcastaracottage.com; map p.230. Appealing wooden house split into three separate self-contained apartments, two with two bedrooms, one a studio (US$70). All are lovingly decorated and with many personal touches courtesy of the owners, and each has a kitchen, mosquito nets, safe and private patio. Plants and trees surround the property, giving it a secluded feel despite being only a 2min walk from the beach, and the Tamarind cottage in particular is great for kids. ☞ US$90

★**Castara Retreats** Northside Rd ☎766 3656, in UK ☎07841 645238, ⓦcastararetreats.com; map p.230. Ranged across the hill on the Castara's southwest side, and with gorgeous views over the beaches, bay and village, this collection of airy wooden studios and one- or two-bedroom apartments (the latter US$203–365) with private porches and sundecks comprise easily one of the most appealing places to stay in the whole island. All are thoughtfully designed, with spacious, modern kitchens equipped with quality wares that make cooking a pleasure, and are decorated with simple style. The lovely gardens attract plenty of birdlife, there's a gorgeous open-air yoga deck, the staff are welcoming and efficient and the owners go to great lengths to promote sustainable tourism in the village. Great restaurant and bar, too (see page 232). ☞ Studios US$128

The Naturalist Second Bay Rd ☎639 5901, ⓦnaturalist-tobago.com; map p.230. Right on the beach, tucked into the corner of Big Bay, with some lovely all-wood one-bed apartments upstairs (US$125–150) with full kitchen, a/c, fan and TV; the standard rooms downstairs are a little older. Rates include breakfast. ☞ US$50

Sea Level Second Bay Rd ☎660 7311 or ☎369 7165, ⓦtobago.de; map p.230. Just up the hill from the *Naturalist*, but still close to the beach, this guesthouse is a good budget choice. Rooms are comfortable and offer good value; all have kitchen, balcony, mosquito nets and fan, and some have sea views. ☞ US$45

LITTLE BAY

★**Alibaba's Sea Breeze** ☎686 7957, ⓦalibaba-tours.com; map p.230. Four en-suite apartments occupying the best location in Little Bay: close to the beach and with immaculate views of Castara Bay. All suites have private balconies, well-equipped kitchens, fans and mosquito nets over the bamboo four-poster beds. The friendly owners are a great source of information and also run one of Tobago's most professional tour operators (see page 202). ☞ US$90

5

Angel Retreat ☎685 4101 or ☎748 9704, ⓦangel-retreat.com; map p.230. This concrete block on the hillside just up from the beach is a bit of an eyesore, but the en-suite apartments with a/c, living area, kitchen and TV are very spacious, and there's a swimming pool (the only one in the village). Second- and third-floor apartments have verandas with sea views. ☎ US$100

The Beach House ☎660 7702, ⓦtobagobeachhouse.com; map p.230. Cute little wood-built house with a one-bedroom apartment upstairs (US$105) and two studios downstairs (which can interconnect), set almost on the sands of Little Bay. All have appealing decor, nets over the beds, full kitchens, hammocks and a balcony overlooking the water, and the rates are very reasonable. ☎ Studios US$65

Boatview Apartments ☎483 0964 or ☎668 3587, ⓦbit.ly/BoatCastara; map p.230. In a lovely location overlooking the waters of Little Bay, these spacious, fan-cooled studio apartments are excellent value, with kitchen and a huge balcony overlooking the bay, bedecked

with hummingbird feeders. The owners run the popular *Boathouse* bar/restaurant and are very friendly and hospitable, and a mine of local info. ☎ US$70

Lillibets Little Bay ☎760 6357, ⓦlillibets.com; map p.230. Built into the hillside above Little Bay and accessible via a steep wooden staircase behind *Angel Retreat* (so not suitable if you have mobility issues), these four suites come with a separate living area, cable TV, a/c, full kitchen, mosquito nets and private bathroom. The views from this elevated spot are excellent, enjoyed from a communal balcony with hanging chairs and bird feeders. ☎ US$80

★ **SeaScape** Little Bay ☎1 559 287 9270 (in US), ⓦseascapetobago.com; map p.230. Gorgeous wooden building perched high above Little Bay and reachable via steep steps, with two luxurious apartments that offer fabulous views from the balconies and bedrooms. Both are beautifully appointed with high-spec kitchen, netted beds and safe; the larger apartment is split-level, with one of its two en-suite bedrooms upstairs. ☎ US$195

EATING

There may not be a huge amount of choice when it comes to eating in Castara, but there are several places offering excellent and inexpensive local cooking often featuring supremely fresh local fish. Note, however, that with a couple of exceptions (*Cheno's* and *Caribbean Kitchen*), **opening hours** are more of a guide than a given; many places simply shut up shop if things are quiet.

Boathouse Little Bay ☎483 0964; map p.230. English/Tobagonian-run restaurant whose daily changing menu (lunch TT$70–90, dinner TT$120–135) includes local dishes such as coconut curried shrimp, river crayfish, fresh fish or curried goat with sides such as breadfruit cheese, herbed cauliflower and curried pumpkin, plus lunchtime burgers and wedges or toasted sandwiches (TT$70), and good home-made pizzas on Sun (TT$90–120). It's a lovely spot for a drink overlooking the water, and becomes the focal point of the village on Wed nights, with African drumming, limbo and dancing (TT$25). Dinner available Mon, Wed & Fri; book ahead. Mon, Wed & Fri 9.30am–10pm, Tues & Thurs 9.30am–5pm, Sun 10am–5pm.

★ **Caribbean Kitchen** Castara Retreats, Northside Rd ☎766 1010, ⓦcastararetreats.com; map p.230. Set on a covered veranda, bedecked with fairly lights and affording stunning panoramic views over Castara Bay (especially lovely if enjoyed at sunset with one of their seriously good cocktails in hand), this is the most upmarket choice in town. With a mission to offer something different from the usual fare that's done so well down in the village, the food here is a blend of local and international cuisine; starters (TT$55–75) range from fishcakes with tamarind sauce to home-made spinach and ricotta ravioli, while main-dish (TT$110–150) highlights include super-fresh fish, succulently grilled and served with fresh salsa; jerk chicken, curried lamb and black-bean burger. Don't miss the silky mousse made with Tobago chocolate or home-

made ice cream for dessert. Daily 11am–10pm.

★ **Cascreole** Big Bay ☎721 5700; map p.230. Right on the beach with tables set on a wooden deck built above the sand, this is one of the nicest locations in town. The cooking is great, too, with mains (from TT$75) such as fish in coconut sauce or chicken with pineapple served with tasty sides like aubergine gratin and stewed pigeon peas. They sometimes do a Thurs night beach bonfire with dinner and music (TT$100 per person), which is lots of fun. Mon–Tues & Thurs–Sat noon–3pm & 6.30–10pm.

Cheno's Northside Rd ☎704 7819; map p.230. This friendly diner, with tables in a little courtyard off the main road as you enter Castara from the south, is the village's best breakfast spot. Saltfish or eggs and bacon with coconut bake are excellent (around TT$50); they also serve coffee, cakes, home-made ice cream and reasonably priced local dinners (TT$65–100) of fish, chicken and crab, and host the odd party night. Daily 8am–1pm.

D'Almond Tree Big Bay ☎683 3593; map p.230. Set back from the sea but right on Big Bay beach, with tables on an open-sided deck, this is a nice little spot for Creole cooking (curry shrimp/goat, catch of the day, baked chicken and so on; from TT$80). Opening times can be erratic and service a little slow; no alcohol but you can bring your own. Mon–Sat 6–10pm.

Marguerite's Northside Rd ☎710 6645; map p.230. Across the street from *Cheno's*, with tables in an open-sided dining room, and offering local cooking with a bit of a twist); expect shrimp, fish, goat and chicken cooked with unusual veg combinations (mains from TT$80). No alcohol licence, but you can bring your own. Mon–Sat 11am–3pm & 6–9pm.

Shirma's Northside Rd ☎798 3409; map p.230. Right on the main road between the two beaches, *Shirma's* is a tiny little place that serves as a rum bar come the evening, and also offers simple local lunches (from TT$40) such as

stew chicken or fish with provisions, mac pie and the like. Fri nights feature BBQ pork/chicken and hearty soups on Sat; in the mornings (7–11am), Ria takes over to cook up lovely breakfasts (TT$50–80), including full English omelettes or bacon with pancakes, local-style tomato/ aubergine choka or saltfish buljol and smoked herring with home-made bread. Daily 7am–10pm.

DRINKING

There are a couple of friendly **rum shops** on Castara's main street, and a more ambient bar on the way down to the main beach, but the highlights of Castara's evening entertainment are the Wednesday drumming session at the *Boathouse* on Little Bay (see page 232), which is sometimes lively on other evenings too; and the Thursday night beach bonfire and DJ session at *Cascreole* restaurant (see page 232).

T'Keyah's Place Big Bay Rd ☎490 4368; map p.230. Run by the genial Marvin, this is a lovely spot for a drink, set back from the beach but with tables set out on a raised

open-air veranda. Icy cold beers, inexpensive rum drinks, friendly atmosphere and a very laidback feel. Daily 11am– late.

DIRECTORY

Banks There's an ATM at the First Citizens Bank on a ridge above the main road as you exit the village to the north; however, bear in mind that it runs out of cash fairly frequently.

Shopping Castara's few general-purpose shops are on the

main street through town; all sell basic food provisions. For fruit and veg, check out Bingi's stall at the corner of Depot Rd. Alcohol is available from Codrington's rum shop just by the Second Bay Rd turn-off.

Englishman's Bay

To find the beach, look out for the blue and white sign (opposite a WASA building) marking a left-hand turn and the gravel track which leads to the small car park

Northeast of Castara, houses, shops and most of the traffic melt away, and the Northside Road is flanked by enormous tufts of whispering, creaking bamboo, broken occasionally to reveal marvellous views of jungle-clad hills. The next worthy beach, about 3km along the Northside Road, is **Englishman's Bay**, hidden from the road by a thick cover of bush. Utterly ravishing and virtually undeveloped, the bay offers a perfect crescent of pure yellow sand, deep blue water and an offshore reef – from the sea, the forested hillside appears completely untouched, as the bush drips right down to the sand. The bay remains delightfully remote, the quintessential "deserted beach" destination of many a pleasure boat cruise. There are no lifeguards here, but beach chairs can be rented from *Eula's*.

EATING   ENGLISHMAN'S BAY

Eula's Café by the Sea ☎639 6408. Adjacent to the car park and right on the beach, *Eula's* serves somewhat overpriced hot meals including roti, chicken and fish

(mains around TT$100), as well as cold drinks, ice cream and a nice selection of crafts. Daily 10am–6pm.

Parlatuvier

East of Englishman's Bay, Northside Road climbs upward and inland, passing through the diminutive community of **Parrot Hall** after about 3km before descending to reveal one of the most arresting views on the island: **Parlatuvier** is another crescent of pearly sand flanked by an absurdly pretty hillside scattered with palms, terraced provision grounds and ice-cream-coloured houses; you can get a great view over the village from the car park adjacent to *Glasgow's Bar* (see page 234). The pier in the middle of the bay is testament to Parlatuvier's dedication to fishing, as are the gulls that roost on the rocks at either side of the bay, patiently awaiting the return of the boats. **Swimming** here is a vigorous experience as waves are usually quite strong and the water deepens sharply from the sand; be careful as there is no lifeguard on duty, and what with the fishing paraphernalia, it's not really a place to lay down a towel and sunbathe.

ACCOMMODATION AND EATING   PARLATUVIER

Culture Foods Parlatuvier Village ☎298 8870. Adjacent to the parking area by the community centre in the western side of the village, this bar/restaurant offers cold beers and simple lunches such as fish broth or catch of the day for around TT$60. Daily 11am–5pm.

★ **Glasgow's Bar** Northside Rd ☎380 8900. In pole position overlooking Parlatuvier, this two-storey bar offers spectacular views down over the bay, and is a great place to chat to locals over a few drinks. The adjacent cookshop also offers chips and chicken lunches (from TT$30). Daily 10am–late.

★ **Gloucester Place** Northside Rd ☎639 5476, in US ☎252 571 0224, ⌨gloucesterplace.com. Set high above the sea on the main road just east of Parlatuvier, this is fantastically peaceful place with precipitous gardens lush with fruit trees and an infinity pool overlooking the ocean. Decorated with Caribbean artworks, the spacious main house operates as a B&B (Nov–April only), and has three a/c en-suite double rooms and access to the lounge and kitchen; there's also a separate self-contained two-bedroom cottage (open year-round), hanging over the cliff and with great views from the balcony. Guesthouse US$130, cottage US$145

Bloody Bay

Lifeguards daily 10am–5pm • Changing facilities TT$1 • Turn left at the T-junction signposted for the Forest Reserve and Roxborough

The last accessible beach on the leeward coast before Charlotteville is **Bloody Bay**, roughly 2km beyond Parlatuvier and named after a battle between English soldiers and African slaves in 1771 that was fierce enough to turn the sea crimson with blood; Dead Bay River, which runs across the sand and into the sea, is named for the same event. The beach itself is fine brown sand, strewn with pebbles and driftwood and frequented by no one except the odd fisherman. From here, directly opposite the bay and clearly visible 5km out to sea, the **Sisters Rocks** form an attractive cluster of tiny, verdant islands; it's also fun to explore the river which flows into the sea at the north end of the bay. A string of luridly painted buildings on the beach house changing facilities and a restaurant, but do detract a bit from the formerly unspoilt beauty of the place.

EATING AND DRINKING   BLOODY BAY

★ **Sunshine** Northside Rd ☎337 4160. This locally run restaurant and bar is a great place to stop off for a meal, with succulent Creole-style fish, chicken pork and goat with all the trimmings – rice, coocoo, callaloo, stewed peas and salad – for around TT$65; shrimp and lobster (from TT$150) are also available. Staff are supremely friendly and the little gazebos overlooking the valley and sea make a great spot for a few drinks. Daily 7am–10pm.

L'Anse Fourmi

East of Bloody Bay, Northside Road continues to the lofty village of **L'ANSE FOURMI**, a one-street town that's remote enough to make the sight of a tourist a talking point; there are a couple of **bars** in which to refresh yourself. Beyond the village, it's trees rather than houses that line the coast road to Charlotteville.

Tobago Forest Reserve

Swinging inland from the Northside Road at Bloody Bay, the Roxborough–Parlatuvier Road connects the leeward and windward coasts, running straight through the **Tobago Forest Reserve** and the central mountain range. Construction of the road began in 1958, prior to which the two sides of the island were only linked by small trails.

5

RAINFOREST GUIDES

Tempting as it may be to walk through the Forest Reserve alone, it's far better to hire a **guide**: you won't lose your way, guides can point out things you may otherwise miss, such as bachac ants carrying their leaf shreds back to the nest, and you'll learn a lot more about forest dynamics. During daylight hours, **registered guides** wait at the entrance to Gilpin Trace (registered individuals all have an ID badge), and you can also visit as part of a longer tour. Most forest guides (usually ex-foresters) are from nearby villages such as Parlatuvier and Roxborough, and all of them are far cheaper than the hotel-arranged guides, charging about TT$160 for a 1hr 30min trip, TT$240 for 2hr 30min, or TT$300 for the 3hr hike down to Bloody Bay. Reliable, certified guides include: Dexter James (☎660 7852 or ☎757 0761), who lives in the second house after the Northside Road/Parlatuvier–Roxborough Road junction; Fitzroy Quamina (☎660 7836 or ☎344 1895); Junior Thomas (☎660 7847 or 344 5431); Darlington Chance (☎660 7828 or ☎318 8034); and the only female guide, Shurland James (☎660 7883 or ☎294 3470). All guides also offer walks to local waterfalls, and night walks into the Reserve (prices negotiable).

In addition to the local guides mentioned above, there are several other reputable guides who offer rainforest tours (see page 202).

However, **Hurricane Flora** (see page 236) ravaged it mercilessly five years later, and the road was not repaired until the mid-1990s. Now it's a beautifully quiet half-hour drive through the rainforest; lined with pioneer ferns and parrot-apple trees, the tarmac is in generally good shape (though watch out for a few water-damaged spots) and traffic is rare.

The reserve itself acquired its status as the oldest protected rainforest in the western hemisphere during the plantation era, when British scientist Stephen Hales began researching the relationship between rainfall and trees and communicated his findings to Soame Jenyns, a British MP responsible for the development of Tobago. At the time, plantations were concentrated in low-lying parts of the island, but the estates began encroaching on the more precipitous forest areas, felling trees for fuel or clearing land to make way for yet more sugar cane. It took Jenyns ten years to convince Tobago's planters that if they continued to cut down the forest, the island would soon be incapable of supporting the smallest of shrubs, let alone a massive sugar plantation. Ultimately, he was successful, and on April 13, 1776, 14,000 acres of central Tobago were designated a protected Crown Reserve.

Gilpin Trace

The main point of access into the Forest Reserve is the **Gilpin Trace**, marked by a painted sign 3km along the Roxborough–Parlatuvier Road. The 5km trail into the forest from here is well marked and maintained, though often very muddy regardless of the weather – the forest gets around 380cm of rain each year. You'll be offered rubber boots to rent for TT$20 on the approach to Gilpin Trace, and it's a good idea to accept (bring your own socks). The trail takes about two and a half hours to walk at a leisurely pace, taking you through some spectacular forest dotted with huge termite nests, with lianas and vines blocking out most of the light. **Birdlife** is most active early in the morning, so birdwatchers should aim to be on the trail by about 6am. Later in the day, you might see the odd hummingbird, mot-mot or woodpecker, if you're lucky. Typically, tour guides will take you past three small waterfalls – none are suitable for swimming – before turning back. If you follow the trail to its end, you'll come out of the forest just after the reserve boundary, towards the windward side, approximately 3km north of Roxborough – remember that it is a steep uphill walk along the road back to the start of the trail if you've parked there.

5

HURRICANE FLORA

On September 30, 1963, **Hurricane Flora** swept over Tobago and completely devastated the island. Most of the banana, coconut and cocoa plantations were wiped out, and large tracts of the forest reserve laid to waste, with 30m trees toppling like matchsticks. Flora left behind thirty dead, hundreds injured and sixty percent of the island's fragile board houses razed to the ground. Moriah, Concordia, Argyle and Richmond were more or less demolished, roads were impassable and there was no mains water or electricity outside Scarborough for more than six weeks.

A **relief fund** helped to repair the worst of the damage, and the United Nations provided foodstuffs that fed the population for nearly a year, while other Caribbean islands pitched in, too. You can still see the effect of the hurricane in the **Forest Reserve** today, as there are few of the really huge trees that formerly made up the forest – much of those you see today are relatively small specimens that grew after Flora (or were saplings at the time). The hurricane also had a profound influence on Tobago's future; a tentative agricultural economy was abandoned, and the island began to devote its energy to tourism. Tobagonians still remember Flora with a shudder, and – though T&T does get hit by some ferocious tropical storms – thankfully hurricanes are very rare this far south and a similar event has not occurred since.

The windward coast

Rugged and continually breathtaking, Tobago's southern shoreline is usually referred to as the **windward coast**. It's spanned by the narrow, winding Windward Road, which sticks close to the sea and provides fantastic views of choppy Atlantic waters and tiny spray-shrouded islands. The parade of languid coastal villages here is a complete contrast to the more developed southwest, and though there is the odd guesthouse on or around the main road, this isn't the most enticing area to stay – tides and strong undercurrents make some of the most attractive-looking **beaches** unsuitable for swimming, and where they're not, the often muddy water can be a bit off-putting. Nonetheless, the coastline between Scarborough and the **King's Bay**, where the road swings inland on its way to Speyside, does make for a fantastically scenic drive, with plenty of roadside bars and diners in which to stop off and have a beer or some lunch. There are one or two diverting attractions, the most popular of which is a refreshing dip at **Argyle Waterfall**, one of the prettiest in the island, alongside the chance to learn more cocoa cultivation and chocolate-making via an estate tour and production demonstration at the **Tobago Windward Chocolate Company** base. Beyond **Roxborough**, the largest settlement on the windward coast, the road swings inland and upwards, swooping spectacularly down to the sea again at **Speyside**, best known for its fantastic snorkelling and scuba diving, and the only place on the coast with any kind of tourist development.

Mount St George

A couple of kilometres east of Scarborough, the Claude Noel Highway ends abruptly just after the Dwight Yorke Stadium, named after the Tobago-born soccer hero who made his name playing with Manchester United. The last fast and straight section of road then sweeps past the glorious **Hillsborough Bay** (also known as **Hope Bay**) about 2km later; although the long stretch of windswept sand looks inviting, stick to paddling and enjoying the breeze – the riptides are dangerous. Past the beach and over a narrow bridge, the road swings round a sharp corner and into tiny **MOUNT ST GEORGE**, on the eastern side of this large bay, its roadside houses fronted with attractive flowered gardens. There's no discernible sign that this was once Georgetown, the island's first British **capital**, named in honour of King George III. The British began to develop Georgetown after they captured the island in 1762, building houses and a base (now destroyed) for the House of Assembly, which held its inaugural meeting here in April 1768. British occupation was short-lived, however; by 1769, they shifted the capital to Scarborough. There's still one tenuous connection to sovereignty in the town, though – set at the top of a breezy hillock overlooking the village below is the official residence of the prime minister, a seldom-used, whitewashed structure that's closed to the public.

Granby Point

Just beyond Mount St George, you'll pass Studley Park Quarry on your left, a busy commercial enterprise that's steadily eating into the surrounding hillsides. Beyond the unassuming village of **Studley Park**, home to Tobago's municipal dump, a right-hand turn onto a short gravel track leads to the sea at **Granby Point**. The track ends at a car park where you'll find a small children's playground. A flight of concrete steps leads off the car park and through the trees to **Fort Granby**, originally built by the British around 1765 to protect Georgetown and briefly occupied by the French between 1781 and 1787. Nothing remains of the original fortification – the cannons are long gone, replaced by pretty gazebos, mown lawns and picnic tables – but the views of the sea and nearby **Smith's Island** are fantastic. There's a small bar in the car park at the base of the steps, serving drinks and basic meals.

Goodwood

As the Windward Road swings into the tiny village of **GOODWOOD**, with its appealing gingerbread houses and neat playing field, you'll begin to see the views for which the windward coast is famous – starting with a spectacular panorama of the unravelling coast and distant **Richmond Island**. There's a track leading from the centre of Goodwood down to the **beach**; the palm trees and greyish sand are nothing to shout about, but it's nevertheless a pleasant place for a stroll, and a popular swimming spot with locals.

Pembroke

A Lilliputian-sized village which spreads down to the sea from the road, **PEMBROKE** is a friendly place with a smattering of rum bars and a pretty clapboard Anglican church set on cliffs overlooking the Atlantic. As the road dips down again, there's a right-hand turn to the **beach**, which is mostly dedicated to fishing, but nice enough for a swim. Pembroke is the venue for the annual **Salaka Feast** celebrations, now an important part of the Heritage Festival (see page 35), and staged in the purpose-built **Pembroke Heritage Park**. A kind of African thanksgiving to the ancestors, the feast commemorates the community's founding by the first slaves brought to the area, and honours obeah spirits (see page 251) through dancing, singing, storytelling, drumming and offerings of fruit and other foods, followed by plenty of eating and drinking.

Tobago Windward Chocolate Company

Louis d'Or • ☎ 493 4358, ☎ bit.ly/TWChoc • Tours (2hr) TT$200

Though most of the producers driving the resurgence of T&T's chocolate industry are in Trinidad, the small-scale **Tobago Windward Chocolate Company** is leading the way for community-based chocolate-making in Tobago. Part of the Alliance of Rural Communities (see page 38), an umbrella group that supports and fosters community chocolate-making, the operation was set up in 2017 by residents of the Roxborough, Delaford and Louis d'Or communities. Products include delicious cocoa-tea balls, made from 100 percent locally grown and processed Trinitario "fine or flavour" cocoa bean (see page 238), a 60 percent cocoa bar, and another bar laced with sesame seeds

5

in a novel take on Tobago's traditional bene ball sweets. You can call ahead to arrange a fascinating **tour**, which includes a trip through the cocoa groves of the Cameron Estate in Roxborough, combined with a cup of cocoa tea and a demonstration of the chocolate-making process at the co-operative's base in the Louis d'Or/Betsy's Hope Multipurpose Community Centre, just off the Windward Road at the tiny village of Louis d'Or. Full-day visits (priced according to what you want to do) allow a more in-depth introduction to the local chocolate industry, and include a delicious lunch of traditional Tobago cuisine.

Argyle Waterfall

Daily 9am–4.30pm, last tour at 4pm • TT$60 adults, TT$30 children • ☎ 660 4154, ⊛ argylewaterfall.org

A few kilometres further east along the Windward Road beyond Belle Garden will take you to the entrance road to the much-visited **Argyle Waterfall**, the island's highest cascade, tumbling 54m out of the greenery into a deep pool.

Just past the entrance, you pay the entrance fee at the Roxborough Estate Visitor Service Co-Operative booth; there's also a café selling soft drinks and snack. To **access the falls**,

---

COCOA MOTION

The Roxborough environs are **cocoa** country; just west of the town, a turnoff from the Windward Road cuts straight through the old Roxborough Estate, formerly one of Tobago's largest cocoa plantations, its lichen-covered groves still maintained and reaped by small-scale local owners. Cocoa was once big business in Trinidad & Tobago, with French and British settlers establishing plantations throughout both islands from the mid-eighteenth century onwards, and making healthy profits from the export of T&T's unique **Trinitario "fine or flavour" cocoa beans**, widely acknowledged to be some of the very best in the world. However, the industry began a slow decline here in the twentieth century, as profits decreased, the local workforce turned away from agriculture (oil and gas became the mainstay of the country's economy) and foreign interests turned their attentions to the cheap labour markets in Africa (Côte d'Ivoire is currently the world's largest producer of cocoa beans).

In recent years, though, cocoa cultivation and home-grown chocolate-making has undergone a fantastic renaissance in T&T; in Tobago, this was initially led by the nearby **Tobago Cocoa Estate** (see page 239), though the community-based **Tobago Windward Chocolate Company** (see page 237) is now blazing a trail for smaller-scale producers. Over in Trinidad, there's a growing buzz surrounding the many local operators who have revived cocoa and chocolate production, promoting an ethical, sustainable business model based on fair trade as well as making some truly superb products. Cocoa growers in Lopinot (see page 130), Brasso Seco (see page 121) and Grande Riviere (see page 142) are producing fantastic dark chocolate from locally grown beans, infusing their bars with coffee, cinnamon or cocoa nibs to delectable effect. Chocolatiers such as **Cocobel** (see page 92) offer tasting sessions that allow you to appreciate the subtle nuances of beans from different parts of the island, and have earned huge local kudos for their delicious handmade chocolates, while small-scale outfits such as **Sun Eaters Organics** (see page 31) have pioneered the production of 60 and 70 percent cocoa bars as well as cocoa powder and cocoa nibs. It's well worth seeking out the delicious creations of other **local producers**, too, such as the delectable chocolates made by **Gina's Truffles** (☎ 794 6202, ⊛ bit.ly/GinaChoc) and organic bars from **Omarbeans** (☎ 685 3457, ⊛ bit.ly/Omarbeans), which are on sale at the Cocoa Pod and *Adam's Bagels* in Port of Spain (see pages 92 and 88); in Tobago, you can buy Trinidad bars alongside locally made confections at **Tobago Chocolate Delights**, just outside Scarborough (see page 227).

If you want to delve deeper into the Trinbago chocolate industry, you can tour a working cocoa estate such as San Antonio (see page 160), or joining one of the fantastic **Bean to Bar tours** offered by Alliance of Rural Communities (ARCTT; ⊛ bit.ly/ARCTnT; see page 38) members in Tobago's Belle Garden and Trinidad's Brasso Seco and Grande Riviere, or the Hot Trinbago Cocoa tours co-ordinated from *Café Mariposa* in Lopinot (see page 131).

follow the easily passable cocoa-tree-lined path to a grassy car park. Official guides wearing blue, green or yellow Argyle Waterfall shirts will be waiting here to walk with you to the falls (the guide's services are included in the entrance fee, although a tip is expected), giving a brief history of the Roxborough Estate and pointing out birds and flowers on the way.

The falls themselves are a pleasant fifteen-minute walk from the car park, and you can hear the water long before you reach it. Argyle is one of Tobago's most accessible cascades, but to see the best parts you'll have to exert yourself a little and climb up the right-hand side along steep and sometimes bushy paths. There are **three main waterfalls**; the second is particularly strong – increased flow during the rainy season (June–Nov) creates a constant fine mist that soon soaks you to the skin. The second tier is also great for a dip in a natural jacuzzi, as there are plenty of rocky seats on which to perch and get a pounding shoulder massage. If you're feeling energetic, climb up even further to the deepest swimming pool – and the smallest section of waterfall – where you can dive or swing in Tarzan-style on a vine.

Tobago Cocoa Estate

Tours (1hr; for groups of 10 or more only) Dec–April Fri 11am • TT$90 • ☎ 390 2021, ⓦ tobagococoa.com • From the Windward Rd, the access road to Argyle Waterfall meets a T-junction; right is to the falls, while the left-hand turning winds a pretty but potholed route up into the hills and to the estate gates

An extensive cocoa plantation overlooking a gorgeous valley with views down to the Atlantic, the **Tobago Cocoa Estate** is devoted to cultivation of Trinidad Select Hybrid or "fine or flavour" cocoa. In 2009, the estate began production of its own chocolate bars (actually made in France rather than on the island, using beans processed here), and their products have since won numerous prestigious awards (the "Laura" bar took the World Gold medal at London's International Chocolate Awards in 2017, to name just one). If you're here at the right time of year and are able to make up a party of ten or more (call ahead in case you can join up with others), you can take a **tour** of the estate, which covers the fermentation and drying process of the beans, as well as the history of cocoa production in Tobago via some historical displays; the tour concludes with a taste of their products, and the opportunity to buy them.

THE BELMANNA UPRISING

Disgusted with the low pay and abysmal working conditions that dogged the ailing sugar industry after emancipation, African plantation workers from the Roxborough Estate **rebelled** in 1876, burning down the estate manager's home and rioting in the streets; in the ensuing melee, one of their comrades, a female labourer named Ti Piggy, was killed by police. Enraged, the workers surrounded the police station and demanded that the chief officer, **Constable Belmanna** – whom they held responsible for the death – should come out and confront them. Unwisely, he did; the mob descended, mutilating his body and beating him to death. As the unrest continued, the workers' ranks swelled with sympathizers from surrounding villages. Hopelessly outnumbered, the police could do little but retreat and call for external assistance; it came a week later in the form of a British warship, which transported hundreds of the dissenters to Scarborough, where they were slammed into jail and put on trial, most receiving a life sentence or banishment from the island.

The riot left self-governed Tobago in turmoil. Feeling they had completely lost control of the island and its predominantly black population, and fearing total chaos, the Legislative Council swiftly washed their hands of the whole affair and handed the running of Tobago back to the British. On January 1, 1877, Tobago became a **Crown colony**, but the Belmanna repercussions were not to be quelled so easily. Continual unrest that followed throughout the island contributed to the final collapse of the sugar industry and the overall economic decline which led to the official coupling of Trinidad and Tobago in 1889, with Tobago becoming a ward of Trindad a decade later.

5

Roxborough

ROXBOROUGH is the largest town along the windward coast. Its main road runs parallel to the sea, although – unlike almost everywhere else on the windward side – there are also a few residential streets stretching inland. A parade of small shops is interspersed with the odd dilapidated and semi-abandoned building, giving the town a rather run-down appearance. It's a laidback and peaceful place, although that hasn't always been the case. In the hard times that followed emancipation, Roxborough was the scene of the infamous and bloody **Belmanna Riots** (see page 239), a rebellion that was to have a far-reaching effect on Tobago's system of governance. Apart from filling up your petrol tank or picking up a takeaway lunch, there's no real reason to linger; the flotsam-strewn **beach** is nothing special.

DIRECTORY ROXBOROUGH

Roxborough has the only **petrol station** on the windward coast, a huge affair just west of town close to the turn-off for the Roxborough–Parlatuvier Rd. There's also an **ATM**, on the sea side of the road about midway through the village, and several small **cookshops** on the main road offering basic local lunches.

King's Bay

Lifeguards on duty daily 10am–5pm • Changing facilities TT$1

Turning inland east of Roxborough, the Windward Road swings through the hilltop village of **Delaford**, making one almighty bend at the outskirts to reveal a breathtaking view of the spiky coconut plantation surrounding the beautiful, deep blue **King's Bay** below. The **beach** here is one of the few along the windward coast to provide changing facilities, and offers gentle waters, reefs and fine dark sand; nonetheless, it's almost always deserted save for the lifeguards. There are also six attractive gazebos on a strip of grass next to the beach which make good spots for picnicking, and a small café selling snacks and drinks. The profusion of First Peoples artefacts found here, on display at the Tobago Museum (see page 224), indicate that King's Bay was once the site of a large settlement; some suggest that the bay is named after Amerindian cacique (chief) King Peter, though it's more likely that that honour goes to King Peter's Bay on the Caribbean coast.

EATING AND DRINKING KING'S BAY

King's Bay Café Delaford ☎ 392 8585. Overlooking the bay on the main Windward Rd, with tables on a tiny breeze-cooled veranda that affords gorgeous views over the water, this friendly place has long been the windward coast's favourite lunch stopoff. Despite a change of ownership the menu of Creole-style fish or chicken lunches (from TT$50) remains reliable. Mon–Sat 7am–9pm.

Speyside and around

The last sizeable village on the windward coast, **SPEYSIDE** is not as pretty as nearby Charlotteville, with just a thin slip of grey-sand beach, but then most people come here to explore the fantastic offshore reefs rather than to laze on the sand. Despite its emergence as a **scuba-diving** paradise and the easy accessibility of nearby reefs for some of the best **snorkelling** on the island, Speyside is a soporific kind of a place with a very end-of-the-road feel. The smattering of hotels seem to only ever have a couple of guests, with most of the activity confined to the dive shops and the tour buses that stop off at lunchtime to disgorge visitors at ever-popular *Jemma's* restaurant.

Speyside lookout

Though Speyside itself isn't particularly scenic, it's hard not to be blown away by the amazing coastal view from the **lookout** point on its western outskirts, just before the Windward Road descends into the village proper. This lofty spot affords a marvellous panorama of the village, the turquoise reef-studded waters of Tyrrel's Bay and the emerald-green hillocks of Little Tobago and Goat Island, the former a renowned birdwatching spot. There's good forest hiking to be had along Murchiston Trace, a tiny road that strikes off to the right from the Windward Road just before the Speyside lookout; ask in Speyside for a local guide.

Speyside village
The Windward Road hits the coast in the centre of Speyside; turn right past the playing field to the **beach** facilities, though the skinny slip of sand isn't particularly inviting; turning left takes you into what could loosely be termed the tourist strip, containing several shops, hotels and restaurants, including the famous *Jemma's* – built around a tree overlooking the sea. Just past the crumbling *Manta Lodge* hotel, the road forks; left takes you across the island's interior and on to Charlotteville, while the right turn to Batteaux Bay runs past the ruins of a coral-stone building and colonial-era **waterwheel** – both being slowly overtaken by the foliage. There are a couple of benches under the almond trees at the sea's edge here, and following the rocky path up the small hillock opposite the ruins brings you to a nice lookout point with a couple more benches.

Batteaux Bay and the northeast
Site of the luxurious *Blue Waters Inn* (see page 243), and the departure point for glass-bottom boat tours to Little Tobago and the Speyside reefs (see page 243), the deliciously blue waters, white sands and rich reefs of **Batteaux Bay** are a much more inviting prospect for a swim than Speyside's main beach. Though the hotel is built right on the sand, the beach itself is public, and you can use the hotel's bathrooms if having lunch or drinks at the restaurant and bar; they're also happy for diners to have a dip in the lovely waterside swimming pool.

Beyond Batteaux, the road to picturesque **Delmont** and **Starwood** bays is often impassable by car; you can walk it, but bear in mind that swimming at both is dangerous because of strong currents.

Goat Island
Of the two misshapen islets sitting 5km or so out from Speyside in Tyrrel's Bay, **Goat Island** is the closer. The white house nestled in its centre was built as the Tobagonian holiday home of Caribbean devotee Ian Fleming, author of the James Bond novels, who once owned the island. Both house and island now belong to the government and are closed to the public. However, birdwatchers and hikers flock to the larger Little Tobago, a kilometre further out to sea.

Little Tobago
The most easterly point of the T&T republic, the two-square-kilometre outcrop of **Little Tobago** has been known as "Bird of Paradise Island" since the beginning of the twentieth century, when it was bought by keen ornithologist Sir William Ingram. In 1909, Ingram transported 24 greater birds of paradise (*Paradisaea apoda*) from Aru island in New Guinea and installed them in the island, though they slowly died out thanks to hurricanes and hunters. When Ingram died in 1924, his heirs gave Little Tobago back to the government on the condition that it receive protected status. It has remained a **bird sanctuary** ever since, inhabited only by one of the Caribbean's largest **sea-bird colonies**, which includes impressive flocks of frigate birds, boobies, terns and the spectacular red-billed tropicbird. You'll also hear the crows and clucks of feral cocks and chickens brought here by the now-departed resident caretaker, who was unable to round up his private flock before leaving the island. Most people visit the island as part of a glass-bottom boat tour (see page 243), but birdwatchers can also arrange specialist tours with the island's eco-oriented tour companies (see page 202). There are no facilities on Little Tobago, so bring water and snacks with you.

5

SCUBA DIVING

Tobago is one of the best **scuba-diving** spots in the southeastern Caribbean, yet it has relatively few divers visiting its dazzling coral reefs, volcanic formations and marine wrecks. The island is internationally recognized for the exciting and challenging **drift dives** caused by the Guyana current, which results from the confluence of the Caribbean Sea and the Atlantic Ocean. The seas around Tobago are home to 300 species of South Atlantic **coral** and a variety of spectacular multicoloured **fish**, not to mention larger species such as **stingrays**, **manta rays**, **sharks**, **dolphins**, **turtles** and **squid**. Rarer species such as toadfish and shortnose batfish are also occasionally spotted. Adding a touch of history to underwater encounters are the sunken ships that litter the sea floor.

There are many dive shops in Crown Point thanks to the sheer volume of visitors in the southwest (see page 205), but **Speyside** is the island's premier diving destination, with a variety of spectacular sites surrounding the offshore islands: **Goat Island** is popular for drift dives; **St Giles** for its rocky pinnacles and underwater canyon; and there's a reasonable chance of seeing manta rays on dives around **Little Tobago**.

TOP 5 TOBAGO DIVE SPOTS

Japanese Gardens, Speyside. Gorgeous hard and soft corals.
Kelliston Drain, Speyside. Home to the world's largest brain coral and frequented by manta rays.
London Bridge, Charlotteville. Underwater arch with whooshing currents and lots of fish.
M.V. Maverick, Mount Irvine. Purposely sunk in 1997, and home to spectacular coral and bonito.
Sisters Rocks, Parlatuvier. Exciting drift diving offshore of Bloody Bay – with the sea shelf falling to 667m – and large pelagic fish including hammerheads.

DIVE OPERATORS

Tobago's **diving industry** was only established in the 1980s but since then scuba-diving operations have multiplied with many hotels, beaches and guesthouses sporting their own centres. Prices vary slightly between operators; in general one to three dives cost about US$50 each, half-day resort courses US$95, five-day PADI Open Water certification courses US$480 and Advanced Open Water from US$450. When deciding who to dive with it's worth consulting the **Association of Tobago Dive Operators** (☎ 660 5445, ⊕ tobagoscubadiving. com), who list certified scuba-diving operators. Always check for the prominent display of a dive affiliation, such as NAUI, PADI, SSI or BSAC. Tobago has a **recompression chamber** in Roxborough (☎ 660 4000). Recommended local operators include:

Blue Caribbean Environmental Conservation Charlotteville ☎ 355 8616, ⊕ bluecaribbean conservation.org. Non-profit outfit offering diving courses and volunteer programmes.
Blue Waters Dive'N Blue Waters Inn, Batteaux Bay, Speyside ☎ 660 5445, ⊕ bluewatersinn.com. Well-regarded outfit in pole position for the Blue Waters jetty.

Environmental Research Institute Charlotteville Charlotteville ☎ 788 3550 or ☎ 497 9705, ⊕ eric-tobago. org. Aka ERIC, this not-for-profit dive school has a research arm dedicated to working toward marine conservation, run by a team of marine biologists and ecologists.
Extra Divers Speyside Inn, Speyside ☎ 660 4852, ⊕ extradivers-worldwide.com. Solid in-hotel dive shop, popular with German visitors.

All the boats dock at a small (and rather wobbly) jetty facing the mainland, from where you get beautiful views of Speyside and Pigeon Peak above, one of Tobago's highest points at 576m. Just up from the dock, the THA have built a handsome wooden structure slated to hold a museum at some distant point in the future. Beyond here, several **trails** cut during the island's brief spell as a cotton plantation thread into interior and up to a gazebo offering gorgeous views of the island's rocky coastline and the nesting grounds of the red-billed tropicbird.

ACTIVITIES   SPEYSIDE AND AROUND

Scuba diving and snorkelling Speyside's dive shops (see above) rent snorkel equipment for around US$10/day; however, the best snorkelling is on the far-off reefs visited by the glass-bottom boats

Glass-bottom boat tours Run by Frank's (☎ 660 5438) and Top Ranking (☎ 660 4904, ⓦ toprankingtobago.com), glass-bottom boats are a good way to see the reefs if you don't want to get wet, but also take you closer to the best snorkelling as well. Trips cost US$30 and include a walk around Little Tobago and a stop for snorkelling (equipment provided); you can also get shorter glass-bottom tours of the reef for a little less, and longer cruises around St Giles Island (US$65). Both operators can pick you up from Speyside and Charlotteville hotels and transport you to the departure point at *Blue Waters Inn*.

ACCOMMODATION

There's a good spread of accommodation in Speyside, from inexpensive to upmarket, but unless you're here for the diving or to ensconce yourself at *Blue Waters Inn*, livelier Charlotteville (just 10min drive away on the Caribbean coast) makes a much more pleasant base.

Bird's Nest Main Rd ☎ 660 5438, ⓔ rose_phil67@ hotmail.com. Close to the *Birdwatcher's* restaurant, and run by the same family, this sea-facing bungalow on the inland side of the road has two immaculately clean and spacious apartments with a/c and full kitchen; one has two double beds, the other a double and a bunk bed. There's a shared porch looking over to the ocean. ⓦ US$60

★ **Blue Waters Inn** Batteaux Bay ☎ 660 4341, ⓦ blue watersinn.com. Speyside's largest and grandest hotel, set around stunning Batteaux Bay and separated from the village by a steep road. Recently refurbished, rooms are spacious and luxurious, with sleek modern furnishings, a/c, porch/balcony and a sea view; there are also one- and two-bedroom bungalows (US$500/US$795). There's a pool, excellent restaurant (see below), bar, games room, dive shop and tennis court as well as 46 acres of lush tropical grounds with two nature trails. Rates include breakfast. ⓦ US$296

Speyside Inn Main Rd ☎ 660 4852, ⓦ speysideinn. com. Simple and nicely styled with great bay views, this diving hotel on the main road is kept busy with visiting enthusiasts, many from Germany, and offers a block of rooms facing the bay; all have a private balcony and a/c. There's a pool on a deck set back from the road, plus a good restaurant on site (see below; rates include breakfast) and a well-run dive shop. ⓦ US$144

Top Ranking Hill View Guesthouse Top Hill St, off Main Rd ☎ 660 4904 or ☎ 682 3622, ⓦ topranking tobago.com. Set in a large pink house on the hillside above town, this is a quiet and appealing place to stay, with friendly owners who also operate one of the Speyside glass-bottom boats. The spotless a/c rooms have kitchenette and ceiling fan, plus a porch or balcony with lovely views down over the bay. Free one-way beach shuttle, and car rental available. ⓦ US$70

EATING AND DRINKING

Speyside isn't exactly a metropolis, even during the high season, and in the low season, you'll find the town pretty much deserted as some of the cafés and dive operators close up shop. Nonetheless, there are a couple of good local **restaurants**, as well as some more upmarket choices in the hotels.

Birdwatcher's Main Rd ☎ 660 5438. Brightly painted café at the sea's edge, next door to *Jemma's*, with an indoor dining room and a more pleasant outdoor eating area overlooking the water. Friendly staff serve all the usual staples of Creole chicken and fish with tasty sides (lunch from TT$70, dinner from TT$110), although there are usually only one or two choices on any given day. Daily 11am–9pm.

★ **Blue Waters Inn** ☎ 660 4341, ⓦ bluewatersinn. com. This in-hotel restaurant and bar is a lovely place for a frosty cocktail or a meal even if you're not a guest, with tables set on an open-sided deck overlooking Batteaux Bay. The lunch menu (mains TT$60–90) runs from wraps, salads and burgers with fries to tacos and Creole-style fish or chicken – no surprises but well done and reasonably priced. Dinner is often a buffet (around TT$250), with mains such as chicken with passion fruit. Daily 7.30am–10pm.

★ **Jemma's Seaview Kitchen** Main Rd ☎ 660 4066. A popular stopoff on round-the-island tours, with dining areas on several levels built around the boughs of a tree, and offering fantastic sea views and ocean breezes. The Creole food is reliably tasty and pretty reasonably priced: breakfast (from TT$25) is eggs, bacon or local fish dishes, while lunch and dinner menus (mains TT$70–150) include grilled, curried or stewed fish, baked chicken in a mushroom or barbecue sauce, curried goat, plus shrimp and lobster, and lovely sides of breadfruit pie, tannia fritters or aubergine casserole; burgers, fried fish and sandwiches with chips (TT$50) are also available. No alcohol on sale, as the owners are Jehovah's Witnesses, but you can bring your own. Mon–Thurs & Sun 8am–8pm, Fri 8am–4pm.

Speyside Inn Main Rd ☎ 660 4852. With tables on a covered patio overlooking the sea, this hotel restaurant is worth a try, and is often the busiest spot in Speyside after dark (though that's not saying much). The reasonably priced dinner menu might feature mains of fish Creole or mango chicken (TT$120–140), while for lunch (TT$45–

115) there's fish salad, shrimp pasta or sandwiches and burgers. Daily 7.30–9.30am, noon–3pm & 6.30–9pm. **Speyside Overlooking** Windward Rd ☎ 686 6365. In a fantastic position with the panoramic views of the bay unfolding below, this is a scenic spot for a beer, natural juice or ice cream, or to enjoy local fish or chicken dishes (from TT$70). Daily noon–10pm.

Flagstaff Hill

The Windward Road strikes inland from Speyside's eastern outskirts on its way from the Atlantic to the Caribbean coast, climbing steeply upwards through the island's central spike before plummeting down to the opposite shoreline. Tobago's most easterly portion of tarmac marks the last sign of "civilization"; northeast of here, the land is completely undeveloped, with no electricity or piped water for the hardy handful of small-scale farmers, bush hunters and fishermen who live here. Just before the descent to the Caribbean, there's a signposted turn-off for **Flagstaff Hill**, with the paved road sweeping past some very fancy homes. At the crest of the hill, the road opens up to reveal a wide grassy area dotted with benches and overlooked by a lofty communications tower and mobile phone mast. The wind whistles through the metal and the **views** are absolutely superlative: Tyrel's Bay, with Little Tobago and Goat Island to one side, and to the other, Man O' War Bay, Booby Island, Cambleton Battery and, much further out, Sisters Rocks. This excellent vantage point was once used by British and French soldiers, who used mirrors to warn their colleagues stationed at Cambleton Battery below of an approaching ship.

Charlotteville

Tumbling willy-nilly down a hillside to a horseshoe bay of calm Caribbean waters where frigate birds swoop over the fishing boats, absurdly pretty **CHARLOTTEVILLE** looks its very best as you approach the village on the Windward Road. Snugly situated under the protective headlands of **Man O' War Bay**, the village is one of Tobago's foremost fishing communities – more than sixty percent of the island's total catch is brought in by local fishermen. Bordered on each side by steep forested hills, Charlotteville has an isolated feel, although this is in fact one of Tobago's largest settlements. It's also one of its oldest, first settled by Amerindians and then by the Dutch in 1633 – for many years the bay was known as Jan De Moor Bay after an early Frisian occupant. During the plantation era, the area was divided into two successful estates, Pirate's Bay and Charlotteville; sugar shipments made regular departures from the bay, and the village prospered. In 1865, both estates were purchased by the Turpin family, who still own much of the surrounding land. Today, tourism plays its part – albeit as second fiddle to fishing – in sustaining the local economy, and the village is popular with independent types who come for the quiet beaches and laidback charm. If you're seeking peace, quiet and great beaches, it's hard not to become utterly besotted with Charlotteville.

The hole-in-the-wall shops and sprinkling of restaurants that make up Charlotteville's centre line the road along the beach, while the streets that stretch inland and uphill, spreading back from a central playing field, are mostly residential. Slap in the centre of the village is the newly upgraded **Fishermen's Co-Operative**, where the day's catch is weighed, scaled and sold; adjacent to it, half-built and with ugly fences shielding the site from the road, is the hulking shell of the **Charlotteville Beachfront Mall**, an incongruous addition to the village and a source of much contention from locals who say its dimensions and design are completely inappropriate, and from vendors whose shops and businesses were illegally demolished to make way for the build. Legal wrangles had halted construction at the time of writing, and an end date for the project's completion was up in the air (as was a clear official vision of what the finished structure will look like). Beyond the site, the bay view opens up, the sea wall dotted

BUSTIN' THE BAMBOO

In Charlotteville and other rural Tobago communities, music at open-air celebrations, Christmas/Old Year's festivities and the annual Heritage Festival is often given an ear-splitting percussive accompaniment. Loved by small boys for the incredibly loud, cannon-like explosion that's produced, the tradition of **bustin' the bamboo** remains a popular – if rather dangerous – pastime. To achieve the desired earth-shaking report, the prospective buster must first have the know-how to select a piece of bamboo of the correct age and durability with at least four or five internal joints, and then cut the section so that joints seal each end. A hole is pierced at one end, and the bamboo is filled with pitch oil (kerosene) from a slit at the opposite end. The fuel is lit and fanned until it heats up sufficiently to blow out the remaining joints, which creates the resounding boom and often results in the loss of eyelashes and moustaches.

with benches and the beach mostly taken up with fishing boats and nets drying on the sand. The long concrete **pier** offers a lovely perspective back over the village, and is a great spot from which to watch the sun set.

Man O' War Bay Beach

Lifeguards daily 10am–5pm • Changing facilities daylight hours, TT$1

There's little to actually do in Charlotteville but enjoy the sea, whether you arrange a **fishing** trip aboard one of the many pirogues which moor up in the bay, or just while away the hours on the fine yellow sand of **Man O' War Bay Beach** – site of Tobago's most popular fisherman's fete, held to celebrate St Peter's Day. The best stretch of sand in Man O' War Bay is five minutes' walk west of the town centre, where you'll find changing/shower facilities as well as a beach bar and restaurant (see page 247). The bay itself is clean, calm and inviting, with good snorkelling.

Pirate's Bay

Charlotteville's main street veers away from the coast at the eastern end of the village, but a dirt track continues along the shoreline to the town's – and, for many, Tobago's – most attractive beach, **Pirate's Bay**. After walking for about fifteen minutes along the steep track you'll come to a long concrete stairway, at the bottom of which you're rewarded with a stunning horseshoe of calm emerald-green water and fine yellow sand, with a backdrop of trees, ferns and foliage. A tumbledown fisherman's hut is the only building in sight, and there's even a freshwater rinse, courtesy of a stream trickling down from the hills. The bay's translucent waters offer good **snorkelling**, especially on the left-hand side.

The seventeenth-century buccaneers after whom it was named may have gone, but the bay still has its freebooters, a large colony of **frigate birds**, which feed by snatching recently caught fish from the beaks of smaller sea birds. These, and other birds such as terns and pelicans, can be found at St Giles Island a few kilometres to the north, but strong currents make it difficult for small boats – and thus birdwatchers – to get there.

If the walk (or the stairs) seem like too much hard work, you can usually arrange for one of the village's fishermen to drop you at the beach and pick you up. Though the track is partially driveable, it's best to leave your car in town – the only place to park is also the only turning spot, so leaving your vehicle there means anyone else will have to reverse back down the hill.

Cambleton Battery

No set hours • Free

Reached via a steep and potholed lane striking off from the main road at the western outskirts of Charlotteville, **Cambleton Battery** was built by the British in 1777, who

5

placed two cannons here to defend against attack from marauding American warships; the sweeping views of Charlotteville, Booby Island and Pirate's Bay explain why they chose this site. It's now a popular cooling-off spot for locals, who lime away under the shade of the gazebo.

ARRIVAL AND INFORMATION   CHARLOTTEVILLE

By bus Buses from Scarborough (see page 226) stop opposite the Fishermen's Co-Operative; ask around to get details of departure times of buses back to Scarborough.

ACTIVITIES AND TOURS

Blue Caribbean Environmental Conservation ☎ 355 8616, ⓦ bluecaribbeanconservation.org. Non-profit diving outfit down the beach toward the swimming area.

Environmental Research Institute Charlotteville ☎ 788 3550 or ☎ 497 9705, ⓦ eric-tobago.org. Set between the beach and the road as you enter the village, ERIC offer eco-oriented beach excursions (US$50), marine birdwatching (US$150) and snorkelling at Pirates Bay

(US$25) and from a boat (US$40) as well as diving courses (see page 242).

Workshop Sea Tours ☎ 660 6281 or ☎ 727 3989, ⓦ workshopseatours.com. Opposite *Sharon and Pheb's* restaurant, this locally run operation offers half-day fishing trips (US$250) as well as offshore island tours and bird- and dolphin-watching expeditions (prices negotiable) and island tours such as to Argyle Waterfall (from US$45).

ACCOMMODATION

Big Fish Man O' War Bay ☎ 660 5717 or ☎ 687 2467, ⓔ thebigfishsuites@hotmail.com. Upstairs from *Sharon and Pheb's* restaurant, with gorgeous views over the village and bay from the private porches out front. Apartments are well maintained and have a/c, cable TV , fridge and microwave; there's also a shared kitchen, and you're just steps from the beach facility. 🛜 US$60

★ **Charlottevilla** Northside Rd, Cambleton ☎ 639 6331 or ☎ 687 2467, ⓦ charlottevilla.com. A handsome two-storey building opposite the road to the beach facilities on the outskirts of town, newly refurbished and well maintained, with two one-bedroom apartments on the ground floor and a two-bedroom unit (US$160) taking up the top floor, with its wraparound veranda. All have fans, full kitchen, lovely wooden furnishings, mosquito-netted beds and washing machine and dryer. 🛜 US$80

★ **Cholson Chalets** Man O' War Bay ☎ 639 8553, ⓦ cholsonchalets.com. The most atmospheric option in town, set in beautifully maintained old green-and-white houses overlooking the beach at the Pirate's Bay end of town. The six simple apartments have a deliciously antiquated feel with their muslin curtains, wooden floors and furniture passed down through the owner's family; those on the top floor (US$88) are the nicest. All have fans, private bathroom, kitchenette and cable TV. 🛜 US$66

★ **Man-O-War Bay Cottages** Man O' War Bay ☎ 660 4327, ⓦ man-o-warbaycottages.com. With easily the best location in town, in a shady grove of trees right on

the beach, these basic wooden one- to three-bedroom cottages (the latter US$85–120) may not have many modern conveniences, and could do with a bit of sprucing up, but you get lulled to sleep by the sound of the waves and the breeze swishing through the trees above, and are just steps from the water. All the cottages are spacious with ceiling and standing fans, hot water and kitchen. 🛜 US$65

Nicoville Spring St ☎ 639 8553, ⓦ cholsonchalets. com. In a good location just behind *Cholson Chalets* and managed by the same owners, the studio and one- and two-bedroom apartments here are decently priced. All have standing fans, hot and cold water and kitchenette, and those at the top overlook the playing field. 🛜 Studio US$40, one-bedroom US$55

Ocean View 11 Mission Rd ☎ 660 4891 or ☎ 620 0452. These small, spotless apartments done in typical Tobagonian decor are perched on Charlotteville's hillside, with wonderful views over Man O' War Bay from the balcony. Each has a/c, cable TV, en-suite bathroom, fully equipped kitchen and a shared balcony from which to gaze out over the town and bay. 🛜 US$60

Top River Pearl 32–34 Spring St ☎ 660 6011 or ☎ 354 7427, ⓦ topriver.com. Set away from Charlotteville's main seafront area, these airy en-suite apartments have kitchenettes, balconies and ceiling fans, and a large communal sundeck complete with hammocks and views of the bay. Top-floor apartments are a little more expensive, and you can pay a daily charge for a/c, too. 🛜 US$60

EATING AND DRINKING

Charlotteville's supermarkets stock only basic provisions, but you can buy fresh fish daily from the Fishermen's Co-Operative. The village isn't blessed with swanky **restaurants**, but there are plenty of places cooking up inexpensive and

5

delicious local food; bear in mind that the opening hours below are merely a guideline; many places shut up shop if things are quiet, so it's well worth calling ahead to arrange dinner.

★ **G's** Bay St. Right on the roadside opposite *Sharon and Pheb's*, with tables on a covered terrace overlooking the beach, *G's* is a nice spot for a sunset rum and coke or beer from the adjoining bar. The Creole food – baked chicken, fish with all the trimmings, fish and chips – is delicious and fresh, with a fish lunch at around TT$50. Daily 10am–10pm.

★ **Gail's** Bay St ☎ 688 5492 or ☎ 660 4316. Prepared by the charming Gail herself, this is a lovely little spot for dinner, with tables on a terrace just across from the water and close to the Pirate's Bay track. The Creole food is well seasoned and nicely presented, with fish and chicken starting at around TT$80 including a soup starter. Breakfast and lunch are also available with prior notice. Mon–Sat 7pm–late.

Sharon and Pheb's Bay St ☎ 660 5717. This local institution is the always reliable and with good service.

For breakfast, there's saltfish or fried fish with coconut bakes and cocoa tea, plus eggs, bacon and the like, while lunch and dinner rests on staples such as barbecue chicken and Creole fish, served with tasty sides (scallop potatoes, mixed veg and the like) on an attractive veranda raised a little above street level. Mains TT$60–150. Mon–Sat 8am–10pm.

★ **Suckhole** Man O' War Bay beach facility ☎ 288 5820. Perfect little beach bar in an unbeatable location overlooking the swimming area at Man O' War Bay, decorated with fishing nets and maritime paraphernalia. It's a great place for a lunch (chicken TT$60, fish TT$70, shrimp TT$180) of fish or jumbo shrimp in coconut curry sauce, Creole-style chicken or just a burger and fries, all served up a range of sides (steamed veg, onion rings, rice thick-cut fries and the like). Good rum punch and ice-cold beers, too. Daily 10am–6pm (lunch noon–3pm).

DIRECTORY

Charlotteville has a police station, health centre and branch of **First Citizens bank** (with an ATM) on the inland side of the playing field In the town centre, opposite the library. There are a couple of small **supermarkets** (usually Mon–Sat 8am–9pm, Sun 8am–3pm) on the main street, and fruit and veg are sold in the bandstand opposite the pier on Saturday mornings. The **petrol station** (Mon–Sat 6am 8pm) is next to the Fishermen's Co-Op.

FORT KING GEORGE, SCARBOROUGH

Contexts

History

Trinidad was the first Caribbean island to be populated, having been settled by Amerindians from South America as early as 5000 BC. The first incomers were peaceful farmers and fishers who called their new home "Ieri", the land of the hummingbird, but were joined after 1000 AD by more warlike tribes.

The Amerindians and European conquest

When **Christopher Columbus** "discovered" Trinidad in 1498, the Amerindian population of some 35,000 had created a structured society, with organized villages along the coastline presided over by caciques (chiefs) and a self-sufficient economy that exploited the abundant natural resources and extensive trade with the South American mainland. Sighting the three peaks of the Trinity Hills, Columbus named the island **Trinidad**, landing at Moruga on the south coast. Despite an initial skirmish with the local tribes, Columbus's sailors considered them the friendliest in the Caribbean islands. This didn't suit the Spanish **slave traders** who followed hot on Columbus's heels; despite protests from Spanish priests such as Bartolomeo de las Casas, they exaggerated the Amerindians' occasional ritual **cannibalism** to justify enslaving them.

The first permanent **Spanish settlers** came to Trinidad in 1592, establishing the small town of San José – present-day St Joseph – complete with governor's residence, *cabildo* (council chamber) and church. Although this fledgling capital was sacked in 1595 by **Sir Walter Raleigh** as he headed for South America in search of El Dorado, it was quickly rebuilt, and the colony survived, despite its vulnerability to foreign attacks and pirate raids, growing tobacco and cocoa for export to Europe. In 1687, Capuchin monks arrived from Spain, setting up several **missions** around the island. Alongside the proselytizing, the missions were also a means to control the Amerindians through the *encomienda* labour system, a kind of semi-slavery in which they were forced to work on plantations and build more churches.

To evade this threat to their way of life, some Amerindians moved to the interior, while others fought back – in 1699, Amerindians in San Rafael rebelled against Spanish missionaries attempting to forcibly convert them and subject them to *encomienda*. Three priests and then-governor José de León y Echales were killed, and the reprisals were savage: Spanish troops slaughtered the region's entire Amerindian population in what's now known as the **Arena Massacre**. Amerindians were further threatened by European diseases to which they had no resistance, and by the end of the eighteenth century, some three centuries after Columbus's arrival, the indigenous population had been all but wiped out.

Spanish Trinidad

Despite all the depredations they visited upon the Amerindians, the Spanish had neither the desire nor the resources to develop Trinidad, treating it as little more than a convenient watering-hole en route to the riches of South America. Their governors were left to do as they pleased – illegal trading of goods and slaves was commonplace – and due to its poor defences, the island suffered repeated attacks from French, Dutch and English **pirates**.

5000 BC	1498	1592
Amerindian peoples cross over from the South American mainland and establish settlements on Trinidad and Tobago.	Christopher Columbus makes a brief stop on Trinidad, naming the island after three hills in its southeast corner.	Spanish settlers establish a capital at present-day St Joseph, and claim Trinidad as a colony of Spain.

BANWARI MAN

The **Banwari Trace** archeological site, on the southern fringes of the Oropuche Lagoon in southwest Trinidad (see page 180), can lay claim to being the oldest human settlement discovered anywhere in the Caribbean. The site is thought to have been occupied by the so-called Ortoiroid peoples (the name taken from the nearby Ortoire river) for two thousand years (between 5200 and 3200 BC). Excavations by members of the Trinidad & Tobago Historical Society in 1969 uncovered a huge array of artefacts buried in a midden that have provided valuable information on the migration patterns of Amerindians from the South American mainland to the Caribbean, as well shedding light on the lifestyle and diet of Trinidad's First Peoples.

The most significant discovery was a human skeleton, known as **Banwari Man**, found lying just 20cm below the surface in the typical Amerindian crouched burial position, and estimated to be around 5000 years old; the remains are now kept at the Department of Life Sciences in the University of the West Indies' St Augustine campus. Other artefacts unearthed in the midden include sharpened animal bones and bevelled peccary teeth thought to have been used as fish hooks or to tip hunting spears; conical pestles and grinding stones used for preparing plant-based foods; stone tools, from knives to scrapers; and a host of shells (shellfish having been a mainstay of the Ortoiroid diet).

When Don Pedro de la Moneda arrived from Spain to take up the governorship in 1757, he found his St Joseph residence practically in ruins, and decamped to Port of Spain.

Eventually, though, the Spanish realized that if they didn't develop this neglected colony, somebody else would. Issued in 1783, the **Cedula of Population** was designed to encourage fellow Catholics – **French planters** suffering Protestant discrimination in British Grenada and Martinique – to settle in Trinidad; the amount of land they were allocated depended on the number of slaves they brought with them. Immigrants of mixed European/African race (termed "**Free Coloured**" by the Spanish) who brought slaves could also receive land (though only half as much as their white counterparts), thus opening the way for the development of a property-owning middle class of non-whites, whose ancestors still run much of Trinidad's big business today.

To implement the Cedula, Spain despatched a new governor, **José Maria Chacón**, in 1784. The economy flourished under his energetic administration, and people of French and African descent came to dominate the population. The island's culture also became increasingly French: it was during this period that **Carnival** was introduced, the French language created a local patois, and a society based on aristocratic principles of birth and connections developed.

As the repercussions of the **French Revolution** gave rise to civil and international wars throughout the West Indies, many more French – both republicans and royalists, white and mixed-race – sought refuge in neutral Trinidad, but to Chacón's alarm, they brought their ideological conflicts with them. Increasingly anxious, the governor reported to Madrid that some of the newcomers' radical ideas were encouraging the slaves to "dream of liberty and equality".

The British conquest

Keen to augment their sizeable list of Caribbean colonies, the British seized upon the idea that Trinidad had become a nest of republicans and "bad people of all

1580–1841	1783
Tobago changes hands 31 times as Dutch, Latvian, British and French colonists fight for ownership. The British establish plantations and bring in African slaves.	The incentives of Spain's Cedula of Population see mixed-race "Free Coloured" and French white immigrants establish a plantation culture in Trinidad.

descriptions", despatching an invasion fleet under **Sir Ralph Abercromby** in 1797. The island had few defences: just five ships compared to the British force of eighteen, and only two thousand soldiers – many of whom had deserted – against seven thousand. The Spanish surrendered with hardly a shot fired, scuttling their own ships in Chaguaramas harbour, and Chacón was recalled to Spain in disgrace.

Abercromby's terms of defeat were lenient – residents could retain their property and Spanish law would remain in force – but his choice of governor, **Thomas Picton**, was not. Left in charge with near absolute powers, Picton instituted a reign of terror, deporting and executing suspected subversives (mostly slaves and "Free Coloureds") on the flimsiest evidence, with confessions frequently obtained under torture. Followers of African religious traditions were persecuted especially harshly; those suspected of practising **obeah** (see below) were hauled before a tribunal, and whipped, hanged, mutilated or burned to death if found guilty. By 1802, Picton's activities had become an embarrassment to the British government, then facing an influential anti-slavery lobby at home, and he was demoted.

Trinidad presented a unique administrative conundrum for the British, however. Their other Caribbean possessions were governed by colonial assemblies, but this wasn't an option for Trinidad – any such body would inevitably be dominated by planters, who would never agree to share power with "Free Coloureds", despite the fact that many of the latter were substantial property owners and thus difficult to exclude from government under British law. The island therefore remained a **Crown colony**, governed by French and Spanish law, with directions issued straight from the colonial office in London.

OBEAH

A retention of African animist traditions, **obeah** (from the Ashanti *obayfor*, meaning witchcraft or magic) is the belief in a spiritual power that can influence events in the temporal world, curing disease, providing good fortune or wreaking revenge. Though dismissed by most as mumbo-jumbo, obeah still lingers on in Trinidad and Tobago via common superstitions and practices passed down over the generations. In rural areas, you'll often see **blue bottles** placed over front doors or in gardens to ward off the evil spirits known as jumbies (see page 253) or protect against the evil eye or **maljo** (*mal yeux*), and there are still those who enlist the services of an **obeah man** (or woman), also known as an **ojhaman** or **seer-man** in the Indian community, usually a respected figure dispensing herbal medicines rather than a sinister character cooking up bubbling potions under a full moon. During the plantation era, every slave community had a herbalist who doled out concoctions for all kinds of ailments, and elements of these traditions remain strong in Trinbagonian attitudes to health. As spiritual and physical problems are seen as being connected, practitioners might prescribe plants, herbs, roots and barks alongside shop bought substances such as red lavender to be infused into the skin through a bush bath, said to get rid of "blight" or *maljo* or turn around a run of bad luck; or advise an internal cleanse and purge by way of a dose of cooling herbs such as wild senna, caraili, mauby or pawpaw bark, followed by a cleansing dose of aloes or castor oil. Less commonly (as such practices are illegal in Trinidad and Tobago), special circumstances such as a case of unrequited love or a feud may see an obeah practitioner paid to invoke or dispel a curse, which is done through a ritual to bring on the desired effect – called **"working obeah"** – that is reversible only by a more powerful practitioner.

1797	1802	1834
Britain captures Trinidad from Spain; heavy-handed governor Thomas Picton is demoted in 1802 and Trinidad is designated a Crown colony.	Spain formally cedes Trinidad to Britain under the Treaty of Amiens; Tobago follows suit in 1814.	Slavery is abolished between 1845 and 1917; some 145,000 indentured workers arrive from India to fill the labour gap.

Emancipation and beyond

Though life for the **slaves** on Trinidad and Tobago's estates was no less brutal than in any of the British colonies, the islands never developed into the full-blown plantation societies of Jamaica or Barbados. Rather than the massive estates established elsewhere, plantations in T&T were relatively small-scale, and the British touted Trinidad as a "model" colony thanks to the introduction of a few tentative measures that attempted to curb the worst of the planters' abuses. Nonetheless, it was a miserable life for the Africans, who resisted by organizing secret societies with their own militias and carrying out several **rebellions**.

Indentureship

The British abolished the slave trade in 1807, though this meant nothing to those still toiling on T&T's estates; and even after the **Act of Emancipation** in 1834, freed Africans were required to serve as apprentices for a further six years. When the apprenticeship system was abolished in 1838, many former slaves moved to urban areas, leaving the planters desperately short of labour, and the British government sanctioned the immigration of **indentured labourers** from India as a means of easing the situation on the estates. In May 1845, the first 225 workers arrived aboard the *Fatel Rozack*; by 1917, when the indenture system ended, some 145,000 Indians, mainly from Calcutta, had come to T&T. Fleeing poverty and the increasingly harsh British rule, the immigrants were signed up to work for five years in return for their passage home. (In 1854 the indenture was extended to ten years, and after 1895 the immigrants had to pay a proportion of their return passage.)

Though indentureship was better regulated and monitored than slavery, the working and living conditions of labourers and slaves were practically indistinguishable. Indentured workers lived in unsanitary single-room barrack houses where disease was rife, and plantation owners failed to honour pledges on wages and working conditions. Nonetheless, many stayed on at the end of their indentureship, accepting land in lieu of a passage home. Known then and today as "**East Indians**" to differentiate them from the "West Indians", they formed the lowest rung of society, working in the agricultural sector scorned by ex-slaves and establishing tight-knit communities that maintained the religious and cultural traditions of their homeland (much to the resentment of the African population, whose ancestors had been afforded no such indulgence). The white ruling class, however, painted the Indians as heathens and barbarians – in 1884, 22 Indians were shot dead by police and hundreds wounded as they tried to enter San Fernando during the annual Hosay festival parade, while East Indian children were considered illegitimate until 1945 as Muslim and Hindu marriages were not recognized.

Despite this persecution, Indian immigrants contributed greatly to Trinidad's developing national identity. Just as the Europeans had brought Carnival, which was taken up and enriched by former slaves, Indians introduced their own festivities and culture. Muslims introduced **Hosay** (see page 72), Hindus brought the festival of light, **Divali**, while Indian foods such as roti and curry have become staples for all Trinbagonians.

Immigrants arrive

Trinidad and Tobago's ethnic mix was further enriched by immigrants arriving from other parts of the world. Several companies of **black American soldiers** who fought for

1889	**1903**	**1941**
Economic woes see Tobago made a ward of Trinidad.	The Red House burns during the Water Riots in Port of Spain; Arthur Cipriani and Uriah Butler lead a newly politicized labour movement.	The American government lease Chaguaramas, the Bocas Islands and Waller Field to use as military bases.

JUMBIES IN TRINBAGO FOLKLORE

The stuff of many a spooky tale, as well as a good few vintage calypso tunes, jumbies – the local name for ghosts – are still very much part of the folklore of Trinidad and Tobago and the wider Caribbean. The characters below represent some of the most enduring characters.

Douens The malevolent spirits of unbaptized children, these sinister genderless waifs have backward-facing feet and hide their featureless faces beneath a wide-brimmed straw hat. They lurk in places where real children play; superstitious parents never call their child's name in the open, lest the douens remember it and lure the child away.

La Diablesse An attractive female devil, La Diablesse wears the floppy hat and flowing gown of French colonial times, and lures men deep into the forest, never to return. At fetes, her frenzied dancing outshines the other women and attracts the men. The only way to distinguish her is by her feet; one is normal, the other a cloven hoof.

La Gahou Also known as *lugarhoo*, this spirit feeds on fresh blood. Iron chains slung about its body rattle and drag along the ground, and its sheaf of sticks functions as a whip; it can alter its form (usually becoming a jackass or dog) as well as changing size from minute to monstrous. A pair of scissors opened to resemble a cross and a Bible placed at the head of the bed are said to force the beast to revert to its human form.

Mama D'Leau Spirit and protector of rivers and lakes, Mama D'Leau sits naked at the edge of rivers, incessantly combing her long hair. Beneath the water, she has the lower body of a snake, which she uses to pull passing men to a watery death.

Papa Bois Tall and strong, his hair entwined with leaves, Papa Bois is guardian of forest trees, birds and animals. He imitates animal calls, leading hunters deep into the bush to become hopelessly lost.

Soucouyant This female vampire lives in villages as a reclusive old woman. At night, she sheds her skin to travel the country in the form of a ball of fire searching for victims, her skin kept in an overturned mortar bowl until her return at daybreak. She can only be stopped by dousing the skin in salt, which prevents her from re-entering it, or dropping piles of rice in homes and at crossroads; she is compelled to pick each pile up one by one until sunrise brings about her discovery.

Britain in its 1812 war against the US were given grants of land in southern Trinidad, where they founded villages named after the units in which they had served while, after emancipation, freed slaves from other **Caribbean islands** were attracted to Trinidad by the relatively high wages for labourers. **Africans** liberated by the British Navy on anti-slave patrols settled in urban areas, becoming craftsmen and construction workers and establishing strong communities that maintained their own cultural institutions and heritage. The first **Chinese immigrants** arrived in 1853 as part of another attempt by the government to meet the continuing labour shortage on the plantations. The plan failed on account of the high transport costs and an appalling mortality rate among the immigrants; those who survived tended to become shopkeepers, and their descendants constitute a small but visible minority today. **Portuguese** labourers were also brought to the country in the mid-1800s, but the practice was short-lived as the employment of Europeans in manual work was seen as a threat to the established racial hierarchy.

Except for a handful of **Jews** who arrived during World War II, the last group of immigrants to join Trinidad's melting pot were the **Syrians** who came in 1913, seeking refuge from religious persecution in the Lebanon. Though they only account for 0.1 percent of the country's population, their business acumen has given them a high profile, and they remain a tight-knit and influential community today.

1945	1956	1958
Universal suffrage is granted, though the islands' legislative council is afforded only limited powers by the British.	Dr Eric Williams founds the People's National Movement (PNM); his election victory marks the start of a thirty-year reign for the PNM.	Trinidad and Tobago joins the West Indies Federation, inaugurated in Chaguaramas but dissolved in 1962 after Jamaica leaves.

AFRICAN RELIGIONS

Centred upon the acceptance of a synthesis between the spiritual and temporal worlds, and the belief in spirits or gods which organize and animate the material world, T&T's **African-based religions** combine Christianity with elements of traditional West African belief systems brought to the island by enslaved peoples.

SPIRITUAL BAPTISTS

The most visible sect is the **Spiritual Baptist** faith, which was established in the late nineteenth century by American ex-slaves who had fought for the British in the War of 1812. Then known as **Shouter Baptists** thanks to their propensity for loud and demonstrative worship, the sect was frowned upon by the British, who banned membership through the Shouters Prohibition Ordinance of 1917. Years of campaigning finally saw the law repealed in 1951, an act that's commemorated in the **Shouter Baptist Liberation** national holiday on March 30.

A well-organized faith, Spiritual Baptists have **churches** throughout Trinidad and Tobago which, as well as the usual pews and altar, feature a **centre pole** decorated with flowers, jugs of water and candles to harness and attract the spirits. Services usually involve purification rituals designed to cast out jumbies (evil spirits; see page 253) that might be lurking in the church: lighted candles are placed in front of doors and windows, incense is lit, brass bells are rung and perfumed water strewn about. Bible readings precede chants and handclapping, which intensify as a kind of hyperventilation known as **adoption** brings about **spirit possession**, accompanied by bell-ringing and chanting called **trumpeting the spirit**, the origin of the "shouter" tag. Those who "catch the power" may gesticulate, speak in tongues or relay the spirit's message in plain English. The characteristic white robes and colourful headwraps worn by followers (which signify their dedication to a particular saint or spirit) are a notable part of the Trinbago Sunday scenery; you may also see outdoor **baptisms**, where white-clad converts are ritually dipped into rivers or the sea.

ORISHA

A Yoruba religion driven underground during British rule, **Orisha** (also Orisa or Shango) centres upon worship of several deities – orishas – who are seen to have a distinct influence upon the living and must therefore be (depending on the situation) respected, pacified, praised, worshipped or feared through ritual dances, chants, drumbeats, offerings and prayer. Each orisha's personality is described in stories that reveal their activities on earth, with each assigned an individual drumbeat, colour, day of the week, favourite food and liquor, sacrificial animal (usually a chicken or goat) and an association with a Christian saint; this last tradition allowed Orisha to be syncretized with Christian festivals when the faith was outlawed. Orisha worship takes place in a **palais**, usually an open-roofed structure decorated with the symbols of individual orishas – daggers, cutlasses, hammers, jugs of water and ritual items such as olive oil for anointing, and offerings of flowers, fruit and foods. Known as **feasts**, most ceremonies take place over several days, and begin with the specialized drum patterns that summon the deities. Drumming, dancing, chanting and hyperventilation encourage possession of devotees by various orishas, while food or rum may be offered to honour the spirits that descend.

Into the twentieth century

Trinidadian society remained deeply stratified along race and class lines for most of the nineteenth century, with white planters firmly at the top of the heap, but in the 1880s and 1890s, reform movements began to challenge the status quo. An improved national education system and an enlarged franchise inspired the formation of **political**

1962	1970	1974
Trinidad and Tobago is granted its independence, with Eric Williams as the country's first prime minister.	The Black Power movement gains widespread support, and a state of emergency is declared after a brief army mutiny in support of the protests.	Vast oil reserves are discovered just off Trinidad's east coast.

pressure groups linked to the international labour movement, from the Trinidad Workingmen's Association (TWA) and East Indian National Association to the Pan African Association, which lobbied the British Colonial Office for an elected governing body for the island.

In 1899, Britain made ailing **Tobago** a ward of Trinidad, though the latter still had no effective form of self-government (for more on the history of Tobago, see chapter 5). Resentment came to a head over the introduction of new water rates, and in 1903 a protest meeting in Port of Spain's Woodford Square erupted into a **riot**. Eighteen people were shot dead by the police, and the Red House – seat of the colonial government – was burned to the ground. Although Britain finally agreed to an **elected assembly** for Trinidad and Tobago in 1913 (albeit one with very limited powers), it was still more than ten years before the first Legislative Council convened in the rebuilt Red House.

Trinidad's burgeoning **oil industry** and the aftermath of **World War I** further politicized the populace. High inflation led to strikes, resulting in increased cooperation between Africans and Indians, while fuel was added to the fire by Trinidadian soldiers who returned from the Great War with stories of discrimination at the hands of the British. The tide had finally turned, with socialism, national independence and the concept of black consciousness, as promoted by Jamaica's Marcus Garvey, now firmly planted in the public mind. In 1925, TWA president **Arthur Cipriani** was elected to the new legislative council, campaigning hard for workers' rights and securing some important concessions, including compensation for industrial injuries. His reformist politics had little effect on the underlying balance of power, however; wages were actually falling, malnutrition was widespread, living conditions grim and industrial accidents appallingly common. As the world economy nosedived into the **Great Depression** of the 1930s, Cipriani found himself outflanked by a new generation of radicals such as the charismatic **Uriah Butler** (see page 185), who formed the **British Empire Workers** trade union in 1935.

The road to independence

During World War II, Trinidad's socioeconomic character was altered radically by the presence of the **US military**, who leased Chaguaramas, the Bocas Islands and Waller Field in 1941 to provide a strategic base for their Caribbean fleet. The Americans improved Trinidad's infrastructure and exposed the population to high-level technology for the first time, while the **high wages** paid for the construction of buildings and roads lured workers from the agricultural sector and led to the decline of many estates. The Americans' racial attitudes, cruder than the more subtle prejudice of the British, and the aura of easy money that attracted many Trinidadian women, caused plenty of resentment, however, and further increased the desire for independence.

The rise of the PNM

Universal suffrage was granted in 1945, and the 1946 and 1950 elections were won by political parties linked to the trade unions, but Britain was not prepared to hand over total control while radical labour politics dominated the political arena. In January 1956, a group of black intellectuals formed the **People's National Movement**

1976	1981
Trinidad and Tobago become a republic, with new President, Ellis Clark, replacing Britain's Queen Elizabeth as head of state.	Falling oil prices trigger a recession, and George Chambers becomes prime minister following the death of Eric Williams.

(PNM) under the leadership of Oxford-educated historian **Dr Eric Williams**. The party's black nationalist policies and the charismatic leadership and immense intellectual authority of "the Doctor" gained widespread support among a population tired of colonial government and the divisions within the labour movement; their only serious opposition was from the **People's Democratic Party** (PDP), later the **Democratic Labour Party** (DLP) supported primarily by rural Hindus. After a controversial campaign that raised racial tension by portraying the PDP as reactionary Hindus, the PNM won a tentative victory in the 1956 election; they were to remain in power for the next thirty years, with Williams as prime minister until his death in 1981.

Caribbean unity and racial division

Many Caribbean leaders saw West Indian confederacy as the way forward for the region's tiny territories, and initially Williams was an enthusiastic proponent of the idea. In 1958, the **West Indies Federation** was launched at Chaguaramas, but political rivalries and the reluctance of larger islands to subsidize smaller ones resulted in a watered-down Federation with no tax-raising powers. When Jamaica voted to leave in September 1961, Williams announced that "one from ten leaves nought"; Trinidad followed suit, and the Federation was swiftly dissolved.

The early 1960s saw the PNM adopting a radical stance, booting out the US military in 1961 and campaigning vigorously for independence, while politics split further along racial lines, with government the preserve of Afro-Caribbeans, and opposition that of East Indians. After **Independence** was finally granted in 1962, things further degenerated when the PNM created a new constitution without consulting the DLP. Autonomy from the "motherland" had done little to change the colonial structure of T&T's society, and the electorate became increasingly disenchanted with their new-found "freedom".

The Black Power years

The late 1960s were marked by repeated unrest. The American **Black Power** movement caught the imagination of many disaffected young men and women, and in 1970 its supporters launched a wave of marches, protests and **wildcat strikes** that shook Trinidad to the core. Businesses and banks were bombed, and when the police shot dead a protester named **Basil Davis** in April 1970, 30,000 people took to the streets for his funeral. Facing a possible general strike, Eric Williams declared a state of emergency and arrested several Black Power leaders, only to be faced by an **army mutiny** at the Teteron base in Chaguaramas, staged by officers outraged at government heavy-handedness. It was only quashed when coastguard vessels prevented the soldiers from marching on Port of Spain by shelling the main road; rumours abounded that a bloody coup had been averted and plans had been discovered for mass executions of "enemies of the people".

Black gold, recession and radicalism

The Black Power crisis proved cathartic. Many whites had fled the country; those who remained could no longer expect the deference to which they had

1986	1990	1991
A.N.R. Robinson's National Alliance for Reconstruction (NAR) win the general election. Economic woes see the dollar devalued.	The Jamaat-al-Muslimeen stage a short-lived coup, holding Robinson and several of his cabinet hostage for six days before surrendering.	The PNM return to power under Patrick Manning.

been accustomed, while the government encouraged locals to be trained for jobs previously occupied by expatriates. The country was teetering on the edge of **bankruptcy**, with the PNM remaining in office primarily thanks to divisions in the opposition. "We are winning by default," PNM minister Hector McLean observed dryly. But salvation was ahead in the form of **oil**. Just as the world was sliding into the oil crisis of 1973–74, vast reserves were discovered off Trinidad's east coast, and T&T found itself swimming in money overnight. Ambitious public projects were undertaken and the country settled back to enjoy the boom years. But this sudden wealth had its downside as people got used to the easy life: productivity fell and agriculture dwindled, while **corruption** thrived.

When oil prices fell in the 1980s, the economy went into **recession**, unemployment rose sharply and inflation soared. In 1981, Williams died a disillusioned man with his policies in ruins; his former finance minister George Chambers took over the reins. As the population became increasingly dissatisfied, the opposition parties started to unify. In 1986, the PNM was ousted by the **National Alliance for Reconstruction** (NAR), led by A.N.R. Robinson, who had resigned from Williams' government in 1970 following the Basil Davis debacle. The NAR tried to resolve some of the more pressing problems facing the country, but within a year the government was breaking up into factions. Harsh economic measures, including **devaluation** of the TT dollar and a stringent IMF-inspired recovery programme, were widely seen as undemocratic and beneficial only to the rich. In 1990, the radical Muslim group **Jamaat-al-Muslimeen** (see page 62) attempted to overthrow the government, holding Robinson and several of his cabinet hostage. Though the coup was crushed after a six-day siege, the government's authority was irreparably undermined, and the following year the PNM returned to power under **Patrick Manning**.

The UNC and the return of the PNM

In the early 1990s increased oil revenues during the Gulf War helped the PNM stabilize the economy and pay off the IMF, but the 1995 election split the country down the middle, with the PNM and the Indo-Trinidadian **United National Congress** (UNC) both winning seventeen seats. The two NAR representatives held the balance of power, and used it to support the UNC, making lawyer and former union leader **Basdeo Panday** the country's first East Indian prime minister. Although the 2000 election returned the UNC to power with nineteen seats, Panday's government lasted just ten months; in October 2001, three UNC MPs defected to the opposition, and with their majority removed, the UNC were forced to call an election. Another hung parliament ensued, with both the PNM and UNC returning 18 of the 36 total seats each. Though the UNC won more votes, President A.N.R. Robinson appointed Patrick Manning as leader, but with no clear mandate to govern Manning called another election; in October 2002, he returned to office with a decisive majority.

Politricks and corruption

In 2006, the political waters were muddied by the formation of a new party, the **Congress of the People** (COP), fronted by former UNC leader **Winston Dookeran** and

1995	2000–2002
The NAR throw in their lot with the United National Congress (UNC) to form a coalition government.	The UNC win the 2002 election, but political shenanigans and a hung parliament leads to elections in 2001 and 2002, when Manning's PNM manage a decisive victory.

representing the first credible alternative to the two-party dominance of the UNC and PNM since the ill-fated NAR. Both the COP and the UNC did moderately well in the 2007 elections, but this new split in the opposition allowed the PNM to limp to victory with just 46 percent of the vote. Though the COP didn't gain any parliamentary seats, the party soldiered on, scoring many points among Trinbagonians for its efforts to distance itself from the race-based voting of the past (with Indians traditionally siding with the UNC and black Trinbagonians with the PNM). The UNC, meanwhile, struggled under the increasingly erratic reins of Basdeo Panday, and internal elections in early 2010 saw him replaced by **Kamla Persad-Bissessar** as UNC leader, marking the end of Panday's 33-year political career and an era in Trinidadian politics.

Patrick Manning, too, was coming under fire both for his increasingly dictatorial style of leadership and for the PNM's culpability in the scandal surrounding the state-owned Urban Development Company of Trinidad and Tobago (**UDeCOTT**). The PNM pumped millions of dollars into ever more lavish UDeCOTT projects, including Port of Spain's waterfront complex and the National Academy of the Performing Arts, but in March 2010 executive chairman **Calder Hart** resigned after it was revealed that lucrative contracts had been given to a company owned by his wife's family. The entire board were fired the following month in the wake of a Commission of Enquiry report that pointed to irregularities in numerous projects, from the TT$700 million Brian Lara Stadium in Tarouba to the TT$368 million Ministry of Legal Affairs Tower in Port of Spain. Reeling from the effects of the scandal, Manning called an early election in May 2010, with detractors arguing that he was going to the polls only to avoid an imminent vote of no confidence. The opposition were finally able to unite under the banner of the **People's Partnership** (PP), with Persad-Bissessar as their candidate for Prime Minister.

A new decade – and more corruption

A **landslide victory** for the PP ensued, making Kamla Persad-Bissessar the republic's **first female Prime Minister**. She sought to distance the new coalition administration from the despotic ruling style of Manning's PNM, creating a Ministry of the People to allow public grievances to be aired and announcing a raft of policies that included an assault on poor environmental practices and a rethink of water resource management. However, despite an election campaign that championed zero tolerance on corruption, the PP came under fire early on thanks to a perceived conflict of interest concerning **Austin "Jack" Warner**, appointed by Persad-Bissessar as Minster of Works and Transport while holding the post of Vice-President of FIFA. By 2011, allegations of ongoing corruption saw Warner resign from his FIFA position, and by 2013 he had also fallen foul of the PP, leaving to form his own political party, the Independent Liberals. In May 2015 he was indicted by the US Department of Justice, accused of wire fraud, racketeering and money laundering, though legal challenges mean he hadn't yet been extradited for trial at the time of writing.

The PNM, meanwhile, were left in disarray by the PP's victory. Vilified by his party for having lost the election and the ongoing corruption scandals, Patrick Manning resigned as PNM leader and was replaced by his arch-rival, **Keith Rowley**. Though Persad-Bissessar remained in power for a full five-year term, her administration was no

2004	2010
Brian Lara recaptures the record for the highest individual score in Test cricket with his 400 not out for the West Indies.	Reeling from corruption scandals, Patrick Manning calls a snap election; Kamla Persad-Bissessar becomes the republic's first female prime minister.

less bedevilled by allegations of corruption and financial mismanagement, and the **2015 general election** saw the PP roundly beaten by Keith Rowley's PNM.

Current issues

One of the most pressing problems facing Trinidad and Tobago is **crime**, particularly the kidnapping of high-profile businesspeople and the violent fallout from Trinidad's uneasy status as one of the Caribbean's main transhipment points for South American cocaine. Until the 1970s, the country was relatively free of violent crime; today, it's a rather different picture. In 2000, 119 **murders** were reported in T&T; today, the figure averages at around 500 per year. Patrick Manning's PNM government unleashed various initiatives, including a series of cripplingly expensive airships equipped with state-of-the-art surveillance gear that patrolled the skies above (and waters around) Trinidad, while the PP imposed a three-month state of emergency in 2011 to try and tackle the problem, but such initiatives have had little long-term effect, and crime remains one of the main challenges facing each successive administration.

Another matter of pressing concern is **corruption**, with financial scandals hitting the headlines with depressing regularity. The People's Partnership were inevitably tainted by Jack Warner's spectacular fall from FIFA grace, while Rowley's PNM administration have been no less immune to allegations of corruption: detractors pointing to wanton expenses claims from several PNM ministers as well as conflicts of interest concerning the acquisition of new vessels for T&T's ailing inter-island ferry service and in regard to construction firms appointed for new roadbuilding projects.

On a more positive note, Trinidad and Tobago continue to enjoy the status of having the most **stable economy** in the Caribbean thanks to the republic's reserves of oil and natural gas, which account for around forty percent of GDP and eighty percent of exports, and provided something of a buffer from the global economic downturn; equally, T&T's external debt is relatively insignificant compared to other Caribbean nations. The income generated from oil and gas is increasingly being used to develop other sectors, including manufacturing, finance, services and tourism, though as reserves are being fast depleted – it's widely agreed that they'll be exhausted within twenty years – there is a real need to diversify the economy. And despite its natural riches, T&T remains a very **polarized** nation, where high-tech malls co-exist with board shacks where inhabitants live without electricity or running water, and where political loyalties are still very much divided according to ethnicity. Such inequality and racial division has created an uneasy tension in this country of extremes.

2012	2018
Keshorn Walcott, a 19-year old from Toco, becomes the first black man to win an Olympic gold for javelin.	Former High Court judge Paula-Mae Weekes becomes T&Ts first female head of state, succeeding Anthony Carmona after his five-year term as president.

Carnival

Trinidad's fabulous Carnival has its origins in the Roman feast of Saturnalia, a midwinter celebration of birth, renewal and inversion of the norm. This developed, during the Middle Ages, into the Feast of Fools, in which the pretensions of the Catholic Church were scabrously mocked despite the Church's best efforts to suppress it. These traditions survive in the ethos of Trinidad and Tobago's modern-day Carnival, which both maintains a healthy dose of fight-the-power satirical rebellion and serves as a last bacchanalian binge (carne vale loosely translates as "farewell to flesh") before the fasting period of Lent.

Carnival through the years

Introduced to Trinidad by **French planters** in the late eighteenth century, Carnival was initially the preserve of the white Creole establishment. A comparatively decorous affair, it consisted of masked balls that allowed the gentry a brief fictive escape from the "cares" of power and respectability: the men would dress as "negres jardins" (field labourers), the women as "mulatresses", representing their slaves or their husbands' mulatto mistresses.

African mas

Carnival was also celebrated in semi-secret by slaves on the plantations; after **emancipation** in 1834, free Africans took their own Carnival procession onto the streets in bands, protected by groups of *batonniers* or stick men. Continuing the tradition of inversion, some costumes satirized the affectations and eccentricities of the French Creoles, with men dressing as **Dame Lorraines**: caricatured planters' wives with fancy gowns and exaggerated breasts and buttocks. Other characters – the little demon known as **jab jab** and the stilt-walking **moko jumbie** – drew on West African traditions and folklore. The parade was enlivened by the use of percussion instruments and the introduction of **canboulay**, which celebrated the end of the difficult and dangerous pre-harvest burning of sugar-cane fields by parading through the streets with flaming flambeaux – the name is derived from the French *cannes brûlées*, or burning cane.

Inversion and prohibition

Disapproving of what they saw as the "desecration" of the Sabbath by the first day of Carnival, the British authorities decreed in 1843 that the festivities could not begin until Monday morning. Since no time was specified, carnivalgoers started celebrating on the stroke of midnight, and today's anarchic **Jouvert** parade was born. Many of the masquerades acted out in the street processions took the form of trenchant **satires** of the colonial government, and in 1846 the authorities attempted to prohibit the wearing of masks. Carnival found defenders in unexpected quarters, however: the French planters, keen to defend their own traditions in the face of increasing Anglicization; and the "Free Coloured" middle class, whose desire for respectability kept them aloof from Carnival itself but who saw attempts to control it as an assertion of white domination.

Carnival continued to provide an outlet for irreverence and satire through the nineteenth century, with outrageous parodies of British **sailors** stationed on the island, as well as characters representing underworld archetypes, such as **jamettes** (prostitutes) and transvestite **pissenlets** (literally "wet-the-bed"). Bands organized **drumming** and **kalenda** (stickfighting), none of which went down too well with the colonial administrators from Victorian Britain. In 1877, police chief **Captain Arthur Baker** began a campaign to tame Carnival, but when he attempted to ban the canboulay outright in 1881, the so-called **Canboulay Riots** broke out (commemorated today in a dawn re-enactment on the Friday before Carnival). Undeterred, the authorities went on to prohibit what had become known as "jamette Carnival" on the grounds of its lewdness. African-style drumming was banned in 1884, while canboulay and stickfighting – seen respectively as a fire hazard and an incitement to violence – were outlawed a year later under the **Peace Preservation Act**.

Structure and competition

Carnival was not so easily quashed, though it continued in a more sedate manner. Social protest was channelled into the emerging labour movement, and Carnival became an officially tolerated safety valve for social pressures, with the black middle class joining in. During the 1890s, the festival became increasingly organized and socially acceptable with the introduction of a **competition** for best band, and in 1921, the calypsonian Chieftain Douglas opened the first organized **calypso tent** to preview the songs that would be heard in the forthcoming Carnival.

During **World War II**, Carnival was suspended by the colonial government as a possible threat to public order, and when it returned on VE Day 1945, it marched to the sound of a different beat – the **steel pan**, fashioned from oil drums brought to the island by the US military. As the national independence movement gained momentum, Carnival flourished alongside. Recognizing its importance to Trinidad's cultural identity and sense of nationhood, Eric Williams established the National Carnival Commission in 1957 to organize and promote the festivities, and set up the Calypso King competition.

Bikinis, beads and creative mas

Though parades during the 1970s saw masquerade bands exploring topics such as racism and white control of the economy, and **Peter Minshall**'s fabulous presentations in the 1980s and 1990s took mas to a new creative level (see page 98), Carnival

---

ESSENTIAL CARNIVAL VOCABULARY

Bands These are not musical bands, but an organized group of costumed masqueraders that parade trough the streets on Carnival Monday and Tuesday to the sound of soca blasted from huge music trucks.

Chipping Slow, shuffling dance cum-walk with a rhythm dictated by the music from trucks and steel bands.

Fete A large open-air party or concert held during the run-up to Carnival

Jump up To dance in the parade.

Mas Short for masquerade.

Mas camp The headquarters of Carnival bands, where costumes are made and displayed, and where you can register to play mas (see page 70).

Old mas Traditional Carnival characters such as jab jabs, imps and sailors.

Play mas To join a Carnival band and take part in the costumed parade.

Road march The soca song played the most at the judging points along the Carnival route – the winner gets the coveted road march title for that year.

Rhythm section The classic accompaniment of Jouvert, as well as the "engine room" that drives a steel band, this is a percussion group who "beat iron"– scrapped brake drums from cars or vans played with metal rods alongside cowbells, shakers and anything that can make a rhythm.

Wining The classic hip-wiggling, gyrating Trini dance, which comes in many variations: be prepared to wine, and be wined on, at any point during Carnival.

today is more about fun than politics, satire or social inversion. **"Pretty mas"** bands of revellers decked out in identikit costumes of feathers and beads are now the order of the day, and given the high price tag and exclusive aura of the prevailing all-inclusive mas bands, many now argue that Carnival has turned full circle, with the parades the sole preserve of the rich. Equally, though costume construction has traditionally been highly specialized and skilled, the drive to cut costs means that most bikini mas isn't even made in T&T these days, instead being imported from the Far East. Nonetheless, designers such as **Brian MacFarlane** and **K2K** have brought out contemporary bands with a creative edge, and since 2017 the **Lost Tribe** offshoot of pretty-mas behemoth Tribe has been producing imaginative and inspired costumes. And with smaller outfits continuing to create gorgeous sailor and fancy Indians mas, and the wonderful **Touch D Sky** taking moko jumbie mas to another level, it seems that the unique skills of Trinidad's mas-makers are likely to be continued in future generations.

Carnival today

To the eye of an uneducated onlooker, the two explosive days of the main Carnival parades might appear a chaotic spectacle, but underpinning the whole event is an order and structure that is the culmination of exhaustive preparations. The countdown begins in late summer, when the large mas bands (see page 80) hold **launches** for their Carnival designs. Once Christmas is out of the way, things get serious. The big steel bands open up their yards for visitors to watch practice sessions, calypsonians perform their Carnival compositions in "tents" in Port of Spain and around the country, and each week features a bewildering choice of pre-Carnival **fetes** (see page 91), from raucous affairs featuring foam and powder paint to seriously classy all-inclusives where tickets starting at TT$500 – with the high-end events costing double that.

Kiddies' Carnival to Dimanche Gras

On the Saturday before Carnival weekend, the parades in Port of Spain kick off with the **Red Cross Children's Carnival**, with kids displaying their costumes at the Savannah; the following day, there's a children's parade along Western Main Road in St James. The Sunday sees the popular **Panorama semi-final** at the Savannah, which sees crowds of aficionados descend to watch the bands perform, and is usually a bigger event than the final itself. It's also the day to take in some **traditional mas**, with characters from blue devils to Dame Lorraines, jab jabs and midnight robbers parading from South Quay to Adam Smith Square on the two Sundays preceding Carnival; there are often additional parades too. (Another blue devil parade, which some equate as the highlight of Carnival, takes place on Carnival Monday itself up in Paramin, where wild posses of blue devils take to the streets in the afternoon and continue well into the night.) Sometime in the week preceding the main parades, the finals of the **national stickfighting competition** are staged at the Savannah, with bois-bearing combatants duelling it out to exciting effect.

On the weekend immediately preceding the main Monday and Tuesday parades, "Fantastic Friday" sees a re-creation of the **Canboulay Riots** at 5am in downtown Port of Spain, and the **Soca Monarch** competition in the evening, while on Saturday there's another **Children's Carnival** parade from South Quay to the Savannah, which makes way for the **Panorama** finals later that day. On Sunday evening, the **Dimanche Gras** competition includes the crowning of the **King and Queen of the Bands** and the all-important **Calypso Monarch**.

Jouvert

Carnival officially starts at 4am on the Monday morning with **Jouvert** (see page 71) or dirty mas, when participants dress in macabre or satirical home-made costumes, or join a mud band and smear themselves with mud, grease, body paint or liquid

TEN COMMANDMENTS OF PLAYING MAS

- Get to Trinidad in time to **collect your costume early** and make any necessary adjustments; you can buy supplies at several shops in Port of Spain (see page 91). Listen to the radio, tap into the year's soca on YouTube and go to some fetes so you know all the year's big tunes before you hit the road.
- **Cut your toenails** very short to minimize damage from the pummelling they'll take on the road, and wear quality, well-fitting, worn-in footwear and absorbent sports socks.
- If you're going to wear **tights** with your costume, get them early before shades and sizes run out. Buy two pairs in case of snags, and cut the toes off to avoid damaging your nails. Micles in West Mall and Samaroo's (see page 91) have a good selection.
- Build up your stamina with some **exercise** before the main event; some of the larger mas bands organize pre-Carnival walks and runs.
- Take souvenir selfies before you leave home when everything's looking fresh; on the road, consider taking a basic **mobile handset** rather than your smartphone, cheap sunglasses (designer shades inevitably fall off when you're dancing and get trodden on), and a small and easy-to-carry bag for phone, keys, money etc.
- Eat a good breakfast before setting out, don't skip lunch, and **drink water** throughout the day. Alternate alcoholic drinks with something soft.
- No matter what your skin colour, start Carnival Monday and Tuesday by dousing yourself in factor 50 **sunblock**. Take some with you, and re-apply it regularly. Aerosol sunblock is easier than cream.
- Prearrange how you'll be **getting home** on both days – book a cab, or designate a driver. Try to find out where your band will be finishing to simplify pick-ups.
- Everyone loosens up a bit come Carnival, but don't lose sight of your **common sense**. Stick with your friends, don't accept drinks from strangers, and if you can't find a toilet en route, don't head off alone down dark alleys.
- **Smile** for the cameras, wine, wave, chip and jump – it's Carnival!

chocolate before taking to the streets in an anarchical expression of Carnival's darker side. This wild party lasts into the daylight hours of Monday, and even if you're not playing with a Jouvert band, it's still a good idea to wear old clothes, as revellers delight in getting everyone as dirty as possible. Certainly, it's a time to leave your inhibitions (and your valuables) at home.

The main parades

Once the bacchanal of Jouvert has dispersed, the **Carnival Monday** parade begins by 10am, when the mas bands take to the streets, with masqueraders wearing either parts of their costume, a hotpants/shorts and T-shirt combo or more elaborate "Monday Wear" (these days local designers offer special Monday Wear collections each year), and dancing along to the accompaniment of steel pan bands or monstrous trucks bearing columns of speakers. **Tuesday** is Carnival's big day, kicking off at 7am and with masqueraders dressing in full costume and parading through the streets as loudly and proudly as they can. All bands follow set routes, with judging points along the way where panels of experts (and crowds of spectators) wait to mark those competing for **Band of the Year**. The main "stage" and judging point, where each band struts as much of its stuff as possible, is the Queen's Park Savannah in Port of Spain (and in Tobago, Scarborough's Market Square). Some of the larger, more upmarket bikini bands nowadays forego the Band of the Year title, eschewing the Savannah for "**Socadrome**", an alternative display space in the Jean Pierre Complex on Wrightson Road, which was established in 2014.

Carnival's **las' lap** kicks in at dusk on Carnival Tuesday when everything becomes just a bit more frantic as the last hours of the event are made the most of, with large bands such as Harts and Tribe continuing the party at the Socadrome. As night draws in, Carnival officially ends and the countdown to next year's event begins.

Music

Trinidad and Tobago's music scene is one of the most exciting and influential in the Caribbean, inextricably linked to the annual Carnival celebrations which give the islands' homegrown genres a stage in which to shine. Downtempo, lyrically based calypso (more traditionally known as kaiso) is very much alive thanks largely to the festival's performance "tents" and Calypso Monarch competition, while the fetes – and the parades of Caribbean carnivals throughout the region and the world – reverberate to the faster, more contemporary-sounding soca. And since it was invented by industrious Trinidadians in the early twentieth century, the lilting tinkle of the steel pan has become synonymous with the region.

However, T&T's musical spectrum is a broad church: at Christmas, you'll hear the Spanish guitars and nasal crooning of **parang**, while East Indian festivals such as Hosay and Phagwah take place to the sound of frenetic **tassa** drumming. Jamaican dancehall reggae is extremely popular here, with a host of local artists offering their take on the genre, while **rapso** fuses calypso-style political lyrics, hip-hop beats and distinctly Caribbean basslines. There's also a healthy "alternative" scene, with a slew of great local **rock** bands such as Orange Sky and Jointpop, which blend classic guitar riffs with calypso and reggae.

Calypso to soca

The heart of T&T's music scene and one of its greatest cultural exports, **calypso** represents far more than catchy melodies and witty lyrics. Most older Trinbagonians are expert scholars of the genre, using the most obscure quote to illustrate an argument and singing along to classic compositions without skipping a single nuance. Though calypso is less of a national obsession these days, each crop of compositions is still closely analysed and discussed until the messages become ingrained in the national consciousness. While foreigners often equate the genre with the glib Caribbean clichés of Harry Belafonte's *Day-O (The Banana Boat Song)* or *Island in the Sun*, Trinbagonians see calypso as their most accessible form of **social commentary**. Calypsonians use double entendre and allegory to make points that would get a politician arrested for libel or a pop singer for lewdness, and over the years, their lyrics have addressed every phase of T&T's development, commenting on shifts in society and attitudes towards love, sex, marriage, masculinity, race and religion – not to mention politics.

Calypso has its roots in the songs of praise and derision performed in Africa by travelling troubadours known as **griots**. Slaves on the sugar plantations used song as a means of covert communication as well as a rhythmic accompaniment to their back-breaking work, and their **cariso** – a forerunner of calypso – was also a form of entertainment for the planters; notorious Diego Martin estate owner Pierre Begorrat could be tempered only by the sweet verses of **Gros Jean**, his personal **chantuelle**, as these nascent calypsonians were known. After emancipation, when the chantuelles were finally able to express themselves as free men, they entertained Carnival revellers with insurgent and satirical lyrics. However, the British found their uninhibited displays unsettling and associated calypso with vulgarity and **civil disobedience**, a stigma that remained for many years. Clashes between revellers and colonial officers, as well as objections from the upper classes to "obscenity" in lyrics, led to the prohibition of African drumming in 1884. In the absence of drums, musicians were forced to be inventive, and created the **tamboo bamboo** – tuned sticks of bamboo beaten on the ground – to provide a legal rhythm for their mas and calypso.

Calypso's golden era

Calypso – also known by its Africanized name, **kaiso** – evolved rapidly in the early twentieth century: English replaced French patois, and brass and string instruments took over from the basic rhythms of the tamboo bamboo. Armed with suitably boastful sobriquets, calypsonians such as **Atilla the Hun**, **Growling Tiger**, **Lord Invader**, **Lord Melody** and **Chieftain Douglas** refined their art and turned professional, performing for paying audiences at makeshift venues in downtown Port of Spain known as **tents**. Though veiled in metaphor and double entendre, much of the early material was as risqué and **controversial** as it is today; sex, religion, race and satirical portrayals of public figures were the meat of calypsos that usually included the patois disclaimer "**sans humanité**" – "without mercy".

During the 1930s, calypso also found an overseas audience, largely through the efforts of white appropriators who played a kind of calypso-lite in America's jazz clubs. In Trinidad, calypso gradually gained a level of social acceptance, but the colonial government still had a vested interest in controlling what they perceived to be subversive lyrics, and the 1934 **Theatre and Dance Halls Ordinance** enabled the censorship of so-called "offensive" compositions and the outright prohibition of pieces deemed particularly seditious; in reality, any calypso seen to undermine British rule (or champion black culture) was swiftly banned. Calypsonians were required to submit their compositions for government inspection before public performance, and officers stationed in the tents ensured that songs met with British approval. Unsurprisingly, calypsos from this time (which you'll still hear today) are often anti-colonial and anti-European.

The Yankee dollar

During World War II, calypso got another boost through the support of **American troops** stationed at Chaguaramas. Entertainment-hungry soldiers responded enthusiastically to calypso-based nightclub floorshows and the tents were packed to the rafters, the lyrics now accompanied by sophisticated **brass bands**, and calypso's success overseas undermined British suppression. The genre flourished, though the soldiers' preference for comedy and frivolity over politics or picong (mocking banter, usually completely unintelligible to foreign audiences) led to a trivialization of the lyrics. The brawling, fornicating habits of the soldiers didn't go unnoticed, however, and calypsonians adeptly

---

PARANG

Created by the combined influences of Spanish missionaries and Venezuelan cocoa workers, the Christmas-time sound of **parang** is one of the last vestiges of Spanish influence in Trinidad. During the season, which starts in October and ends with Epiphany (Jan 6), *parranderos* perform *aguinaldos*, sentimental Spanish songs accompanied by rapid, Mediterranean-style strums on guitars and four-stringed mandolins and cuatros, with violin, box bass, tambourines, maracas and other percussion instruments providing backup. Traditionally, *parranderos* went from house to house during the festive season, but these days most performances take place in bars and clubs.

Parang's Spanish lyrics can be romantic or humorous, though many are devoted to religious themes such as the exploits of saints and the birth of Jesus. Whatever the lyric, the music is always infused with a sense of joyous **celebration**, and the festivities are enhanced by the consumption of Spanish-derived dishes such as pastelles, arepas and strong draughts of rum or poncha creme, a rum-laced eggnog.

Though the parang tradition has waned a little in recent years, it still remains strong in communities dominated by people of Spanish and Amerindian ancestry, such as Paramin, Lopinot, Santa Cruz, San Raphael and St Joseph; and if you visit T&T around Christmas, you'll hear plenty of parang and the more contemporary soca-parang on the radio.

documented the morally bereft Port of Spain society during American occupation. An infamously cynical take on the American presence, Lord Invader's *Rum and Coca-Cola* (see page 95) was one of the best of these biting commentaries; ironically, a cover version by the Andrews Sisters sold five million copies in the US, though Maxine Andrews later commented that none of the sisters gave a moment's thought to the lyrics, which just "went over our heads". Denied a share of the profits, Invader successfully sued.

Dominated by **Mighty Sparrow** and the inimitable late **Lord Kitchener**, calypso grew in popularity throughout the 1950s and 1960s. Tourists descended on T&T to experience this latest craze first-hand and the tents went from strength to strength, with new venues springing up each year. In 1956, Dr Eric Williams' newly elected PNM government created the **Calypso King** competition, and Sparrow swept to victory with the classic *Jean and Dinah*, which gloried in the fact that local women would have to fall back on Trini men now that US soldiers had departed. Crowned monarch so many times that he was eventually barred from competition and given the special title of "Calypso King of the World", Sparrow continued to overshadow his competitors, and calypso lyrics settled into two strands: political praise or picong, and salacious references to love and sex.

Soca on the rise

Though independence in 1962 prompted a slew of calypsos infused with optimism, the late 1960s saw militant lyricists such as **Valentino**, **Black Stalin** and **Mighty Chalkdust** delivering incisive commentaries on post-colonial society. But despite some innovations – **Calypso Rose** became the first female "king" in 1978, and the competition was renamed **Calypso Monarch** – the 1970s turned out to be a decade of stagnation for calypso. As the anti-establishment, pro-black themes of Jamaican roots reggae held sway over Caribbean musical tastes and sensibilities, calypso lyrics sank to an all-time low of banality. From the early 1980s onwards, **soca** (see page 267) began to overshadow its parent during Carnival season, its more danceable style proving irresistible to revellers, but calypso returned to its roots in the middle of the decade via the sensitive, thoughtful work of **David Rudder**, who in 1986 secured an unheard-of triple victory in the Young King, Calypso Monarch and Road March competitions with his beautiful *Bahia Girl*.

Calypso today

Calypso chugged on through the 1990s and into the new millennium, with the Dimanche Gras performances of artists such as **Shadow**, **Singing Sandra**, **Sugar Aloes** and **Gypsy** becoming increasingly extravagant, with props and costumes that make each delivery into a piece of mini theatre. In 2010, **Kurt Allen** caused a sensation by singing his winning composition *Too Bright* dressed as a vagrant and surrounded by a full set that re-created Woodford Square; his lyrics, meanwhile – a scathing criticism of the incumbent PNM government and the opposition – marked a return to the glory days of the genre. Female calypsonians such as **Karen Ashe**, who took the monarch title 2011, are also making their mark, while stalwarts of the genre are still making some great music, as demonstrated by **Chalkdust**'s 2017 win with *75 Can't Go Into 12*. Thanks to each year's fantastic performances in the Junior Calypso Monarch competition, the future of calypso seems a lot brighter these days.

The adult Monarch competition, meanwhile, is still underpinned by the **tents** (see page 34), where an older crowd of enthusiasts disentangle the metaphors and squeal at jokes that are often unintelligible without a good knowledge of Trinbago affairs and gossip. Most calypsonians concentrate on two numbers during the season, usually one with a political slant and another with a more light-hearted theme, be it picong or sex; whether they get to perform them both is up to the audience – after the first few verses, each artist leaves the stage, returning only if the claps and catcalls are deemed loud enough to bring them back on. These days, the most established tents have a permanent location and a roster of well-known artists supplemented by the year's crop of promising newcomers; line-ups change annually.

Soca

Most attribute the birth of **soca** to the great calypsonian **Lord Shorty** (later known as Ras Shorty I after he converted to Rastafarianism), who died in 2000. Distressed at the moribund state of 1970s calypso, he made a conscious decision to breathe new life into the genre. The Indian instrumentation and souped-up rhythmic structure of what he called **sokah** was an infinitely more danceable form that fitted right in with the disco craze, and when he unveiled his song *Indrani* in 1973, it took T&T by storm.

Since Blue Boy's *Soca Baptist* became the Road March (the most heavily played tune as mas bands pass judging points on the Carnival route) of 1980, soca has dominated Carnival and become the music of choice among a nation of professional feters, sustained by some four hundred new releases per year. From November or December onwards, soca artists put out their new material; by the time they perform them at the Carnival fetes, everyone knows the year's crop of music well, waving their rags when commanded or launching into the dances that accompany some of the most popular songs.

In 1993, the soca/calypso dichotomy was officially recognized when a separate **Soca Monarch** competition was set up. For many years, the Soca Monarch show on Fantastic Friday represented the climax of the soca madness that envelops pre-Carnival Trinidad, drawing huge flag-waving crowds, with competitors using pyrotechnics and ever more elaborate sets in extravagant and electric performances. The early years were dominated by **Super Blue**, who returned to become a joint winner (alongside soca superstar Machel Montano) of the Power Soca section in 2013 with *Fantastic Friday*; his daughter, **Fay-Ann Lyons**, became the first female Soca Monarch in 2009. Other notable Power Soca champions include Lyons' husband, **Bunji Garlin**, the ever-present **Iwer George**, and above all, **Machel Montano**, who won for five years running between 2011 and 2015. However, recent years have seen Bunji, Fay-Ann and Machel opt out of competing in Soca Monarch, and as a result the show has become a bit of a marathon, featuring endless hours of mediocre acts and drawing far smaller crowds. Nonetheless, recent winners such as sweet-singing crooner **The Voice** have been allowed to shine, while the **Groovy Soca** category, a slightly slower and more mellow affair, still sees strong performances from the likes of **Olatunji** and **Kerwin Du Bois**.

Otherwise, the soca scene's biggest star is still Machel Montano. Having shot to fame in 1986 with *Too Young to Soca* while still in primary school, Machel (now self-styled as The Monk) went on to form the band **Xtatic**, a conglomeration of artists within which he was always the most prominent. Machel still dominates the T&T soca scene, claiming most of the **Road March** titles in recent years and establishing his hugely popular Machel Monday show as an essential date in the Carnival feting calendar. He has also found some international success, often via collaborations with a range of artists from Doug E Fresh to Angela Hunte, and dancehall stars Beenie Man, Vybes Kartel and Shaggy.

Other names to look out for include Machel's former protégé **Patrice Roberts**; **Destra Garcia** (one of the genre's few enduring female artists); ladies' favourites **Kes the Band** and **Benjai**; the ever-reliable **Shal Marshall** and **Blaxx**; and **Maximus Dan**, who made a sensational return to the scene in 2017 as MX Prime, voicing the **Ultimate Rejects'** enduringly popular Road March smash *Full Extreme*. Soca's big names also include a strong contingent from other Caribbean islands, such as **Skinny Fabulous** from St Vincent, or **Mr Killa** and **Talpree** from Grenada; Barbados has produced many soca legends, too, from **Rupee** to **Alison Hinds**. **Arrow**, the man behind the world's most overplayed soca hit *Hot, Hot, Hot*, actually hails from Montserrat.

Chutney soca

With sparse, fast soca-style beats mixed with sitars, thumping *dholak* drums and vocals that lean heavily on traditional Indian singing styles, **chutney** is a contemporary take on classical Indian music and *filmi* movie songs. Sung in a mixture of Hindi and English, lyrics tend towards the light-hearted (often with a good dollop of sentimentality), while chutney fetes have become a showcase for sensual dance steps that combine athletic wining with the delicate arm and hand movements of classical Indian dance. However, many older Hindus dislike chutney, finding the overtly sexual dancing and sometimes risqué lyrics distasteful.

Established in 1996, the **National Chutney Soca Monarch** competition is the annual focus for chutney artists, and the finals (usually held at Skinner Park in San Fernando) now attract up to 20,000 enthusiasts. Classic chutney performers include the wonderful **Drupatee Ramgoonai**, **Sonny Mann** and the late **Sundar Popo**, while contemporary big-name acts include the smooth **Rikki Jai** (multiple winner of the Chutney Monarch competition) and **Ravi B**, a chief proponent of the so-called "rum songs" that the genre has become known for in recent years. Today, chutney is by no means the preserve of the East Indian community alone; big chutney acts regularly headline at Carnival fetes, while many black Trinidadian stars, from Machel Montano to Olatunji, employ chutney-style instrumentation in their music.

Steel pan

Said to be the only new acoustic instrument invented in the twentieth century, the **steel pan** evolved from the Trinbagonian talent for using readily available materials as percussion instruments. During the Carnivals of the 1930s, tamboo bamboo-led kalinda music was supplied by bands of young men from deprived areas such as Port of Spain's Laventille and Belmont, who were unanimously viewed as "bad johns" or thugs by the more fortunate. With names such as Desperadoes and Invaders, these loosely organized bands supplemented the tamboo with **rhythm sections**, beating steel rods against anything from brake drums and buckets to dustbin lids to create a danceable beat. It was only a matter of time before someone realized that discarded saucepans or biscuit tins – and later the oil drums brought over by US troops – could be hammered into concave sections that produced rough notes; these early raw materials explain why steel drums are known as **pans**. The first pan was played at some point in the late 1930s by either – depending upon who you believe – **Winston "Spree" Simon** of the John John band (now Carib Tokyo), who tapped out *Mary Had a Little Lamb*, or **Neville Jules** of Hell Yard (now Trinidad All Stars) who managed the basic chords of a calypso called *Whoopsin, Whoopsin*.

By the end of the war, experimentation had produced basic pans with up to fourteen notes, and the 1946 Carnival was dominated by the ringing of steel bands. However, the associations of **violence** lingered, and the panyards that sprang up throughout the East–West Corridor were widely viewed – probably quite correctly – as seething dens of iniquity. Feuds were common, and in 1950 a bloody pitched battle between Invaders and Tokyo had Carnival revellers running for cover. Calypsonian Blakie documented the clash: "It was bacchanal/Fifty Carnival/Fight for so, with Invaders and Tokyo/When the two bands clash/Mamayo, if yuh see cutlass/Never me again/To jump in a steelband in Port of Spain."

Steel pan gets organized

Soon after the clash between Invaders and Tokyo, the violence tailed off and the movement gained respectability (and respect) as the music became more polished and complex. Soon, bands of up to 200 pannists were playing a sophisticated repertoire of classical pieces as well as calypso, and the nation's dedication to pan began in earnest. In 1950, the **T&T Steelband Association** (now **Pan Trinbago**; ⊕pantrinbago. co.tt) was established to promote and coordinate the movement, setting up a round of competitions that eventually led to the first annual **Panorama** tournament in 1963; twenty-odd years later, the steel pan was officially declared the national instrument.

These days, Panorama is a hugely popular affair that involves almost all of T&T's steel bands and attracts big crowds to its semi-finals and finals, held at Port of Spain's Queen's Park Savannah. To qualify for the event, bands must get through the preliminary stage, with judges visiting panyards in the various **regional zones**. Those that qualify take part in the semi-finals at the Savannah, and the final list battle it out on the Saturday before the main parade.

The steel band

Transforming an oil drum into a shiny, playable **steel pan** demands skill and experience. All pans other than the bass must first be **cut** to size, and a 5lb sledgehammer is used to beat the unopened end into a convex shape. The pan is then **heated** over a wood fire; oil is used to **temper** the metal, and a coating of **chrome** gives a better surface and a shiny finish. The **tuner** then takes over, marking the notes and beating them out with a hammer and chisel, an extremely specialized process that's usually achieved with the help of a keyboard. A finished chrome-coated tenor pan will sell for as much as US$1500, powder-coated versions around US$800.

In contemporary bands, different types of pan produce a variation of tones. The main melody is held by the **tenor** (or soprano) pan, which has the largest range of notes. **Guitar** and **cello pans** provide the background harmonies, and the booming **bass pan** underpins it all. Most contemporary bands are comprised of between fifty and two hundred volunteer pannists, who play one or two harmonic pans; with up to six instruments, bass pannists have to be pretty dextrous, twisting around to reach the right notes. And no steel band would be complete without its rhythm section or **engine room**, as the percussion section is known. In addition to a conventional drum kit, cowbells, shakers and scrapers, there is the **iron**: assorted bits of metal beaten with iron rods.

Each band is led by an **arranger**, who will adapt music from a variety of sources for the steel band. Though some arrangers work with more than one band, there are several long-standing relationships, such as Len "Boogsie" Sharp with Phase II Pan Groove or Pelham Goddard with Exodus. Though most bands used to play it safe and enter Panorama with calypsos familiar to audience and judges alike, many now enter original compositions, or even adapt recent pop hits.

Reggae

As in the rest of the Caribbean, **reggae** has made massive inroads in Trinidad and Tobago, and at Carnival time you'll even see the current hottest acts from Jamaica gracing the stage at soca fetes, especially as guest performers in Machel Montano's sets. There's also a lively **local reggae** scene, with artists such as **Marlon Asher, Prophet Benjamin** and **King David** leading the way, while local DJ families such as **Matsimela** play regularly at parties and clubs. Reggae has also lent its influence to soca, with many artists employing Jamaican vocal styles (and language and accent), while soca rhythms have become increasingly intertwined with **dancehall** from Jamaica; indeed, Jamaican artists usually release songs voiced on the most popular soca rhythm tracks of the year, either solo or in collaboration with Trini vocalists.

Rapso

A fusion of African-style drumbeats, soca melodies and spoken calypso-esque vocals infused with the militancy of 1990s hip-hop, **rapso** is a highly politicized genre that, while it has its followers, has always retained something of an underground feel. The genre's originator is generally considered to be **Lancelot "Kebu" Layne**, who released *Blow Away* in 1970 and *Get Off My Radio* in 1971. In 1976, "Mother of Rapso" **Cheryl Byron** became the first rapso artist to perform in a calypso tent, while **Brother Resistance** emerged as the "Father of Rapso" in the 1980s, and has become something of a spokesman for the genre, famously describing it as "the power of the word in the rhythm of the word". Rapso's popularity increased in the 1990s with the emergence of a host of new artists, though stalwarts such as Resistance, **Ataklan** and **3Canal** remain the movement's most popular proponents, fusing poetic, haunting lyrics that centre upon black empowerment and resistance to oppression with stinging, drum- and bass-dominated rhythms.

Ecology and wildlife

Joined to the South American mainland during the Ice Age when sea levels were lower, Trinidad and Tobago only became separate entities when movements of the Caribbean tectonic plates submerged the Orinoco Delta some 10,000 years ago. The islands owe their immense environmental diversity to this period of attachment, which has left them with many South American plants, animals and birds alongside the flora and fauna found elsewhere in the Caribbean. Few places of relative size harbour such variety.

A wide range of **habitats** support T&T's wildlife; **Tobago** boasts the oldest protected rainforest in the western hemisphere along its main ridge of mountains, as well as marshes and lagoons in its southwestern tip, a network of thriving offshore reefs and the bird sanctuaries of Little Tobago and the St Giles islands. In **Trinidad**, the rich wetlands at Nariva Swamp are home to several plant and animal species found nowhere else in T&T, while Caroni Swamp offers easy access to mangroves and their inhabitants. The dry, treeless prairie at Aripo – the island's only remaining true savanna plain – sustains unusual plants and orchids as well as birdlife. Trinidad's hills are afforded some government protection, and contain three state reserves: the Northern Range Sanctuary, the Valencia Wildlife Sanctuary in the northeast and the Trinity Hills Wildlife Sanctuary in the southeast. However, there are only a handful of game wardens and rangers to defend the forests, and with quarrying and industry constantly encroaching on virgin land, the island's wildlife is under constant threat. For more on the challenges faced by local environmentalists, check out Environment Tobago (ⓦenvironmenttobago. net), Papa Bois Conservation (ⓦbit.ly/PapaBoisTT), Fishermen and Friends of the Sea (ⓦffostt.com) and the Trinidad and Tobago Field Naturalists' Club (ⓦttfnc.org).

Trees and shrubs

Although T&T's **woodlands** are disappearing at a significant rate, they still make up around 40 percent of the country's total land area. The various forest types include littoral woodland, deciduous seasonal woodland, rainforest and swamp forests; higher elevations see **montane** forest – wet and cool with plenty of epiphytic growth – while the stubby 2m canopy of **elfin** forest occupies only the highest mountain peaks.

About **350 species** of tree grow in T&T, including the exotically named pink bark, gustacare, crapaud, saltfishwood, sardine, purpleheart, bloodwood, hairy cutlet and the naked Indian, which gets its somewhat politically incorrect name from its peeling brown bark. Forests are mostly made up of **mora**, **teak**, **mahogany**, **cedar**, **cypress**, **Caribbean pine** and **balata**; the latter produces a milky latex used to coat golf balls. Immediately noticeable, the **bois cano** has large, deeply lobed leaves that dry into a distinctive claw shape; and the mighty 40m **silk cotton** or kapok tree (its fruits contain the cotton-like kapok) boasts an impressive girth of buttressed roots spreading elegantly to meet the ground – Amerindians used entire trees for their dugout pirogues. With its spectacular spreading branches, **samaan** are often planted as shade trees, while the **banyan** looks more like a collection of interweaved vines than a tree, as its boughs produce aerial roots that form secondary trunks when they reach the ground. The **tree fern**'s diamond-patterned trunk and top-heavy crown of fern-like leaves lend a primeval aspect to high altitude forests.

Ornamental trees

A host of **ornamental** trees turn T&T's forests into a patchwork of colour during the dry months (roughly Dec–May), when the intense orange-red flowers of the mountain

immortelle compete with two varieties of **poui**, which shed their leaves to make way for cascades of dusky-pink or bright yellow blossoms. The **cassia** also produces prolific cascades of deep yellow or pink. Covering a flat, wide-spreading crown, the deep red **flamboyant** or poinciana blooms in August as well as April; during the dry season, half-metre pods full of rattling seeds dangle from the leafless branches.

Flowering sporadically throughout the year, the 15m **African tulip** or "flame of the forest" produces clusters of deep red blooms along outer branches; unopened buds in the centre of the flower are sometimes used as natural water pistols, as they contain a pouch of water which spurts out at speed when pressure is applied. Creating patches of mauve throughout Trinidad's forests, the crown of the **crepe myrtle** is usually smothered with blooms, while **bauhinia** or orchid tree and **jacaranda** add to the purple hues.

Fruit trees

Among the huge variety of **fruit trees**, the most easily recognizable are the many varieties of **mango**, with their rounded, dense crown of long, leathery leaves over a short trunk. **Banana** plants are not trees in the strict botanical sense; their huge, tattered leaves grow from a central stem of overlapping leaf bases. Covered by large purple bracts, the flowers hang from the main stem and eventually develop into fruit. Stands of **plantain** are similar, with larger, less tattered leaves and bigger, more robust fruit. Equally easy to recognize, **pawpaw** (papaya) has a long hollow stem with large splayed leaves and fruit growing out from the top of the trunk.

Still grown in groves for export and local chocolate production (see page 238), **cocoa** is easily identifiable by its lichen-smothered trunk and dark green shiny leaves; the 20cm ridged oval pods grow from the trunk and turn from light green to brown, yellow, orange or purple when ripe. Covered with a sweet white gloop, the beans inside can be sucked when raw, but must be fermented, dried and roasted to produce cocoa powder. **Cashew** trees, with their strongly veined oval leaves, are common; the familiar nut pokes out of the bottom of a sweet-tasting, pear-shaped red fruit, whose shell produces an oily liquid that is a skin irritant.

The lifeblood of many a craft vendor, the fruits of the **calabash** tree grow to more than 35cm in diameter and are hollowed out and made into bowls, bags and all manner of souvenirs. Employed as a vegetable but classified as a fruit, **breadfruit** was brought to the Caribbean by Captain Bligh aboard the HMS *Providence* as food for plantation slaves, and is common throughout T&T. With spreading branches decorated by large serrated leaves, the spherical fruits are lime-green and pockmarked. Its close cousin is the chataigne or **breadnut**, a similar tree with smaller, spiky fruits that are eaten roasted.

PALM COUNTRY

Commercial plantations on both islands have made the **coconut** T&T's most prevalent palm. It's an incredibly versatile tree; the water and meat are consumed fresh at the jelly stage, while the flesh of older coconuts is grated and used in baking or immersed in water and strained to produce the coconut milk that flavours a thousand local dishes. Coconut oil is used in soap, cosmetics and cooking; the leaf fronds thatch roofs and make hats or floor mats; the husks are used to make floor buffers; and pieces of hard shell are made into jewellery and cups.

Of the many ornamental varieties, the 30m **royal palm** is a graceful specimen with a grey, ruler-straight trunk; it's often used to mark out driveways. Similar but even taller at an average of 40m, the **cabbage** palm has thicker, messier looking fronds, while the squat, spiky-leafed **cocorite** is one of the most common forest species. The ultimate in tropical splendour, the **traveller's palm** is actually a member of the banana family – the name refers to mini-ponds at the base of the trunk that provide a convenient water source. Fronds fan out from the base in an enormous peacock's tail shape as high as 10m.

Coastal trees and palms

Trinidad's swamps of red, black and white **mangrove** trees, with their dense tangle of aerial roots, help protect coastal communities from storm surges, filter sediments that smother reefs and provide a nursery for fish and crustaceans. Common seashore plants include the wide-spreading **Indian almond** and **sea grape**, both with broad, deep-veined leaves that turn a pretty deep red as they mature. Definitely one to avoid, the **manchineel** tree grows to about 15m with a wide spreading canopy, yellow flowers and apple-like green fruits. All parts of the tree are extremely **poisonous**: even standing below a manchineel during rain incurs blistering from washed-down sap; those in oft-visited stretches of coastline sometimes have an identifying warning plaque or stripe of white paint around the trunk.

Plants and flowers

Of T&T's various **wild plants**, the **jumbie bead vine** produces distinctive red and black seeds used in craft items and as good luck charms; they are said to ward off evil spirits, and a bead kept in a purse will keep it filled with money. A variety of mimosa with scratchy stems, **ti Marie** is known as "the sensitive plant" for its ability to curl back its leaves at the slightest touch; you'll see patches of it on lawns throughout the islands.

The largest of the epiphytes that grow along tree branches, electricity wires and any available surface is the **wild pine bromeliad**, a spiky-leafed relative of the pineapple that produces a battered-looking red flower. These "air plants" are not parasites – they draw their nutrients from the humid, mineral-rich atmosphere – but water reserves trapped between the leaves (which provide a habitat for insects and frogs) can mean that smothered tree limbs sometimes collapse under their weight. Other epiphytes include 200 different species of **orchids**, which grow on living or dead plant or tree matter and in lowland savannas such as Aripo in eastern Trinidad. In the lowland forests, distinctive epiphytes include the **monkey throat**, whose flower is a perfect primate facsimile, and the pendulous **jackspaniard**, with its trailing wasp-like petals; the common **lamb's tail** grows horizontally from large trees, and has attractive maroon-flecked green petals with a white and pink stamen.

T&T's 2300-odd varieties of **flowering plant** provide beds, borders and hedges with a splash of colour, and you'll often see several varieties of multicoloured **croton** leaves in between the blooms. The national flower is the **chaconia**, a spectacular crimson poinsettia which you'll see throughout the forests, but the ubiquitous **bougainvillea** is the most common ornamental, its red, white, orange, purple and pink papery bracts spilling out into intensely coloured clumps. Distinguishable by its protruding pollen-tipped stamen, **hibiscus** takes on an abundance of hues and shapes – the lacy **coral** variety has clusters of tiny curling red petals and a red frill at the end of the stamen. A dark-leafed shrub with clusters of small red flowers, **ixora** is another popular ornamental that flowers throughout the year.

Flamboyant **tropical flowers** are grown commercially in T&T and also flourish in the wild. Brush-like **ginger lilies** are one of the most common exotics; the deep pink or red bracts hide the insignificant true flower, and the shiny, banana-like leaves are used in florists' arrangements. A close relative, the **torch ginger**'s deep crimson cluster of thick waxy petals makes an impressively showy head. However, the queen of local exotics – and the symbol of the PNM political party – are the forty vividly coloured varieties of **balisier**, all members of the heliconia family, which include the aptly named **lobster claw** and the red, yellow and green **hanging heliconia**, which looks like a series of fish hanging from a rod. Equally prevalent are the artificial-looking **anthuriums**, a shiny, heart-shaped red, pink or white bract with a long penile stem or spadix protruding from the centre. The flashy **bird of paradise**, a blue and purple flower that resembles a bird's head graced by a deep orange crest, is rarer.

Wildlife

With more than 100 species of **mammal** roaming the forests and flats (not including T&T's ubiquitous 50,000-plus goats) hunting has long been a popular pastime and wild meat is consumed with gusto whenever available, with little thought to the devastating effect on animal populations. Most hunters go after the most common animals; the smallest quarry is the herbivorous **agouti**, a rabbit-sized brown rodent that looks like a long-legged guinea pig and feeds on fruits and leaves; and its larger relative the **lappe** or **paca**, which has longer legs and a pattern of stripes and spots on its fur. Equally desirable for the pot is the **manicou** or **opossum**, an unattractive cat-sized marsupial with a rat-like tail and a long snout that forages for scraps and carrion. The nine-banded **tattoo** (armadillo) is increasingly rare, as is the brown-coloured **red brocket deer** (extinct in Tobago) and the **quenk**, an aggressive wild hog. Another threatened species, the metre-long **ocelot** wildcat has been extensively hunted for its beautiful spotted pelt.

Otters live in and around the Madamas and Paria rivers in Trinidad, but shy away from humans. Trinidad's cutest water-dwelling mammal, the herbivorous West Indian **manatee** or sea cow, grows up to 4m long and can live for fifty years. However, the destruction of its swampland habitat by development and by drainage for agriculture has decimated local populations, with around forty still living in the protected Nariva Swamp.

The islands' largest **monkey** colonies also live in Nariva; with red-furred, hulking frames and a bulbous, bearded larynx, troops of up to fifteen **red howlers** defend their territory with the eerie, deafening roars that prompted their name. Smaller **weeping capuchins** live in the tree-tops in troops of up to twenty, and are able to use basic tools to crack open nuts and occasionally express their irritation at human intrusions by raining down a volley of sticks on curious heads. Around seventy species of **bat** inhabit T&T's forests and caves, most living on a diet of insects, fruit, nectar and pollen. The two notable exceptions are the vampire bat, which prefers a more gruesome food source, creeping up on sleeping livestock and drinking their blood; and the frog-eating bat, which distinguishes between poisonous and edible species by listening to mating calls.

Reptiles and amphibians

The largest of the seventy species of **reptile** is an endemic sub-species of the **spectacled caiman**, a 3m alligator with an elongated snout that inhabits swamps, rivers and dams, and feeds on fish and birds. Among the 47 different types of **snake**, only four are venomous. With the girth of a man's arm and a length of up to 3m, the **fer-de-lance** is particularly aggressive, and is identifiable by its pointed head, yellow underside and chin, and orange-brown triangular markings. The **bushmaster** is slightly longer (up to 4m) with a burnt-orange skin distinctly patterned by dark brown diamonds, with smaller diamonds of orange within. Its venom can be lethal to the young, old or infirm, but deaths are incredibly rare and most bites afflict farmers working habitually in the bush; all hospitals carry antivenin. Both snakes are known as mapepire (pronounced "*mah*-pee-pee") and inhabit forest areas. The two varieties of poisonous **coral snake**, the common and large coral snake, are smaller, rarer and less aggressive; they're easy to spot, with black skin and red and white rings around the body. Known as macajuel (pronounced *makka*-well), **boa constrictors** – including anacondas – are T&T's largest snakes, and can grow up to 10m in length. Most are patterned with brown diamonds that provide camouflage. They are not venomous, but can easily crush a small mammal in their powerful coils.

Among more than twenty species of lizard are **gecko**, usually referred to as zandolie or ground lizards. The **twenty-four-hour lizard** gets its name from a local myth which warns that if you disturb one, it will attach itself to your body and remain there for 24 hours – at the end of which you die. The bright green, spiky-backed, herbivorous

iguana is a favourite quarry of hunters, especially if it's carrying eggs; unsurprisingly, it spends most of its time hiding from human captors in leafy tree-tops. The metre-long, dark brown **matte lizard** relies on speed to stay out of the cooking pot, raising itself onto its hind legs to accelerate to 11kph in two seconds.

T&T's most common **amphibian** is the crapaud (pronounced "crappo"), a warty, hand-sized toad with a loud, booming croak. The colostethus is a frog that provides a night-time chorus reminiscent of a demented guinea pig. Trinidad's only endemic species, the **golden tree frog**, lives in epiphytic plants that cling to the rainforest trees of the island's two highest mountains, El Tucuche and El Cerro del Aripo. In addition to the land turtle or morrocoy, five species of **sea turtle** lay their eggs on T&T's beaches: the green turtle, the olive ridley, the hawksbill, the loggerhead and the giant leatherback (see page 142).

Birds

With more than 485 types of **birds** recorded on the islands, Trinidad and Tobago ranks among the world's top ten in terms of numbers of species per square mile, and offers some of the best birdwatching in the Caribbean. The national birds are the scarlet ibis (Trinidad) and the cocrico (Tobago), both of which adorn the republic's coat of arms. A native of Venezuela and best seen at the Caroni Swamp, and resplendent with deep crimson plumage, the **scarlet ibis** typifies the eye-catching colours of local species, while the golden-brown, pheasant-like **cocrico** has a fleshy, bright red turkey-style wattle at its throat and a raucous, incredibly loud call that echoes through Tobago's hills in the pre-dawn hours.

The sugar-water feeders at most hotels are a great way to see smaller birds at close quarters. Seventeen species of brightly coloured **hummingbirds** have been recorded in T&T, of which the most frequently seen are the copper-rumped and white-necked jacobin varieties, both with fabulous iridescent feathers. The most unusual hummer is the 6cm **tufted coquette**, Trinidad's smallest bird and the third smallest in the world, with a red and yellow body, dark wings and a beautiful deep orange crest. Look out too for the stunning **ruby-topaz**; males boast deep orange tailfeathers and a bright red swathe on the head.

OILBIRDS

Squat, mottled-brown and whiskered, **oilbirds** have the honour of being the world's only nocturnal fruit-eating birds, and Trinidad supports eight breeding colonies. Spending the daylight hours inside the caves in which they nest, oilbirds are unusually gregarious; up to forty will huddle on a single ledge, squawking and picking through each other's feathers for parasites. Mature birds venture into the open only at night, using **sonar** to assist their manoeuvres through the forests in search of palm, laurel and camphor fruits, and often travelling as far as 120km from the colony in each foray. Fruits are swallowed whole and the seeds regurgitated, and their in-flight consumption is an important agent of reforestation.

Oilbirds rear one brood of **young** each year, laying between two and four eggs over several days in nests constructed from regurgitated, cement-like matter that rapidly turns the snowy-white clutch a dirty brown. The parents share the 32-day incubation between them, after which the blind, featherless fledglings emerge, remaining immobile for up to three weeks and feeding on partially digested fruit pulp. Development is slow: a patchy cover of downy feathers grows after 21 days, and young birds don't fledge until they are 100 to 120 days old.

A young oilbird weighs twice as much as a mature one, due to the high fat content that gave rise to its name. Amerindians and Capuchin monks used to boil the fledglings down for their **oil**, which they then used to fuel cooking fires and make flambeaux; Amerindians also called the oilbird *guacharo*, "the one who wails and mourns", on account of the rasps, screams, squawks and snarls that make up its call – an eerie sound that also inspired the bird's French patois sobriquet, *diablotin* (devil bird).

Both jet-black, the blunt-beaked **smooth-billed ani** and the **shiny cowbird**, with a sharper beak and beady yellow eyes, are the local equivalent of pigeons. The audacious 10cm black-and-yellow **bananaquit** is supposed to subsist on nectar, but has become a frequent visitor to hotel breakfast tables, dipping its sharp little beak into fruits and sugar bowls. Seen wherever there are cattle, white **egrets** roost on ruminating rumps in a mutually rewarding relationship that provides the egret with a constant supply of insects and the cow some relief from bloodsuckers.

In the forests and flats, distinctive birds include: **white-bearded manakins**, which are one of several species of bird in Trinidad that perform intricate courtship displays in designated areas known as leks; and intensely coloured **woodpeckers**, **antbirds**, **trogons** and **tanagers** – the palm tanager is a cool olive with black flecks on its wings, while the bay-headed variety is a brilliant emerald with a russet head. Various **honeycreepers** display dazzling hues of turquoise and black; the purple variety's near-black feathers only show their true colours in the sunshine.

Of larger birds, common varieties include multicoloured **toucans**, **parrots**, **yellow orioles** and the crow-like **crested oropendola**, black with a yellow tail, cream beak, beady blue eyes, a truly exotic call and a marvellous way of building nests: metre-long, teardrop-shaped constructions of dry grass that hang in groups from tree boughs. Though it can be hard to spot the **bearded bellbird**, you'll certainly hear its penetrating "bok, bok" call in the hill forests. Birds of prey include the **peregrine falcon**, as well as several kites and hawks, including the **ornate hawk-eagle**, the largest of the lot. The ubiquitous **vultures** – locally known as corbeaux – perform a necessary function by devouring dead animals.

Tobago sustains a few species not seen regularly in Trinidad, such as the **red-crowned woodpecker**, **rufous-tailed jacamar** and the **white-tailed sabre-wing**. The smaller island is also the best place to see **blue-crowned mot-mots** (locally called king of the woods), with deep orange breasts, green-blue heads and long flowing tail feathers. Offshore of both islands, **boobies** and **brown pelicans** trawl for fish, the latter diving from great heights into the sea and scooping up its quarry in its large pouched bill. However, if a **frigate bird** is around, smaller sea birds often lose their catch, as the frigate feeds on stolen goods snatched from the beak of more efficient fishers.

Insects and spiders

With 92 varieties of **mosquito** in T&T, and far too many kinds of **cockroach** (ranging from 7cm dark brown beasts to the rare albino variety), you could be forgiven for doing your best to stay well away from the country's invertebrate life, but many species are vital to the local ecosystems. More than 600 varieties of **butterfly** flit between local flowers, ranging from the 2cm crimson-and-black red devil to the commonly seen 7cm, bright blue morpho or emperor and the cocoa mort bleu, which is brown and mauve with eye-like spots on the wings.

Armies of black, brown or red bachac or **leaf-cutting ants**, with almost triangular heads and sharp, sizeable pincers, are divided into ranks. Large workers trim entire shrubs into coin-sized pieces and carry them on their backs to the nest, while smaller workers fend off any potential predators; the leaf-pieces are then shredded and chewed into compost for the cultivation of the fungus that feeds the colony. A single nest may discard as much as 20 cubic metres of waste material in five years, banking it up over the subterranean colony, which houses up to 2.5 million ants. Living in equally complex societies that can number one billion per colony, **termites** attach their large, irregular earthen nests to the sides of trees.

Aside from the spindly-limbed specimens that you'll see indoors, the largest common spiders are black and red **orb-web spinners**, about 8cm long including the legs, and which spin the classic hexagonal web. More unusual is the **trapdoor spider**, which conceals its forest-floor burrow with a hinged doorway, springing out to drag in passing prey. Ten species of **tarantula** range from a delicately hued violet and brown to hairy

---

ATTACK OF THE LIONFISH

The waters around T&T have seen an influx of the orange-and-white-striped **lionfish** in recent years, an invasive species with spectacular venomous spines that has made its way along the Caribbean chain from the south Atlantic, probably after being released from private aquariums. Voracious eaters with no natural predators in Caribbean waters, lionfish spawn every three days and have had a devastating effect on the marine environment here, drastically reducing numbers of tropical reef fish such as parrot and snapper. Efforts are underway to control the population, with local divers coordinating culls and educating fishermen about how delicious lionfish are to eat, but little headway has been made thus far.

---

and black, and can measure between 8 and 15cm (including the legs). Apart from a bird-eating variety, most are nocturnal insect hunters that construct their basic, messy-looking web tunnels on grassy banks or in dead wood.

Marine life

Sediment flows from the South American mainland via the Orinoco River have prevented the build-up of extensive **reefs** around Trinidad, but the waters off Tobago, where visibility ranges from 12 to 50m, hold some of the richest in the Caribbean, though many are suffering the depredations of overfishing, pollution and the coral bleaching caused worldwide by rising sea temperatures. Among the sixty or so **coral** varieties found in T&T waters are rotund brains, patterned with furrowed trenches; branching umber elkhorn and staghorn; stalagmite-like pillar coral; and cool green star coral. Extremely striking are the groups of intricate **soft coral** sea plumes, sea whips and purple sea fans, while brilliant yellow **anemones** as well as red, brown, purple and green **sponges** provide a splash of colour, some growing in excess of 1m in diameter. Caribbean spiny **lobsters** and green or spotted moray **eels** lurk in the crevices between corals.

Sand flats and seagrass fields between the reefs host spiny black **sea urchins**, as well as a round white variety with shorter spines. Long, thin and off-white, **sea cucumbers** sift through the sea floor to feed on deposited nutrients, while **starfish** and **queen conch** snails move slowly along the seagrass blades, vacuuming up organisms that live there.

The reefs harbour a huge variety of multicoloured **tropical fish**, including parrot fish, electric-blue Creole wrasse, queen and French angel fish, striped grunts and spiny puffer fish – which balloon in size if threatened – as well as tarpon and trigger fish.

Of larger marine species, giant 7m **manta rays** are sometimes seen around Speyside in Tobago; smaller eagle, spotted and Atlantic torpedo rays, and southern stingrays are more common (Castara's Big Bay is great for spotting rays in the shallows). **Dolphins** and **porpoises** are common, and docile, 15m **whale sharks** are occasional visitors, feeding on plankton and small fish. Other large fish include reef, tiger and nurse sharks; plus grouper, dolphin fish, kingfish (wahoo), tuna, blackjack, marlin, blue cavalli, sailfish, bonito and barracuda. During nesting season, T&T's beaches are also used as nesting sites by **turtles**, most notably giant leatherbacks (see page 142).

Books

The reviews below cover some of the best available books written about Trinidad and Tobago. All are readily available internationally and in T&T, where you'll also find many more specialized titles not listed here. To delve deeper into writing from Trinidad and Tobago, check out Peepal Tree Press (⊕peepaltreepress.com), which publishes works by almost fifty writers of T&T descent, while the Reviews section of Caribbean Beat magazine (⊕caribbean-beat.com) gives a rundown of newly published books on/ from the region each month. Of the books highlighted here, authors and individual titles marked with a ★ are especially recommended.

FICTION

★ **Lisa Allen-Agostini and Jeanne Mason (eds)/ Earl Lovelace and Robert Antoni (eds)** *Trinidad Noir* and *Trinidad Noir: The Classics*. The first of these companion anthologies explores T&T's dark side via works by contemporary authors such as Sharon Millar, Vahni Capildeo, Kevin Baldeosingh, Tiphanie Yanique and Keith Jardim; the second provides a wonderful introduction to some of the T&T's finest writers, with stories and poetry from the likes of C.L.R. James, Derek Walcott, Samuel Selvon, V.S. Naipaul, Michael Antony and Wayne Brown alongside newer names from Elizabeth Walcott-Hackshaw to Barbara Jenkins.

Michael Anthony *Cricket in the Road and Other Stories* collects concise, thought-provoking short stories, rich in descriptive detail. Anthony's novel *In the Heat of the Day* is centred on the industrial unrest that led to the 1903 water riots, while *The Year in San Fernando* is an acute portrayal of San Fernando in the 1940s, seen through the eyes of a teenage boy on a year's sojourn from his village home. Perhaps his best book, though, is the coming-of-age novel ★ *Green Days by the River*.

Robert Antoni *My Grandmother's Erotic Folk Tales, Carnival* and *As Flies to Whatless Boys*. *Folk Tales* offers outlandish stories of life on Corpus Christi (aka Trinidad) under US military occupation during World War II, as told by a saucy 97-year-old to her grandson, while the powerful *Carnival* moves from New York to Port of Spain and the Trinidad rainforest, touching on love and the island's historical prejudices along the way. Perhaps his greatest work is the fantastic ★ *Whatless Boys*, a magnificent *tour de force* that describes the journey to and settlement in Trinidad of a band of idealistic English pioneers led by a charismatic swindler. His earlier *Blessed is the Fruit* and *Divina Trace* are well worth checking out, too.

Kevin Baldeosingh *The Autobiography of Paras P* and *The Ten Incarnations of Adam Avatar*. A hilarious satirical novel, *Paras* is a brilliant light read; ★ *Adam Avatar* is much more

powerful stuff, a retelling of Caribbean history from the inside by way of the central character's many incarnations, from an Amerindian to a white prostitute and a mixed-race slave-owner.

Roslyn Carrington *A Thirst for Rain*. Love story set in the St Ann's foothills, centred around food seller Myra and her relationship with saga boy Slim, ex-stickfighter Jacob and teenage daughter Odile, with some fabulous descriptions of Port of Spain.

Barbara Jenkins *Sic Transit Wagon*. A beautiful and sometimes sad collection of short stories that evoke the essence of Trini-ness, all lovingly written.

★ **Earl Lovelace** *The Dragon Can't Dance* and other novels. A passionate examination of the motivation behind Carnival – if you only read one book about Trinidad, *Dragon Can't Dance* should be it. In *The Wine of Astonishment*, Lovelace highlights the persecution of the Spiritual Baptists, while *The Schoolmaster* offers a powerful and superbly handled allegory of colonialism. *Salt*, which won the Commonwealth Writer's Prize in 1997, is a stunning commentary on freedom from oppression, while *Is Just a Movie* explores the lives of residents of a small backwater village in Trinidad.

Shiva Naipaul *The Chip-Chip Gatherers*. A darkly funny tale of the machinations of the one rich man in a poor rural community. His novel *Fireflies* chronicles with empathy and ironic humour the moral, financial and spiritual decline of a rich and influential Indo-Trinidadian family.

★ **V.S. Naipaul** *A House for Mr Biswas*. Mr Biswas – a newspaper journalist trapped by poverty into living with his domineering in-laws – struggles to establish his own identity. *In a Free State*, which won the Booker Prize in 1971, explores the changing roles and attitudes of people transplanted from their homelands, while *Miguel Street* paints a picture of community life in Trinidad through the eyes of a child. *The Middle Passage* looks at the effects of colonialism on five societies in the Caribbean and South America.

TRINBAGO'S LITERARY GREATS

Given T&T's diverse cultural heritage, opaque dialect and witty, imaginative use of language, it's no surprise that the islands boast a rich **literary heritage**. A radical 1930s journal featuring poetry and short stories by a host of young Trinidadian writers and intellectuals, *The Beacon* was at the forefront of the emerging literary tradition, but Trinbagonian literature really flourished after World War II. **Samuel Selvon**'s wryly humorous novels chronicle both the experience of growing up in Trinidad and the trials and tribulations of an emigrant in London, while those of **Earl Lovelace** are a lyrical celebration of Trinidadian life and culture, its "shacks that leap out of the red dirt and stone, thin like smoke, fragile like kite paper balancing on their rickety pillars as broomsticks on the edge of a juggler's nose" (*The Dragon Can't Dance*).

The late 1950s saw the appearance of Trinidad's most acclaimed novelist, Nobel Prize-winner **V.S. Naipaul**, who grew up in Chaguanas and Port of Spain, and won a scholarship to study English at Oxford University in 1950. He wrote his first book, *The Mystic Masseur* (1957), at the age of 23 while working for the BBC Caribbean Service in London, but it was his fourth, *A House for Mr Biswas*, that made his name in 1961. Naipaul's ironic treatment of the snobbery, corruption and small-mindedness of Trinidadian life has earned him an ambivalent reputation in his homeland, however, as has his legendary irascibility and misogynistic comments about women writers. His brother **Shiva Naipaul** also garnered substantial literary acclaim with books such as *Fireflies* (1970) and *Beyond the Dragon's Mouth* (1984), before his sudden death of a heart attack at the age of 40 in 1985.

Trinidad's best-known poet, the Nobel Prize-winner **Derek Walcott** (1930–2017) was actually born in St Lucia, but lived in Port of Spain for decades, establishing the Trinidad Theatre Workshop there (see page 67). An accomplished and prolific lyric poet, Walcott drew on the Elizabethan tradition, using both traditional rhyme and metre and free verse to explore issues of exile and identity and evoke the rich, heady atmosphere of the Caribbean.

Elizabeth Nunez *The Limbo Silence*. The tale of a Trinidadian girl's efforts to integrate into an all-white school in Wisconsin during the Civil Rights movement. In *Bruised Hibiscus*, set in a Trinidadian village, the murder of a white woman reunites two childhood friends who are forced to relive memories of witnessing abuse by plantation owners. *Prospero's Daughter* offers a post-colonial retelling of Shakespeare's *The Tempest*, while *Even in Paradise* swings between Trinidad, Barbados and Jamaica in exploring racism and family.

★ **Monique Roffey** *White Woman on a Green Bicycle*, *Archipelago* and *House of Ashes*. A beautifully written chronicle of an expat couple in Trinidad, *White Woman* describes a husband's passion for the country and its people alongside his wife's battles with racial politics, humidity and isolation, which she vents through writing letters to a wonderfully imagined Eric Williams. Via a boat journey from Chaguaramas to the Galapagos, *Archipelago* is a tender lament to a man coming to terms with the death of his infant son, while *House of Ashes*, set in the fictional island of Sans Amen, explores the events of the 1990 coup in Trinidad. All are gripping and absorbing throughout.

Lawrence Scott *Ballad for the New World and Other Stories* is a clever collection evoking the experiences of a white boy growing up in pre-Independence Trinidad with

ironic humour and sensitivity. Set on a leper colony off Trinidad's coast, *Night Calypso* revolves around the troubled life of an orphan who goes to live with the island's doctor.

★ **Samuel Selvon** *The Lonely Londoners*. A classic and powerful account of West Indian immigrants adjusting to the climate, racism and big-city life of 1950s London. Its sequel, *Moses Ascending* (Heinemann), is an ironic tale of an apathetic Trinidadian's experience of the Black Power movement and race relations in 1970s London.

★ **Amanda Smyth** *A Kind of Eden*. A ruthless and gripping portrayal of a middle-aged British policeman working in Trinidad, whose various preoccupations have a devastating effect on his family when they visit Tobago together: perhaps best read after you get home. Moving between the eponymous coastal village in Tobago, Port of Spain and Tamana in eastern Trinidad, her earlier *Black Rock* offers an interesting take on T&T just after World War II, with post-colonial racial politics at the heart of the action.

★ **Derek Walcott** *Omeros*. An extraordinary *tour de force* that draws on Homer's *Odyssey* to produce a vast Caribbean epic of the dispossessed. Many of the works in Walcott's *Collected Poems 1948–1984* evoke the sights and sounds of Trinidad, including the famous *Laventille*, dedicated to V.S. Naipaul.

HISTORY AND CULTURE

★ **Stefan Falke** *Moko Jumbies: The Dancing Spirits of Trinidad*. Gorgeous coffee-table book capturing the beauty and energy of moko jumbies (stilt-walkers) from the

Keylemanjahro School in Cocorite, from practice sessions to glorious Carnival shots.

James Ferguson *A Traveller's History of the Caribbean*.

Concise and well-written overview that provides a good introduction to the region's history.

Patrick Leigh Fermor *The Traveller's Tree*. Written in the late 1940s, this classic account of a Caribbean tour has an interesting section on Trinidad, describing Port of Spain with an eagle eye and analysing the island's history, as well as its music and the "saga boy" fashions of the time.

James T. Houk *Spirits, Blood & Drums: The Orisha Religion in Trinidad and Tobago*. An anthropological study of the Orisha religion.

C.L.R. James *Beyond a Boundary*. Classic autobiographical book on cricket which extends into life and society in Trinidad in the 1920s.

John Newel Lewis *Ajoupa*. A marvellously idiosyncratic and enthusiastic account of the unique architecture of Trinidad and Tobago, illustrated by the author's superb line drawings. Hard to find outside Trinidad, but a must if you're interested in local architecture.

Peter Mason *Bacchanal! Carnival, Calypso and the Popular Culture of Trinidad*. A little dated, having been published in 1998, but packed with interviews with the calypsonians and costume designers behind Trinidad's Carnival.

John Mendes *Cote Ce, Cote La*. The original dictionary of Trinbagonian words, with sections on Carnival and proverbs and drawings by Carnival designer Wayne Berkley. Widely available on the islands.

Harvey R. Neptune *Caliban and the Yankees*. Fascinating account of the social and economic effects of the American bases at Chaguaramas and Waller Field during World War II, touching on everything from race and sexual politics to the response of calypsonians.

Colin A. Palmer *Eric Williams and the Making of the Modern Caribbean*. Contemporary take on the "father of the nation" and still the most influential figure in the republic's political history, from his days as a Howard University professor and author to his battle for an independent T&T and his years as the country's prime minister.

★**Alex Smailes** *Trinidad and Tobago*. Gorgeous coffee-table photo journal of Trinidad, with an incisive introduction to T&T history and culture by Jeremy Taylor and lovely reproductions of Smailes' photographs in the four sections, Carnival, Land, Water and People. The best visual souvenir on the market.

Vincent Tothill *Trinidad Doctor's Office*. The diaries of a Scottish doctor who signs up for a stint in Trinidad via the Colonial Office, this witty and often sad book offers a fascinating insight into Trinidadian society during the early twentieth century.

★**Derek Walcott and Peter Doig** *Morning, Paramin*. A visual and literary treat, Walcott's poetry accompanies Peter Doig's fabulous paintings in an ode to the pair's friendship and to life and love in Trinidad.

GUIDEBOOKS AND FIELD GUIDES

Solomon Baksh *Trinidad and Tobago*. Essential diving and snorkelling guidebook, with detailed descriptions of all the best dive sites on the islands.

Comeau, Guy, Hesterman and Hill *T&T Field Naturalists' Club Trail Guide*. Widely available in T&T, this is the definitive guide to hiking trails in Trinidad and Tobago with detailed descriptions and sketch maps, and useful sections on local geology and preparing for a hike.

★**Richard Ffrench** *A Guide to the Birds of Trinidad and Tobago*. Definitive guide to T&T's birdlife, including information on habitat, habits, appearance and calls as well as a description of the islands' natural history and environment. The pocket-sized version, with pictures and descriptions of 83 common species, is handy for travellers.

Martin Kenefick, Robin L. Restall and Floyd E. Hayes *Birds of Trinidad and Tobago*. Newer than the classic Ffrench guide, with plenty of colour plates and detailed descriptions.

G.W. Lennox and S.A. Seddon *Flowers of the Caribbean; Fruits and Vegetables of the Caribbean; Trees of the Caribbean*. Slim and handy reference volumes with glossy, sharp colour pictures and concise accounts.

Language

T&T's rich and varied vocabulary stems as much from a love of wordplay as it does from the republic's tumultuous history. Though English is the main language, Amerindians, the Spanish and the French have all left their mark, in both place names and common parlance, and in the Trinidadian village of Paramin in Trinidad, French Creole (or patois) is still spoken by elders. Meanwhile, Spanish surfaces in parang lyrics, and Hindi is widely used in Indian communities.

The nation's diverse ethnic mix has also influenced **Creole English**; Trinis will say "it making hot" as the French would say "Il fait chaud". Terms such as *pommecythere* (golden apple) and *dou dou* (sweetheart, from the French *doux doux*) are commonplace, and **French patois** phrases are still part of the vernacular; *tout bagai* and *toute monde* are catch-alls meaning "everything". **Hindi** words, such as *dougla* and *aloo* (potato), have also entered the local lexicon.

Other idiosyncrasies include a habit of using the part to refer to the whole, calling an arm a hand, or a leg a foot – when someone breaks their arm, for example, they'll say "meh han break". People will also describe the afternoon as evening – it's common to be greeted with "good evening" at 3pm, while "goodnight" is used as a greeting.

Finally, bear in mind that language use here is often oblique and allusive. **Double entendres** are ubiquitous, especially in calypsos, with an endless supply of euphemisms – from "brush" to "hard work" to "saltfish" – employed to refer to sex or genitalia. If you're not well versed in local slang you'll need a Trini interpreter to appreciate the subtleties of many songs.

Glossary

Abir Pink dye thrown around by (and among) participants of the Hindu Phagwah festival.

Ajoupa Amerindian building with a palm-thatch roof and walls of clay and cow manure.

All fours Popular card game, often played for money.

Allyuh Everyone, as in "Allyuh not tired yet?"

Babash An illegal, extremely potent bootleg white rum, also called bush rum and mountain dew.

Bacchanal A rowdy event or social commotion, or just general scandal.

Bachac Large, black-brown leaf-cutting ant, which gives a painful nip.

Bad John Old-time term for a man of violent or criminal reputation.

Bamsie Bottom; backside, a staple of soca songs: "wine yuh bamsie".

Bandit A thief or criminal.

Bareback Term for a man who's not wearing a top.

Bath suit Swimsuit.

Bazodee State of confusion, usually caused by being attracted to someone of the opposite sex.

Beastly Used to describe an extremely cold beer.

Big yard Trinidad's largest panyard: the Savannah at Carnival time.

Bobol Corruption, embezzlement; a **bobolee** is a person easily taken advantage of, as well as an effigy of an unpopular public figure which you'll see strung up on fences and at roadsides around Easter time, and is treated to a piñata-like thrashing.

Boldfaced Being pushy or demanding.

Boof To lambast or scold someone: "He get a real boof for staying out last night".

Bounce Fist-to-fist greeting – you'll often be asked to "gimme a bounce nah?"

Brass band The bands that back live acts at fetes, usually featuring a good brass section; traditionally, soca and calypso songs hinge on a repeated brass refrain.

Broughtupsy Solid, proper upbringing – to have "no broughtupsy" is to have no manners and class.

Bumper Another word for backside, usually a woman's.

Bush Generic term for forests and undeveloped countryside. Also medicinal herbs used in a "bush bath" or "bush tea".

COMMON TRINBAGO EXPRESSIONS

Cockroach have no right in fowl party Don't involve yourself in situations where you're unwelcome or out of place.

Crapaud smoke yuh pipe You are in big trouble.

Every bread have it cheese Everyone, regardless of their background or appearance, will find a matching partner in the end.

Fruit doh fall far from de tree Aka, "like father, like son".

Get cage before yuh ketch bird Before you can ensnare a woman, you need a house to put her in.

If you play with dog, you must get fleas Hanging out with lowlifes will eventually rub off on you.

Man plans, God laughs It doesn't matter what you plan to do, things never work out the way you want them to.

Now yuh cookin' with gas When you finally understand or work out how to do something.

When cock get teeth Pigs might fly.

Yuh cyar play sailor an' fraid powder If you're going to be controversial you have to accept the consequences (a sailor mas traditionally includes a heavy coating of talcum powder on the face).

Zandolie fin' yuh hole Know your place and stick to it.

Buss To do something; eg to "buss a lime". Also describes an unsuccessful event ("De fete buss after Machel perform").

Cascadura Scaly black fish with folklore associations; if you eat it, you're destined to end your days in Trinidad.

Chip-chip Mollusc found on Trinidad's beaches; see pacro.

Chunkalunks Term of endearment, usually for a partner or a child.

Chupidee Something or someone idiotic.

Cocoa panyol/coco payol Originally used to describe Venezuelans who moved to Trinidad in the nineteenth century to work on the burgeoning cocoa and coffee estates, but often deployed to describe anyone or anything of mixed origin these days.

Commesse Confusion, controversy, scandal.

Cook up Food prepared in one pot, usually outside, such as pelau.

Coolie Derogatory term for someone of Indian descent.

Creole A broad term describing a person of mixed European and African descent born in T&T. Also classic Caribbean food, such as callaloo and coocoo.

Cut eye A nasty look, also a "bad eye".

Cutlass Machete.

Dingolay To wind down low or dance unreservedly.

Dotish Stupid, ridiculous-looking. Sometimes "dotishness" as well.

Dou dou Sweetheart.

Dougla Person of mixed Indian and African parentage. Does not have offensive connotations.

Dreevay Waste time.

East Indian A Trinbagonian of Indian descent.

Ent Used at the end of a statement to mean "is that not so" or "that's true isn't it?"

Fatigue Witty repartee.

Fete A large, open-air party or concert; the biggest are held around Carnival time.

Flambeaux A flaming kerosene torch used by oyster salesmen to advertise their wares.

Flask A half-bottle of rum.

Fresh-water Yankee Mocking term for Trinbagonians who use foreign mannerisms picked up during trips to the US.

Friending Having a sexual relationship with someone.

Gallery Veranda or porch outside one's home; to "gallery" is to show off.

Get on bad To dance and jump up with abandon at a fete.

Hops Light, fluffy bread rolls.

Horning Two-timing, being unfaithful to your partner.

Horrors Lots of problems, bad vibes caused by anger.

Hoss Good/best friend: "She's my real hoss".

Ital Rastafarian term meaning natural or pure, often used to refer to meatless food cooked with no salt.

Jackspaniard Large, aggressive wasp which delivers a vicious sting; also called a jep.

Jagabat Promiscuous woman.

Jamette Woman of questionable morals.

Jamishness Wild, unabandoned dancing/behaviour at Carnival time.

Jumbie Spirit or ghost, also a night person.

Jump-up Frenetic party.

Kaiso Old-time word for classic calypso music.

Kicksee Funny.

Lackeray Gossiping.

Laginiappe Pronounced "lan-nyap": a little extra, a bonus.

Las' lap Final parade of revellers on Carnival Tuesday before the abstinence of Lent begins.

Licks To lash or hit someone.

Lickser Person who gets free things through devious means.

Lime To socialize with friends on the street, in a bar, in a person's house, by a river, anywhere. T&T's favourite pastime.

Lyrics Flirtatious sweet talk, usually from a man to a woman.

Maaga Skinny, slim.

Macafouchette Leftovers from a meal; or a meal cobbled together from leftovers.

Maco A busybody prying into other people's business; also used as a verb.

Make style Show off.

Maljo Evil eye.

Malkadi Epilepsy. Having a fit.

Mamaguy Verb meaning to fool someone with smart talk that makes false promises: "Don't try to mamaguy me!".

Mampy Fat woman.

Mas Short for masquerade, used to describe playing in a costume band at Carnival.

Mauvais langue Damaging gossip.

Navel string Placenta, buried by the superstitious under a fruiting mango tree to ensure a prosperous life. Also used to denote someone's roots or a place they frequent, as in "yuh navel string's not buried in Carnival fete!".

Ol' talk Idle chatter.

One time Immediately, now: "pass the pepper one time".

Outside man/woman A person with whom one commits adultery.

Pacro Sea barnacle cooked up into "pacro water", a thin broth said to have aphrodisiac qualities.

Pampalam Backside.

Pan The steel drum as a musical instrument.

Panyard Home base of steel pan bands.

Papa yo! An expression of surprise.

Pappy show From puppet show, meaning nonsense, something inconsequential and ridiculous.

Parlour Small grocery store or bar.

Petit carem Dry spell in the middle of the rainy season, usually in September.

Picong The tradition of making fun of someone through an exchange of witty comments.

Piper Crack user.

Pitch oil Kerosene.

Posey Chamberpot. Sometimes placed on the stage by audiences at calypso tents to demonstrate displeasure with a performance; equally, used as a makeshift cup (filled with straight rum) during Jouvert.

Pressure General term for stress or problems, as in "it real pressure, man".

Puja Indian prayer or offering to the gods.

Puncheon High-proof rum.

Ras Dreadlocks or a person with them.

Real Plenty: "It have real people in the party!".

Reds Someone of African descent but with a light skin colour; also known as high brown.

Rucktion Confusion, bacchanal.

Saga boy Flashy dresser, now a little outdated.

Scruntin' Penniless, broke.

Sea bath To go for a swim in the sea.

Semi-demi Something unexpected, a little bit of magic.

Skin out To splay ones legs, usually when dancing.

Skin teet To smile.

Slackness Impolite, crude and low-down behaviour.

Sound system A crew of DJs operating the decks and providing the huge speaker boxes at fetes and parties.

Spranger Crack user, petty thief or volatile person.

Steups The Trini version of a "tut", a steups is kissing or sucking the teeth to indicate irritation, disapproval or derision.

Storm Getting into a fete without paying by climbing over the fence, sweet-talking the doorman, etc.

Stupidness The preferred term to describe ridiculous, slack, time-consuming actions or behaviour.

Sweet hand Used in reference to someone who cooks very well.

Sweet to bad Very good: "the curry duck was sweet to bad".

Sweetman A man who is financially supported by a woman.

Swizzle stick A whisk used for stirring callaloo or juicing fruits to make punch.

Tabanca The depression caused by the ending of a love affair. In extreme states, "tabantruck".

Tan-ta-na Excitement, confusion.

Tantie Aunt.

Tapia Hut made with thatch and mud walls.

Thick Pronounced "tik", and usually used to refer to the (pleasant) plumpness of a woman.

Ting A thing, woman or a euphemism for all kinds of eventualities – "tings a gwan".

Tittivay Waste time or stir up trouble.

Tobago love Disguising your feelings for a loved one, possibly due to finding it difficult to express your emotions; also the actions of a couple who quarrel all the time.

Tout bagai/tout monde Everything.

Trace A road or street that once was or still is a dirt track.

Travel A journey using public transport.

Vaps To behave in an overexcited manner; also to indicate something that happens suddenly or a sudden change of mind/mood.

Vex Angry or annoyed.

Vex money Extra money to take out with you, in case you have an argument with your partner and have to pay your own way home.

Wajang A hooligan.

Wapie A card game.

Warahoon Person behaving in a wild or crazy manner.

Wassi Lewd, uninhibited behaviour and dancing at fetes; wining down to the ground.

We is we You are among friends.

Wine To dance by rotating hips and bottom in an erotic manner. Your "wining bone" is what allows you to move with suitable sensuality.

Wotless Worthless, no good.

Yard fowl Chickens raised in someone's backyard.

Small print and index

A ROUGH GUIDE TO ROUGH GUIDES

Published in 1982, the first Rough Guide – to Greece – was a student scheme that became a publishing phenomenon. Mark Ellingham, a recent graduate in English from Bristol University, had been travelling in Greece the previous summer and couldn't find the right guidebook. With a small group of friends he wrote his own guide, combining a contemporary, journalistic style with a thoroughly practical approach to travellers' needs.

The immediate success of the book spawned a series that rapidly covered dozens of destinations. And, in addition to impecunious backpackers, Rough Guides soon acquired a much broader readership that relished the guides' wit and inquisitiveness as much as their enthusiastic, critical approach and value-for-money ethos. These days, Rough Guides include recommendations from budget to luxury and cover more than 120 destinations around the globe, from Amsterdam to Zanzibar, all regularly updated by our team of roaming writers.

Browse all our latest guides, read inspirational features and book your trip at **roughguides.com**.

Rough Guide credits

Editor: Edward Aves
Cartography: Carte, Katie Bennett
Managing editor: Rachel Lawrence
Picture editor: Michelle Bhatia

Cover photo research: Sarah Stewart-Richardson
Senior DTP coordinator: Dan May
Head of DTP and Pre-Press: Rebeka Davies

Publishing information

This seventh edition published in 2018 by
Rough Guides Ltd

Distribution

UK, Ireland and Europe
Apa Publications (UK) Ltd; sales@roughguides.com
United States and Canada
Ingram Publisher Services; ips@ingramcontent.com
Australia and New Zealand
Woodslane; info@woodslane.com.au
Southeast Asia
Apa Publications (SN) Pte; sales@roughguides.com
Worldwide
Apa Publications (UK) Ltd; sales@roughguides.com
Special Sales, Content Licensing and CoPublishing
Rough Guides can be purchased in bulk quantities
at discounted prices. We can create special editions,
personalised jackets and corporate imprints tailored to
your needs. sales@roughguides.com.

roughguides.com
Printed in China by CTPS
All rights reserved
© Rough Guides, 2018
Maps © Apa Digital AG and Rough Guides Ltd
All rights reserved. No part of this publication may be
reproduced, stored in or introduced into a retrieval system,
or transmitted in any form, or by any means (electronic,
mechanical, photocopying, recording or otherwise) without
the prior written permission of the copyright owner.
A catalogue record for this book is available from the
British Library
The publishers and authors have done their best to
ensure the accuracy and currency of all the information
in **The Rough Guide to Trinidad & Tobago**, however,
they can accept no responsibility for any loss, injury, or
inconvenience sustained by any traveller as a result of
information or advice contained in the guide.

Help us update

We've gone to a lot of effort to ensure that the seventh
edition of **The Rough Guide to Trinidad & Tobago** is
accurate and up-to-date. However, things change – places
get "discovered", opening hours are notoriously fickle,
restaurants and rooms raise prices or lower standards. If
you feel we've got it wrong or left something out, we'd like
to know, and if you can remember the address, the price,
the hours, the phone number, so much the better.

Please send your comments with the subject line
"Rough Guide Trinidad & Tobago Update" to mail@
uk.roughguides.com. We'll credit all contributions and
send a copy of the next edition (or any other Rough Guide
if you prefer) for the very best emails.

Readers' updates

Thanks to all the readers who have taken the time to write in with comments and suggestions (and apologies if we've
inadvertently omitted or misspelt anyone's name): Andrew J. Gordon; Edward Stiel; Reid Smoot.

Acknowledgements

Author: Huge thanks to all in Trinidad and Tobago who
helped, supported and limed this book into existence,
particularly Dexter, Aaron and Soleil, and my Trini family:
Lynette, Dale, Gillian and Dean Lewis, Skye Hernandez,
Anna Carlsson, and Daddy Frank, Eugene and Francine
Romany. Many thanks also to my longtimes, Gunda
Harewood and Lara and Briony Baden-Semper; and to
Jillian and Jada Fourniller; Fay Patrick; Mark and Zena
Puddy; Gillian Goddard; Stephen Broadbridge; Piero

Guerrini; Courtenay Rooks; Judy Gemmet; Sean Clark
and all at *Plantation Beach Villas*. Thanks to editor par
excellence Edward Aves and all-seeing eye for the small
things, and for being so much fun to work with. And finally
thanks also to those who were there at the beginning of
the T&T guide, twenty years ago: the inimitable Dominique
De-Light; and the Dagnino family: Josie, Natasha, Nick and
Sasha, and especially Angelo, who is sadly missed.

ABOUT THE AUTHOR

Polly Thomas has been travelling to the Caribbean since her teens, and lived in
Port of Spain, Trinidad, for five years. As well as writing articles about the region's
food, music and travel attractions, she has authored guidebooks to Jamaica, St
Lucia and Antigua and Barbuda as well as T&T. She currently lives in London.

Photo credits
(Key: T-top; C-centre; B-bottom; L-left; R-right)

Index

Main references are in **bold** type

Map symbols

The symbols below are used on maps throughout the book

—	International boundary	◆	Point of interest	▲	Mountain peak/hill	♀	Church (regional map)
– – –	Chapter boundary	✉	Post office	⌃	Mountain range	♙	Monastery
	Highway	✚	Hospital	◠	Cave	♙	Mosque
	Main road	ⓘ	Information office	～	Reef	♣	Hindu temple
	Minor road	🅿	Parking	⚘	Waterfall	✚	Church (town map)
– – – –	Footpath	⛽	Petrol station	∴	Ruins	◻/◔	Market
— -	Ferry	⚑	Golf course	♜	Fortress	▮	Building
	Waterway	☂	Beach	♦	Museum	▱	Park
✈	Airport	🦃	Turtle nesting site	☉	Statue	⊞	Cemetery
★	Transport stop	🐦	Bird sanctuary	☗	Lighthouse	◻	Beach
☆	Viewpoint	☂	Palms	🍾	Distillery	~~	Swamp
⑧	Bank						

Listings key

■ Accommodation

● Eating

■ Drinking/nightlife

● Shopping